The Economics of the Welf

The Economics of the Welfare State

Third Edition

NICHOLAS BARR

Stanford University Press
Stanford, California
1998

Stanford University Press
Stanford, California
© 1987, 1993, 1998 Nicholas Barr
Originating publisher: Oxford University Press
First Published in the USA by Stanford University Press, 1987
Second edition published 1993
Third edition published 1998

Cloth ISBN 0–8047–3551–4
Paper ISBN 0–8047–3552–2
LC 98–60890

For my Mother and Father

PREFACE TO THE THIRD EDITION

The world has changed since the first edition was published in 1987. At that time the Thatcher and Reagan administrations were in their pomp in the West, and the Communist threat was still regarded as very real. Possibly as a result, the issue of the market versus the state was something of a Punch and Judy debate between the two polar extremes. With the end of the cold war has perhaps come a more balanced view. The enormous virtues of private markets for most commodities is now appreciated in the former Communist countries—at least those of Central and Eastern Europe—while governments in the West are more open to the idea that private markets are not always and everywhere a complete answer. In part this has come about as the ideological pendulum has swung a bit, but it has also resulted from experience of the problems which arise if markets are not properly regulated—scandals over mis-sold pensions, worries about 'mad cow disease', and the continuing problems of the US health-care system being cases in point.

Like previous editions, this book is not just about Britain but at least as much about the underlying economic theory of the welfare state which applies to all industrial countries, to transition countries, and also to many middle-income developing countries. As previously, though an economics book, it is written to be accessible to readers in related areas: the theory in Chapters 3–6 is summarized in an appendix at the end of each chapter; and algebra, where used, can be skipped, since the results are always explained verbally.

The main thrust of the argument remains unchanged: the welfare state, whatever its distributional objectives, *also* has an important efficiency function; it does things which markets would either not do at all, or would do badly.

The arguments in support of that view have been updated in various ways. New or expanded theoretical discussion concerns the distinction between risk and uncertainty, analysis of the administrative costs of insurance, and problems of imperfect information on the demand side of the insurance market. The discussion of poverty and inequality brings out more fully the key role of choice in assessing whether differences in income reflect inequality or not, and there is additional discussion of why estimates of poverty and inequality can vary so much.

New or expanded items on the policy agenda include broader discussion of the challenges to the welfare state arising out of demographic change, global competition, changes in family structure, and changes in the structure of jobs, and continuing debates about the welfare state (is it desirable; is it any longer feasible?). Specific new topics include long-term insurance to cover disability and residential care in old age; the impact of genetic screening on medical insurance and life insurance; expanded discussion of the desirability—or otherwise—of competitive insurance; and additional analysis of the nature of social insurance (including discussion of unemployment and retirement as risks

Preface to the third edition

which, to some extent, are social constructs). Throughout the book gender aspects of the welfare state, such as the increasing feminization of poverty, have been brought out more fully.

Discussion of health (and, similarly, of education) has been reoriented to give added emphasis to health (the outcome) as opposed to health care (one of its determinants). In the case of education, outcomes include not only technical expertise but also attitudes and values. The move towards quasi-markets for health care and education is discussed and evaluated. And the discussion of higher-education finance has been largely rewritten to take account of events over the 1990s and the report of a major Committee of Inquiry into higher education.

The quickest way to get the book's major messages is to read Chapters 1 and 15; the next quickest is to read those chapters plus the concluding sections of Chapters 4 (economic theory), 11 (cash benefits), and 12, 13, and 14 (health, education, and housing, respectively). For those who want to read round the subject, three volumes are, in many ways, companions to this one. Howard Glennerster's (1997) book discusses the detailed finances of the welfare state; Glennerster and Hills (1998) is a detailed assessment of British developments since the mid-1970s; and Barr (1994), written by a mix of academic writers and World Bank staff, covers ground very similar to this book for the transition countries of Central and Eastern Europe and the former Soviet Union.

As with earlier editions, my colleagues and friends in the LSE's Centre for the Analysis of Social Exclusion have been generous in letting me pillage their bookshelves, their writings, their brains, and their time, especially Phil Agulnik, Martin Evans, Howard Glennerster, John Hills, and Julian Le Grand. I owe a continuing debt also to my students. They ask awkward questions (all the time), see things in clearer ways (often), or provoke me into seeing things in clearer ways (sometimes). I am also grateful for advice, comments, and help from Gary Burtless, Richard Jackman, Frank Levy, Branko Milanovic, Dilia Montes, and Richard Scheffler; and I would be even more grateful to Polly Toynbee, whose columns from the *Independent* litter my desk, if she would publish them as a collection of essays. My work on higher-education finance, summarized in Chapter 13, grows out of a joint enterprise with Iain Crawford over the past ten years; I have also learnt a lot from Mark Blaug and Bruce Chapman. Once more, my biggest debt is to Gill, who has listened patiently to my ruminations, made many suggestions, and (with distressing accuracy) told me when I was wrong. None of them should be implicated in errors which remain.

Nicholas Barr

September 1997

viii

PREFACE TO THE SECOND EDITION

The friendly reception the first edition received was very gratifying, and I regret that it has taken so long till the appearance of the second. Much has happened in the intervening years both in Britain and elsewhere, particularly in the formerly Communist countries (one reason why the second edition has not appeared till now is that I spent two years with the World Bank working on the design of social safety nets in Central and Eastern Europe and the former Soviet Union).

The demise of Marxism faces those countries with the problem of the appropriate division of responsibility between the state and the private sector—the central theme of this book. The economic argument and strategic policy conclusions remain the same as in the first edition: that the welfare state (i.e. income support, health care, education, and housing), quite apart from its distributional and other objectives, has a major efficiency role. To the extent that this is so, it is no longer public involvement *per se* which is controversial but only its precise form and the choice of its distributional objectives. It is therefore not surprising, as discussed in Chapter 15, that the welfare state weathered the storm of the 1980s in the UK and the USA intact and was, in many ways, strengthened. . . .

Though the main thrust of the argument has not changed, there are a number of significant changes from the first edition. Chapter 1 contains a new section on the objectives of the welfare state. The theoretical discussion is strengthened by new sections in Chapter 4 on public choice and government failure, and on the boundary between the market and the state, and in Chapter 5 by a new section on social insurance, and by extended discussion of the problems caused by asymmetric information.

Policy analysis includes discussion of three major UK developments: the 1988 social-security reforms; reform of the National Health Service in the aftermath of the 1989 White Paper, and changes to school and university education under the 1988 Education Reform Act. In addition, the analysis of targeting in Chapter 10 has been extended, and there is a new section assessing the arguments for child benefit. Chapters 12 and 13 on health care and education have been completely reorganized. Chapters 12, 13, and 14 now discuss health care, education, and housing, respectively, and all have a common structure. Alongside discussion of ongoing reforms, the chapters include additional material on international comparison of health-care systems and a new section on the reform of higher education, including discussion of student-loan schemes. The References have been brought up to date, and expanded to include more international material.

Readers in a hurry can find the major arguments in Chapters 1 and 15, plus the concluding sections of Chapter 4 (economic theory), Chapter 11 (cash benefits), and Chapters 12, 13, and 14 (health care, education, and housing, respectively). Readers in less of a hurry may want to look at a number of other books and articles which are, in many ways, companion volumes. My colleague, Howard Glennerster's (1992) book sets

Preface to the second edition

out the detailed finances of the welfare state. Barr and Whynes (1993) invite a range of authors to cover the welfare state from a variety of different perspectives. Barr (1992) sets the arguments in a broader OECD context.

My thanks are due to all the colleagues and friends who helped with the first edition. My specific thanks for help with this revision (without implicating them in errors which remain) are to Howard Glennerster and John Hills, to Alan Thompson for guiding me through the morass of UK cash-benefit institutions, and to Martin and Peggy Baer for letting me share their rural idyll for a good part of the writing. My greatest debt is to Gill, for her support and encouragement, and for tolerating the sound of the nocturnal keyboard in hotels throughout Central and Eastern Europe.

Nicholas Barr

November 1992

PREFACE TO THE FIRST EDITION

There is a large literature on different aspects of the welfare state and a substantial body of economic theory which bears on the issues involved. One of the main purposes of this book is to draw together these diverse sources into a unified whole. Two general conclusions emerge. First, the issues raised by the welfare state fit very naturally into the conventional theoretical framework used by economists. Secondly, public involvement in institutions of the general sort which comprise the welfare state (i.e. income support, health care, education, and housing) can, for the most part, be justified rather strongly in efficiency terms, quite independent of debates about social justice. To the extent that this is so, it is no longer public involvement *per se* which is controversial but only its precise form and the choice of its distributional objectives.

Throughout the book the main arguments are contrasted with those arising from different perspectives, especially from socialists and from libertarians such as Hayek and Friedman. The debate with the latter two is particularly fruitful. The difference between their views and a liberal defence of the welfare state rests less on ideology than on economic theory. Specifically, the theory set out in this book assigns a prominent role to technical problems with markets, with particular emphasis on information problems which are largely left out of account in most libertarian writing. These, more than any other theoretical consideration, are crucial to establishing the important efficiency role of the welfare state.

Though written specifically for economics specialists, the needs of a diverse readership are kept in mind throughout the book. The early theoretical chapters (3–6) in particular assume a working knowledge of intermediate microeconomic theory. To help readers with little economics, each of these chapters has a non-technical appendix, with the aid of which the rest of the book should, for the most part, be intelligible. Algebra is used where necessary to pin down some important concepts precisely; but the results are always explained verbally so that the equations can be skipped by those who are prepared to take their conclusions on trust. As a result the book should be accessible to readers in related academic areas (e.g. social administration, public policy, and political economy) and to professionals in such fields as medicine and education. Familiarity with British institutions is not essential; they are described in separate sections which can be consulted as desired. The important arguments do not depend on institutional knowledge and should therefore make sense to readers in (or from) other countries. The principles developed are applicable to all industrialized economies and, where possible, examples and parallels from other countries are given. The Glossary explains the meaning of technical terms, and disentangles some differences of usage in various countries. The central arguments are summarized in Chapters 1 and 15, buttressed by the concluding sections

Preface to the first edition

of Chapter 4 (economic and political theory), 11 (income support), 13 (health care and education), and 14 (housing).

The origins of the book lie in lectures given over the years to students at the London School of Economics and in a series of seminars in Tokyo and Osaka under the sponsorship of the Kansai Economic Research Centre. I have been lucky in my audiences —they have never failed to disagree, to challenge, and to ask thoroughly awkward questions.

My list of specific debts is large because I launched draft chapters liberally, and my colleagues are generous. My friends and mentors Alan Day and Alan Prest read the complete manuscript in draft, and had a major influence on its final shape. The book as a whole also owes a great deal to Christine Sarson-Gale, who contributed substantively to a number of chapters. Many other people have given valuable comments on drafts of one or more chapters: Brian Abel-Smith, Patricia Apps, Tony Atkinson, David De Meza, Howard Glennerster, Gervas Huxley, Kurt Klappholz, Julian Le Grand, Peter Levin, Jane Lewis, Robin Naylor, Joseph Pechman, David Piachaud, Sally Sainsbury, Christine Whitehead, and Basil Yamey. Dilia Montes gave helpful research assistance; Hilary Parker typed and retyped with superb efficiency, without fuss, and without ever overshooting a deadline; and Alma Gibbons and her colleagues taught me to use the word processor, and promptly and cheerfully bailed me out of a number of tight corners. I thank them all most warmly without implicating them in errors which remain.

Nicholas Barr

1986

CONTENTS

Contents

PART 4. EPILOGUE

15. Conclusion

DETAILED CONTENTS

PART 1. CONCEPTS

Detailed contents

PART 2. CASH BENEFITS

PART 3. BENEFITS IN KIND

Detailed contents

PART 4. **EPILOGUE**

LIST OF FIGURES

LIST OF TABLES

ABBREVIATIONS

AC	average cost
AFDC	Aid to Families with Dependent Children
ATR	average tax rate
CPAG	Child Poverty Action Group
DES	Department of Education and Science
DfEE	Department for Education and Employment
DHSS	Department of Health and Social Security
DoE	Department of the Environment
DoH	Department of Health
DRG	diagnosis-related group
FIS	Family Income Supplement
GGE(X)	general government expenditure, excluding certain items
GP	general practitioner
GPV	gross present value
HAG	Housing Association Grant
HEFCE	Higher Education Funding Council for England
HMO	health maintenance organization
HRA	Housing Revenue Account
LEA	Local Education Authority
LIS	Luxembourg Income Study
LSE	London School of Economics
MC	marginal cost
MPC	marginal private cost
MPV	marginal private value
MSC	marginal social cost
MSV	marginal social value
MTR	marginal tax rates
MV	marginal value
NBER	National Bureau of Economic Research
NCIHE	National Committee of Inquiry into Higher Education
NHS	National Health Service
NIC	National Insurance Contribution
NPV	net present value
OAI	Old Age Insurance

Abbreviations

OASI	Old Age and Survivor Insurance
OASDI	Old Age, Survivor, and Disability Insurance
OASDHI	Old Age, Survivor, Disability, and Health Insurance
OECD	Organization for Economic Cooperation and Development
PAC	Public Assistance Committee
PAYG	Pay-As-You-Go
PI	Pareto improvement
PPO	preferred provider organization
PVB	present value of benefits
PVC	present value of costs
QALY	Quality Adjusted Life Year
RAWP	Resource Allocation Working Party
RI	Rawlsian improvement
SERPS	state earnings-related pension scheme
SI	Socialist improvement
SLC	Student Loans Company
UGC	University Grants Committee

Justice is the first virtue of all social institutions, as truth is of systems of thought. A theory however elegant and economic must be rejected or revised if it is untrue; likewise laws and institutions no matter how efficient and well-arranged must be reformed or abolished if they are unjust. John Rawls, 1971

Let us remember that it [*laissez-faire*] is a *practical rule*, and not a doctrine of science; a rule in the main sound, but like most other sound rules, liable to numerous exceptions; above all, a rule which must never for a moment be allowed to stand in the way of any promising proposal of social or industrial reform.
J. E. Cairnes, 1873

Part 1
CONCEPTS

CHAPTER 1

Introduction

[The duties of the state are] . . . first . . . that of protecting the society from the violence and invasion of other independent societies . . . second . . . that of protecting, as far as possible, every member of the society from the injustice or oppression of every other member of it . . . third . . . that of erecting and maintaining those publick institutions and those publick works which, though they may be in the highest degree advantageous to a great society, are of such a nature, that the profit could never repay the expence to any individual or small number of individuals.

Adam Smith, 1776

1. The approach

1.1. The central argument

One of the wellsprings of this book was the exuberant insistence of various of my students and colleagues that economics appeared largely irrelevant to major issues of social policy. They had a point, and this book—like previous editions—is an attempt both to remedy their grievances and to assert the importance of economics. To address the concern about relevance, I try to relate economic theory to different notions of social justice and to the historical development of the welfare state. In stressing the importance of economics, two results stand out. First, the welfare state is not a subject apart, but fits very naturally into the framework of economic analysis. Secondly, the theoretical arguments support the existence of the welfare state not only for well-understood equity reasons but also very much in efficiency terms. This, it turns out, is an area in which economic theory is capable of strong results which can justify the general idea of the welfare state and, to a surprising extent, can do so without resort to ideology.

Given the size of the subject, this book of necessity is an attempt to paint a broad canvas in the hope that readers, even if they do not accept all the answers, will at least be directed to the right battleground. The book addresses two broad questions: what theoretical arguments can justify the existence of the various parts of the welfare state in a modern industrialized economy; and, given these arguments of principle, how sensible (or otherwise) are the specific arrangements in the UK[1] and in other countries?

The approach is best illustrated by two questions which permeate throughout:

1. What are the *aims* of policy?
2. By what *methods* are those aims best achieved?

Question 1 is very broad ranging. There is general agreement that the major aims of policy in Western societies include *efficiency* in the use of resources; their distribution in accordance with *equity* or *justice*; and the preservation of *individual freedom*. These aims, however, can be defined in different ways, and may be accorded different weights. To a utilitarian,[2] the aim of policy is to maximize total welfare; to Rawls the aim is social justice, defined in a particular way; libertarians make their main aim individual freedom, and socialists their prime concern equality. Beveridge's goal was the conquest of what he called the five giants of want, disease, ignorance, squalor, and idleness. The answer to question 1 is explicitly normative and largely ideological. The objectives of the welfare state are discussed in more detail in Section 2.2.

In contrast, once question 1 has been answered, question 2 should be treated not as *ideological* but as *technical*—that is, it raises a *positive* issue. Whether a given aim should be pursued by market allocation or by public provision depends on which of these methods more nearly achieves the chosen aim. Market allocation is neither 'good' nor 'bad'—it is useful in some instances—for example, private markets for food are generally effective in achieving the aim that people should not starve; in others, however (it is argued in Chapter 12 that health care is one), the market mechanism works less well, and a system with substantial state intervention can be more efficient and just. Similarly, public provision is neither good nor bad, but useful in some cases, less so in others. One of the questions throughout is which method is the more useful in different areas of the welfare state.

The distinction between aims and methods is fundamental, and bears reinforcement. Consider two central questions which all societies face:

• How much redistribution (of income, wealth, power, etc.) should there be?
• How should the economy best be run (i.e. the market system, central planning, or a mixed economy)?

The first question is clearly ideological and normative; it is an aims question and so properly the subject of political debate. But, *once that question has been answered*, the second question is largely one of method (i.e. a positive issue) and more properly the subject of technical than political discussion. This approach is explained in detail in Chapters 3 and 4, and summarized in the concluding section of Chapter 4.

---

[1] The United Kingdom (UK) is Great Britain and Northern Ireland (Act of Union with Ireland 1800; Government of Ireland Act 1920). Britain (or Great Britain) consists of England, with Wales and Scotland (Act of Union with Scotland 1706).

[2] Utilitarianism and other theories of society, including those of Rawls and libertarian and socialist writers, are discussed in Chapter 3.

1.2. Organization of the book

Part 1 sets the scene, starting in Chapter 2 with a discussion of the historical development of the welfare state in the UK, including some comparison with other countries, particularly the USA. The three chapters which follow are the theoretical heart of the book: Chapter 3 discusses various definitions of social justice and their different implications for the welfare state; Chapter 4 sets out the economic theory of state intervention and Chapter 5 the theory of insurance. Chapter 6 discusses problems of definition and measurement, particularly as they apply to poverty and inequality. To help readers who are diffident about their theoretical background, each of the conceptual chapters (3, 4, 5, and 6) has a non-technical appendix which summarizes the essential material; and technical terms are explained in the Glossary.

Three major threads developed in Part 1 run through the rest of the book: the social-welfare-maximization problem; alternative definitions of social justice; and measurement problems. The social-welfare-maximization problem (set out in Chapter 4) is the conventional starting point for economic theory. An important theorem states that under appropriate assumptions a competitive market equilibrium will allocate resources efficiently. It is argued that, where these conditions hold, the role of the state, if any, is limited to income redistribution; conversely, where these conditions fail, there may be efficiency grounds for intervention in a variety of forms. The second major theme is social justice. The definition chosen will determine the weights assigned to different individuals, with major implications for the form and extent of intervention—for example, whether people with no income should be supported at subsistence or at some higher level. The third thread, discussed in Chapter 6, concerns problems of definition and measurement. Many variables are hard to define and, once defined, hard to measure. A crucial and recurrent difficulty is that utility[3] is not measurable. This makes it hard both to measure living standards and to compare them. Costs or benefits—of health care or education, for example—may also be hard to measure.

As far as possible, each chapter in Parts 2 and 3 has a similar layout to clarify the structure of the argument. Each chapter discusses in turn: the *aims* of policy; the *methods* by which they might be achieved—that is, the theoretical arguments about intervention for reasons of efficiency and social justice; *assessment* in the light of this theoretical discussion of the appropriateness (or otherwise) of the UK and other systems, including discussion of the empirical literature; and *reform*.

Part 2 analyses cash transfers. Chapter 7 briefly describes the finances of the welfare state. Chapter 8 looks at unemployment, sickness, and disability benefits, Chapter 9 at retirement pensions, and Chapter 10 at non-contributory benefits, in each case starting with the theory and then assessing the practice. Chapter 11 considers a variety of reform strategies. Part 3 discusses provision in kind. Chapter 12, on health, analyses the theoretical arguments for public production and allocation, assesses the effectiveness

---

[3] See the Glossary.

of the UK National Health Service in comparison with systems in other countries, and discusses alternative ways in which health care might be organized. Chapters 13 and 14 cover similar ground for education and housing, respectively.

The conclusions of the book are summarized in Chapter 15, which picks up some of the questions asked at the end of this chapter. Readers in a hurry can get an idea of the book's approach and its main conclusions by reading Chapter 15 and the concluding sections of Chapters 4 (economic and political theory), 11 (income support), and 12, 13, and 14 (health care, education, and housing, respectively).

2. The welfare state and its objectives

2.1. Defining the welfare state

We shall see in Chapter 6 that important concepts such as poverty and equality of opportunity are hard, if not impossible, to define in principle, and even harder to measure. The concept of the welfare state similarly defies precise definition, and I make no serious attempt to offer one (see the Further Reading). Even Richard Titmuss (1958) ducked the problem—that book is called *Essays on 'The Welfare State'* (his quotes). As he later put it, 'I am no more enamoured today of the indefinable abstraction 'The Welfare State' than I was some twenty years ago when . . . the term acquired an international as well as a national popularity' (Titmuss 1968: 124). Three areas of complication stand out (for fuller discussion, see Glennerster 1997: ch. 1).

1. *Welfare derives from many sources in addition to state activity*. Individual welfare derives not only, nor necessarily primarily, from state institutions, but from at least four sources.

- *The labour market* is arguably the most important, first through *wage income*. Full employment is a major component of welfare broadly defined. High levels of employment and rising labour productivity over the 1950s and 1960s were at least as much an equalizing force as redistribution.[4] In addition to wage income, firms (individually or on an industry-wide basis, voluntarily or under legal compulsion) provide *occupational welfare* in the face of sickness, injury, and retirement.
- *Private provision* includes voluntary private insurance and individual saving.
- *Voluntary welfare* arises both within the family and outside, where people give time free or at a below-market price, or make voluntary charitable donations in other forms.
- *The state* intervenes by providing cash benefits and benefits in kind. In addition, it contributes through various tax concessions to the finance of occupational and private provision.

---

[4] As discussed in Chapter 2, Section 5.1, full employment was one of Beveridge's central assumptions.

2. *Modes of delivery* are also diverse. Though a service may be *funded* by the state, it does not follow that it must necessarily be publicly *produced*. The state can produce a service itself and supply it to recipients at no charge (e.g. health care under the National Health Service); or it can pay for goods produced in the private sector (e.g. free drugs under the National Health Service); or it can give individuals money (either explicitly or in the form of tax relief) to make their own purchases (e.g. tax relief in some countries for private medical insurance premiums). The issue of 'privatization', as we shall see in Chapter 4, Section 6, is more complex than is often recognized in public discussion.

3. *The boundaries of the welfare state are not well defined.* Though the state's role should not be exaggerated, neither should it be understated. Some typically excluded expenditure (e.g. public health and environmental policies) is very similar in purpose to activities which are included.

Welfare is thus a mosaic, with diversity both in its source and in the manner of its delivery. Nevertheless the state, through various levels of government, is much the most important single agency involved in the UK, and in most industrialized countries (for a survey of the welfare state in ten OECD countries, see Barr 1992). Throughout the book the term 'welfare state' is used as a shorthand for the state's activities in four broad areas: cash benefits; health care; education; and food, housing, and other welfare services.

In broad terms the modern UK welfare state comprises cash benefits and benefits in kind. The latter embrace a wide range of activities, including education, medical care, and more general forms of care for the infirm, the mentally and physically handicapped, and children in need of protection. Cash benefits have two major components.

1. *Social insurance* is awarded without an income or wealth test, generally on the basis of (*a*) previous contributions and (*b*) the occurrence of a specified contingency, such as becoming unemployment or reaching a specified age.

2. *Non-contributory benefits* are of two sorts. '*Universal*' benefits are awarded on the basis of a specified contingency, without either a contributions or an income test. There is no convenient shorthand for such benefits. They are often referred to (Margaret Gordon 1988: 37) as 'universal' and, reluctantly, I shall follow that usage. Major examples in the UK are child benefit and the National Health Service (discussed in Chapters 10 and 12, respectively). *Social assistance* is awarded on the basis of an income test. It is generally a benefit of last resort, designed to help individuals and families who are in poverty, whether as an exceptional emergency, or because they are not covered by social insurance, or as a supplement to social insurance.

In practice the UK welfare state can be taken to comprise, at a minimum, the publicly provided benefits (representing about 25 per cent of gross domestic product) shown in Figure 1.1, together with the contributions which pay for them. Cash benefits follow the pattern described above. National insurance is payable to people with an adequate contributions record; benefits cover, *inter alia*, unemployment, sickness (short- and long-term), and retirement, of which the last (about 18 per cent of social spending) is much the largest. Non-contributory benefits include child benefit (a weekly cash payment to

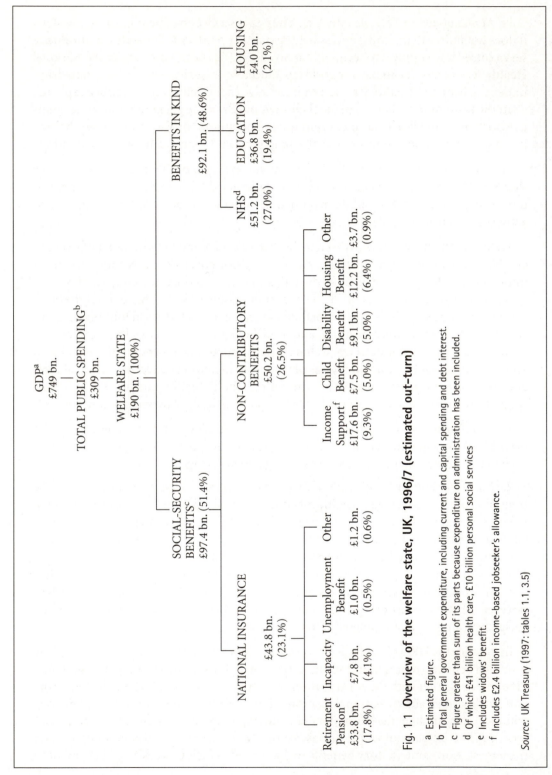

GDP[a]
£749 bn.

TOTAL PUBLIC SPENDING[b]
£309 bn.

WELFARE STATE
£190 bn. (100%)

SOCIAL-SECURITY
BENEFITS[c] (51.4%)
£97.4 bn.

NATIONAL INSURANCE
£43.8 bn.
(23.1%)

Retirement Pension[e]
£33.8 bn.
(17.8%)

Incapacity
£7.8 bn.
(4.1%)

Unemployment Benefit
£1.0 bn.
(0.5%)

Other
£1.2 bn.
(0.6%)

NON-CONTRIBUTORY
BENEFITS
£50.2 bn.
(26.5%)

Income Support[f]
£17.6 bn.
(9.3%)

Child Benefit
£7.5 bn.
(5.0%)

Disability Benefit
£9.1 bn.
(5.0%)

Housing Benefit
£12.2 bn.
(6.4%)

Other
£3.7 bn.
(0.9%)

BENEFITS IN KIND
£92.1 bn. (48.6%)

NHS[d]
£51.2 bn.
(27.0%)

EDUCATION
£36.8 bn.
(19.4%)

HOUSING
£4.0 bn.
(2.1%)

Fig. 1.1 **Overview of the welfare state, UK, 1996/7 (estimated out-turn)**

a Estimated figure.
b Total general government expenditure, including current and capital spending and debt interest.
c Figure greater than sum of its parts because expenditure on administration has been included.
d Of which £41 billion health care, £10 billion personal social services
e Includes widows' benefit.
f Includes £2.4 billion income–based jobseeker's allowance.

Source: UK Treasury (1997: tables 1.1, 3.5)

the parent or guardian of every child), and income support (i.e. social assistance for people with little or no other income). The major benefits in kind are the National Health Service (27 per cent of total social spending), education (19 per cent), and housing (2 per cent, plus substantial additional expenditure on cash assistance with housing costs).

2.2. The objectives of the welfare state

The objectives of social institutions, as in any other area of economic policy, are efficiency, equity, and administrative feasibility. In this context, however, it is useful to adopt a more detailed categorization.

EFFICIENCY has at least three aspects.

1. *Macro-efficiency*. The efficient fraction of GDP should be devoted to the totality of welfare-state institutions—for example, policy should seek to avoid distortions which lead to cost explosions.

2. *Micro-efficiency*. Policy should ensure the efficient division of total welfare-state resources between the different cash benefits, different types of medical treatment, and different kinds of education.

3. *Incentives*. Where institutions are publicly funded, their finance and the construction of benefits should minimize adverse effects (*a*) on labour supply and employment, and (*b*) on saving.

Objectives 1–3 are different aspects of *allocative efficiency*, sometimes—particularly in the context of health care and education—referred to as *external efficiency*. As an example, if the objective of health policy is to maximize the health of the population, external efficiency is concerned with producing the quantity, quality, and mix of health interventions (including preventive care and education about diet and life style) which bring about the greatest improvement in health.

SUPPORTING LIVING STANDARDS, the second strategic aim, has at least three components.

4. *Poverty relief*. No individual or household should fall below a minimum standard of living. The aim could be to *eliminate* poverty or to *alleviate* it. As discussed in Chapter 6, there is no analytically satisfactory way of defining a poverty line, so that the definition of the minimum standard is largely normative. Once the poverty line has been decided, the effectiveness of the system is measured by statistics relating to *how many* people are below the poverty line ('headcount' measures), by *how much* ('poverty-gap' measures), and for *how long* (life-cycle and intergenerational matters) (see Atkinson 1987*b*, 1995*a*: ch. 3).

5. *Insurance.* No one should face an unexpected and unacceptably large drop in her living standard. This is a major objective of unemployment benefits and most health-related benefits. Its success is measured by the replacement ratio, which shows a person's income when on benefit in comparison with her previous income.

6. *Income-smoothing.* Institutions should enable individuals to reallocate consumption over their lifetime. As discussed in Chapter 9, individuals can redistribute from themselves at one stage in the life cycle to themselves at another (an actuarial private pension scheme); or such redistribution could be notional (an unfunded state pension scheme which embodies an intergenerational social contract (Samuelson 1958)). Alternatively, there could be tax-funded provision, with no pretence of individual contributions, to groups whose stage in the life cycle suggests that they are likely to be financially constrained (e.g. benefits for families with young children).

Objectives 5 and 6 are different aspects of the broader aim of *economic security*. Objective 5 concerns unexpected reductions in living standards (i.e. it is mainly an insurance objective); objective 6 concerns predictable falls in income (i.e. it is more a savings objective). Both objectives therefore have an efficiency as well as an equity dimension.

THE REDUCTION OF INEQUALITY, in contrast, is almost entirely an equity issue.

7. *Vertical equity.* The system should redistribute towards individuals or families with lower incomes. This aim is contentious. All income-tested benefits contribute to it to a greater or lesser extent; so, secondly, do non-means-tested benefits whose recipients disproportionately have lower incomes (e.g. the UK flat-rate pension). A third form of redistribution arises where the benefit formula favours lower-income individuals. 'Free' provision of a tax-funded service (e.g. health care in the UK) is also generally redistributive. The success or otherwise of benefits in reducing inequality is assessed by inspection over time of aggregate inequality measures, though with all the caveats noted in Chapter 6.

8. *Horizontal equity.* Differences in benefits should take account of age, family size, etc., and differences in medical treatment should reflect only factors which are regarded as relevant (e.g. whether or not the patient has dependants), but not irrelevant factors like ethnic background.

SOCIAL INTEGRATION. So far the objectives have been conventional economic ones. Some commentators include broader social goals.

9. *Dignity.* Cash benefits and health care should be delivered so as to preserve individual dignity and without unnecessary stigma (Meade 1978: 269). Beveridge emphasized the importance of contributions in this context: 'The popularity of compulsory social insurance today is established, and for good reason; by

compulsory insurance . . . the individual can feel assured that [his] needs will be met . . . by paying . . . a contribution, he can feel that he is getting security not as a charity but as a right (Beveridge Report 1942: para. 296).

10. *Social solidarity*. Cash benefits and health care should foster social solidarity—a frequently stated goal in mainland Europe. So far as possible, benefits should depend on criteria which are unrelated to socioeconomic status. Retirement pensions are an example; so is medical care in many countries. Additionally, benefits should be high enough and health care good enough to allow recipients to participate fully in the life of the society in which they live—an aim which relates closely to the objective of poverty relief.

ADMINISTRATIVE FEASIBILITY has two aspects.

11. *Intelligibility*. The system should be simple, easy to understand, and as cheap to administer as possible.

12. *Absence of abuse*. Benefits should be as little open to abuse as possible.

PROBLEMS of definition and measurement abound. Efficiency objectives 1–3 have precise analytical definitions, but measurement problems—particularly the incidence of taxes, contributions, and benefits—make it difficult to assess how far they are achieved. How do we define a poverty line in objective 4; and how large a drop in living standard is 'unacceptable' (objective 5)? The appropriate extent of vertical redistribution and a workable definition of horizontal equity (objectives 7 and 8) have occupied economists, philosophers, and political theorists almost since the dawn of time, and have plagued policymakers at least since the British Poor Law Act of 1601. Even 'equality' is difficult to define unambiguously (Okun 1975: ch. 3; Le Grand 1982: ch. 2), especially in the context of benefits in kind like health care. Concepts such as 'dignity', 'stigma', and 'social solidarity' (objectives 9 and 10) are hard to define and raise major measurement problems. Writers like Hayek (1976) argue in addition that the term 'social solidarity' is devoid of meaning, and that its pursuit is both pointless and dangerous. These problems are discussed in some detail in Chapters 3–6.

Even were these problems assumed away, a second set of difficulties arises, in that some objectives are inherently in conflict and others may be. The trade-off between efficiency and distributional objectives is no less intractable for its familiarity; the same is true of the trade-off between horizontal equity and administrative simplicity. Other objectives conflict almost by definition. Income-smoothing implies that an individual with higher earnings should receive higher benefits, which sits uneasily with the requirement that benefits should redistribute towards those with lower incomes, and with the objective that benefits should contribute to social solidarity. On one interpretation of equity everyone should receive benefits proportional to their past contributions, but that, again, conflicts both with redistribution towards lower incomes and with social solidarity. The choice of objectives and of priorities between them is a fundamental normative issue.

3. A changing world: Challenges and responses

A number of trends, though they may have been discernible for a long time, have major implications for the design of the welfare state (for a review, see Esping-Andersen 1996*a*) and recur throughout the book.

DEMOGRAPHIC CHANGE. Life expectancy has increased in all industrial countries while birth rates have declined, simultaneously increasing the number of older people and reducing the number of younger workers. As a result, from about 2005 onwards, the ratio of people over 60 to those of working age will increase sharply. If present policies continue unchanged, spending on pensions and health care in some countries is set to double. Policies to accommodate these changes are discussed in detail in Chapter 9.

GLOBALIZATION. The trend to globalization has at least two roots. First, since 1970 the international trade regime has become more and more open. Secondly, as a result of technological change, an increasing amount of economic activity is, in Quah's terminology, 'dematerialized'—that is, it is in the form of encoded binary bits (computer programs, e-mail messages, music videos, and the like) rather than in solid form such as a Boeing 747. One of many implications of this trend, according to Quah (1996: 7), is that 'international trade becomes not a matter of shipping wine and textiles . . . but of bouncing bits off satellites'. In these circumstances, national boundaries become less relevant.

For both sets of reasons, globalization reduces the capacity of any country to act independently in designing its institutions, including its welfare-state arrangements. Countries with expensive welfare states, it is argued, will increasingly be at a competitive disadvantage relative to those with more parsimonious ones. At the same time, however, demands on the welfare state are rising: there are more old people, and in many countries rising numbers of unemployed; in addition, as discussed below, there are more lone-parent families, and increasing numbers of low-paid and part-time workers.

CHANGES IN FAMILY STRUCTURE. Family structures have changed in several ways. First, they have become more fluid. The institutions of the immediate post-war period assumed an archetypal nuclear family: the main (frequently the only) source of income was the wages of the husband; and husband and wife stayed married, so that the husband's pension entitlement also covered his wife. Though not wholly valid even then, the assumption was true enough to form the basis of most social policy. Today, in contrast, many more marriages end in divorce; and parenthood is less closely tied to marriage. These changes have major implications for social policy, particularly so far as child support and pension arrangements for women are concerned.

A second set of changes arises from the increasing number of women who have jobs outside the home: 'one of the greatest challenges for the future welfare state is how to harmonize women's employment with family formation. Women demand employment and greater economic independence; [and] the family is more likely to be flexible, and less likely to be poor, if it can rely on two earners . . .' (Esping-Andersen 1996*a*: 26–7).

CHANGES IN THE STRUCTURE OF JOBS. The nature of work is also changing. Post-industrial employment tends to favour professional and highly skilled occupations. The demand for unqualified workers is lower than in the past and, in consequence, their wages are low and their employment often precarious and part-time. There are worries about increasing polarization between a core of skilled workers and a peripheral workforce. Contributory social insurance is of doubtful relevance to the latter group.

RESULTING CHALLENGES AND RESPONSES. Two challenges stand out. A problem—both for economic policy and social policy—is the possibility that the strategic design of the welfare state is, at least in part, based on a past social order with stable, two-parent families, with high levels of employment, and where most jobs were full-time and relatively stable.

Secondly, the conflict between economic growth and equality has become sharper over the years. 'The harmonious coexistence of full employment and income equalization that defined the postwar epoch appears no longer possible' (Esping-Andersen 1996*a*: 4). There is a major debate, discussed in Chapter 15, Section 2.2, about why this is so.

Despite much public discussion of a 'crisis' of the welfare state, change by the mid-1990s consisted mainly of marginal adjustments to existing systems. Esping-Andersen (1996*a*) distinguishes three broad approaches to economic and social change since the first oil shock of the 1970s.

The first (broadly that in the Scandinavian countries, and particularly in Sweden) was to try to increase the demand for labour through active labour-market policies and increased public-sector employment. The problem with this approach was its cost (see Lachman *et al.* 1995). By the mid-1990s, Sweden faced major fiscal problems at a time of rising pressure on public jobs. Part of the response was a move towards wage flexibility and a reduction, albeit marginal, in benefits.

A second approach—that in the rest of mainland Europe—tried to reduce the supply of labour, notably through early retirement. In many ways this is the Scandinavian solution by a different route: instead of finding jobs, frequently in the public sector, for people who would otherwise be unemployed, this approach tries to open up jobs by offering early retirement, either explicitly or through the award of a disability pension. The cost in this case is not that of public employment but of public pensions. The approach is coming under increasing fiscal pressure.

The third approach—broadly the Anglo-Saxon model (the UK, USA, Australia, and New Zealand)—sought to increase the demand for labour by liberalizing labour markets, not least through increased wage flexibility. This approach has two advantages: it does not face the heavy fiscal cost of the Scandinavian or mainland European arrangements; and employment growth in the Anglo-Saxon countries over the 1980s was significantly higher than in the rest of the OECD. The besetting problem of the approach is rising inequality and poverty, particularly among unskilled workers and single-parent households.

Concepts

This book is primarily about what economic theory tells us about how to respond to these challenges. The resulting debates are drawn together in the concluding part of the final chapter.

FURTHER READING

The diversity of sources of welfare is discussed by Glennerster (1997: ch. 1). Titmuss (1958) and Briggs (1961*a*) attempt to define the welfare state; see also Esping-Anderson (1990). On the idea of welfare, see William A. Robson (1976), Pinker (1979), and Higgins (1981).

Esping-Andersen (1996*b*) gives a wide-ranging overview of the challenges facing welfare states across a broad range of countries, including the former Communist countries, Latin America, and the newly industrializing countries of East Asia. See also Blank (1994), OECD (1994), and, for a view of Sweden which does not pull its punches, Lindbeck (1994, 1997*b*).

CHAPTER 2

The historical background

The principle of *laissez-faire* may be safely trusted to in some things but in many more it is wholly inapplicable; and to appeal to it on all occasions savours more of the policy of a parrot than of a statesman or a philosopher.

J. R. McCulloch, 1848

The poverty of the poor is the chief cause of that weakness and inefficiency which are the cause of their poverty.

Alfred Marshall, 1885

The UK welfare state is neither the outcome of the Second World War nor simply the creation of the first post-war Labour government. Its roots are ancient and complex. Christian charity to relieve poverty has gradually (though even today not wholly) been taken over by state action. And state activity has grown over the years from small scale to large; from local to central; from permissive to mandatory; and from piecemeal to complex and interrelated. From this tangle, however, four events stand out: the *Poor Law Act* 1601 and the *Poor Law Amendment Act* 1834 were the main legislative bases of poverty relief before the twentieth century; the *Liberal reforms* of 1906–14 represented a substantial departure from *laissez-faire* capitalism and so can be argued to form the basis of the welfare state; and the *post-war legislation* of 1944–8 set the foundations of the welfare state as we know it today.

It should be clear that the question 'how did the welfare state come about?' is vast, so discussion is limited in two important ways. No attempt is made at complete coverage; the story is confined for the most part to the experience of the UK, with only a sideways glance at other countries, notably the USA. The question is also controversial; I shall sketch out the major areas of historical dispute, but make no attempt at resolving them. The chapter is organized chronologically, discussing seriatim the period up to the end of the nineteenth century (Section 1); the Liberal reforms of 1906–14 (Section 2); developments in the UK between the two world wars (Section 3); inter-war poverty relief in the USA (Section 4); the Second World War and its immediate aftermath in the UK (Section 5); and developments since 1948 in the UK and the USA (Section 6). Section 7 draws the threads together by considering the forces which created the welfare state.

1. Early days

1.1. Poor relief

Among the early motives for public poor relief in Britain were the fear of social disorder and chronic labour shortages in the years after the Black Death of 1348–9. As a result, the state attempted, *inter alia*, to control wages and labour mobility in the Statute of Labourers 1351 and the Poor Law Act 1388. Tudor legislation grew away from this repressive and not very effective regime:

In 1576 the concept of 'setting the poor on work' was enshrined in statute law where it was to remain for something like three and a half centuries. If the able-bodied required assistance they had to work for it, and in the 1576 Poor Relief Act [magistrates] were instructed to provide a stock of raw materials on which beggars could work in return for the relief they received.

(Fraser 1984: 32)

THE 1601 POOR LAW ACT, built on the 1576 Act, adopted a twofold approach: each parish was required to assume responsibility for its poor; and different treatment was prescribed for three categories of pauper. The 'impotent poor' (the old and the sick) were to be accommodated in 'almshouses'; the able-bodied were to be given work in a 'house of correction' (not at first a residential workhouse); and those who refused to work were to be punished in this 'house of correction'. The idea was that paupers not able to work should be cared for and the able-bodied should be given work; neither regime was intended to be punitive.

This arrangement worked moderately well for nearly 200 years; but eventually its institutions, locally financed and adapted to a pre-industrial economy, came under pressure from population growth, increased social mobility, industrialization, and economic fluctuations. By 1795 food shortages and inflation resulting from war and bad harvests had spread poverty from the unemployed to those in work, giving rise to various local initiatives, notably the Speenhamland system which supplemented wages with an 'allowance' based on the price of bread. The novelty of these changes was that they extended aid to people in work. Poor relief, whether under the Poor Law *per se* or under a local variant, carried less social stigma than it was later to acquire.

These arrangements soon came under attack. Bentham believed that they caused moral degeneracy among recipients. Malthus argued that poor relief would cause excessive population growth, and Ricardo that it would depress wages and thereby exacerbate poverty. Possibly more important than these theoretical arguments was the escalating cost of relief, partly due to rising prices (especially of bread), and also because of rising unemployment as soldiers returned from the Napoleonic Wars. As a result, the costs (which were met from local revenues) rose sharply.

THE POOR LAW REPORT AND THE POOR LAW AMENDMENT ACT 1834 were consequences of this philosophical and financial climate. A Royal Commission was set up in 1832. Its report, which was *laissez-faire* in tone, was written by Nassau Senior and Edwin Chadwick, a former secretary to Bentham. The intellectual background to the report, and particularly the position of the classical economists on the Poor Law, is often misunderstood. It is true that Malthus and Ricardo, worried by population growth and shocked by the earlier effect of the Poor Law, advocated its gradual repeal. But it is *not* the case that Nassau Senior (who was, according to Robbins, more in the mainstream of classical thought) was against poor relief. In Senior's view, 'the great test which must be applied to any project of state action in regard to relief is the question *whether it has any tendency to increase that which it is proposed to diminish*' (Robbins 1977: 128, emphasis in original). Thus, he supported public provision for orphans, the blind, and the disabled, including provision of medical treatment and hospitals. He was not in favour of abolishing relief for the able-bodied and their dependants, but insisted on the principle of 'less eligibility'—that is, that relief should be limited to an amount and administered in a manner which left the recipient worse off than the employed.

The Poor Law Report was entirely consistent with this approach when it argued that the new system should contain three elements (often referred to as 'the Principles of 1834'): the notion of less eligibility, the workhouse test, and administrative centralization. Less eligibility was the central doctrine of 1834. It was not intended to apply to the old or sick, but only to the able-bodied whose indigence, it was argued, would be encouraged by higher benefits.[1] The workhouse test (i.e. relief conditional upon living in the workhouse) was not a principle, but simply a means of enforcing less eligibility. As far as possible, the workhouse would provide a standard of living lower than that of the lowest worker. Additional restrictions were imposed, including the strict segregation of husbands, wives, and children. The purpose of centralization was to avoid local corruption and incompetence; to ensure uniformity; to enhance cost effectiveness; and to promote labour mobility. The difference between the 1601 Poor Law and the Principles of 1834 is important. The former was intended to give work to the able-bodied without stigma; the latter discouraged claims for relief by making its receipt highly unpleasant and also stigmatizing.

The Poor Law Amendment Act followed quickly in the wake of the Poor Law Report. Despite controversy among historians, it is now clear that, though the intention of the Act was largely (though in important respects not fully) to implement the recommendations of the report, the effect of the Act in practice was less than appeared in principle. The Poor Law Commission (in whom the powers of central government were vested) was never able to bend local administration of the Poor Law to its will, particularly in respect of enforcing the workhouse test. But in other respects, it is argued, the implementation of the Act had more unpleasant effects than was intended by its architects (Bowley 1937: pt. II, ch. 2). Many people were forced to accept the harsh conditions of the workhouse, and many others endured appalling privation to avoid it. Because of

---

[1] Readers may note more than a passing similarity between these arguments of more than 150 years ago, and the more recent debates discussed in Sections 6 and 7. Some commentators argue that part of the Poor Law spirit persists—e.g. the decline in unemployment benefit relative to other benefits in the UK in the 1980s can be interpreted as a case of less eligibility.

its very cruelty, however, the system became over time a force for change, and thus the 1834 Act may be seen as one of the roots of later developments.

1.2. Other early social legislation

Notwithstanding the philosophical underpinnings of the Principles of 1834, *laissez-faire* was increasingly eroded over the nineteenth century.

FACTORY LEGISLATION. The first Factory Act, passed in 1802, protected women and children by limiting hours and regulating working conditions. Althorp's Factory Act 1833 tightened the rules and, probably of greater long-run importance, appointed four inspectors to enforce its provisions. The latter was implicit acknowledgement of the right of the state to regulate certain social conditions.

EDUCATION. The role of the state in education started more gradually (Edwin West 1970; Fraser 1984: ch. 4). Most schools in the early nineteenth century were charitable and reflected the prevailing ethos of social deference, Christian morality, and voluntarism. The Sunday school movement had an important role in teaching reading, often with the Bible as the only text. State intervention started in 1833 with a grant to Protestant schools for school-building—i.e. as financial help for voluntarism—and from 1847 a grant was paid for a limited scheme of teacher-training. As government involvement grew, a Royal Commission was established, though its recommendations were largely superseded by the Education Act 1870, which gave every child the right (at least in principle) to some form of schooling. School Boards were empowered (but not compelled) to provide elementary education, financed by a mixture of central and local revenues. The resulting system was a compromise in which the new board schools coexisted with the voluntary sector. Later developments made elementary school attendance compulsory between 5 and 10 (Mundella's Education Act 1880) and virtually free (the Fee Grant Act 1891).

Thus a process of gradual accretion over the nineteenth century led to a system of primary education which was compulsory and largely publicly funded. Of the many explanations of these changes one in particular is a recurring theme—the *national-efficiency* argument, which justified state involvement in education on the grounds that it made labour more productive, thus contributing to economic growth. It is also argued that the 1870 Act was encouraged by the extension of the franchise in 1867, creating a need to educate the growing electorate.

PUBLIC-HEALTH ACTIVITIES were the third breach in *laissez-faire* (Fraser 1984: ch. 3; Finer 1952: chs. 5, 7, and 8). In the first half of the nineteenth century, urbanization (largely the result of the Industrial Revolution) and population growth caused cities to grow rapidly, leading to a housing shortage and, connected with it, a sanitation problem. The poor in particular were afflicted by typhus and tuberculosis; and a series of cholera epidemics, being water-borne, attacked everyone, including the middle classes with their ready access to water supplies.

This was the problem. The solution again involves Edwin Chadwick (1842), whose *Inquiry into the Sanitary Condition of the Labouring Population of Great Britain* was remarkable for the high quality of its statistical analysis. Chadwick originally advocated sewage disposal as a public enterprise on the grounds that ill health, by causing poverty, added to the cost of the Poor Law. The report, however, included wider grounds for intervention. Its main recommendation (though based on a faulty theory of the transmission of cholera) was that sewage should be separated from other water through the use of glazed pipes. The report met considerable opposition, both technical and based on financial, ideological, and political arguments. As a result, legislation was delayed and initially ineffective. After several false starts, the Public Health Act 1875 established clear duties for local authorities, and remained the basis of most public-health activities until 1936.

This, then, was the situation in the 1870s. The state was slowly becoming involved in increasing areas of social and economic life; but, though the classical economists supported much of the new legislation, the prevailing doctrine was still largely *laissez-faire*.

2. The Liberal reforms

2.1. The origins of the reforms

The next major development was the period of the Liberal reforms between 1906 and 1914.[2] Historians have debated at length this burst of activity so much at variance with the ideology of the nineteenth-century Liberal Party. Hay (1975) distinguishes three influences in particular which historians regard as underlying the reforms: pressure from below, changing attitudes to welfare provision, and institutional influences.

PRESSURE FROM BELOW. There is a measure of agreement that working-class political pressure was one of the origins of the reforms, though the relationship is far from simple. If reform was so popular, why was it not a major election issue; and why the long lag between electoral reform in 1867 and social reform in 1906–14? Pelling (1979: 18) deals with the problem by denying the premiss, arguing that working-class pressure was negligible:

The members of the working class as a whole, cynical about the character of society as they knew it, were yet fearful of change which would more likely be for the worse than for the better. They advanced into the twentieth century with little expectation of social improvement being engineered by political means, and none at all of the 'welfare state' as we know it today.

---

[2] This section draws on Hay (1975). See also the Further Reading.

Concepts

Hobsbawm (1964) argues that it was only unorganized workers who opposed reform. Nor was working-class pressure necessarily important for all the reforms.

CHANGING ATTITUDES to welfare provision among the political élite arose *inter alia* out of the national-efficiency issue. The argument at its simplest was that economic growth depended on a healthy, educated workforce. In dramatic contrast with the Principles of 1834, a speaker in parliamentary debate could argue: 'The future of the Empire, the triumph of social progress and the freedom of the British race depend not so much upon the strengthening of the Army as upon fortifying the children of the State for the battle of life' (*Hansard* (Commons), 18 Apr. 1905, col. 539, quoted by Bruce 1972: 152–3). The influence of the national-efficiency arguments is debated. At a minimum they made social reform politically respectable.

A second reason for greater acceptance of intervention was a changed attitude towards poverty. Social surveys by Rowntree (1901) and Booth (1902) and the study of the health of Boer War recruits yielded much empirical information. The effects of these data on attitudes were complex; they suggested that poverty was more widespread than had been believed, and that not all poverty, even among the able-bodied, was due to moral defect. They also raised doubts about the effectiveness of private philanthropy.[3]

A third influence was the rise of collectivism. The 'Old Liberalism', which was opposed to state intervention, had twofold roots in the 'natural-rights' individualist philosophy of writers like Spencer (1884) and in utilitarianism.[4] Between 1860 and 1900, however, several philosophers, though in no sense advocating collectivism, suggested that the traditional definition of individual freedom as *absence of coercion* was too narrow. It was argued (e.g. Hobson 1909: pt. II, ch. II) that 'positive freedom' should include not only economic freedom but also a measure of *economic security*. It followed that the state, in advancing individual freedom, should adopt an active role in social reform. This was the 'New Liberalism' (Freeden 1978).

In the context of these changing ideas the German example became important. Between 1883 and 1889, largely as a counter to socialist agitation, the German government under Bismarck had created a broad system of social insurance under which compulsory contributions gave entitlement to a system of guaranteed benefits, thereby removing the threat of the means test and poor house. The scheme was investigated by Lloyd George, and had a major influence on the shape of the National Insurance Act 1911 (discussed below).

INSTITUTIONAL INFLUENCES on the reforms included pressure groups such as the Friendly Societies, which represented the idea of working-class self-help. It is also argued that bureaucracies like the civil service exerted an independent influence. McDonagh (1960)

---

[3] For the view that poverty was 'discovered' much earlier, see Himmelfarb (1984).

[4] The important distinction between a natural-rights and a utilitarian defence of individual freedom is discussed at length in Chapter 3, which also discusses the ideas of collectivist writers.

describes a process whereby, as awareness of a problem grew, a body of experts would be set up to investigate. As a result of its findings, awareness of the problem increased, and so did the volume of resources devoted to combating it. Experts thus contributed not only to the *manner* in which social problems were tackled, but also to the *range* of issues regarded as the proper province of public policy.[5]

The reforms were central rather than local mainly because of the reluctance of central government (despite several official inquiries) to reform local-authority finance in the light of regional inequalities, and the failure of local revenues to rise in step with expenditure.[6] Finally, the reforms were outside the Poor Law partly because the latter was financed locally; partly to sidestep the long-established vested interests of local Poor Law institutions; and partly because of popular hostility towards the old system.

2.2. The new measures

Whatever their causes (about which historians continue to argue) and motives (discussed below), the reforms of 1906–14 were substantial by any standards and particularly so in the context of the times. The new measures concerned children, pensions, unemployment, health, and fiscal policy.

CHILDREN. The Education (Provision of Meals) Act 1906 permitted (but did not compel) local authorities to provide school meals for needy children; the Education (Administrative Provisions) Act 1907 introduced medical inspection of schoolchildren; and the Children Act 1908 made it a punishable offence for parents to neglect their children. The motives for these Acts were partly humanitarian and partly on national-efficiency grounds.

PENSIONS. The Old Age Pensions Act 1908 'introduced a new principle into social policy. Hitherto relief had been provided . . . from *local* funds and only after a test of destitution. Now for the first time payments were to be made, as of right, from *national* funds . . . within strict limits of age and means, but with no test of actual destitution' (Bruce 1972: 178, emphasis in original). The Act introduced a non-contributory pension of five shillings (25 pence) per week for people over 70 whose income was below £31 per year, though it excluded previous recipients of Poor Law relief, and some people on moral grounds.[7]

---

[5] The government-failure literature discussed in Chapter 4, Section 5, argues that these forces can go too far and create inefficient upwards pressure on the size of government.

[6] The owner of my borrowed copy of Hay has written 'so what's new?' in the margin.

[7] History is full of small anomalies. An additional reason for the pensions legislation, according to Pelling (1979: 11), was 'a loosening of the Treasury's purse strings (because of) the temporary lull in the naval building race, which was due to the destruction of Russian battleships in the Russo-Japanese War . . . Thus in a sense it was Admiral Togo, the victor of Tsushima, who laid the groundwork of Old Age Pensions and deserves to be remembered as the architect of the British Welfare State.'

Concepts

UNEMPLOYMENT AND MINIMUM WAGES. Various earlier proposals to resolve the growing problem of unemployment had met with little success (see Harris 1972). Any acceptable solution had to meet four criteria (Hay 1975: 50–1). It had to 'make the minimum alterations in the normal workings of the labour market to satisfy individualists, economists and industrialists'. Secondly, 'it . . . had to be largely self-financing in order to avoid unacceptable increases in direct taxation or the reintroduction of tariffs'. It had to be separate from the Poor Law to avoid the need to discriminate between the 'deserving' and 'undeserving' poor. Lastly, it had to be sufficiently attractive to head off any socialist threat. The resulting package had three elements: voluntary labour exchanges would assist the normal working of the labour market; there was to be a limited scheme of unemployment insurance; and a Development Fund would finance counter-cyclical public-works expenditure, mainly by local authorities.

The scheme of unemployment insurance was limited: it applied only to a narrow range of industries; only workers earning less than £160 per year were covered; and benefits were low, to discourage deliberate unemployment. A variety of other industrial legislation, including the Trades Disputes Act and the Workmen's Compensation Act in 1906, and the Trade Boards Act 1909, gave the government limited power to set minimum wages. It was recognized that unemployment and sickness were interrelated, so the National Insurance Act 1911 also contained health insurance. The combined package was financed by a weekly contribution of 9*d.* (3.75 pence), of which 4*d.* (1.67 pence) was paid by the worker, the rest by the employer.

HEALTH. Whereas unemployment insurance, according to Hay, was largely the result of working-class pressure, health insurance arose more from considerations of national efficiency. Prior to 1911 there were voluntary hospitals for those who could afford to subscribe to them; for others Poor Law hospitals offered free and (for the most part) non-stigmatizing health care (Abel Smith 1964: ch. 15). The 1911 Act did little to change these arrangements. Cover was extended only to the breadwinner, who was entitled to a sickness (i.e. cash) benefit, free medical treatment and drugs from a panel doctor, and access to a sanatorium.

FISCAL POLICY. The fiscal controversies of the period concerned tariffs (which are not the issue here), and progressive income tax. The traditional economic argument was that taxation should be based on the principle of 'equal sacrifice' (implying a poll tax), or of 'equi-proportional sacrifice' (implying a proportional tax). Both approaches ruled out redistribution through the tax system. By the turn of the century, however, there was limited support for redistribution through tax-financed public expenditure. Edgeworth justified progressive taxation by appeal to the 'least-aggregate-sacrifice' principle under which *marginal* rather than *total* sacrifice was to be equalized. Equal marginal sacrifice plus the assumption of diminishing marginal utility of income together imply progressive taxation.

A different line of argument by people like Hobson (1908) was that monopoly elements resulted in a suboptimal income distribution, leading to under-consumption. By thus attributing unemployment to under-consumption which could be remedied by income redistribution, Hobson foreshadowed Keynes some thirty years before the publication of *The General Theory*. Others, notably socialists, saw progressive taxation as an issue of social justice, a subject to which we return in Chapter 3.

BRIEF ASSESSMENT. In assessing the reforms, two hotly debated issues arise: what was their motive (discussed in Section 7.1); and were they particularly radical? It can be argued (Marsh 1980: 17) that the virtually simultaneous introduction of old-age pensions, unemployment insurance, sickness benefits, and progressive taxation, supported by the interventionist philosophy of the New Liberalism, constituted a fundamental break with earlier economic and political doctrines.

However, a closer look at the individual programmes gives a less clear answer. The pension scheme, albeit non-contributory, was to some extent means-tested, and applied only to individuals over 70 who had never received poor relief and were not excluded on moral grounds. Its main purpose, it can be argued, was to improve national competitiveness by weeding out inefficient labour (the national-efficiency argument again). Unemployment insurance was based in part on a weekly employee contribution of 4*d*. (i.e. lump sum and therefore regressive), and applied only to a few relatively skilled workers in some industries. Sickness benefits were financed by the same contribution, with similar coverage; and the health-care benefits applied only to the breadwinner. It can be argued, therefore, that the reforms were relatively minor and had limited coverage; and that only the pension scheme was substantially redistributive from rich to poor. The New Liberalism, from this viewpoint, was not very new; it still accepted capitalism unquestioningly, and in that sense was only a reinterpretation of the Old Liberalism. As we shall see in Section 4, strikingly similar issues arise in considering the novelty (or otherwise) of the 1935 US Social Security Act.

Nor, in conclusion, were the Liberal reforms in any way unique. Germany, as we have seen, had introduced social insurance in the 1880s, motivated in part by fears of social unrest. New Zealand introduced non-contributory pensions in 1898, *inter alia* for reasons of national efficiency, in the face of increased international competition on an economy highly dependent on its exports. By 1908 Denmark, Ireland, Austria, Czechoslovakia, and Australia also had social legislation of some sort. The Liberal reforms, though one of the earlier examples of nationally organized income support, were not the first; nor did they represent a major discontinuity either with previous arrangements or with developments in other countries.

3. The First World War and the inter-war period in the UK

3.1. Housing

In contrast with the eventful years between 1906 and 1914, the period thereafter was largely a time of stagnation in social policy, with the important exception of housing. There were also major changes in unemployment insurance (Section 3.2).

THE ROOTS OF STATE INVOLVEMENT. In housing, probably more than any other part of the welfare state, past policies, notably during and after the First World War, have a crucial bearing on more recent institutions. Before 1914, virtually all housing was provided by the private market. By and large the system worked well for those who could afford it, but for the lowest income groups, particularly in large cities, it led to overcrowding and squalor (Gauldie 1974). In a strictly technical sense the housing market cleared, but policy-makers found the result unacceptable both for reasons of public health and public order, and for more charitable motives. Early legislation had little effect, mainly because it imposed no *duty* on local authorities to remedy poor housing. Though working-class housing conditions continued to cause concern in the latter part of the nineteenth century, the response was limited mainly to philanthropic efforts (see Merrett 1979).

By 1918, however, for at least three reasons, housing had become a problem for which existing methods were no longer regarded as adequate. First, there was an acute housing shortage because of falling supply (due to the cessation of building during the First World War, and the deterioration of older property) and rising demand (because people were living longer and marrying earlier, and mobility among young people was increasing). Secondly, this shortage was regarded as politically too sensitive to be left to private charity and discretionary local action. In 1918 large numbers of soldiers were demobilized, and there were fears of social unrest (the Russian Revolution having occurred in the previous year). Lloyd George's promise in November 1918 'to make Britain a fit country for heroes to live in' was seen as a commitment on which it would have been politically dangerous to renege.

The third reason why housing was thought to warrant government action was because intervention had already occurred, through the imposition of rent control in 1915 as an emergency wartime measure. As we shall see in Chapter 14, rent control is rather like smoking—if one never starts one can do without, but once started it is hard to give up. By 1918 many people were unable to pay the market price of housing, which had risen sharply because of the shortage; at least as important, controlled rents had already assumed an aura of 'fair' rents.

Since immediate decontrol was politically impossible, the government chose to assume some responsibility for people dependent on renting at the lower end of the market, through direct provision of housing at rents equivalent to controlled rents.

RESULTING ACTION. The resulting Housing and Town Planning Act 1919 (the Addison Act) contained three provisions: local authorities were invested with the *duty* of remedying housing deficiencies in their areas; house-building was to meet *general* needs rather than concentrating only on slum clearance; and the operation received a central government subsidy which underwrote the entire cost of house-building in excess of the product of a penny rate.[8] In contrast with nineteenth-century thought, the Act embodied three new principles—central supervision, compulsion, and subsidy. It had three long-term effects: the acceptance of housing as a legitimate area of government intervention, in the sense of public production as opposed only to regulation; the provision of accommodation at a subsidized rent, implying a view of housing as a social service; and the delivery of service by local authorities. The Act, together with rent control, laid a foundation for housing policy which lasted well into the post-war period.

The Addison Act met with some success. However, generous subsidies, when the capacity of the building industry was already stretched by private-sector demand, led inevitably to soaring costs; and, when the post-war boom faltered, the resulting public-spending cuts (the so-called Geddes axe) halted expenditure under the Act. Chamberlain's Housing Act 1923 reduced the subsidy and laid the burden of excessive costs on local revenues. But the subsidy was too small to help the worst off, and the scheme was used mainly by private builders for moderately priced houses for the middle class and the more affluent section of the working class. The hope that a process of 'filtering up' would free cheaper housing for the less well off remained unfulfilled, partly because controlled rents reduced housing mobility (a recurring theme). The Labour government of 1924 recognized that the subsidies were failing to reach the people who needed them most (another recurring theme). The Wheatley Act 1924 increased the subsidy on condition that it was used for houses to be let at controlled rents subsidized from local revenues. This stimulated local-authority building, and the Wheatley and Chamberlain schemes operated side by side, finally coming to an end in 1933 when it was felt that the housing shortage had been resolved.

In sum, the First World War and its aftermath saw the introduction of rent control and the provision of subsidized housing by local authorities. But not everyone shared in the gains. Though the overall size of the housing stock increased, there remained a shortage of accommodation at rents the poor could afford. In particular, much local-authority housing remained beyond the reach of poorer workers, who still relied largely on the private sector, a fact recognized by the 1938 Housing Act which continued rent control on smaller houses. It can be argued that the continuation of rent control perpetuated the initial shortage; there remained little incentive for the private sector to provide rented accommodation for the less well off. And the continuing story of local-authority housing (Chapter 14) was one of considerable subsidy, uneconomic rents, and long waiting lists persisting into the 1990s.

---

[8] i.e. the revenue raised by increasing local rates (property taxes) by 0.4 pence in the pound.

3.2. Unemployment insurance

From 1920 to 1940 unemployment never fell below one million and reached a peak of over three million, in the face of which unemployment insurance qua insurance virtually collapsed. The story in many other countries involves similar problems, similar debates, and, in broad terms, similar solutions (Kaim-Caudle 1973). The case of the USA is taken up in Section 4.

DEVELOPMENTS IN THE 1920s. The Unemployment Insurance Act 1920 extended the 1911 Act to more workers, and also paid an allowance for dependants. It was introduced hastily in the face of rising unemployment after the war, not least among demobilized soldiers. The Act was doomed to failure, since rising unemployment inevitably undermined the insurance aspect of the scheme. This led to continual juggling with contribution and benefit levels, and to a series of devices which sought to preserve the fiction of insurance while in reality paying benefits not financed by contributions, thereby violating the insurance principle. The payment of such benefits out of the insurance fund was partly because the locally financed Poor Law could not cope with mass unemployment and, equally important, because the unemployed strenuously resisted the Poor Law. The realization grew only slowly that insurance has problems even with short-term unemployment, and is totally inadequate in the face of long-term or mass unemployment (a central topic of Chapters 5 and 8).

As a result of the report of the Blanesburgh Committee, two benefits were introduced in 1927. Standard benefit was paid as an insurance benefit of indefinite duration to anyone who had made *any* contributions. Transitional benefit was payable as of right to those who did not satisfy even the minimal requirements of the insurance scheme, provided that they were 'genuinely seeking work'. Both benefits were paid from the insurance fund. Transitional benefit protected the unemployed from the Poor Law, which was reorganized in 1929, when the powers of the Guardians were transferred to Public Assistance Committees (PACs) run by local authorities.

In 1930 the Labour government changed the regulations for transitional benefit in two ways: they made the benefit a charge on the Consolidated Fund (i.e. general government revenues) rather than the insurance fund; and they relaxed the 'genuinely seeking work' clause. As a result, the numbers receiving transitional benefit doubled within two months, at a cost of £19 million in its first year, just as the economic crisis came to a head.

THE 1931 CRISIS AND THE BENEFIT CUTS. By the late 1920s one strand of policy was concerned with how unemployment benefits should be arranged and financed; another concentrated on the economic crisis more generally, and particularly on how unemployment could be reduced. Economic radicals, most obviously Keynes, with support from the Liberal Party and from various politicians in other parties, favoured expansionary public-works expenditure. Economic conservatives such as Prime Minister Ramsay MacDonald and Chancellor Philip Snowden followed the traditional orthodoxy, supporting expenditure cuts, a balanced budget, and lower government borrowing.[9] In the 1931 crisis the economic conservatives dominated. The decision to preserve the gold standard by stringent fiscal and monetary policy, particularly a cut in unemployment benefit, split the Labour Cabinet and led to the formation of a National Government under Ramsay MacDonald. In the face of expenditure cuts, unemployment and controversy mounted.

The rapid escalation of benefit payments at a time of economic crisis led to immediate action. Benefits were cut by 10 per cent from 17s. (85 pence) to 15s. 3d. (76 pence) in 1931. Standard benefit was limited to twenty-six weeks, and the administration of transitional benefit (renamed transitional payment) was transferred to the local PACs, though still paid from central funds.

It is a matter of controversy whether *real* benefits fell, since prices had also declined. Between 1921 and 1931 the overall price of consumer goods fell by about 28 per cent, and those of food, clothing, and fuel and light by even more. Compared with 1927 (when standard and transitional benefits were introduced), the price of consumer goods fell by 8 per cent, though the price of housing increased by 2 per cent (Feinstein 1972: tables 61, 62). Possibly of greater importance as an explanation of the anger engendered by the cuts was the manner of their implementation. The role of the PACs in this context was crucial, and had ramifications for the relief of poverty which survive to the present. Eligibility for benefit was tightened, though with regional variation, which was itself a further cause of anger. The interpretation of the 'genuinely seeking work' condition became more harsh. Additionally, from 1931, in sharp contrast with arrangements after 1927, the PACs administered transitional payment on the basis of the stringent Poor Law *household* means test, which 'like the workhouse before it, was destined to leave an indelible mark on popular culture . . . long after its official demise . . . Receipt of transitional payment through the PACs in effect put the unemployed right back on to the Poor Law' (Fraser 1984: 194).

It is often not appreciated that the desperate plight of many of the unemployed in the 1930s was not typical of the country as a whole. The unemployment rate varied widely between regions, and long-term unemployment was concentrated in a limited number of decaying areas. While the unemployed suffered, living standards rose substantially for those in regular work.

THE UNEMPLOYMENT ACT 1934 was based on the report of the Holman Gregory Royal Commission in 1932, whose main recommendation was the complete separation of unemployment insurance proper from measures to support the long-term unemployed. The Act, consequently, was divided into two parts. Part I extended compulsory insurance to more workers; restored benefits to their level prior to the 1931 cut; organized contributions on the basis of one-third each from worker, employer, and government; and established an independent committee to run the scheme, with responsibility only for those receiving *insurance* benefits. Part II dealt with unemployment assistance for people with no insurance cover, or whose cover had expired. Benefits were paid from

---

[9] The parallel with debates fifty years later is striking.

general government funds, and run on a *national* basis by the newly established Un-employment Assistance Board. Payment was on the basis of need, in the light of family circumstances. The principle of less eligibility was finally laid to rest. Sixteen years after the end of the First World War, the UK had a system of unemployment relief which worked reasonably smoothly.

The social measures of the 1906–14 period were inadequate for the mass unemployment of the inter-war years. The Widows, Orphans and Age Contributory Pensions Act 1925 (extended by a further Act in 1929) introduced the first national scheme of contributory pensions; the 1911 health-insurance scheme was enlarged; and there was action on housing. For the most part this legislation was a product of the 1920s. In the 1930s the welfare state was in abeyance, and new measures were little more than crisis management. The main lesson for the future was that *laissez-faire* capitalism could not solve the problem of unemployment—in this area, too, state intervention was necessary. When intervention came, in the form of rearmament and war production, the unemployment problem disappeared—an unhappy way of ending an unhappy period in British social policy.

4. Inter-war poverty relief in the USA

4.1. The roots of the 'New Deal'

It is instructive at this stage briefly[10] to discuss contemporaneous events in the USA, where government involvement in income support (at least at the federal level) began late by international standards. There was no American equivalent of the Liberal reforms, nor any analogue to the broadening of the UK welfare system during and after the First World War. Until 1935 it was accepted that, except in times of disaster, no able-bodied person need be without work. Public assistance was regarded as charity, and its receipt generally carried stigma. Until the 1930s such aid as existed came mainly from state and local government, though private schemes also had a limited role. By 1929 approximately 75 per cent of all relief derived from public funds, mostly local. *Until 1933 the federal government paid no grants and organized no programmes for relief or insurance, except for its own employees.* Emergency appropriations were made occasionally in the face of local disasters, but *no federal relief had ever been granted to the unemployed.*

Eligibility requirements and benefit levels varied widely by locality. Common among eligibility rules were taking the 'pauper's oath', disenfranchisement (in fourteen states), residency requirements, and the condition that recipients live in almshouses (US National Resources and Planning Board 1942: 26–8). In states where relief was granted to people outside almshouses, payments were very low; and many localities gave benefits only in kind.

---

[10] For additional detail, see the Further Reading.

A detailed explanation of why these arrangements changed sharply in the 1930s lies outside the scope of this chapter and is, in any case, a matter of controversy. I shall do no more than set out the main questions. First, why did income support at a national level begin in the USA later than in almost any other industrialized country[11] and, moreover, at a level which by international standards was low?[12] The arguments are complex (for an overview, see Higgins 1981: ch. 4). Most writers concentrate on one or more of three sets of factors: the influence of ideology (see Section 7.1); the cultural and political heterogeneity of the USA (Gronbjerg *et al.* 1978; Katznelson 1978); and the influence of pressure groups (Menscher 1967; Derthick 1979; Weaver 1982: ch. 4).

A second question is why the 1930s legislation took the shape it did. To a minor extent it was influenced by the experience of other countries, notably the UK, Germany, France, Sweden, and Canada. Considerably more important was the desire to head off more radical proposals. Douglas (1925) advocated a system of family allowances for dependants. The Townsend Plan in the early 1930s called for a monthly pension of $150 for everyone over 60. Simultaneously, Huey Long was pursuing his populist campaign to 'share our wealth'. The Social Security Act 1935 was in part 'a compromise measure to blunt the political appeal of the enormously expensive and essentially unworkable Townsend Plan' (Pechman *et al.* 1968: 32).

Why, finally, did reform occur when it did? Well before the 1930s, pressures for change were emerging out of various long-run developments, notably technological innovation, the decline of the family farm, and decreasing average household size (Wilensky and Lebeaux 1965: 341–8). However, the crisis of the 1930s brought developments to a head. As unemployment mounted after 1929, local expenditure on relief rapidly outstripped declining tax revenues; and emergency assistance by states ran into similar problems, so that federal participation became inevitable. Under Title I of the Emergency Relief and Construction Act 1932, $300 million in federal funds were made available for loans to states to help in their relief efforts.[13]

4.2. The Social Security Act 1935

Between 1933 and 1935 the federal government played an increasing financial and administrative role. The Civilian Conservation Corps, the Public Works Administration, and the Federal Civil Works Administration organized public works; the Federal Surplus Relief Corporation distributed surplus commodities to the needy; and the Federal Emergency Relief Administration supervised federal grants to states for unemployment relief. This last had the greatest impact, both at the time and through its influence on subsequent legislation. The use of federal funds gave federal government

---

[11] By 1930, twenty-seven countries had public schemes of poverty relief of some sort. Among industrialized countries only Norway, Japan, and Switzerland started later than the USA (Pechman *et al.* 1968: app. C).

[12] Why, to use Wilensky and Lebeaux's (1965) concept, did the USA adopt a *residual* model of welfare? We return to this issue in Section 7.1.

[13] Repayment of these loans was eventually waived.

a measure of influence over the state programmes, in particular on benefit levels and administration, and these features were carried over into the permanent legislation.[14]

THE 1935 SOCIAL SECURITY ACT created what, for the USA, was a broad-ranging scheme. It established two major insurance schemes and three major forms of assistance, administered by a new Social Security Board whose powers and duties were set out in Title VII of the Act.[15]

Federal Old Age Benefits (Title II) were financed by contributions from employees and employers under Title VIII and, as originally envisaged, were to be run largely on actuarial lines with respect to both benefit levels and financing (as we shall see shortly, neither resolve was effected).

Federal assistance to states for unemployment compensation was granted under Title III, financed by taxes levied on employers under Title IX. Unlike the pension scheme, which was federal, unemployment insurance was organized by states, which had wide discretion over the precise form of their arrangements. Though the scheme (being insurance) provided no benefits for individuals currently out of work, this was much the most controversial part of the Act, many employers being bitterly opposed to any form of unemployment compensation. Nevertheless, by 1937 all the states and territories had such a scheme.

Old Age Assistance (Title I) provided for means-tested cash payments to the elderly through federal grants to states with approved schemes. It was envisaged that costs would decline as the insurance benefits under Title II became payable. By 1940, fifty-one jurisdictions offered Old Age Assistance.[16]

Aid to the Blind (Title X) provided federal grants to approved state plans of aid to the needy blind. By 1940, forty-three states qualified for federal funds.

Aid to Dependent Children (Title IV) paid federal grants to states giving cash assistance to families with needy children 'under the age of 16 (or under the age of 18 if found by the State agency to be regularly attending school) . . . deprived of parental support or care by reason of the death, continued absence from the home, or physical incapacity of a parent'.[17] By 1949, forty-two jurisdictions had schemes of this sort which qualified for federal funds.[18]

THE 1939 AMENDMENTS to the Social Security Act stressed its welfare objectives and broadened its scope. The strict actuarial principles of the 1935 legislation were diluted; insurance benefits became payable to dependants of aged recipients, and to widows and children of workers covered by the scheme; payments were to begin in 1940 rather than

[14] For further details of the emergency programmes, see US Federal Emergency Relief Administration (1942), and US National Resources and Planning Board (1942: 26–7).

[15] For the wording of the Act itself, see Social Security Act, 14 Aug. 1935, ch. 531, 49 Statutes at Large 620, or, for an edited version, R. B. Stevens (1970: 167–80).

[16] The forty-eight continental states, plus Washington DC, Alaska, and Hawaii.

[17] Social Security Act 1935, Title IV, section 406(*a*). Phrase in parentheses added by an amendment in 1939.

[18] A further eight states (Alaska, Connecticut, Illinois, Kentucky, Mississippi, Nevada, South Dakota, and Texas) operated schemes without federal funds (US National Resources and Planning Board 1942: 83).

1942; benefits were tied to average earnings over a minimum period, thus breaking the link with lifetime contributions; and the earnings test prescribed by the 1935 Act was slightly liberalized before the first benefits were paid.[19] The financial basis of the scheme also changed. The intention of accumulating an actuarial fund was abandoned, and benefits for the elderly and their dependants were paid almost entirely out of current contributions (i.e. the scheme was organized on a Pay-As-You-Go (PAYG) rather than a 'funded' basis, an issue discussed at length in Chapter 9).

BRIEF ASSESSMENT. To a greater extent than the Liberal reforms, the Social Security Act can be criticized as in certain respects timid. The Act, admittedly, was an improvement on earlier arrangements: the range of benefits was broader, the age requirements for retirement more liberal, and the eligibility restrictions on residence and citizenship less stringent; and benefits were paid in cash, this being a condition of the federal contribution to state schemes.

In important respects, however, 'the . . . Act may be reasonably regarded as a conservative legislative solution to a difficult and explosive problem' (Pechman *et al.* 1968: 32). First, though the federal government ensured some uniformity, state programmes still varied widely in terms of benefit levels and eligibility requirements. Secondly, the insurance arrangements were severely constrained: in 1940 only about 60 per cent of workers were covered; benefits were intended originally to bear a fairly simple relationship to contributions, thus ruling out any substantial redistribution (though this aspect was relaxed somewhat by the 1939 amendments); and the insurance benefits were subject to an earnings test. Thirdly, the assistance measures were categorical—that is, they granted aid only to individuals falling into one of the three categories: aged, blind, or dependent child—since it was felt that only these groups should ever require assistance.

The importance of the original Social Security Act, it can be argued, lies less in its content, which was in many ways rather conservative, than in the reform process itself: first, the Act gradually brought about public acceptance of income support as a permanent institution; secondly, and very relevant to reformers elsewhere, the use of carefully designed subsidies to states enabled the federal government to impose some uniformity on state programmes.

5. **The Second World War and its aftermath**

5.1. Wartime activity

POLICY. The final climacteric in the development of the welfare state occurred in the years 1940–8. The Second World War was a total war; *everyone's* life was affected, and this, it

---

[19] These changes were based on recommendations in US Advisory Council on Social Security (1938), which contains valuable background information. For details of the legislative history, see Myers (1965: ch. 4) or, more briefly, Pechman *et al.* (1968: app. B).

is argued, led to important changes in attitude. The totality of the war effort forced the UK government to adopt powers (rationing and the direction of labour, for example) on a scale hitherto unknown. It also reduced social distinctions; unlike the divisive unemployment of the 1930s, food shortages and bombs affected all social classes (though not all areas) equally. The pressure of common problems prompted the adoption of common solutions. Attitudes were changed also by increased awareness of social problems as social classes mingled during the war. In the armed services men who would otherwise have led separate lives were thrown together. Evacuation, too, 'was part of the process by which British society came to know itself, as the unkempt, ill-clothed, undernourished and often incontinent children of bombed cities acted as messengers carrying the evidence of the deprivation of urban working-class life into rural homes' (Fraser 1984: 210).

As well as planning for the future, there was some action on social policy as a direct result of the war, including action on school meals, the transformation of the Unemployment Assistance Board, and dramatic changes in the organization of health care. As a result of wartime food shortages, school meals and school milk, previously a form of charity, became a normal feature of school life. The needs of wartime diversified the activities of the Unemployment Assistance Board (renamed the Assistance Board). In particular, wartime inflation adversely affected pensioners, and legislation in 1940 allowed the Board to pay supplementary pensions on the basis of need. By 1941 it dealt with ten pensioners to every one unemployed person. It also helped others who fell outside the traditional categories—victims of bombing, evacuees, dependants of prisoners of war, etc. As a direct result of the war, the Assistance Board became a generalized relief agency and so foreshadowed the National Assistance Board of 1948.

From 1939 onwards there were two sorts of hospital patient. Some received emergency treatment, which was free, and financed and organized nationally. Others had to take their turn, as previously, in a voluntary or municipal hospital. Payment in the latter two cases was generally through membership of a contributory scheme to a voluntary hospital, or through a means test (Abel Smith 1964: ch. 26). Initially only military personnel fell into the emergency category, but wartime exigencies extended the services to an ever-widening group of people. This served as an example of large-scale, state-financed health care and also exposed the deficiencies of the old system.

PLANNING FOR THE POST-WAR PERIOD. The Beveridge Report (1942) has pride of place on the planning front. It was based on three assumptions: that a scheme of family allowances would be set up; that there would be a comprehensive health care service; and that the state would maintain full employment. The report envisaged a scheme of social insurance which would be 'all-embracing in scope of persons and of needs. . . . Every person . . . will pay a single security contribution by a stamp on a single insurance document each week. . . . Unemployment benefit, disability benefit [and] retirement pensions after a transitional period . . . will be at the same rate irrespective of previous earnings' (ibid. 9–10). Benefits were to be paid also for maternity, and to widows and orphans. Coverage was to be compulsory and (in contrast with the 1935 US Social Security Act) universal in respect of individuals and risk. Flat-rate contributions would give entitlement to flat-rate, subsistence benefits; there would be no means test; and the scheme was to be administered nationally.

The 1944 White Paper, *Social Insurance* (UK Government 1944), accepted most of these recommendations, and became the basis of the National Insurance Act 1946. In the same year two other major White Papers were published. *A National Health Service* (UK DoH 1944) envisaged 'a comprehensive service covering every branch of medical and allied activity' providing free treatment on a universal basis, financed out of general taxation. *Employment Policy* (UK Department of Labour 1944) was very much a Keynesian document. It committed the government to 'the maintenance of a high and stable level of employment', brought about, where necessary, by counter-cyclical deficit spending. The economic radicals of 1931 had finally come into their own.

The major piece of social legislation during the war was the Education Act 1944, based on Butler's 1943 White Paper (UK Board of Education 1943), which set the foundation for post-war education. It created a comprehensive national system of what the Act called primary, secondary, and further education. Primary and secondary education were to be free up to school-leaving age, which was to be raised to 15 in 1945[20] and to 16 as soon as possible thereafter.

ASSESSING BEVERIDGE. The original Beveridge proposals have four central characteristics (see Harris 1977 for fuller discussion).

- *Strategic*. The true novelty of the proposals was their replacement of the old, haphazard system by a coherent *strategy* embracing social insurance, family allowances, national assistance paid out of central revenues, the National Health Service, and (possibly crucially) a presumption of high employment. Thus the Report was not a ragbag of recommendations, but a set of proposals which fitted together as a strategic whole.

- *Universal*. Coverage was mandatory for everyone with an employment record. The motivation was not a predilection for collective provision, but Beveridge's insistence that this was the only way to avoid the gaps experienced during the Great Depression.

- *Actuarial*. The proposals were modelled as closely as possible on private, actuarial insurance: flat-rate benefits were based on flat-rate contributions related to the average risk, and his original proposal was that the state pension scheme should be funded.

- *Parsimonious*. Beveridge argued that the main insurance benefits should be at or above the poverty line, so that recipients would not need to apply for means-tested benefits. For incentive and fiscal reasons, however, he advocated a parsimoniously defined poverty line, with a stringent test to ensure that unemployment was genuine.

---

[20] The school-leaving age had been set at 14 under Fisher's Education Act 1918.

Concepts

The emphasis on poverty relief is particularly important. The Beveridge approach concentrates on poverty relief, in sharp contrast with the Bismarck approach (earnings-related contributions giving entitlement to earnings-related benefits), with their explicit emphasis on income-smoothing.

5.2. Policies 1946–1948

The 1945 Labour government was armed with a large parliamentary majority and a stack of White Papers, many of which had met with Conservative approval during the wartime coalition. Under the Family Allowance Act 1945 a payment of 5 shillings (25 pence) was made for the second and subsequent children in each family. The benefit was universal and paid out of general taxation.

The National Health Service Act 1946, based on the 1944 White Paper, established a national system of comprehensive health care available universally at no charge. The system was financed from general taxation, except for a small proportion from national-insurance contributions. The detailed arrangements (Abel Smith 1964: chs. 27–9) involved considerable discussion with the medical profession.

The National Insurance Act 1946 was based on the 1944 White Paper, which in turn followed closely the recommendations of the Beveridge Report. All insured persons were required to buy a weekly stamp (to which the employer also contributed), whose cost varied by age, sex, and marital and employment status. An employed person was eligible for flat-rate benefit under seven heads, including unemployment, maternity, sickness, widowhood, retirement, and a death grant to cover funeral costs. Beveridge had envisaged that it would take twenty years to build up entitlement to a full retirement pension, but in the event the Labour government implemented full pensions from October 1946.

Alongside the National Insurance Act was the National Insurance (Industrial Injuries) Act 1946, which entitled those injured at work to various benefits (usually at a higher rate than sickness benefit), financed by an identifiable component of the national-insurance contribution. Because the scheme was compulsory it was possible to pool risks across industries with higher and lower accident rates (see Chapter 5, Section 4.1).

The National Assistance Act 1948 established a safety net for those whose needs were not covered (or not fully covered) by insurance. The Act, like the other major Acts, was universal in approach. The old Assistance Board became the National Assistance Board, administering means-tested benefits to those not in full-time work, whose income was below subsistence. In doing so it assumed the residual functions of the local PACs left over from the Poor Law, which were explicitly repealed by the Act.

The legislation of 1944–8 was, on the whole, successful. If the welfare state has any official birthday, it is 5 July 1948, when the provisions of the National Insurance, Industrial Injuries, National Assistance, and National Health Service Acts came simultaneously into effect, family allowances and higher pensions having been implemented in 1946. With unemployment below 250,000, the insurance fund made a surplus of £95 million in its first year, but the National Health Service cost more than anticipated.

There is considerable debate about the importance, or lack of it, of the Second World War in bringing about this legislation. Some writers (Titmuss 1958: ch. 4; Marshall 1975) regard the war as a sine qua non for subsequent events, others (Glennerster 1995: ch. 1) as merely one of a long chain of formative influences.

6. **Post-war developments in the UK and USA**

This section reviews and briefly compares post-war developments in the UK and USA, concentrating mainly on cash benefits. Discussion of health care, education, and housing is deferred to the relevant chapters. For fuller assessment, see Glennerster (1995).

6.1. The UK

At risk of oversimplifying, the post-war story can be divided into two phases defined by the watershed of the 1976 economic crisis. The first period saw consolidation and extension, the second a series of attempts to restrict the growth of social spending.

CONSOLIDATION AND EXTENSION. The contributions regime was the first to show stress. An implication of a self-balancing fund is that total contributions must match total benefits. Since contributions (being flat-rate) could not exceed the reach of a low-paid worker, benefits, too, had to be low. In a fundamental reform, the 1975 Social Security Act replaced the weekly stamp with an earnings-related contribution for all employed persons. One effect of the changes was to enable the insurance system to redistribute from rich to poor (see Chapters 8 and 9).

National-insurance benefits remained broadly unchanged for twenty years. During the later 1960s and early 1970s there was much political wrangling over a series of proposed pension reforms. The Social Security Pensions Act 1975—one of the most important pieces of social legislation since 1948—was in some ways a blend of these proposals (see UK DHSS 1974). It introduced wide-ranging earnings-related pensions and, for the first time, gave a statutory basis for the indexation of benefits, which were intended to rise in line with average earnings.

The system of family support advocated by Beveridge remained largely intact until the late 1970s. It had two strands: a taxable family allowance for the second and subsequent child in any family; and an income-tax allowance for all children. The resulting system was complex and did not give the greatest benefit to the poorest families (such interrelations between the tax and benefit systems will be a recurring theme). To avoid these difficulties the Child Benefit Act 1975 (a remarkable year for social legislation) abolished family allowances and child tax allowances, replacing them with child benefit, a weekly, tax-free cash payment in respect of *all* children in the family, with an additional payment for single parents (see Chapter 10).

Concepts

Assistance benefits are also discussed in Chapter 10. The National Assistance Board was abolished in 1966, and a Supplementary Benefits Commission with wide discretionary powers established. Contrary to Beveridge's expectations, there was a large increase over the years in the number of recipients.

The 1960s saw the 'rediscovery' of poverty (Abel Smith and Townsend 1965), including poverty among working families, who were normally not eligible for supplementary benefit. One response was the introduction in 1971 of family income supplement, a cash benefit for working families with children. The scheme's success was limited by problems with take-up (i.e. potentially eligible families not applying), and (again) anomalous inter-actions between the tax and benefit structures. At certain income levels, for instance, a family was eligible for family income supplement, but also liable for income tax.

More generally, the years after 1960 saw a proliferation of assistance benefits. Some directly parallelled the insurance scheme (e.g. pensions for people too old to have an adequate post-1948 contributions record); others were means-tested; and the relation between different benefits, and between benefits generally and the tax system, became complex and muddled, raising problems of the 'poverty trap' discussed in detail in Chapter 10, Section 3. By the early 1970s there were over fifty benefits outside national insurance (UK Select Committee on Tax Credit 1973: 47–8).

A snapshot of the welfare state in the mid-1970s shows a system with earnings-related contributions, with the major benefits at least partially earnings-related and indexed to average wages, and with a growing array of assistance benefits. The welfare state, it must have appeared to its proponents, was coming into full flower. The seeds of retrenchment, however, had already been sown. The effects of the first oil shock in late 1973 included rapidly accelerating inflation. The economic situation deteriorated rapidly, forcing the government sharply to tighten its macroeconomic policy as part of the conditions for a standby loan from the International Monetary Fund in 1976. The later 1970s were times of tight spending limits. The first Thatcher government took office in 1979.

ATTEMPTED RETRENCHMENT. By the late 1980s the picture was different (for a more detailed account, see Martin Evans 1998). The concerns of the 1960s and 1970s were coverage and adequacy of benefit; those of the 1980s were efficiency, labour-market incentives, and fiscal constraint. Unemployment benefit became less generous through a series of cumulative changes (Atkinson 1995a: ch. 9, app.); indexation became less generous by tying the major benefits to changes in prices rather than earnings; and a series of measures tipped the balance increasingly towards means-tested benefits (Martin Evans 1998: tables 7.3 and 7.15).

A 'fundamental review' of income transfers (UK DHSS 1985a, b) set out with radical intentions, including privatizing all pensions except the basic pension. In the event (UK DHSS 1985c), the main changes were to reduce the state pension for individuals retiring after the turn of the century (see Chapter 9, Section 5) and to allow individuals to opt out of the state earnings-related scheme and occupational schemes and instead to have a personal pension. The review also introduced changes to income-tested benefits, mainly through measures to alleviate the poverty trap (Chapter 10, Section 3).

The real income of the population as a whole increased by 36 per cent between 1979 and 1990. However, inequality increased to such an extent that the poorest 10 per cent of the population were 13 per cent absolutely worse off in 1993/4 than they had been in 1979, while the real income of the richest decile rose by 60 per cent (Hills 1997: 37). Though poverty can be measured in different ways (Chapter 6, Section 2), poverty increased unambiguously (see Chapter 6, Section 2.3, and Chapter 10, Section 3.4).

It is widely believed that attempts at retrenchment (*a*) were driven by ideology and (*b*) reduced the size and scope of the welfare state. The evidence (Glennerster 1995: ch. 1; Glennerster and Hills 1998) does not support that view. Though ideology was doubtless part of the story, external factors—successive oil shocks, increasing global pressures (Chapter 1, Section 3), and ageing populations (Chapter 9)—were more potent driving forces. Furthermore, notwithstanding a contrary policy intention, successive Thatcher administrations did not reduce the share of national income devoted to welfare-state spending. The detailed story is taken up in the relevant chapters.

6.2. The USA

The US story, too, can be presented in two phases. Living standards rose fairly rapidly from the late 1940s until 1973, thereafter growing much more sluggishly.

EXPANSION. Developments in the USA in the 1940s lay outside the social-security system. The Full Employment Act 1946, which represented a considerable departure from previous policies, imposed on federal government the (implicitly Keynesian) responsibility for the maintenance of full employment.

In the years after 1950 the insurance scheme was steadily broadened to the point where, together with various related programmes, virtually all workers and their dependants were covered. The parallel extension of risks covered is conveniently summarized by the changing name of the scheme: the 1935 Act concentrated on Old Age Insurance (OAI); survivor benefits were added in 1939 (OASI); disablement benefits in 1956 (OASDI); and various health benefits for the elderly and the poor in 1965 (OASDHI) (for legislative details, see R. B. Stevens 1970: 758–75).

The benefit regime established by the 1935 Act was also liberalized: there were proportionately larger increases for lower-income workers (increasing the scheme's redistributive impact); benefits for survivors and dependants were raised relative to those for the insured person (increasing the support given to families); and the rules about the age of retirement were relaxed.

There was considerably less change in the system of assistance benefits. Aid to the Permanently and Totally Disabled was established in 1950; and Aid to Dependent Children (renamed Aid to Families with Dependent Children) was liberalized in various ways in the 1960s. Of particular note, states were given the option after 1962 of paying benefit not only where the father was absent or disabled, but also where he was unemployed.

Concepts

Health care for recipients of assistance ('medicaid') was introduced in 1965, at the same time as its inclusion for the elderly under the main insurance scheme ('medicare'), with major implications for expenditure on health care (see Chapter 12, Section 4.1).

The 1960s saw a 'welfare explosion'—a dramatic expansion in the size and cost of Aid to Families with Dependent Children. The increase was particularly great in the states with the largest cities, especially in New York and California. 'Governor Reagan complained last night that California's "permissive" welfare system is encouraging teenaged girls to become pregnant and subsidizing hippie communes at poor folks' expense. "The Age of Aquarius smells a little fishy," he told a sympathetic audience of conservative Republicans' (*San Francisco Chronicle*, 14 Sept. 1970, p. 37). The phenomenon evoked considerable concern, particularly because it coincided with a period of low unemployment and sustained economic growth (see David Gordon 1969; Barr and Hall 1981).

Poverty became a major political issue in the 1960s for the first time in thirty years, not just as a defensive response to the escalating numbers receiving assistance but also for more positive reasons, at least during President Johnson's 'War on Poverty' (US President's Commission on Income Maintenance Programs 1969). With hindsight, however, the response was long on words but muted in action. There were a number of experiments with negative income tax (see the Further Reading to Chapter 11), but changes *ex post* were small.

THE GROWTH SLOWDOWN. Two overarching facts explain much of US social policy since 1973: growth slowed down, and inequality increased sharply, as discussed in more detail in Chapter 6, Sections 2.3, 4.3. In principle, more—and more redistributive—transfers might have been able to protect the poor. In practice, the USA provides income transfers to working-age people only parsimoniously (Burtless 1987 describes how eligibility requirements for unemployment benefit tightened; for fuller assessment, see Blank 1997*a*: ch. 3). Americans of working age are thus very dependent on earnings; and, since there is no equivalent of family allowance, American children are very dependent on their parents' earnings. The combined effects of stagnating growth, rising inequality, and parsimonious transfers thus led inexorably to an increase in poverty. The poverty rate fell from 22 per cent of the population in 1950 to 11 per cent in 1973; over the following two decades, notwithstanding a 27 per cent increase in real per capita income, it increased to 14.5 per cent (Gottschalk 1997). The composition of the total changed sharply, with less poverty among the elderly (reflecting expanding social security and private pensions) and more among children (reflecting rising numbers of single-parent families). Welfare reform in 1996, shifting much of the responsibility for poverty relief to states, did nothing to reverse the trend (see Blank 1997*b*).

In 1965, Wilensky and Lebeaux (1965: pp. xvi–xvii) argued that the 'United States is more reluctant than any rich democratic country to make a welfare effort appropriate to its affluence. Our support of national welfare programs is halting; our administration of services for the less privileged is mean. We move toward the welfare state but we do it with ill grace, carping and complaining all the way.' Thirty years later, little had changed: 'Government transfer programs had little effect in ameliorating the trend towards inequality. If anything, these programs become less effective in redistributing incomes to low-income families after 1979' (Burtless 1996a: 289).

6.3. Comparative issues

Four strategic issues are the subject of much of the rest of the book: the role of employment; the importance of social insurance; the relation between the benefit and tax systems; and the continued and substantial reliance on means-tested benefits.

A high level of employment was initially seen in both countries as the primary method of income support. The UK government committed itself to such policies in its wartime White Paper (UK Department of Labour 1944). The US analogue was the Full Employment Act 1946. The retreat from these commitments and the increased emphasis on labour-market flexibility in both countries in the 1980s is discussed in Chapter 1, Section 3.

Social insurance was the major line of defence. The coverage of the UK 1946 National Insurance Act was broader in three important ways than the US Social Security Act as amended in 1939: it dealt with contingencies such as sickness and maternity, which were not covered by US legislation; its coverage was virtually universal with respect to individuals; and, as its name implied, it was a *national* scheme (so, too, were assistance payments). In contrast, the US system (apart from federal retirement and disability insurance and, later, health insurance for the elderly) was organized by states.

The original intention of both Acts was to emulate private, actuarial insurance, both generally, and particularly in the way pensions were to be paid from an accumulated fund. But political pressures and favourable demographic and economic trends resulted instead in pensions paid largely out of current contributions, starting in 1940 (USA) and 1946 (UK); and over the years political pressure led to further erosion of actuarial principles, as the coverage of both schemes was broadened and the relation between contributions and benefits relaxed. The overall result, in a UK context, was considerable erosion of the Beveridge strategy. The extent to which such benefits are (or should be, or can be) true insurance is one of the main topics of Chapters 5, 8, and 9.

Tax expenditures (see Chapter 7, Section 1.1) served in both countries to buttress social insurance. Parallel to public pensions, for instance, was the tax relief granted to private schemes. Both methods provide income support for the elderly, though often with very different distributional consequences. That tax expenditures should properly be included in any assessment of income support has long been recognized in the academic literature, though awareness of the issue by politicians has come more slowly. Income tax is relevant also because of the increasing overlap between taxpayers and benefit recipients. Some social-insurance benefits are taxable, an issue of acute relevance when (in sharp contrast with the 1940s) most earners are above the income tax threshold and where husband and wife pay income tax as separate individuals. The overlap is crucial also in connection with income-tested benefits, as we shall see in Chapters 10 and 11.

Reliance on means-tested benefits continued in both countries (and in many others) on a substantial—and latterly a growing—scale, despite the existence of wide-ranging social insurance and tax expenditures, and notwithstanding Beveridge's expectation that the assistance measures would become residual. This was partly because in the UK many of the insurance benefits were below the subsistence level established by national assistance (thus violating what Beveridge regarded as an essential ingredient of his proposals), and partly because of problems with take-up. As a result, means-tested assistance continued in both cash (income support, Aid to Families with Dependent Children) and kind (free medical prescriptions in the UK, 'medicaid' and food stamps in the USA).

The persistence of these benefits, and the large numbers of people involved, demonstrate that insurance and related measures were only partially successful in abolishing 'want'.[21] Studies in both countries (Hills 1997; US Panel on Poverty and Public Assistance 1995) showed continuing and widespread poverty, partly due to factors outside the direct scope of income support (e.g. racial discrimination). But poverty was also found among the elderly and the unemployed, to whom social insurance was directly relevant.

Finally, as we have seen, there were two substantial differences. There remained a complete absence in the USA of any analogue of child benefit, notwithstanding the many countries which had such arrangements (France introduced the first scheme before the First World War).[22] Nor, despite attempts at major reform in the early 1990s, was there anything remotely resembling the UK National Health Service. This remains true in the late 1990s.

7. Concluding issues: From the past to the present

7.1. Interpreting the forces creating the welfare state

Given the variety of influences on the welfare state, it is not surprising that there is controversy over their relative importance. The key issue is whether the dominant factor was ideology or the nature of the industrial process. The ideological debate concentrates on the motives underlying social legislation. A *liberal* (as defined in Chapter 3, Section 1) interpretation of history attributes the development of the welfare state to the quest for social justice, and sees the events described earlier as progress along a road towards the good society. Fraser (1984: 157) writes of Lloyd George's 1909 'People's Budget' that '[here] was the essence of the novel approach: financial policy geared to the social needs of the people; the budget as a tool of social policy'.

---

[21] This is not to imply that income-testing is *necessarily* a sign of a failing system of income support. The Australian system uses means-testing, but more to exclude the rich than to try to include only the poor. For a summary of social-security institutions worldwide, see US Department of Health and Human Services (1997).

[22] For a review and international comparison of family allowances, see Ditch *et al*. (1997) and Kamerman and Kahn (1997).

Marxists, *per contra*, did not see the welfare state as arising out of a concatenation of disparate events, and certainly not as the result of a quest for social justice. They argue that the primary motive of social legislation was the protection and preservation of the capitalist system. The welfare state, according to this view, fills two roles: it helps to meet the needs of the capitalist industrial system for a healthy, educated workforce; and it is the 'ransom' paid by the ruling élite to contain social unrest. To a Marxist, the Liberal reforms were very limited and intended mainly to preserve the existing economic system. Unemployment, sickness, and health benefits under the 1911 National Insurance Act applied only to limited classes of worker; and some historians argue that one of the main motives of the 1908 Pension Act (the only substantially redistributive measure) was to weed out of the workforce older men and women whose presence was reducing Britain's industrial efficiency in the face of international competition. These different views of the welfare state are discussed in more detail in Chapter 3, Section 5.3.

Ideology, then, can be argued to have fostered the development of the welfare state either in the quest for social justice or as 'capitalist conspiracy'. But is ideology actually very important? The *theory of convergence* (see the Further Reading) is based on detailed studies of how welfare states (under whatever name) have arisen in different countries. The theory is based on two propositions: that all countries, whatever their dominant ideology, have over time developed similar industrial structures, and that a welfare state in one form or another is an inevitable concomitant of that industrial structure. The theory therefore bases its argument on technological determinism. At its strongest, it asserts that the dominant force in the development of the welfare state is industrialism—and, more recently, global pressures—and, by implication, that ideology is largely irrelevant.

Ideology or technological determinism? I make no serious attempt to judge the two theories. However, the world is a complicated place, and I have a profound suspicion of almost any unicausal explanation of anything. Most industrial countries face similar problems of unemployment and pockets of poverty, so it is not surprising that many have adopted broadly similar solutions; the logic of industrialism clearly has some validity. Similarly, the technical problems with private markets discussed in Chapters 4 and 5 afflict all industrialized countries.

But ideology also appears to play a part, if only in determining whether a country adopts a *residual* or an *institutional* model of welfare. The former accords welfare a role only when market or family structures break down; the latter regards it as an integral part of modern industrial society (Wilensky and Lebeaux 1965: 138–9; Higgins 1981: 41–5). Thus a 'capitalist' country like the USA has (and has always had) a system of income support and social services which is small relative to its population and national income (though it has a wide-ranging system of publicly provided education). A 'socialist' country like Sweden has a highly articulated welfare state; Denmark and New Zealand (which were not highly industrialized) were among the first countries with a public system of old-age pensions; and Saskatchewan was the first Canadian province to have publicly organized health insurance.

It is clear, in conclusion, that the forces which created the UK (or any other) welfare state are diverse and complex. The question 'how did it come about?' has no easy answer.

7.2. What was created?

The nature of what was created, as we have just seen, is a matter of controversy. Is the welfare state a step in the direction of the good society (discussed in detail in Chapter 3, Section 3), an expensive and demeaning road towards totalitarianism (Chapter 3, Section 2), or a cynical device to prop up the capitalist system (Chapter 3, Section 4.2, 5.3)? Setting these issues to one side, the successes of the post-1948 arrangements are twofold and clear. There is, first, a comprehensive system of income support, with insurance arrangements underpinned by a broad safety net in the form of income support (i.e. means-tested social assistance), which is organized nationally and for which *everyone* is potentially eligible. Many other countries have considerably less comprehensive systems. The second major success—at least thus far—has been the National Health Service, which 'brought to all the most obvious and immediate benefits. To many it *is* the Welfare State, and every survey . . . has shown how much it is . . . valued and taken for granted as part and parcel of British life' (Bruce 1972: 330).

The failures are also fairly clear. It is striking how many current and prospective problems have their roots or their parallels in the past. The inter-war difficulties with unemployment insurance raised questions about the extent to which unemployment is an insurable risk (see Chapters 5 and 8); the introduction of state pensions in 1908 was motivated in part by demographic problems (Chapter 9); the British antipathy to means-testing (Chapters 10 and 11) is strongly influenced by the folk memory of the stringent household means test between the wars; the post-war distributional complexities arising out of the interaction between family allowances and child tax allowances will emerge in many guises; the housing measures during and after the First World War were a direct contributory cause of continuing difficulties with housing (Chapter 14); and the exploding costs of medical care in the USA (Chapter 12, Section 4.1) stem in part (though far from wholly) from the design of 'Medicare' and 'Medicaid', introduced in 1965.

Over and above these problems is the fact, despite the relative success of the cash benefit system, that poverty, far from being eliminated, has risen since the early 1980s. In part this is because the poverty line has moved up as living standards and expectations have risen; but for many the issue is not just one of *relative* poverty, but of uncertainty and harsh discomfort.

For some, the most important problem of all is the pressure to retrench. The 'welfare consensus' on both sides of the Atlantic weakened during the 1980s, though the roots of the attack, at least in the USA, go back further (Wilensky and Lebeaux 1965: pp. xxxii–xxxvii). The change in attitude is highlighted by the contrast between the 1944 employment White Paper (UK Department of Labour 1944), committing the government to counter-cyclical demand management, and the 1997 Conservative election manifesto which argued that unemployment should be tackled by expanding 'workfare' and by seeking to impose the lowest tax burden of any major European economy. Notwithstanding greater emphasis on employment levels by the Labour government elected in 1997, the high summer of 1948 has passed. And though no one has a monopoly of wisdom, to some commentators at least, the Principles of 1834 (Section 1.1) come rather readily to mind, thereby completing a historical circle.

FURTHER READING

Good general texts on the historical development of the UK welfare state are Bruce (1972), Marshall (1975), Thane (1982), and Fraser (1984); for the period since 1945 Glennerster (1995) and Timmins (1996); and, for a detailed account since the mid-1970s, Glennerster and Hills (1998).

Contemporary discussion of the 'New Liberalism' can be found in Hobson (1909); for more recent analysis of economic and political thought at the time, see Robbins (1977) and Freeden (1978). For a brief introduction to early poor relief, see Rose (1972); on the principle of *laissez-faire*, Taylor (1972); and on the Liberal reforms, Gilbert (1973) (compendious) or Hay (1975) (brief). The early debates on unemployment are detailed in Harris (1972) and a history of health care prior to 1948 is given in Abel Smith (1964). A brief official historical account is given in UK DHSS (1985*a*: ch. 3).

The origins of the modern welfare state are discussed explicitly by Harris (1977) (a magisterial biography of Beveridge) and Titmuss (1958) (who stresses the influence of the Second World War). The proposals contained in the Beveridge Report (1942) are still well worth reading, as are those for the National Health Service in UK DoH (1944). Detailed historical statistics for the UK from 1855 to 1965 can be found in Feinstein (1972). For the modern institutions, see Tolley (1996).

For contemporary accounts of US developments in the 1930s, see Douglas (1939), US Federal Emergency Relief Administration (1942), and US National Resources and Planning Board (1942). For retrospective analysis, see Witte (1962), Schottland (1963), or Altmeyer (1966); and, for later debates, Tobin (1968) and US President's Commission on Income Maintenance Programs (1969) (a remarkable document). Details of US legislation are given in R. B. Stevens (1970). On recent developments, see Blank (1994; 1997*a*, *b*), Karoly and Burtless (1995), and US Panel on Poverty and Public Assistance (1995).

For differing interpretations of the origins of the welfare state, including discussion of the theory of convergence, see Higgins (1981: ch. 4) and Mishra (1981: ch. 3) for a summary; and, for specific views, Wilensky and Lebeaux (1965) and Rimlinger (1971). A more general international comparison is given in Kaim-Caudle (1973). For a compendious summary of institutions internationally, see US Department of Health and Human Services (1997).

CHAPTER 3

Political theory:
Social justice and the state

The fundamental issue [of the welfare state] is not economic. It is moral . . . The issue is the responsibility of people to manage their own affairs . . . Is it not the case that while adults manage incomes children receive pocket money? The operation of the welfare state tends to reduce the status of adults to that of children.

Peter Bauer, 1983

[The] major evil [of paternalistic programs] is their effect on the fabric of our society. They weaken the family; reduce the incentive to work, save and innovate; reduce the accumulation of capital; and limit our freedom. These are the fundamental standards by which they should be judged.　　Milton Friedman, 1980

Traditional socialism was largely concerned with the evils of traditional capitalism, and with the need for its overthrow. But today traditional capitalism has been reformed and modified almost out of existence, and it is with a quite different form of society that socialists must now concern themselves.　　Anthony Crosland, 1956

1. Theories of society

A society is a cooperative venture for the mutual advantage of its members. It generally contains both an identity of interests and conflicts of interest between individuals and groups. The institutions of any society (e.g. its constitution, laws, and social processes) have a profound influence on a person's 'life chances'. The purpose of a theory of society is to offer principles which enable us to choose between different social arrangements. In analysing the welfare state it is helpful to distinguish three broad types of theory: libertarian; liberal; and collectivist.[1]

---

[1]　Readers with a limited background in political theory can find the gist of the argument in the Appendix at the end of the chapter.

LIBERTARIANS (discussed in Section 2) are in many ways the direct descendants of the 'Old Liberalism' of the nineteenth century (Chapter 2, Sections 1.1, 2.1), although, as we shall see, there are important differences between 'natural-rights' and 'empirical' libertarians. The former (e.g. Nozick) argue that state intervention is *morally wrong* except in very limited circumstances. The latter, including writers such as Hayek and Friedman and proponents of the 'New Right' arguments such as Margaret Thatcher, are the modern inheritors of the classical liberal tradition;[2] they argue against state intervention not on moral grounds, but because it will *reduce total welfare*. Both groups analyse society in terms of its individual members (as opposed to the group or social class), give heavy weight to individual freedom, and strongly support private property and the market mechanism. As a result, the state's role *vis-à-vis* taxation and redistribution is severely circumscribed.

LIBERAL theories (Section 3) are the modern inheritors of the 'New Liberalism' (Chapter 2, Section 2.1). They find their philosophy in utilitarianism (Section 3.1) and in writers like Rawls (Section 3.2); their policy advocates in people such as Beveridge, Keynes, and Galbraith; and their practitioners in politicians such as Harold Macmillan and John Kennedy. The theory has three crucial features. First, societies are analysed in terms of their individual members. Secondly, 'private property in the means of production, distribution and exchange [is] a contingent matter rather than an essential part of the doctrine' (Barry 1973: 166)—that is, the treatment of private property is explicitly regarded not as an end in itself, but as a means towards the achievement of policy goals. Finally, liberal theories contain 'a principle of distribution which could, suitably interpreted and with certain factual assumptions, have egalitarian implications' (ibid.)—that is, in certain circumstances income redistribution is an appropriate function of the state. This book, as Chapter 4 will amplify, is firmly in the liberal tradition.

COLLECTIVIST theories, too, are varied. *Marxist* theory (Section 4.2) draws its philosophy from Marx and its policies from writers such as Laski, Strachey, and Miliband. The theory sees industrial society as consisting of social classes, defined narrowly in terms of their relation to the means of production. Private property has only a limited role, and the allocation and distribution of resources in accordance with individual need is a primary concern of the state. *Democratic socialists* (Section 4.1) present an intermediate case. They derive their philosophy from writers like Tawney, and find their policy advocates in, for example, Crosland and Titmuss, and their practitioners in politicians such as Clement Attlee and Harold Wilson. Though sharing to some extent the egalitarian aims of Marxists, their analysis has much in common with liberal thinking.

In practice the theories blur into each other like the colours of the rainbow. Should Bill Clinton be regarded as a liberal, or is there an admixture of the empirical libertarian? Should

---

[2] There is a confusing ambiguity in the use of the word 'liberal'. In the nineteenth century it was used as a label for *laissez-faire* thinkers such as Bentham and Nassau Senior (Chapter 2, Section 1.1); and today a writer like Friedman, in calling himself a liberal, is using the term in the same way. I shall, throughout, refer to such writers as libertarians.

Tony Blair be thought of as a democratic socialist or as a liberal coming from a socialist background? But it is useful for exposition to discuss them as separate entities, especially when contrasting their implications for policy (Section 5). Nevertheless, their differences and similarities are complex, and involve subtleties well beyond the scope of one brief chapter. The purpose here is limited to sketching the ideological debate only in outline. Knowledgeable readers will, I hope, be forgiving.

2. Libertarian views

It is necessary to return briefly to nineteenth-century debates (Chapter 2, Sections 1.1, 2.1). The ideology of *laissez-faire* derived from two very different philosophical roots. When modern writers such as Hayek and Friedman advocate free markets and private property, they follow Hume (1770), Adam Smith (1776), Bentham (1789), and Mill (1863) in doing so on a *utilitarian* or *empirical* basis, out of a belief that such institutions maximize total welfare. Nozick, in contrast, follows Spencer (1884) by defending private property on *moral* grounds, as a *natural right* (see Robbins 1978: 46 *et seq.*). Though not completely watertight, the distinction between the two views (exemplified by the first two quotes at the head of the chapter) is crucial to debates about policy (Section 5), and so merits closer attention.

NATURAL-RIGHTS LIBERTARIANS. To Nozick (1974) everyone has the right to distribute the rewards of his own labour. He calls this *justice in holdings*, which has three elements. A person is entitled to a holding if he has acquired it (*a*) through earnings (so-called justice in acquisition), or (*b*) through the inheritance of wealth which was itself justly acquired (justice in transfer). Holdings which fall under neither principle cannot be justified, hence (*c*) government may redistribute holdings acquired illegally (the principle of rectification).

These propositions support the libertarian predilection for a minimalist or 'night-watchman' state with strictly circumscribed powers: the state can provide one and only one public good—namely, the defence of our person and property, including the enforcement of contracts; but other than correcting past wrongs it has no legitimate distributional role. Nozick regards taxation as theft (since it extracts from people money (legitimately acquired) which they would otherwise have allocated in other ways), and also as slavery, in that people are forced to spend part of their time working for government.

EMPIRICAL LIBERTARIANS. Hayek's theory has three strands: the primacy of individual freedom; the value of the market mechanism; and the assertion that the pursuit of social justice is not only fruitless (because there is no such thing) but actively harmful. Freedom to Hayek (1960: ch. 1) and other libertarians is defined narrowly as absence of coercion or restraint; it includes political liberty, free speech, and economic freedom. The central argument of Hayek (1944) is that the pursuit of equality will reduce or destroy liberty.

To Hayek the market is beneficial because it protects individual freedom and also because of its economic benefits. '[It is] a procedure which has greatly improved the chances of all to have their wants satisfied, but at the price of all individuals . . . incurring the risk of unmerited failure . . . It is the only procedure yet discovered in which information widely dispersed among millions of men can be effectively utilised for the benefit of all' (1976: 70–1). These advantages arise only if prices and wages are allowed to act as signals which tell individuals where to direct their efforts. A person's reward is that which induces him to act in the common good; it will often bear no relation to either his individual merit or his need.

Hayek's view of social justice contrasts sharply with that of Rawls. According to Hayek, a given circumstance (e.g. winning the lottery or dying young) can be regarded as good or bad, but can be described as just or unjust 'only in so far as we hold someone responsible for . . . allowing it to come about' (ibid. 31). Thus something is just or unjust *only if it has been caused by the action or inaction of an individual or individuals.* The market, in contrast (ibid. 64–5), is an impersonal force like 'Nature', akin to an economic game with winners and losers, whose outcome can be good or bad, but never just or unjust. To Hayek, therefore, the whole notion of social justice is 'a quasi-religious superstition of the kind which we should respectfully leave in peace so long as it merely makes those happy who hold it' (ibid. 66). However, 'the striving for [social justice] will . . . lead to the destruction of . . . personal freedom' (ibid. 67). The reason is that

the more dependent the position of individuals . . . is seen to become on the actions of government, the more they will insist that the governments aim at some recognisable scheme of distributive justice; and the more governments try to realise some preconceived pattern of desirable distribution, the more they must subject the position of the different individuals . . . to their control. *So long as the belief in 'social justice' governs political action, this process must progressively approach nearer and nearer to a totalitarian system.* (ibid. 68, emphasis added)

For Friedman, too, the primary value is individual freedom. Hence,

the scope of government must be limited. Its major function must be to protect our freedom both from the enemies outside our gates and from our fellow-citizens: to preserve law and order, to enforce private contracts, to foster competitive markets. Beyond this major function, government may enable us at times to accomplish jointly what we would find it more difficult . . . to accomplish severally. However, any such use of government is fraught with danger. We should not and cannot avoid using government this way. But there should be a clear and large balance of advantages before we do. (1962: 2–3)

To Friedman and Hayek the state has no distributional role, other than for certain public goods and for strictly limited measures to alleviate destitution.

This line of thinking re-emerged in the 1970s and 1980s in the arguments of the New Right (see George and Wilding 1994: ch. 2). British adherents of this approach see Keynes and Beveridge as unhelpful influences. In the USA, writers like Murray (1984) argue that social benefits have exacerbated poverty and should largely be abolished. The New Right puts great faith in individuals and little faith in government. The market, according to their view, is the best coordinator of vast amounts of decentralized information and is thus efficient. It benefits consumers because competitive pressures maximize choice, minimize costs, and reduce the power of providers. It does not depend on the goodwill of service providers and hence, it is argued, accords better with the realities of human nature. Accordingly, the New Right advocates a larger role for markets and a severely circumscribed role for the state.

3. Liberal theories of society

Liberal theories are sometimes referred to as the 'Middle Way', which, according to George and Wilding (1994: ch. 3) starts from three premises very different from the New Right. First, capitalism is regarded as more efficient than any other system; secondly, though efficient, capitalism has major costs in terms of poverty and inequality; thirdly, government can ameliorate those costs. As a result, according to this view, a combination of capitalism and government action jointly maximizes efficiency and equity. This approach derives from two strands of thinking: utilitarian writing and, more recently, the writing of the philosopher John Rawls.

3.1. Utilitarianism

The utilitarian arguments which form the basis of much of this book derive from the 'New Liberalism' of the early twentieth century (Chapter 2, Section 2.1), which was itself firmly rooted in the nineteenth-century classical tradition. Thus modern utilitarians have common intellectual roots with empirical libertarians.

THE THEORY. The utilitarian aim is to distribute goods so as to maximize the total utility[3] of the members of society. 'Goods' are interpreted broadly to include goods and services, rights, freedoms, and political power. Maximizing total welfare has two aspects: goods must be produced and allocated *efficiently* (discussed in Chapter 4); and they must be distributed in accordance with *equity* (though not necessarily equally). The equitable distribution is shown in Figure 3.1. Total income to be distributed is *AB*. Individual A's marginal utility (read from left to right) is shown by the line *aa*, and is assumed to diminish as his income rises. Individual B's marginal utility, which declines from right to left, is shown by the line *bb*. Total utility is maximized when income is shared equally; A's income is *AC*, and B's is *BC*.

Utilitarianism can therefore justify redistributive activity by the state in pursuit of an egalitarian outcome, but this result depends crucially on two conditions. First, A and B

---

[3] Synonymously, to maximize total happiness or total welfare.

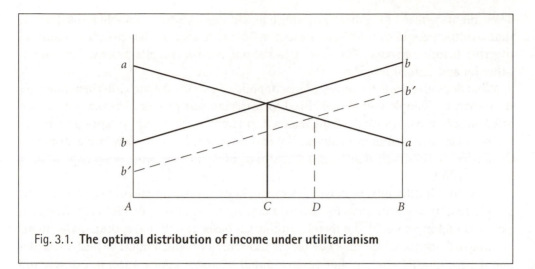

Fig. 3.1. **The optimal distribution of income under utilitarianism**

must have identical marginal utility of income functions.[4] If B's marginal utility is shown by $b'b'$, then the distribution which maximizes total welfare is unequal, since A now has an income of AD. Secondly, utilitarianism can fully specify the optimal distribution only where the utility of A and B can be measured cardinally (see the Glossary).

CRITICISMS include questions such as: is utility capable of precise definition; does interpersonal comparison of utility have any meaning; and whose utility counts (e.g. future generations, animals, etc.)? These issues are set to one side to focus on two fundamental criticisms.

An unjust outcome. Utilitarianism can sanction injustice by justifying harm to the least well-off if this maximizes total utility. 'The trouble with [utilitarianism] is that maximising the sum of individual utilities is supremely unconcerned with the interpersonal distribution of that sum' (Sen 1973: 16). Formally, suppose that individual B in Figure 3.1 derives less pleasure from life than A because he has major health problems. His marginal utility is shown by the line $b'b'$, and the optimal distribution of goods by point D. Thus B should receive *less* income than A because of his health problems. This outcome is criticized as being unjust.

The impossibility of a Paretian liberal. Consider two desirable objectives: individual freedom (which includes the idea that an individual is the best judge of her own welfare), and maximizing total welfare. Sen (1970, 1982) (see also Sen and Williams 1982, and Brittan 1995: ch. 3) argues that it is not always possible to achieve both objectives simultaneously —that is, individual freedom may not be compatible with simple utilitarianism. The argument goes as follows.

Suppose that my action imposes a cost on other people, not in economic terms (e.g. polluting their garden with dense smoke) but because *they* have views about *my* actions.

---

[4] Strictly, several other technical conditions are necessary—e.g. that the underlying social-welfare function is symmetric and concave (see Chapter 6, Section 1.2).

They might think it wrong that I have long hair. More generally, they might think it wrong that wealthy people should have a yacht in Monte Carlo, or that people should live together before marriage. Thus the action of one person can affect the welfare of another for aesthetic or moral reasons.

What does this imply for public policy? If policy-makers take such interdependencies into account, 'people will be penalized for carrying out private personal acts which affect others only because thinking makes it so' (Brittan 1995: 74). Accepting such preferences can make utilitarianism an illiberal doctrine, because they 'are a disguised form of coercion which arise from a desire to regulate the way other people spend their lives . . .' (ibid.).

To avoid this difficulty, policy-makers may choose to ignore the preferences of some people (e.g. those who wish to impose mandatory haircuts). In that case, however, policy is no longer decided *only* on a utilitarian basis; it will incorporate judgements about which forms of interdependence are allowable and which not. The heated debates about appropriate public policy (if any) about personal appearance, soft drugs, and sexual behaviour illustrate the point.

3.2. Rawls on social justice

Rawls in some ways is Nozick's liberal counterpart. Nozick is a natural-rights defender of liberty. For Rawls the natural right, and hence the prime aim of institutions, is *social justice*: thus 'each person possesses an inviolability founded on justice that even the welfare of society as a whole cannot override' (1972: 2). Justice, to Rawls, has a twofold purpose: it is desirable for its own sake on moral grounds; but also, and importantly, institutions will survive only if they are perceived to be just. Rawls argues that there exists a definition of justice which both is *general* (i.e. not specific to any particular culture) and can be derived by a process which everyone can agree is fair. The resulting principles deal with the distribution of goods, interpreted broadly to include also liberty and opportunity.

THE ORIGINAL POSITION is Rawls's starting point. He invites us to contemplate a group of rational individuals, each concerned only with his own self-interest, coming together to negotiate principles to determine the distribution of goods. They are free agents in the negotiation, but they must abide by the resulting principles. Rawls thus uses the convention of a *social contract*.

In this situation no discussion between interested parties will yield principles of justice which command universal acceptance. Rawls therefore abstracts the negotiators from their own society by placing them behind a *veil of ignorance*. They are assumed to be well informed about the general facts of the world—psychology, economics, sociology—but each is *deprived of all knowledge about himself*—that is, of his natural characteristics or endowments, his position in society, and the country or historical period into which he is born. The negotiators seek to advance their own interests, but are unable to distinguish them from anyone else's.

The role of the veil of ignorance is best illustrated by example. To distance ourselves from personal interests we (i.e. citizens through our elected representatives) may decide that aircraft hijackers' demands should never be met, even if innocent lives are lost. We do this in order to save even more lives in the long run; and we establish this doctrine in advance of the event (i.e. behind the veil of ignorance) because if it were our personal loved ones who were kidnapped we would be likely to do anything to save them, irrespective of the possible consequences for others in the future.

The negotiators can consider any principle of justice—for example, the just action is that which is in the interests of the stronger, or that which ennobles the species or that which maximizes total utility. According to Rawls, the rational negotiator will reject these because under each he might systematically be underprivileged. The only rational choice is to select principles in terms of what Rawls calls the 'maximin rule', which maximizes the position of the least well-off individual or group. The negotiators do this because 'for all they know they may turn out to be the least privileged inhabitants of a country like [pre-reform] South Africa' (McCreadie 1976: 117).

The original position, together with the veil of ignorance, plays two distinct roles. First, it is an analytical device, which 'reduc[es] a relatively complex problem, the social choice of the principles of justice, to a more manageable problem, the rational individual choice of principles' (Daniels 1975: p. xix). Secondly, and possibly of greater importance, Rawls sees the procedure as a *moral justification* of the resulting principles—they will be seen to be fair, he argues, because they are selected in a manner which is both rational and fair, hence his term 'justice as fairness'.

THE PRINCIPLES OF JUSTICE which follow are those which Rawls claims would be chosen rationally and unanimously by the negotiators. Because of the veil of ignorance, they will choose to maximize liberty for everyone. Hence:

The first principle (the 'liberty principle'). 'Each person is to have an equal right to the most extensive basic liberty compatible with a similar liberty for others' (Rawls 1972: 60).

The negotiators then turn to the distribution of goods other than liberty. Each will reject any principle of distribution which could leave him disadvantaged or exploited.

The negotiators may consider a principle that mandates a thoroughly equal distribution of goods . . . But they will soon come to realise that they stand to benefit by the introduction of certain inequalities . . . For example, giving a rural [doctor] an airplane would make him relatively advantaged, but even—and perhaps especially—the least advantaged among the rural populace stand to benefit as a result, and thus should sanction such inequality.   (Gorovitz 1975: 281)

Hence:

The second principle (the 'difference principle'). 'Social and economic inequalities are to be arranged so that they are both (a) to the greatest benefit of the least advantaged and (b) attached to offices and positions open to all under conditions of fair equality of opportunity' (Rawls 1972: 83).

Concepts

The possibility of a conflict between the two principles is ruled out by a *priority principle*, which gives the first principle absolute priority over the second. A reduction in the liberty of the least well off cannot be justified even if it is to their economic advantage. Subject to these priorities the two principles can be regarded as a special case of a simpler, more general conception of justice, in which 'all social primary goods—liberty and opportunity, income and wealth . . . are to be distributed equally unless an unequal distribution of any or all of these goods is to the advantage of the least favoured' (ibid. 303). At its simplest, the distribution of goods between individuals A and B in Figure 3.1 should be that shown by point *C* unless any other distribution benefits the less advantaged of the two.[5] If goods are not so distributed, any policy which improves the position of the less well off would be an improvement according to Rawls.[6]

RAWLS AND UTILITARIANISM. Rawls is an explicit opponent of utilitarianism. He regards it as illogical (in as much as it would be rejected by rational negotiators in the original position) and as unjust (in that it can sanction injustice in the interests of maximizing total welfare). The two theories can have very different implications. Suppose a given policy change makes at least one person better off without making anyone else worse off. This is an increase in Pareto efficiency,[7] and hence desirable to utilitarians even if the individual thus benefited were rich. Rawls's difference principle, in contrast, would oppose the policy unless it were also (though not necessarily only) to the advantage of the least well off. Thus an efficient answer in Paretian terms will not always be a just answer in a Rawlsian sense (though, as argued in Chapter 4, Section 2.2, it may be possible to find a distribution which is both efficient and just).

CRITICISMS OF RAWLS'S THEORY are summarized only briefly. It has been argued that the negotiators would be unable to make any decisions behind the veil of ignorance. According to Nisbet (1974: 112),

[the negotiators] don't know much of anything—anything, that is, that we are justified by contemporary psychology in deeming requisite to thought and knowledge of any kind whatever. Nevertheless, Professor Rawls is shortly going to put his happy primitives through feats of cerebration that even the gods might envy. Out of the minds of his homunculi, these epistemological zombies who don't know their names, families, races, generation or societies of origin, are going to come principles of justice and society so vast in implication as to throw all present human societies into a philosopher's limbo.

Miller (1976) (discussed shortly) similarly argues that removing *all* cultural knowledge will immobilize the negotiators; but failure to do so, though permitting them to make a decision, will result in a culture-bound definition of justice.

---

[5] Under the lexical extension of the difference principle any policy should benefit the worst off; if he is indifferent, it should benefit the next worse off, and so on. Rawls thus admits a policy which benefits *only* the best off, provided that everyone else is indifferent to it.

[6] Formally, a utilitarian social-welfare function (see Chapter 4, Section 1) does not constrain the way individuals are weighted; a Rawlsian social-welfare function gives infinite weight to the least-advantaged individual or group.

[7] See Chapter 4, Section 2.1, and the Appendix to Chapter 4, paras. 2–4.

The first principle is criticized[8] because Rawls's list of liberties may be too narrow, because the principle of toleration (e.g. of diversity of goals) inherent in Rawls's definition of liberty may reflect class bias, and because some issues are left unresolved—for example, what liberty should be accorded racists? Additionally, Barry (1973: 6) and Hart in Daniels (1975: p. xxx) dispute the priority given to liberty. Poor people might well be willing to trade some liberty for greater social or economic advantage. The second principle is criticized for its crucial dependence on maximin, which, it is argued (Arrow 1973*a*; Letwin 1983: 22–9), is the optimal outcome only under very restrictive assumptions.

MILLER'S ANALYSIS OF SOCIAL JUSTICE. A final criticism of Rawls is that he developed not a *general* theory of justice but a liberal theory. Miller (1976) argues that a completely general theory of justice is logically impossible, and that in this respect Rawls was bound to fail. According to Miller, social justice has three distinct elements:

- *rights*—e.g. political liberty, equality before the law;
- *deserts*—i.e. the recognition of each person's actions and qualities;
- *needs*—i.e. the prerequisites for fulfilling individual plans of life.

The 'deserts' aspect implies, ceteris paribus, that someone who works longer hours should receive more pay, and the 'needs' aspect that an individual incapable of work should not be allowed to starve. Though admitting the difficulty of precise theoretical definition, Miller argues that each element is a logically distinct principle embodying a particular type of moral claim.

It is easy to see that rights and deserts can be reconciled (e.g. a person should have the right to keep all her income if she has earned it legally); similarly, rights and needs can be compatible (e.g. a person should be entitled to health care if she is ill). But conflict can arise between desert and need: if I am rich and healthy and you are poor and ill, then either I am taxed (and do not receive my deserts) to pay for your medical treatment, or you receive no treatment (hence your need is not met) so as to protect my deserts.

The essence of Miller's argument is that the definition of social justice depends crucially on the type of society being discussed. In a pure market economy, justice will be defined in terms of rights and the requital of deserts. A collectivist defines justice as distribution according to need.

Miller thus argues that the different principles of justice are connected to wider views of society. He criticizes utilitarians and Rawls because they take no explicit account of the conflicting claims of rights, deserts, and needs, but blur them into a single, indistinct whole. Miller also criticizes the view implicit in Rawls that there is a single conception of justice upon which everyone's definition will converge, arguing instead that justice comprises conflicting principles, the relative weights attached to which may vary sharply between different societies. 'The whole enterprise of constructing a theory of justice on the basis of choice hypothetically made by individuals abstracted from society is mistaken, because these abstract ciphers lack the prerequisites for developing conceptions

[8] See Daniels (1975: pp. xxviii–xxix) and the chapters therein by Hart, Scanlon, Daniels, and Fisk.

of justice' (Miller 1976: 341). Or if they do manage to make choices, it must be in terms of culturally acquired attitudes. In short, the negotiators in the original position will be immobilized unless they have some knowledge of the nature of the society for which they are choosing rules of justice. Finally, 'Rawls individuals are given the attitudes and beliefs of men in modern market societies, and it is therefore not surprising that the conception of justice they . . . adopt should approximate to the conception . . . dominant in those societies' (ibid. 342). Hence, he argues, Rawls fails to develop a *general* theory of social justice; such generality is not possible.

4. Collectivist views

4.1. Democratic socialism

Collectivist writers agree on the importance of equality. They regard resources as available for collective use, and consequently favour government action; but historically they have disagreed about whether socialist goals could be achieved within a market order. Some writers advocate a mixed economy which blends private enterprise and state intervention; Marxists (discussed in Section 4.2) argue that this is not possible; that capitalism is inherently unjust; and that socialism is possible only where the state controls the allocation and distribution of most resources.

SOCIALIST AIMS vary widely, but three—equality, freedom, and fraternity—are central. Equality is a variant of the vertical equity aim discussed in Chapter 1, Section 2.2, and fraternity of the social solidarity aim. It is recognized that these aims can clash; and different writers accord them different weight; but together they make up the socialist definition of justice. In Miller's terms, the dominant themes are rights and needs, with deserts assigned a smaller role.

There is a measure of agreement (Tawney 1953, 1964; Crosland 1956) that the crucial element of justice is equality, which to socialists is an active concept. Equality of opportunity on its own may be insufficient (Tawney 1964; Laski 1967: ch. 4; Hattersley 1987), since substantial inequality of outcome may persist. Positive equalizing measures are needed, though not necessarily complete equality of outcome (see Daniel 1997).

Such emphasis on equality bears closely on Miller's concept of need. Weale points out that 'in some political arguments . . . the assumption is made that to distribute according to need is to satisfy the claims of equality' (1978: 67), but suggests (ch. 5) that the relationship is rather more complicated. For present purposes we need note only that equality and meeting need are closely related concepts, though not logically equivalent.

The socialist concept of freedom is broad. It embraces the free exercise of individual choice (which is possible only if there is no poverty and no substantial inequality of wealth and power), and extends from legal and political relations to economic security. Thus individuals should have some power in relation to their conditions of work, including stability of employment, and should not be subject to the arbitrary power of others. In sharp contrast with libertarian views, socialists regard government action as an essential and active component of freedom.

The third major value is fraternity. To a socialist this means cooperation and altruism rather than competition and self-interest. Altruism (e.g. Titmuss 1970) is a recurring theme.

SOCIALIST CRITICISM OF THE FREE MARKET starts with the motive given to individuals to pursue personal advantage rather than the general good, and denies the libertarian assertion that the former brings about the latter. Secondly, the market is regarded as undemocratic, inasmuch as some decisions with widespread effects are taken by a small power élite, and others are left to the arbitrary distributional effects of market forces. Thirdly, the market is unjust because it distributes rewards which are unrelated to individual need or merit, and because the costs of economic change are distributed arbitrarily. Fourthly, the free market is not self-regulating; in particular, left to itself, it is unable to maintain full employment. Lastly, the market has not been able to abolish poverty, let alone inequality. In sum,

production is carried on wastefully and without adequate plan. The commodities and services necessary to the life of the community are never so distributed as to relate to need or to produce a result which maximises their social utility. We build picture palaces when we need houses. We spend on battleships what is wanted for schools. . . . We have, in fact, both the wrong commodities produced, and those produced distributed without regard to social urgency.   (Laski 1967: 175)[9]

Socialists have generally been in broad agreement over aims, but have parted company over the best way of achieving them. Though the distinction is far from watertight, it is useful for exposition to contrast the 'fundamentalists' (largely Marxists), who reject capitalism, with what—at least since the collapse of Communism in Central and Eastern Europe and the former Soviet Union—has become the mainstream, which holds that the ills of society can be corrected within a broadly capitalist framework.

DEMOCRATIC SOCIALISM. Mainstream writers see two great changes in the capitalist system: first, government today has a large role to play in economic life as well as in other areas; secondly, the classic entrepreneur has largely disappeared, the ownership of modern corporations being both diffuse and largely separate from the people who manage them. It is argued in consequence (see the quote by Crosland at the head of the chapter) that capitalism has been 'tamed', and that the resulting mixed economy, with an active role for government in the distribution of goods, income, and power, is fully compatible with socialist objectives.

Latterly, at least in the UK, democratic socialism appears to have moved closer to liberalism, with more worry about the trade-off between efficiency and distributional

---

[9] Having read this paragraph, it is instructive to reread the diametrically opposite quote from Hayek (1976: 70–1) in Section 2, on the virtues of the market. The two were on excellent personal terms.

objectives, and hence less crisp adherence to older definitions of equality. Daniel (1997) puts it bluntly.

The current academic and political climate has come a long way from the ambitions of George Bernard Shaw, and even those set out in Labour's 1974 Manifesto which called for 'a fundamental and irreversible shift in the balance of power and wealth . . . far greater economic equality—in income, wealth and living standards . . . and an increase in social equality . . . [through] full employment, housing, education and social benefit'.

It is an illustration of how attitudes to equality have changed that this declaration seems absurdly extreme.   (pp. 23–4)

There is not enough political will to see through an aggressive direct attack on money inequalities . . . It seems clear that the focus will be on redistributing opportunities, not income—an emphasis on preventive medicine, through boosting skills, not invasive surgery, through higher taxes. (p. 25)

4.2. Marxists

This is not a Marxist book and I am no Marxist writer, so this section seeks only to sketch out as much Marxist thought as is necessary to contrast it with other theories (see George and Wilding 1994: ch. 5, and the Further Reading). In considering the Marxist view of capitalism, we need to turn our minds to three things: the contrast between the Marxist approach and that of conventional economic analysis; its analysis of the exploitation of labour; and its view of the role of government in supporting capitalism.

THE MARXIST APPROACH differs substantially from that of the classical political economists such as Adam Smith (1776) and Ricardo (1817), for whom the production of commodities was largely independent of the society in question. This approach has continued to dominate economic thinking. It is argued that conventional economic theory is applicable to the USA, to the UK, to Sweden, and to the former Communist countries; and such economic analysis is seen as almost entirely separate from political and social arrangements. Thus to Sweezy (1942: 5), 'economic theorising is primarily a process of constructing and interrelating concepts from which all specifically social content has been drained off'. A key part of Marx's thought, in contrast, is that the economic, political, and social structure of a society is determined largely by its dominant *mode of production*. It is argued that the capitalist mode of production will result not only in a particular form of economic organization, but also (and inevitably) in a particular and inequitable structure of social class and political power.

THE EXPLOITATION OF LABOUR UNDER CAPITALISM is a central tenet of Marxist thought. Conventional economic theory sees individuals as selling their labour services (more or less) freely in a (more or less) competitive market; the wage is established when the demand for labour equals its supply, which, under competitive conditions, results in a wage rate equal to the marginal product of labour. Capital, similarly, receives its marginal product, which, under competitive conditions and in the long run, is equal to the 'normal' rate of profit plus any premium for risk. Under certain conditions[10] these payments to factors exhaust the product leaving no surplus; thus, it is argued, there is no exploitation. In a Marxist analysis of the labour market this *apparently* free exchange of labour services (called *labour power*) for the wage is seen as a key feature of the capitalist mode of production. But for most people the sale of their labour power is their only means of subsistence, since other methods (e.g. the cultivation of common land) are largely blocked. Thus, 'in the capitalist mode of production the worker is *forced* to sell his/her labour power because he/she has no substantial savings or independent access to the means of production . . . Hence the relations of production are *enforced* through the institution of the labour market' (Ginsburg 1979: 21, emphasis added). Because of this compulsion, the capitalist can extract *surplus value* from the labour he employs.

Marx's argument is complex, but in essence exploitation arose because the capitalist was obliged to pay only a weekly wage sufficient to support the worker and his family at around subsistence, but could then extract as much output as possible by imposing long working hours. The surplus value is the difference between the value of a worker's output and his wage and is, according to Marx, much greater than that necessary to yield a 'normal' rate of profit. Individuals whose only source of income is the sale of their labour thus have less power than the (fewer) people who own wealth or have independent access to the means of production. Marx argued that this inequality of power is inevitable in a capitalist society, and consequently the more powerful few are able to exploit labour by extracting its surplus value, hence enjoying a disproportionate share of output.

Because of its exploitative nature, Marx's attitude to capitalism 'was one of total rejection rather than reform and much of his intellectual effort went into proving that the capitalist system was both unworkable and inhuman' (Mishra 1981: 69). The heart of the argument is that the capitalist mode of production causes conflict between one class (the large, poor, exploited working class) and another (the small ruling class, which derives power from wealth and/or political influence), and that conflict between these classes is inherent and inevitable.

THE ROLE OF GOVERNMENT IN A CAPITALIST SOCIETY. Given this position, it is necessary to ask why capitalism has survived despite the numerical superiority of the working class. The first reason, according to Marxists, relates to *economic* power, which is concentrated in a small number of hands. The second is the distribution of *political* power. The ruling class dominates government decisions, Marxists argue, both because of its economic power and because members of the economic élite share a common education and social class with the political élite. Accordingly, government in a capitalist society always favours the ruling élite (Miliband 1969: chs. 4–6). Thirdly, there is the power of the ruling class over *ideas*. The arguments are complex and the details controversial (see Strachey 1936;

[10] Euler's theorem states that paying all factors their marginal product will lead to product exhaustion under constant returns to scale. This can occur either where the production function exhibits constant returns to scale at all levels of output or at the point of minimum long-run average cost.

Miliband 1969: ch. 8). From this prop to capitalism derives the Marxist emphasis on 'consciousness raising'.

All three factors constitute the Marxist explanation of the continuance of capitalism despite class conflict. But there is disagreement whether the resulting structure supports capitalists by furthering the interests *only* of the ruling class, or whether the state, rather more broadly, supports the entire capitalist *system*, with benefits also for the working class. Gough (1979: 13–14) criticizes some Marxist writers for ignoring the effects of class conflict; he argues that in order to protect the capitalist system in the face of working-class pressure, the welfare state has been extended, with gains not only for the ruling élite, but also for workers.

THE MARXIST STATE. The next step is to outline the Marxist definition of a just society and the role of government necessary for its achievement. Marxists share the socialist triad of liberty, equality, and fraternity, though with some differences in interpretation and in their relative weights. Liberty is a much more active concept than the mere absence of coercion. It cannot exist where economic or political power is distributed unequally, nor where the actions of the state are biased (Laski 1967: ch. 4; Miliband 1969: ch. 7); freedom, moreover, includes a substantial measure of equality and economic security. To a Marxist, therefore, freedom and equality are two essential and intermingled aspects of social justice. This contrasts very sharply with the liberal perspective, in which the potential conflict between freedom and equality creates the central problem of political economy.

Equality to a Marxist does not necessarily imply complete equalization. According to Laski (1967: 157), 'the urgent claims of all must be met before we can meet the particular needs of some'. Once this basic condition has been met, differences in rewards should depend on effort or ability. It can therefore be argued that the Marxist aim is not equality but meeting need, which, as we have seen (Weale 1978), is a related but logically distinct objective. In Miller's terms, the Marxist definition of justice is based largely on needs, with rights somewhat secondary and with a small place for deserts.

Finally, we turn to the methods advocated by Marxists for the achievement of these aims. It is clear that their view of society, particularly the emphasis on economic equality and analysis of class conflict, implies a highly active role for government. They stress the importance of nationalizing the means of production, both because profits though produced socially generally accrue to a few large shareholders, and because private ownership of productive resources is incompatible with the Marxist definition of freedom. Though not a panacea, nationalization is regarded as essential to the achievement of Marxist aims, including industrial democracy, which is seen as a necessary concomitant of political democracy. An additional purpose is to ensure that industry is run for social rather than private benefit.

A Marxist society, therefore, would combine public ownership and government planning with wide-scale participation by workers in decisions affecting their lives. Libertarians argue that there is too much planning in the welfare state, Marxists that there is not enough—planning, they argue, far from reducing individual freedom, enhances it. It is logical that each side should reach the conclusion it does—planning reduces freedom defined by libertarians as the absence of coercion, but (if successful) enhances freedom defined by socialists to include some guarantee of economic security.

5. Implications for the role of the state

5.1. Theoretical issues

This section compares the theories, and discusses their implications for policy generally (Section 5.2) and the welfare state in particular (Section 5.3).

CRITICISMS OF LIBERALISM BY LIBERTARIANS centre largely on the definition of individual freedom. The liberal concept includes economic security, so that social justice embraces needs as well as rights and deserts. Libertarians criticize the inclusion of needs (at any rate above subsistence) because the resulting institutions (e.g. taxation) reduce efficiency, abridge natural rights (Nozick), and are part of a slippery slope towards totalitarianism (Hayek). Several counter-arguments are possible. The first concerns Hayek's argument that it is not possible to define social justice. As we shall see in Chapter 6, many concepts, including poverty and inequality, are hard, if not impossible, to define; but this does not imply that no such phenomenon exists. Defenders of Rawls would argue, in addition, that the priority of the liberty principle is explicit protection against the Hayekian slippery slope; and also that redistribution does not violate individual rights where it was agreed behind the veil of ignorance, as part of the social contract.

CRITICISMS OF LIBERALISM BY COLLECTIVISTS arise, first, because of the greater collectivist emphasis on needs. Additionally, collectivists adopt a broader definition of freedom. As a case in point, Daniels (1975) criticizes Rawls's liberty principle, because it underestimates the effect of economic inequality on political liberties; as a result, the two principles may be incompatible. Marxists also criticize liberal theories because they leave out class conflict.

CRITICISMS OF LIBERTARIANISM. There is no opposition by liberals to markets *per se*. But they attack the libertarian emphasis on *free* markets, which can distribute resources unjustly by failing to meet individual need. More specifically, Hayek (1976: 64–5) has a view of markets as a game with winners and losers; but it can be argued that it is a game without rules, like a boxing tournament in which participants are not divided into different classes by weight. To liberals this violates the assumption of equal power on which, *inter alia*, the advantages of a market system depend (see Chapter 4, Section 3.2). Collectivists criticize the libertarian definition of freedom as too narrow, and regard equality and economic security as inseparable aspects of freedom (contrast Hayek 1944: ch. 9, and Laski 1967: 520). In addition, Marxists reject the market system entirely.

CRITICISMS OF COLLECTIVISM. Natural-rights libertarians, in consequence, entirely reject collectivist views, since attempts to redistribute resources equally or in accordance with need are seen as violations of individual freedom. Empirical libertarians and liberals criticize collectivism not because it includes meeting need as an objective, but because it gives it pride of place.

A different line of criticism is that collectivism (particularly when combined with central planning and state ownership) is inefficient—as shown, for instance, by the growth slowdown after 1960 in the countries of Central and Eastern Europe and the former Soviet Union (see Estrin 1994; World Bank 1996: ch. 1). The major purpose of the late 1980s revolution throughout the region was to replace central planning by a market system, with the objectives of improved efficiency and increased individual freedom. It is important, however, not to misinterpret these events. It can be argued that collectivism defined, as by Marxists, in terms of its *methods* (e.g. state ownership and control) has been discredited. Democratic socialism, however, is defined in terms of its *aims*—for example, the pursuit of more or less egalitarian goals. This form of socialism, which blurs into a liberal analysis, remains firmly on the agenda.

5.2. Policy implications

PRIVATE PROPERTY is inviolate only to natural-rights libertarians like Nozick (1974: ch. 7), for whom justice in holdings implies total freedom for the individual to allocate as she chooses those resources which she has justly acquired. To Marxists, resources are available collectively to be distributed according to need; hence their emphasis on public ownership, and the view that 'property is theft' (see Laski 1967: chs. 5 and 9).

To liberals, private property and public ownership are a pragmatic matter, and government should be free to adopt whichever mix of the two is most helpful in achieving its aims. Rawls maintains that his two principles are compatible with either private or public ownership of resources, or with a mixed economy. Empirical libertarians accord private property a major but not overriding role; and democratic socialists allow it a more important role than formerly.

TAXATION to Nozick means that an individual will work (say) three days a week for himself, and two days compulsorily for the government; to Nozick, therefore, it is taxation, not private property, which is a form of theft. It is, however, mistaken to attribute this view to all libertarians. The necessity of taxation was always acknowledged by the classical liberals (Robbins 1978: ch. 2), albeit with some reluctance because of the consequent interference with liberty. The modern inheritors of this position such as Hayek and Friedman and the New Right concede the necessity of some taxation for the provision of public goods (narrowly defined) and for poverty relief (generally at subsistence).

To collectivist writers (Tawney 1964: 135–6) taxation for any social purpose is entirely legitimate. Liberals, also, regard taxation as an appropriate means towards policy objectives, though they are concerned about its disincentive effects particularly on labour supply and capital formation, and more generally with selecting an optimal trade-off between efficiency and social justice (Atkinson and Stiglitz 1980: lectures 12–14).

REDISTRIBUTION. Distributive justice is not a problem for everyone. To Marxists, resources are available for collective allocation on the basis of need, which is given clear priority. Natural-rights libertarians like Nozick concentrate entirely on rights and deserts. Resources are produced by *individuals*, who thereby acquire the right to allocate them; the question of *societal* allocation does not arise. Distributive justice is therefore removed entirely from the agenda.

Other groups have difficulties with distribution precisely because they are concerned with both desert and need. Empirical libertarians may oppose progressive taxation; but they do not take an absolute line against redistribution, accepting public action to relieve destitution. Utilitarians favour redistributive activity which increases total welfare, but are concerned about the trade-off with efficiency. Rawls, too, is not a complete egalitarian, since privilege is acceptable where it improves the position of the least well off. For general discussion, see Brittan (1995: ch. 12).

PUBLIC PRODUCTION raises similar arguments. Libertarians countenance provision by the state of at most a limited class of public goods such as law and order, and even those only if no method of private supply can be found (Hayek 1960: 223; Friedman 1962: ch. 2). In complete opposition, Marxists regard it as a function of the state to supply all basic goods and services, and to distribute them in accordance with individual need. To liberals the issue of public versus market production and allocation is a pragmatic question of which method is more effective—the subject of most of this book.

5.3. Attitudes towards the welfare state

The welfare state is a complicated set of institutions, so it is not surprising that attitudes towards it are complicated (for detailed discussion, see George and Wilding 1994).

NATURAL-RIGHTS LIBERTARIANS like Nozick regard a welfare state of any sort as an anathema, seeing its pursuit of the spurious (or immoral) goal of equality as an unacceptable violation of individual liberty.

EMPIRICAL LIBERTARIANS such as Hayek and Friedman require careful discussion. The distinction between an institutional welfare state, which pursues substantially redistributive goals, and a residual welfare state was discussed in Chapter 2, Section 7.1. The former is strongly opposed by all libertarians. It is seen as a coercive agency which stifles freedom and individualism and courts the risk of totalitarianism through the amalgamation of economic and political power under central planning, in contrast with their separation in a market system. It also creates inefficiency because at a zero or subsidized price demand is excessive, because government monopoly is insulated from competition, and because of the distortionary effects of the taxation necessary to finance it.

A residual welfare state has much more limited aims. It is recognized that a free society based on private property and competitive markets is likely to distribute income unequally. Limited state activity may therefore be appropriate to relieve destitution and to provide certain public goods. Empirical libertarians consider this rather austere welfare state as essential to their conception of a civilized society. It is therefore not inconsistent when they attack existing social arrangements in the strongest terms (see Hayek 1960, and the quote from Friedman at the head of this chapter), but support more limited welfare institutions (see Friedman 1962: chs. 6, 12; Willetts 1992: ch. 10; George and Wilding 1994: ch. 2).

LIBERALS AND DEMOCRATIC SOCIALISTS tend unambiguously to support the welfare state (George and Wilding 1994: chs. 3, 4). To Beveridge (1944: 254) it was necessary 'to use the powers of the State, so far as may be necessary without any limit whatsoever, in order to avoid the five giant evils'.[11] Writers like Gilmour (1992) argue that the welfare state is not just an outcome of working-class pressure nor a creation of the post-war Labour government but an all-party creation deeply rooted in British history.

For most socialist writers, however, the welfare state is not a complete solution to society's ills, but only a step along the way.

For [Democratic Socialists], the welfare state is a significant staging post in the transition from laissez-faire capitalism to socialism . . . They have always understood and accepted that this transition . . . would be both gradual and slow for they have consistently rejected any other form of transition but the parliamentary process. . . . Social policy plays a very special role in this transition . . .   (George and Wilding 1994: 74)

It is not surprising that liberals and socialists share some common ground. Robson (1976: 17), citing Hobhouse, writes:

The liberal . . . stands for emancipation, and is the inheritor of a long tradition of those who have fought for liberty, who have struggled against government and its laws or against society because they crushed human development . . . The socialist stands for solidarity of society, for mutual responsibility and the duty of the strong to aid the weak . . . On this analysis the ideals of the liberal and socialist were seen as complementary rather than conflicting.

MARXISTS disagree among themselves (George and Wilding 1994: ch. 5). Is the welfare state *only* an instrument of capitalist oppression, or does it *also* represent a progressive outcome of working-class pressure? Under the first view, the welfare state is at best irrelevant, a 'ransom' paid by the dominant class, and an institution dealing with symptoms rather than causes of economic and social problems; at worst, the welfare state is actively malign, in that it has sustained the capitalist system. 'Social control . . . has to do with

---

[11]   Want, disease, ignorance, squalor, and idleness—see the discussion in Chapter 1, Section 1.1.

the maintenance of order and the reduction of social conflict and tension. From the viewpoint of the ruling classes this often means reducing the workers' hostility towards the capitalist regime . . .' (Mishra 1981: 82). This, according to some Marxists, is the major purpose of the welfare state.

Other Marxist writers see the welfare state as serving the interests of the capitalist class *and* those of workers. A central insight (Gintis and Bowles 1982) is the contradictory position of the welfare state in a modern capitalist economy; the former is based on rights (e.g. of citizenship) and needs, the latter recognizes claims on resources based on deserts (e.g. through the ownership of property). Thus Gough (1979) sees the state not as a neutral umpire, nor as acting *merely* in the interests of the capitalist class (as opposed to the capitalist *system*), but as responding to pressure: from the working class to meet needs and extend rights; and from capital to foster capital accumulation.

The welfare state thus has contradictory functions. 'It simultaneously embodies tendencies to enhance social welfare, to develop the powers of individuals, to exert social control over the blind play of market forces; and tendencies to repress and control people, to adapt them to the requirements of the capitalist economy' (Gough 1979: 12).

As a result it is not surprising that some Marxists have ambivalent attitudes. Is the welfare state an 'agency of repression, or a system for enlarging human needs and mitigating the rigours of the free-market economy? An aid to capitalist accumulation and profits or a "social wage" to be defended and enlarged like the money in your pay packet? Capitalist fraud or working-class victory?' (ibid. 11).

Whether the welfare state contributes to justice is clearly a matter of perspective, and hence susceptible of no definitive answer. Miller (1976: 343–4) admits that 'readers with a yearning for Rawlsian "moral geometry" may . . . find this [conclusion] disappointing. Can there be no . . . arguments of universal validity that hold good across social and historical barriers? This is indeed a pleasant prospect, but since there seems little hope of it being realised, I conclude that we shall have to make do with more modest results.'

It is, nevertheless, instructive to conclude with a few words on who can usefully talk with whom, and about what. It is not possible to enter debate with natural-rights defenders of free markets and the nightwatchman state, save by disputing their values, nor with Marxists, to whom the evils of the market system are axiomatic. But dialogue *is* possible between empirical libertarians, liberals, and democratic socialists. Writers such as Hayek and Friedman share common roots in nineteenth-century classical liberalism with the largely utilitarian arguments of this book. Their position rests less on an ethical than on a theoretical and empirical view about the institutions likely to maximize total utility. The distinction is vital. The issues dividing a liberal defence of the welfare state from the views of empirical libertarians are not moral but largely factual. The main thrust of the argument is that technical problems with markets as both a theoretical and an empirical matter are much more pervasive than Hayek and Friedman allow. These are the grounds of the debate; the theoretical heart of the argument is the subject of Chapter 4.

FURTHER READING

For more detailed discussion of the ideas in this chapter and their application to the welfare state, see George and Wilding (1994).

Libertarian ideas are set out by Nozick (1974) (a natural-rights defence), Hayek (1944, 1960, 1976), Friedman (1962), and Friedman and Friedman (1980). For an appreciation of Hayek, see Brittan (1995: ch. 6). The intellectual roots of these ideas are discussed by Robbins (1978).

The liberal approach is analysed by Barry (1973) and Miller (1976). On utilitarianism, see, for instance, Sen (1973). On the impossibility of a Paretian liberal, see Sen (1982), Sen and Williams (1982), and for a summary of the main arguments, Brittan (1995: ch. 3). For an introduction to Rawls (1972), see Gorovitz (1975) (one of the best teaching articles I have read, and one to which readers are most warmly referred). For more detailed commentary, see the contributions in Daniels (1975), and Sen (1992: ch. 5); for liberal critiques, Barry (1973) and Miller (1976); and for cogent libertarian criticism, Nisbet (1974). McCreadie (1976) offers an interesting application to the UK National Health Service.

A simple introduction to socialist thought (and also to the other theories of society) is by George and Wilding (1994), and discussion in greater depth by Crosland (1956), Tawney (1964) (a defence of equality), Laski (1967), and Miliband (1969).

The classic exposition of Marxist economic theory is Sweezy (1942). See also Mandel (1976), J. Harrison (1978), and Desai (1979). Marxist attitudes to the welfare state are discussed by Ginsburg (1979), Gough (1979), and Mishra (1981).

On arguments about equality, see the essays in Franklin (1997) (a defence of equality) and Letwin (1983) (a libertarian critique of egalitarianism).

Gender aspects of the welfare state are discussed by George and Wilding (1994: ch. 7), Sainsbury (1994), and Anne Phillips (1997).

Appendix: Non-technical summary of Chapter 3

1. Chapter 3 discusses various theories of society—libertarianism, utilitarianism, Rawlsian arguments, and socialism. In practice the theories blur into each other like the colours of the rainbow, but it is useful for exposition to talk about them as separate entities.

Libertarian theories

2. To libertarians (Section 2), as their name implies, the primary aim of institutions is individual liberty, and the best method of achieving its economic dimension is through the operation of private markets. *Natural-rights libertarians* like Nozick (1974) defend a minimal (or 'night-watchman') state on ethical grounds; *empirical libertarians* such as Hayek and Friedman out of a belief that such a regime will maximize total welfare. For natural-rights libertarians the state has no legitimate distributional role at all; to empirical libertarians its distributional activities are strictly circumscribed.

3. Hayek argues in addition that the pursuit of social justice is not only fruitless because there is no such thing, but also dangerous because it will destroy the market order which is both efficient and the only guarantee of personal freedom. According to Hayek (1976), a given circumstance is just or unjust only if it has been caused by the action/inaction of a *named* individual or individuals. The outcome of impersonal forces ('Nature') can be good or bad, but never just or unjust. The market is seen as an impersonal force, akin to an economic game with winners and losers, and so the market-determined distribution of goods can be neither just nor unjust. The notion of social justice therefore has no meaning. Its quest, however, is dangerous according to Hayek, because once governments start to interfere with the market-determined distribution a process is set in motion which progressively approaches totalitarianism.

Liberal theories

4. Liberal theories (Section 3)—e.g. utilitarianism and Rawlsian thinking—contrast with libertarian views first by allowing the state a greater distributional role, and secondly through a weaker presumption that the free market is necessarily the best means of production and distribution. The treatment of property rights is not an end in itself, as with libertarians, but a means towards the achievement of stated policy aims. In certain circumstances this can justify a mixed economy.

5. The utilitarian aim is to distribute goods so as to maximize the total utility of society's members (Section 3.1). Where individuals have identical marginal utility of income functions, this occurs when income is shared equally (Figure 3.1). Utilitarianism thus enables statements to be about the optimal distribution of goods (which in certain circumstances can be egalitarian), and so legitimates a redistributive role of the state.

6. This approach is criticized by Rawls and others because it can justify harm to the least well-off individual or group, if this raises total utility.

Concepts

7. Rawls, in contrast, makes justice the primary aim of policy (Section 3.2) (for a very clear introduction, see Gorovitz 1975). Rawls defines social justice in terms of two principles, the first dealing with the distribution of liberty, the second with that of other goods. Taken together they imply that all goods (interpreted broadly to include liberty and opportunity) should be distributed equally unless an unequal distribution is to the advantage of the least well-off individual or group. No policy should be undertaken, according to Rawls, unless it benefits also (though not necessarily only) the least well-off. Again, there is a legitimate, and generally egalitarian, redistributive role for the state.

8. The theories of utilitarians and Rawls can have different policy implications. Suppose a given policy change makes at least one person better off without making anyone worse off. This is a Pareto improvement (see Chapter 4, Section 2.1); hence utilitarians would regard the policy as desirable, even if the individual thus benefited were rich. Rawls's principles of justice would oppose the policy unless it were also to the advantage of the least well-off. Thus an efficient answer in a Paretian sense is not always just in a Rawlsian sense (see Chapter 4, Section 2.2).

Socialist theories

9. The main socialist aims are equality, freedom, and fraternity. These values can conflict, and different writers accord them different weight. But there is general agreement about the importance of equality, which is closely related (though not logically equivalent) to the further socialist aim of meeting need.

10. Despite agreement about their aims, and in their diagnosis of the failings of the free market, socialists are divided over how best to achieve them, most fundamentally over the role, if any, of the market system.

11. Democratic socialists (Section 4.1) argue that institutional changes, not least the enlarged role of government in economic life, have greatly reduced the evils of capitalism and made it possible to harness the market system to socialist goals. Adherents of this view accept a role for private property and the market mechanism, though modified in both cases by state intervention—i.e. like liberals they feel that their aims are likely to be best achieved by some sort of mixed economy.

12. Other socialists, e.g. Marxists (Section 4.2), argue that private ownership and the market system are inherently in conflict with socialist aims. In particular they regard the market as exploitative and therefore incompatible with equality. Marxists therefore reject capitalism outright, whether or not it makes up part of a mixed economy, and give the state a primary role in production and allocation, as well as in distribution and redistribution.

Attitudes towards the welfare state

13. The appropriate role of the state depends crucially on the underlying theory of society (Sections 5.1 and 5.2), as also do attitudes towards the welfare state (Section 5.3).

14. Natural-rights libertarians reject all but minimal intervention and are unambiguously hostile to the welfare state, which they regard as a coercive agency which stifles freedom and individualism, and encourages waste and inefficiency in pursuit of the spurious and dangerous goal of social justice.

15. Empirical libertarians have a broadly similar attitude towards a large-scale welfare state with substantial redistributive goals. They do, however, recognize that a free society based on private property and competitive markets is likely to distribute income unequally, and are therefore prepared to support an austere welfare state whose primary aim is the relief of destitution.

16. The main support for the welfare state comes from liberals and democratic socialists, in the latter case unreservedly, because it is seen as an equalizing force. For liberals its existence is a contingent question: they support the institutions of the welfare state where (and only where) they contribute more than alternative arrangements to the achievement of society's aims. In such cases their support is unreserved.

17. Marxists are generally hostile to the welfare state, though with some controversy. 'Hardline' commentators regard it as an actively malign agency which serves *only* (or mainly) as an instrument of social control, to protect the continued existence of the capitalist system. Other writers argue that, though the welfare state is indeed a 'ransom' paid by the dominant class, it *also* represents a genuine improvement in working-class conditions.

18. Finally, who can talk with whom, and about what? No debate is possible between liberals and natural-rights libertarians, on the one hand, or between liberals and Marxists, on the other. Debate *is*, however, possible between liberals and libertarians such as Hayek and Friedman, who argue less from a moral position than from an empirical view about the institutions likely to maximize total utility. The main thrust of this book is that technical problems with markets, as both a theoretical and an empirical matter, are much more pervasive than Hayek and Friedman allow. In other words, the issues which separate a liberal defence of the welfare state from the views of empirical libertarians are at least as much factual as ideological.

CHAPTER 4

Economic theory 1:
State intervention

Every individual . . . generally . . . neither intends to promote the public interest, nor knows by how much he is promoting it. By preferring the support of domestic to that of foreign industry he intends only his own security; and by directing that industry in such a manner as its produce may be of the greatest value, he intends only his own gain, and he is in this, as in many other cases, led by an invisible hand to promote an end which was no part of his intention.   Adam Smith, 1776

[The] market needs a place, and the market needs to be kept in its place. It must be given enough scope to accomplish the many things it does well. It limits the power of bureaucracy . . . responds reliably to the signals transmitted by consumers and producers . . . Most important, the prizes in the market place provide the incentives for work effort and productive contribution . . . For such reasons I cheered the market; but I could not give it more than two cheers. The tyranny of the dollar yardstick restrained my enthusiasm.   Arthur Okun, 1975

I see the critical failing in the standard neoclassical model to be in its assumptions concerning information . . . however, while it is the informational assumptions underlying the standard theory which are perhaps its Achilles heel, its failures go well beyond that: The assumptions concerning completeness of markets, competitiveness of markets, and the absence of innovation are three that I stress.   Joseph E. Stiglitz, 1994

1. The formal structure of the problem

We now change gear and move from the world of political philosophy to economic theory.[1] The main aim is to develop a framework which (*a*) explains and (*b*) justifies (or fails

---

[1] Non-technical readers can find the gist of the argument in the Appendix at the end of the chapter.

to justify) the fact that the state produces and/or allocates some goods such as health care and education, but leaves others like food for the most part to the private market. The main issues concern economic efficiency and social justice. Section 1 sets out the formal structure of the problem. Section 2 shows that the efficiency aim is common to all theories of society, but that redistributive goals depend crucially on which definition of social justice is chosen. The next step (Section 3) is to consider the conditions in which the market will allocate efficiently, and appropriate forms of intervention where those conditions fail. The pursuit of social justice (Section 4) raises such questions as: why does redistribution occur; should it be voluntary; should it be in cash or in kind; and what role (if any) should the state adopt to bring about equality of access, opportunity, or outcome? One set of counter-arguments to government intervention comes from the 'government-failure' analysis, discussed briefly in Section 5. As a precursor to policy discussion in later chapters, Section 6 sets out the logic of privatization. Section 7 pulls together the major threads running through Chapters 3 and 4 by discussing the appropriate boundary between the market and the state, summarizing the main theoretical argument of the book, and establishing the areas of debate with its opponents, particularly libertarian writers such as Hayek and Friedman.

The conventional starting point for economic theory is the social-welfare-maximization problem. The aim of policy is to maximize social welfare subject to the three basic constraints of tastes, technology, and resources, i.e.

Maximize: $$W = W(U^A, U^B) \tag{4.1}$$

Subject to:
$$\left. \begin{array}{l} U^A = U^A(X^A, Y^A) \\ U^B = U^B(X^B, Y^B) \end{array} \right\} \text{Tastes} \qquad \begin{array}{l} (4.2) \\ (4.3) \end{array}$$

$$\left. \begin{array}{l} X = X(K^X, L^X) \\ Y = Y(K^Y, L^Y) \end{array} \right\} \text{Technology} \qquad \begin{array}{l} (4.4) \\ (4.5) \end{array}$$

$$\left. \begin{array}{l} K^X + K^Y = \bar{K} \\ L^X + L^Y = \bar{L} \end{array} \right\} \text{Resources} \qquad \begin{array}{l} (4.6) \\ (4.7) \end{array}$$

The aim in equation (4.1) is to maximize social welfare, W, as a function of the utilities of individuals A and B, U^A and U^B (thus the problem is a joint maximization of efficiency and social justice). The utilities of individuals A and B are constrained by their consumption of goods X and Y (equations (4.2) and (4.3)); consumption is constrained by equations (4.4) and (4.5), which show the production functions for X and Y in terms of the inputs of capital, K, and labour, L; the inputs used to produce X and Y are constrained by the total availability of capital and labour, $\bar{K}$ and $\bar{L}$ (equations (4.6) and (4.7)).

The problem as formulated relates to a *first-best economy*. This implies one of two situations: either there is no impediment to efficiency, and also an optimal distribution of endowments; or government can counter problems of inefficiency or maldistribution with first-best policies (e.g. through lump-sum taxation). An important theorem discussed in Section 3 establishes the (first-best) assumptions under which a competitive market will allocate resources efficiently. Where these conditions hold, the state has no role except possibly a distributional one.

The conditions, however, are stringent, as is the assumption that lump-sum taxation is feasible. A *second-best economy* faces additional constraints: imperfect information is a recurring theme, e.g. if U^A is not well-defined with respect to X^A. As a result, unrestricted markets may be inefficient or inequitable, and intervention may improve matters. Externalities are another problem. If U^A depends on X^B we have a consumption externality which constitutes a constraint additional to those in equations (4.2) to (4.7). This may justify intervention in various forms. We return to these issues in Sections 3 and 4.[2]

2. Why economic efficiency is one of the aims of policy

2.1. The concept of economic efficiency

Since the concept of efficiency[3] is fundamental to the whole book, this brief introduction is included in the main body of the chapter rather than relegated to the Appendix. Technical readers should proceed directly to Section 2.2.

Economic efficiency[4] is about making the best use of limited resources given people's tastes. It involves the choice of an *output bundle*

$$X^* = (X_1, X_2, \ldots, X_N) \qquad (4.8)$$

(where X_i is the output of the ith good) with the property that any deviations from these quantities will make at least one person worse off. The intuition is shown in a partial equilibrium framework in Figure 4.1: the optimal quantity of any good, ceteris paribus, is that at which the value placed by society on the marginal unit equals its marginal social cost.[5]

For a general equilibrium three conditions must hold simultaneously.[6]

1. *Productive efficiency* means that activity should be organized to obtain the maximum output from given inputs. This is what engineers mean when they talk about efficiency. It is about building a hospital to a specified standard with as few workers as possible standing around waiting for something to do. It is also about the choice of

---

[2] For a compendious survey of the literature on first- and second-best analysis within the social-welfare-maximization framework, see Atkinson and Stiglitz (1980: lectures 11–14).

[3] Non-technical readers should consult (in ascending order of difficulty) the relevant chapters (see the following footnotes) in Le Grand *et al.* (1992), Baumol and Blinder (1997: ch. 3), Stiglitz (1993*b*: chs. 2, 4), Estrin and Laidler (1995: ch. 30), or Varian (1996: ch. 1).

[4] Referred to synonymously as Pareto efficiency, Pareto optimality, allocative efficiency, or external efficiency.

[5] See Le Grand *et al.* (1992: ch. 1) or Stiglitz (1993*b*: chs. 7, 13).

[6] See, in ascending order of formality, Estrin and Laidler (1995: ch. 30), Varian (1996: chs. 28, 29), or Varian (1992: chs. 17, 18).

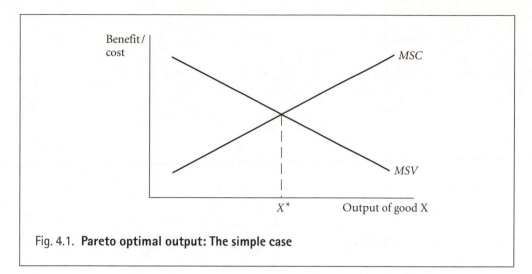

Fig. 4.1. **Pareto optimal output: The simple case**

technique, taking the prices of inputs into account. The transformation curve $Y_0 X_0$ in Figure 4.2 shows the maximum quantities of the two goods that can be produced with available resources. Productive efficiency means that production is at a point on—rather than inside—the transformation curve. Thus all points on the transformation curve conform with productive efficiency.

This, however, is not enough for allocative efficiency, which requires two additional conditions to hold.

2. *Efficiency in product mix* means that the optimal combination of goods should be produced given existing production technology and consumer tastes. The fact that it is possible to build a hospital cheaply is not *per se* justification for building it. The resources involved could perhaps give the local population greater satisfaction if used to build a school; or the land could be used as a park, and the money saved by not building a hospital used to reduce taxes.

Formally, production is not at *any* point on the transformation curve in Figure 4.2, but at the specific point *a*, at which the ratio of marginal production costs (i.e. the slope of the transformation curve) is equal to the ratio of marginal rates of substitution in consumption (i.e. the slope of the 'social' indifference curve, *I–I*).

3. *Efficiency in consumption* means that consumers should allocate their income in a way which maximizes their utility, given their incomes and the prices of the goods they buy—in formal terms, the marginal rate of substitution must be equal for all individuals.

The meaning of the third condition is analysed further in the Edgeworth box in Figure 4.3. The size of the box shows the total output to be divided between individuals A and B, $O_A X^*$ of good X and $O_A Y^*$ of good Y, where the quantities X^* and Y^* are those in Figure 4.2 (hence fulfilling efficiency in production and in product mix). The output allocated to A is measured from the origin O_A, and that to B from O_B; at point *g* the two individuals share output equally. The contract curve, represented by the line $O_A O_B$,

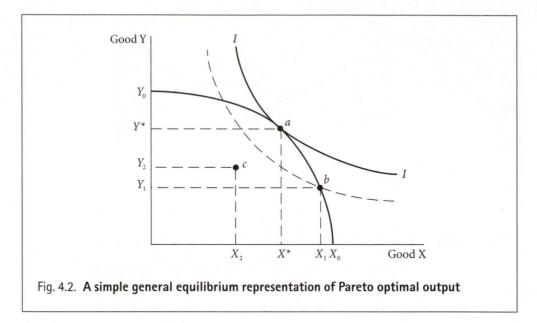

Fig. 4.2. **A simple general equilibrium representation of Pareto optimal output**

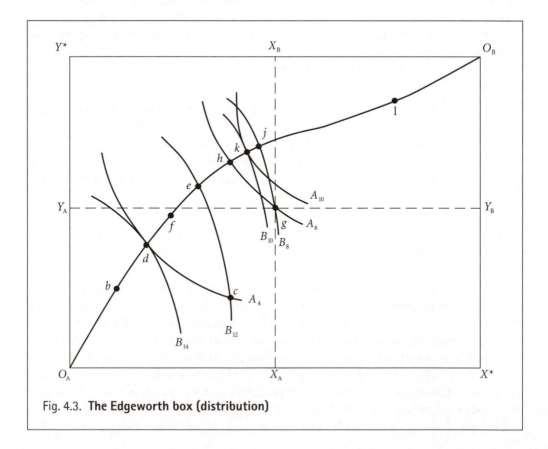

Fig. 4.3. **The Edgeworth box (distribution)**

shows those combinations of X and Y at which the marginal rate of substitution between the two goods is the same for both individuals. Any movement away from the contract curve makes at least one person worse off. Hence any point on the contract curve constitutes an efficient allocation.

Thus in Figure 4.2, point c is neither productively nor allocatively efficient. Point b, like all other points on the transformation curve, conforms with productive efficiency. Only point a conforms with both productive and allocative efficiency. Thus allocative efficiency conforms simultaneously with all these requirements. It will depend on external conditions (more resources are devoted to hotels on the Mediterranean than in Murmansk); it will depend on tastes (the French spend more on food than the English; the English spend more on gardens than the Germans; Hungarians consume more paprika than anyone else); it will depend on the age of the population (more resources are spent on schools in a country with many children); it will depend on income levels (private ownership of cars and personal computers is more widespread in better-off countries). The argument in favour of markets, discussed in detail in Section 3, is that they can automatically achieve this efficient result.

The concept of a *Pareto improvement* is important for the analysis which follows. Suppose the initial allocation is shown by point c in Figure 4.3; then individual A on indifference curve A_4 is 'poor' and B on indifference curve B_{12} 'rich'. If trade moves the allocation to point d, then B is better off (he has moved to the higher indifference curve B_{14}) and A is no worse off; this is a Pareto improvement. Similarly, a move to the allocation shown by e makes A better off without harming B; and a move to an intermediate allocation like f benefits both parties. Thus any move from the distribution shown by c to any distribution on the contract curve between d and e, including points d and e themselves, increases efficiency and constitutes a Pareto improvement.[7] The next question is which of these allocations is socially optimal.

2.2. The relevance of efficiency to different theories of society

The relationship between efficiency and social welfare is shown in Figure 4.3.[8] We have seen that a move from point c to a point like e is a Pareto improvement. The next step is to show that this is not just a utilitarian result. In each case two questions are considered: (*a*) given an initial suboptimal allocation, what constitutes a welfare improvement; and (*b*) what is the optimal distribution of goods, i.e. what allocation is both efficient and socially just? Two results are established: economic efficiency, in the sense of a movement to an appropriate subset of the contract curve, is an important aim under *all* the

---

[7] For an amusing and informative example taken from a prisoner-of-war camp, see Radford (1945).

[8] The issue can be approached also via a utility-possibility frontier, which can be derived as a simple transformation of the contract curve in Figure 4.3; see Estrin and Laidler (1995: ch. 32), and, for fuller treatment, Atkinson and Stiglitz (1980: lecture 11.2).

Concepts

definitions of social justice discussed in Chapter 3; and in a first-best economy no distribution can be socially just unless it is also efficient.

These, however, can be murky waters. Pareto efficiency incorporates two value judgements: social welfare is increased if one person is made better off and nobody worse off, and individuals are the best judge of their own welfare. As discussed in Chapter 3, Section 3.1, these assumptions can be problematic. Thus 'Pareto-type definitions . . . are not uncontested . . . for they incorporate values that are less innocuous that might be at first apparent' (Le Grand 1996: 152; see also Le Grand 1991a: ch. 3). This section (and Barr 1985, from which it largely derives) abstract from these problems.

THE FIXED–FACTOR CASE assumes an Edgeworth box of given size, and also that the conditions for efficiency in production and in product mix hold. This is equivalent to discussing a first-best solution.

Libertarianism.[9] Welfare is increased by any Pareto improvement, which to writers like Nozick is the only source of welfare gain. Thus a movement from c in Figure 4.3 to any point on the contract curve between points d and e (including the end points) increases welfare.

Natural-rights libertarians have little to say about the optimal distribution of goods. If the initial distribution is at c, then any point on the contract curve between d and e is optimal, provided that c accords with Nozick's idea of justice in holdings, and that the movement from c to the contract curve is the result of individual utility maximization through voluntary trading in a competitive market system. More generally, depending on the initial distribution, *any* point on the contract curve can be an optimum. Empirical libertarians such as Hayek and Friedman support this conclusion, save that they accept redistributive activity up to (but not beyond) a guarantee of subsistence— that is, they would have nothing to say about movements along the contract curve between points b and l, if these show subsistence for individuals A and B, respectively.

Utilitarians aim to maximize total utility. Again, any Pareto improvement, such as a move from c to the contract curve between (and including) points d and e, will increase welfare.

Is any point on the contract curve superior to any other, i.e. do movements *along* the contract curve raise welfare? The utilitarian answer, which is often misunderstood, depends on whether utility is ordinally or cardinally measurable. When utility is cardinally measurable and A and B have identical marginal utility of income functions (as in Figure 3.1), welfare is maximized by starting from an equal distribution of goods, shown by point g in Figure 4.3. From this egalitarian endowment, Pareto improvement is possible; under the stated assumptions total utility will be highest at point k. Individuals A and B are on indifference curves A_{10} and B_{10}, respectively; each enjoys ten units of utility (because utility is cardinally measurable); and (because marginal utility of

[9] The libertarian theory of society is discussed in Chapter 3, Section 2. Utilitarianism, Rawls, and socialism are discussed in Chapter 3, Sections 3.1, 3.2, and 4, respectively, and in the Appendix to Chapter 3.

income declines) total utility is lower at all other points on the contract curve. In these circumstances a move *along* the contract curve from a point like *e* towards *k* constitutes a utilitarian welfare improvement.

This egalitarian outcome, however, depends on A and B having identical marginal utility of income functions. If A is a gloomy guy and B is a cheerful chappie, social welfare is maximized at a point like *d*, and with roles reversed at a point like *l*. The same logic applies when utility is measurable only ordinally, but here, though we know that the optimum distribution is at a point like *k* (or *d* or *l*), we cannot say which point because we cannot compare the utility of the two individuals. Note that the latter conclusion is fundamentally different from the libertarian argument that there is no ethical difference between points on the curve like *d*, *k*, and *l*.

Rawls's aim is to distribute resources in accordance with social justice. Starting again from point *c*, a movement to *e* is a Rawlsian improvement (RI) because it benefits the less advantaged individual A. But a movement from *c* to *d*, though a Pareto improvement (PI), is *not* RI because it violates Rawls's principle that matters are to be arranged to the benefit of the least advantaged. A movement from *c* to a point between *d* and *e* is RI (and PI), because it benefits A at least to some extent. In addition, a movement from *c* to points between (and including) *e* and *k*, though it is not PI (since individual B is made worse off), is RI because it benefits the less-advantaged A. Hence a movement from *c* to the contract curve between *d* and *e*, *including* points *d* and *e*, is PI; RI excludes point *d*[10] and includes points between *e* and *k*. The conclusion is that, if we are off the contract curve at a point like *c*, there will always be a subset of the contract curve which is RI. Thus, in a first-best economy *all Rawlsian socially just distributions lie on the contract curve*.

According to Rawls, goods should be distributed equally, unless any other distribution benefits the least well off. Hence the just distribution is generally point *g*, and the optimum outcome point *k*—that is, a single, known, and (generally) egalitarian point. Any movement along the contract curve towards *k* is an unambiguous improvement.

Socialism. Under one interpretation resources should be shared equally. A movement from *c* to *e* raises the welfare of (poor) individual A, thereby reducing relative inequality. Such a move is a socialist improvement (SI). But a movement from *c* to *d* helps only (rich) individual B. If output is fixed (i.e. ruling out the case where B uses the extra resources to bring about economic growth to the advantage of A), this increases relative inequality and is therefore not SI. A movement from *c* to an intermediate point like *f* is arguable. I shall define (though others may disagree) SI to refer to any movement which increases individual A's *relative share* of output, thereby reducing inequality. Suppose *f* is the point on the contract curve at which A's relative share is the same as at *c*. We can then interpret as SI a movement from *c* to any point on the contract curve between (and including) *e* and *k*, and arguably also to any point between *e* and *f* (excluding point *f* itself). *SI is thus a subset of RI*, and all first-best solutions which are just in a socialist sense lie on the contract curve; and, like Rawls, socialists will favour any movement along the contract curve towards *k*.

---

[10] Unless the lexical extension to the difference principle applies (see Chapter 3, note 5).

Concepts

RELAXING THE FIXED-FACTOR-SUPPLY ASSUMPTION complicates matters because of the resulting need, in the absence of lump-sum taxation, to analyse policies in a second-best economy. It is a standard proposition (Atkinson and Stiglitz 1980: 343) that lump-sum transfers, being based on characteristics exogenous to the taxpayer, can bring about any desired distribution of income or goods without efficiency loss. Taxes related to income, however (including any indirect tax whose payment rises with income), are not lump sum, and generally cause inefficiency, *inter alia* through their effect on individual labour supply. But attempts to achieve social justice (such as a movement from e to k in Figure 4.3) involve redistribution; hence taxation must inevitably be income related. As a result, any practicable system of taxation may cause inefficiency in production and/or product mix. Thus there may be a trade-off between efficiency and equity.

This trade-off is analysed formally in the optimal taxation literature[11] in terms of the social-welfare-maximization framework set out in Section 1. The distribution which jointly optimizes efficiency and social justice depends on two sets of factors: the efficiency costs of redistribution (mainly a technical matter depending, *inter alia*, on the compensated elasticity of factor supply); and the relative weights attached to efficiency and equity (primarily an ideological matter).

When account is taken of the efficiency impact of redistribution, it may not be possible, for instance, to move from point c to point e. The only feasible possibilities might be:

- a movement to a point like b, which is efficient and leaves total production unaffected, but which, in most theories of society, is less just than the distribution shown by c; or

- a movement to a distribution less unequal than b. In this case redistributive taxation will cause efficiency losses, generally by reducing output (i.e. attempts to move from c towards e will shrink the size of the box in Figure 4.3).

In the face of this trade-off there will be different views about the desirability of an increase in efficiency, which will not be seen as a welfare gain if its equity cost is 'too' high. To some libertarians equity has a zero weight; a movement from c to b will therefore increase both efficiency and welfare. To utilitarians the weight given to social justice is an open question. A given efficiency gain may or may not increase welfare; and the utilitarian optimum will not necessarily be efficient (i.e. utilitarians are prepared to sacrifice some efficiency in the interests of greater justice). Rawlsians and socialists give social justice more weight, and will therefore generally accept a higher efficiency cost to achieve a just distribution. Note, however, that no theory of society gives social justice complete priority. Even a Marxist would resist the pursuit of distributional objectives if the resulting efficiency costs reduced output to zero.

CONCLUSIONS focus particularly on the relationship between efficiency and social welfare. The overall conclusion is that the analysis of this chapter is general in its application.

---

[11] See, in ascending order of formality, Stiglitz (1988: ch. 20), Cullis and Jones (1998: chs. 15, 16), and Atkinson and Stiglitz (1980: lectures 11, 12).

Conclusion 1: the meaning of efficiency: an increase in efficiency (e.g. a movement from point *c* to a point on the contract curve) has the same meaning in all theories of society.

Conclusion 2: welfare improvements: welfare is increased under all the theories of society by a movement from a point like *c* to an appropriate subset of the contract curve. Additionally, a movement from *c* to a point between *e* and *f* (excluding *f*) is SI *and* RI *and* PI. *Efficiency gains of this sort raise social welfare under all the theories of society discussed in Chapter 3*. Where such a movement is feasible, this conclusion is valid whether factor supply is fixed or variable.[12]

Conclusion 3: the optimal distribution in a first-best economy: for any of the theories of society discussed earlier *all first-best socially just distributions are also Pareto efficient*. Efficiency in this case is a necessary condition for social justice.

Conclusion 4: the optimal distribution in a second-best economy: in this case an increase in efficiency may be possible only at the expense of social justice. Whether such an efficiency gain raises social welfare depends on the relative weights accorded efficiency and equity, weights which will generally vary with different theories of society. Thus, the second-best optimum distribution may be a point which is not Pareto efficient.

3. Intervention for reasons of efficiency

3.1. Types of intervention

Discussion so far has concerned the *aims* of policy. The next step is to consider *methods*. This section discusses the circumstances in which market allocation is efficient and, if it is not, the types of intervention which might be justified. The analysis here (and for most of the book) looks mainly at static efficiency, though in later chapters issues of economic growth (i.e. dynamic efficiency) are discussed where relevant.

The state can intervene in four ways: regulation, finance, and public production, which all involve direct interference in the market mechanism; and income transfers, which may have indirect effects.

REGULATION. The state interferes with the free market through large numbers of regulations. Some (e.g. those concerning alcohol sales or shop-opening hours) have more to do with social values than economics. But many are directly relevant to the efficient or equitable operation of markets, especially where knowledge is imperfect. Regulation of *quality* is concerned mainly with the supply side—for example, hygiene laws relating to the

---

[12] As discussed earlier, this does *not* imply that the definition of efficiency is value free. The assertion here is weaker: that a subset of Pareto improvements, though not value free, is consistent with all the theories of society discussed in Chapter 3.

production and sale of food and pharmaceutical drugs; laws forbidding unqualified people to practise medicine; and consumer protection legislation generally. Regulation of *quantity* more often affects individual demand—for example, the requirement to attend school, mandatory automobile insurance, and compulsory social-insurance contributions. Examples of *price* regulation include minimum wages and rent control.

FINANCE involves subsidies (or taxes) applied to the *prices* of specific commodities or affecting the *incomes* of individuals. Price subsidies affect economic activity by changing the slope of the budget constraint facing individuals and firms. They can be partial (e.g. for public transport or local-authority housing) or total (e.g. free pharmaceutical drugs for the elderly in the UK, and under medicare in the USA). Similarly, prices can be affected by a variety of taxes (e.g. on pollution or congestion). Income subsidies raise different issues which are discussed shortly.

PRODUCTION. Though regulation and finance modify market outcomes, they leave the basic mechanism intact. Alternatively, the state can take over the supply side by producing goods and services itself; in such cases the state owns the capital inputs (e.g. school buildings and equipment) and employs the necessary labour (e.g. teachers). Other (more or less pure) examples are national defence and (in the UK) most health care. It is important to be clear that finance and production are entirely separate forms of intervention, both conceptually and in practice. The distinction is of considerable relevance to privatization, discussed in Section 6.

INCOME TRANSFERS can be tied to specific types of expenditure (e.g. education vouchers or housing benefit) or untied (e.g. social-security benefits). First-best transfers take the form of a lump sum, and therefore affect economic activity by changing the incomes of the individuals, with no extra-market effect on product or factor prices. As we saw in Section 2.2, however, redistributive transfers in practice are not of this sort, and so cannot be regarded in efficiency terms as wholly neutral.

3.2. The assumptions under which markets are efficient

This section is in some respects the theoretical heart of the book. The so-called *invisible hand theorem* asserts that the market clearing set of outputs, X_M, will automatically be the efficient output bundle X^* in equation (4.8) if and only if a number of assumptions hold. These (henceforth collectively called the *standard assumptions*) concern perfect competition, complete markets, the absence of market failures, and, crucially, perfect information. Where all the assumptions hold there is no justification for intervention on efficiency grounds, but if one or more fails the resulting market equilibrium may be inefficient, and state intervention in one of the forms described above may be appropriate.

PERFECT COMPETITION

Perfect competition must hold in product and factor markets, and also (and importantly) in capital markets. The assumption has two essential features: economic agents must be price-takers; and they must have equal power.

PRICE-TAKING implies a large number of individuals and firms, with no entry barriers in any market. The assumption can fail—for example, in the presence of monopoly, monopsony, or oligopoly—and appropriate intervention can increase efficiency. It is a standard proposition (Hirshleifer 1980: 348 *et seq.*) that a monopolist can be given an incentive to produce the efficient output either through the imposition of a maximum price (i.e. *regulation*) or via an appropriate *price subsidy* (with or without the addition of a lump-sum tax). Where imperfect competition takes the form of oligopoly, other forms of regulation may be appropriate (e.g. the Monopolies and Mergers Commission in the UK and anti-trust legislation in the USA).

EQUAL POWER is not violated if some individuals have higher incomes than others and so have more 'dollar votes'. In all other respects agents must have equal power—there can be no discrimination. The assumption is frequently breached, and hard to correct. In some areas (e.g. safety legislation in factories) the state intervenes through *regulation*. Others, such as having friends in high places (which socialists regard as a major cause of inequality), have no easy solution; nor does outright discrimination—for example, by race or sex. Legislation (i.e. regulation) in these areas has met with only limited success.

COMPLETE MARKETS

Complete markets would provide all goods and services for which individuals are pre-pared to pay a price which covers their production costs. This is not always the case. The market will generally fail completely to supply public goods (discussed shortly). Missing markets arise, secondly, because certain risks are uninsurable (Chapter 5). Thirdly, capital markets may in some circumstances fail to provide loans (student loans are discussed in Chapter 13). Fourthly, there may be no futures market—that is, it may not be possible to make a contract now to buy or sell a commodity on given terms at some time in the future. Finally, a commodity may not be supplied because a complementary market is absent. This is a particular problem if large-scale activities need to be coordin-ated—for example, in the case of urban renewal projects. Where there are missing mar-kets, state intervention (often, though not always, in the form of public production) will generally be necessary if the commodity is to be supplied.

NO MARKET FAILURES

This assumption can be violated in three major ways: public goods, external effects, and increasing returns to scale, discussed in more detail in the Appendix.

Concepts

PURE PUBLIC GOODS exhibit three technical characteristics, non-rivalness in consumption, non-excludability, and non-rejectability, which together imply that the market is likely to produce inefficiently, if at all. Once a public good is produced, non-excludability makes it impossible to prevent people from using it, hence it is not possible to levy charges (this is the *free-rider* problem); in such cases the market may fail entirely. Non-rivalness implies that the marginal cost of an extra user (though *not* of an extra unit of output) is zero. The efficient price should therefore be based on individual marginal valuations of the good—that is, on perfect price discrimination; where this is not possible, the market is likely to be inefficient. If a public good is to be provided at all, the appropriate form of intervention is generally *public production*.[13]

EXTERNAL EFFECTS are a closely related phenomenon. They arise when an act of agent A imposes costs or confers benefits on agent B for which no compensation from A to B, or payment from B to A, takes place. Formally, a technological externality arises when A's utility function or production function is interrelated with B's. It is a standard proposition[14] that, in the presence of an external cost, the market clearing output will generally exceed the efficient output, and vice versa for an external benefit. The market itself can sometimes solve the problem, (*a*) through merger of the relevant parties (Meade 1952) or (*b*) where property rights are well defined, through negotiation between the parties concerned (Coase 1960). The latter, however, is not always possible—for instance, where property rights are not enforceable (air pollution) or where transactions costs are high because large numbers of people are involved (traffic congestion). In such cases, intervention may be warranted through either (*c*) *regulation* or (*d*) an appropriate Pigovian *tax or subsidy*. The choice of method depends on a complex of factors. Taxation/subsidy is the usual solution if the intention is marginally to change levels of consumption or production. But regulation may be useful where the aim is to enforce at least a minimum level of some activity (compulsory automobile insurance), or to restrict it below some maximum (mandatory pollution controls) or where measurement problems prevent assessment of the appropriate tax/subsidy.[15]

INCREASING RETURNS TO SCALE at all levels of output imply that average cost will exceed marginal cost, as in Figure 4.4. The consequent long-run losses will drive competitive firms from the industry, which will either become monopolized or (if even a monopolist makes losses) will cease to exist at all. Intervention can take one of two forms.

---

[13] See, in ascending order of difficulty, Baumol and Blinder (1997: ch. 13), Estrin and Laidler (1995: ch. 31), Stiglitz (1993*b*: ch. 7), Stiglitz (1988: ch. 5), Musgrave and Musgrave (1989: chs. 4, 5), or Varian (1996: ch. 34). The classic exposition of the theory of public goods is Samuelson (1954).

[14] On the welfare effects of externalities, see, in ascending order of difficulty, Le Grand *et al.* (1992: ch. 2), Baumol and Blinder (1997: ch. 13), Stiglitz (1988: ch. 8), Estrin and Laidler (1995: ch. 31), Varian (1996: ch. 31), and Varian (1992: ch. 24).

[15] For discussion in the context of environmental issues, see Stiglitz (1988: ch. 8), Stephen Smith (1992), and the various contributions in the special issue 'Public Finance and the Environment', *International Tax and Public Finance*, 2/2 (Aug. 1995).

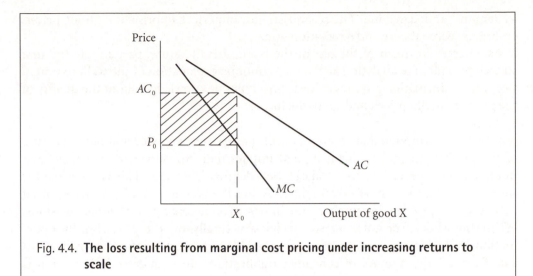

Fig. 4.4. **The loss resulting from marginal cost pricing under increasing returns to scale**

The industry could remain private, buttressed by an appropriate lump-sum subsidy $(AC_0 - P_0)X_0$ in Figure 4.4;[16] or it could be nationalized and similarly subsidized. The appropriate intervention, therefore, is *subsidy* or *public production* or both.

PERFECT INFORMATION

The analysis of imperfect competition and market failures has two noteworthy features: for the most part it has a long pedigree in the economic literature; and it justifies regulation and subsidy but (with the exception of public goods) gives no efficiency argument for public production. Two conclusions follow (for fuller discussion, see Barr 1992: section III (A)): when applied to the welfare state, these traditional arguments give little justification, at least in utilitarian terms, for large-scale, publicly organized welfare-state services; and, to the extent that they support such institutions at all, they justify only a *residual* welfare state.[17]

A more recent body of theory focuses on the extent to which consumers and firms are well informed. Simple theory assumes that consumers know what goods are available and their nature. The assumption can fail because economic agents may have imperfect knowledge of the *quality* of goods or their *prices*. The literature thus has two strands. The first analyses the effects of imperfect information about quality: consumers might be badly informed (e.g. about the quality of an automobile), so might producers (e.g. about the riskiness of an applicant for insurance). The resulting literature investigates such topics

---

[16] Though the taxation necessary to finance the subsidy would itself be distortionary unless levied on a lump-sum basis.
[17] Chapter 2, Section 7.1 explains the distinction between a residual and an institutional welfare state.

as 'lemons' and signalling. The second strand, imperfect information about prices, embraces search theory and reservation wages.[18]

As emerges in much of the rest of the book, this literature, particularly the first strand, provides the analytical key to the economic explanation of the welfare state.[19] Complete information requires at least three types of knowledge: about the quality of the product, about prices, and about the future.

QUALITY. The assumption that economic agents have perfect knowledge about the nature of the product (including factor inputs) implies that individuals have well-defined indifference maps, and firms, similarly, well-defined isoquants. This is plausible for some goods (e.g. food), but less so for others. When the assumption fails, the market itself may solve the problem by supplying the information necessary for rational decisions. When I buy a house I do not know whether it is structurally sound, but I can buy the information by hiring the services of a surveyor. More generally, information is available from a large number of consumer publications. In such cases intervention is unnecessary.

Other types of information failure may justify regulation. Consumers usually have sufficient knowledge about the characteristics of food to choose a reasonably balanced diet, but may be imperfectly informed about the conditions in which the food was prepared. The state therefore intervenes with hygiene laws (i.e. *regulation*), whose effect is to improve consumer information, thereby increasing efficiency.

Where the information failure is small, regulation may suffice. Where information is seriously deficient, however, market outcomes *may* be less efficient than some sort of administrative solution. Markets are generally more efficient:

(*a*) the better is consumer information,

(*b*) the more cheaply and effectively it can be improved (e.g. computer magazines),

(*c*) the easier it is for consumers to understand available information,

(*d*) the lower are the costs of choosing badly, and

(*e*) the more diverse are consumer tastes.

Commodities which conform well with these criteria are food and such consumer durables as hi-fi, personal computers, and automobiles. As discussed later, health care conforms less well: consumer information is often poor; people generally require individual information, so that the process will not be cheap (violating (*b*)); much of the information is highly technical (violating (*c*)); and the costs of mistaken choice can be high (violating (*d*)). In these circumstances, there may be a justification for *public production and allocation*.

---

[18] The quality literature has its roots in classic articles by Arrow (1963) and Akerlof (1970). See Stiglitz (1987), Phlips (1988: ch. 2), and Hirshleifer and Riley (1992) for surveys and, for fuller discussion, Stiglitz (1989). For a survey of the literature on imperfect price information, see Mortensen (1986) and Phlips (1988: ch. 3).

[19] It has also led to major advances in other areas, as suggested in the quote by Stiglitz at the head of the chapter. See the references in the previous note.

PRICE. Rational choice requires also that agents are perfectly informed about prices—that is, that they face a well-defined budget constraint. This is plausible for commodities like clothes, less so for things like car repairs. Where the assumption fails, the market, again, may supply the necessary information—for example, a house or a piece of jewellery can be professionally valued. In such cases the services of the valuer improve knowledge about prices, and so increase efficiency. Where the market does not resolve the problem, state intervention via *regulation* may be necessary—for instance, a requirement to issue price lists.

It should be noted that rational choice depends on both indifference/isoquant map and budget constraint; hence perfect information is needed about the nature of the product *and* about prices—neither on its own is sufficient. The two together have a critical efficiency role: it is conventionally argued, not least by writers such as Hayek and Friedman, that the advantages of competition are the maximization of consumer choice and the minimization of cost. Without perfect information, however, agents are unable to exercise their consumer sovereignty rationally; nor can they tell whether competitive cost reductions are associated with an unacceptable reduction in quality. An important conclusion follows—that *the efficiency advantages of perfect competition are contingent on perfect information.*

THE FUTURE. Intertemporal utility maximization requires perfect information also about the future. I know that I will need food this week and again next week, and shop accordingly; but I do not know how much furniture I will consume over the next ten years nor how many cars, because I do not know whether my house will catch fire or my car be involved in an accident. In such cases, the market solution is to offer insurance, which gives me certainty, since any losses I suffer will be made good by the insurance company. However, as discussed in Chapter 5, technical problems (due largely to information failures in insurance markets) can make private insurance inefficient or impossible. In these circumstances *public funding* might be appropriate.

3.3. Policy implications

LESSONS FROM ECONOMIC THEORY. It is important to be clear about what has been said, and what not said, about the size of the public sector. As a theoretical proposition, the market allocates efficiently when *all* the necessary assumptions hold. In such cases intervention on efficiency grounds is neither necessary nor desirable. Where one or more of the assumptions fails, it is necessary in each case to ask three questions:

- Can the market solve the problem itself?
- If not, which type of intervention—regulation, finance, or public production—or mix of interventions might improve efficiency?
- Would intervention be cost effective?

Concepts

As a practical matter, the necessary conditions rarely apply *fully*; it is generally sufficient that they are broadly true. Competition may operate with a relatively small number of suppliers and minor forms of consumer ignorance can often be ignored. Nevertheless, the market's efficiency advantages are tempered by the possibility of market failure and, completely separately, by the fact that it can lead to inequitable outcomes.

A second lesson is that a prima-facie case for intervention—because one or more assumptions fails significantly—translates into a case for action only if intervention can improve on an imperfect market outcome. Intervention, in short, must be cost effective. This is more likely the more effective is government. Government failure is discussed in Section 5.

Thirdly, the size of the public sector depends also on demand. If there are only two goods, food (produced privately) and education (produced publicly), the optimal size of the public sector will depend on preferences over food and education, and will vary over time and across countries. Thus the size of the public sector has a political as well as a technical dimension.

MARKET SUCCESS. Food, by and large, conforms with the standard assumptions. People generally have sufficient information to buy a balanced diet; food prices are known, not least because food is bought frequently; and most people know roughly how much they will need over a given period. Food production and (especially) distribution are competitive; and there are no major market failures. A possible violation is ignorance about the conditions under which food is produced and about its ingredients. The state therefore intervenes with hygiene regulations; it may also require packaging to display ingredients and a 'sell-by' date. Since such regulation can readily be understood, it enhances consumer information, leaving the private market to operate efficiently. Even where there are reservations about the effectiveness of hygiene regulations, consumer choice and market allocation are more efficient than any alternative, not least because of the enormous diversity of consumer tastes. It is not surprising that there are no serious advocates of a national food service.

Clothing, too, mostly conforms with the assumptions. It can, however, be argued that people are less well informed about the quality of clothing than about food. Yet there is less regulation about the quality of clothing, not least because the costs of mistaken choice are generally much lower than with food. The exceptions—for example, safety clothing and crash helmets—for precisely that reason *are* regulated. Except for these latter cases, it can be argued that, even where an assumption fails, intervention is not cost effective.

Consumer goods such as televisions, washing machines, kitchen appliances, and personal computers fit into the same pattern. The market supplies much information through consumer magazines, newspaper articles, and consumer programmes on radio and television; and aggrieved individuals can seek legal redress. Minor consumer ignorance is ignored where the costs of mistaken choice are small. Where the potential costs of poor quality are larger (e.g. electrical appliances which might catch fire), the appropriate form of intervention is regulation.

Cars raise two sets of issues. On the production side the arguments are similar to those for smaller consumer goods, a key feature being the extent of consumer information about quality. In particular, consumers cannot easily check that a car's brakes and steering are safe and its tyres well designed. Given the high costs of mistaken choice, regulation of such safety features is stringent and continually evolving. So far as the use of cars is concerned, regulation mainly addresses the external costs my driving imposes on others if I drive unsafely (e.g. drink-drive laws), or operate a car in unsafe mechanical condition (worn tyres).

MARKET FAILURE. Since much of the rest of the book discusses areas where—to a greater or lesser extent—markets fail, this section takes only one illustration, health care (discussed in detail in Chapter 12). With health care, consumer information can be highly imperfect, since much medical treatment is complex and technical. In addition, knowledge of prices is scant. Nobody knows how much health care they will need and, as shown in Chapters 5 and 12, there are major technical (again, largely information) problems with private medical insurance. It is also argued that health care is not competitive. Finally, some medical care can generate externalities. What type of intervention is then appropriate? Information failures and the lack of competition justify regulation; the externality, coupled with major insurance problems, may justify public funding; and a strong (though not overriding) argument for public production and allocation arises out of serious problems with both consumer information and private insurance.

These arguments, though applied in this book to the components of the welfare state, are completely general, and it is instructive to apply them to past or present public enterprises well outside the welfare state, such as railways, electricity, telephones, steel, coal and airlines, and to reform in Central and Eastern Europe and the former Soviet Union.

4. Intervention for reasons of social justice

Different definitions of social justice (or equity) were discussed in Chapter 3. The main questions in this section are different—namely: why does redistribution occur; should it be in cash or kind; and is there enough redistribution?

4.1. Why does redistribution occur?

COERCED REDISTRIBUTION. According to writers such as Downs (1957) and Tullock (1970),[20] the 'poor', acting as individuals or as part of a coalition, use their voting power to enforce redistribution from the 'rich'. Downs assumes that politicians seek office for reasons of income, status, and power, and therefore choose policies which maximize the

---

[20] See also Buchanan and Tullock (1962), and, for a non-technical introduction, Tullock (1976).

votes they receive at the next election; and that citizens vote for the party whose programme promises them the highest expected utility. Since the income distribution in most countries contains relatively few people with high incomes and many with lower incomes, governments maximize votes by redistributing from the rich, thereby gaining the (many more) votes of those with lower incomes.

The logic of the argument is that the system will redistribute towards equality. That equality is not reached is attributed to three countervailing pressures: fear of the efficiency losses of high taxation; the fact that the rich generally have more power; and the fact that the poor might want some inequality to remain, in the hope that they might some day themselves be rich.

Tullock discusses how different income groups might form voting coalitions, noting in particular that any coalition of at least 51 per cent of the electorate must contain not only the very poor but also many in the middle-income group. His theory therefore offers an explanation of the commonly observed phenomenon (Le Grand 1982) that public expenditure on the poor is often lower than on the middle-income group (which tends, for example, to make more intensive use of the educational system). There is a direct relationship between these arguments and the government-failure analysis discussed in Section 5.

VOLUNTARY REDISTRIBUTION. According to Downs (1957) and Tullock (1970), redistribution is motivated by selfishness and enforced by political coercion. Hochman and Rodgers (1969), in contrast, recognize the possibility of altruistic motives. Their theory seeks to explain both voluntary giving, and the fact that people with high incomes may vote for political parties which propose to tax them more heavily to finance redistributive policies. At the heart of this approach lies the notion that individual welfares are interdependent.

The simplest explanation of *voluntary* redistribution is based on a particular type of externality. Assume a two-person world with representative 'rich' and 'poor' individuals, R and P. If R is concerned with P's utility as well as his own, both may gain by a gift from R to P. Where redistribution makes some people better off without making anyone worse off, transfers from rich to poor may be justified on quasi-efficiency grounds.[21]

Formal analysis. In the simplest case R and P each has a utility function which is dependent only on his own income. Thus

$$U^R = f(Y^R) \tag{4.9}$$

and

$$U^P = f(Y^P) \tag{4.10}$$

where U^R and U^P are the utilities of the rich and the poor man, respectively, and Y^R and Y^P their incomes. But now suppose that R's utility depends not only on his own income, but also on P's. Then,

---

[21] For a fuller exposition, see Hochman and Rodgers (1969). A similar approach treats the size distribution of income as a public good; see Thurow (1971).

$$U^R = f(Y^R, Y^P), f_1 > 0, f_2 \geq 0 \qquad (4.11)$$

where f_1 and f_2 are the partial derivatives of U^R with respect to Y^R and Y^P, respectively. There is an externality since *ceteris paribus* R's utility rises with P's income.[22] In this situation redistribution from rich to poor can be rational: it will raise P's utility (because his income goes up) and also R's utility (because of the increase in P's income) so long as

$$\frac{\partial U^R}{\partial Y^P} - \frac{\partial U^R}{\partial Y^R} \geq 0 \qquad (4.12)$$

where the first term shows the increase in R's utility as a result of the increase in P's income, and the second the reduction in R's utility because of the reduction in his own income. Voluntary redistribution from R to P will be rational so long as the first term exceeds the second.

Criticisms of voluntarism. This approach leaves no distributional role for the state through compulsory taxation unless voluntarism can be shown to be suboptimal. Two such arguments have been proposed. The first concerns the problem of free-riders, which can arise when the model is extended from the two-person case to the *n*-person. Suppose that it is not the income of specific *individual* poor people which affects the utility of the rich, but the *overall* distribution, which then displays all the characteristics of a public good.

Each individual in society faces the same income distribution. No one can be deprived of the benefits flowing from any particular income distribution. My consumption of whatever benefits occur is not rival with your consumption. In short, the income distribution meets all the tests of a pure public good. Exclusion is impossible; consumption is non-rival; each individual must consume the same quantity. The same problems also occur. *Each individual has a vested interest in disguising his preferences concerning his desired income to avoid paying his optimal share of the necessary transfer payments.* (Thurow 1971: 328–9, emphasis added)

Hence, 'It can be argued that private charity is insufficient because the benefits from it accrue to people other than those who make the gifts . . . [We] might . . . be willing to contribute to the relief of poverty, *provided* everyone else did' (Friedman 1962: 191, emphasis in original).

The extent of free-riding depends on the nature of the externality. If what matters to the rich is the *income of the poor*, it may be rational for them to vote for redistributive taxation, which is compulsory and so avoids free-riding. I shall refer to this as 'voluntary compulsion'. Since it is, up to a point, imposed by the rich upon themselves, this is a very different argument from the 'coercion via the ballot box' of Downs and Tullock. If, however, the rich derive utility from the *act of giving*, free-riding is less of a problem.[23]

---

[22] In formal terms we are relaxing the assumption that the social-welfare function is additive—see Chapter 6, Section 1.2.

[23] For precisely this reason, many charitable organizations now attempt to reduce free-riding by assigning a specific, named family to the giver. Attempts have been made to defend voluntarism against the free-rider argument. See Sugden (1983*b*), Andreoni (1989, 1990), and, for a survey, Jones and Posnett (1993).

A second and completely separate criticism of voluntarism is that, if redistribution were *only* that which the rich volunteered, it might be suboptimal even in the absence of free-riders. Suppose the initial situation is shown by point *d* in Figure 4.3, and the social welfare maximizing distribution by point *k* (as for Rawls or a socialist). The rich might be prepared through voluntarism to move the distribution from *d* to *f*, or through compulsory taxation to *e*. But if the income externality is 'exhausted' at *e* then a movement to *k*, though possibly raising *total* utility, would reduce the utility of the rich. In such a case voluntary transfers would be insufficient to bring about the egalitarian distribution advocated, for example, by Rawls.

It follows, in conclusion, that voluntary redistribution *alone* will be suboptimal unless one believes *both* that free-riding is not a problem *and* that the optimal amount of redistribution is that which the rich wish to volunteer.

4.2. Should redistribution be in cash or kind?

What, if any, are the arguments for redistribution in kind (i.e. transferring commodities directly to the poor at zero or non-market prices)?

ECONOMIC ARGUMENTS. The efficiency case for overriding consumer sovereignty has two legs.

- Where consumer information is poor *and* an agent's decisions likely to be better, the consumption decision might be more efficient if made on the individual's behalf by an agent. This is the efficiency case for 'merit goods', discussed below, where individual preferences are overridden—for example, parents cannot choose not to send their children to school.

- Even where it might be *desirable* to override preferences, it is *possible* only where the individual cannot subvert the agent's choices. This requires that (*a*) the commodity is not easily tradeable (otherwise the individual could sell the good and use the money to finance a different consumption mix), (*b*) the commodity is not easily fungible in family income (otherwise, if given free food, I could buy whisky with the money I would otherwise have spent on food), and (*c*) it not easy to reject the good.

There are two additional reasons why policy-makers might wish to override consumer sovereignty. First, individuals may have unequal power, leading to horizontal inequity. In some societies a daughter's income is transferred to her husband's family whereas a son's income stays in his parents' household. Parents may therefore give daughters less education or feed them less well. In such circumstances, the freedom of parents might partly be overridden—for instance, through school-feeding programmes. Secondly, consumer sovereignty might be overridden in extreme cases of supply-side disruption (food rations in wartime). The problem is less that market allocation is inefficient, than that it is more inequitable than policy-makers regard as tolerable.

This suggests that, in strict economic terms, the use of in-kind transfers for distributional purposes is very circumscribed unless they are also justified on *efficiency* grounds.

POLITICAL ECONOMY ARGUMENTS. The counter-argument suggests that it may sometimes be politically easier to redistribute in kind.

Formal analysis. In equation (4.11), the utility of the rich person depends both on his own income, and that of the poor man. But suppose the externality is caused not by P's *income* but by his *consumption*. Then,

$$U^R = f(Y^R, C^P) \tag{4.13}$$

where C^P is P's consumption. However, not all increases in C^P will raise the utility of the rich—consumption of alcohol by the poor might not do so. It is necessary to disaggregate so that,

$$C^P = G^P + B^P \tag{4.14}$$

where G^P is 'good' consumption by the poor (children's clothing, basic food), and B^P is 'bad' consumption (whisky, welfare Cadillacs), where 'good' and 'bad' are defined by the rich.

From equations (4.13) and (4.14) we have

$$U^R = f(Y^R, G^P, B^P) \quad f_1 > 0, f_2 \geq 0, f_3 \leq 0 \tag{4.15}$$

where f_1, f_2 and f_3 are the partial derivatives of U^R with respect to Y^R, G^P and B^P, respectively. R's utility increases with his own income, and with 'good' consumption by P, but decreases with P's 'bad' consumption. In this situation, transfers of 'good' consumption take place as long as

$$\frac{\partial U^R}{\partial G^P} - \frac{\partial U^R}{\partial Y^R} \geq 0 \tag{4.16}$$

where the first term shows the increase in R's utility resulting from the increase in P's 'good' consumption, and the second is the decrease in R's utility because of the decrease in his own income.

Merit goods. School education is compulsory, irrespective of the wishes of parents or children. As discussed above, if the standard assumptions hold, there is no efficiency justification for merit goods. Figure 4.5 shows how their existence can be explained in political economy terms by a consumption externality. Suppose individual P initially faces the budget constraint $Y_P Y_P$ and maximizes utility by choosing point a. Now compare a cash transfer with a compulsory in-kind transfer. Suppose that the cash transfer shifts P's budget constraint outward to $Y_1 Y_1$ so that he maximizes utility at point b. Alternatively, a compulsory transfer of $Y_2 - Y_P$ units of education shifts P's budget constraint to $Y_2 Y_2$, and utility is maximized at c. Given the choice, a rational poor person will favour the in-kind transfer, since c is on a higher indifference curve than b.

Now consider matters from the viewpoint of individual R. It is clear that the in-kind transfer is more costly (i.e. measuring along the horizontal axis, the in-kind transfer consists of $Y_2 - Y_P$ units of education, whereas the cash transfer buys only $Y_1 - Y_P$ units). However, though R gives up more *income* to finance the in-kind transfer, he might give up less *utility*. In the presence of a consumption externality, an income transfer can

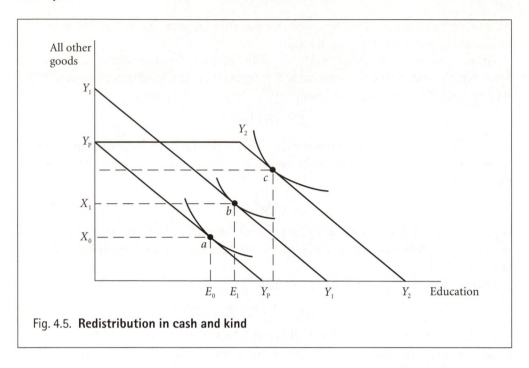

Fig. 4.5. **Redistribution in cash and kind**

reduce the utility of the rich both *per se* and because it might be used by the poor to finance 'bad' consumption. Transfers in kind, though costing more in financial terms, have the advantage, from R's point of view, that they are entirely 'good' consumption. If f_2 in equation (4.15) is large and positive, and f_3 large and negative, then R too might prefer the in-kind transfer.

In this case social welfare might be higher with in-kind transfers, despite the absence of any efficiency reasons for public production or allocation, simply because both rich and poor prefer it that way.

4.3. Horizontal equity

Discussion thus far has concentrated mainly on *vertical equity*—that is, the redistribution of income or consumption from rich to poor. Social justice also involves *horizontal equity*, which concerns goals like minimum standards for certain goods and services, or equal access to them, and equality of opportunity.[24]

MINIMUM STANDARDS are a form of regulation, and can therefore be justified only by the failure of one or more of the standard assumptions. This can occur in three ways. Where agents have imperfect information, they are generally unable to make rational choices; a case can be made on this basis for minimum standards concerning food hygiene,

---

[24] For the place of horizontal equity in the social-welfare-maximization framework of Section 1, see King (1983).

schools, and hospitals. Secondly, if agents have unequal power, they might not be able to enforce their decisions; this justifies, for example, regulations about safety standards at work. Finally, there may be externalities. If my house has inadequate sewage disposal, the resulting public-health hazard is an argument for appropriate building codes.[25]

If the standard assumptions hold, however, consumers are able to make rational choices, and to enforce them, provided that they have sufficient income to do so. In such cases, concern with the quality of consumption should manifest itself in income transfers rather than minimum standards, except, possibly, in the presence of consumption externalities. The latter, however, is a dangerous argument, since minimum standards imposed on the poor 'for their own good' (i.e. 'good' consumption) may end up harming the poor if pitched at a higher level than is justified in efficiency terms (see Chapter 14, Section 5.2 for the case of housing standards).

EQUAL ACCESS. Where the standard assumptions hold, the only cause of unequal access is shortage of income. But action to ensure equal access may be justified in particular by imperfect information or unequal power.[26] A case in point is 'know-how', inequality of which is a major cause of inequality generally. Know-how includes understanding the value of education; knowing your entitlements under the National Health Service; knowing your legal rights; and also, more generally, your social and professional contacts. In the face of such inequality the state can intervene through regulation (e.g. legislation against discrimination); through subsidy (e.g. legal aid for people with low incomes); or through public production (e.g. the provision of compulsory, free education, which is supposed to be of an equal standard for all).

EQUALITY OF OPPORTUNITY is closely related to equal access. We return to the issue in Chapter 6, Section 3.1.

4.4. Is there enough redistribution?

We saw in Section 2.2 that social justice is concerned with movements along the contract curve towards the optimal distribution. What is that distribution; and have we achieved it?

Libertarians[27] see the optimal distribution as the result of competitive market forces on legally acquired endowments. They support the relief of destitution through voluntary charity, which writers like Nozick regard as the only legitimate method, all redistributive taxation being coercive. It follows from earlier discussion that, if the free-rider problem is non-trivial, voluntary giving will be suboptimal even in libertarian terms.

---

[25] In the light of these theoretical arguments it is noteworthy that much early social legislation in Britain was concerned with factory conditions and public health—see Chapter 2, Section 1.2.

[26] For a powerful theoretical analysis of how the failure of the equal-power assumption leads to discrimination against women, see Apps (1981) and Apps and Rees (1996).

[27] See note 9.

Empirical libertarians such as Hayek and Friedman allow taxation to bring incomes up to subsistence if voluntary giving fails to do so, not least because of the free-rider problem, which Friedman explicitly accepts (see the quote in Section 4.1). However, as discussed in the next section, most libertarians argue that benefits are too high, and therefore that we have *too much* redistribution (for fuller discussion, see Brittan 1995: ch. 12).

Utilitarians are unsure which distribution maximizes social welfare because of the impossibility of measuring utility cardinally. They are therefore unclear whether there has been too much redistribution or not enough.

Rawls argues unequivocally that goods should be distributed equally unless any other distribution is to the advantage of the least well off. This is not the actual situation, and therefore there has been too little redistribution. Rawls disagrees with the Downs–Tullock argument that democratic politics have resulted in excessive redistribution, arguing that voting and other political activity in practice takes place outside the veil of ignorance. Negotiation is therefore hindered by special pleading, particularly because the rich generally have greater power. The resulting distribution is nowhere near the Rawlsian optimum. Socialists, too, are clear that their goal of equality has not been reached.

5. Public choice and government failure

THE ARGUMENT. Inman (1987) and Mueller (1989) survey the public-choice literature, of which this section is a very brief account (see also the Further Reading). There are four explanations of the extent of and growth in government activity. The role of government (*a*) in dealing with market failures and (*b*) as redistributor of income and wealth has been the major focus of this chapter and the previous one. The literature analyses in addition (*c*) the response of government to the electorate in the form of coalitions of voters or through pressure groups, and (*d*) the role of bureaucrats. The government-failure arguments point to the latter two as important distorting influences. The essence of the argument is that government actions are based on self-interest rather than on maximizing social welfare.

The influence of the electorate operates in various ways. The coercion-via-the-ballot-box arguments were discussed in Section 4. Writers such as Buchanan and Tullock (1962) and Tullock (1970, 1971) argue that most transfers from the rich are captured by the middle class through their electoral power as median voters or acting as interest groups. Other arguments stress the broader role of interest groups on redistributive transfers (e.g. the poverty lobby). Interest groups use their lobbying power to bring about redistribution also through regulation. It is argued that regulators are frequently 'captured' by those whom they are supposed to regulate (Stigler 1971; Posner 1975; Pelzmann 1976). According to this view, regulation (e.g. of the medical profession) is an entry barrier which allows the extraction of monopoly rent.

Distortions can arise also within government. Public agencies may partly be run for the benefit of the bureaucrats who run them (Niskanen, 1971). Such 'organizational slack', it is argued, occurs because politicians cannot fully monitor the actions of utility-maximizing officials.

For one or more of these reasons, it is argued, the size of the public sector may be inefficiently large; or its composition may be distorted to meet the needs of the bureaucracy, powerful interest groups, voters in marginal constituencies, etc.

ASSESSMENT. These insights, however, should not be overstated. Even within a strict utilitarian framework, as discussed in Section 4, writers such as Friedman (1962) and Hochman and Rodgers (1969) explain tax-financed redistribution in ways which do not rely on electoral coercion. Interest groups may enhance efficiency (Becker 1983, 1985). Regulation *may* result in monopoly rents (e.g. doctors in some countries) but, as discussed in Section 3.2, it also serves to protect imperfectly informed consumers (e.g. regulation of medical training).

The power of bureaucrats can be overstated and their motivation misunderstood (Dunleavy 1985). Organizational slack should not be exaggerated: it is reduced by competition between agencies; it can be exploited only where the true benefits and costs of the agency are hard to measure; increases or enlarged departments can be monitored; voters may be able to vote with their feet against high local taxation (Tiebout 1956); and bureaucratic utility maximization can just as easily lead to *less* government (Treasury officials under Margaret Thatcher won favour by cutting expenditure). In addition, organizational slack may be more pronounced where the state regulates private activity than with public production: as discussed in Chapter 12, Section 4.1, countries where private, fee-for-service medical care is publicly funded find it more difficult to contain costs than those with public production.

Nor do the government-failure arguments necessarily apply equally everywhere. Tullock's (1971) claim that benefits go disproportionately to the middle class may be more true of the USA than elsewhere. In Germany and Sweden, for instance, the lowest-income quintile in the mid-1980s received net transfers of about 10 per cent of GDP.

The borderline between the market and the state is discussed further in Section 7.1.

6. From theory towards policy: The issue of privatization

THE CONCEPT OF PRIVATIZATION is by no means simple. A good can be *financed* publicly or privately, and it can be *produced* in either sector; thus there are four cases. Food is generally financed and produced in the private sector (Box 1 of Figure 4.6); at the other extreme, most school education is produced publicly and paid out of tax revenues (Box 4). Two intermediate cases are frequently overlooked. Public transport is produced in the public sector but financed by charges on the private sector (Box 2). Other goods are produced privately but sold to the public sector, including many inputs to the National

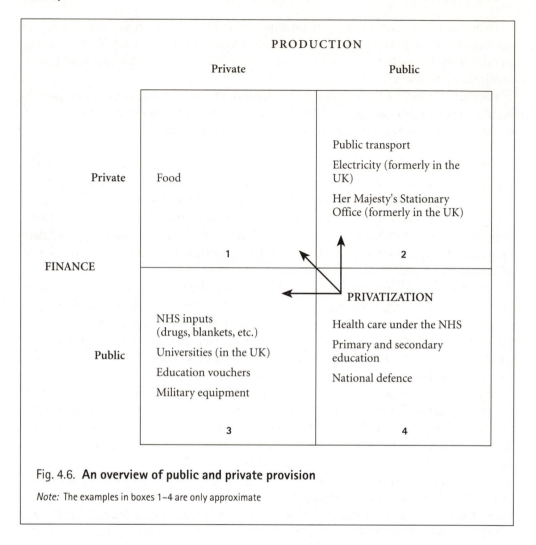

Fig. 4.6. **An overview of public and private provision**

Note: The examples in boxes 1–4 are only approximate

Health Service—for example, drugs, blankets. Those who favour privatization often mean a movement from Box 4 to Box 1. But it can be any movement up and/or to the left in Figure 4.6.

This analysis, unfortunately, is too oversimplified to be of much use. Markets in reality are virtually never purely private: food is subject to regulation about quality, and its price is distorted *inter alia* by agricultural subsidies; and it may be purchased out of transfer income (social-security benefits), or provided without charge (free school meals). Nor are there many pure cases of free public provision—for example, charges are levied under the National Health Service for prescriptions and dentistry.

To clarify the situation, even keeping matters as simple as possible, it is necessary to distinguish not only (*a*) in which sector *production* takes place and (*b*) which sector *finances* it, but also the influence of *regulation* on decisions about production and consumption, in particular on (*c*) the total quantity produced of any good and (*d*) how much each individual consumer will receive. These are illustrated in Table 4.1, though the analysis is still far from exhaustive. The first part shows different examples of private production. Row 1 (which corresponds to Box 1 in Figure 4.6) shows the pure private case—for example, food purchased out of non-transfer income. Production is private, and total supply determined by producers; individuals decide how much to consume, and pay for it themselves. Row 2 is identical except that individual consumption is financed by the state. The simplest case is food purchased out of transfer income; other examples are food stamps, Medicare, and Medicaid in the USA. Row 3 illustrates a private market subject to regulation. In row 3(*a*) the individual-consumption decision is made by the state (mandatory automobile insurance); in row 3(*b*) the state puts a ceiling on total production, though allocation to individuals remains private (very roughly the case of health care in Canada). Row 4 illustrates private production modified by both regulation and finance (i.e. roughly Box 3 in Figure 4.6). In row 4(*a*) production decisions are wholly private (e.g. education vouchers). Row 4(*b*) shows the case where allocation and finance are wholly public, but production itself takes place in the private sector (National Health Service inputs such as blankets and X-ray machines, certain types of military equipment).

The second half of the table looks at public production. In row 5(*a*) output is produced in the public sector but allocated and financed privately (public transport); in row 5(*b*) supply is determined publicly, but demand decisions and finance are private (pay beds in Health Service hospitals). These cases approximate Box 2 in Figure 4.6. Row 6 illustrates public production and allocation with private finance—for example, social insurance. Row 7 illustrates public production and finance, though the individual consumption decision is private—for example, secondary education after minimum school-leaving age. The case of pure public production is shown in row 8 (i.e. Box 4 in Figure 4.6); examples include (as approximations) compulsory school education, the National Health Service, and national defence.

We can now see what privatization means. Libertarians favour private production under column (1), producer and consumer sovereignty under columns (2) and (3), and private finance under column (4). They would therefore choose row 1 or, failing that, the private market underwritten by income transfers, shown in row 2. Privatization can therefore be seen as an upward movement in the table from a lower line to a higher.

THE ISSUES. How, then, should specific proposals for privatization be analysed? It was argued in Section 3 that where the standard assumptions all hold there are no efficiency grounds for intervention, and distributional objectives are generally best approached through income transfers.

The issues raised by the privatization debate (see the Further Reading) fall naturally into this framework. It is necessary to consider the extent to which any activity conforms with the standard assumptions. And in this context information problems assume considerable importance. Because of technological change over the century, the optimal scale of many types of industry is large; and in any large organization information

Table 4.1. **Public and private provision: A more complete view**

Type of allocation	Production (1)	Regulation — Decision about total production (2)	Decision about individual consumption (3)	Finance (4)	Examples
1. Pure private (= Box 1 in Figure 4.6)	PRIVATE	PRIVATE	PRIVATE	PRIVATE	Food purchased out of non-transfer income
2. Private market plus state finance (income subsidy)	Private	Private	Private	Public	All consumption of privately produced goods purchased out of transfer income; food stamps, Medicare, and Medicaid (USA)
3. Private market plus regulation					
(a) regulation of individual consumption	Private	Private	Public	Private	Mandatory automobile insurance
(b) regulation of total supply	Private	Public	Private	Private	Health care (Canada, approx.)
4. Private production, state regulation and finance (= Box 3 in Figure 4.6)					
(a) supply wholly private	Private	Private	Public	Public	Education vouchers
(b) total supply determined by state	Private	Public	Public	Public	Inputs for NHS and national defence
5. Public production, private allocation and finance (= Box 2 in Figure 4.6)					
(a) total supply determined by private demand	Public	Private	Private	Private	Public transport
(b) supply wholly public	Public	Public	Private	Private	NHS pay beds
6. Public apart from private finance	Public	Public	Public	Private	National insurance (UK), health-care insurance (Canada, approx.)
7. Public apart from private consumption decision	Public	Public	Private	Public	Post-compulsory education
8. Pure public (= Box 4 in Figure 4.6)	PUBLIC	PUBLIC	PUBLIC	PUBLIC	NHS, national defence

Note: The examples are only approximate.

(i.e. management) problems are likely to arise whether the industry is public or private. It is, therefore, not surprising that 'the fundamental problems concerned with the control of public utilities are very similar, irrespective of whether they are in the public or private sectors' (Webb 1984: 99).

Whatever the answers about privatization, the technical dimension of the analysis should not be obscured by ideology,[28] an observation which leads naturally to the final part of the chapter.

7. Conclusion: Economic and political theory

7.1. Drawing the borderlines between government and markets

This section brings together the analysis of Chapters 3 and 4. The efficiency arguments for intervention were set out in Section 3, and the government failure counter-arguments in Section 5. The important contribution of the public-choice literature is the idea that analysis of government should treat its activities as endogenous. It does not, however, follow that the social-welfare outcome of the political market place is necessarily inferior to that of conventional markets. Markets can be efficient or inefficient; so can governments. Thus market failure is a counterpoint to government failure.

Inman's (1987) survey concluded:

Markets fail. They fail for the fundamental reason that the institution of market trading cannot enforce cooperative behavior on self-seeking, utility-maximizing agents, and cooperative behavior between agents is often required for beneficial trading. In each instance of market failure . . . agents were asked to reveal information about their benefits or costs from trades with no guarantee that that information would not be used against them. Without that guarantee, information is concealed, trades collapse, and the market institution fails.   (p. 672)

While democratic processes do not generally guarantee an efficient allocation of social resources, *we cannot go the next step and conclude that collectively-decided allocations . . . are inferior to individually-decided market allocations.*   (p. 727, emphasis added)

neither the institution of markets, or voluntary trading, nor the institution of government, or collectively decided and enforced trading, stands as *the* unarguably preferred means for allocating societal resources. Each institution has its strengths and its weaknesses.   (p. 753, emphasis in original)

The 'New Right' properly criticizes a naïve predisposition towards state intervention at the slightest sign of problems in private markets; but to argue that public-sector

---

[28] As an example of how ideology can bias logic, note the tendency for proponents of free markets to regard 'managers' as 'good' and 'administrators' as 'bad' ('bureaucrats' being a term of abuse for everyone). In many respects, however, managers, administrators, and bureaucrats all do broadly the same job and face similar problems. Calling them by different names with differing emotive connotations does little to advance the argument.

inefficiency *automatically* implies that private markets raise social welfare is to make the same mistake. Decisions about the borderline between market and state involve judgement, so that different interpretations are possible. Le Grand (1987*b*), with echoes of Tullock (1971) (though from a very different perspective), argues that the UK welfare state has been 'captured' by the middle class, and goes on to suggest that this is a matter for ambivalence. It is 'bad' because the welfare state's major benefits should go to the poor; but it is 'good' because it keeps the articulate middle class as consumers of the welfare state, thus creating pressure to maintain standards. The arguments above suggest that we should not be ambivalent: as subsequent chapters explain, many parts of the welfare state are a response to pervasive technical problems in private markets, and therefore serve not only the distributional and other objectives listed in Chapter 1, Section 2.2 (poverty relief, vertical and horizontal equity, dignity and social solidarity), but also efficiency objectives such as income-smoothing and the protection of accustomed living standards in the face of uninsurable risks and capital-market imperfections. As such, the welfare state exists quite properly both for lower-income groups *and* for the middle class. In the Wilensky and Lebeaux (1965) sense discussed in Chapter 2, Section 7.1, there is an *efficiency* case for a universal welfare state.

7.2. Achieving policy aims: A liberal view

The vital distinction between the *aims* of policy and the *methods* available to achieve them should by now be clear. Aims include social justice and economic efficiency: the definition of social justice will vary with different theories of society (Chapter 3); economic efficiency has broadly the same meaning in all theories of society (Section 2). Methods embrace income transfers and direct intervention in the market through regulation, finance, and public production. The resulting form of economic organization, at one extreme, is the free market (with or without redistribution) and, at the other, central planning and public production of all basic goods and services (with or without charges). In between are different types of mixed economy involving both private markets (with or without intervention in the form of regulation and finance) and public production.

The central argument of this book is that the proper place of ideology is in the choice of aims, particularly in the definition of social justice and in its trade-off with economic efficiency; but, *once these aims have been agreed*, the choice of method should be regarded as a *technical* issue rather than an ideological one. Whether a particular good or service is provided publicly or privately should depend on which method more nearly achieves the chosen policy objectives. The issue of market versus state provision is thus a contingent matter rather than an item of dogma, and in that sense this book is firmly in the liberal tradition.[29]

---

[29] For a classic defence of the mixed economy on broadly similar grounds, see Okun (1975).

How, then, should we choose between different methods? The analysis of Section 3 suggests:

Proposition 1: efficiency. Where one or more of the standard assumptions fails, state intervention in the form of regulation, finance, or public production may increase economic efficiency. If none of the assumptions fails, efficiency is generally best achieved without intervention.

Proposition 2: social justice. Setting political-economy arguments (Section 4.2) to one side:

(*a*) Only efficiency arguments can justify intervention other than cash redistribution. If no efficiency justification exists, social justice is likely to be served best by *income* transfers.

(*b*) But if analysis suggests that efficiency will be furthered by public production and allocation of any good or service, then social justice can be enhanced by *in-kind* transfers (e.g. redistribution via free education or health care).

There are three possible exceptions to Proposition 2. The first is political-economy arguments, which may support transfers in kind even where there are no efficiency grounds for public production or allocation. The second concerns the role of giving. There is no technical argument against having a market for babies. But most societies rule this out on ethical grounds. It is argued, for instance, that health care might more appropriately be regarded as a gift than a purchase, and Titmuss (1970) makes a cogent argument for blood to be treated in this way.

The optimal taxation literature (see the Further Reading) offers the third exception. The taxation necessary to finance income transfers may reduce labour supply; if so, a given distributional objective *may* be possible at lower efficiency cost by subsidizing the *prices* of goods consumed by the poor. The result requires (*a*) that such goods are consumed only (or mainly) by the poor, and (*b*) that their consumption is not strongly complementary to leisure.

From a purely theoretical viewpoint, this suggests that the two propositions can be criticized for their 'piecemeal' approach—that is, for discussing conformity with the standard assumptions in a given area while implicitly assuming that they hold in all other areas. This ignores second-best considerations (Lipsey and Lancaster 1956). Several defences are possible. First, in a limited number of cases the approach is *theoretically* valid (Davis and Whinston 1965). Secondly, the measurement problems involved in applying the approach to policy are intractable, so that 'the rules of first-best optimality, coupled with the caveat of second-best . . . constitute part of the fund of guidelines from which good, if not perfect, policy might be formulated' (Winch 1971). Thirdly, none of the areas covered by the welfare state conforms closely with the two conditions at the end of the previous paragraph.

Finally, I want to nail a wholly fallacious line of argument. In one form it runs, 'we must have a National Health Service because otherwise the poor could not afford adequate health care'—an argument which does the cause of its proponents little service. The fallacy is that if inability to pay were the *only* difficulty, there would not be a *market-allocation problem* but an *income-distribution problem*, which could be solved by income transfers, as currently with food. The justification for the National Health Service, as argued in Chapter 12, lies not in Proposition 2(*a*) (which applies to food) but in Proposition 2(*b*).

Even more woolly is the assertion that 'we must have a National Health Service because everybody has a right to health care'. The fallacy lies in the word 'because'. It can equally be argued that everybody has a right to good nutrition, yet there are few advocates of a national food service. The statement confuses aims with methods. There is wide acceptance of the value judgement that people have a right to adequate nutrition and health care. These are *aims*; but the existence of these rights does not, per se, have any implications for the best method of achieving them. As we shall see, there are good reasons why the UK has a National Health Service but not a national food service—entitlement to food and health care, however, is not one of them.

7.3. The debate with libertarians

Propositions 1 and 2 would meet with general agreement from liberals and democratic socialists. Marxists would reject them for the reasons discussed in Chapter 3, Section 5. They accept the idea of social justice, but argue that too little has been done to achieve it. The efficiency arguments embodied in Proposition 1 are in large measure rejected because the market system, though possibly in some respects efficient, is the fundamental *cause* of the failure to achieve social justice.

The debate with empirical libertarians such as Hayek and Friedman is in many ways the most interesting and, given current policy concerns, the most relevant. The less interesting part of the argument is ideological. Libertarians reject almost in their entirety the social-justice arguments of Section 4, and in consequence reject Proposition 2. Hayek argues (Chapter 3, Section 2) that there is no such thing as social justice, and that its quest risks eventual totalitarianism. Libertarians argue— largely for the government-failure reasons set out in Section 5—that there is too much redistribution, and that redistribution in kind is even more dangerous than transfers in cash. Taken as an ideological view, little counter-argument is possible, save to assert a different set of values.

The debate over efficiency is much more important. As we saw in Chapter 3, Section 2, empirical libertarians are the direct descendants of Classical liberalism (compare the views in Friedman (1962: ch. 2) on the role of the state with those of Adam Smith quoted at the head of Chapter 1). Writers such as Hayek and Friedman therefore admit a limited role for the state in the presence of market failures, and both accept a very restricted welfare state. Beyond this, however, both would resist the efficiency arguments of Section 3. State intervention, it is argued, is often the *cause* of imperfect information rather than its result (e.g., if there were a competitive market for health care, people would acquire better information, in part because market institutions would arise to supply it). They support intervention to break monopolies or near-monopolies in product and (particularly) factor markets, and argue that domestic monopolies of tradeable goods need not be a problem if there are no barriers to foreign trade. As a result they argue that state intervention is excessive.

In sum, libertarians such as Hayek and Friedman accept the analytical framework of Section 3, but interpret facts differently. To that extent the debate is empirical. But it is also (and importantly) theoretical. What is not in dispute is the aim of maximizing social welfare, nor the existence of imperfections in the form of monopolies, externalities, public goods, and increasing returns to scale. The critical difference, as suggested in Section 3, is that the analysis of Hayek and Friedman takes little account of information problems. These afflict consumers of increasingly complex products, and managers of increasingly large-scale enterprises, and they include technical—again largely information—problems in insurance markets (Chapter 5). The existence of information problems, more than any other theoretical consideration, suggests that a properly designed welfare state is much more than an instrument of social justice. It also has a major efficiency role.

FURTHER READING

The most comprehensive treatment of the subject matter of this chapter is Atkinson and Stiglitz (1980; lectures 11–18), Stiglitz (1989, 1993*a*), or, at a less technical level, Stiglitz (1988: chs. 3, 4). For a gentler introduction to the economic theory of markets and welfare economics, see Le Grand *et al.* (1992: chs. 1, 2), Stiglitz (1993*b*: chs. 2, 4, 7, 13), Baumol and Blinder (1997) (elementary); Estrin and Laidler (1995: chs. 27–30) or Varian (1996) (intermediate, non-mathematical); and Varian (1992: chs. 17, 18, 21, 22, 24) (more advanced). Barr (1994*a*) covers similar theoretical ground at a non-technical level with particular reference to the former-Communist countries of Central and Eastern Europe and the former Soviet Union. For a lucid, non-technical discussion of efficiency, equity, and their trade-off, see Okun (1975) (a classic, strongly recommended defence of the mixed economy) and Le Grand (1991*a*: ch. 3) and, for a wide-ranging set of essays, Brittan (1995). References to the literature on information problems are given in the Further Reading at the end of Chapter 5.

For a simple introduction to the theory of externalities, see Le Grand *et al.* (1992: ch. 2) and Stiglitz (1993*b*: ch. 7); and, for fuller discussion of market failures, Stiglitz (1988: chs. 4, 5, 8) and Johansson (1991: ch. 5). A complete technical account of the optimal taxation literature and the trade-off between efficiency and equity is given by Atkinson and Stiglitz (1980: lectures 11–18); for less technical discussion, see Stiglitz (1988: ch. 20) or Cullis and Jones (1998: chs. 15, 16).

Different definitions of equity are discussed in Chapter 3; for an excellent brief summary, see also Le Grand (1984). A non-technical introduction to the theory of coerced redistribution through the ballot box is given by Tullock (1976), and in more complete form by Downs (1957) and Tullock (1970). The theory of voluntary (Pareto optimal) redistribution is developed by Hochman and Rodgers (1969); see also Thurow (1971). For general discussion of the economics of charity, see Sugden (1983b) (a simple introduction), and for a more complete treatment

Concepts

Sugden (1982, 1984) and the discussion in Collard (1983) and Sugden (1983*a*). The literature on the economics of charity is surveyed by Jones and Posnett (1993) and the references therein.

The large literature on public choice is surveyed by Inman (1987), Dunleavy (1991), Horn (1996), and J. Stevens (1993). For broader perspectives, see Mueller (1997), and for shorter summaries, Estrin and Laidler (1995: chs. 33–5), Stiglitz (1988: ch. 6), and Johansson (1991: ch. 6).

For argument about privatization in the context of the welfare state, and public enterprise generally, see the contributions in Le Grand and Robinson (1984). For more general discussion, see Stiglitz (1988: chs. 7, 11, 13), Vickers and Yarrow (1988), Boardman and Vining (1989), Galal (1994), and Megginson *et al.* (1994). On privatization in Russia, see Boycko *et al.* (1995), and, in the former Communist countries more generally, World Bank (1996: ch. 3). Le Grand and Estrin (1989) discuss the relationship between the market system and the achievement of socialist objectives.

Appendix: Non-technical summary of Chapter 4

1. Chapter 4 sets out the economic theory of state intervention, with particular emphasis on why intervention might foster efficiency and/or social justice (also referred to as equity).

The efficiency objective

2. *The meaning of economic efficiency.* Efficiency is concerned with making the best use of limited resources given people's tastes and available technology. A key underlying concept is that of *resource scarcity*—that is, if resources (labour, capital, raw materials, land) are used for one purpose they cannot be used for another (this is what economists mean by *opportunity cost*). Since those resources are limited, it follows that output is limited. Thus it is not possible to satisfy everyone's demands completely: policy should seek to satisfy people as much as possible—that is, should seek to use limited resources as effectively as possible. This is precisely what economic efficiency is about. As discussed in section 2.1, the efficient (or Pareto optimal) output of any good is the quantity which maximizes the excess of benefits over costs. This is the output X^* in Figure 4.1 at which the value placed by society on the marginal unit of output equals its marginal social cost (see Le Grand *et al.* 1992: 9–14).

3. *A Pareto improvement* (i.e. an increase in efficiency) takes place if any change in production or distribution makes one person better off without making anyone else worse off.

4. *Efficiency and ideology.* Section 2.2 shows that an increase in efficiency can raise welfare under any of the theories of society discussed in Chapter 3. The aim of efficiency is therefore common to all these ideologies, though the weight attached to it will vary when its achievement conflicts with distributional goals.

Intervention for reasons of efficiency

5. The state can intervene in four ways (Section 3.1).
   - *Regulation* mainly concerns the quality of supply (e.g. hygiene laws relating to food, minimum building standards) and regulation of individual demand (e.g. the legal requirement to attend school, compulsory membership of national insurance).
   - *Finance* can involve subsidies (or taxes) which change the price of specific commodities. Subsidies can be partial (e.g. local-authority housing) or total (e.g. free drugs under the National Health Service).
   - *Public production* covers national defence, education, and (in the UK) most health care.

These three types of intervention all involve direct interference in the market mechanism.
   - *Income transfers* do not do so directly, but enable recipients to buy goods of their choice at market prices—for example, elderly people receive a retirement pension with which they buy food.

6. *The invisible-hand theorem* asserts that markets are automatically efficient if and only if a number of assumptions hold (Section 3.2). These conditions (collectively called the standard

Concepts

assumptions) are discussed in paragraphs 7–16 below, which, together with paragraphs 22–6, summarize the theoretical heart of the book. The conditions relate to perfect information, perfect competition, and the absence of market failures.

7. *Perfect information* implies, first, that consumers and firms should be well informed about the nature of the product, and also about prices. This is plausible for some goods (e.g. food and clothing), less so for others (e.g. health care). Where the assumption fails, several solutions are possible: the market itself may develop institutions to supply information (e.g. professional valuers, consumer magazines); or the state may respond with regulations (e.g. hygiene laws in the case of food); where information problems are serious the market might be so inefficient that public production might be a better answer.

8. Individuals need perfect information also about the future, so as to make rational choices over time. This is broadly true of food (since I know that I will need to eat tomorrow, next week, next month); it is not true with motor cars, because I do not know whether my car will be involved in an accident. The market can frequently cope with this sort of uncertainty through the mechanism of insurance (the main topic of Chapter 5). But private insurance can be inefficient or impossible, largely because of information problems in insurance markets. Thus some risks (e.g. unemployment) are not insurable. In such cases public funding may increase efficiency.

9. *Perfect competition* must apply in all input and output markets and also to capital markets (i.e. access to borrowing). Two conditions must hold: individuals must be price-takers; and they must have equal power.

10. Price-taking implies free entry and exit into/from an industry with a large number of consumers and firms, none of whom individually is able to influence market prices. Where the assumption fails (e.g. in the case of a monopoly), intervention generally involves regulation (e.g. a price ceiling) or an appropriate mix of taxation and subsidy.

11. Equal power is violated by any difference (apart from differences in individual incomes) in the ability of individuals to choose their consumption. The assumption rules out all forms of discrimination; where it fails, solutions (to the extent that they exist) are usually based on regulation.

12. *Market failures* arise in three forms: public goods, external effects, and increasing returns to scale.

13. *Public goods* in their pure form exhibit three technical characteristics: non-rivalness in consumption; non-excludability; and non-rejectability. Private (i.e. 'normal') goods are rival in consumption in the sense that if I buy a cheese sandwich there will be one sandwich less available for everyone else; excludability means that I can be prevented from consuming the cheese sandwich until I have paid for it; and rejectability implies that I do not have to eat it unless I wish to. Not all goods display these characteristics, the classic example being national defence. If the Royal Air Force is circling over the UK, the arrival of an additional person does not reduce the amount of defence available to everyone else (non-rivalness in consumption); nor is it possible to exclude the new arrival by saying that the bombs will be allowed to fall on him until he has paid his taxes (non-excludability); nor is the individual able to reject the defence on the grounds of pacifist beliefs (non-rejectability). Similar considerations apply wholly or in part to roads, public parks, and television broadcast signals.

14. In discussing public goods, an important distinction should be noted. For a private good the marginal cost associated with an *extra unit of output* and the marginal cost of an *extra user* are

one and the same thing—if it costs £1 to produce an extra cheese sandwich, it also costs £1 to provide for an extra cheese-sandwich-consumer. But this identity does not hold for public goods—the marginal cost of, for example, an extra hour's broadcasting is positive and generally large, whereas the marginal cost of an extra viewer is zero. This has important implications. If a public good is provided at all, non-excludability makes it impossible to charge for it (this is the *free-rider* problem); in such cases the market will generally fail entirely. Non-rivalness implies that the marginal cost of an extra user (though *not* of an extra unit of output) is zero, and therefore the efficient price should be based not on costs, but on the value placed by each individual on an extra unit of consumption. Since this is impractical, the market is likely to produce an inefficient output. Thus the market is either inefficient or fails altogether; if the good is to be provided at all, it will generally have to be publicly produced.

15. *External effects* arise when an act of individual A imposes costs or confers benefits on individual B, for which no compensation from A to B or payment from B to A takes place, or, more formally, when A's utility or production function is interrelated with B's. The effect of externalities is to create a divergence between private and social costs and benefits. As a result, the market output in the presence of an external cost will generally exceed the efficient output, X^* in Figure 4.1, and vice versa for an external benefit. On occasion the market can resolve this inefficiency itself. Coase (1960) shows that, where the law assigns unambiguous and enforceable property rights, the externality problem may be solved by negotiation between the parties concerned. But this is not always possible—for instance, where property rights are not enforceable (air pollution) or where large numbers of people are involved (traffic congestion). In this case intervention may be justified either through regulation (e.g. mandatory filtering equipment) or via an appropriate tax (sometimes referred to as a Pigovian tax) on the activity generating the external cost (see Le Grand *et al.* 1992: ch. 2; Stiglitz 1993*b*: ch. 7).

16. *Increasing returns to scale* arise when doubling all inputs leads to more than twice the output. If a production function exhibits increasing returns to scale at all levels of output, average cost will always exceed marginal cost, as in Figure 4.4. It follows that at an output of X_0 the marginal cost price P_0 is less than average cost, AC_0. Hence competitive pricing results in an inherent loss, shown by the shaded area. If firms in a competitive industry make long-run losses, they will leave the industry, which will either become monopolized or, if even a monopolist is unable to make a profit, cease to exist. The result, therefore, is a suboptimal output or a failure by the market to produce at all. Two solutions are possible: paying firms a lump-sum subsidy equal to the loss associated with competitive pricing; or nationalizing the industry and paying an identical subsidy. The appropriate intervention is therefore subsidy or public production, or both.

17. The market will allocate efficiently only when *all* the assumptions in paragraphs 7–16 hold, in which case no intervention on efficiency grounds is necessary. Where one or more of the assumptions fails, it is necessary in each case to consider which type of intervention (regulation, finance, or public production) is most likely to improve efficiency.

Intervention for reasons of social justice

18. Section 4.1 sets out two broad explanations of why redistribution occurs. To libertarians it is enforced on the rich by the voting power of the poor. Utilitarians argue that the rich may *choose* out of altruistic motives to vote for political parties which propose to tax them more heavily to finance redistributive policies.

Concepts

19. In certain circumstances there may be political-economy arguments for direct in-kind transfers—for instance, of education. The formal analysis (based on the idea of a consumption externality) is shown by the voting model in Section 4.2. Suppose the utility[30] of a representative rich individual, R, rises with his own consumption, and also with the consumption of a representative poor man, P. In particular, suppose that R's utility rises with 'good' consumption by P (e.g. education), but falls with P's 'bad' consumption (e.g. whisky), where 'good' and 'bad' are defined by R. In this circumstance it might be rational for R to offer P an education costing (say) £1,000, but to offer a cash transfer of only £200 (since P might spend the latter in part on 'bad' consumption). Faced with these offers, P might prefer the in-kind transfer to the lower cash sum (see Figure 4.5)—that is, both rich and poor might vote for compulsory in-kind transfers.

Privatization

20. The term 'privatization' is more complicated than many of its users realize (Section 6). As a first approximation, commodities like food are *produced* and *financed* privately whereas, at the opposite extreme, most education is produced in the public sector and paid for out of tax revenues. But intermediate cases are possible (Figure 4.6). Some goods are publicly produced, but are financed by user charges (e.g. public transport); others are paid from tax revenues but produced in the private sector (e.g. drugs supplied free under the National Health Service).

21. Matters become considerably more complicated when regulation is included. It is then necessary to distinguish not only the sector in which (*a*) production and (*b*) finance take place, but also who decides (*c*) how much in total of any good will be produced and (*d*) how much each individual consumer will receive. Some of these cases are set out in Table 4.1.

Achieving the aims of policy

22. Section 7 draws together the main arguments of Chapters 3 and 4 by repeating the distinction between the *aims* of policy and the *methods* available to achieve them. Aims embrace social justice and economic efficiency; methods include income transfers and direct interference in the market through regulation, subsidy, or public production.

23. The central argument of this book is that the proper place of ideology is in the choice of aims, particularly the definition of social justice and its trade-off with economic efficiency; but, once these aims have been agreed, the choice of method should be regarded as a *technical* issue, not an ideological one. Whether a commodity like health care is produced publicly or privately should be decided on the basis of which method more nearly achieves previously agreed aims. A rationale for choosing between the different methods is given in Section 7.2 in the form of two propositions.

24. *Proposition 1: efficiency.* Where one or more of the standard assumptions fails, state intervention in the form of regulation, finance, or public production may increase economic efficiency. If none of the assumptions fails, the efficiency aim is generally achieved best by the market with no intervention.

---

[30] See the Glossary.

25. *Proposition 2: social justice.* Subject to minor qualifications it is possible to argue:

   (*a*) Only efficiency arguments can justify intervention other than cash redistribution. If no such efficiency justification exists, the interests of social justice are best served by *income* transfers.

   (*b*) But if there exist arguments which suggest that efficiency will be furthered by public production and allocation of any good or service, then social justice can be enhanced by *in-kind* transfers (e.g. redistribution in the form of free education or health care).

26. The two propositions make the issue of market versus state production and allocation a contingent matter, placing this book firmly in the liberal tradition (as defined in Chapter 3, Section 1). The debate between this book and libertarian writers such as Hayek and Friedman is set out in Section 7.3.

CHAPTER 5

Economic theory 2: Insurance

Insurance, *n*. An ingenious modern game of chance in which the player is permitted
to enjoy the comfortable conviction that he is beating the man who keeps the table.
(Ambrose Bierce, 1842–1914)

1. Introduction

The term 'insurance'[1] is used by different people to mean different things.

- as a device which offers individuals *protection against risk*, or
- as an *actuarial mechanism* (equation 5.12), normally organized in the private sector.

The first defines insurance in terms of its objective, the second in terms of a method by which that objective might be pursued. Even where institutions are not insurance in the second sense, they might still be regarded as insurance in that they offer protection against risk.

It is possible to insure against many common mishaps such as burglary, death, or car accidents, against losses caused by bad weather, and for holiday deposits lost through illness. It is even possible to buy life insurance for one's dog or cat. On the face of it this is curious, since insurance companies usually make a profit: thus a representative individual receives less in benefit in the long run than he pays in contributions.

This gives rise to two questions: why do people insure voluntarily; and under what conditions will the private market provide insurance? These questions concerning, respectively, the demand and supply sides of the insurance market are discussed in Sections 2 and 3. Section 4 considers the circumstances in which a market equilibrium will exist,

---

[1] Non-technical readers can find the gist of the argument in the Appendix at the end of the chapter.

and will be efficient. Many of the problems discussed are examples of a more general class of information problem (see the Further Reading). The parallels will be noted as we proceed.

2. The demand for insurance

2.1. Individual demand

Why might a rational individual choose to insure when the expected pay-out is less than his premium payments? The answer, if he is risk averse, is that uncertainty *per se* causes disutility; hence certainty is a commodity yielding positive marginal utility, for which he will pay a positive price. The formal argument starts with the definition of a risk-averse individual as someone with diminishing marginal utility of income, as shown in Figure 5.1.[2] Suppose there is a 'bad' outcome, y_1, yielding utility $U(y_1)$, and a 'good' outcome, y_2, yielding utility $U(y_2)$, occurring with probabilities p_1 and p_2, respectively. The individual's expected income and expected utility are:

$$\text{Expected income: } E(y) = \bar{y} = p_1 y_1 + p_2 y_2. \tag{5.1}$$

$$\text{Expected utility: } E(U) = \bar{U} = p_1 U(y_1) + p_2 U(y_2). \tag{5.2}$$

If $p_1 = p_2 = 0.5$, expected income, $\bar{y}$, is midway between y_1 and y_2 (if $y_1 = £100$, and $y_2 = £1,000$, then $\bar{y} = £550$); and expected utility, $\bar{U}$, is midway between $U(y_1)$ and $U(y_2)$.

It is important to realize that a risk-averse individual can obtain the utility $\bar{U}$ in two entirely different ways.

- It could be obtained as the *expected* utility from an uncertain income of y_1 or y_2. Note that the individual never receives $\bar{y}$; each year she receives *either* y_1 *or* y_2 with corresponding utilities $U(y_1)$ and $U(y_2)$; the expected (or average) outcome is $\bar{y}$.
- Alternatively, she could obtain $\bar{U}$ from a *certain* income y^*, as shown directly by the utility function in Figure 5.1. When a person insures, what she is buying is *certainty*.

A rational individual will be indifferent between (*a*) an expected income $\bar{y}$ arising from uncertain outcomes y_1 and y_2 and (*b*) a lower income y^*, with certainty. The value of certainty is thus

$$V = \bar{y} - y^* \tag{5.3}$$

and a rational individual will pay a net price, ϕ, so long as:

$$\phi < V. \tag{5.4}$$

---

[2] For an introduction, see Estrin and Laidler (1995: ch. 8), Varian (1996: ch. 12), and the Further Reading.

Concepts

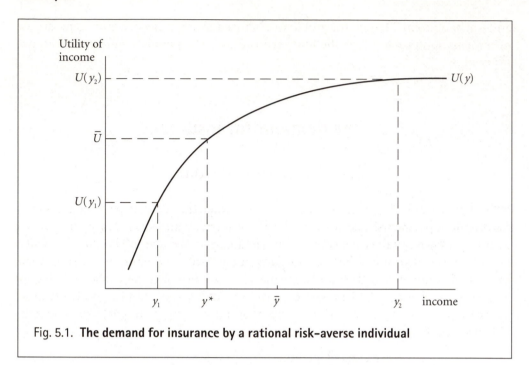

Fig. 5.1. **The demand for insurance by a rational risk–averse individual**

Table 5.1. **Gross and net insurance premiums, and net income in good and bad years (£)**

Income, insurance premium, and benefit	Good year	Bad year
1. Income	1,000	100
2. Insurance premium	550	550
3. Insurance benefit	–	900
4. Net Income ((1) – (2) + (3))	450	450
5. Net Premium ((2) – (4))	100	100

The net price of insurance, ϕ, should be carefully distinguished from the gross premium. The difference is shown in Table 5.1, where the insurance company charges an annual premium of £550, and compensates for up to £900 of lost income. In a 'good' year the individual has an income of £1,000, and pays a gross premium of £550, leaving a net income of £450. In a 'bad' year her income is £100; she pays a premium of £550 but receives compensation of £900. Thus the effect of insurance is to guarantee a net income of £450.

The net premium, ϕ, is the difference between the gross premium and the average pay-out. The latter is the individual's expected loss

$$E(L) = pL \qquad (5.5)$$

defined as the size of the loss, L, times the probability, p, that it will occur. Thus the net price of insurance is

$$\phi = \pi - pL \tag{5.6}$$

where π is the gross premium. In the example, the individual's expected loss is £450; so £450 of the gross premium can be regarded as a form of saving to cover her own losses in the long run. The *net* price of insurance is £100, which the individual will pay so long as it does not exceed the value to her of certainty, V, in equation (5.3). We return to the calculation of insurance premiums in Section 3.1.

2.2. The nature of the product: Insurance as a mechanism for pooling risk

The twin intellectual bases of insurance are the law of large numbers and gains from trade. Under the former, *individuals* may face uncertainty, but society can face approximate certainty—for example, I do not know whether I will die this year, but the death rate for men aged 40 to 60 is known and stable. It is the relative certainty about the *aggregate* probability resulting from the law of large numbers which opens up to individuals the possibility of exploiting gains from trade by agreeing to pool risks.

Suppose each individual's income is a random variable y with mean, μ, and variance, $\mathrm{var}(y)$; there are N such individuals with incomes $y_1, y_2, \ldots, y_N$, respectively. We assume:

- All individuals face the same probability distribution of outcomes.

- y, μ, and $\mathrm{var}(y)$ for each individual are independent of those for every other individual.

In the absence of insurance, the variance (i.e. risk) facing the ith individual is $\mathrm{var}(y_i)$. Now suppose all N individuals put their income into a pool agreeing that each will receive

$$\bar{y} = \frac{1}{N}(y_1 + y_2 + \ldots + y_N). \tag{5.7}$$

This pooling is a form of insurance. The variance for society is

$$\mathrm{var}(y_1 + y_2 + \ldots + y_N) = N\,\mathrm{var}(y)$$

since all incomes are independent and have the same variance. But the variance for the *individual* is smaller. He receives the average income, $\bar{y}$ in equation (5.7) and

$$\text{var}(\bar{y}) = \text{var}\left(\frac{y_1}{N} + \frac{y_2}{N} + \ldots + \frac{y_N}{N}\right)$$

$$= N \, \text{var}\left(\frac{y}{N}\right)$$

$$= \frac{\text{var}(y)}{N} \to 0, \text{ as } N \to \infty.$$

(5.8)

What equation (5.8) shows is that, if N identically distributed and independent incomes are pooled, the variance of average income (and hence the risk to the individual) tends to zero as N tends to infinity. By 'trading' (i.e. pooling), individuals can acquire certainty.

2.3. An example: Annuities

Annuities (i.e. an annual income stream) are another form of pooling. An individual could buy a pension of £y per year for a lump sum A, where A is the present value of the pension stream for the rest of her life, n years, and r is the rate of interest.[3] Thus

$$A = y + \frac{y}{1+r} + \frac{y}{(1+r)^2} + \ldots + \frac{y}{(1+r)^{n-1}}.$$

(5.9)

More generally, the capital cost of a given income stream is

$$A = f(y, n, r).$$

(5.10)

Consider someone with £50,000 accumulated in pension contributions over his working life. He could finance his retirement (twelve years on average, for a 65 year old man in the UK) by consuming this lump sum at a rate of, say, £5,000 per year; but he thereby risks outliving his savings. He can avoid this uncertainty by exchanging £50,000 plus an uncertain lifespan for a pension of £y, with certainty and for life. He is, in effect, making a bet with the insurance company: if he hands over the lump sum and immediately drops dead he loses, but if he lives to 98, he wins. This arrangement is exactly analogous to income-pooling. All retired persons put their lump sums into a pool and draw the average income; those who live longer draw more than those who die younger, but the fund can pay for the long-lived because it is based on average life expectancy.

How large is the annuity? Equation (5.10) can be rewritten as

$$y = g(A, n, r)$$

(5.11)

which shows that the annual payment, £y, for a given lump sum, A, depends on the insurance company's view of n (the applicant's life expectancy) and r (its expected interest rate).

---

[3] See Cullis and Jones (1998: ch. 6) or Stiglitz (1988: ch. 10).

LIFE EXPECTANCY. The insurance company will pay a lower annual income the longer it expects to pay benefit. In principle, this depends on four broad factors.

Age. The younger a person, the longer, on average, he has to live and the smaller the annuity in respect of a given lump sum.

Sex. On average women live longer than men. Other things being equal, a woman will therefore receive a smaller annuity than a man. In practice, many pension schemes pool across men and women, not least for the equity reasons discussed in Chapter 9, Section 4.2.

Health. With annuities, it is the long-lived who are 'bad' risks. But it is easier to detect health problems than to prove their absence, hence companies usually pool across health for annuities. There is no such pooling for life insurance, where it is the short-lived, often with detectable health problems, who are bad risks.

Marital status. Where an annuity is payable also to a surviving spouse, the age difference between husband and wife becomes relevant. If I retire at 65, and my wife is considerably younger, she is likely to outlive me by many years, in which case the payout period, n, is longer, and the annuity correspondingly smaller. However, where a scheme is compulsory (e.g. a pension scheme for school teachers), insurance companies usually pool across men aged 65 irrespective of the age of their wives. This is feasible because for the *group* the average age difference is predictable.[4]

THE RATE OF INTEREST. If changes in the price level are not to affect the real value of an annuity, it is necessary to base calculations on the real rate of interest (i.e. the excess of the nominal interest rate over the rate of inflation). Suppose an individual has accumulated a lump sum of £50,000, and the insurance company expects him to live for 12 years ($n = 12$) and anticipates a real rate of interest of 3 per cent ($r = 0.03$). The actuarial value of an annuity is obtained by substituting these values into equation (5.11) to obtain a value for y. The subject of annuities in the context of pension finance is a major topic in Chapter 9.

3. The supply side

3.1. The supply of insurance

This part of the chapter discusses the price at which the private market will supply insurance, and then turns to a number of technical problems.[5]

THE ACTUARIAL PREMIUM. Suppose that I insure the contents of my house for £1,000, when the probability of being burgled is 1 per cent. From equation (5.5) my expected loss is

---

[4] The fact that such schemes are compulsory is important, an aspect discussed in more detail in Sections 3.2 and 4.2, below.

[5] See, in ascending order of difficulty, Burchardt and Hills (1997: ch. 1), Stiglitz (1988: ch. 12), Culyer (1993), and Rees (1989).

the insured loss, L, multiplied by the probability, p_i, that I will experience the loss. The insurance company knows that on average it will have to pay out £10 per year (i.e. 1 per cent of £1,000). The actuarial premium for the ith individual, π_i, is then defined as:

$$\pi_i = (1 + \alpha)p_i L \tag{5.12}$$

where $p_i L$ is the individual's expected loss, and $(1+\alpha)$ is the loading which the insurance company adds to cover administrative costs (e.g. sending an expert to assess the damage) and normal profit. π is the price at which insurance will be supplied in a competitive market.

The actuarial premium in equation (5.12) rests on a number of conditions on the probability, p_i. Some are strictly technical, others bring us directly back to the issue of perfect information. Problems of either sort can make private insurance inefficient or impossible.

INDEPENDENT PROBABILITIES. Private insurance requires, first, that the probability of the insured event for any individual is independent of that for anyone else. This condition is necessary because insurance depends on the existence in a given period of a predictable number of winners and losers. If, in the extreme, individual probabilities are completely linked, then if one person suffers a loss so does everyone else. Thus actuarial insurance can cope with *individual* shocks but not with *common* or *systemic* shocks. An important problem under this head (discussed in Chapter 9, Section 3) is inflation, which, if it affects any one member of an actuarial pension scheme, will affect all.

PROBABILITY LESS THAN ONE. The relevant probability must be less than one. If not, equation (5.12) simplifies to:

$$\pi = (1 + \alpha)L > L \tag{5.13}$$

and the actuarial premium exceeds the insured loss. I might, for example, have to pay a premium of £1,500 to insure against potential burglary losses of £1,000. Private insurance will not be offered because there will be no demand for it. In economic terms there is no possibility of spreading risk, and hence no gains from trade.

This problem can arise for the chronically ill, where the probability of ill health is equal to one unless insurance is taken out before the condition is diagnosed. Medical insurance usually excludes cover for pre-existing conditions precisely because the probability of needing treatment is too high to insure. Advances in genetic screening will create major problems: the more and better the information about a person's future health, the greater the extent of pre-existing, and hence uninsurable, conditions (see Chapter 12, Section 3.1, and, for fuller discussion, Barr 1995).

We have seen (Chapter 4, Section 3.2) that market efficiency requires perfect information on the part of consumers and firms. Firms may face problems in a number of ways: employers may not be well informed about the quality of labour, nor lending institutions about the degree of riskiness of prospective borrowers. A particular class of information problem concerns insurance markets.

KNOWN PROBABILITIES. The relevant probability must be known or estimable. Insurance addresses *risk*, but cannot cope with *certainty* (the previous condition) nor with *uncertainty*, the issue here. If the insurer does not know the probability, it is not possible to calculate a premium from equation (5.12), making private insurance impossible. An important example concerns long-term insurance contracts. In the long run a known risk can become unknown (i.e. can turn into uncertainty). Thus private insurers are generally unable to offer contracts which index pensions against future inflation, *inter alia* because it is not possible to estimate the probability distribution of different levels of future price change (Chapter 9, Section 3.1). Similar problems arise for insurance for long-term residential care (Chapter 9, Section 3.1).

Further problems are caused by asymmetric information, where the supplier of insurance has less information than the customer. Specifically there should be no *adverse selection*, and no *moral hazard*. The former arises where the purchaser can conceal from the insurer that he is a high risk—for example, it may be possible for people to conceal potential ill health from medical insurers. Adverse selection thus arises where there is *hidden knowledge*. Moral hazard arises where there is *hidden action*—that is, situations where (slightly to oversimplify) the customer can costlessly manipulate the probability of the insured event. Pregnancy, for example, can be the result of deliberate choice (Chapter 12, Section 3.1). Thus the probability cannot be regarded as exogenous, and individual medical cover will generally exclude the costs of a normal pregnancy.[6]

3.2. Asymmetric information

Adverse selection and moral hazard are central to efficiency arguments about the welfare state, and so merit further discussion.[7]

ADVERSE SELECTION is a manifestation in insurance markets of the more general concept of 'lemons' (Akerlof 1970). The purchaser of insurance may have a much better idea than the supplier that he is a 'lemon' (i.e. a poor risk), and may conceal the fact from the insurer in order to choose a policy which would be unattainable if the insurer were perfectly informed.

Akerlof's competitive analysis was extended by Rothschild and Stiglitz (1976) to cover strategic behaviour by firms.[8] Point *A* in Figure 5.2 shows the income of an uninsured individual when working and when unable to work because of illness. Under simplifying assumptions (e.g. no administrative costs), a rational individual will insure

---

[6] But many policies will cover the extra costs of complications because the probability of *complications* is exogenous.

[7] The literature starts from Arrow (1963), followed by Akerlof (1970), Pauly (1974), Rothschild and Stiglitz (1976), and Stiglitz (1983). For an overview, see Stiglitz (1993*a*).

[8] For further discussion see, in ascending order of difficulty, Atkinson (1989: ch. 7), repr. in Barr and Whynes (1993: ch. 2), Culyer (1993), and Rees (1989).

Concepts

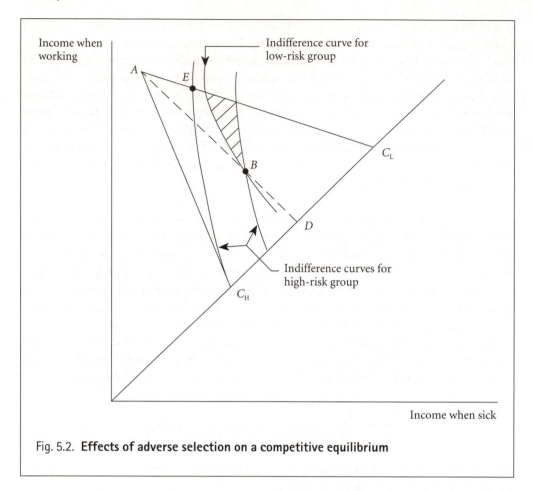

Fig. 5.2. **Effects of adverse selection on a competitive equilibrium**

fully, so that income (net of the insurance premium) will be the same when ill as when working, i.e. at a point on the 45-degree line.

Known probabilities. Suppose that there are two groups of people, low risk with a probability of illness p_L, and high risk with a probability P_H. Suppose, initially, that the insurer can distinguish the riskiness of individuals and can therefore match policies to individual risk. Thus:

$$\pi_L = (1 + \alpha)p_L L. \tag{5.14}$$

$$\pi_H = (1 + \alpha)p_H L. \tag{5.15}$$

Low-risk individuals pay a premium π_L and can trade from A on favourable terms. They give up little income in premiums when working and receive generous benefits when ill. They can buy any insurance contract along the line AC_L and, under the stated assumptions, will choose the contract (i.e. a pair of incomes when at work and ill, respectively) shown by point C_L. High-risk individuals face the less-favourable terms shown by AC_H, and will choose point C_H. Where insurers cannot distinguish high- from low-risk applicants, they can respond in several ways.

Pooling equilibrium. One option is to charge a premium based on average risk:

$$\bar{\pi} = (1 + \alpha)[\theta p_H + (1 - \theta)p_L]L \qquad (5.16)$$

where p_H and p_L are the (now unobserved) probabilities of high- and low-risk individuals, respectively, and θ and $(1 - \theta)$ the proportions of high- and low-risk individuals buying insurance. The locus of potential insurance contracts is illustrated by the line AD in Figure 5.2.

If low risks buy less cover and high risks more at an average premium, $\bar{\pi}$, the resulting policies are less efficient than would exist with individually tailored policies, π_L and π_H. Consider the contract shown by B. Any contract in the shaded area above B would (*a*) be preferred by the low-risk group, and (*b*) still be profitable. However, the pooling equilibrium (i.e. a common premium for all applicants) at B is not stable—if any company offered such a contract, another company could bid away the low-risk group by offering a policy in the shaded area above B. This instability applies to any other contract along AD.

Separating equilibrium. Suppose instead that the insurer tried to offer separate policies to the two groups. It cannot verify the riskiness of each individual. It might, however, appeal to *self-selection* by offering policies which incorporate incentive structures such that customers' market behaviour reveals their true probability (see Ravallion and Datt 1995 for analysis of such self-selection in different contexts). Thus the policy offered to the low-risk group along AD must lie to the left of point E (anywhere to the right would attract high-risk applicants). As Figure 5.2 is drawn, however, low-risk individuals prefer the pooling contract shown by B to any contract between A and E. The problem in this case is that no separating equilibrium exists. Even if it did, it would still be inefficient because low-risk individuals cannot buy complete cover.

Outcomes of adverse selection. Attempts by insurers to recruit good risks and avoid bad risks is known as *cream-skimming*. Paradoxically, however, though insurers fear that mainly bad risks will buy cover, the outcome is gaps in coverage for *low risks*. In the face of adverse selection, the market is either inefficient or fails entirely. The ultimate outcome is sensitive to the assumed behaviour of insurer and insured (see Dasgupta and Maskin 1986; Hellwig 1987). A partial solution is to restrict the range of choice the insured is allowed—for instance, making membership compulsory to prevent low risks opting out of a pooling equilibrium (i.e. seeking to move into the shaded area above point B). If preferences are sufficiently similar, the welfare loss from compulsion may be small.

MORAL HAZARD. At its strongest, the condition that there should be no moral hazard requires that both the probability, p, and the insured loss, L, should be exogenous to the individual. Slightly less stringently, moral hazard can be avoided so long as individuals can influence p or L only at a cost to themselves greater than the expected gain from so doing. Where the assumption fails, customers can affect the carrier's liability without its knowledge.

Concepts

Pauly (1974) considers the case of individual expenditure on a preventive activity, z, which can reduce the probability of the insured event. From a social point of view, the efficient level of z is where its marginal cost is equal to the marginal reduction in insured losses. But if losses are fully insured and the insurance company cannot monitor individual preventive activity, the private incentive is to spend little or nothing on it—people, in short, will behave differently if they are insured. At its simplest, my extra spending on z reduces my premium by only an infinitely small amount: the main beneficiaries are other insured people who now pay slightly lower premiums. As a result of this type of externality, Pauly argues, individuals face private incentives to under-invest in preventive activities.

Pauly's analysis is sensitive to one strong assumption—namely, that all losses, *including* non-material losses, are insurable. If that assumption is relaxed, there are several possible outcomes, of which Pauly's is only one. To show the effects of uninsurable psychic losses, it is useful to distinguish four cases.[9]

Case 1: Endogenous p_i, but only at substantial psychic cost. An example is suicide. Here the problem of moral hazard is more apparent than real. It is possible to influence the probability of dying, but generally only at a high utility cost to the person concerned. People do not commit suicide *only* to make their legatees rich. (It is true that someone intending to commit suicide *for other reasons* might do so; but that is a problem of adverse selection, to deal with which most policies exclude cover during the first year of the policy). Because individuals cannot insure against the psychic cost to themselves of death, insurance is incomplete. Moral hazard in such cases does not cause a problem.

Case 2: Endogenous p_i, with no substantial psychic cost. People might drive less carefully if they are insured, or buy fewer fire extinguishers, since insurance reduces the cost to the insured individual of those unwelcome events. In this case, the Pauly result holds: moral hazard does not make insurance impossible but causes inefficiency, since people take less care than if they had to bear the full loss themselves.

Case 3: Endogenous p_i, with substantial psychic gains. This is the case of voluntary pregnancy or elective health care (e.g. a hair transplant). Here the insured outcome is not an undesired exogenous event but a deliberate act of consumer *choice*. Individuals can control at small cost the probability, p_i, in equation (5.12), and the insurance company can calculate neither the expected loss nor the actuarial premium. This is a far cry from an insurable risk. Such activities are generally uninsurable for individuals, though the problem can sometimes be sidestepped where insurance is compulsory. If, for example, all workers in the steel industry are compelled to join a particular scheme, the insurer can impose a pooling solution based on the average expected number of births. In contrast, if insurance were voluntary, a disproportionate number of intending parents might join, raising issues of adverse selection as well as moral hazard.

---

[9] For fuller discussion of moral hazard, see Stiglitz (1983), Rees (1989), or Culyer (1993).

Case 4: Endogenous L at zero or low cost (the so-called *third-party-payment problem*). Here it is not the probability, p_i, which is endogenous but the size of the insured loss. To see intuitively what is going on, contrast behaviour in a conventional restaurant with that in an 'all-you-can-eat-for-£9.95' restaurant. In the case of medical care, for instance, if an insurance company pays all medical costs, neither patient nor doctor is constrained by the patient's ability to pay. The marginal private cost of health care is zero for both doctor and patient, even though social cost is positive. The results of this form of moral hazard are twofold: because of the divergence between private and social costs, consumption of health care (and consequently the insurance payout) is inefficiently large (Chapter 12, Section 3.1); and there is an upward bias in insurance premiums.

Similarly, suppose automobile insurance pays for all car repairs. I then have an incentive both to drive recklessly (*p* endogenous) and to have my car repaired lavishly (*L* endogenous). The result of this type of moral hazard, once more, is inefficiency in the form of over-consumption.

Thus moral hazard creates incentives to over-consumption on the demand side (cases 2 and 3) or supply side (case 4). The problem is fundamental: the more complete the cover and the lower the psychic loss from the insured event, the less individuals have to bear the consequences of their actions and the less, therefore, the incentive to behave as they would if they had to bear their losses themselves. A number of devices try to reduce the problem, either through regulation or through incentives.

- *Inspection* (a form of regulation) is frequently used for damage claims (e.g. for house contents or automobile repairs). The carrier inspects the damage and pays benefit only in respect of what it regards as the true insured loss.

Incentive mechanisms share the cost between the individual and the insurer.

- Frequent claimants (e.g. accident-prone car drivers) pay *higher premiums*.
- *Deductibles* make the insured person pay the first £*X* of any claim.
- With *coinsurance* the insured person pays *x* per cent of any claim.

None of these, however, faces the individual with the full marginal financial cost of making good the loss.

In analytical terms, adverse selection and moral hazard both derive from information failure. Neither would arise if the insurer could 'get inside the head' of insured persons (i.e. could read their thoughts), hence ruling out both hidden knowledge and hidden action.

4. The insurance market as a whole: Private and social insurance

4.1. The existence and efficiency of private insurance markets

THE EXISTENCE OF PRIVATE INSURANCE MARKETS requires three conditions.

1. There must be positive demand. From equation (5.3) this requires that

$$V = \bar{y} - y^* > 0.$$

This condition holds only if some individuals are risk averse.

2. It must be technically possible to supply insurance—that is, none of the problems discussed previously must make private insurance impossible.

3. It must be possible for insurance to be supplied at a price which the individual is prepared to pay—that is, the demand price must exceed or equal the net supply price. From equation (5.4) this requires

$$V = \bar{y} - y^* \geq \phi.$$

Equation (5.6) defines the net premium as the gross premium, π, minus the expected benefit, pL:

$$\phi = \pi - pL.$$

Hence, from equation (5.12),

$$\phi = \alpha pL.$$

Thus, a market for insurance exists only if

$$\bar{y} - y^* \geq \alpha pL. \tag{5.17}$$

Insurance can be supplied at an acceptable price only where the individual's risk aversion (represented by the difference between $\bar{y}$ and y^*) is sufficient to cover the insurer's administrative costs and normal profit, shown by αpL.

SHOULD INSURANCE BE COMPETITIVE? The three conditions hold for the examples of private insurance in Section 1. Consider the case of a head teacher who wants to insure against the loss to the parish if it rains on the day of fund-raising event. Since she wants to insure, it follows that she is risk averse, hence the demand condition holds. Nor are there technical problems on the supply side; the probability of rain on a given day is known and less than one; there is no adverse selection (since she cannot hide rainfall statistics from the insurer) and no moral hazard (since she cannot influence the weather). Finally, administrative costs are low, since it is easy to establish whether or not the weather was bad, and so insurance can be provided at a low net price. Thus private insurance is technically possible.

Is competitive insurance desirable? It was argued in Chapter 4 that an unrestricted private market allocates resources efficiently provided that the standard assumptions hold. These conditions apply equally to insurance. Perfect information is relevant to people who buy insurance, and to the companies that supply it. Where both sides of the market are well informed, competition provides consumers with their desired type and mix of policies and ensures that suppliers make no long-run excess profits. In such cases—for example, automobile insurance and burglary insurance—competition is both possible and desirable.

The strength of this argument is not diminished by the fact that the necessary conditions do not always hold, creating areas where the case for competitive actuarial insurance is weaker or non-existent. Three types of problem stand out.

1. *Imperfectly informed consumers.* With long-term contracts, buyers may not be well informed about the details of the cover they will need many years hence (e.g. long-term residential care insurance); and with technically complex contracts (e.g. pensions) people may not understand the issues fully. In some instances the market may supply the necessary information, for example, through insurance brokers. Where information problems are serious, however, the benefits from competition are diminished and may largely disappear. Competitive insurance is likely to be inefficient; it may also create inequities (for example, inappropriately sold pensions policies). These issues are taken up in later chapters (see also Burchardt and Hills 1997).

2. *Imperfectly informed insurers.* The resulting problems were discussed in detail in Section 3. Competitive pressures can create problems in the form of cream-skimming, gaps in coverage, and third-party incentives to inefficiently high spending.

3. *Administrative costs.*[10] From equation (5.12), the higher the administrative loading, α, the less likely that people will buy insurance. As equation (5.17) shows, the effect of α is to drive a wedge between people's risk aversion, $\bar{y} - y^*$, and the net return, pL, they derive from insurance. As a result, risk-averse individuals, whose welfare could be increased by insuring, do not buy insurance.

This outcome is not necessarily inefficient: an individual's risk aversion may be slight, and *some* administrative costs are unavoidable. The administrative costs associated with individual policies include:

- marketing costs, e.g. advertising, sending out applications, etc.;
- processing costs, e.g. the costs of matching premiums to individual risk;
- reimbursement costs, i.e. the costs of processing individual claims; and
- forgone economies of scale which a larger company might enjoy.

---

[10] For fuller discussion, see Culyer (1993: 156–7).

Concepts

These costs are efficient (and hence competition is desirable) if they generate significant welfare gains by enabling insurers to offer policies which match individual preferences more accurately. They are inefficient, however, if (a) their costs outweigh the welfare gains from individually tailored policies or (b) some other form of organization would be cheaper. With badly informed consumers, for example, the welfare gains from improved individual choice are likely to be low; thus social insurance, which has no marketing costs, low costs (because of standardization) of processing and reimbursement, and economies of scale, may be more efficient.

Where any of these problems arises, private insurance may be (a) inefficient or (b) not supplied at all. The central point of later discussion is that difficulties often arise because two sets of needs—those of actuarial insurance and those of social-policy—do not match. The solution is not to berate insurers for failing to meet social-policy objectives, still less to ignore social-policy needs because insurance, for technical reasons, cannot meet them. What is needed is a bridge between the two sets of objectives. Such a bridge may involve regulating or subsidizing private insurance or it may involve public funding through social insurance or taxation. These issues arise repeatedly, particularly for unemployment insurance (Chapter 8, Section 2.2), the protection of pensions against inflation (Chapter 9, Section 3.1) and medical insurance (Chapter 12, Section 3.1).

PREMIUM DIFFERENTIALS. Earlier discussion of adverse selection poses the question of whether efficiency requires that differences in individual probabilities should *always* result in different premiums. Suppose I am burgled more often than my brother. This could be because I am unlucky (a *random* difference), or because I live in London, which has a high crime rate, and he lives in the country (a *systematic* difference).

To define more precisely what we mean by random and systematic differences, suppose that individual probabilities vary randomly, i.e.

$$p_i = \bar{p} + \varepsilon_i \tag{5.18}$$

where p_i, the observed probability of the ith individual being burgled, comprises a 'true' or average probability, $\bar{p}$, and a random component, ε_i. If is truly random, and hence has a zero mean, the average probability, $\bar{p}$, is simply the mean of the observed probabilities, p_i, i.e.

$$\bar{p} = \frac{1}{N}\sum p_i. \tag{5.19}$$

Now consider two groups of individuals: $p_{11}, p_{12}, \ldots, p_{1M}$ are the observed probabilities facing the M individuals in group 1, and $p_{21}, p_{22}, \ldots, p_{2N}$ those of the N people in group 2. From (5.19) we can calculate the average probability for individuals in group 1, $\bar{p}_1$, and similarly for group 2. We can then argue that, if $\bar{p}_1 = \bar{p}_2$ any difference in probabilities between individuals in the two groups is random. However, if $\bar{p}_1$ is significantly greater than $\bar{p}_2$, differences in the probabilities are *systematic*. It is then appropriate to talk of high- and low-risk individuals, with average probabilities $p_H (= \bar{p}_1)$ and $p_L (= \bar{p}_2)$, respectively. Thus:

Conclusion 1. The efficient price of insurance should not reflect random differences in probabilities.

Conclusion 2. But where the decision to insure is voluntary, efficiency requires that suppliers should seek to discover who is high and who is low risk, and charge premiums accordingly, as in equations (5.14) and (5.15).

In contrast, where insurance is compulsory, it might be possible to pool high and low risks and charge everyone the average premium (equation (5.16)), since low-risk people cannot choose not to insure. Thus, for example, the 1946 National Insurance Act (Chapter 2, Section 5) applied pooling explicitly both to individuals and to risks. All employed men of working age paid the same lump-sum contribution to buy entitlement, *inter alia*, to the same unemployment benefit, even though some groups (e.g. doctors) were less likely to be unemployed than others (e.g. construction workers). All individuals paid an average premium (equation (5.16)); and, because contributions were compulsory, it was not possible for overcharged low-risk individuals to opt out. Analytically, the low-risk group paid an actuarial premium (equation (5.14)) plus an unavoidable lump-sum tax, and the high-risk group paid an actuarial premium shown by equation (5.15) and received a lump-sum transfer. Thus a system which charges a compulsory average premium irrespective of risk can alleviate problems of adverse selection.[11] Another example (Chapter 9, Section 4.2) is the pooling of men and women in pension schemes, despite the fact that on average women live longer. In contrast, automobile insurance is also compulsory, but there is no pooling across groups—people with worse accident records generally pay higher premiums. We can therefore add:

Conclusion 3: if insurance is compulsory, charging all categories of risk the same premium causes little inefficiency in *insurance* markets, though it might cause secondary inefficiency in related activities.

FALLACIOUS EQUITY ARGUMENTS appear in a number of guises. The first is that insurance is inequitable because it redistributes from those who do not make claims to those who do. This assertion merits little discussion. The whole point of insurance is that people do not know whether they will need to claim (i.e. whether the 'good' or the 'bad' outcome will occur). A rational risk-averse individual increases her utility by choosing a lower income with certainty (y^* in Figure 5.1), in preference to a higher expected income, $\bar{y}$. Insurance can bring about this increase in utility precisely because the individual is a net contributor in a 'good' year and a net beneficiary in a 'bad' year.

A second fallacious argument is that 'private insurance is inequitable because the poor cannot afford adequate cover'. This proposition can be attacked in a number of ways.

---

[11] It might, however, cause inefficiency in other ways: standard policies do not allow for differences in preferences; and a common structure of premiums for employers might lead to inefficient expansion of risky industries.

First, if the *only* difficulty is that the poor cannot afford cover, the problem is one not of market allocation but of income distribution, and can be solved by cash redistribution. Secondly, who decides what level of cover is 'adequate'? Public provision on these grounds can be justified only where there are efficiency problems with private insurance, or if the poor have imperfect information. The arguments developed earlier, in particular the two propositions in Chapter 4, Section 7.2, apply equally to insurance.

4.2. Social insurance

SOCIAL INSURANCE AS A RESPONSE TO INFORMATION FAILURE. Arrow argues that, where markets fail, other institutions may arise to mitigate the resulting problems, sometimes through public production and sometimes through private institutions using non-competitive allocation mechanisms: 'the failure of the market to insure against uncertainties has created many social institutions in which the usual assumptions of the market are to some extent contradicted' (Arrow 1963: 967). In other words, as discussed in the first paragraph of this chapter, institutions (public or private) may arise which are insurance in the sense of protecting against risk, even if they are not insurance in a narrow actuarial sense.

The Arrow arguments and their subsequent elaboration contrast strongly with those of Hayek (1945). Both writers started from the assumption of asymmetric information. To Hayek the fact that different people know different things is an argument *in favour* of markets. He argued (analogous to the existence of skill differences) that the market makes beneficial use of such differences by allowing gains from trade to be exploited. Arrow showed that the market is an inefficient device for mediating certain important classes of differences in knowledge between people. Nor is the Arrow view idiosyncratic. The Rothschild and Stiglitz (1976) and similar arguments were discussed in Section 3.2. Lucas (1987: 62), in discussing unemployment, reached an identical conclusion:

Since . . . with private information, competitively determined arrangements will fall short of complete pooling, this class of models also raises the issue of *social insurance*: pooling arrangements that are not actuarially sound, and hence require support from compulsory taxation. The main elements of Kenneth Arrow's analysis of medical insurance are readily transferable to this employment context.   (emphasis in original)

Social insurance thus derives from two sources. The need for insurance arises because in industrialized countries employment is largely a binary phenomenon (i.e. a person is either employed or unemployed) and retirement, similarly, is a discrete event. Thus the risks against which social insurance offers protection are to some extent a social construct.[12] Second, on the supply side, information failures provide both a theoretical *justification of* and an *explanation for*, a welfare state which is much more than

---

[12] Atkinson (1995a: ch. 11) stresses the importance of labour-market institutions. On retirement, see Hannah (1986).

a safety net. A central argument in later chapters is that private insurance cannot cover contingencies such as unemployment, inflation, and important medical risks. Social insurance is one response.

THE NATURE OF THE BEAST. An important characteristic of most social insurance is that membership is compulsory, thus preventing low risks from opting out (though partial opting out may be allowed for some benefits). Compulsion makes possible the three generic forms of organization described in Chapter 1, Section 2.1, all of which are insurance in the sense of offering protection, but which diverge increasingly from insurance in conventional actuarial terms.

- *Social insurance* (i.e. benefits based on a contributions record and the occurrence of a specified contingency) takes two broad forms. Quasi-actuarial contributions are related to the average risk (e.g. the flat-rate weekly contribution of the UK scheme between 1948 and 1975); this is a pure pooling equilibrium. Income-related contributions break the link with individual risk; the contribution in this case looks like an earmarked tax.

- *'Universal' benefits* abandon the attempt to mimic private insurance. Tax-financed benefits are awarded on the basis of specified contingencies without a contributions or income test (the flat-rate retirement pension in some countries, health care in some countries including the UK).

- *Social-assistance benefits* are awarded on the basis of specified contingencies and an income test.

Administration can be by the state at central level (as mostly in the UK) or at a lower level (as for most programmes in the USA, and for health care in Australia, Canada, and Sweden). Alternatively, administration can be hived off to private-sector institutions such as friendly societies or trades unions (as with unemployment compensation in Sweden and medical care in Germany); in such cases the private sector is acting, in effect, as an agent of the state.

The social-insurance arrangements just described are based on private institutions: benefits are conditioned on an implicit or explicit contributions record and on the occurrence of a specified event, frequently related to employment status, in that one of their major purposes is to replace lost earnings.

Social insurance, however, differs from private insurance in two important respects. First, because membership is generally compulsory, it is *possible* (though not essential) to break the link between premium and individual risk; a pooling solution is therefore an option. Secondly, the contract is usually less specific than private insurance, with two advantages: protection can be given against risks which the private market cannot insure (Chapter 8 argues that unemployment is one); and the risks can change over time. Atkinson (1995a: 210) points out that 'the set of contingencies over which people formed probabilities years ago may have excluded the breakdown of the extended family, or the development of modern medicine, simply because they were inconceivable'.

Concepts

Thus social insurance, in sharp contrast with actuarial insurance, can cover not only *risk* but also *uncertainty*. Social insurance, in various guises, will appear repeatedly in later chapters.

FURTHER READING

Burchardt and Hills (1997: ch. 1) give an excellent, non-technical introduction to the economics of insurance. See also, in ascending order of formality, Stiglitz (1993*b*: ch. 6), Estrin and Laidler (1995: ch. 8), Varian (1996: ch. 12), Rees (1989), or Varian (1992: ch. 11). For discussion in the context of cash benefits, see Stiglitz (1988: ch. 12), and in the context of medical insurance Culyer (1993). Barr (1995) discusses the implications of genetic screening for insurance.

On information problems more generally, see Varian (1992: ch. 25) for an overview. For compendious discussion, see Hirschleifer and Riley (1992) and Stiglitz (1993*a*). The classic articles are by Arrow (1963) (who discusses medical insurance), on adverse selection by Akerlof (1970) and Rothschild and Stiglitz (1976), and on moral hazard by Pauly (1974) and Stiglitz (1983). For surveys of the literature on imperfect information about quality, see Stiglitz (1987: 1993*a*) and Phlips (1988: ch. 3), and on imperfect information about price, Phlips (1988: ch. 2).

Appendix: Non-technical summary of Chapter 5

1. Chapter 5 discusses the demand and supply of insurance, and some problems which can arise on the supply side of a private insurance market (for a simple introduction, see Burchardt and Hills (1997: ch. 1)).

2. The term 'insurance' is used by different people to mean different things. Two meanings above all should be distinguished. Insurance can be defined (*a*) as a device which offers individuals *protection against risk*, and/or (*b*) as an *actuarial mechanism* (as defined in equation (5.12), below) which the private sector can organize. The first defines insurance in terms of its purpose, the second in terms of a method by which that purpose might be pursued. Even where institutions are not insurance in the sense of (*b*), they might still be regarded as insurance in that they offer protection against risk.

The demand and supply of insurance

3. Uncertainty reduces the utility of an individual who is risk averse; hence certainty has a positive value, and a risk-averse individual will be prepared to pay a positive price for it. When I take out insurance, the commodity I am buying is *certainty* (e.g. that if my car is stolen it will be replaced). The formal argument is presented in Section 2.1.

4. The supply of insurance is discussed in Section 3.1. Suppose that the probability, p, of being burgled is 1 per cent; and that if I am burgled my loss, L, will be £1,000. On average, therefore, I can expect a loss of £1,000 once every 100 years. In annual terms my expected loss is $p \times L = 1\%$ $\times £1,000 = £10$—that is, the insurance company knows that on average it will have to pay me £10 per year. Formally, an *actuarial premium*, π, is defined as

$$\pi = (1 + \alpha)pL \qquad (5.12)$$

where pL is the expected loss of the individual buying insurance, and $(1 + \alpha)$ is the insurance company's mark-up of α per cent to cover its administrative costs and normal profit. π is the price at which insurance will be supplied in a competitive market.

Technical problems on the supply side

5. Private insurance will be inefficient or non-existent unless the probability, p, in equation (5.12) meets five conditions (Sections 3.1 and 3.2). First, the probability of a given individual being, for example, burgled must be *independent* of the probability of anyone else being burgled. What this means (roughly speaking) is that insurance depends for its financial viability on the existence in any year of a predictable number of winners and losers.

6. Secondly, p must be *less than one*. If $p = 1$ it is certain that my car will be stolen; hence there is no possibility of spreading risks, and the insurance premium will equal or exceed the cost of a new car. This problem can arise for the chronically or congenitally ill, for whom the probability of ill health equals one unless insurance is taken out *before* the condition is diagnosed.

Concepts

7. A third condition is that p must be *known or estimable*. If it is not, insurance companies will be unable to calculate an actuarial premium, and private insurance will be impossible. This problem can arise for policies with a long-time horizon, where risk (which is insurable) turns in the long run into uncertainty (which is not). The private market, for example, is generally unable to supply insurance against future inflation because the probability of different levels of future price increases cannot be estimated.

8. Fourthly, there must be *no adverse selection*, which arises when a purchaser is able to conceal from the insurance company the fact that he is a poor risk. If the insurance company cannot distinguish high- and low-risk customers, it will have to charge everyone the same premium, based on the average risk. As a result, low-risk individuals will face an inefficiently high premium and may choose not to insure even though, at an actuarial premium, it would be efficient for them to do so. This problem arises particularly in the case of medical insurance for the elderly.

9. Finally, there must be *no moral hazard*. The problem can arise in two ways: first, where the customer is able costlessly to manipulate the probability p in equation (5.12) that the insured event will occur; and, secondly, where the customer can manipulate the size of the loss, L. The latter difficulty is conventionally called the *third-party-payment problem*.

10. There are numerous ways in which consumers can manipulate the relevant probability. The chances of developing appendicitis are beyond individual control, and so medical insurance for this sort of complaint is generally possible. In contrast, the probability of becoming pregnant, and visits to one's family doctor, can both be influenced by individual actions and are therefore generally not well covered by private medical insurance. Where the problem is serious, the supplier is unable to calculate the actuarial premium, and private insurance may be impossible.

11. The third-party-payment problem does not make insurance impossible, but causes over-consumption. The problem is particularly relevant to health care. If an individual's insurance pays all medical costs, then health care is 'free' to the patient. Similarly, on the supply side, the doctor knows that the insurance company will pay her charges; she is therefore not constrained by the patient's ability to pay. As a result, both doctor and patient can act as though the cost of health care were zero. This is inefficient: it causes over-consumption and creates upward pressure on insurance premiums.

12. The problems discussed in paragraphs 5–11 can cause inefficiency, and may make private insurance impossible. Both difficulties are relevant to unemployment insurance (Chapter 8, Section 2.2), to the protection of pensions against inflation (Chapter 9, Section 3.1) and to medical insurance (Chapter 12, Section 3.1).

CHAPTER 6

Problems of definition and measurement

To criticise inequality and to desire equality is not . . . to cherish the romantic illusion that men are equal in character and intelligence. It is to hold that, while their natural endowments differ profoundly, it is the mark of a civilised society to aim at eliminating such inequalities as have their source, not in individual differences, but in its own organisation. (R. H. Tawney, 1964)

Common prosperity cannot and never will mean absolute egalitarianism or that all members of society become better off simultaneously at the same speed . . . Such thinking would lead to common poverty.

(People's Republic of China, Central Committee's Decision on Reform of the Economic System, 1984)

1. Measuring welfare

Measurement problems are a recurring theme.[1] They are illustrated here in the context of poverty (Section 2) and inequality (Sections 3 and 4). Two sets of issues are discussed: how do we define poverty and inequality; and how do we measure them in principle and in practice? It is helpful to start by considering the definition and measurement of welfare for individuals and for society as a whole.

---

[1] Non-technical readers may omit Sections 1.2, 4.1, and 4.2. The gist of the argument is in the Appendix at the end of the chapter.

1.1. Individual welfare

DEFINING INDIVIDUAL INCOME

WEALTH AND INCOME. The theoretical concept of income is complex and the literature vast (see the Further Reading). For present purposes it is possible to simplify matters by considering income as the flow deriving from a stock of wealth. Individual wealth can arise, broadly, in three forms. *Physical wealth* consists of consumer durables such as houses, machines (e.g. cars, television sets), Picassos, and Persian rugs. *Financial wealth* includes shares, government bonds, and bank accounts.[2] *Human capital* is wealth embodied in individuals as a result of skill and training, and has two quite separate sources: it is the result of past investment in education and training (which is what most people mean when they talk about human capital); it also arises from 'natural talent'. The latter requires explanation. Obvious examples are Shakespeare and Mozart, whom most of us could not emulate, however much training we had. The concept, however, is much broader. The talent of a road sweeper, for example, consists mainly of muscle and an ability to put up with simple routine; and a major item under this head is the ability to walk, dress, wash oneself, etc. (which forms of human capital may be denied to individuals with serious health problems).

Each type of wealth yields a flow of income. Physical wealth produces non-money income in the form of a flow of services (e.g. housing, or televisual services), but can also yield money income (e.g. a house to a landlord, or an automobile to a taxi driver). Financial wealth yields money income (e.g. the annual flow of interest from a £1,000 bank account). Human capital produces income in several forms. Suppose an individual divides his time between 'work' and 'leisure'.[3] When he is working, his human capital yields money income (i.e. wages), and, non-money income like job satisfaction (which can be positive or negative); and, when not working, he receives non-money income through the enjoyment of leisure (again positive or negative), and also in the form of own production (household chores, gardening, etc.).

FULL INCOME, Y_F, consists of the flow of services from *all* individual wealth, i.e. money income, Y_M, plus all forms of non-money income, Y_N:

$$Y_F = Y_M + Y_N \tag{6.1}$$

where money income comprises wage and non-wage money income (e.g. dividends and interest),[4] and non-money income includes job satisfaction, the flow of services from

---

[2] It is legitimate to include both physical and financial wealth for *individuals*. But, for society as a whole, care is needed to avoid double counting, which would arise if, for example, Ford factories and Ford shares were both included in the definition of wealth.

[3] The distinction between work and leisure is in many respects suspect (see, e.g., Apps and Rees 1996). But it does no harm to retain the distinction for present purposes, and makes the exposition clearer.

[4] This definition leaves unanswered the difficult question of whether, and to what extent, capital gains should be included in income. See Prest and Barr (1985: ch. 13, sect. 4).

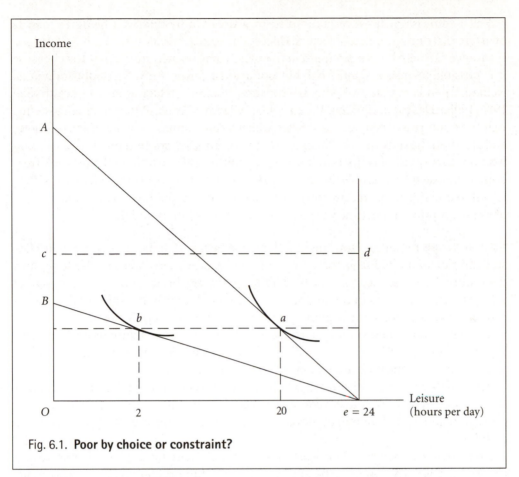

Fig. 6.1. **Poor by choice or constraint?**

physical wealth, the value of own production, and, importantly, the enjoyment of leisure. For given prices, full income thus defined is a measure of an individual's *opportunity set*.

The word 'opportunity' is crucial. The opportunity set measures the individual's *potential* consumption, including leisure. In Figure 6.1 the lines eA and eB show the earning opportunities of individuals A and B, respectively. A and B are both poor as conventionally measured, since their income, shown by points *a* and *b*, is below the poverty line *cd*. However, A's full income, including the value of leisure, shown by *OA* is well above the poverty line; B's full income, *OB*, is not. A is 'poor' because *by choice* he works for only four hours per day; B is poor *despite* working twenty-two hours per day.[5] By defining full income as the return to *all* forms of individual wealth it is possible to construct a measure of consumption opportunities which makes theoretical sense.

---

[5] See Atkinson and Stiglitz (1980: 260–1) on the importance of including leisure, and Le Grand (1984) on the central importance of choice in assessing individual welfare.

Concepts

Full income is not, however, a complete measure of individual well-being. Even in its own terms, it omits important factors. Uncertainty can be a major source of welfare loss. Insurance can help but, as discussed in Chapter 5, may be incomplete, not least because it is possible to insure against risk but not against uncertainty. Secondly, individual welfare depends not only on potential consumption but on factors such as health (Sen 1985, 1995a; Dasgupta 1993: ch. 4). Sen (1985; 1992: ch. 3) extends the argument to define well-being in terms of people's 'capabilities', which includes important dimensions of choice and freedom. 'Just as the . . . "budget set" in commodity space represents a person's freedom to buy commodity bundles, the "capability set" . . . reflects the person's freedom to choose from possible livings' (Sen 1992: 40). While noting these criticisms, they are set to one side in the discussion which follows, since even the more limited concept of a consumption opportunity set cannot easily be put into practice.

THE HAIG–SIMONS DEFINITION. How might full income be translated into practice? The classic definition of individual income is by Simons (1938: 50), also called the Haig–Simons definition: 'Personal income may be defined as the algebraic sum of (1) the market value of rights exercised in consumption and (2) the change in the value of the store of property rights between the beginning and the end of the period.' More simply, 'income in a given period is the amount a person could have spent while maintaining his wealth intact' (Atkinson 1983: 39). The word 'could' is important. My income is increased if my *potential* to consume is raised, whether or not I actually choose to consume more.

The Haig–Simons definition has twofold importance: it indicates how income might be measured in practice; and it is comprehensive (and therefore theoretically sound) because it includes the following types of income which are omitted from conventional definitions.

Non-pecuniary benefits from work. Where fringe benefits are marketable (e.g. a chauffeur-driven car), they can be valued fairly easily. But problems arise where benefits are non-marketable and/or a mixture of 'work' and 'leisure'. Is a business trip abroad work, or leisure in disguise, or a mixture of the two? And how should 'enjoyment' of the trip be valued? The measurement of job satisfaction raises obvious problems. All these non-pecuniary benefits are part of 'rights exercised in consumption', and their market value forms part of the Haig–Simons definition.

Own production includes goods I have produced for myself (e.g. building an extension to my house) which could in principle be part of market production, and also the consumption of unpaid services produced by others within the household sector (e.g. cooking, cleaning, child-minding).[6] Both forms of activity give rights over consumption, and their market value is properly included in the Haig–Simons definition. Income under this head also includes leisure, whose value to an individual is not less than the earnings thereby forgone, £X.

Imputed rent is the market value of the services deriving from physical assets, notably consumer durables and owner-occupied houses.

---

[6] In formal terms these two sorts of activity correspond to production for own consumption and production for trade within the household sector (see Apps and Rees 1996).

Capital gains and losses, according to Haig–Simons, are part of income, since they constitute a change in the value of the store of property rights. An individual with a £1,000 asset which appreciates over the period to £1,100 would be able (assuming no inflation) to spend an extra £100 without reducing her wealth. Thus capital gains should be included as part of income *in the period in which they accrue*, whether or not they are realized; and capital losses should be deducted from income as they accrue.

MEASURING INDIVIDUAL INCOME

The next step is to consider how a theoretically sound definition of income might in practice be measured. This raises three sets of problems.

WHAT DO WE INCLUDE IN INCOME? A version of Haig–Simons which might be workable is the sum of wage income, non-wage money income, fringe benefits, imputed rent, and realized capital gains. But this measure deviates from full income as defined in equation (6.1) through the omission of job satisfaction, extra-market production, and forgone income taken as leisure, and also because capital gains are not measured as they accrue. Further problems arise in attributing to individuals the benefits of publicly provided goods and services (e.g. education, roads).

Because non-money income is largely unmeasurable, it is necessary to focus on money income. This would not matter if money income were a good proxy for full income, but in practice the proportion of income arising in non-money form varies widely and unsystematically across people. Non-observability of parts of full income prevents a complete characterization of the individual opportunity set, forcing us to use the unreliable yardstick of money income. Full income is useful less as a guide to policy than as an explanation of why conventional definitions of poverty and inequality, based on money income, have only limited validity as measures of welfare.

THE INCOME UNIT. What is the relation between household income and individual welfare? Part of the story—the comparison of households of different sizes—is discussed in Section 3.3. The other part concerns relations within a household. Consider the case of a man, a woman, and two children, whose only source of income is £20,000, earned by the man. Regarded as a family, four people share an income of £20,000; no one is poor; nor is there necessarily substantial inequality. But if the man is regarded as a separate unit, the woman and child have no income; they are counted as poor; and there is substantial measured inequality. Thus the narrower the definition of the income unit, the greater are measured poverty and inequality.

The heart of the problem is the difficulty of measuring how income is shared. Since this is unobservable, policy is frequently based on the observable but not strictly relevant fact that two people are married, and thereby infers (rightly or wrongly) that income is shared. This is a strong assumption and one which is clearly unsatisfactory. The large literature on industrialized (Okin 1989; Sainsbury 1994; Sutherland 1997) and poorer countries (Dasgupta 1993: ch. 11) confirms widespread gender inequality. Any measure of income, however complete, will fail to capture important aspects of the distribution of welfare within households.

OVER WHAT TIME PERIOD IS INCOME MEASURED? Problems arise because income rarely flows continuously. Consider a salesman who earns £400 per week in commission but receives no wage; during the year he works fifty weeks, earning £20,000, and in the remaining two weeks, because of illness, earns nothing. If income is measured over a year he is not poor, but on a weekly basis he is poor for two weeks. For some purposes (e.g. setting a level for student support) it might be appropriate to use a long-run notion like permanent income. On the other hand, if a student with no family support or job applied for social assistance during the summer vacation, it would not be very helpful to refuse benefit because he had a high expected lifetime income. In cases of immediate need, the relevant definition of income is usually short run.

1.2. Social welfare

Similar arguments apply at an aggregate level. A comprehensive measure of national income would include both money and non-money income.

'We cannot measure . . . national achievement by the gross national product. For the gross national product includes air pollution and advertising for cigarettes, and ambulances to clear our highways of carnage . . . It swells with equipment for the police to put down riots in our cities; and though it is not diminished by the damage these riots do, still it goes up as slums are rebuilt on their ashes . . . And if the gross national product includes all this, there is much that it does not comprehend. It does not allow for the health of our families, the quality of their education or the joy of their play . . . It allows neither for the justice in our courts, nor for the justice of our dealings with each other . . . It measures everything, in short, except that which makes life worthwhile.'[7]

More formally, the *social-welfare function* in equation (4.1) is the explicit relation between aggregate welfare and the welfare of the individuals who make up society. If U^i, the utility of the ith individual, depends on his income, y^i, then social welfare, W, can be expressed as

$$W = W(U^1(y^1), U^2(y^2), \ldots, U^n(y^n))$$ (6.2)

or, more simply, as

$$W = W(y^1, y^2, \ldots, y^n).$$ (6.3)

Thus $y^1, \ldots, y^n$ measure the welfare of each of the n individual members of society; these are aggregated into a measure of social welfare through the function W. Social welfare functions are categorized in terms of their formal properties (see Cowell 1995: 35–41),

---

[7] Speech by Robert Kennedy in 1967, reported by Newfield (1978: 59–60).

an explanation of which is a necessary prelude to the discussion of aggregate inequality in Section 4.

PROPERTY 1: NON-DECREASING. Let social welfare in state A be $W_A = W(y^1, y^2, \ldots, y^{iA}, \ldots, y^N)$ and, in state B, $W_B = W(y^1, y^2, \ldots, y^{iB}, \ldots, y^N)$. In other words, the distribution in states A and B differs only because the ith individual has a higher income in state B than in state A. Then a social welfare function is non-decreasing if and only if

$$W_B \geq W_A \text{ if } y^{iB} \geq y^{iA}. \tag{6.4}$$

Non-decreasing implies that, if any individual's income rises, social welfare cannot decrease.

PROPERTY 2: SYMMETRIC. A social-welfare function is symmetric if

$$W(y^1, y^2, \ldots, y^n) = W(y^2, y^1, \ldots, y^n) = \ldots = W(y^n, \ldots, y^2, y^1). \tag{6.5}$$

Social welfare depends on the distribution of income, but not on who gets which income—that is, social welfare is unchanged if two people 'swap' incomes. This is equivalent to assuming that all individuals have identical utility functions.

PROPERTY 3: ADDITIVE. A social-welfare function is additive if

$$W(y^1, y^2, \ldots, y^n) = \sum_{i=1}^{n} U^i(y^i) = U^1(y^1) + U^2(y^2) + \ldots + U^n(y^n). \tag{6.6}$$

This is the utilitarian social-welfare function, under which social welfare is the sum of the utilities experienced individually by members of society. Additivity implies that a person's utility is a function of his income alone, independent of anyone else's income—a strong assumption which rules out the possibility of welfare interdependence discussed in Chapter 4, Section 4.1, and which also rests uneasily with the relative definition of poverty discussed shortly.

These three properties taken together have important implications. If a social-welfare function is non-decreasing, symmetric, and additive, it has the general form

$$W = U(y^1) + U(y^2) + \ldots + U(y^n) \tag{6.7}$$

where: (*a*) (in contrast with equation (6.6)) U is the same for each individual (a consequence of symmetry); and (*b*) $U(y^i)$ increases with y^i (because the social-welfare function is non-decreasing).

Equation (6.7) makes it possible to use $U(y^i)$ as an index of social welfare. If there is an increase in the income of the ith individual, the increase in social welfare will be

$$U'(y^i) = \frac{dU(y^i)}{dy^i} \geq 0. \tag{6.8}$$

The welfare index $U(y^i)$ is *not* an ordinary utility function. It shows the social marginal valuation or *welfare weight* of changes in the ith person's income. To show why $U'(y^i)$ is the welfare weight, consider a tax/transfer scheme which leads to a series of (small) changes in individual incomes, $\Delta y^1, \Delta y^2, \ldots, \Delta y^n$. The resulting change in social welfare is the total differential ΔW; and, if the social-welfare function takes the simple form of equation (6.7), then

$$\Delta W = U'(y^1)\Delta y^1 + U'(y^2)\Delta y^2 + \ldots + U'(y^n)\Delta y^n \qquad (6.9)$$

and the terms $U'(y^i)$ act as a system of weights when summing the effects of the scheme on social welfare. The next step is to discuss what value the weights might take. This brings us to:

PROPERTY 4: CONCAVE. A social-welfare function is concave if the welfare weight always decreases as y^i increases—that is, concavity implies diminishing social marginal utility of income. A £1 increase in income raises social welfare more if it goes to a poor than to a rich man; thus a small redistribution from rich to poor raises social welfare. For some purposes it is useful to know how concave a social-welfare function is—that is, how rapidly the welfare weight falls as an individual's income rises. Thus:

PROPERTY 5: CONSTANT RELATIVE INEQUALITY AVERSION. A social-welfare function has constant relative inequality aversion (or constant elasticity) if the utility index $U(y^i)$ has the specific form

$$U(y^i) = \frac{1}{1-\varepsilon} \, y^{i(1-\varepsilon)} \qquad (6.10)$$

where ε is a non-negative *inequality aversion parameter*. The welfare index in equation (6.10) has the property that a 1 per cent increase in someone's income reduces her welfare weight by ε per cent whatever her income (i.e. by 1 per cent from £100 to £101 or from £10,000 to £10,100). The larger is ε, the more rapid the decline in the welfare weight as income rises, hence the name 'inequality aversion parameter'. We return to these issues in more detail in Section 4.2.

2. Poverty

Attempts to define a value-free poverty line (Section 2.1) face a series of largely intractable problems. The first concerns the choice of *indicator of welfare*, specifically (*a*) *what* indicator of consumption opportunities, and (*b*) *whose* income, i.e. the issue of the income unit. A second set of issues concerns which *concept of poverty* should be used. A third issue is how should poverty be *measured* (Section 2.3).

2.1. Defining poverty

WHICH INDICATOR OF WELFARE? Individual consumption opportunities should be measured in terms of full (i.e. money plus non-money) income. Because this is not possible, it is necessary to turn to more measurable indicators. Three measures are common: actual consumption of a specific bundle of goods, total expenditure, and total money income. Each has its difficulties, of which the following is the barest of summaries.[8] The first approach requires a definition of the appropriate consumption bundle, and, when that difficult task has been accomplished, leads to a multidimensional (and hence complex) definition of poverty. Expenditure is difficult to measure and needs adjustment for inefficient spending.

Money income is a flawed measure of individual welfare.[9] Three problems were discussed in Section 1.1: the unsystematic relation between money income and full income; the definition of the income unit; and the time period over which income is measured. None has an unambiguous answer, so any definition of poverty in terms of money income is somewhat arbitrary, a point reinforced in Section 3.2.

All three measures—consumption, expenditure, and income—face an additional and major problem. They all look only at *ex post* magnitudes, totally ignoring the issue of choice illustrated by Figure 6.1. I may eat no meat and have low expenditure and income, and so be poor according to all three measures. But if by choice I am a vegetarian ascetic, then my *potential* living standard may exceed the poverty line. For these and other reasons, and notwithstanding a large body of work on measuring individual welfare, Ravallion (1996: 1331) concludes that 'even the best . . . measures found in practice are incomplete on their own'.

WHOSE INCOME? This is the issue of the income unit. There are two core issues: income-sharing within households (Section 1.1), and the treatment of households of different size (Section 3.3). Again, there is no wholly satisfactory solution.

WHAT CONCEPT OF POVERTY? Even if these problems had been solved, major problems remain. In particular, should poverty be regarded as an absolute or a relative concept? With an *absolute* definition a person is poor if her money income is too low to keep her alive and healthy. Early studies (see the Further Reading) attempted to define poverty 'objectively' by reference to basic nutritional requirements. There are serious objections to this approach. People have different nutritional requirements, so that no universally applicable standard is possible; nor is it reasonable to expect people to fill these requirements at minimum cost. Philosophically, the idea of an absolute poverty line stems from times when it was natural to think in subsistence terms; but this can be argued to be out of place, at least in industrial countries, when people live well above subsistence, and where the concept of deprivation is applied to emotional and cultural standards as well as to physical ones.

Under a *relative* definition, with deceptive simplicity, a person is regarded as poor if he feels poor. The definition of poverty will vary by time and place according to prevailing

---

[8] For fuller discussion, see Atkinson (1987*b*; 1989: ch. 1), Sen (1987), Chaudhuri and Ravallion (1994), and Ravallion (1996), and the references therein.

[9] See Townsend (1979); and, for a trenchant critique, Piachaud (1981). See also the Further Reading.

living standards; and whether or not a person feels poor will depend in part on what he sees around him. It is argued, for example, that the collapse of the Berlin Wall was hastened because the citizens of East Berlin could watch West German television and see how high Western living standards were in comparison with their own.

An absolute poverty line will remain fixed at subsistence; with a relative definition it will tend to rise with living standards generally. In the latter case it is argued (Townsend 1979) that a person is poor if he cannot participate in the sorts of activities pursued by the generality of the population (this is known as a participation poverty standard). Thus a person without access to television is culturally deprived, and increasingly in richer countries a child is deprived if she does not have access to a computer. A relative poverty line has to increase to include such items.

A different line of argument for real increases in the poverty line is that over time incomes rise; hence the demand for inferior goods falls, and they tend to disappear from the market. 'The paradox of affluence is that [it] actually creates, as a by-product, a new poverty . . . [M]ore people have cars, so that buses carry fewer passengers at higher fares, and services are cut . . . The more people who have central heating, the harder and dearer it becomes, as the number of coal merchants dwindles, for the others to buy coal' (*Sunday Times*, 19 Sept. 1982). In such cases it is necessary to raise the poverty line so that people can buy the next cheapest substitute (for further discussion, see Sen 1983).

Formally, an absolute definition of poverty is more appropriate the greater the extent to which the utility of rich and poor depends only on their own incomes, and a relative definition is more appropriate the greater are income externalities. Suppose the relevant utility functions are

$$U^R = f(Y^R) \tag{6.11}$$

$$U^P = f(Y^P) \tag{6.12}$$

where U^R and U^P are the utilities of a representative rich and poor person, respectively, and Y^R and Y^P their incomes. This is the case implied by an additive social-welfare function (equation (6.6)), and an absolute definition of poverty might be appropriate. But if the utility functions are

$$U^R = f(Y^R, Y^P) \quad f_1 > 0, f_2 > 0 \tag{6.13}$$

$$U^P = f(Y^R, Y^P) \quad f_1 < 0, f_2 > 0 \tag{6.14}$$

(where f_1 and f_2 are the partial derivatives of utility with respect to Y^R and Y^P, respectively), we have an income externality of the type discussed in Chapter 4. Section 4.1, and both rich and poor might prefer a poverty line which rose over time.

The conclusion is that there is no unambiguous definition of poverty, a topic to which we return in Section 5.

2.2. Poverty and inequality

Absolute poverty and inequality are separate concepts which should not be confused. Absolute poverty refers to a standard of living below some benchmark. The unbroken income distribution in Figure 6.2 shows a substantial number of poor people (i.e. the area *A*), a large number of middle incomes, and few high incomes. Inequality is concerned not with the absolute living standard of the poor, but with the *differences* between income groups; the dotted distribution shows more inequality (but less absolute poverty) than the unbroken one. Various measures of this dispersion are discussed in Section 4.

The difference between poverty and inequality is illustrated more fully in Table 6.1, which shows the average income in two societies of the poor (the lowest two-thirds of incomes), the rich (the top third), and the average income of rich and poor together. In society 1 the poor have an average income of £6,000, which is one-third of the average income of the rich, £18,000. In society 2 (which is identical in all respects except

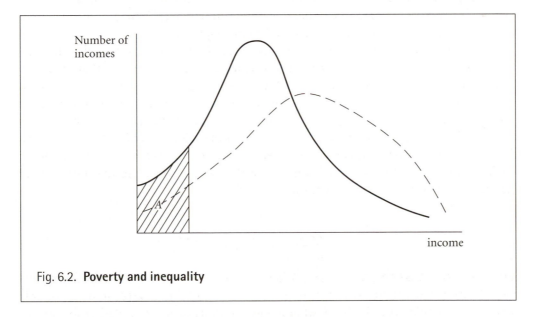

Fig. 6.2. **Poverty and inequality**

Table 6.1. **Poverty and inequality in two different societies**

Average income	Society 1	Society 2
Average income of the poor (²/₃ of population)	£6,000 (¹/₃ income of rich)	£9,000 (¹/₄ income of rich)
Average income of the rich (¹/₃ of population)	£18,000	£36,000
Average income of rich and poor together	£10,000	£18,000

income) the average income of the poor, £9,000, is one-quarter of the average income of the rich, £36,000. In society 2 the poor have a higher standard of living than in society 1 (i.e. there is less absolute poverty), but are further behind both the average income and the standard of living of the rich (i.e. there is more inequality).

It is instructive to ask which society the poor would choose. Suppose a representative poor person has the utility function shown by equation (6.12); his utility depends on his own income, and his rational choice is society 2. In contrast, with equation (6.14), his utility increases with his own income but decreases as that of the representative rich person rises. If the externality (shown by f_1) is sufficiently strong, it will be rational for a poor person to choose society 1, in which the difference between rich and poor is smaller.

The distinction between poverty and inequality is important because it might not be possible to reduce both. A supply-side argument is that poverty can be alleviated by reducing the taxation of the rich, thereby encouraging economic growth and making possible further redistribution from rich to poor (i.e. reducing the top rates of tax might change society 1 into society 2). The relevance of this argument (whose truth is an empirical question) is its implicit assumption that the real enemy is absolute poverty rather than inequality—that is, it assumes an individual utility function of the form of equation (6.12). In consequence, policy design is concerned with poverty relief (objective 4 in Chapter 1, Section 2.2), but not with inequality reduction (objective 7).

Alternatively, policy which aims to 'squeeze the rich until the pips squeak' implicitly assumes that inequality rather than poverty is the main enemy—that is, that the utility of the poor is shown by equation (6.14). But, if the argument of the previous paragraph is true, then any attack on inequality might aggravate absolute poverty through the effect of higher taxation in reducing economic growth and hence the size of the tax base (i.e. attacking inequality might convert society 2 into society 1). The policy conclusion is not that attacks on inequality *will* increase absolute poverty, but that they might, making it important to be clear about the relative weights given to the objectives of poverty relief and inequality reduction.

2.3. Measuring poverty

EMPIRICAL DEFINITIONS OF THE POVERTY LINE. Policy-makers cannot refuse to establish a poverty line just because there are conceptual problems;[10] and it is possible to infer roughly what the state thinks by looking at what it does. First, is poverty regarded as absolute or relative? With an absolute definition, the major benefits would have about the same real value today as in 1948, when the Beveridge arrangements came into effect. In fact, until the mid-1980s, benefits kept pace with changes in pre-tax average earnings.[11] Thus poverty is regarded as a relative concept, and this remains true, notwithstanding a

---

[10] See Atkinson (1995*a*: ch. 3) and Ravallion (1996) for the state of play on methodology in the mid-1990s.

[11] Since the real burden of taxation rose substantially over the post-war period, this implies that the real level of benefits *rose* relative to *post-tax* average earnings.

decline in the relative value of the major benefits since 1986.[12] The European Commission uses an explicit relative poverty line of 50 per cent of national average income (European Commission 1991).

Turning to the other issues posed earlier, the definition of the income unit for benefit purposes is fairly broad. Couples in the UK pay income tax on an individual basis; in contrast, the incomes of individuals living together are usually aggregated for benefit purposes, irrespective of marital status. In comparing families of different sizes, the poverty line for much of the post-war period was about 20 per cent of pre-tax average earnings for a single person, around 30 per cent for a married couple, and 40–5 per cent for a family of four. Thus the implied adult equivalents (see Section 3.3) for a single individual, a couple, and a family of four are 100, 150, and about 200, respectively. Finally, the time period over which income is measured for awarding cash benefits is frequently short. For some benefits it is necessary only to show that one has no current income; for others evidence of the previous five weeks' income is required.

These are the state's answers to the various definitional questions (see Barr 1981 for the earlier period; Martin Evans 1998 for more recent trends). They are valid to the extent that over the years they have acquired the force of social convention; but they should not be regarded as having any particular intellectual merit.

HOW MUCH POVERTY? Since it is not possible to define poverty even for an individual, it is not surprising that there are no unambiguous answers about the extent of poverty overall. Aggregate poverty measures grapple with three dimensions of the problem: *how many* people are poor (the headcount measure); by *how much* they fall below the poverty line (the poverty-gap measure); and *how long* are they poor—that is, is poverty transient or persistent?

The poverty headcount. Given a poverty line of £X per week, how many people are poor? Even this simple question has no simple answer. Using the number of recipients of social assistance gives an underestimate, since not everyone who is eligible for benefit receives it.[13] Thus the number of poor people in the UK is larger than the number receiving income support (5.7 million[14] in 1995/6), but without additional information we do not know how much greater. As a result, estimates have to be constructed from sample surveys

The headcount, even were an accurate figure to be obtained, has major failings (Sen 1976). It does not show how far people fall below the poverty line, and thus gives only a partial picture. Worse, a transfer of £100 from someone well below the poverty line to someone only £50 below *reduces* poverty as measured by the headcount.

The poverty gap attempts to remedy these deficiencies. It considers the total shortfall from the poverty line, divided by (*a*) the poverty line or (*b*) total income. Index (*a*) gives

---

[12] The retirement pension for a single person rose in real terms from £24.46 in 1948 to £58.85 in 1995 (April 1995 prices); it hovered on either side of 20% of average earnings from 1948 till 1986, thereafter declining to 17.5% in 1995 (UK DSS 1995a: table 5.1).

[13] The issue of these so-called 'take-up rates' is discussed in Chapter 10, Section 3.

[14] This figure refers to the number of *recipients*. When account is taken of their dependants, the total number supported wholly or in part by income support is about 70% higher.

Concepts

a measure of the average depth of poverty, (*b*) the relative cost of relieving it. Both approaches have been criticized (see Atkinson 1996), not least because a transfer from a poor person to a poorer person does not increase measured poverty.

To address this problem, Foster (1984) proposes a poverty gap which gives greater weight to larger shortfalls. He suggests a measure

$$P_A = (1 - Y/P)^A \tag{6.15}$$

where Y = family income and P = the poverty line. The value $A = 0$ gives the headcount; $A = 1$ gives an unweighted poverty gap; $A = 2$ gives a higher weight to greater shortfalls.

The duration of poverty. If most people dip into poverty only briefly, the problem is smaller than if poverty is long term. Yet current household circumstances are uninformative about longer term prospects. A static analysis (i.e. a snapshot at a single instant) gives no information about the (usually very different) characteristics of the persistently poor and the transient poor, and hence gives no guide to the (usually very different) policy measures. There is now a growing literature (Chaudhuri and Ravallion 1994; Jarvis and Jenkins 1997; Ravallion *et al.* 1995) on poverty dynamics, which seeks to disentangle persistent from transient poverty.

EMPIRICAL EVIDENCE. The fact that a definitive measure of poverty is not possible does not mean that empirical work is not useful, merely that care is needed in interpreting results.

Country studies. After 1980, poverty headcounts rose sharply in the UK. Using the European Commission poverty line of 50 per cent of average income, poverty increased from 4.4 million people in 1979 to 10.4 million ten years later, the latter figure embracing 19 per cent of the population and 22 per cent of children (Atkinson 1995*a*: 292). Hills (1997: 37; see also Martin Evans 1998: fig. 7.14) concludes that the poorest decile lost not only in relative terms but absolutely. Much of this poverty is persistent: Atkinson *et al.* (1983) found that nearly half of their sample of poor people came from poor parents (see also Atkinson, 1989: chs. 4, 5). Over the twenty years from the mid-1970s, the composition of the poor changed: the number of pensioners in the bottom quintile of income recipients declined, while families with children and households with economically inactive people increased (Martin Evans 1998).

Poverty rose also in the USA. The facts are simple (Gottschalk 1997; see also the Further Reading): after 1973, growth slowed while inequality increased. Because of these trends, combined with a parsimonious benefit structure, the poverty rate increased from a low of 11.1 per cent of the population in 1973 to 14.5 per cent in the mid-1990s. As in the UK, poverty fell among the elderly and rose for children. In both countries, poverty increased partly because of the response by government to economic and demographic forces (see Chapter 1, Section 3.1). We return to the topic in Chapter 10, Section 3.4.

Comparative studies. Many of the problems of international comparison have been addressed over the 1980s by the availability of microdata (i.e. data on individuals) from the Luxembourg Income Study (LIS), which covers various countries of the OECD,

Central and Eastern Europe, and the former Soviet Union. Microdata have the two overriding advantages of comparability and completeness: it is possible to choose income units, income definitions, and equivalence scales, facilitating systematic comparison; and the data include income from all sources, including private pensions and savings. The disadvantage is that such data are available only with a lag.

Smeeding (1997: table 1; see also Danziger and Jäntti, forthcoming) concluded that the post-transfer poverty headcount in the early 1990s was highest in the USA, and was also high in Australia and the UK. Income poverty was considerably lower in the mainland Western European countries. Smeeding (1997: table 4) also comments on the feminization of poverty, which in virtually all the OECD countries disproportionately affected older single women and single-parent families (see also Oppenheim and Harker 1996: ch. 5).

Modelling poverty. The approaches discussed so far are broadly descriptive. Targeting (Chapter 10, Section 3.1), however, can be helped by more detailed knowledge of the characteristics of the poor—for example, are they disproportionately old, or living in certain areas. One way of constructing the necessary poverty profiles is to run a regression of the poverty measure (e.g. whether the person is in receipt of social assistance) against a variety of household characteristics. This approach can be useful in identifying characteristics on which to condition benefits and also to simulate possible changes in anti-poverty policy. For fuller discussion, see Ravallion (1996). Discussion of empirical evidence is resumed in Chapter 10, Section 3.4.

3. Inequality 1: Individuals and families

This section discusses equality (as with poverty, no wholly satisfactory definition is possible), and then turns to inequality between individuals (Section 3.2) and families (Section 3.3).

3.1. Defining equality and inequality

DIFFERENT DEFINITIONS OF EQUALITY. The first question is: equality of what? In principle the answer is easy—individuals are equal if they face identical opportunity sets—that is, face the same full income in Figure 6.1. But full income cannot be measured, so matters in practice are more complex. Le Grand (1982: 14–15; 1991a: ch. 5) distinguishes five possible definitions. The simplest, *equality of final income*, implies that individuals are equal if they have the same level of money income plus income in kind. But complications arise in measuring income in kind. Should there be *equality of public expenditure* (i.e. spending on, say, health care is the same for everybody); or *equality of use* (e.g. everyone is allocated the same quantity of health care); or *equality of cost* (e.g. everyone faces the same cost of using the National Health Service, which implies that people visiting their

Concepts

doctor should be compensated for any lost earnings); or *equality of outcome* (e.g. health care is allocated so that, as far as possible, everyone enjoys equally good health)? All have valid claims as definitions of equality; all are different.

Similar problems arise when we try to define 'equality of opportunity'. An individual's income according to Atkinson and Stiglitz (1980: 267) depends on three sets of factors: his *endowments* (e.g. of human capital or inherited wealth); his *tastes* with respect to work and leisure, consumption and saving, risk, etc.; and his *luck*, since the outcome of choices is often stochastic. Thus two individuals with identical tastes and opportunity sets may experience very different outcomes—'some people work for a firm that goes bankrupt; some people invest early in Rank Xerox' (ibid.).

EQUALITY OF OPPORTUNITY is best approached in several steps.

First step: equality of opportunity exists if

$$Y_F = K \text{ for all } i \quad i = 1, 2, \ldots, N \tag{6.16}$$

where Y_F is full income as defined in equation (6.1), and includes a time dimension. Equation (6.16) states that full income should be the same for all N individuals in society. The obvious problem is that no account is taken of the stochastic element in individual income. Equality of opportunity implies that people should have an equal *chance*—that is, it is an expected value not an absolute value which should be equal. Hence:

Second step: equal opportunity can be said to exist if

$$E(Y_F) = K \text{ for all } i. \tag{6.17}$$

Here equality of opportunity requires only that expected income should be the same for all individuals. This is an adequate definition of equality of opportunity in terms of *full* income, which captures all aspects of the individual opportunity set. In practice, however, measurement problems force us to use money income, which varies not only with the individual opportunity set, but also with individual choices (see Figure 6.1); and differences in income resulting from different choices need not imply inequality. Hence, if Y is money income:

Third step: equal opportunity exists if

$$E(Y|C_i) = K_i \text{ for all } D_i. \tag{6.18}$$

Equation (6.18) requires explanation. As discussed in Section 3.2, some characteristics may affect money income without causing inequality; these include age, and any differences in individual choice which are the result of differences in tastes, and so are referred to as C (choice) characteristics. But if money income varies systematically with other characteristics (social class, race, sex, parental money income), we would regard society as unequal. These are the D (discrimination) characteristics. Equation (6.18) states that equality of opportunity exists if the expected value of money income is the same for all individuals with given C characteristics, but must be invariant to their D characteristics.

At first glance equation (6.18) seems to offer a workable definition of equality of opportunity. But it contains two strategic difficulties. First, using money income as an indicator of welfare raises problems even if we control for age and tastes. Equality of opportunity must apply both to cash income and to income in kind; yet, as discussed earlier, equality of access when discussing distribution in kind can be ambiguous. In addition (Section 1.1), any measure of welfare based on material well-being is incomplete; some non-material aspects can be analysed in economic terms as violations of the perfect-information and equal-power assumptions (Chapter 4, Section 3.2), but they stand in their own right as independent sources of inequality.

Secondly, even if full income were measurable, there remains the problem of distinguishing a C from a D characteristic. There is broad agreement that social class, race, and sex are D characteristics; and it might be argued that laziness and a long-time horizon are C characteristics. But what about 'natural ability'? If ability is entirely exogenous (i.e. 'innate'), differences in ability can be regarded as the luck of the draw, giving rise to the stochastic element of Y. Society might take no action where people do well (e.g. the state does not confiscate the high incomes of gifted musicians or athletes), but may compensate people who do badly (e.g. someone born with a long-term health problem). A completely different case arises if ability is at least partly endogenous—for example, induced by differences in the quality of education. Ability is then in part a D characteristic, and positive discrimination might be justified.

Thus people can be unequal for two very different reasons. If incomes differ because of discrimination, 'society' is unfair, and appropriate action might involve changing the structure of society (see the quote by Tawney at the head of the chapter). In contrast, inequality can arise because of random differences in luck (i.e. 'life' can be unfair), captured by the stochastic element in equation (6.18). Bad luck may require remedial action, but does not imply that society is unfair.

The last word should go to Okun (1975: 76, reprinted in Atkinson, 1980), who summarizes the problem with customary eloquence.

The concept of equality of opportunity is far more elusive than that of equality of income . . . [It] is rooted in the notion of a fair race where people are even at the starting line. But . . . it is hard to find the starting line. Differences in natural abilities are generally accepted as relevant characteristics that are being tested in the race rather than as unfair headstarts and handicaps. At the other extreme, success that depends on whom you know rather than what you know is a clear case of inequality of opportunity. And it seems particularly unfair when the real issue is whom your father knows.

The inheritance of natural abilities is on one side of the line of unequal opportunity, and the advantages of a family position are clearly on the other. But much of the territory is unsettled.

3.2. Measuring inequality between individuals

Inequality between individuals is best approached by considering A and B, with money incomes of £20,000 and £10,000, respectively, and asking why they might in fact be *equal.* There are three reasons why differences in money income might have no bearing on an individual's opportunity set, and so be irrelevant to issues of equality.

DIFFERENT CHOICES can cause differences in money incomes in two ways. A and B have *different tastes about money income* (i.e. different indifference maps in Figure 6.1) if they have different leisure preferences. Suppose A likes champagne and foreign travel, and B likes walking across the hills with his dog. A (with money-intensive consumption preferences) might choose to work longer hours; and B might work fewer hours (i.e. enjoy more leisure) and/or choose work with more job satisfaction (i.e. higher non-money income). Both A and B are maximizing their utility, and there is no case for regarding them as unequal simply because one has higher money income. Secondly, there can be *differences in acquired skills* (hence different budget constraints in Figure 6.1): suppose A has chosen to forgo income early in life in order to acquire skills, while B has not. A's higher income is a return to her investment in human capital. Again there is no reason to suppose that there is any inequality provided (and the proviso is crucial) that A and B had the *same opportunity*, including access to information, to acquire skills (for further discussion, see Le Grand 1984).

AGE. Suppose A earns twice as much as B because she is 40 years old and highly skilled, whereas B is 20 years old and an apprentice. Suppose, further, that when B is 40 he will earn as much as A does now. In this case, the difference in money income is simply a life-cycle effect, and no long-term issue of inequality arises.[15]

THE TIME DIMENSION. If A and B have fluctuating incomes, A might earn £20,000 and B £10,000 this year, with the positions reversed next year. Taking the two years together, there is no inequality. More generally, inequality is greater if a rich person systematically has rich descendants and a poor person poor ones, an issue directly related to the earlier distinction between persistent and transient poverty.

It is possible also to ask the question in reverse. Suppose A and B each has money income of £15,000. That does not necessarily mean that they are equal. They might face different price levels; more importantly, A might have a larger family than B and so, it might be argued, has a lower standard of living. This raises issues of how to compare families of different sizes.

The conclusion is that money income is a misleading indicator of inequality. *This does not imply that there is no inequality in society—just that money income is bad at measuring it.*

---

[15] The need to control for age is particularly important in analysing the distribution of wealth. Consider a society where everyone has identical earnings, of which 10% are saved to finance retirement. The resulting wealth distribution is highly unequal: young people have no wealth (because they have not yet started to save); people aged 98 have very little wealth (because they have spent all their savings); and people aged 64 have substantial wealth (because they have been saving all their working lives and have yet to start dissaving).

3.3. Measuring inequality between families

If it is not possible to compare the living standards of two individuals, we are likely to make even less headway with families of different sizes. Families with the same standard of living have 'equivalent' incomes, from which can be derived equivalence scales. Suppose a couple with an income of £15,000 have a child; what increase in money income is necessary to leave them as well off as before? The issue is important. Buhmann *et al.* (1988) found that different equivalence scales had a significant impact on measured inequality.

The logic of the problem is illustrated by the following arguments.

- The *consumption argument* states that, if a couple have a child, per capita income in the household falls, and the couple need a higher money income to maintain their standard of living. If there are no economies of scale in household formation, a 3-person family has an adult equivalent of 3; if there are economies of scale (e.g. it costs no more to heat a house containing three people than two), it will be (say) 2. In either case, larger families require a higher income. The question is—how much higher?

- The *utility argument*, along revealed preference lines, asserts that a couple will have a child by choice only if it raises their utility. In the extreme, where two people with perfect information have a child by choice, their utility is increased, and they can maintain a given standard of living with *less* money income. More generally, the utility associated with a child reduces the additional income necessary to maintain a given living standard. This approach might be useful for better-off families,[16] but the consumption argument might be more appropriate for a low-income family.

If one person needs one unit of income, a two-person family will need (say) 1.75 units to achieve the same standard of living, and a three-person family (say) 2.25 units. More recent studies[17] encapsulate the equivalence scale in a single parameter. Economic well-being, or 'adjusted' income, W, is related to gross disposable family income, D, and family size, S, where:

$$W = D/S^E. \tag{6.19}$$

The equivalence elasticity, E, varies between 0 and 1. A value of zero implies no adjustment for family size (closer to the utility argument above), a value of one implies per capita income (a family of three people will need three times the income to maintain a given standard of living).

Atkinson, Rainwater, and Smeeding (1995) distinguish four approaches to setting a value on E, illustrating—yet again—that there is no unambiguously 'correct' answer.

- *Statistical scales* are developed to count people at or below a given standard of living—for example, the scales used by the European Commission or the US Bureau

---

[16] Some couples are prepared to pay large amounts to adoption agencies or for medical treatment to cure infertility.
[17] See Buhmann *et al.* (1988), Coulter *et al.* (1992), Atkinson (1995a: chs. 2, 4), and Atkinson *et al.* (1995: ch. 2).

of Labor Statistics to count the low-income population. Atkinson, Rainwater, and Smeeding (1995) report a median value for such scales of $E = 0.72$—i.e. close to per capita.

- *Programme scales* are used for defining social assistance and similar benefits for families of different sizes. Here the median value of E is 0.59, implying some economies of scale in household formation.

- *Consumption scales* are based on observed spending patterns. For example, if food spending rises proportionately with family size but housing expenditure does not, then an increase in family size in effect raises the price of an improved diet relative to improved housing; *ceteris paribus* there will, therefore, be substitution towards housing. An implication is that families need not be fully compensated for increases in food costs. The median value of E in this case is 0.57, very close to that of the programme scales.

- *Subjective scales* attempt to measure the utility associated with different income levels—i.e. the utility approach discussed above. Predictably, the median value of E, 0.25, is lower than for scales which do not attempt to capture the utility associated with a child.

4. Inequality 2: Aggregate measures

4.1. The descriptive approach

This section discusses the measurement of inequality in society as a whole,[18] starting with simple representations of the income distribution, and proceeding to more complex measures and a brief review of empirical studies. The aim is to construct a scalar representation of income differences within a given population. Ideally it would take on values between zero (if everyone had the same income) and one (if one person had all the income), making it possible to answer questions like: how much inequality is there in the UK today; how much more than ten years ago; is it less than in the USA? Any such overall measure of inequality rests on two ingredients:

- What is the unit defined to be equal or unequal—for example, the individual, family, or household? Here we talk only of 'individuals' and abstract from issues of household size and definition.

- Inequality of what—for example, income, wealth, power? The literature generally looks at 'income', which usually means money income.

An inequality measure combines knowledge of the 'incomes' of 'individuals', though we shall see that its usefulness is qualified both by conceptual difficulties and measurement problems.

---

[18] See Cowell (1995: chs. 1, 2) or, for broader discussion, Sen (1992).

6. Problems of definition and measurement

THE FREQUENCY DISTRIBUTION AND ASSOCIATED MEASURES. The simplest starting point is the *frequency distribution*, which shows the number of income recipients at each level of income. It can be represented as a continuous function, as in Figure 6.2, or as a histogram. The frequency distribution has the advantage of being simple and easy to interpret, especially in the middle-income ranges. But it is weak at the tails; the left-hand tail should include negative incomes (e.g. business losses), and the right-hand tail has been severely truncated.

A simple yet dramatic way of representing the income distribution is *Pen's parade*,[19] in which each person (i.e. income recipient) marches past the onlooker. The parade takes an hour and each person's height corresponds to his pre-tax income (a person with average income having average height). This representation is vivid; it shows up the tails well; and we can see not only the distribution, but also who is where in it. It does not, however, lend itself readily to quantification.

There are several measures of inequality based on the frequency distribution, of which this section discusses only the most important. A natural way of trying to capture aggregate inequality is by a summary measure of dispersion like the *variance*

$$V = \frac{1}{n} \sum_{i=1}^{n} (y_i - \mu)^2 \tag{6.20}$$

where y_i is the money income of the ith individual, μ is average income, and there are n income recipients. The advantage of the variance is twofold: it considers the whole distribution, and measured inequality is reduced by any redistribution which brings an individual's income closer to the mean. Its main disadvantage is its sensitivity to the absolute level of income; if all incomes double (or are expressed in dollars at an exchange rate of $2 = £1), inequality does not change but V quadruples.

This problem is avoided by the *coefficient of variation* defined as

$$C = \frac{V^{0.5}}{\mu}, \tag{6.21}$$

which is the variance normalized on average income. The advantage of C is its independence of scale. But it has a number of difficulties, not least that it is neutral to the income level at which transfers take place—that is, transferring £100 from an individual with an income of £1,000 to one with an income of £500 has the same effect on C as a £100 transfer from a person with an income of £1 million to one with £999,500.

If we want to give greater weight to transfers to lower incomes, one procedure is to take some transformation such as the logarithm which staggers income levels. The *variance*

---

[19] See Pen (1971), reprinted in Atkinson (1980: 47–55), for an entertaining and non-technical description of the income distribution.

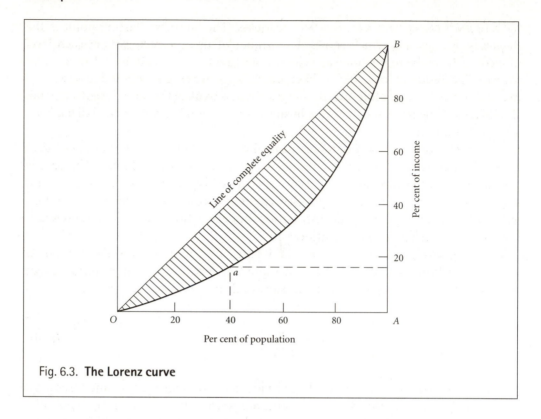

Fig. 6.3. **The Lorenz curve**

of the logarithm of income has the added advantage of scale independence.[20] For this reason the variance of the logarithm of income

$$H = \frac{1}{n} \sum_{i=1}^{n} (\log y_i - \log \mu)^2 = \frac{1}{n} \sum_{i=1}^{n} \log \left(\frac{y^i}{\mu} \right)^2 \qquad (6.22)$$

has been used as an inequality measure. H has the advantages that it is invariant to the absolute level of income, is sensitive to income transfers at all income levels, but gives greater weight to transfers to lower incomes. There are also disadvantages. The measure (in common with V and C) considers only differences of income from the mean; and it squares those differences. Both procedures are somewhat arbitrary. In addition, H may not be concave at higher income levels—that is, H can rise in the face of some transfers from rich to poor.[21]

THE LORENZ CURVE was devised explicitly as a representation of inequality. Though the approach is old (Lorenz 1905), it is a powerful device, intimately connected with an important theorem by Atkinson discussed in Section 4.2. In Figure 6.3 the horizontal axis shows the percentage of individuals or households, the vertical axis the percentage of total

[20] If income, say, doubles, this simply adds a constant to all logarithms of income, which cancel when calculating deviations from the mean.

[21] Concavity and other properties of social-welfare functions are discussed in Section 1.2.

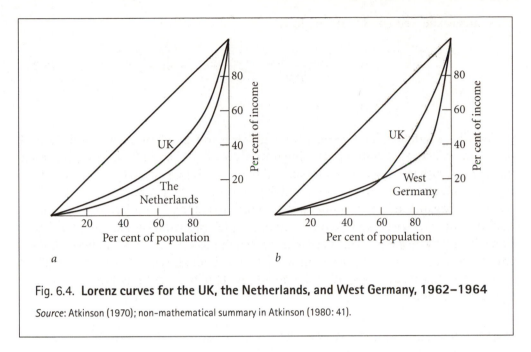

Fig. 6.4. **Lorenz curves for the UK, the Netherlands, and West Germany, 1962–1964**

Source: Atkinson (1970); non-mathematical summary in Atkinson (1980: 41).

income. The Lorenz curve is shown by the line *OaB*. Each point shows the share of total income received by the *lowest x* per cent of individuals; thus point *a* shows that the bottom 40 per cent of individuals receive 17 per cent of income.

The Lorenz curve will coincide with the diagonal *OB* if income is distributed completely equally (because only then will the lowest 50 per cent of individuals receive 50 per cent of total income, and so on); and the greater the degree of inequality, the further the curve will lie from the diagonal. If the Lorenz curve for the UK lies entirely inside that for the Netherlands (as in the historical example in Figure 6.4*a*), we can say that income inequality is lower in the UK; but where the curves cross (as in the historical comparison between the UK and West Germany in Figure 6.4*b*), an ambiguity arises. Lorenz curves thus give only a partial ordering of outcomes.[22]

The Gini coefficient is based on the Lorenz curve; diagrammatically it is the ratio of the shaded area in Figure 6.3 to the triangle *OaB*. If incomes are distributed completely equally, it will be zero; and, if one person has all the income, it will be unity. Formally, the Gini coefficient is defined as half of the arithmetic average of the absolute differences between *all* pairs of incomes, the total then being normalized on mean income:

$$G = \frac{1}{2n^2\mu} \sum_{i=1}^{n} \sum_{j=1}^{n} \left| y^i - y^j \right|.$$ (6.23)

[22] Shorrocks (1983) attempts at least partly to resolve the ambiguity. He constructs a 'generalized Lorenz curve' by scaling up the conventional Lorenz curve by the mean of the income distribution. While the measure is often successful at resolving ambiguity, it does so only because of strong assumptions about the weight given to absolute living standards. Weakening those assumptions greatly reduces the ambiguity-resolving power of the construct.

Concepts

This can also be written (Sen 1973: 31) as

$$G = 1 + \frac{1}{n} - \frac{2}{n^2 \mu} (y^1 + 2y^2 + \ldots + ny^n) \qquad (6.24)$$

for $y^1 \geq y^2 \geq \ldots \geq y^n$.

The Gini coefficient has several advantages. It is independent of the absolute level of income, avoids the arbitrary squaring procedure of V, C, and H, and compares each income not with the mean but with every other income, as equation (6.23) makes clear. Its disadvantages are twofold. It gives ambiguous results when Lorenz curves cross. The second disadvantage is more subtle, and we return to it later. Formulation (6.24) shows that the Gini coefficient is a weighted sum of people's incomes, with the weights determined solely by the person's *rank order* in the distribution. Thus y^1 (the highest income) enters the term in parentheses with a relative weight of 1, y^2 (the second highest income) with a relative weight of 2, and so on. This is an entirely arbitrary social-welfare function.

GENERAL CRITIQUE OF THE DESCRIPTIVE MEASURES. To set the scene for subsequent discussion, it is helpful to bring out four sets of criticisms which apply to all the descriptive measures.[23]

1. They lack generality. V, C, and H all incorporate the arbitrary procedures of squaring differences from the mean.

2. They all incorporate an *implicit* and *arbitrary* social-welfare function with built-in welfare weights. With V and C a given transfer from a relatively higher to a relatively lower income always has the same effect; the implied social-welfare function values all reductions in inequality equally, even if redistribution is from a millionaire to a semi-millionaire. For H the implied social-welfare function embodies weights derived from the logarithm function, which again might not be one's chosen weights. The social-welfare function underlying the Gini coefficient, as equation (6.24) shows, embraces weights based on rank order.

3. The descriptive measures give only a partial ordering of outcomes. This is obviously true of intersecting Lorenz curves and hence of the Gini coefficient. The same problem arises with the other measures.

4. In addition to these conceptual difficulties, all the measurement problems discussed earlier in the context of poverty apply equally to measures of inequality.

---

[23] For trenchant criticism of virtually all summary measures, see Wiles (1974: esp. pp. 7–12). He advocates the ratio of the average income of someone in the top 5% of incomes to the corresponding average for the lowest 5% as the least bad summary statistic. As discussed in Section 4.3, Smeeding (1997) uses this approach to measure 'social distance.'

4.2. Inequality measures based on a social-welfare function

Normative measures start explicitly from a social-welfare function. This section discusses an important theorem by Atkinson, its implications, and the Atkinson inequality measure.[24]

THE ATKINSON THEOREM on Lorenz ranking is remarkable for its generality. Assume:

1. States A and B have income distributions given by $(y^{1A}, y^{2A}, \ldots, y^{nA})$ and $(y^{1B}, y^{2B}, \ldots, y^{nB})$, respectively.
2. Total income is the same in states A and B.
3. W is a social-welfare function which is non-decreasing, symmetric, additive, and concave (see Section 1.2).

Then: the Lorenz curve for B lies wholly inside the Lorenz curve for A *if and only if* $W_B > W_A$ for *every* social-welfare function with the four properties listed in assumption 3. To amplify, the theorem tells us:

1. If the Lorenz curve for B lies wholly inside that for A, then: (*a*) welfare in state B is higher than in state A; we can say this *without knowing what the social-welfare function is*; (*b*) the income distribution is unambiguously more equal in state B; (*c*) the Gini coefficient compares distributions unambiguously; and (*d*) all the conventional summary measures (e.g. V, C, and H) give the same result.
2. Conversely, if social welfare is higher in state B, then we know that Lorenz curve B must lie strictly inside Lorenz curve A.
3. As a corollary, if Lorenz curves cross: (*a*) we cannot say whether inequality is greater in state A or B; (*b*) the Gini coefficient gives an ambiguous comparison; and (*c*) different inequality measures give different results.

These conclusions link the (descriptive) Lorenz curve to the explicitly normative world of the social-welfare function. But the result is still not sufficient, both because not all Lorenz curves are non-intersecting, and because we still want a *numerical* measure of inequality. Atkinson (1970) approached the issue by considering the Lorenz curves in Figure 6.4. The theorem enables us to say unambiguously that the distribution of income was less unequal in the UK than in the Netherlands. Figure 6.4*b* shows that the share of lower incomes was higher in West Germany than in the UK, but at higher incomes there was less inequality in the UK. By inspection, the area between the Lorenz curve and the diagonal was greater for West Germany than the UK, so that the Gini coefficient shows

---

[24] See Cowell (1995: ch. 3), which also discusses other approaches, by Dalton (1920) and Theil (1967). For a simple introduction, see Atkinson (1983: 54–9). See also the Further Reading.

Concepts

that the UK is *less* unequal than West Germany. But a measure which gives greater weight to lower incomes would show that the UK is *more* unequal.

Atkinson draws two major conclusions:

1. Where Lorenz curves cross it is necessary to compare one income group with another. *Thus the degree of inequality cannot in general be compared without introducing values about the distribution* in the form of welfare weights for different income levels. This should be done *explicitly* via a social-welfare function, in contrast with descriptive measures, which all embody implicit but unstated weights.

2. Only where Lorenz curves do not intersect is it possible (subject to assumption 3 of the theorem) to avoid the necessity of explicit welfare weights; in this case all the descriptive measures will agree.

THE ATKINSON INEQUALITY MEASURE considers distributional values explicitly. It is based on a social-welfare function with the five properties discussed in Section 1.2—that is, non-decreasing, symmetric, additive, concave, and with constant relative inequality aversion, ε, as in equation (6.10), as an explicit representation of distributional values. The Atkinson measure is given by

$$A = 1 - \left[\sum_{i=1}^{N} \left(\frac{y^i}{\mu} \right)^{1-\varepsilon} f(y^i) \right]^{1/(1-\varepsilon)} \qquad \varepsilon \neq 1 \qquad (6.25)$$

where y^i is the income of individuals in the ith income range (N ranges altogether), $f(y^i)$ is the proportion of the population with incomes in the ith range, and μ is mean income. A will be zero *either* if $y^i = \mu$ for all i (i.e. if income is equally distributed), *or* if $\varepsilon = 0$ (i.e. if policy is concerned only with the absolute level of income, not its distribution). The greater the deviation of y^i from μ and/or the higher the value of ε the greater the value of A.

There is a natural connection between ε and the theories of society discussed in Chapter 3. If $\varepsilon = 0$, society is indifferent to inequality (the Libertarian position), and A is zero. If $\varepsilon = \infty$, society is concerned only with the position of the lowest individual or income group, as advocated by Rawls. Socialists, too, would choose a high value. Utilitarians set no *a priori* limits, but choose the value which maximizes total welfare. In general the place of ε between the two extremes determines the importance of redistribution from richer to poorer: as equation (6.25) shows, the deviation of y^i from μ is weighted by the exponent $(1 - \varepsilon)$, rather than the arbitrary squaring formula of $V, C,$ and H.

The meaning of ε is shown by Atkinson's 'mental experiment', subsequently elaborated as Okun's 'leaky bucket'. Consider taking £100 from a rich man and giving a proportion £x to a poor man, the rest leaking away in efficiency losses (disincentives, administration). How far can x fall (i.e. how leaky can the bucket be) before we no longer regard the redistribution as desirable? The answer determines ε.[25] The higher is ε, the lower x

---

[25] ε is determined from the formula $1/x = 2\varepsilon$; see Atkinson (1983: 58).

Table 6.2. **Values of the Atkinson inequality measure for the UK, the Netherlands, and West Germany**

Value of ε	UK (1964)	The Netherlands (1962)	West Germany (1964)
0.5	0.12	0.15	0.17
1.0	0.24	0.29	0.29
1.5	0.34	0.42	0.38
2.0	0.43	0.52	0.45
3.0	0.55	0.66	0.54

Note: For explanation, see pp. 153–4.

Source: Atkinson (1970); non-mathematical summary, in Atkinson (1980: 42).

can be (i.e. the more egalitarian the view, the more 'leakiness' is tolerable): if $\varepsilon = 1$ it is fair to take £100 from a rich person and give £50 to a poor person; if $\varepsilon = 2$ it is sufficient if the poor man receives £25.

The Atkinson measure can be interpreted both as an inequality measure *and* as an index of the potential welfare gains from redistribution. Consider the proportion of present total income necessary to achieve the same level of welfare if it were equally distributed. If $A = 0.3$, we can say that, if income were equally distributed, we should need only $(100 − 30)\% = 70\%$ of present national income to achieve the same level of social welfare. Alternatively, the gain from redistributing to equality is equivalent to raising national income by 30 per cent. The welfare gain is higher (*a*) the greater the value of ε, and (*b*) the more unequal the pre-existing distribution.

Table 6.2 (taken from Atkinson 1970) shows the value of A for the UK, the Netherlands, and West Germany. Measured inequality is greater the higher is ε; consequently the welfare gains from redistribution to complete equality in the UK rise from 12 per cent of national income when $\varepsilon = 0.5$ to 43 per cent when $\varepsilon = 2$. The table also shows that inequality in the Netherlands is unambiguously greater than in the UK for all values of ε, as shown by the non-intersecting Lorenz curves in Figure 6.4*a*. West Germany is more unequal than the UK for $\varepsilon < 3$; but when inequality aversion is high, West Germany is less unequal because of its greater equality at lower incomes.

The Atkinson measure thus has powerful advantages. Conventional measures like the Gini coefficient obscure the fact that a complete ranking of states is possible only where the form of the social-welfare function is specified, and the social-welfare functions implicit in conventional measures are often arbitrary, if not unacceptable. The Atkinson measure avoids both difficulties—a complete ranking of states is possible, though precise knowledge of the social-welfare function is unnecessary.

The main criticism of the measure is not operational but philosophical—namely, its basis on an additive, individualistic social-welfare function—that is, on the assumption that social welfare is a (more or less) simple sum of individual utilities. This is restrictive: it rules out the sort of welfare interdependence discussed in Chapter 4, Section 4.1; and it ignores non-material sources of well-being.

4.3. Inequality: Some empirical results

PROBLEMS WITH EMPIRICAL WORK on the distribution of income are ubiquitous.

1. Virtually all studies are based on the current money income of households or tax units. This procedure raises serious difficulties for all inequality measures:
   - It generally omits a significant fraction of non-money income (Section 1.1) and is therefore inherently a poor measure of individual opportunity sets. Additionally, cross-country comparisons may omit certain dimensions of inequality, e.g. differences in political freedom.
   - It fails to exclude differences in money income which have no bearing on inequality, e.g. life-cycle factors and individual choice (Section 3.2).
   - Adjustments for differences in the size and composition of different households, if any, face the problems described in Section 3.3.

2. Summary measures of inequality raise the following conceptual problems:
   - Conventional measures are subject to the criticisms set out at the end of Section 4.1.
   - The Atkinson measure is based on the assumption of additivity.
   - Trends over time need to be interpreted in the light of structural change. For example, an increase in the size of a poor group—e.g. students or old people—will appear to increase inequality even though the position of each student or pensioner is unchanged.

3. Data problems:
   - Information on income by type or level of income, or type of recipient, might be scant.
   - The definition of income might change over time, or be incompatible with those of other countries.
   - Estimation is generally based on income classes, and so neglects dispersion within each class; the use of more disaggregated data generally increases measured inequality.

EMPIRICAL EVIDENCE. The absence of any definitive measure of inequality does not mean (nor should it) that empirical work is useless, merely that it should be interpreted with all the earlier caveats in mind.

Country studies. The downward trend in inequality over the twentieth century was reversed in the years after 1980. Indeed, the UK and USA stand out for the sharpness of the increase in inequality over the 1980s. In the UK 'the Gini coefficient . . . rose by 10 percentage points . . . between 1977 and 1990. The latest years . . . begin to suggest that this rise halted in the early 1990s, but it is too early to judge whether a new turning point has been reached . . .' (Hills 1996a: 3). The increase, which is far from completely understood, has multiple causes, including increased inequality in wages; the changing role of women's earnings in family income; increasing self-employment (whose outcomes are more diverse than for employment income); changes in the benefit regime; changes in the distribution of wealth; and differential costs of living. These are all discussed in the various contribution to Hills (1996*b*); see also the Further Reading. Part of the story is increasing returns to skills; another is the extent to which households are increasingly polarized into 'work-rich' (two or more workers) and 'work-poor' (no full-time workers).

In the USA, as in the UK, inequality increased sharply. In 1973 an American at the ninety-fifth percentile received slightly less than twelve times as much as an American at the fifth percentile. By 1993 the equivalent figure was over twenty-five (Burtless 1996*a*: 272; see also the Further Reading). There is controversy about causes. Part of the story was demographic trends, in particular the increase in the number of single-parent families. Labour-market trends reinforced the effect: Danziger and Gottschalk (1995) (see also Gottschalk 1997) argue that the greater part of the increase in inequality among people of working age is due to increased earnings inequality of family heads. Fischer *et al.* (1996), contradicting earlier work by Murray, argue that increased inequality in the USA is largely the result of badly designed and parsimonious public policy.

Comparative studies. Inequality across countries has been estimated using the data from the Luxembourg Income Study discussed in Section 2.3 (see Atkinson *et al.* 1995: table 4.8, and the Further Reading). One result which stands out is that, of the countries studied, in the mid-1980s only the UK and USA had a Gini coefficient over 30 per cent.[26] Atkinson (1995*a*: 63) suggests two conclusions:

First, certain groupings may be made. The Scandinavian countries, Benelux and West Germany have apparently distinctly less inequality in disposable income; Southern Europe and Ireland have distinctly higher inequality, with France and, to some extent, the UK and Italy, occupying an intermediate position . . . Secondly . . . continuing progression towards *reduced* inequality was in the 1980s the exception rather than the rule.

Smeeding investigates inequality in terms of 'social distance', which he defines as the ratio of the incomes of the rich (people at the ninetieth percentile) to those of the poor (those at the tenth percentile). He reports (1997: fig. 1) that, in the early 1990s, this ratio was highest in the USA (5.78), UK (4.67), and Australia (4.3) and lowest in the Nordic countries (the Swedish ratio was 2.78). France (3.48) and Germany (3.21) straddled the average of 3.42.

The former Communist countries. Problems here are even more complex (see Atkinson and Micklewright 1992). Prior to reform, prices were often not market prices (e.g. subsidized food) and much income was received in kind (e.g. free holidays). Reform has increased inequality (World Bank 1996: ch. 4; see also Milanovic 1998). Part of the increase—reflecting the introduction of market-determined wages and similar growth-promoting changes—was both necessary and desirable. Thus, by the mid-1990s, countries such as Poland and Hungary had Gini coefficients approaching

---

[26] The other countries in the comparison were Australia, Belgium, Canada, Finland, France, the Netherlands, Norway, and Sweden.

(though still below) the OECD average. In contrast, Russia had a Gini coefficient approaching 50 per cent, well above that in any OECD country.

The distribution of wealth should be mentioned, if only to stress its importance. Some empirical studies are listed in the Further Reading. If anything the problems are even worse than with income. Some problems are conceptual (e.g. what should be included in personal wealth). Others are measurement problems (e.g. the valuation of estates at death). Many are problems of both concept and measurement (e.g. whether accrued pension rights should be included as part of personal wealth and, if so, how they should be valued).

5. Conclusion

DESCRIBING OUTCOMES. The main conclusion is that there is no scientifically 'correct' measure of poverty or inequality.

The following lead to more people being counted as poor—that is, to higher measured poverty:

- a higher poverty line;
- a narrower definition of income (e.g. excluding home-grown produce);
- a narrower definition of the income unit (i.e. excluding the income of the extended family);
- a larger adjustment for household size; smaller economies of scale in household formation imply a value of E (equation (6.19)) closer to one, leading to per capita adjustment or close to it, thus giving a higher weight to children;
- a shorter time period over which income is measured.

Measured inequality, similarly, will be higher with a narrower definition of the income unit, a shorter period over which income is measured and when based on a more continuous income distribution (the wider the bars of a histogram, the more inequality *within* groups is omitted).[27]

All these problems are compounded when comparing across countries (see Atkinson, 1995*a*, ch. 4). Country A can have less measured poverty or inequality than country B because of (*a*) differences in the distribution of pre-transfer incomes or (*b*) more generous transfers, or (*c*) because poverty and inequality are measured differently (i.e. the difference could be a statistical artefact).

Since well-informed commentators can (and do) make different assumptions about the elements of (*c*), it is not surprising that estimates of poverty and inequality vary widely. These are not just technical issues but involve important social judgements. A higher weight for children will find more poor children and fewer poor old people than

[27] The relation between measured inequality and adjustment for household size is more complex; see Coulter *et al.* (1992).

with a poverty line in which children receive a lower weight. Similarly, a broader definition of the income unit assumes that older people share the resources of younger family members and thus finds fewer poor old people. In short, measuring poverty and inequality involves inescapable value judgements.

EVALUATING OUTCOMES. Why does any of this matter? Measuring poverty is important because poverty is costly. It is costly in equity terms for most of the theories of society discussed in Chapter 3. It is also costly in efficiency terms: poverty is associated with ill health; and ill health is associated with poor learning outcomes (this is the national efficiency argument in Chapter 2, Section 2); poverty is also associated with crime, imposing external costs on society more broadly (Chapter 8, Section 2.1).

Measuring inequality is also important. In contrast with poverty, it is possible to have *too little* inequality. Incentives are important for static and dynamic efficiency; a flat income distribution generally requires both a fairly flat wage distribution and job security. The growth slowdown in the Communist countries of Central and Eastern Europe and the former Soviet Union show the resulting devastating efficiency costs. *Too much* inequality, however, can also be costly. As with poverty, this is partly for equity reasons. But there is also growing evidence (Deininger and Squire 1996) that, at least in developing countries with very high rates of inequality, a reduction in inequality is associated with increased growth rates.

FURTHER READING

For an overview of the problems of defining and measuring income, poverty and inequality, see Atkinson (1983) (compendious and non-mathematical) and Sen (1992); and for wide-ranging collections, Atkinson (1980, 1989, 1995a).

The classic works on defining and measuring income are Fisher (1930: 3–35), Simons (1938: 41–58), Hicks (1946: 171–81), and Kaldor (1955: 54–78).

The classic historical studies of poverty are by Rowntree (1901) and Booth (1902); for follow-up studies, see Rowntree (1941) and Rowntree and Lavers (1951); for an assessment, Briggs (1961b); and for reworking and updating, Atkinson *et al.* (1983). For more recent discussion of the definition and measurement of poverty, see Sen (1985), Piachaud (1987, 1993) and Atkinson (1987b; 1989: chs. 1, 2). Orshansky (1965) discusses the calculation of a poverty line for the USA.

On poverty in the UK, see Atkinson (1989: ch. 3), Hills (1997), and for a review of evidence between 1974 and 1995, Martin Evans (1988). Poverty among women and poverty and race are discussed by Oppenheim and Harker (1996: chs. 5, 6). On the USA, see Blank (1994, 1997a: ch. 1), Danziger and Gottshalk (1995), Karoly and Burtless (1995), US Panel on Poverty and Public Assistance (1995), Gottshalk (1997), and Levy (1998). For comparative analysis, see Atkinson (1995a: ch. 4), Smeeding (1997), and Danziger and Jännti (forthcoming). On poverty in the former Communist countries, see World Bank (1996: ch. 4) and Milanovic (1998). For broader international discussion, see World Bank (1990, 1992) and the contributions in van de Walle and Nead (1995).

Concepts

The meaning of 'equality' is discussed by Okun (1975: ch. 3) and Le Grand (1982, 1984, 1991a: ch. 5). For a simple introduction to the literature on adult equivalents, see Atkinson (1983: ch. 3) and for fuller discussion, Coulter *et al.* (1992) and Atkinson *et al.* (1995).

Aggregate inequality is illuminated in Pen (1971) (reprinted in Atkinson 1980), and discussed more generally by Atkinson (1983); see also Sen (1992). Cowell (1995) discusses aggregate inequality measures (and also contains a useful introduction to social-welfare functions). The classic article on the Atkinson inequality measure is Atkinson (1970), reprinted with a non-mathematical summary in Atkinson (1980: 23–43) (for a simple introduction, see Atkinson (1983: 54–9)). For the 'leaky-bucket' experiment, see Okun (1975: 91–100) (another piece of vintage Okun to which the reader is warmly recommended); and, for a witty and highly critical review of most inequality measures, Wiles (1974).

Inequality in the UK is discussed in UK Royal Commission on the Distribution of Income and Wealth (1979: ch. 2; reprinted in part in Atkinson 1980: 71–8). On increases in inequality over the 1980s, see Atkinson (1995a: chs. 1, 2, 1996) and Goodman *et al.* (1997), and, for discussion of the causes of this increase, Hills (1996b) and Atkinson (1997). Trends in the USA are discussed by Danziger and Gottshalk (1995), Karoly and Burtless (1995), Burtless (1996a, b), and Gottshalk (1997). On a major debate over causes, see Fischer *et al.* (1996).

The results of comparative studies of inequality are presented by Gottschalk (1993), Atkinson *et al.* (1995), Gottschalk and Smeeding (1997), and Smeeding (1997). On inequality trends in former-Communist countries, see Atkinson and Micklewright (1992), World Bank (1996: ch. 4), and Milanovic (1998).

On analysis of the distribution of wealth, see UK Royal Commission on the Distribution of Income and Wealth (1979) and, for more recent analysis, Banks *et al.* (1996) and Hamnett and Seavers (1996).

Appendix: Non-technical summary of Chapter 6

1. Chapter 6 discusses problems which arise in defining and measuring the key concepts of income, poverty, and inequality.

Income

2. The only theoretically sound definition of individual income (Section 1.1) is *full income*, Y_F, which consists of money income, Y_M, plus all non-money income, Y_N (e.g. job satisfaction, the value of own production, and the enjoyment of leisure), i.e.

$$Y_F = Y_M + Y_N. \tag{6.1}$$

The inclusion of non-money income, including the enjoyment of leisure, is crucial. Full income defined this way is a broad measure of an individual's *potential* consumption—i.e. of her power to consume goods (including leisure) if she so chooses. As such it is a form of generalized budget constraint.

3. The measurement of income (Section 1.1) is bedevilled by several sets of problems. First, money income is used as a proxy for full income because it is not possible to measure most forms of non-money income. The fact that there is no systematic relation between Y_M and Y_N makes money income an unreliable yardstick of consumption opportunities, and therein lies the origin of many of the problems of defining and measuring poverty and inequality. A second difficulty concerns the definition of the unit whose income we are measuring—e.g. whom does the income unit include, and how should the incomes of families of different sizes be treated? Finally, over what time period should income be measured? The conclusion is that a theoretically sound definition of income faces intractable measurement problems.

Poverty

4. In principle poverty should be defined in terms of full income. Its measurement therefore faces all the problems described in para. 3. But, even if these were solved, it would still be necessary to decide whether poverty, however measured, should be defined in absolute or relative terms (Section 2.1). *Absolute poverty* means that a person's money income is too low to keep him alive and healthy. Early studies hoped in this way to measure poverty 'objectively', an approach which is increasingly out of favour, at least in developed economies. *Relative poverty* implies that a person is poor if her standard of living deviates substantially from the average of the society in which she lives—i.e. if she cannot participate in 'normal' life.

5. Poverty (in an absolute sense) and inequality are two entirely separate concepts (Section 2.2). Absolute poverty relates to a standard of living below some benchmark, inequality to the *difference* between the incomes of poor and non-poor. The distinction is important, because policies aimed at one might aggravate the other. It is, therefore, necessary to be clear whether poverty relief or inequality reduction is the major objective.

Concepts

Inequality

6. EQUALITY OF OPPORTUNITY (Section 3.1) would be hard to define even if full income could be measured. The main problem is to decide which causes of income differences matter. Systematic differences due to race, sex, or social class are generally regarded as examples of inequality. But ambiguity can arise when differences are due to 'natural ability', depending on whether or not it is influenced by differences in the quality of education. Equality of opportunity is not, however, violated by random differences in income (i.e. luck).

7. These problems are compounded because in practice it is necessary to use money income as a proxy for individual welfare. Differences in money income can overstate inequality between individuals A and B for at least three reasons (Section 3.2): they may have different tastes and hence have made different choices (e.g. about leisure); they may be at different stages in their life cycle (e.g. A fully trained, B an apprentice); and the difference in their incomes may be the result of random fluctuations. Other factors can understate inequality. None of this implies that there is no inequality in society—just that money income is bad at measuring it.

8. Further problems arise when comparing the incomes of families of different sizes (Section 3.3). One argument is that, if a couple has a child, per capita household income will fall; it follows that larger households need higher money income than smaller households to maintain an 'equivalent' standard of living. Alternatively, if a couple has a child by choice, it can be argued that, though per capita money income falls, the couple's *utility* rises because otherwise they would not have had the child. In the latter case a larger household does not necessarily need a higher money income to maintain a given living standard. Again, the problem arises because it is not possible to measure full income; and again there is no wholly satisfactory solution.

9. Section 4 discusses measures of the overall degree of inequality in society. These measures, to the extent that they are valid, enable us to answer questions like: is the UK today more unequal than ten years ago; is it more unequal than the USA?

10. A widely used measure is the *Lorenz curve* (Section 4.1). In Figure 6.3 the horizontal axis shows the percentage of individuals/households, the vertical axis the cumulative percentage of total income. The Lorenz curve is shown by the line OaB. Each point on the curve shows the share of total income received by the *lowest x* per cent of individuals. Thus point a shows that the bottom 40 per cent of individuals receive 17 per cent of income. If income is distributed completely equally, the Lorenz curve will coincide with the diagonal (i.e. the lowest 50 per cent of individuals receive 50 per cent of income, and so on). Thus the greater the degree of inequality, the further the Lorenz curve will be from the diagonal, and vice versa.

11. The *Gini coefficient* is an inequality measure based on the Lorenz curve; diagrammatically it is the ratio of the shaded area in Figure 6.3 to the triangle OaB. It follows that the Gini coefficient will vary between zero (if income is distributed completely equally) and one (if one person has all the income).

12. The use of the Gini coefficient as a measure of inequality is subject to a variety of criticisms (Section 4.3). First, it is based on the current money income of individuals or households: this omits all non-money income (paras. 2 and 3); it fails to exclude differences in money income which have no bearing on inequality, e.g. life-cycle factors and individual choice (para. 7); and it faces difficulties over differences in household size (para. 8). Secondly, the data on money income are not always accurate, complete, or consistent over time or across countries. Finally, the Gini

coefficient raises a number of conceptual problems. These are discussed in Section 4.2 together with the Atkinson inequality measure, which treats inequality in a more sophisticated way, and hence avoids some of the problems of the Gini coefficient.

13. The main message of paragraph 12 for non-technical readers is that the Gini coefficient, though widely used and useful in some circumstances, is in no way definitive as a measure of over-all inequality.

Part 2
CASH BENEFITS

CHAPTER 7

Financing the welfare state

Taxes, after all, are the dues that we pay for the privileges of membership in an organised society.

(Franklin D. Roosevelt, 1936)

Thrift should be the guiding principle in our government expenditure.

(Mao Tse-tung, 1893–1976)

1. The structure of the UK government accounts

1.1. Conceptual issues

This chapter discusses the finances of the welfare state, and is somewhat more institutional than the rest of the book. The subject is vast, and the account here no more than a very brief summary of the ground covered in detail by Glennerster (1997). National insurance and other cash benefits are discussed in Section 2, and the rest of the welfare state, mainly the National Health Service, education, and housing, in Section 3. Section 4 considers a number of important methodological issues. This section describes the structure of UK government accounts. As a backdrop it is necessary to bring out a number of conceptual points.

THE BOUNDARIES OF THE PUBLIC SECTOR have to be established, *inter alia* between the government sector and public corporations, and between government, on the one hand, and companies and the personal sector, on the other. The task is more complex than is apparent (Prest and Barr 1985: ch. 8). It is not possible to define such boundaries unambiguously; careful judgement is needed; and any definition, however carefully constructed, will be open to criticism.

LEVELS OF GOVERNMENT ACTIVITY. The most obvious distinction is between central and local government. For instance, total spending by central and local government is *not* the simple sum of their respective expenditures. Part of central spending is a grant to local authorities, which then forms part of local spending. In producing overall public-sector accounts, as in Table 7.1, care is needed to avoid double counting.

GOVERNMENT ACTIVITY ON CURRENT, CAPITAL, AND FINANCIAL ACCOUNT. It is necessary to distinguish receipts on current account (mainly from taxes on income and expenditure), receipts on capital account (e.g. from capital taxation and the sale of capital assets), and financial receipts (mainly revenue from government borrowing). Similar distinctions arise on the expenditure side.

TYPES OF GOVERNMENT EXPENDITURE. It is vital to distinguish:

- absorption of goods and services, which (taking education as an example) includes (*a*) current spending (i.e. public consumption in the form of teachers' salaries), and (*b*) capital spending (i.e. public investment, such as the costs of building new schools).
- Transfer payments, which include (*c*) current grants to the personal sector (e.g. student scholarships), and (*d*) capital grants to the private sector (e.g. contributions to the cost of university building).[1]

Chapter 4, Section 3.1, set out the four generic forms of state intervention—regulation, finance, public production and income transfers. Government absorption of goods and services corresponds with public production. Transfer payments take two very different forms. The first is explicit transfers, as discussed above, including all state cash benefits. Secondly there are:

TAX EXPENDITURES—that is, implicit public expenditure in the form of tax reliefs. Cash assistance to help tenants with their rent is an explicit transfer, mortgage-interest tax relief for owner-occupiers an implicit transfer. Both assist with accommodation costs, and both ultimately make up part of private-sector spending. Tax relief for private pensions is similarly a form of transfer.[2] But tax expenditures do not appear in conventional public-spending figures, and their distributional implications have been criticized. Both issues assume special relevance in the context of pensions (Chapter 9) and housing (Chapter 14) (for detailed discussion, see the Further Reading).

1.2. Government revenue and expenditure

THE REVENUE PROPOSALS of government are set out each year in the Budget, and more formally in the *Financial Statement and Budget Report* and the Finance Bill. It is a long-standing principle of UK public finance that, in general, all central government revenues,

---

[1] These are transfer payments from the viewpoint of government, because universities are regarded as part of the private sector.

[2] Though valuation problems may arise—see UK Board of Inland Revenue (1983).

Table 7.1. Income and expenditure of central and local government, UK, 1996/7 (est.) (£bn.)

Revenue	(1)	(2)	(3)	(4)
Central government				
Taxes on income		100.8		
Income tax	68.1			
Corporation tax	26.1			
Other	6.6			
Taxes on expenditure		83.3		
VAT	47.5			
Fuel duties	17.4			
Taxes on alcohol and tobacco	13.5			
Other	4.9			
Other taxes		19.2		
Vehicle excise duties	4.3			
Oil royalties	0.7			
Business rates	14.2			
Total central government tax revenues			203.3	
Interest and dividends			8.1	
Other			10.5	
TOTAL CENTRAL–GOVERNMENT REVENUE				221.9
National–insurance contributions				45.2
Local government				
Council Tax		9.9		
(Current grants from central government)		(58.1)		
(Capital grants from central government)		(3.2)		
Other receipts		3.9		
TOTAL LOCAL–GOVERNMENT REVENUE				13.8
Total general government receipts				280.9
Public–sector borrowing requirement				27.6
GENERAL GOVERNMENT RECEIPTS AND BORROWING				308.5

Expenditure	By department (5)	By function (6)
Social security[a]	76.9	97.5[b]
Health and personal social services	34.0	51.2[b]
of which health care		(41.1)
Education and Employment	14.8	36.9[b]
DoE—local government	31.3	
DoE—other	8.4	
DoE—housing		4.0[b]
DoE—environment		9.8
Defence	22.1	21.1
Home Office	6.6	
Law, order and protective services		16.5
Transport	4.9	9.0
Other departments	19.3	62.5
Scotland, Wales, and Northern Ireland	29.6	
Local authorities, self-financed spending	13.3	
Allowance for shortfall	−0.6	
Control total	260.6	
Cyclical social security	14.3	
Central–government debt interest	22.2	
Accounting adjustments	10.3	
GGE(X)	307.4	
Privatization proceeds	−4.5	
Other adjustments	5.6	
GENERAL GOVERNMENT EXPENDITURE	308.5	

[a] Spending on all contributory and non-contributory cash benefits.

[b] See Tables 7.5, 12.1, 13.1, and 14.1 for breakdowns of total spending for social security, health, education, and housing, respectively.

Sources: UK Treasury (1996: tables 1.5, 4A.3, 4A.4 and 4A.6; 1997: table 3.5).

Cash benefits

whatever their source, are paid into the *Consolidated Fund*, from which all central government expenditure is made. The only major exception is the *National Insurance Fund*, discussed in Section 2.2.

The income of a local authority derives from two main sources: grants from central government (i.e. from the Consolidated Fund), whose complexities lie well outside the scope of this book, and local taxation. For present purposes, as Table 7.1 shows, the most important aspect of local finance is the size of the central-government grant (nearly 3.5 times local revenues in 1996/7), which raises major issues for the relationship between central and local government, particularly in the light of tight control by central government of the revenue-raising powers of localities (see Glennerster 1997: ch. 5).

Table 7.1 gives an overview of the income and expenditure of government. The three main blocks of revenue relate to central government, national-insurance contributions, and local government.[3] Central-government revenue in 1996/7 was £222 billion, mainly from current taxation. Taxes on income, administered by the Inland Revenue, raised £101 billion, nearly 70 per cent from income tax, making it the largest single revenue source. Taxes on expenditure, mostly administered by Customs and Excise, raised £83 billion. In addition to tax revenues, central government also received £8 billion, *inter alia* from interest and dividends.[4] National-insurance contributions (£45 billion) are discussed in more detail in Section 2.

Local-government receipts from Council Tax (the only tax levied by local authorities: see Kneen and Travers 1994) were £10 billion. Rents, mainly from local-authority housing, and dividends and interest raised another £4 billion. In addition, there are central-government current and capital grants (£61 billion in 1996/7). To avoid double counting, these intra-governmental transfers are omitted from the totals.

Total current and capital receipts were £281 billion, to which are added financial receipts (i.e. public-sector borrowing) of £28 billion, bringing the total revenue of all levels of government to £309 billion.

THE SPENDING PROPOSALS of government are set out each year in a series of departmental reviews (UK DfEE 1997a; UK DHSS 1997; UK DoE 1997; UK DoH 1997; UK Treasury 1997a) and debated by Parliament. There has been much discussion over the years about the planning of public spending and its control (see the Further Reading), in part because of the increased costs of the welfare state. The departmental reviews in their current format give a detailed breakdown of public spending,[5] and are the source of many of the later tables.

The 1996/7 control total for expenditure (Table 7.1) was £261 billion, to which are added cyclical social security (e.g. to assist people who are unemployed) of £14 billion,

---

[3] All figures in Section 1.2 are rounded to the nearest £billion.

[4] This £8 billion does *not* include proceeds from the sale of assets, which appear as a negative item on the *expenditure* side in the government accounts.

[5] The departmental reviews, and their predecessors, the Public Expenditure White Papers, have been the subject of considerable criticism. Since 1980 planning has been in 'cash' terms—i.e. departments are allocated a specific sum, irrespective of subsequent price changes. This makes planning of expenditure easier, but creates great difficulties for *volume* planning (i.e. for resource allocation)—see Glennerster (1997: ch. 4).

and interest on the national debt of £22 billion. GGE(X) represents general-government expenditure excluding certain items, notably privatization proceeds and spending financed by the National Lottery (one of the items in 'Other adjustments'). Total spending by all levels of government was £309 billion. The breakdown of this total is given by department (column 5) and by function (column 6). To illustrate the difference, social security—much the largest item—comprised spending by the department (£77 billion), to which needs to be added, *inter alia*, cyclical spending on social-security, and social-security spending in Scotland, Wales, and Northern Ireland, which appear under the budgets of those departments. The total figure in the right-hand column, £98 billion, represents all spending in the UK on national insurance and other cash benefits.[6] Continuing with the right-hand column, defence spending was £21 billion,[7] health (including personal social services) £51 billion, and education, £37 billion, deriving only in part from the budget of the education department.[8]

One point to emerge immediately is the sheer size of the welfare state, however defined (and it consists at a minimum of cash benefits, health, education, and housing). In Table 7.2 these are divided into social services (approximating to the last three) and current grants to the personal sector (approximating cash payments). Figures are given also for defence and debt interest in current and constant prices in 1920, 1948, and 1996/7. There is always room for judgement about the definition of the welfare state; and the price index is subject to the usual caveats; the figures should therefore be regarded as no more than indicative. Several broad results emerge:

1. The welfare state has assumed an increasing proportion of public spending; in 1920 it absorbed about 28 per cent of total government expenditure, only marginally greater than debt-interest payments and about 1.75 times defence spending; the picture had not changed enormously by 1948; but by 1996/7 the welfare state made up over 60 per cent of public spending, and nine times defence spending.

2. Government spending doubled as a percentage of gross national product, from 21 per cent in 1920 to 41 per cent in 1996/7.

3. A consequence is the sharp increase in the welfare state as a percentage of gross national product, from under 6 per cent in 1920 to 10 per cent in 1948, and to 25 per cent in 1996/7.

4. In real terms (1996/7 prices), expenditure on the welfare state rose from £7 billion in 1920 to £24 billion in 1948 and to £190 billion in 1996/7, representing a twenty-five-fold increase since 1920, and a seven fold real increase since 1948. The resulting

---

[6] As explained in the Glossary, there is an ambiguity in the use of the term 'social security'. In the USA it generally refers only to retirement benefits; in the UK it refers to *all* contributory and non-contributory cash benefits, and in mainland Europe to all cash benefits and health care. The term will be avoided where possible. Where its use is inevitable it will be used in the UK sense.

[7] The figure for defence in the right-hand column is slightly smaller than the departmental figure because some spending by the department appears under other functions heads. For example, expenditure on sending officers to university appears as part of education spending.

[8] Disaggregated figures are given in Tables 7.5 (cash benefits), 12.1 (health), 13.1 (education), and 14.1 (housing).

Table 7.2. Gross domestic product and spending by central and local government, UK, 1920, 1948, and 1996/97

Item	1920				1948				1996/7			
	£m. current prices (1)	£m. 1996/7 prices (2)	% of government spending (3)	% of GDP (4)	£m. current prices (5)	£m. 1996/7 prices (6)	% of government spending (7)	% of GDP (8)	£m. current prices (9)	£m. 1996/7 prices (10)	% of government spending (11)	% of GDP (12)
Defence	186	4,036	16	3.3	743	14,657	19	6.3	21,100	21,100	6.8	2.8
Social services[a]	169	} 7,248	28	5.9	541	} 23,573	31	10.1	92,100	} 189,600	61.5	25.3
Current grants to the personal sector	165				654				97,500			
Debt interest	320	6,944	27	5.6	553	10,909	14	4.7	22,200	22,200	7.2	3.0
Total government current spending	1,182	25,649	100	20.8	3,862	76,183	100	32.6	308,500	308,500	100	41.2
GROSS DOMESTIC PRODUCT[b]	5,688	123,430	–	100	11,837	233,501	–	100	749,000	749,000	–	100

[a] Current spending on goods and services.
[b] Market prices.

Sources: Feinstein (1972: tables 12, 13, 33, 35, 65); UK DSS (1995a: table 1.1); Table 7.1.

expenditure, however, is still well below the European average as a proportion of national income (see Esping-Andersen 1996*b*: table 1.1).

2. **Cash benefits**

2.1. Individual national-insurance contributions

Current arrangements are the outcome of various changes since 1948 (Chapter 2, Section 6). There are three types of contributor for national-insurance purposes: employed persons, the self-employed, and the non-employed, as summarized in Table 7.3 (for details, see Tolley 1996: ch. 2).

EMPLOYED PERSONS. Class 1 contributions are paid by both employee and employer. There is a *lower-earnings limit* (£62 per week in 1997/8), set at the level of the basic retirement pension (Chapter 9, Section 1), and an *upper-earnings limit* (£465 per week in 1997/8), set at 6.5–7.5 times the lower-earnings limit. Someone with total earnings below the lower-earnings limit pays no contributions. People with higher earnings pay 2 per cent

Table 7.3. **National–insurance contribution rates, 1997/8**

Class of contribution	Contribution rate
Class 1 (employed earners), not contracted out[a]	
Employee contribution[b]	
on first £62.00	2%
on balance up to £465.00	10%
Employer contribution	
under £62.00	—
£62.00–£109.99	3%
£110.00–£154.99	5%
£155.00–£209.99	7%
over £209.99	10%
Class 2 (self-employed, flat-rate)	
Self-employed persons with profits in excess of £3,480 per year	Flat-rate contribution of £6.15 per week
Class 3 (voluntary contributions by non-employed persons)	
Non-employed persons	Flat-rate contribution of £6.05 per week
Class 4 (self-employed, earnings related)	
Self-employed persons	6% of profits between £7,010 and £24,180 per year[c]

[a] Contracted-out rates for employees are 2% of earnings up to £62 per week and 8.4% of the balance up to £465. For employers, contracted out rates are 3% below those shown for employees in salary-related (i.e. defined benefit) schemes and 1.5% less for employees in money purchase (i.e. defined contribution) schemes.
[b] Men aged 65 or over and women aged 60 or over do not pay employees' contributions. However, employers' contributions are payable.
[c] Half of the Class 4 contribution is deductible for income-tax purposes.

of earnings up to the lower-earnings limit and 10 per cent of earnings between the lower- and upper-earnings limits. Individuals contracted out of the state earnings-related pension scheme into an occupational scheme (Chapter 9, Section 1) pay contributions at a reduced rate (8.4 per cent in 1997/8).

A full contribution year requires a total contribution of at least that due on fifty-two times the lower-earnings limit. A person who is unemployed, ill, or caring for children or a disabled person, if he would otherwise fall below this minimum, is given a *credit*— that is, no contribution is paid, but future benefits are awarded as though the appropriate percentage contribution had been made on earnings equal to the lower-earnings limit.

Unlike income tax and the other types of national-insurance contribution, the income limit for Class 1 contributions is a *weekly* exemption. Thus, someone earning £61.50 in some weeks and £62.10 in others would pay contributions in weeks where earnings were £62.10, even if her average for the year was under £62. These contributions are not refundable, in sharp contrast with the operation of income tax in similar circumstances. Uneasy relationships like this have generated pressure for an integrated system of income tax and national-insurance contributions (Chapter 11, Section 3.2).

The basic employer Class 1 contribution in 1997/8 was 10 per cent of the employee's gross weekly earnings with no upper limit. For lower earnings the employer contribution was payable at a lower percentage rate (Table 7.3); and a lower contribution was payable in respect of contracted-out employees.

Both employee and employer Class 1 contributions are collected together with income tax. They help to pay for national-insurance benefits; part of the contribution is channelled to the National Health Service.

THE SELF-EMPLOYED pay both Class 2 and Class 4 contributions. The Class 2 contribution is flat rate (£6.15 in 1997/8), paid in the form of a weekly stamp. Class 4 contributions are a percentage (6 per cent in 1997/8) of a self-employed person's profits between certain limits, collected by the Inland Revenue as part of the individual's income-tax assessment. Half of the contribution is deductible for income-tax purposes. Class 2 and 4 contributions do not entitle a self-employed person to the full range of benefits available to an employee. There is no support while unemployed, no earnings-related retirement pension, and no entitlement to redundancy pay.

A person who is both employed and self-employed is potentially liable to pay Class 1, Class 2, and Class 4 contributions, subject to an annual ceiling on total contributions (see Tolley 1996: ch. 2).

THE NON-EMPLOYED, broadly, are not current members of the labour force—for example, students or married women who are not employed or self-employed. To maintain an unbroken contributions record, such a person can pay a voluntary flat-rate Class 3 contribution (£6.05 per week in 1997/8). The payment of Class 3 contributions gives no right to immediate benefit, but may protect future entitlement. As discussed further in Chapter 9, Section 1, a woman (or in certain circumstances a man) staying at home to look after young children or a disabled person can avoid breaks in her contributions record without paying Class 3 contributions because she receives home responsibilities protection—that is, receives a credit for her contribution.

2.2. The National Insurance Fund

National-insurance benefits are paid from the National Insurance Fund, and all other central government benefits from the Consolidated Fund. The distinction is important for operational purposes and for understanding the structure of government accounts but has less economic significance.

REVENUE. On the revenue side, the relation between the two funds is straightforward. The income of the National Insurance Fund (Table 7.4) derives mainly from the contributions of the various classes of insured persons. Virtually all other central-government revenues go into the Consolidated Fund.

In 1996/7 total net contributions were £42 billion, the great bulk from Class 1 contributions. There was also a transfer of £2 billion from the Consolidated Fund. The interest item (£480 million in 1996/7) is earned on current revenue and on the accumulated surplus (£7.5 billion) shown at the bottom of the table. At various times there has been debate about the proper role of the Fund, though a surplus of some sort is desirable for a number of reasons: to bridge short-term imbalances (the end-year balance in Table 7.4 represents under nine weeks' outgoings); to cushion a growing increase in contribution rates to finance pensions; and to assist with public-sector borrowing (which last aspect has drawn a certain amount of political fire). Whether the Fund should be organized

Table 7.4. **Account of the National Insurance Fund, Great Britain, 1996/7 (est.) (£m.)**

Income		
Contributions (net)	41,884	
Treasury grant	1,925	
Compensation for payments on statutory sick pay and statutory maternity pay	524	
Income from investments	480	
Other	158	
TOTAL REVENUE		44,971
Expenditure		
Benefits	41,956	
Transfer to Northern Ireland	75	
Personal pensions	2,027	
Administration, etc.	1,066	
Other	169	
TOTAL EXPENDITURE		45,293
BALANCE CARRIED FORWARD		7,513

Source: UK DSS (1997: table 1c).

Cash benefits

Table 7.5. **Cash benefits, UK, 1996/7 (est.) (£m.)**

Contributory benefits (paid from the National Insurance Fund)			
Retirement pensions (including lump-sum payments)		32,671	
Widows' benefit, etc.		1,086	
Unemployment benefit (cyclical)		606	
Sickness and invalidity		8,127	
Industrial-injury benefits		740	
Maternity allowance and statutory maternity pay		544	
			43,774
Non-contributory benefits (paid from the Consolidated Fund)			
Non-contributory retirement pension		56	
War pensions		1,419	
Disability benefits			
Attendance allowance	2,421		
Invalid care allowance	768		
Severe-disablement allowance	893		
Disability living allowance	4,361		
Disability working allowance	25		
Other	658		
		9,126	
Income support (cyclical)		13,734	
Income support for the elderly		3,895	
Family benefits			
Child benefit	6,724		
One parent benefit	348		
Family credit	2,047		
Other	343		
		9,462	
Social fund		252	
Housing benefit		12,209	
			50,153
Administration			
Contributory benefits	1,056		
Non-contributory benefits	2,328		
Other	159		
			3,543
TOTAL SOCIAL–SECURITY BENEFITS			97,470

Sources: UK Treasury (1997: table 3.5; UK DSS 1997: table 1).

on actuarial lines (i.e. have a reserve sufficient to pay all expected future liabilities) is a central topic in Chapter 9.

Two general points should be noted. First (Table 7.1), total gross contributions in 1996/7 were £45 billion; hence the revenue of the National Insurance Fund was 20 per cent of central government revenue from all other sources; only income tax produced significantly more revenue. In effect there is a third estate alongside the Inland Revenue and Customs and Excise. Secondly, the budgetary procedures for this revenue differ from those for public spending generally; for example, the accounts of the National Insurance Fund are kept separate from the general accounts.

EXPENDITURE. On the expenditure side, matters are less tidy. In principle, benefits from the National Insurance Fund (e.g. for unemployment) are paid only to individuals with an appropriate contributions record, while similar benefits paid from the Consolidated Fund are awarded on the basis of other criteria, such as low income or number of children (e.g. child benefit). In practice, however, there are many linkages and interactions because many individuals receive benefits from both sources, so that it is often necessary to discuss them together.

Expenditure on cash benefits is set out in Table 7.5. Much the largest is the retirement pension (£33 billion in 1996/7). Spending on the elderly went up steadily over the years, accounting for over one-third of increases in state-benefit spending between the mid-1970s and mid-1990s. In addition, spending on private benefits rose considerably (see Martin Evans 1998: table 7.14). The remaining insurance benefits cover unemployment, sickness (i.e. relatively short-run health problems), invalidity (i.e. long-term and permanent health problems), and widowhood. Total spending on the insurance benefits was £44 billion.

EXPENDITURE ON NON-CONTRIBUTORY BENEFITS in 1996/7 was £50 billion, of which nearly three-quarters was on income support (£18 billion), housing benefit (£12 billion), and child benefit (£7 billion). Income support is payable to individuals/families whose income after receipt of all other benefits is still below the poverty line; it thus constitutes the final safety net on the cash side of the welfare state. Housing benefit assists with housing costs. Child benefit is a tax-free cash payment in respect of each child, payable weekly to (usually) the mother. All three benefits are discussed in Chapter 10.

3. Benefits in kind

This section surveys very briefly the finances of the National Health Service, of the state educational system, and of local-authority housing (for details, see Glennerster 1997: chs. 10–13). As we shall see in Chapter 12, the original intention of the National Health Service that all health care should be free has largely been realized. Medical attention is generally free, with the exception of certain items (e.g. prescriptions) for which charges, generally below full cost, apply to some people. Of total spending on the National Health Service, 81 per cent comes from general taxation, about 12.5 per cent from national-insurance contributions, and 2.4 per cent from charges (UK DoH 1997*d*: table 2.3). Table 7.1 shows that total spending on health care in 1996/7 was £41.1 billion (for further detail see Table 12.1). The National Health Service, clearly, is not a contributory scheme, and any assessment of its finances must discuss the tax system as a whole (see Section 4).

State education (discussed in Chapter 13) is supplied largely without charge. Historically it was both produced and financed locally. Table 7.1 shows that spending on education and related activities in England was £36.9 billion (for further detail see Table 13.1). Though most education spending is at the local level, the extent of central government grants to local authorities means that it is largely financed from the

Consolidated Fund. I shall abstract from most of the central versus local debates as they apply to education (and the National Health Service and local-authority housing) and discuss education for the most part as a non-contributory scheme financed from general taxation, and differing from the National Health Service only to the extent that there is a larger role for local government (see the Further Reading).

Table 7.1 shows that net expenditure on housing in England in 1996/7 was £4 billion, with substantial involvement by both central and local government (see Table 14.1 for further detail). This figure *understates* public involvement in housing: first, it is a net figure, and therefore excludes capital receipts from the sale of housing and land; secondly, it omits other forms of housing expenditure, e.g. housing benefit, which appear as part of spending on cash benefits; thirdly, the tax relief for owner-occupiers, like all tax expenditures, is an invisible item in government accounts (they serve simply to reduce the revenue from income tax in Table 7.1). The importance of tax expenditures in any systematic analysis of public spending is emphasized by their scale. Mortgage interest tax relief in 1996/7 was £2.6 billion (see Table 14.2), to which should be added the value of capital-gains tax relief. Housing expenditure thus broadly defined is set out in Table 14.2.

In 1995 about 19 per cent of households lived in local authority housing (Hills 1998: table 5.11). Until the early 1990s, local-authority rents generally failed to cover current housing costs, the shortfall coming from local-taxation and a central subsidy. Historically, therefore, local authority housing was financed partly out of 'contributions' (i.e. rents), partly out of local taxation, and partly from the Consolidated Fund. The system is assessed in Chapter 14.

4. Assessing the welfare state

4.1. Incidence considerations

Assessing the efficiency and redistributive impacts of the welfare state is a vast undertaking which raises both methodological and measurement problems (see Atkinson and Stiglitz 1980: lecture 9). This section limits itself to outlining some of the issues of principle, leaving more detailed discussion to later chapters. Two aspects assume special relevance: the notion of tax incidence; and the importance of considering benefits and taxes together.

THE SIMPLE TAX INCIDENCE ARGUMENT is illustrated in Figure 7.1, which analyses the partial equilibrium incidence of a housing subsidy. Suppose the housing market is in equilibrium at price, P_0 and quantity, X_0. A specific rent subsidy shifts the supply curve vertically downwards to S–subsidy; this reduces the price paid by the tenant from P_0 to P_1 (i.e. only a small reduction), and increases the price received by the landlord substantially from P_0 to P_2.

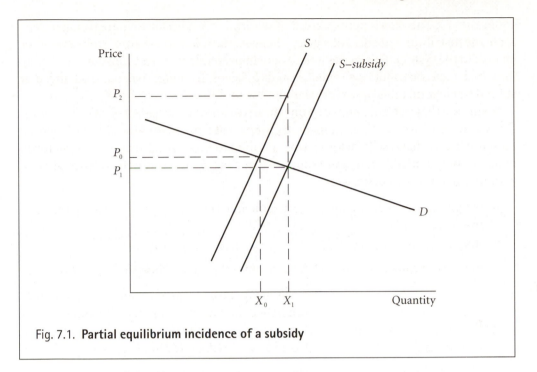

Fig. 7.1. **Partial equilibrium incidence of a subsidy**

The result is that, if landlords are rich and tenants poor (not that this is necessarily the case), then a seemingly redistributive housing subsidy might of itself be regressive. Similarly, suppose that labour is supplied inelastically to the market (empirically plausible for primary workers).[9] A reduction in income tax or the national-insurance contribution can be analysed as a labour subsidy, and Figure 7.1 shows how the subsidy reduces unit wage costs to the employer from P_0 to P_1 (since P_1 is on the demand curve for labour), and increases the wage received by the employee from P_0 to P_2 (since P_2 is on the labour-supply curve). In this case the tax reduction benefits mainly the employee. But the result is reversed where labour supply is elastic.

THE GENERAL EQUILIBRIUM INCIDENCE ARGUMENT. However, to be sure of the efficiency of any policy or of its redistributive effects, it is necessary also to see how the *general* equilibrium of production, consumption, and distribution is affected. There has been some work on applied general-equilibrium analysis (see the Further Reading), though no detailed analysis of the impact of the welfare state.

The discussion of incidence concentrates on the effect, ceteris paribus, of tax/expenditure changes on the relative position of different income groups. The crucial words are ceteris paribus and the *relative* position of individuals or groups (see Prest and Barr

---

[9] The primary labour force consists of 'breadwinners'—i.e. people who would normally be in the labour force full-time. It consists traditionally of men aged 18 to 65 and unmarried women aged 18 to 60. The secondary labour force consists of people who are not *necessarily* full-time members of the labour force—e.g. people under 18, people past retiring age, and married women.

Cash benefits

1985: 101–5). The ceteris paribus condition is important because we are trying to separate the distributional effect of a given change in tax (or expenditure) from any other change in the system. This makes it necessary in principle to introduce a countervailing tax which (*a*) is distributionally neutral and (*b*) keeps the budget balance unchanged. It should be clear that this procedure is fraught with difficulty.

Assuming that this can be done by one means or another, the effect of a tax change on the relative position of different income groups will depend on several sets of factors. Suppose individual A sells factor *m*, which is used to make good *x*, and B sells factor *n*, which is used to make good *y*; and suppose that a tax change raises the relative price of *x*. Individual A is then better off:

1. the greater the increase in his pre-tax income (i.e. the greater the rise in the relative price of *m*);

2. the smaller the taxes he pays;

3. the greater the extent to which he consumes (relatively cheaper) *y* rather than *x*.

The first two items together determine A's net disposable income, and are often jointly referred to as the 'sources' side; the third item concerns the 'uses' side. The three factors show the effect on relative incomes of a tax change considered in isolation. To complete the distributional picture, it is crucial to add that A will be advantaged relative to B also:

4. The greater the benefit derived by A (relative to that received by B) from goods/ services provided by government out of the taxes paid by A and B.

It should be clear that discussion of distributional effects which limits itself to tax changes on their own (i.e. 2 above) looks at only part of the picture, and one which may be completely altered by other changes, particularly under 3 and 4.

4.2. Redistribution: A preliminary discussion

THE MEANING OF PROGRESSIVITY is illustrated by an individual's average tax rate—that is, his tax bill as a proportion of his total income. A tax is progressive if the average rate is higher for someone with a higher income. Suppose that an individual can earn £4,000 tax free per year, and pays tax at a marginal rate of 25 per cent on anything above this. Someone earning £4,000 pays no tax; someone earning £8,000 pays £1,000 (12.5 per cent of his income); and someone with £16,000 pays £3,000 in tax (18.75 per cent of his income). Thus the tax (which is a stylized version of the UK system) is progressive, even though most people face the same marginal rate of 25 per cent.[10]

In assessing the progressivity of a tax it is necessary, in addition to its formal structure, to know the number of people affected: a tax of 25 per cent on income up to £50,000 and 100 per cent thereafter may sound highly progressive, but if nobody has income over £50,000 the tax in practice is proportional. It is also necessary to know the extent to which

---

[10] Whether the degree of progression is the *right* one is an entirely different question.

180

the formal tax rates apply in practice: a tax is less progressive than it appears if the highest rates are never applied—that is, if tax avoidance or evasion[11] are proportionately more frequent at higher incomes. These considerations apply equally to benefits, whose distributional effects have become more complicated because state benefits have increasingly been subject to tax while contributions to private pensions attract tax relief.

CONSIDERING TAXES AND BENEFITS TOGETHER. The discussion in Section 4.1 suggests two implications. First, in assessing the finance of the welfare state it may be necessary to consider simultaneously a variety of taxes contributing to the Consolidated Fund, the National Insurance Fund, and local revenues. Suppose a government tries to help the poor by increasing the employer national-insurance contribution relative to the employee contribution. The discussion underlying Figure 7.1 suggests that it is of no analytical consequence whether a tax is imposed on the buyer or seller. In the case of national insurance, it is therefore (except in the very short term) the combined employer and employee contribution which matters; any attempt to increase one and reduce the other is little more than window dressing.

Secondly, it is frequently the *overall* system which is important. The issue is complex (see the Further Reading), but for present purposes the crucial point is that taxation and expenditure should be considered together. At its simplest, a scheme which uses a proportional tax to subsidize mink coats will usually be regressive; the same tax used to finance poverty relief is progressive.

In principle the logic is simple. Consider a commodity (e.g. health care) which is publicly supplied without charge, and financed by a specific contribution. This arrangement is redistributive from rich to poor *if (rich) individual A pays more in contributions than (poor) B, if each consumes the same quantity; it is also progressive if A consumes twice as much as B, but pays more than twice as much in contributions*.

In practice matters are more complicated because it is hard to identify precisely which contributions/taxes have paid for the commodity—that is, which tax(es) would be reduced or abolished if it were no longer publicly supplied. It might be argued that health care is redistributive so long as A (who consumes twice as much as B) pays more than twice as much in taxes. But this implicitly assumes that health care is financed by a proportionate share of all taxes. The definition in the previous paragraph must therefore be qualified: health care is financed progressively if A consumes twice as much as B, but pays more than twice as much in whatever taxes are used to finance it.

REDISTRIBUTIVE IMPLICATIONS. These various aspects must be borne in mind in considering the extent to which the welfare state is financed progressively. This is done for unemployment and sick pay in Chapter 8, Section 3.2, for pensions in Chapter 9, Section 5.2, and for the major non-contributory benefits in Chapter 10, Section 3.4. These benefits all redistribute from rich to poor to a greater or lesser extent. Nevertheless, as discussed

---

[11] Tax avoidance is legal (e.g. reducing one's tax liability via a mortgage); tax evasion is illegal (e.g. concealing part of one's income).

in Chapter 1, Section 3, and Chapter 6, Sections 2.3 and 4.3, poverty and inequality both increased over the 1980s.

The redistributive effects of the National Health Service and the educational system are discussed in Chapter 12, Section 4.3, and Chapter 13, Section 4.3, and of local-authority housing in Chapter 14, Section 4. It was traditionally thought that all three systems redistributed from rich to poor, but Le Grand (1982) argued the contrary. The core of his argument is that, though these benefits are financed progressively, in that the rich pay more towards them in taxes and contributions than the poor, they are used even more progressively so that the overall result can be regressive. For example, if the rich pay twice as much in taxes as the poor to finance education, but use it proportionately ten times as much, then it is not the rich who subsidize the poor, but the other way round. We return to these arguments in Chapters 12, 13, and 14.

Thus there is a limited presumption that at least the cash side of the welfare state is progressive. But any such view is rendered somewhat tentative by incidence considerations; by conceptual difficulties (e.g. the validity of the Gini coefficient); and by measurement and data problems.

FURTHER READING

Glennerster (1997) covers the ground of this chapter in much greater detail. For a historical perspective, see Peacock and Wiseman (1967).

Conceptual problems with government accounts are discussed in Prest and Barr (1985: chs. 8 and 9). On the concept and measurement of tax expenditures, see McDaniel and Surrey (1984), Surrey and McDaniel (1985), and, in a UK context, Willis and Hardwick (1978).

For data on public spending, see *The Government's Expenditure Plans*, and for taxation and spending together the *Financial Statement and Budget Report*. For general data, see *National Income and Expenditure* (the 'Blue Book'). All are published annually by HMSO.

On the planning and control of public expenditure, see Glennerster (1997: ch. 4), and, for more general discussion, Corry (1997).

The institutions of national-insurance contributions (and other state benefits) are described in Tolley (1996); this work is published annually. On the finances of social security, the National Health Service, personal social services, and education see the relevant chapters in Glennerster (1997) and of housing, ibid., ch. 13, and Hills (1991).

The theory of tax incidence is set out in Stiglitz (1988: ch. 17), Kay and King (1990: ch. 1), and Cullis and Jones (1998: ch. 7), and, more formally, in Atkinson and Stiglitz (1980; lectures 6, 7). For empirical studies, see Aaron and Pechman (1981) and Pechman (1985). The pioneering work on applied general equilibrium analysis is Harberger (1962); for later developments, see Ballard *et al.* (1985) and Piggott and Whalley (1985, 1986).

For methodological discussion of the distribution of public expenditure, see Peacock and Shannon (1968), Prest (1968), and Le Grand (1987c). For empirical analysis of redistribution (and its pitfalls), see the Further Reading to Chapter 6.

CHAPTER 8

Contributory benefits 1: Unemployment, sickness, and disability

> The plan covers all citizens without upper income limit, but has regard to their different ways of life; it is a plan all-embracing in scope of persons and of needs.
>
> (The Beveridge Report, 1942)

1. Introduction and institutions

1.1. The issues

AIMS AND METHODS. Historically the main aim of cash benefits was *poverty relief* (objective 4 in Chapter 1, Section 2.2), in particular the prevention of *absolute* poverty. Motives were controversial, ranging from altruism to capitalist oppression (Chapter 2, Section 7.1, Chapter 3, Section 5.3, and Chapter 4, Section 4.1), but with widespread agreement about the aim itself. Over the twentieth century other aims have become important. Policy has aimed at alleviating *relative* poverty. *Insurance* (objective 5) is concerned with protection in the face of stochastic contingencies such as unemployment or ill health). *Income smoothing* (objective 6) relates to life-cycle effects such as retirement or the presence of dependent children. The objective of *inequality reduction* is more controversial, particularly the aim of redistribution from rich to poor. Other aims discussed in Chapter 1, Section 2.2, concern *efficiency* and *ease of administration*. These aims all recur in the following chapters.

More specifically, unemployment benefit and sickness benefit both contribute to the insurance objective. If the benefit formula is weighted towards the lower paid, they also contribute to poverty relief and to vertical redistribution. One of the major purposes of explicit social-insurance contributions is to give recipients an entitlement to benefit, thereby fostering social solidarity. If properly constructed, the benefits minimize adverse labour-supply effects, thereby contributing to the incentives objective. In addition, in that unemployment is uninsurable in private markets (a major argument in this chapter), state-organized unemployment compensation can contribute to the micro-efficiency objective.

The methods available for income protection vary enormously, but schemes can usefully be classified into three types—private, public, and mixed. Pure private arrangements include the voluntary purchase of actuarial insurance and voluntary charity. Mixed schemes involve public participation in private arrangements through regulation (e.g. minimum standards for private insurance) and/or through finance. The latter frequently takes the form of tax expenditures (Chapter 7, Section 1.1)—for example, tax relief for private pension contributions. Public schemes embrace the forms of institution discussed in Chapter 1, Section 2.1 *Social insurance* is awarded on the basis of a contributions record and the occurrence of a specified contingency, such as unemployment or being above a specified age. *Social assistance* is financed from taxation and awarded on the basis of a means test. '*Universal*' *benefits* are awarded on the basis of a specified contingency (e.g. having dependent children), without either a contribution or an income test.

Which method is preferred depends on the relative weights given to different aims, which in turn depends on political perspective. Libertarians make a sharp distinction between two forms of income transfer.

- Under actuarial insurance an individual provides for his *own* benefits through his previous contributions, and can therefore legitimately choose any desired level of benefit.

- Under a non-contributory scheme, his benefits are paid by *others*. In this case the aim of cash transfers should be to prevent *absolute* poverty—that is, benefits should be at subsistence.

To a libertarian the preferred methods for achieving these aims are voluntary private insurance and private charity, respectively.

Socialists, in contrast, see income transfers as contributing to their egalitarian aims, and therefore favour publicly organized transfers to prevent *relative* poverty and to reduce inequality. Liberals take an intermediate line. We saw in Chapter 6, Section 2.1, that poverty cannot be defined analytically, so its definition is largely ideological. The alleviation of poverty, however defined, can be via insurance (private or public, voluntary or compulsory); through cash transfers out of tax revenues; via private charity; or through whatever mix of these approaches best meets stated aims. The pros and cons of these methods are the subject of Part 2 of the book. This chapter looks at social insurance. Retirement pensions raise a number of separate issues which are discussed in Chapter 9. Chapter 10 looks at non-contributory benefits and Chapter 11 discusses reform strategies.

QUESTIONS about national insurance are of two sorts. The first (Section 2) is whether it should be national (i.e. publicly provided). This in turn raises questions about the circumstances in which people insure voluntarily, and those where it might be appropriate for the state to make insurance compulsory and/or to provide insurance itself. The second issue (Section 3) is the effectiveness of the existing system, including its effects on work effort and saving. Where necessary, different benefits are discussed separately. The major conclusions about cash benefits are set out at the end of Chapter 11.

NON-ECONOMIC ARGUMENTS. Three types of argument are commonly adduced to justify publicly provided cash transfers. The first is that 'the state has a duty to protect its less fortunate members', or that 'everyone has a right to protection from catastrophic income loss'. Both value judgements are widely accepted. Both, however, beg the crucial question of *how* individuals are most effectively helped. It is precisely this issue which is the main subject of this chapter and the next. The second type of argument is that 'without national insurance the poor could not afford adequate cover'. The weakness of this position was discussed in Chapter 4, Section 7.2. If there are no technical problems with private insurance, the market can supply it efficiently. In such cases, distributive aims are generally best achieved through income transfers.

A third argument is that 'it is immoral for insurance companies to profit from people's misfortunes'. This is tenable as a value judgement. But it has been argued (Chapter 4, Section 7.2) that the question of public-versus-private production and allocation is less a moral issue than a technical one. Hence insurance against income loss should be publicly provided if that is more efficient and/or just; but, where private insurance is more efficient, equity aims can generally be achieved through income transfers. We do not, after all, say that food should be publicly provided because it is immoral for food manufacturers to exploit the fact that without it people would starve.

1.2. Institutions

National insurance refers to benefits payable to people with the necessary contributions record; in economic terms it is an insurance scheme against income loss due to events such as unemployment, ill health, or old age. The development of the Beveridge system after 1948 was discussed in Chapter 2, Section 6.1, and contribution arrangements in Chapter 7, Section 2.1. This section summarizes current benefit institutions very briefly (for detailed discussion, see Tolley 1996 and the Further Reading). Table 8.1 shows the level of some of the major benefits.

UNEMPLOYMENT. In 1996 unemployment benefit and means-tested income support for the unemployed were replaced by *jobseeker's allowance* paid at a flat rate (£49.15 in 1997/8 for a single person aged 25 or over) to people who are capable of work, available for work, and actively seeking work. Benefit is paid on the basis of *either* a contributions record *or* a means test—that is, the benefit cuts across the traditional divide between contributory and non-contributory benefits. The contributory benefit is payable for a maximum of six months.

Cash benefits

Table 8.1. **Main National Insurance benefit rates, 1997/8**

Type of benefit	Weekly benefit
Jobseeker's allowance (contributions based)	
Person age 16–17	£29.60[a]
Person aged 18–24	£38.90[a]
Person aged 25 or over	£49.15[a]
Married couple (under pension age)	£69.30[a]
Statutory sick pay	
Standard rate	£55.70[a]
Maternity benefits	
Statutory maternity pay	
First 6 weeks	90% of earnings
Thereafter	£55.70[a]
Incapacity benefit (under state pension age)	
Short term: lower rate	£47.10[a]
Short term: higher rate	£55.70[a]
Long term, basic rate	£62.45[a]
Disability benefits	
Disability living allowance	
Care component	£13.15–£49.50
Mobility component	£13.15–£34.60
Disability working allowance	
Single person	£57.85
Couple or lone parents	£77.15
Industrial injuries benefit	
Disablement pension (aged over 18, 100% rate)	£101.10[a]
Retirement pension	
Basic state retirement pension	
Single person	£62.45[a]
Married couple	£99.80[a]
State earnings-related pension	earnings-related
Non-contributory retirement pension	
Single person	£37.35[a]
Married woman	£22.35[a]
Widow's pension	
Widow's payment (lump sum)	£1,000.00
Widowed mother's allowance	£62.45[a]
Widow's pension	£62.45[a]
Miscellaneous benefits	
Guardian's allowance (in addition to child benefit)	£9.90–£11.20

[a] Benefit subject to income tax.

HEALTH-RELATED ABSENCE FROM WORK. Sickness benefit, introduced in the first wave of post-war institutions, has been replaced by a range of benefits.

Statutory sick pay is administered by employers. Benefit, which depends on a contributions record and is taxable, is paid at a weekly rate (in 1997/8) of £55.70. Various groups are excluded, *inter alia* those below the lower earnings limit, the self-employed, and people over pensionable age. In addition, benefit is not payable in respect of the first three days of absence. A medical certificate is required only where sickness lasts more than seven days. Someone who is still unwell after twenty-eight weeks is eligible for incapacity benefit, discussed shortly.

Statutory maternity pay is directly analogous. Benefit, which is taxable, is paid by employers on the basis of a contributions test for up to eighteen weeks, for the first six weeks at 90 per cent of the person's average weekly earnings, and thereafter at a flat rate.

Both statutory sickness payments and statutory maternity payments are made by employers, who deduct outgoings from their monthly national-insurance contribution receipts. The advantage of this approach is the administrative ease of subjecting benefit to tax and national-insurance contributions. Both benefits, however, continue to be paid from the National Insurance Fund. Thus both are publicly funded, with administration hived off to employers.

Incapacity benefit has three components. Short-term incapacity benefit is paid at the lower rate for up to twenty-eight weeks to people (e.g. self-employed or unemployed) who cannot claim statutory sick pay. Someone whose health problems persist beyond twenty-eight weeks is eligible for short-term incapacity benefit at the higher rate. A person who is still ill after a year receives long-term incapacity benefit (£62.45 per week in 1997/8). Eligibility for the first twenty-eight weeks is assessed on the basis of an 'own-occupation' test—that is, an assessment by an Adjudication Officer of whether the person is incapable of carrying out his normal job. After twenty-eight weeks, the 'all-work' test is normally applied—that is, whether the person is capable of carrying out other, less demanding, work.

Severe disablement allowance is a tax-free benefit for someone who has not been able to work for at least twenty-eight consecutive weeks because of ill health, whose contributions record does not entitle him to incapacity benefit.

COPING WITH DISABILITY. Several benefits assist with the extra costs of living independently, and for that reason are often paid irrespective of a person's income or contributions record.

Disability living allowance is a tax-free benefit, normally payable without a contributions test or an income test. The benefit has two components: the care component, payable at one of three weekly rates, is awarded to people who are physically or mentally disabled to the point where they need help caring for themselves; the mobility component offers assistance to individuals who are unable or virtually unable to walk. The benefit is normally awarded only to people under 65. Eligible individuals can receive either or both components.

Attendance allowance is the analogue to disability living allowance for people whose need for help with personal care because of illness or disability starts when they are 65 or over. The benefit is tax free and awarded without a contributions test.

Disability working allowance is a tax-free benefit awarded on the basis of an income test, in some ways analogous to family credit (see Chapter 10, Section 1). It is awarded to someone whose income is below a specified limit, whose disability (physical or mental) puts him at a disadvantage in finding a job or restricts his earning potential, and who is working for at least sixteen hours a week.

Cash benefits

Industrial injuries disablement benefit. Someone who is disabled because of an accident at work or industrial disease is eligible for industrial injuries disablement benefit, which is tax free, and payable for the entire duration, temporary or permanent, of any loss of faculty, whether or not the person is unable to work. Benefit is payable when statutory sick pay/sickness benefit ceases, or from three days after the accident if there is no incapacity for work. Various additional payments can be made where injury is exceptionally severe (see Tolley 1996: ch. 16).

CARING FOR OTHERS. A range of benefits is available at least partially to compensate people who care for others.

Invalid care allowance is a taxable benefit for someone of working age who is caring for a severely disabled person (i.e. someone who is receiving one of the major health-related benefits).

Guardian's allowance (£11.20 per week in 1997/8) is paid for each child in addition to child benefit. The benefit is paid where the parents of a child are dead (or, in certain circumstances, where only one parent is dead), to anyone who looks after a child as part of his or her family.

Increases for dependants. The level of many of these benefits may be increased if the beneficiary has dependants (adult or child) whom he or she supports. In the latter case, child benefit is normally payable in addition.

Benefit levels are reviewed regularly. Most benefits are uprated according to a statutory formula; some are increased on an ad hoc basis; most are increased annually. Total spending in 1997/8 was £97 billion (Table 7.5). Sickness and disability benefits, together with retirement and widows' pensions, make up nearly 96 per cent of direct national-insurance disbursements.

2. **Theoretical arguments for state intervention**

2.1. Efficiency 1: Regulation

Are efficiency and social justice assisted by state involvement in insurance markets in the ways just described? In particular, would individuals in a private market buy the *socially* efficient quantity of insurance against income loss? This breaks down into three separate questions: (*a*) why do people insure at all; (*b*) why does the state make membership of national insurance compulsory; (*c*) why does the state provide such insurance itself?

The first question was answered in Chapter 5—a rational risk-averse individual will insure voluntarily so long as the value of certainty exceeds the net cost of insurance. Why, secondly, is membership of national insurance compulsory? The standard argument for voluntarism is that it is efficient for an individual to make her own decision so long as she bears fully the costs of so doing. If I do not insure my Picasso, society regards this as my prerogative. Similarly, it might be argued that I should be free not to insure against income loss because of unemployment or ill health. If I then lose my job and starve that is my fault.

The flaw in the voluntarism argument in this case is that it overlooks the external costs which non-insurance can impose on others. Suppose someone chooses not to insure, and then loses his job. If society bails him out by paying a non-contributory benefit, the external cost falls upon the taxpayer. Alternatively, if he is given no help, he may starve, which imposes costs on others in a variety of ways. First, non-insurance may bring about not only his own starvation, but also that of his dependants. There are also broader costs, including any resulting increase in crime, and the financial costs of disposing of his body, or the health hazards if it were left where it fell. Additionally, though more arguably, it is possible to specify a psychic externality, where people do not like the idea of a society which allows people to starve. If so, the individual's death from starvation imposes external costs by reducing the utility of others directly.[1]

Where an activity causes an external cost, one form of intervention is a Pigovian tax.[2] Here, however, the aim is not marginally to influence consumption decisions through marginal price changes, but to prevent non-insurance. Making insurance compulsory (i.e. regulation) is likely to be a more effective way of achieving this.

In sum, the major efficiency argument for compulsory membership is that uninsured losses due to unemployment, illness, or industrial injury may impose costs on others, including dependants such as spouses and children. There is an analogy with automobile insurance, which is also compulsory in most countries. But, quite correctly on efficiency grounds, compulsion is limited to insurance to cover the damage I might inflict on *others*. I can choose whether to take out insurance to cover damage to my *own* car or person.

2.2. Efficiency 2: Public provision

To continue the analogy, the state makes car insurance compulsory, but does not supply insurance itself. Why, then, does it provide national insurance? This question brings us back to the discussion in Chapter 5, Section 4.1, of the circumstances in which private-insurance markets are efficient. The end of this section considers the demand conditions. However, it is useful to look first at the supply conditions: the relevant probability must be independent across individuals, less than one, known or estimable, known equally to all parties (i.e. no adverse selection), and exogenous (i.e. no moral

---

[1] This psychic cost would not arise if members of society had different utility functions—another manifestation of the impossibility of a Paretian liberal (see Chapter 3, Section 3.1).

[2] See, in ascending order of completeness, the Glossary, the Appendix to Chapter 4, para. 15, and/or Chapter 4, Section 3.2.

hazard). Efficiency arguments about the appropriateness of public provision hinge on whether these five assumptions hold for the risks covered by national insurance.

UNEMPLOYMENT INSURANCE. We need to consider separately each of the assumptions discussed in Chapter 5, Section 3.

1. Whether individual probabilities of becoming or remaining unemployed are independent is a matter of high controversy. Simple Keynesian theory suggests that unemployment reduces demand and contributes to further unemployment, thus making unemployment a common risk. Those who believe in a natural rate of unemployment deny this conclusion except in the short run. Individual probabilities may be partly correlated, though this problem alone is unlikely to make private insurance impossible.

2. The overall probability of being unemployed is less than one, though for some sectors of the labour force, such as unskilled young people, it may be too high for private insurance to be viable. Individuals returning to the labour force after a long break in employment, and unemployed school-leavers cause additional problems.

3. The average probability of being unemployed is well known—it is simply the aggregate unemployment rate. There is also considerable knowledge of the probability of unemployment for subgroups of the labour force.

4. Adverse selection: a private insurance company could in principle ask about an applicant's previous employment record. This is not a complete solution, however: the process is costly; verification is not always possible; and not everyone has a past employment record.

5. Much the greatest problem with private unemployment insurance is moral hazard. The insured individual may be able to influence, first, the probability of *entering* unemployment by bringing about his own redundancy ('I'll work for you this week for nothing if you'll then make me redundant'). Secondly, and of greater importance, he can influence the probability of *leaving* unemployment—that is, the duration of unemployment.

A key question is how costly (financial and psychic) it is for an individual to remain unemployed. Since psychic costs are unobservable, it is not possible to distinguish two cases:

- The psychic cost to the individual is high (case 1 in Chapter 5, Section 3.2), and unemployment is caused by a lack of jobs.
- The cost is low (case 3), and the individual remains unemployed to some extent by choice.

The first is an insurable risk; the second is not—the insurer is imperfectly informed and, as discussed shortly, the problem is worse for unemployment than for most other risks.

As we shall see (Section 3.1), the relationship between the level of benefits and the level and duration of unemployment is hotly disputed. It should be noted, however, that to say that individuals with insurance devote more time to job search is not *necessarily* to imply inefficiency. In principle, the efficient duration of unemployment for the *i*th individual, x_i, is that period which he would rationally choose if he had to finance his unemployment from accumulated savings or by borrowing in a perfect capital market. Inefficiency arises when an individual chooses to be unemployed for longer than x_i because insurance has reduced the marginal cost to him of so doing. It was for this reason that Beveridge insisted on full employment, because 'the only satisfactory test of unemployment is an offer of work' (Beveridge Report 1942: 163).

We saw in Chapter 5, Section 3.1 that an actuarial premium is calculated as

$$\pi_i = (1 + \alpha)p_i L \tag{8.1}$$

where p_i is the probability of the *i*th individual becoming or remaining unemployed, L is the unemployment benefit, and $(1 + \alpha)$ is the loading to cover the insurance company's administrative costs and normal profit. Moral hazard of the sort described above means that p_i can be manipulated by the insured individual, making it impossible for the insurance company to calculate a premium.

The theory is borne out by empirical evidence. There are no private policies I can buy to top up the (low, flat-rate) UK state unemployment benefit (the analogue for sick pay appears regularly in my junk mail). Nor, for such white-collar schemes, is it possible to argue that private schemes have been driven out by the existence of a state scheme. It is true that unemployment benefit in Sweden is organized by trade unions (Bjorklund and Holmlund 1989); but the system (*a*) is heavily regulated, and is buttressed (*b*) by a complementary public insurance scheme and (*c*) by income-tested unemployment assistance.

A second source of support for the impossibility of *general* private unemployment insurance arises from an attempt by Beenstock and Brasse (1986) to show the opposite. They discuss mortgage protection policies, offered *inter alia* in the UK and the USA, which make mortgage repayments during unemployment. Such policies have three salient characteristics. They are open, by and large, only to the best risks: owner-occupiers tend to be in more secure jobs, and so have a lower-than-average probability of *entering* unemployment; they are also more mobile (since owner-occupiers are generally less affected than renters by housing market rigidities), increasing the probability of *leaving* unemployment. Secondly, such policies can typically be started only at the time the mortgage is taken out, on the grounds that few people will seek to buy a house if they know their job is at risk; this reduces adverse selection. Thirdly, owner-occupiers tend to have higher-than-average earnings, and so face lower replacement rates, thus minimizing moral hazard. Mortgage protection policies are therefore limited to the best risks, impose restrictions which minimize adverse selection, and sidestep the worst problems of moral hazard. Such policies are genuinely private insurance, but they offer no basis whatever on which to generalize. A careful study by Burchardt and Hills (1997: ch. 4) reaches the same conclusion.

Thus unemployment is not a risk which accords well with the model of actuarial insurance. First, as discussed in Chapter 5, Section 4.2 (see also Atkinson 1995*a*: ch. 11),

Cash benefits

the risk itself is a social construct arising out of the nature of employment in industrial labour markets. Secondly, the probability is to some extent endogenous to the individual. Thus it is not surprising that earlier schemes under the 1911 National Insurance Act and during the 1920s ran into trouble (Chapter 2, Sections 2.2 and 3.2). The theoretical conclusion, supported by empirical evidence, is twofold:

- If income support is to exist for the unemployed, it will have to be publicly provided. This outcome can be supported on *efficiency* grounds because of information problems in insurance markets, of which problems no mention is made in Hayek's (1960: ch. 19) attack on publicly provided benefits. The libertarian predilection for private markets and voluntarism in this instance is untenable.
- The resulting institutions do not look actuarial. The argument in Chapter 5, Section 4.2, suggests that no other result is possible.

SICK-PAY INSURANCE. Asking the same questions about sick-pay insurance,[3] the individual probabilities of absence from work because of ill health are unrelated, except during a major epidemic (i.e. the likelihood of my missing work for health reasons is independent of your state of health). Except for the chronically ill, the probability of absence is less than one, and can be estimated. There is no major problem of adverse selection, since a private insurance company can ask about an applicant's previous health and absenteeism. Nor is there a serious problem of moral hazard. The probability of missing work is broadly exogenous, since making oneself genuinely ill is costly, and pretended illness can, at least up to a point, be policed by requiring claimants to provide a doctor's certificate.

Thus there is no substantial technical difficulty with private sick-pay insurance, and such institutions exist in many countries. The only efficiency justification for public provision is through a two-step argument:

1. There are economies of scale to be derived from running unemployment and sick-pay insurance jointly, not least because it is administratively cheaper to collect both contributions simultaneously.
2. Unemployment benefits must be publicly provided for technical reasons.

Given 2, it follows from 1 that administrative savings arise from running a public sick-pay scheme alongside unemployment insurance. This argument, though valid, is not overriding.

THE SMALLER NATIONAL-INSURANCE BENEFITS. Voluntary maternity insurance may face problems of adverse selection (i.e. only women intending to become pregnant would insure), making private supply impossible. However, as we saw in Chapter 5, Section 4.1, compulsion can sidestep the problem. Thus, if maternity insurance is compulsory, it would not necessarily have to be publicly provided.

---

[3] Discussion here is concerned with income replacement during health-related absence from work, *not* with insurance against the cost of medical treatment, which is discussed in Chapter 12.

Similar arguments apply to the guardian's allowance, which is payable when one or both parents are dead, and also to increases for dependants more generally. What we are talking about here is a form of life insurance, with which the private market is well able to cope. If private insurance is feasible for the individual, it is also feasible for her dependants (e.g. we saw in Chapter 5, Section 2.3, how an annuity can cover a spouse).

In the case of industrial injury insurance, again, there is no strong efficiency argument for public provision. The probability of injury is independent across individuals, less than one, and can be estimated. Nor do serious problems arise with adverse selection or moral hazard (for instance, it would not generally pay an individual deliberately to injure himself). It is true that some occupations are riskier than others, but this simply means that private insurance would require higher premiums for riskier occupations.

In all these cases, there is an overwhelming case for compulsion but not for public provision. Counter-arguments to the latter position are that there might be administrative economies if all social benefits were organized together; and there might be administrative difficulties in enforcing compulsion if supply were private. The issue of public versus private pensions is deferred to Chapter 9, Section 3.1

DEMAND-SIDE CONDITIONS. Alongside these supply-side considerations, it is necessary also to consider the demand side. Here, the central question is whether purchasers of insurance against income loss due to unemployment, ill health, or old age are well informed. With short-term policies (i.e. this year's premium pays for this year's potential benefit), individuals can acquire information about different policies, as currently with car insurance, perhaps with the advice of an insurance broker. There is a case for regulation of standards, but not for public provision. As discussed in Chapter 5, Section 4.1, the situation may be different for complex long-run policies, for example pensions or long-term care in old age (Burchardt and Hills, 1997). Where information problems are serious, the benefits from competition are diminished and may largely disappear.

Two other arguments have been put forward at various times to explain or justify public provision of national insurance. Marxists argue (Chapter 3, Section 5.3) that such institutions are a form of social control, whose main aim is to prevent social unrest. This argument may *explain* the existence of national insurance, but it does not necessarily *justify* it. In particular, it does not establish why we have publicly organized social insurance rather than, say, non-contributory benefits. It also used to be argued, along Keynesian lines, that national insurance generally, and unemployment benefit in particular, is a built-in stabilizer. But asserting that this might be a consequence (albeit a beneficial one), again, does not necessarily *justify* national insurance.

2.3. Social justice

What are the equity arguments for publicly provided insurance? Horizontal equity is concerned with such goals as minimum standards for certain commodities and/or equal access to them. It was argued in Chapter 4, Section 4.3, that these occur automatically where the assumptions of perfect information and equal power hold. Thus the demand-side conditions, just discussed in the context of efficiency, are also relevant here. Where consumers are well informed there is no case for intervention on horizontal equity grounds; where they are badly informed, the case for publicly organized insurance can be argued on both efficiency and equity grounds.

Similar arguments apply to the equal-power assumption. Where insurance markets are competitive, what matters is not whether individuals have more or less power, but whether they are able to pay an actuarial premium. In the case of car insurance, premiums are generally related to age and previous driving record, but there is no evidence of a systematic relationship between premiums and social class. Similarly, there is no reason to expect substantial discrimination with unemployment and sick-pay insurance. This argument is less strong, however, with complex, long-term policies, for which it can be argued that more articulate people will be better placed to ask assertive questions about the degree of cover offered.

Vertical equity concerns redistribution from rich to poor. The standard argument, that 'the state must provide insurance, because otherwise the poor would not be able to afford adequate cover' is false (Section 1.1). A somewhat more subtle variant is that actuarial insurance cannot redistribute from rich to poor, only from 'lucky' to 'unlucky', and therefore insurance should be publicly provided to redistribute income. Again, the key argument in Chapter 4, Section 7.2, suggests that, without efficiency reasons for provision, distributive goals should be pursued through income transfers except, possibly, where there are consumption externalities (Chapter 4, Section 4.2). In the presence of consumption externalities, the rich may want the poor to consume insurance, and so impose it as a merit good; and the poor may feel less stigmatized by receiving 'insurance benefit' than 'welfare'. Both reasons offer an explanation (though not necessarily a justification) of public provision for reasons of vertical equity.

Finally, it can be argued (Chapters 4, Section 7.2, and Chapter 5, Section 4.1) that, if there are *efficiency* grounds for making membership of national insurance compulsory, it is not inappropriate to finance the scheme so as to redistribute from rich to poor. We return to this issue in the next section.

3. **Assessment of the national insurance system**

3.1. Efficiency and incentives

ARGUMENTS OF PRINCIPLE

This part of the chapter briefly assesses the UK system in the light of earlier theoretical argument (for fuller discussion of the UK, the USA, and other countries, see the Further Reading). The major issues are empirical, but we start with a number of issues of principle: should national insurance be national (i.e. publicly provided); does the state provide the optimal quantity of insurance; and are the resulting institutions insurance?

SHOULD IT BE NATIONAL? The efficiency arguments rest on externalities, justifying compulsion, and technical (mainly information) failures on the supply side of the insurance market and, for longer-term policies, also on the demand side, justifying provision of the major benefits, though with a somewhat weaker argument for sick pay than for the other schemes. If we ignore consumption externalities, the main equity arguments are (a) that the poor may feel less stigmatized by insurance, and (b) that, if insurance is publicly provided for efficiency reasons, it can then be used as a redistributive device. These arguments are compelling. Some areas could, indeed, be returned to the private sector, as considered for short-term sick pay (Prest 1983). However, unemployment is an uninsurable risk and, as argued in Chapter 9, so is unanticipated inflation, with major efficiency implications for public involvement with pensions. Since spending on elderly people and unemployed people makes up over half of all income transfers (UK DSS 1997e: table 5), if we ask 'Should national insurance be national?' the short answer is yes.

DOES THE STATE PROVIDE THE OPTIMUM QUANTITY OF INSURANCE? Where insurance is compulsory and publicly provided, inefficiency arises if the state, through misperception of individual preferences, constructs a larger or smaller than optimal scheme. In a first-best world, the ith individual (assumed rational and risk-averse) will choose to insure against a loss L_i for which she pays the actuarial premium shown in equation (8.1). All N individuals make this utility-maximizing decision, resulting in a vector of optimal insurance purchases

$$(L_1, L_2, \ldots, L_N). \tag{8.2}$$

The L_i vary across individuals depending *inter alia* on their risk aversion.

Will national insurance offer these optimal quantities? The answer must be no, because the insurance offered is a sort of average which does not cater for differences in individual tastes. However, national insurance is less inefficient than the free market outcome, not least because risks like unemployment are uninsurable; and individuals can buy additional insurance against risks such as sickness and disability.

A separate issue is whether there are missing benefits. The case of long-term residential care insurance is discussed in Chapter 9, Section 3.1.

IS IT INSURANCE? On the face of it, national insurance does not look much like insurance, for at least four reasons.

1. Contributions are not related to individual risk. In the scheme envisaged by Beveridge, contributions were geared to the *average* risk, as shown in equation (5.16), and adverse selection avoided by making membership compulsory. This principle was violated because retirement pensions from 1946 onwards were not actuarial (see Chapter 9); because from 1975 contributions by the employed (Class 1) and self-employed (Class 4) were related not to average risk but to the contributor's income; and

because of the existence of credits for the unemployed, and for parents who stay at home to look after young children or a disabled person.

2. Entitlement to benefit does not depend only on the occurrence of the insured event. Benefits (but not contributions) are higher where the contributor has dependants; contributions and benefits taken together are redistributive from rich to poor; and until 1989 pensions in the first five years after normal retirement age were subject to an earnings test (i.e. the pension was rapidly withdrawn for individuals with more than small earnings). In other countries, additional restrictions may be imposed—for example, 'workfare' in various American states requires recipients of unemployment and related benefits to undertake work or training.

3. The scheme is not financed on actuarial lines. As discussed in Chapter 9, state pensions, unlike most private schemes, generally make no provision for future liabilities.

4. The contract is not fully specified, in that the risks covered can change over time. Some people view this as a disadvantage, since the state can renege on past promises. On the other hand, it is an advantage because (as discussed in Chapter 5, Section 4.2) it enables the state to respond to unforeseen risks. Social insurance, unlike private insurance, thus offers protection not only against risk but also against uncertainty.

The conclusion is that national insurance is insurance in the sense that it offers protection against risk (see Gruber 1997), but not insurance in which premiums bear an actuarial relationship to individual risk. In the sense discussed in Chapter 5, Section 4.2, the mechanism is social insurance rather than actuarial insurance. For the reasons given in Section 2.2, no other result is possible.

It is important to be clear that social insurance does not *have* to be redistributive from rich to poor. Its precise form will depend on the objectives of policy. It is perfectly possible to have social-insurance arrangements which closely mimic actuarial arrangements (e.g. the original Beveridge scheme, or a scheme in which both contributions and benefits are strictly proportional to individual earnings). Over the years there has been much confusion about the purposes of social insurance. There are good reasons for thinking of it both as a technical instrument for dealing with market failure *and* as a redistributive device. But the two cases are argued on very different grounds and should be carefully distinguished.

INCENTIVE ISSUES

In discussing the incentive effects of social insurance two questions dominate: is the system itself a contributory cause of unemployment; and does it reduce the rate of saving and capital accumulation (the latter issue being particularly relevant in the case of pensions)?

ARE UNEMPLOYMENT BENEFITS A CONTRIBUTORY CAUSE OF UNEMPLOYMENT? The discussion of moral hazard in Section 2.2 has already hinted at this issue. With a high replacement rate (i.e. the ratio of income when unemployed to post-tax-and-transfer income in work) the low paid may be little worse off (and in the short run perhaps better off) out of work. It is estimated (UK DSS 1997*e*: fig. 32) that about 510,000 workers face replacement rates of 70 per cent and over, creating an 'unemployment trap' whereby an unemployed person has little financial incentive to seek work (this should be contrasted with the 'poverty trap' (Chapter 10, Section 3.2), under which an individual doing at least some work is given no incentive to work longer hours).

The logic of the disincentive argument is appealingly straightforward. Simple theory suggests that higher replacement rates tend to reduce work effort which is financially motivated, an argument which informed policy throughout the 1980s and later. 'When increases in benefits narrow the gap between in-work and out-of-work incomes, work becomes less attractive; the effect is to encourage dependency' (UK DSS 1997: 52).

The quantitative literature is large, complex, and controversial (see Atkinson 1987*a* for a survey). Early studies used aggregate time-series data (Maki and Spindler 1975 for the UK; Grubel and Maki 1976 for the USA), and found that benefits exerted a substantial upward effect on the level of unemployment. The advantage of the time-series approach is its apparent ability to analyse the effects of a policy change. But in practice it is difficult to separate these effects from other influences on unemployment, not least because aggregate data necessitate such devices as representative individuals, replacement rates based on average benefit levels and average tax rates, and so on, which obscure most of the variation between individuals.

Cross-section data have the great advantage of being a much richer source of information on the large differences between individuals, making it possible to estimate the determinants of unemployment with greater precision than the aggregate data allow. The general conclusion of the cross-section studies (see the Further Reading) is that, though the duration of unemployment may be slightly longer at higher replacement rates, the magnitude of the effect is not large.

This consensus, however, conceals a rich collection of difficulties, both of principle and of measurement. The major methodological problem with cross-section analysis is its attempt to extrapolate from individual behaviour to the aggregate economy, a procedure which is valid only where individual responses are not interdependent. Suppose that as someone with a high replacement rate I am choosy about accepting a new job. If everyone else's behaviour is independent of mine, this will increase unemployment. But, if behaviour is interdependent, my choosiness simply means that someone else will take the job I have rejected. In this case the replacement rate determines *who* is unemployed, but not total unemployment. Cross-section analysis does not enable us to distinguish the two cases.

The treatment of benefits also raises substantial problems. Institutional complexities, in particular the interaction of the tax and benefit systems, make it difficult to estimate benefits accurately. One approach is to estimate the individual's potential entitlement; the difficulty here is that the sample may not contain sufficient information (e.g. past contribution records) to make this procedure accurate. Alternatively, it is possible to use actual benefit receipts. This avoids complexity, but causes statistical difficulties where unobserved individual characteristics influence *both* the level of benefit *and* the probability

Cash benefits

of accepting a particular job offer; for example, if I am lazy (unobserved) I may have a poor employment record and consequently receive less benefit *and* be less keen to accept a new job. In view of these difficulties it is not surprising that the precision of the estimates (as measured, for instance, by the statistical significance of estimated coefficients) is often low even by cross-section standards.

A second wave of work (Atkinson and Micklewright 1991; Layard *et al.* 1991; Atkinson 1995*a*: ch. 10) emphasizes cross-country data, making it possible to include institutional differences as explanations of why unemployment was more persistent over the 1980s in most European countries than in the USA and Japan. Particular emphasis is placed on three aspects of the labour market. First are aspects of the benefit structure additional to the replacement rate, such as the maximum duration of benefit, qualification conditions for benefit, the proportion of the unemployed receiving benefit, and the stringency with which the 'actively-seeking-work' condition is enforced. Secondly there are active labour-market policies, such as placement and counselling services, training and job creation.[4] Thirdly there is the structure of the labour market, including the power of trade unions and the extent of centralized wage-bargaining. The conclusion is that, though the replacement rate has an effect, labour supply is influenced more by other aspects of the benefit structure, in particular the maximum duration for which benefit can be received.

The general conclusion, which applies equally to cross-section and time-series studies, is that they lack robustness with respect to the definition of variables, the choice of sample and time period, and the specification of the estimated equation. The simplicity of the original argument disappears the deeper one digs—and the more we learn, the greater the complications of which we are made aware. In short, the hypothesis that unemployment benefits exert a substantial upward effect on the level of unemployment receives little empirical support.

Policy, however, continues to be based on the assumption that unemployment benefits have significant incentive effects. Atkinson and Micklewright (1989) list thirty-eight changes during the 1980s to UK benefits for the unemployed, the great bulk of them making benefits less generous. As Atkinson (1995*a*: 179–80) later summarized the period from 1979 onwards:

Insurance benefits [have] been eroded by . . . the tightening of the contribution conditions [and] the extension of the disqualification period . . . their value has been reduced by the taxation of benefits: and the abandonment of statutory indexation has made the position of recipients insecure. These measures add up to a substantial reduction in the amount and extent of National Insurance benefit paid to the unemployed.

DISABILITY BENEFITS AND LABOUR SUPPLY. Spending on health-related cash benefits rose sharply, by 1996/7, absorbing 18 per cent of total benefit spending (Table 7.5). To the extent that this is a manifestion of more generous benefits, it can be argued that disability benefits

---

[4] See Flanagan (1987) for an account of Swedish policy and Fretwell and Jackman (1994) for discussion of Western experience and its application to Central and Eastern Europe.

reduce labour supply. It is, however, possible to argue the reverse: recipients of disability benefit rose as unemployment increased; taken literally, this means that disability benefit is not a *cause* of unemployment, but a *consequence*. Both theories are almost certainly too simple (see Disney and Webb 1991); the problem of causation remains unsolved.

OTHER INCENTIVE EFFECTS. Pensions and labour supply may also be related if pensions induce early retirement. It is also argued that publicly provided pensions financed out of tax revenues may reduce savings, capital accumulation, and economic growth. Both sets of issues are discussed in Chapter 9, Section 5 (see also the Further Reading to Chapter 9).

3.2. Equity issues

HORIZONTAL EQUITY. It can be argued that national insurance gives everyone equal access to income support. One of the major themes of the Beveridge Report was that national insurance should be comprehensive, unified, and compulsory. This aim has been achieved in that there is no evidence of discrimination in the payment of benefits, nor of substantial maladministration.

However, not all groups receive equal coverage, despite Beveridge's intention to the contrary. Fifty years ago most single-parent families resulted from widowhood, which therefore received extensive coverage, especially where there were young children. It is argued that this group (which today comprises only one in six single-parent families in the UK) is treated generously relative to families separated by other causes, such as divorce. The difficulty (and the prominence of the latter group among the poor) arises largely because benefits are conditioned on cause (e.g. widowhood) rather than outcome (i.e. being a single parent).

Disability benefits have also been criticized. Again, individuals facing similar problems do not necessarily receive similar benefits. Under plausible assumptions a single man could in the past receive twice as much if 100 per cent disabled in an industrial accident as with identical disabilities from a non-industrial cause (Hemming 1984: 119). The introduction of incapacity benefit has gone some way to addressing the worst problems.

There is also criticism that the relative treatment of men and women can be inequitable: some benefits of particular relevance to women (e.g. the universal maternity grant) have been withdrawn, others (child benefit, one-parent benefit, free school meals, and the state earnings-related pension) have become less generous; and childcare costs cannot be offset against earnings for income support (see Oppenheim and Harker 1996: ch. 5, and the Further Reading, and, for institutional detail, Tolley 1996).

VERTICAL EQUITY. How redistributive is national insurance? The major difficulties include conceptual problems (Chapter 7, Section 4) and many of the measurement problems discussed in Chapter 6. A definitive answer requires general equilibrium analysis of the joint incidence of contributions and benefits. No such work exists, so we must be content with more rough-and-ready answers. National-insurance contributions for most people rise disproportionately with income for all except the highest earners (Table 7.3). The state pension is redistributive from rich to poor (Chapter 9, Section 5.2). Unemployment compensation is also redistributive, since people with lower incomes pay smaller contributions, generally for fewer weeks, and receive benefit more frequently than someone with a higher income. The various incapacity benefits are redistributive to the extent that claims are more common among the lower paid. The combined effect of all cash benefits in 1995/6 was to reduce the Gini coefficient by about 16 per cent (UK Office for National Statistics 1997: table C).

Another aspect is whether benefits are pitched at the right level. This raises two further questions. First, and largely an efficiency matter, is whether the level of benefit is that which would have been chosen voluntarily by a hypothetically well-informed, rational individual. This is the issue, discussed earlier, of whether national insurance provides the optimal quantity of insurance. Secondly, are the insurance benefits high enough to keep people out of poverty? If we use the level of income support as the yardstick of poverty, it can be argued that the main national-insurance benefits, which are generally below the income-support level, are too low. We return to the subject in Chapter 10, Section 3.1.

FURTHER READING

A compendious and up-to-date account of institutions (including legal sources) is published annually by Tolley (1996). For institutions worldwide, see US Department of Health and Human Services (1997) (also available at http://www.ssa.gov/statistics/ssptw97.html).

On the theory of insurance, see the Further Reading at the end of Chapter 5. The application to social insurance is discussed by Stiglitz (1988: ch. 13). Barr (1992) applies the arguments in this chapter in a survey of ten OECD countries.

On policy in the UK, see Hills (1997), Atkinson (1995a: chs. 9, 10, 11), and Martin Evans (1998), and, for contrasting perspectives, Commission on Social Justice (1994: 221–45) and Brittan (1995: ch. 11). Baldwin and Falkingham (1994) discuss the ways in which the original Beveridge model no longer conforms with social conditions. Burchardt and Hills (1997) analyse private mortgage protection insurance and insurance covering long-term residential care. On policy in the USA, see Burtless (1987), Card and Freeman (1993), and Myles (1996); in Scandinavia, Stephens (1996); and in Australia and New Zealand, Castles (1996). On problems and policies in the reforming former Communist countries, see Barr (1994b) and World Bank (1996: ch. 4).

On the economics of labour supply, see Ehrenberg and Smith (1994: ch. 6) and Elliott (1990: chs. 2, 3) for textbook discussion, and, for surveys, Ashenfelter and Layard (1986), Heckman (1993), and Bean (1994). For broader discussion of unemployment, see Layard *et al.* (1991); see also Gordon (1997), Stiglitz (1997), and other papers in the symposium in the same issue of the *Journal of Economic Perspectives*.

Taxation and labour supply are discussed by Stiglitz (1988: ch. 19) and, more formally, by Atkinson and Stiglitz (1980: lecture 2); for surveys, see Blundell (1992, 1995).

Incentive issues more broadly are surveyed by Atkinson (1987*a*), Atkinson and Micklewright (1991), Layard *et al.* (1991: ch. 5), and Atkinson and Mogenson (1993). For cogent discussion of the unemployment and poverty traps, see Parker (1995). For a useful *tour d'horizon*, see the American Economic Association symposium papers by Gramlich (1989), Kotlikoff (1989*a*), and Summers (1989). Disney and Webb (1991) discuss the sharp rise in recipients of disability benefit. See the Further Reading to Chapter 9 for references on the incentive effects of pensions.

For a (somewhat depressing) account of the difficulties of reforming the system even in a relatively minor way, see Prest (1983).

On the distributional impact of national insurance, see Martin Evans (1998) and the Further Reading at the end of Chapter 6, and, for discussion of gender aspects, Sainsbury (1994), Oppenheim and Harker (1996: ch. 5), Anne Phillips (1997), and Sutherland (1997).

CHAPTER 9

Contributory benefits 2:
Retirement pensions

'You are old, Father William,' the young man said,
'And your pension has almost run out;
And yet you insist that funding is safe
It's no wonder you're all up the spout.'

'In my youth', Father William replied to his son,
'They told me my savings would grow;
But, now that I'm perfectly sure I have none,
I'd prefer you to Pay as I Go.'
(With apologies to Lewis Carroll)

1. Introduction and institutions

Pensions contribute to many of the objectives in Chapter 1, Section 2.2. Retirement pensions enable individuals to redistribute to themselves over the life cycle, and thus contribute to income smoothing. Invalidity and widows' pensions contribute to the insurance objective. Pensions also contribute to the relief of poverty, particularly long-term poverty, and may also contribute to vertical redistribution. Like other social-insurance benefits, they may also contribute to social solidarity. The relative terms on which men and women receive pensions (e.g. whether there is a common retirement age) raise important issues of horizontal equity.

The questions which arise broadly parallel those of Chapter 8. Section 2 discusses different methods of organizing pensions, and their pros and cons. The efficiency and equity arguments for state intervention, and the effects of different types of intervention, are analysed in Sections 3 and 4. National-insurance pensions and related benefits are assessed in Section 5.

THE 1975 SOCIAL SECURITY PENSIONS ACT (UK DHSS 1974) was one of the most important pieces of social-security legislation since the National Insurance Act 1946 (Chapter 2, Section 5), and, as subsequently amended, is the basis of the arrangements described here (for details, see Tolley 1996: ch. 20).

The contributions side was discussed in Chapter 7, Section 2.1. To qualify for a full pension, an individual must generally have contributed to the current (i.e. post-1975) scheme for at least twenty years, and to the current scheme or its predecessor (i.e. the 1948 scheme) for at least forty-four years (men) or forty years (women). Where this requirement is not met, pension is awarded on a sliding scale. *Home-responsibilities protection* ensures that years spent by a parent at home looking after children or a disabled dependant will not usually result in loss of pension. Thus a woman who drops out of the labour force for fifteen years to look after children has to work for only twenty-five years (i.e. 40−15) to qualify for a full pension.

On the benefits side, the major provisions of the 1975 Act may be summarized as follows, noting subsequent amendments, and in particular a number of important changes (motivated by cost containment) which are to be phased in for people retiring after 2000.

1. The weekly pension comprises the flat-rate *basic component* and the *earnings-related* component, also referred to as the state earnings-related pension scheme (SERPS).

2. The basic component for a single person is about one-fifth of national average earnings. The lower earnings limit (Chapter 7, Section 2.1) for national-insurance contributions is set at the level of the basic pension.[1]

3. For people retiring before 2000, the earnings-related component for someone with a full contributions record is calculated as 25 pence of pension per pound of pensionable earnings between the lower and upper earnings limits. The figure of 25 pence per pound will thereafter decline gradually to 20 per cent for people retiring in or after 2010.

4. The pension is based on the individual's best twenty years, thus improving pensions by omitting years in which earnings were low. For people retiring after 2000, the calculation will be based on the individual's entire contribution record.

5. The same pension formula applies to men and women. Pensionable age is 65 for men and 60 for women. An increase in women's pensionable age will be phased in from 2010, leading to a common pensionable age of 65 by 2020.[2]

6. For someone retiring before 2000, each year of contribution entitles him to earnings-related pension equal to 1.25 per cent of the excess of earnings (or the ceiling, whichever

---

[1] The actual calculations are done on an annual basis, but achieve the same effect as the (simpler) weekly description in the text.

[2] Under the reforms, the key date is 6 April 1950. For women born before that, pensionable age will continue to be 60. Pensionable age for a woman born on 6 May 1950 (i.e. one month after the key date) would be 60 years and one month, for a woman born of 6 June 1950, 60 years and two months, and so on. Thus for women born on or after 6 April 1955 pensionable age will be 65 (see Tolley 1996: app. 20A).

is the lower) over the lower earnings limit. Thus, someone with 20 contribution years receives an earnings-related pension of 25 per cent (i.e. 20×1.25 per cent) of the relevant earnings, in addition to the flat-rate pension. For someone retiring after 2010 (assuming for simplicity that forty years is a full contributions record), each year of contributions entitles him to an earnings-related pension of 0.5 per cent of the relevant earnings; thus someone who has contributed for forty years will receive an earnings-related pension of 20 per cent (i.e. 40×0.5 per cent) of the relevant earnings.

7. A man receives an increase in his pension if he is married unless his wife has a pension in her own right, in which case she receives the full pension to which she is entitled on the basis of her earnings. Where a couple has two contribution records, the surviving spouse receives the basic pension plus both earnings-related components, up to the maximum which could have been earned by a single person. After 2000, the surviving spouse will inherit only half of his or her partner's earnings-related pension.

8. From 1975 the basic component was uprated broadly in line with earnings. Since the mid-1980s (an important change), mandatory uprating has reflected only price increases. The earnings-related component is protected in two ways. First, the earnings on which the pension is calculated are revalued each year in line with the general movement of earnings, so that the earnings-related pension, when first awarded, reflects a person's *real* earnings record. Secondly, the earnings-related component, once in payment, is uprated each year in line with price increases.

9. The pensions of people who work beyond pensionable age are increased by 7.5 per cent (in real terms) for each year by which pension is deferred.

10. Membership of the flat-rate scheme is compulsory. It is possible to contract out of the earnings-related component by belonging to a private scheme—either an occupational pension or a personal pension. Since 1995 (another important change), approved occupational and personal pensions must offer *limited price indexation*—that is, must index pensions for annual rates of inflation up to 5 per cent. The central topic of pensions in the face of inflation emerges repeatedly in subsequent discussion.

Let us take a specific example of the scheme based on 1997 data. Suppose someone retires with a full contribution record, and with average earnings over his best twenty years of £300 per week. If he were single, he would receive a basic pension of £62.45 per week, plus one-quarter of the excess of his average earnings (£300) over the lower earnings limit (£62). His earnings-related pension would therefore be £59.50 per week and the total pension £121.95.

Many people receiving a national-insurance pension are also eligible for income support (Chapter 10, Section 1), including automatic entitlement to benefits like housing benefit. One of the main purposes of the 1975 scheme was to reduce the numbers receiving both retirement pension and means-tested social assistance. Despite improvement since 1975, the problem remains: nearly 14 per cent of pensioners in 1995–6 also received income support (UK DSS 1997: table 7).

WIDOWHOOD. Provision for widows (and in restricted circumstances widowers) takes three forms (see Tolley 1996: ch. 11). *Widowed mother's allowance*, subject to contribution conditions, is payable to a widow with at least one child. *Widow's pension* is payable to a woman who is 45 or over when widowed or when widowed mother's allowance ends. Widows who qualify for neither benefit receive *widows' payment*, a tax-free, lump-sum payment (£1,000 in 1997/8).

PRIVATE PENSION SCHEMES vary widely but are broadly of two sorts: *occupational schemes*, which are organized by employers and frequently offer pensions related to the worker's final salary, and *personal pensions* (see the Further Reading). Private pensions in industrialized countries share some key features. Almost all are *funded*.[3] They are *supplemental*, in that they replace only part of the state pension. They are *constrained* in two ways: individual choice, particularly under occupational schemes, is generally limited; and the conduct of pension companies is regulated to protect consumers. Virtually all private pension schemes are *subsidized* through tax expenditures.[4] Finally, though an increasing number of schemes offer *limited indexation*, virtually none offers complete protection against inflation.

The coverage of private pensions has grown substantially over the years. By 1991, half of all employees, including a growing number of women, belonged to an occupational scheme, 28 per cent had a personal pension, and 20 per cent belonged to the state earnings-related scheme (Dilnot *et al.* 1994: table 2.4). Employers can choose whether or not to offer occupational pensions in place of the state earnings-related scheme; and, where an occupational scheme exists, employees can choose whether to join or, instead, to have their own personal pension, either run by a financial institution or, even more individually, self-managed.

2. Methods of organizing pensions

THE ECONOMICS OF PENSION SCHEMES can be confusing, because writers easily become bemused by its *financial* aspects (i.e. analysis of insurance companies' portfolios of financial assets). I shall try to simplify matters by concentrating on the essential *economic* issues (i.e. the production and consumption of goods and services).

From an individual viewpoint, the economic function of pensions is to redistribute consumption over time. By contributing to a pension scheme, an individual consumes today less than she produces, so as to continue to consume when she has retired and is no longer producing. In principle, an individual can transfer consumption over time in two ways, and in *only* two ways: she can store current production; or she can acquire a claim to future production.

---

[3] i.e. pay benefits out of a previously accumulated fund, as explained in detail in Section 2.

[4] Tax expenditures (see Chapter 7, Section 1.1) for pensions were £13 billion in 1995 (Martin Evans 1998: table 7.14), close to 40% of spending on state pensions.

Cash benefits

One way of ensuring future consumption is to set aside part of current production for future use—for example, by digging a hole in one's back garden and adding to its contents each year tins of baked beans, shoelaces, and soap powder. Though this is the only way Robinson Crusoe could guarantee consumption in retirement, the method in practice has major inefficiencies. Storing current production is costly in terms of the potential return to savings forgone, and also because storage costs for many commodities are high. A second problem is uncertainty—for example, about what quantities to store, what new goods might become available, and how one's tastes might change. Thirdly, some services can be transferred over time by storing the physical wealth which generates them (e.g. it is possible to store housing services by being an owner-occupier); but it is not possible, even in principle, to store services deriving from human capital, medical services being a particularly important example. Organizing pensions by storing current production on a large scale is therefore a non-starter.

The alternative is for individuals to exchange current production for a claim on future output. There are two broad ways in which I might do this: by saving part of my wages each week I could build up a pile of *money* which I would exchange for goods produced by younger people after my retirement; or I could obtain a *promise* that I would be given goods produced by others after my retirement. The promise could be from my son ('Don't worry, dad, I'll look after you when you're old'), or from government. The two most common ways of organizing pensions broadly parallel these two sorts of claim on future production. So-called *funded* schemes follow the first; *Pay-As-You-Go* (PAYG) or unfunded schemes the second.[5]

FUNDED AND PAY-AS-YOU-GO SCHEMES. In a funded scheme (frequently organized in the private sector by insurance companies), contributions are invested in financial assets, the return on which is credited to its members. When an individual retires, the pension fund will be holding all his past contributions, together with the interest and dividends earned on them. This usually amounts to a large lump sum which is converted into an annuity (Chapter 5, Section 2.3), i.e. a pension of £x per year. Funding, therefore, is simply a method of accumulating money, which is exchanged for goods at some later date. Most occupational schemes are of this type.

Funded schemes take many forms, of which two in particular should be distinguished. Under a *defined-contribution* scheme, the contribution rate is fixed, so that a person's pension is determined *only* by the size of the lump sum accumulated during working life. As discussed in Chapter 5, Section 2.3, insurance protects the individual against the risks associated with longevity, but leaves her facing those associated with varying real rates of return to pension assets, including:

---

[5] There are other ways of organizing pensions. The so-called *book* method makes advance provision for pensions on the company's balance sheet in the same way as provision is made for other deferred liabilities (e.g. future tax payments). Money is not transferred out of the company (as with funded schemes) but is retained for use by the company. At the same time a reserve is set up in the balance sheet to reflect the estimated liability. In *cash* terms there is little difference between book reserving and Pay-As-You-Go.

- the risk that her pension portfolio will do better or worse, depending on (*a*) overall economic risk and (*b*) the potential for managerial slack; and

- the risk that unanticipated inflation after retirement will exceed whatever indexation provisions the pension offers.

Under a *defined-benefit* scheme, usually run at a firm or industry level, the firm promises to pay an annuity at retirement; the size of the annuity depends on the employee's wage in her final year (or final few years) of work and upon length of service (a typical formula is one-eightieth of final salary per year of service, up to a maximum of forty years). Thus the annuity is, in effect, wage indexed until retirement. The employee contribution is generally a fraction of her salary. Thus, the employer's contribution becomes the endogenous variable. In a defined benefit scheme, it is the firm or industry which bears the risk in the face of unanticipated changes in the real rate of return to pension assets.[6]

Occupational schemes can be either defined benefit or defined contribution (in the UK, they are mostly defined benefit—see Dilnot *et al.* 1994: table 2.4); personal pensions are all defined contribution. Funded schemes of both sorts have two major implications: in principle they always have sufficient reserves to pay all outstanding financial liabilities (since an individual's entitlement is simply his past contributions plus the interest earned on them); and a representative individual, or a generation as a whole, gets out of a funded scheme no more than he has put in—that is, with funding, a generation is constrained by its own past savings. Other implications emerge throughout the chapter.

Pay-As-You-Go (PAYG) schemes are usually run by the state. They are contractarian in nature, based on the fact that the state has no need to accumulate funds in anticipation of future pension claims, but can tax the working population to pay the pensions of the retired generation. Almost all state pension schemes are PAYG.

From an economic viewpoint, PAYG can be looked at in several ways. As an individual contributor, my claim to a pension is based on a promise from the state that, if I pay contributions now, I will be given a pension in the future. The terms of the promise are fairly precise; they were set out in some detail in Section 1. From an aggregate viewpoint, the state is simply raising taxes from one group of individuals and transferring the revenues thereby derived to another. State-run PAYG schemes, from this perspective, appear little different from explicit income transfers.

The major implication of the PAYG system is that it relaxes the constraint that the benefits received by any generation must be matched by its own contributions. Samuelson (1958) showed that, with a PAYG scheme, it is possible in principle for *every* generation to receive more in pensions than it paid in contributions, provided that real income rises steadily; this is likely when there is technological progress and/or steady population growth.

PRELIMINARY COMPARISON. PAYG schemes have important advantages. First, they minimize impediments to labour mobility, since pension entitlement depends on earnings and years

---

[6] For comparison of defined-benefit and defined-contribution schemes, see Bodie *et al.* (1988).

Cash benefits

Table 9.1. **Financing a Pay–As–You–Go pension scheme in the presence of inflation and growth**

Income, contributions, and real pensions	Period 1	Period 2 (Inflation)	Period 2 (Growth)
	(1)	(2)	(3)
1. Total income of workforce	£1,000	£2,000	£2,000
2. Price index	100	200	100
3. Pension contribution rate	10%	10%	10%
4. Available for pensions	£100	£200	£200
5. Real value of pensions ($=$[row (4)/row (2)] $\times$ 100)	£100	£100	£200

of service but not on how many jobs a person has had. Secondly, full pension rights can be built up quickly, since pensions are paid not by one's own previous contributions, but by those of the current workforce. Thirdly, PAYG schemes are generally able to protect pensions in payment against inflation and, fourthly, they can generally increase the real value of pensions in line with economic growth. Table 9.1 illustrates the latter two points. In period 1 the total income of the workforce is £1,000, so that a contribution rate of 10 per cent yields £100. Suppose by period 2 prices and earnings have risen by 100 per cent (column 2). A contribution of 10 per cent now yields £200, which has a purchasing power of £100 at the old price level, and so maintains the real value of pensions in the face of inflation. Alternatively, suppose (column 3) that economic growth raises earnings to £2,000, while prices stay at their original level. In this case the 10 per cent contribution rate has a *real* yield of £200, and so it is possible to double the real value of pensions.

Against these undoubted advantages must be offset the major problem that PAYG is sensitive to any change in the age structure of the population which reduces the workforce relative to the number of dependants. The crucial variable is the so-called dependency ratio,

$$\frac{P}{W} \tag{9.1}$$

where P is the number of pensioners and W the number of workers. Influences like increased longevity raise the number of pensioners, and longer education reduces the size of the workforce. Lowering the retirement age simultaneously reduces the workforce and increases the number of pensioners. Finally, as we shall see, any large 'bulge' in the birth rate can cause serious difficulties.

Another claimed disadvantage of PAYG finance is that it makes pensioners dependent on the future workforce. This is true. But, as we shall see in Section 3.2, the same is true of funded schemes. In both cases pensioners are dependent on future generations, since both schemes build pensions round claims on future production rather than by storing current production.

The disadvantages of funded schemes tend to mirror the advantages of PAYG. The benefit formula of occupational schemes favours long-serving workers. This is a deliberate feature of such schemes (see Hannah 1986) to encourage loyalty and help management of internal labour markets, but it has the effect of impeding labour mobility. Secondly, it takes a long time to build up full pension rights, because it takes an individual many years to build up a lump sum sufficiently large to generate an annuity which will support him fully in retirement. Thirdly—and fundamental to any discussion of funded schemes—there is the issue of inflation, discussed shortly.

Against these disadvantages, it is often claimed that funding has the major advantage of being insensitive to changes in the dependency ratio. The argument is that a funded scheme always has sufficient resources to pay the pensions of its members, since the present value of a representative pension stream exactly equals past contributions plus interest. It is true that a funded scheme will have sufficient resources to pay all *money* claims against it; but it does *not* follow that funding, on that account, offers pensioners better protection against demographic change. This controversial topic is addressed in detail in Sections 3.2 and 5.1.

PENSIONS AND INFLATION. The issue is particularly relevant to defined contribution schemes. It is important to distinguish (*a*) pensions in build-up, when contributions are still being paid, and (*b*) pensions in payment. Defined contribution schemes can generally cope with inflation during the build-up of pension rights, and with a given rate of *anticipated* inflation once the pension is in payment. But they do not cope well with unanticipated post-retirement inflation. The reason is straightforward. A pensioner under a funded scheme builds up over his working life a lump sum, which he exchanges upon retirement for an annuity. The present value of an actuarial annuity equals the lump sum. From equation (5.11) the annuity thus depends on the lump sum, and on the *real* rate of interest facing the insurance company (i.e. the excess of the nominal interest rate over the rate of inflation). Two cases need discussion.

- *Certainty*: if inflation is 5 per cent each year with certainty, it is an easy matter to offer an annuity which rises by 5 per cent each year. Inflation is no problem.

- *Uncertainty*: as discussed in more detail in Section 3.1, inflation is a common shock and thus an uninsurable risk. A possible escape route where inflation is purely domestic is to hedge through an internationally diversified portfolio of pension assets. Another escape route, from the insurer's perspective, is to offer limited indexation. If the limit is 5 per cent then, so far as the insurer is concerned, the situation is similar to the certainty case, above—the risk of inflation beyond 5 per cent is transferred to the pensioner.

The conclusion is that, once pensions are in payment, private, funded schemes can cope with limited inflation (i.e. can offer indexation up to some pre-specified level). But they face major problems with inflation beyond that level. The point is much more than academic. The price index in the UK in January 1974 was 100; in September 1978, in the wake of the first oil shock, it was 200. With 5 per cent indexation, pensions would have increased from 100 to about 133, rather than to 200. Pensions in payment would have lost one-third of their value. Two points are noteworthy: the loss is permanent—in contrast with pensions during build up, there is no opportunity to make up any of the lost ground; and people are retired today for many more years than previously.

The relative ability of PAYG and funding to cope with inflation is due less to the method of finance *per se* than to the fact that in many instances only the state can guarantee indexed amounts. Funded schemes can cope with inflation if their assets are indexed by the state—for example, where the state sells indexed gilts or where it underwrites directly the indexation component once funded pensions are in payment. However, the part of the return which compensates for inflation is paid out of current tax revenues—that is, on a PAYG basis. More generally, any receipts of funded schemes deriving from current tax revenues, whether the return to indexed government bonds[7] or the tax advantages they currently enjoy, constitute a PAYG element in such schemes.

3. **Efficiency arguments for state intervention**

Section 3.1 discusses efficiency aspects of public-versus-private provision, and Section 3.2 looks at the PAYG-versus-funding controversy. Social justice is discussed in Section 4.

3.1. Public-versus-private provision

To help subsequent discussion, imagine two possible states in retirement: either I am well enough to look after myself (in which case what is relevant is my pension); or I am unwell and need residential care. Though there are many differences in terms of social policy, the economic arguments are directly parallel—the issue in both cases is how I can transfer sufficient resources into the future. Thus pensions and residential-care insurance are usefully discussed together.

PENSIONS. Efficiency requires that individuals buy the *socially* efficient *real* level of pension. The theoretical conditions under which private insurance markets achieve this result were discussed in Chapter 5, Section 4.1. The three major policy issues are why people insure at all, why the state makes membership of a pension scheme compulsory, and why it provides retirement pensions itself.

We know that a rational, risk-averse individual will pay pension contributions (i.e. buy insurance) so long as their net cost does not exceed the value to him of the certainty he thereby derives (Chapter 5, Section 2.1). Membership is compulsory because of the external costs which arise if an individual does not buy pension rights (Chapter 8,

---

[7] See the Glossary.

Section 2.1). The issue of public provision is more complicated. The private market provides pensions efficiently only if the standard assumptions of perfect information, perfect competition, and no market failures hold. Potential problems on the demand side were discussed in Chapter 5, Section 4.1. A central issue is whether buyers of a technically complex financial instrument are well informed. On the supply side, it is necessary to consider separately the five technical conditions (Chapter 5, Section 3) which must hold if the private market is to supply insurance efficiently.

The probability of living to a given age for pensioner A is independent of that for pensioner B; and the probability is known and less than one. Data on mortality rates are reliable in all industrialized countries. Nor is there any problem of adverse selection—by and large people do not know when they are going to die. Moral hazard is not a problem either; suicide is costly to the individual, and works in the insurance company's favour.

The initial conclusion, therefore, is that there is no technical problem with private pension provision. This, however, overlooks inflation. An individual can purchase a future consumption bundle which is efficient in terms of quantity and quality only if she can guarantee the *real* value of her future pension. This can occur without intervention only if the private market can supply insurance against unanticipated inflation. Such insurance is not possible for two reasons.

- The probability distribution of different future levels of inflation is unknown.[8]
- Inflation is a common shock. The probability of pensioner A experiencing a given rate of inflation is *not* independent of that for pensioner B—the rate of inflation facing one pensioner will (by and large) face them all. There is no possibility of winners compensating losers and so insurance is impossible.

Inflation is therefore an uninsurable risk. Thus pensioners cannot insure each other. To what extent might they be able to find protection through some other mechanism—for example, by buying assets whose value keeps pace with inflation? That would be possible without intervention if real rates of return were independent of inflation. As an empirical matter, this is not the case. The dependence is partly the result of distortions elsewhere (e.g. non-indexed tax systems) which could in principle be corrected. However, where an inflationary shock represents other adverse movements in the economy, no private agency can offer a complete hedge against inflation. Bodie's survey points out (1990: 36) that 'virtually no private pension plans in the US offer automatic inflation protection after retirement'. Margaret Gordon's cross-national conclusion (1988: 169) is that 'indexing of pension benefits after retirement . . . presents serious difficulties in funded employer pension plans'.

The conclusion is that private pensions can offer limited indexation, as discussed in Section 2, but protection beyond that must ultimately come from government. Thus there

---

[8] Inflation is not a problem for car repairs, for example, because automobile insurance, unlike pensions, is financed by *current* premiums.

is an efficiency argument, at a minimum, for state intervention to assist private schemes with the costs of unanticipated inflation once pensions are in payment. The state is able to offer such a guarantee because it can use current tax revenues on a PAYG basis. This will introduce a PAYG element into even the purest funded scheme. It should be clear that an indemnity against inflation, if publicly provided, is not true insurance (because it cannot be), but a form of tax/transfer. Since efficiency requires individuals to make decisions about the real value of the pension they purchase, and since the appropriate guarantees against inflation can be given only by the state on a PAYG basis, there is a cast-iron efficiency argument for at least some public involvement with pensions. Whether this should stop at the provision of inflation indemnities for private schemes, or whether the state should step in to provide pensions itself on either a PAYG or a mixed funded/PAYG basis, is an open issue upon which most of the rest of the chapter has a bearing.

RESIDENTIAL CARE. Consider, now, the second case: I need to be looked after in old age. In the past, many people who could no longer care for themselves were looked after by the national health service, hence for the most part paid out of taxation. However, the number of older people is growing. In addition, changes in the finance of the health service, together with tighter access to cash benefits, is making the problem politically salient, as people have been forced to sell their homes to finance the costs of residential care. For both sets of reasons, the suitability of private insurance for financing such care is an important issue.

On the demand side, policies, being long term, are inevitably complex (Burchardt and Hills 1997: ch. 6), calling into question the quality of consumer information. On the supply side, insurers face two of the problems discussed in Chapter 5, Section 3.1. First, they may not know the relevant probability. It might be known today, but may change over the course of a long-run contract: it might decline through medical advances which help me to care for myself; equally, medical progress, by extending my life, might increase the likelihood that I will require care. Thus not even the direction of change is known. Over a long time horizon, the relevant risks shade into uncertainty. Secondly, probabilities may not be independent: a medical advance which does not prevent or cure disability but which prolongs life once a person has become disabled affects the probability of *all* policy-holders.

Thus there are several arguments in favour of social insurance. First, the scope for differences in individual choice is limited. Secondly, these are not risks which fit the actuarial mechanism very well. With social insurance, in contrast, the contract need not be fully specified, making it easier to adapt to changing social and medical circumstances (see also the discussion in Chapter 5, Section 4.1). Thirdly, the costs of residential care are much lower than for pensions because on average people require care for a much shorter period than they require a pension. In the UK today, roughly one in six people requires residential care in old age, and the average duration of such care is two years. Thus a representative person will require care for four months.

3.2. Funding versus Pay-As-You-Go: Theoretical arguments

Having established the case for at least some public involvement, the next question is whether any state scheme should be funded or PAYG and, in particular, what are the relative merits of the two methods in the face of demographic change.

THE DEMOGRAPHIC PROBLEM is analysed by Barr (1979), on which this section draws (see also Falkingham 1989).[9] The root of the problem (Figure 9.1) is the peak in the birth rate in the 1940s, followed by the larger bulge in the 1960s in which more than ten million babies were born. These cohorts of 'bulge' babies will retire between 2010 and 2030, and will have to be supported in old age by the smaller succeeding generations. Specifically, in 1991 about 16 per cent of the population was 65 or over; the projected figure for 2041 is 24 per cent (Hills 1997).

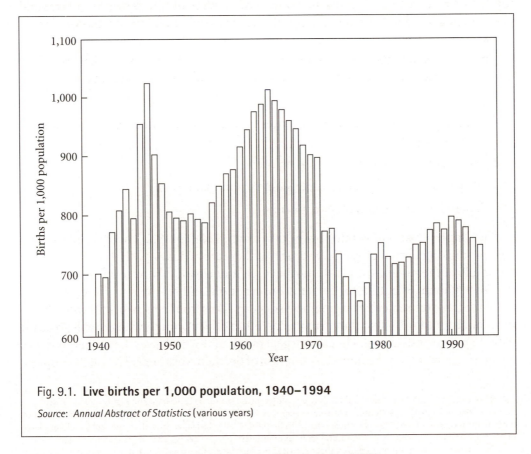

Fig. 9.1. **Live births per 1,000 population, 1940–1994**

Source: Annual Abstract of Statistics (various years)

---

[9] The analysis is similar in spirit to Samuelson (1958).

Cash benefits

The problem is compounded by the maturation of the state earnings-related pension (see Section 1). Even with the reforms discussed in Section 5.1, a worker with an average contributions record will receive a pension almost twice the current flat-rate benefit.

The demographic problem is not unique to the UK. A startlingly similar pattern exists in the USA, in most of the EU countries, and also in Australia, New Zealand, and Japan.[10]

How relevant is funding to the problem? The widely held (but false) view that funded schemes are inherently 'safer' than PAYG is an example of the fallacy of composition.[11] For *individuals*, the economic function of a pension scheme is to transfer consumption over time. But (ruling out the case where current output is stored in holes in people's gardens) this is not possible for society as a whole; the consumption of pensioners as a group is produced by the next generation of workers. From an *aggregate* viewpoint, the economic function of pension schemes is to divide total output between workers and pensioners—that is, to reduce the consumption of workers so that sufficient output remains for pensioners. Once this point is understood, it becomes clear why PAYG and funded schemes, which are both simply ways of dividing output between workers and pensioners, should not fare very differently in the face of demographic change.

THE SIMPLE MODEL highlights the argument under strong assumptions (which are subsequently relaxed). These simplify the analysis without substantially altering the conclusion. They are:

1. Output per head remains constant over time, and is the same whether pensions are funded or PAYG.
2. The number of workers remains constant.
3. Wages are fixed in real terms, pensions in nominal terms.
4. There is no trade with other countries.

The simplest case is illustrated by the first column of Table 9.2. There are 10 workers who produce an output of 1,000. Assume that there are no taxes, so that workers receive the whole of their output; and assume that each unit costs £1. Now suppose that workers use 900 units of output for current consumption, and set the remaining 100 units aside for their retirement. Pension provision can take two forms. Workers can sell 100 units of output for £100 to the current generation of pensioners, who are able to buy it with their own past savings. The current generation of workers saves the money, and uses it when it retires to buy the non-consumption of the then workforce. This, at its simplest,

---

[10] This is a remarkable fact. Why should countries as different as Denmark (Protestant and highly industrialized) and Italy (Catholic and with some largely unindustrialized parts) have a similar pattern of birth rates? Australia, which escaped much of the recession of the 1970s, nevertheless had a declining birth rate. And Japan faces the same problem despite large differences in religion, social organization, and patterns of industry. No one has yet given a satisfactory explanation.

[11] It is a fallacy of composition to assume that because something is true for an individual it will *necessarily* be true on aggregate. For instance, if I stand on my seat in the theatre I will get a better view, but if everybody does so nobody will get a better view.

Table 9.2. **Output and consumption with workforces of different sizes**

Size of workforce, output, and consumption	Period 1	Period 2 (constant productivity)	Period 2 (doubled productivity)
	(1)	(2)	(3)
Size of workforce	10	5	5
Total output = total income of the workforce	1,000	500	1,000
Workers' consumption	900	450	900
Workers' non-consumption	100	50	100

Note: Output is measured in physical units.

is how funded schemes operate.[12] Alternatively, in a PAYG world, 100 units of output are transferred from workers to current pensioners via a 10 per cent tax on the workforce, so that it can afford to consume only 900. When the current workforce retires, it in turn receives 100 units of output.

Under the stated assumptions both schemes can continue indefinitely and both lead to the same three conclusions:

- pensioners can consume only what workers produce but do not consume;
- pensioners always depend on succeeding generations to provide the labour to produce the goods which they consume; and
- under the stated assumptions PAYG and funding lead to identical results.

THE EFFECTS OF A DECLINE IN THE WORKFORCE. The previous assumptions stand, except that the labour force halves. This case is shown in the second column of Table 9.2. With output per worker unchanged (by assumption) output has halved to 500, and workers' consumption to 450, leaving 50 units of output for pensions. Under PAYG, the 10 per cent tax mentioned above leads to exactly this result. With a funded scheme matters are more complicated. The current generation of pensioners is taken to be the previous workforce of 10 in column 1, which has accumulated sufficient funds to buy an output of 100 at the initial price of £1 per unit. If the savings habits of workers do not change, total expenditure will be £450 by workers on current consumption, plus £100 by pensioners out of accumulated funds. The total of £550 is greater than the value at current prices of output of 500. While pensioners get their £100 in *money* safely transferred to their retirement, they will not necessarily receive 100 units of *consumption*.

In economic terms, if there is a large accumulation of pension funds when the workforce is declining, the high level of spending by pensioners out of their accumulated savings will reduce the rate of saving in the economy, and possibly lead to aggregate dissaving. Net pensioner consumption (i.e. the excess of pensioner consumption over

---

[12] In practice things can be more complicated: contributions can come from employers and the government as well as from workers; and contributions may not be entirely at the expense of workers' consumption. These factors complicate the analysis but do not change the logic of the underlying argument.

any pensioner production) is greater than saving by workers (i.e. the excess of workers' production over their consumption at current prices); and at full employment this causes demand inflation, which erodes the purchasing power of pensioners' accumulated funds, and hence their consumption. The precise mechanism of this inflationary process is spelled out in Barr (1979), which shows that, if the labour force halves, then, under the stated assumptions, output will halve, the price level will double, and pensioner consumption will halve. In the extreme, it does me no good to accumulate a huge fund if on the day I retire the last worker flies to Australia—I will have plenty of pound coins, but no mechanism for transforming them into consumption.[13]

RELAXING THE ASSUMPTIONS. Suppose first that workers' wages are not necessarily indexed, nor pensions necessarily fixed in money terms. If the labour force halves (the other assumptions remaining in force), output will halve (column 2 of Table 9.2). This output can be divided between workers and pensioners in different ways; but their joint demand is constrained by total supply. The relative shares of the two groups will depend on such factors as their political and bargaining strengths—that is, whether pensioners are more powerful lobbying for current tax revenues (PAYG) or as the owners of capital. There is no difference of principle between the two methods, only a practical issue.

Suppose, next, that productivity doubles, but is unaffected by the method of pension finance. If the other assumptions still hold, a smaller workforce of 5 can now produce the same output as previously produced by 10 (column 3). Workers can consume 900, leaving 100 for pensioners. The system is in equilibrium, in this case because supply has adjusted. In a world of funding, the growth in output makes possible sufficient extra saving by the smaller workforce to match dissaving by the larger group of pensioners. Under PAYG, a tax at an unchanged rate of 10 per cent enables government to transfer to pensioners the 100 units of output promised to them.

Relaxing the demographic assumptions is straightforward. Suppose that the decline in the working-age population is entirely offset by increases in the labour-force participation of women, and in the retirement age. In this case, column 1 of Table 9.2 applies in period 2, notwithstanding demographic change. The problem is entirely resolved, again on the supply side, for both types of pension scheme, for the same reason as in the previous paragraph. A similar conclusion arises from any combination of increased productivity and labour-force participation which prevents output from falling.

Finally, it is in principle possible to maintain the consumption of both workers and pensioners with goods produced abroad, provided the country has sufficient overseas assets to do so. This could be done with publicly owned stocks of foreign currency (PAYG) or with foreign assets accumulated by pension funds.

Two conclusions emerge.

- If changes in productivity and labour-force participation are independent of the method of finance, then relaxing the assumptions does not change the previous results. In particular, it remains the case that funding and PAYG are not substantially

---

[13] Australian producers would be unlikely to accept pounds in exchange for Australian goods in this situation.

different in their ability to cope with demographic change. This should not be surprising. The task of both schemes is to reduce workers' consumption; PAYG does this by taxing workers, funding by forcing (or allowing) them to save. The only difference is that PAYG makes explicit the notion that pensions involve current resources.

- The crucial variable is *output*. A decline in the labour force causes problems for any pension scheme only if it causes a fall in output; the problem is solved to the extent that this can be prevented.

The choice between PAYG and funding in the face of demographic change is therefore relevant only to the extent that funding (as is sometimes argued) systematically *causes* output to be higher. This is a matter of considerable controversy both theoretically and empirically, and is a central topic in Section 5.1.

OTHER ASPECTS. This section digresses briefly to a number of other issues about PAYG and funding, mainly to make clear that they have little or nothing to do with the central issue of paying for pensions. The main arguments are that funded schemes are safer, give more freedom, and impose greater financial discipline.

The question of safety, as we have seen, turns on whether pensioners as a group are better able to fight for their share of national output as recipients of current tax revenues or as the owners of capital. The PAYG mechanism makes clear both the quarrel over output shares and the dependence of pensioners on the next generation of workers. Funding hides both issues, but does not remove them. It is, indeed, possible for the state to break promises made earlier under a PAYG scheme. But funded schemes are equally vulnerable and equally political (consider the political sensitivity of tax advantages for pension funds).[14] As a practical matter the flat-rate component of the national-insurance retirement pension in the mid-1990s was nearly 2.5 times as large in *real* terms as in 1948. Funded benefits have frequently failed to keep up with inflation (see the quotes from Bodie and Gordon in Section 3.1).

A related argument asserts that taxes in a PAYG world curtail individual liberty. The issue of freedom, however, is raised not by PAYG versus funding but by compulsion versus voluntarism. A compulsory funded scheme gives no more freedom than current arrangements.

A final argument is that funding imposes greater financial discipline. With PAYG, the state makes promises now, but may not have to pay anything till later (e.g. increases under the 1975 Act became fully payable only in 1998). The immediate revenue charge is negligible relative to the potential future liability, leading, it is argued, to irresponsible pension promises (this is an example of government failure discussed in Chapter

---

[14] While on the subject, it should not be imagined that storing current output at the bottom of one's garden gives complete protection against *all* contingencies. The state can always expropriate such output either explicitly, or by a tax on individual wealth, or, more subtly, by engineering inflation and imposing a non-indexed capital-gains tax on an accruals basis. In similar vein, funded schemes run a potential risk of state direction of their investment portfolios, a besetting problem in Latin America (see Mesa-Lago 1990). For specific discussion of the safety of different pension regimes, see Diamond (1996*b*).

4, Section 5). With funding, promises of higher future benefits must be matched by increased contributions immediately, thereby, it is argued, guarding against government failure. Though factually true, these are not necessarily arguments against PAYG. The ability of social insurance (of which PAYG is an example) to respond to changing social and economic circumstances is regarded by many as one of its great advantages. Of course, PAYG can be abused, but—as with automobiles and pain-killing drugs—that is not a watertight argument for abolition.

4. Social justice

4.1. Public-versus-private provision

This section, which closely parallels Chapter 8, Section 2.3, considers the equity arguments for public organization of pensions. Horizontal equity concerns goals like a guaranteed minimum standard of some commodities, or equal access to them. These occur without intervention (Chapter 4, Section 4.3) where individuals have perfect information and equal power, a line of argument which lends little support to public provision of pensions. If individuals did not have perfect information, they would generally be able to buy it. At most there is a case for regulation of minimum standards. The fact that individuals do not have equal power lends further support to minimum standards but, again, there is no argument for public provision.

I have already discussed in Chapter 8, Section 2.3, and elsewhere the weakness of the vertical equity argument that the state should provide pensions because otherwise the poor could not afford them. The earlier conclusions apply equally here—that public provision solely to foster redistribution is justified only by a consumption externality, where the rich confer pensions on the poor as a merit good.

Consumption externalities apart, equity reasons for public provision must appeal to efficiency arguments. In the case of pensions, these arise out of the inability of the private market to guarantee protection against inflation, giving an efficiency justification for public involvement at least in underwriting the indexation component of pensions, and possibly (depending on the outcome of the funding-versus-PAYG debate) of some or all of the pension. In the case of residential care, the argument for public organization of insurance rests on the imperfect information of consumers and (particularly) of insurers. As discussed in Chapter 4, Section 7.2, once a commodity is publicly provided on *efficiency* grounds, it is not inappropriate to finance it redistributively. In addition, the fact that membership is compulsory, by imposing a pooling solution, avoids the worst problems of adverse selection (Chapter 5, Section 4.1); in consequence, premiums based on income rather than individual risk need cause no major inefficiency. These efficiency arguments for compulsion and public provision, taken together, suggest that using publicly organized pensions for distributional purposes does not necessarily cause substantial efficiency losses.

4.2. The redistributive effects of pensions

A pension scheme, depending on its precise construction, can redistribute from young to old, from rich to poor, and from men to women. It will also redistribute over the life cycle. It is necessary to consider PAYG and funded schemes, and in each case to ask three questions: is such redistribution possible; is it inevitable; and to what extent does it occur in practice?

REDISTRIBUTION FROM YOUNG TO OLD. PAYG finance enables a generation as a whole to receive more than the sum of its past contributions. Thus redistribution from the young workforce to the retired generation is *possible*. But it is not *inevitable*, since a PAYG scheme could be organized to pay actuarial benefits. *In practice*, as we shall see in Section 5.2, there has been substantial redistribution from young to old in many countries over the postwar period.

With funded schemes it is necessary to consider separately the cases of stable and unstable price levels. In a world with no inflation, the funded benefits of any generation are constrained by its past contributions, rendering redistribution from young to old impossible. The effect of unanticipated inflation is to bring about unintended redistribution from old to young (and vice versa for unanticipated price deflation).

REDISTRIBUTION FROM RICH TO POOR can, and usually does, occur with PAYG pensions. In many state schemes there is *formula redistribution*, in that individual B with half the income of individual A generally pays half the contribution, but receives a pension which is more than half of A's. The UK system was described in Section 1. In the USA, though the formula has changed from time to time, it has always been explicitly redistributive (Aaron *et al.* 1989: table 2.4). The same is true in the systems of most industrialized countries (Barr 1992: sect. V).

The effect of formula redistribution is partially offset by *differential mortality*, to the extent that the rich live longer than the poor. But redistribution is not inevitable—it is possible to organize a PAYG scheme in which pensions are proportional to contributions.

It might be possible to devise a (compulsory) funded scheme which redistributed from rich to poor. But, where membership is voluntary, the present value of the annuity received by a representative individual must equal the lump sum accumulated over her working years. This implies, *ceteris paribus*, that pensions must be proportional to contributions, thus ruling out systematic redistribution.

REDISTRIBUTION FROM MEN TO WOMEN. The following are all statements of fact referring to the UK:

- The normal retiring age for men is 65, at which age a man has a life expectancy of 77. The average man is thus retired for 12 years.
- The normal retiring age for women is 60, at which age women have a life expectancy of 80, so that the average woman is retired for 20 years.

- It is therefore $\frac{20}{12} = 1\frac{2}{3}$ times as expensive to provide a given weekly pension for a woman as for a man.

- If men and women pay equal contributions and receive equal weekly benefits, there is redistribution from men to women. Since women live longer than men, abolishing the differential retirement age would reduce the subsidy but would not eliminate it.

Redistribution from men to women occurs for these reasons in both funded and PAYG schemes. The phenomenon is widespread, but is particularly strong in the UK, which was an outlier in international terms in having a lower retiring age for women (a subject to which we return in Section 5.2).[15] Two issues arise: is such redistribution inevitable; and is it desirable? On the first point, one could devise a scheme (PAYG or funded) in which women received benefits related to their longevity. A woman could receive a lower monthly pension than a man with an identical contributions record—that is, a definition of equity as a pension stream of equal present value. Alternatively, women could pay a higher contribution and receive the same monthly pension as men—that is, equity consists of women receiving a pension stream with a higher present value, matched by a larger contributions stream. Thus there are two definitions of equity: equal present value, or equal monthly value. Either is defensible, but they are different, hence the equity problem.

Redistribution from men to women in pensions, though not inevitable, is almost universal, partly from a belief that any differential is a form of discrimination. A decision by the US Supreme Court (1978) declared differential pensions unconstitutional even if calculated actuarially (i.e. on the basis of equation (5.11)).[16] Nor is such redistribution necessarily undesirable. Analytically, it occurs because women pay the same premiums as men despite being (from the insurer's viewpoint) worse risks because they live longer. As we saw in Chapter 5, Section 4.1, efficiency generally requires that premiums should be proportional to risk; where insurance is compulsory, however, low-risk individuals are not able to opt out, and charging the same premium for all categories of risk does not cause adverse selection. It is possible that secondary inefficiency might arise—for example, the possible distortion of labour-supply decisions which non-actuarial contributions might cause. To the extent that this is not a substantial problem, the decision whether all classes of risk should pay the same premium can be made mainly on equity grounds. Thus some compulsory schemes do not match premium with risk (unemployment benefits), while others do (automobile insurance).

REDISTRIBUTION OVER THE LIFE CYCLE. A central purpose of pensions is income-smoothing—pensions are a device which allows me to redistribute from myself in my productive

---

[15] The Old Age Pensions Act 1908 established a common retirement age of 70, which was reduced to 65 under the Old Age and Widows and Orphans Contributory Pensions Act 1925. Women's retirement age was reduced to 60 in 1940, partly because of a campaign by women's organizations (for details of the events leading to the change in 1940, see Thane 1982: 245). Women's retirement age will over time be raised to 65; see note 2.

[16] Though tenable on equity grounds, the decision was based on a total failure to understand the nature of insurance.

middle years to myself after retirement. Where none of the earlier types of redistribution occurs, this is the only redistributive effect of pensions. In comparison with PAYG, funded schemes generally have less redistribution from young to old and less from rich to poor. Thus a larger fraction of funded pensions will relate to redistribution over time than to redistribution between people.

5. Assessment of national insurance retirement pensions

5.1. Efficiency and incentives

BACKGROUND QUESTIONS

This section asks whether the national-insurance pension scheme is efficient and equitable, starting with the a priori questions of Chapter 8, Section 3.1: should pensions be national (i.e. publicly provided), are they optimal in quantity and type, and are they insurance?

SHOULD PENSIONS BE NATIONAL? The efficiency arguments for state pensions rest on externalities, justifying compulsion, and technical failures in the insurance market, justifying public provision at a minimum of some sort of indemnity against inflation. It is agreed (*a*) that it should be compulsory for people to belong to a pension scheme, at least up to some minimum level, and (*b*) that efficiency is enhanced where people are able to reallocate consumption over their lifetime. Individual decisions about pensions are therefore more efficient if inflation can be ignored; but only the state can offer a complete guarantee against inflation (i.e. full indexation). Thus there is a role for public provision at least of indexed assets for use by private, funded schemes. The efficiency argument for public provision of the whole pension is less clear-cut.

DOES THE STATE PROVIDE THE OPTIMAL QUANTITY AND TYPE OF PENSION? Only tentative answers are possible.

The first question is whether state action leads to the optimal level of pensions. Martin Evans (1998: table 7.7) shows that about one-third of increased state pension spending between 1973 and 1994 related to rising numbers of pensioners; the remaining two-thirds related to rising real pensions. For this and other reasons, the fraction of pensioners requiring additional means-tested assistance fell over the period from 22 per cent to 14 per cent. For the most part, this outcome results from deliberate government policy. The state has also acted to assist protect private pensions against inflation—for example, by issuing indexed bonds for use *inter alia* by private pension funds.

It can be argued that the increasing role of the state in indexing public and private pensions has contributed to the relative certainty with which individuals can plan for the future, and has therefore increased efficiency, albeit imperfectly because the state scheme makes no allowance for different degrees of risk aversion between individuals.

A second set of questions relates to the efficiency of private institutions. Private pensions in the UK are well established and, for the most part, work well. They have, however, had problems, largely connected with imperfect consumer information. Occupational pensions faced the so-called Maxwell scandal, in which the assets of an occupational scheme were illegally siphoned off for other purposes.[17] Proposals to tighten regulations (UK Pension Law Review Committee 1993) were enacted in the Pensions Act 1995, which set up a new, independent body, the Occupational Pensions Regulatory Authority. With personal pensions the problem was less of an isolated one, but had clear resonances of the problems discussed in Chapter 5, Section 4.1. 'What is clear, even at this early stage, is that there is considerable inefficiency within the personal pensions market because of the high management costs and poor advice offered to savers. Individual purchasers have little chance of gaining full information about the wide array of highly complex long-term financial instruments on offer' (Johnson and Rake 1997: 44).

Long-term-care insurance faces similar problems.

If there is too little information . . . to ascertain whether [long-term-care] insurance products . . . represent value for money, can consumers make an informed choice about purchase?

If insurers likewise suffer from a lack of reliable data . . . premiums may turn out to be higher than they need to be; but if not, insurers may be unable to meet their commitments.

Given this uncertainty, it must be questioned whether private insurance is a suitable way to meet the security needs of a large part of the elderly population. (Burchardt and Hills 1997: 44–5)

What this suggests is *not* that the state necessarily does a better job than the private sector but—as argued in Chapter 4, Section 7.1—that the choice of instruments is subtle and complex. In the case of pensions, the best way forward is to retain private institutions, with state intervention through stronger regulation and, possibly, an element of subsidy. In the case of long-term-care insurance, as argued earlier, there is a strong case for a move towards social insurance, possibly with voluntary private top-up insurance.

ARE PENSIONS INSURANCE? Chapter 8, Section 3.1, pointed out that national-insurance contributions are not geared to risk; that the scheme is not funded; and that rights to benefit are not determined solely by the occurrence of the insured event. In addition, as we shall see in Section 5.2, the scheme redistributes to the poor, and offers credits for people at home looking after young children, and for the unemployed. These arrangements are a considerable departure from the Beveridge scheme, whose lump-sum contributions and benefits ruled out redistribution from rich to poor (assuming, for example, equal life expectancy); and, since the original proposals were for a funded scheme, they would also have ruled out redistribution from young to old.

For these reasons, some writers (for example, Johnson and Stears 1996) have questioned whether the basic pension should continue to be contributory. The counter-argument is that pensions are social insurance, as defined in Chapter 5, Section 4.2: they

---

[17] For claims about the vulnerability of private pensions in the USA, see Bartlett and Steele (1992: ch. 9).

are insurance in the sense of offering protection against risk, but not in the sense of an actuarial mechanism. As discussed in Chapter 8, Section 3.1, social insurance, though it *enables* redistribution from rich to poor, does not *require* it. The extent to which social insurance is redistributive therefore depends on the relative weights attached to the different objectives in Chapter 1, Section 2.2.

INCENTIVE ISSUES

The incentive effects of pensions are the subject of considerable debate. This section makes no attempt to survey the large literature (see the Further Reading) but seeks only to sketch out why the issue is controversial. Two issues predominate: does PAYG restrict saving and output growth; and do pensions reduce labour supply?

PENSIONS, SAVING, AND ECONOMIC GROWTH. It is often regarded as self-evident that saving, and hence economic growth, will be higher with funding than under PAYG. But this assertion requires at least three major qualifications.

1. *Increases in saving, if any, occur only during the build-up of the fund*. It should be clear from column 1 of Table 9.2 that in the long run workers save 100 and pensioners dissave 100, so that net saving is zero.

2. *Does funding increase saving even during the build-up phase?* Opinion is divided. The issue can be posed simply. Suppose that my mandatory pension contribution of 100 is moved from a PAYG scheme to a funded scheme. Two illustrative outcomes are interesting:

- My voluntary savings behaviour (e.g. for retirement or bequests to my children) does not change. Thus my saving increases by 100.
- I reduce my voluntary saving by 100; thus there is no increase in my saving.

The issue, therefore, is the extent to which any increases in mandatory saving are offset by reductions in voluntary saving.

The issue is a very old one. In the context of the 1908 Old Age Pensions Act (Chapter 2, Section 2.2), Sydney and Beatrice Webb (1909: 334) reported that 'some of our witnesses . . . have taken the view . . . that such non-contributory pensions would be likely to discourage thrift and saving'.

Current debate was reopened by Feldstein (1974). His empirical work, based on time-series data, concluded that the US social-security (i.e. pension) scheme (which is PAYG) reduced personal saving by about 50 per cent, thereby reducing the capital stock by 38 per cent below what it would have been in the absence of the social-security system.

Aaron (1982) sets out three theoretical models of the determinants of saving: the life-cycle model (which rules out bequests); the multigenerational model (which allows bequests); and the short-horizon model (which relaxes the assumption that individuals make rational lifetime plans based on (more or less) full information). Feldstein's theoretical analysis can be criticized because it is based on a life-cycle model, in which an increase in PAYG benefits *must* reduce savings; in a multigenerational model increased benefits could instead increase bequests (and hence not reduce savings). Aaron (1982: 28) summarises the theoretical debate by observing

that a person determined to find a respected theoretical argument to support a preconception will find one, and that a person without preconceptions will find a bewildering diversity of answers in economic theory about whether social security [i.e. pensions] is more likely to raise or to lower consumption or labor supply.

To get by this theoretical impasse, one turns with hope to the empirical research . . . As will become clear, most of these hopes remain unfulfilled.

Feldstein's empirical work was also criticized: additional variables such as the unemployment rate or a measure of permanent income tended to reduce the effect on saving, and to destroy its statistical significance; and the results were highly sensitive to the time period over which the relation was estimated. The results were finally discredited by Leimer and Lesnoy (1982), who found an error in some of Feldstein's data. They also pointed out that the results are very sensitive to the way in which people are assumed to form expectations. Subsequent work (Auerbach *et al.* 1989; Auerbach and Kotlikoff 1990) used a seventy-five-period life-cycle general equilibrium model to simulate the effects of demographic change under different pension regimes. The results highlight the key role of expectations (which are largely unmeasurable) on retirement behaviour. Recent work by Gale (1998) argues that the savings offset is larger than previously supposed because of econometric biases in earlier work. Holzmann (1997) reaches a similar conclusion. The debate continues.

3. *Do increased savings lead to increased output?* The third qualification is that an increase in saving does not *necessarily* raise output. There are not one, but three links in the argument that future output will be higher with funding than with PAYG:

- funding leads to a higher rate of saving in the build-up period than PAYG;
- this higher saving is translated into more and better investment; and
- this investment leads to an increase in output.

None of the three links *necessarily* holds. The evidence on the first, as just discussed, is mixed. On the second, increased saving does not necessarily lead to new investment; pension savings could instead be used to buy old masters. So far as the third link is concerned, the objective is to channel resources into their most productive investment use. But it cannot just be *assumed* that pension managers make more efficient choices than other agents. The Government Actuary admitted that he was 'not in a position to judge whether . . . pension fund money is more capable than other money of being deployed in accordance with the long-term national interest' (UK Government Actuary's Department 1978: para. 25). Nor do state-funded schemes necessarily fare better. Experience in Sweden and Japan (where the state earnings-related pensions are funded) suggests that such schemes 'offer powerful evidence that this option may only invite squandering capital funds in wasteful, low-yield investments [which] should give pause to anyone proposing similar accumulations elsewhere' (Rosa 1982: 212).

All three links have to hold before it can be asserted that funding will lead to greater increases in output than PAYG. At best the assertion is not proven.

PENSIONS AND LABOUR SUPPLY. The question here is whether pensions (either PAYG or funded) reduce aggregate labour supply. The problems are similar to those which beset empirical analysis of the labour-supply effects of unemployment benefits (Chapter 8, Section 3.1). On the contributions side, the theoretical analysis of taxation on work effort is generally accepted (see Atkinson and Stiglitz 1980: 23–61 and the Further Reading). The effect of national-insurance contributions is to drive a wedge between gross and net money wages. If workers discount future benefits entirely, contributions have the same effect as an income tax; at the other extreme, where future benefits bear an actuarial relationship to contributions, and are perceived to do so, national-insurance contributions are not a tax but simply the price of insurance, which, like any other price, has little if any distortionary effect on labour supply.

The impact of future benefits, on the other hand, is harder to analyse. They are payable only in certain contingencies, can be changed by legislation, and will depend on, for example, marital status; and it is not possible to borrow against future benefits, which must therefore be weighted by the probability that each type of benefit will be received at some given future date. The weighted benefits must then be discounted to present value using the market rate of interest or, for people who cannot borrow as much as they wish, at a personal rate of time preference. Similar problems arise in valuing pension rights considered as part of personal wealth.

As a result, modelling the effect of pensions on labour supply is complex. Some studies conclude that pensions (both public and private) reduce labour supply, others that pensions have little or no effect on work effort. Up to a point the conflicting results can be explained *inter alia* by differences in model specification, different treatment of benefits and taxes, and different choice of samples (see Atkinson 1987*a*). To a considerable extent, however, the issue is not only unresolved, but may remain so. A study by Mitchell and Fields (1981) used a single body of survey data in four different (and plausible) ways, and found that the US social-security scheme induced workers to retire earlier, or later, or left the retirement decision unaffected.

Though pensions may not affect overall labour supply, employer pension schemes can affect individual decisions: pension design may reduce shirking (Lazear 1986*b*); vesting rules (which specify the length of service before a worker gains title to any pension benefits) may reduce labour turnover (Hannah 1986; Wise 1986); and benefit provisions can encourage older workers to retire early (Stock and Wise 1988).

It is important to be clear that the issue of labour supply, though highly significant, is logically separate from the PAYG-versus-funding controversy. Though different methods of organizing pensions may influence the rate of saving, they affect work effort only if people perceive social-insurance contributions differently from private-pension contributions. What really matters for labour-supply decisions is the size of a person's future pension, the terms on which he can buy it, and the range of choice (e.g. about retirement age). If pensions (of whatever sort) do induce retirement, the simplest solution is to raise the retirement age and/or to give greater financial incentives to defer retirement.

DEALING WITH FUTURE PROBLEMS

Britain's demographic problems are less acute than elsewhere in Europe. In addition, since the mid-1980s the state pension has been tied to changes in prices rather than earnings. The resulting savings will be enough to keep contributions fairly constant despite the ageing population. In many ways, therefore, Britain's pensions 'crisis' is not a crisis at all, but a matter which has largely been resolved (see Hills 1997). This section therefore concentrates more on the logic of dealing with demographic problems than with the British specifics.

POLICIES IN THE FACE OF THE DEMOGRAPHIC PROBLEM. We saw earlier that the Eurotoddlers of the 1950s and 1960s will cause a sharp rise in the dependency rate when they retire in the years after 2010. Any solution to the declining population of working age must reduce the demand for goods and services and/or increase their supply. This implies one (or more) of three outcomes. Demand can be reduced (*a*) by increasing contributions, thereby reducing the average consumption of workers, and/or (*b*) by reducing benefits, thereby reducing the average consumption of pensioners. The UK has adopted (*b*) by deciding to increase pensions in line with prices rather than earnings.

Alternatively, on the supply side, both workers and pensioners can have the consumption they currently expect, so long as (*c*) output rises sufficiently to maintain average consumption per head (hence the emphasis in Section 3.2 on the key role of output). In theory, raising output involves either or both of two strategies. *Increased output per worker* can arise from increases in the quantity and quality of capital, and from increases in the quality of labour. *Increased numbers of workers* can arise from increased labour-force participation by those of working age; from an increase in the retirement age; and/or by importing labour (e.g. 'guestworkers').

In practice, supply-side policies in the face of a declining workforce should therefore include some or all of the following:

1. policies to increase the capital stock and its quality, e.g. robots (which have the added advantage of not requiring pensions);
2. increased investment in labour through education and training;
3. increasing labour force participation by reducing unemployment and by encouraging more married women to join the labour force (e.g. by improving child-care facilities);[18]

---

[18] One aspect of this policy is to make more use of older workers. In the USA the number of men between 55 and 64 in the labour force increased by 2% between 1996 and 1997.

4. raising the retirement age;

5. importing labour, either directly, through immigration, or indirectly, by exporting capital to countries with a young population. A unique opportunity was lost when the UK refused passports to the (mostly young) population of Hong Kong prior to 1997, when the colony reverted to China.

Policy 4 has major advantages. First, it has a powerful effect on pension finance, beneficially affecting both numerator *and* denominator in equation (9.1). Secondly, it has social policy advantages: if men aged 65 have a life expectancy of 77, an increase in men's retirement age from 65 to 67 with no increase in pensions is an implicit reduction in benefits of about 15 per cent, but with the advantage that it works not by reducing living standards in retirement, but by reducing the average duration of retirement. Thirdly, the adjustment to greater life expectancy could come from lower consumption or from longer working life; it seems strange completely to ignore the latter option. For these and other reasons, such policies have been announced in the USA for the years after 2000, and in the UK for women after 2010 (see note 2).

TO WHAT EXTENT IS FUNDING A SOLUTION? Funding is clearly irrelevant to policies 2–5, which can all be pursued by *direct* methods. If funding makes any difference, it can only be if it (*a*) leads successively to an increase in saving, in investment, and in output (i.e. policy 1), *and* (*b*) does so more effectively than any other method of garnering resources and channelling them into productive investment. The stringency of these conditions should be clear from earlier discussion. The evidence on (*a*), both theoretically and empirically, is mixed, inconclusive, and highly controversial, and that on (*b*) is unlikely to be less so. The funding-versus-PAYG controversy can therefore be argued rather to miss the point by concentrating on a method of increasing output which is both indirect (namely, the three steps in (a)) and debatable. Since the issue is one of economic growth, it seems easier and more reliable to adopt direct methods of effecting policies 1–5.

This is *not* an argument against funding; but it *is* an argument against reliance on funding *alone* to address demographic problems. We saw in Chapter 5, Section 2.2 that it is possible to insure against individual risks (e.g. life expectancy), but not against common shocks which affect everyone. Funding and PAYG both offer individuals a measure of certainty about their future, but neither method (indeed, no method) can insure against common shocks. The future is full of uncertainties (about rates of inflation, output growth, birth rates, and the like), which affect pension schemes just as they affect most other institutions. Thus it should not be surprising that there is little to choose between PAYG and funding in this respect. To imagine that funded schemes are substantially better in the face of aggregate uncertainty is to fall for crude mythology.

THE 1985 REVIEW. Not least to deal with demographic change, there was a wide-ranging review of the entire benefit system in the mid-1980s. The state pension was made less generous for people retiring after 2000 (Section 1); and occupational schemes were changed in several ways. The 1986 Social Security Act gave added protection to people leaving a scheme early and/or transferring to a new scheme (i.e. as an aid to labour mobility, occupational pensions were required to have 'portable' benefits).

Contracting-out was liberalized in two important ways. Requirements for employer schemes after 1988 were expressed in terms of defined contributions rather than defined benefits. As discussed in Section 2, this faces the pensioner with the risk of variable returns to pension assets. Secondly, individuals were allowed to opt out of both the state scheme and employer schemes and, instead, to have a personal pension.

These changes had two sets of effects: they reduced the longer-term cost of pension provision, both by making the state scheme less generous and by allowing occupational schemes to move to a defined-contribution basis; and the changes to the state scheme after 2000 reduce the weight given to equity objectives. For instance, the calculation of benefits over a whole working life rather than over the best twenty years works to the disadvantage of individuals with fluctuating incomes, particularly people (mainly women) who have spells in and out of the labour force (for fuller assessment, see Martin Evans 1996a).

A VIEW AHEAD. These trends—downward pressure on state-pension spending and increased emphasis on funding arrangements—are likely to continue. The first is a result of the demographic and global pressures discussed in Chapter 1, Section 3. The second is the result of fiscal incentives encouraging private pensions and is also to some extent the expression of people's choices. By the mid-1990s, for example, 6 million people were contributing to the state earnings-related pension, while 15 million had contracted out and were contributing to occupational or personal pensions. To some extent, therefore, people were voting with their feet. As a result, the more-traditional reform proposals in Commission on Social Justice (1994: 265–85) may be replaced by more radical proposals. Field (1996a), in a book published before he became a social-security minister in the 1997 Labour government, proposed that the state earnings-related pension should be replaced by what he calls a 'stakeholder's pension' scheme, an individual, defined-benefit, funded pension run by the private sector but monitored by government and with some sort of state guarantee. Falkingham and Johnson (1995) offer a set of proposals from broadly the same stable. Similar pressures are leading to similar proposals in the USA (see Diamond 1996a; Gramlich 1996).

5.2. Equity issues

The discussion in Chapter 8, Section 3.2, of equity aspects of national insurance applies equally to pensions. This section concentrates on a number of other issues.

REDISTRIBUTION OVER THE LIFE CYCLE. Hills (1997) (for fuller discussion, see Falkingham and Hills 1995b) looks at the combined effects of taxation and benefits. He finds that of every £1,000 of cash benefits (mostly pensions) paid to a representative person, nearly three-quarters is self-financed. To a significant extent, therefore, the welfare state acts as a 'piggy bank'.

REDISTRIBUTION FROM RICH TO POOR. The system of benefits (Section 1) and contributions (Chapter 7, Section 2.1) together imply considerable formula redistribution (see Section 4.2). At its simplest, from Table 7.3, someone with weekly earnings of £65 pays a contribution of about £2 per week, and someone earning £350 pays about £30. If each received only the basic pension, the 'poor' person would receive fifteen times as much pension per pound of contribution. Because of the earnings-related component, the effect is not as strong as the example suggests; but ceteris paribus there is still redistribution from rich to poor. In 1995/6, the effect of taxes and benefits was to reduce the Gini coefficient for retired households from 66 for original income to 31 for post-tax income (UK Office for National Statistics 1997: table L).

Other factors, however, work in the opposite direction. There is differential mortality, in that the better off have a greater life expectancy (and hence collect their pensions longer) and, a related phenomenon, tend to stay in education longer (and hence start to pay contributions later). Secondly, it is disproportionately the better off who contract out of the state scheme, and this, too, reduces its redistributive impact.

The overall redistributive effect is therefore complex and results are far from definitive. An implication of the life-cycle results just discussed is that about one-quarter of cash benefits are not self-financed. Hills (1997: fig. 12) shows that the 'lifetime poor' are net gainers and the 'lifetime rich' net losers. Alongside redistribution over the life cycle, therefore, the system also redistributes from rich to poor.

REDISTRIBUTION FROM YOUNG TO OLD. The real purchasing power of the UK basic state pension increased by 240 per cent between 1948 and 1995 (UK DSS 1995a: table 5.1), far beyond pensioners' actuarial entitlement. In the USA many retirees receive a social security pension at least twice their actuarial entitlement. Whether this is more equitable than a funded scheme with no such redistributive possibilities is a matter of judgement.

REDISTRIBUTION FROM MEN TO WOMEN can occur in both funded and PAYG schemes as a consequence of differential life expectancy (Section 4.2). This type of redistribution is particularly strong in the UK, which is unusual in having a lower retirement age for women. Taking taxes and all benefits together, Hills (1997) finds that on average women receive a net lifetime gain of about £375 per £1,000 of benefits.

To the extent that this redistribution is caused by the differential retirement age, it is inequitable. First is the anomaly whereby a woman who retires at 65 will receive a higher pension than a 65-year-old man with an identical contributions record, because she has worked beyond her normal retirement age.[19] Secondly, there is the discrimination against women who would prefer to work longer. This is not a trivial matter: the US Age

---

[19] The real pension is increased by 7.5% for each year of work beyond normal retiring age (section 1); thus a woman retiring at 65 receives a pension 37.5% higher than that of an identical 65-year-old man.

Cash benefits

Discrimination in Employment Act 1978, which enables (but does not compel) broad classes of people to defer retirement until they are 70, was enacted not for fiscal reasons but in response to strong political pressure. Thirdly, the earlier retirement age gives a woman fewer years to make up any deficiency in her contributions record. For these, as well as for fiscal reasons, women's retirement age will be increased to 65 (see note 2).

Removing this indefensible anomaly reduces the transfer from men to women but does not eliminate it. What, if anything, could or should be done about it? One answer is to recognise the fact but, having recognized it, to leave it at that. As discussed in Section 4.1, this is defensible, not least because compulsory membership means that the subsidy will not cause inefficiency in insurance markets through adverse selection.[20]

OTHER ASPECTS. Redistribution also takes place between households of different sizes. From Table 8.1, the basic pension for a married couple is 60 per cent higher than for a single person making the same contribution; in the USA the situation is broadly comparable.

Finally, note should be taken of the important relation between accrued pension rights—particularly to the state pension—and the distribution of personal wealth. Because pension rights are distributed more equally than most other forms of non-human wealth, the overall wealth distribution is more equal when they are included. The size of the effect, however, is controversial, depending on (a) precisely which types of pension wealth are included (e.g. how should national-insurance pension rights be treated?), and (b) the valuation placed on entitlements to a future income stream. The latter problem is particularly intractable.[21]

5.3. Conclusion

Empirical investigation suggests that funding is likely to make little difference, if any, to growth rates. The funding solution is indirect in its mechanism, controversial in its outcome, and likely in any case to have only a second-order effect. It would, therefore, be highly dangerous to imagine that simply by embracing funding the demographic problem would be solved. In addition, efficiency arguments of principle point strongly towards a public role at least in underwriting indexation. The efficiency case for continued public, PAYG involvement is therefore strong. Such an argument accepts that it is appropriate for people to use the state as a collective institution for saving and insurance where it is able to perform these functions more cheaply and efficiently than any private alternative. This does not mean that PAYG schemes have never made profligate promises. But the efficiency case for state involvement is, at its very least, a counterblast to the government failure arguments in Chapter 4, Section 5.

---

[20] Voluntary personal pensions do not offer unisex benefits. Reform would require EU-wide action.

[21] The valuation problems involved were discussed briefly in Section 5.1 in the context of labour supply. On the problems of valuing an indexed pension, see UK Select Committee on a Wealth Tax (1975: 665–75). See also the Further Reading.

Aaron (1982) contrasts the absence of conclusive evidence that PAYG schemes have deleterious efficiency effects, with the strong evidence that their equity impact is beneficial, in that they have greatly improved the economic status of the elderly. He concludes that decisions about the future of state pensions should therefore be made mainly on equity grounds.

FURTHER READING

UK institutions are described in Tolley (1996) (published annually; comprehensive, and includes references to the legislation). Private pensions in the UK are analysed by Hannah (1986) and Dilnot et al. (1994); see also Blake (1997) and UK Office of Fair Trading (1997); for US discussion, see Aaron et al. (1989) and Diamond (1996a) and the references in the latter. Systems abroad are discussed by Disney (1996) (a survey of various OECD countries) and World Bank (1994a).

For overviews of the analytics of pensions, see Aaron (1982), Johnson and Falkingham (1992) and Diamond (1995; 1998). Residential care is discussed by Burchardt and Hills (1997); for US discussion, see the relevant chapters in Fuchs (1996).

On the determinants of saving, see Stiglitz (1988: ch. 22), and Atkinson and Stiglitz (1980: lectures 3, 4); for surveys, see Boadway and Wildasin (1994), Blundell (1995), and Robson (1995). On pensions and saving, see Aaron (1982: ch. 4), Diamond and Hausman (1984), Aaron et al. (1989: ch. 4), Kotlikoff (1989b), Dicks-Mireaux and King (1994), and MacKenzie et al. (1997). Empirical studies of the UK include Banks and Tanner (1996), and of the USA, Venti and Wise (1990), Munnell and Yohn (1992), Engen et al. (1994), Gale and Scholz (1994), and Gale (1998).

The effects of pensions on labour supply are surveyed by Aaron (1982: ch. 5), Aaron and Burtless (1984), Lazear (1986a), and Kotlikoff (1989a).

The distributional effects of the UK state pension are discussed by Hills (1997), Falkingham and Hills (1995b), and Martin Evans (1998). For US analysis, see Aaron et al. (1989). See also the Further Reading at the end of Chapter 7.

There is a huge literature on pension reform. For the UK, see Commission on Social Justice (1994: 265–85) and, for somewhat more radical suggestions, Dilnot et al. (1994), Falkingham and Johnson (1995), and Field (1996a). On the USA, see Aaron et al. (1989), Bodie et al. (1996), Diamond et al. (1996) (particularly the contributions by Bosworth (1996) and Burtless (1996c)), Gramlich (1996), and Gordon et al. (1997). On problems and policies in the reforming former Communist countries, see Barr (1994b) and World Bank (1996: ch. 4).

There is also a huge debate. See Atkinson (1995a: ch. 16) (broadly favourable to state schemes), and, for advocates of private schemes, World Bank (1994a) and Feldstein (1996); see also Chand and Jaeger (1996) (who question the fiscal feasibility of rapidly shifting towards funding) and Holzmann (1997) (who questions the size of the savings increase brought about by a move to funding). See also various articles in The *Brookings Review* (Summer 1997), including a debate between Henry Aaron (against radical privatization) and Laurence Kotlikoff and Jeffrey Sachs (in favour).

Discussion of pension rights as part of wealth is contained in UK Select Committee on a Wealth Tax (1975: 665–75) and UK Royal Commission on the Distribution of Income and Wealth (1979: ch. 4). See also Banks et al. (1996) and Hamnett and Seavers (1996).

CHAPTER 10

Non-contributory benefits

Poverty is a great enemy to human happiness; it certainly destroys liberty, and it makes some virtues impracticable, and others extremely difficult.

(Samuel Johnson, 1709–94)

Social security has increasingly become a reactive ambulance, picking up the casualties of social, economic and ideological change. It would be perverse to blame motorway accidents on ambulances, even though they appear every time there is one.

(Martin Evans, 1998)

1. Introduction and institutions

Non-contributory benefits are many and diverse. Their only common feature is that they are all paid from general taxation rather than the National Insurance Fund. The main schemes listed in Table 7.5 are buttressed by many smaller benefits. They differ widely: some are administered centrally, some locally; some are mandatory, others discretionary; some take the form of cash grants for specific purposes (higher-education awards for students), others serve to reduce the price of specific commodities (rent subsidies), others make certain goods available without charge (free pharmaceutical drugs). In many cases the distinction between benefits in cash and in kind becomes blurred, though for present purposes it is not necessary to dwell on them.

As discussed in Chapter 1, Section 2.1, non-contributory benefits are of two sorts: means-tested (i.e. awarded only where income/wealth falls below a prescribed limit), and universal (i.e. awarded without a contributions or income test on the basis of other criteria), a key example of the latter being child benefit. The two sorts of benefit have various of the aims set out in Chapter 1, Section 2.2. The major objective of means-tested benefits is poverty relief; such benefits also contribute to vertical redistribution. The key objectives of child benefit are poverty relief and income smoothing in the face of life-cycle effects. To the extent that the benefit is financed out of progressive taxation, it also contributes to vertical redistribution. If the benefit is awarded to all families without an income test, it assists social solidarity.

This chapter starts by summarizing the institutions of four of the most important of these benefits in the UK (for details, see the Further Reading): income support, housing benefit, and family credit are all means-tested; and child benefit is universal. Section 2 considers the arguments for state intervention; Section 3 assesses means-tested benefits and child benefit, respectively, including a brief survey of empirical evidence.

INCOME SUPPORT is the final safety net, when family income from all other sources falls below a specified minimum. Expenditure is large (£18 billion in 1996/7 (Table 7.5)), exceeding that on any other benefit except the national-insurance pension. The numbers involved are also large: in 1996/7 there were 4.8 million recipients (and over 7.5 million when account is taken of dependants), of whom over 60 per cent were pensioners or unemployed (UK DSS 1997: tables 6, 7). The scheme has changed in various ways since 1948 (Chapter 2, Section 6) and its details are complex. Where a benefit is intended to supplement people's incomes, there are bound to be complications in its interactions with other income sources. Discussion here is restricted to the simplest cases.

Income support is calculated by setting requirements against resources. If the latter are less than the former, the difference is paid as benefit. Additionally, income support acts as a 'passport' to other benefits, including housing benefit, free prescriptions and dental treatment, and free school meals. The scheme is usefully discussed under three heads: eligibility; benefits for those with no income or capital; and the treatment of income.

Eligibility. Anyone aged 18 or over (in limited cases, 16 or over) who is not working for more than sixteen hours per week may be eligible, whether or not he has a national-insurance record or is receiving national-insurance benefit. For those under pensionable age, benefit will normally be conditional on registering for work, with some exceptions such as people with major health problems and single parents of children under 16.

Benefits for those with no income or capital are of two sorts: income support itself, which offers benefit on a weekly basis, and the social fund, from which single payments are made. The determination of income support in any particular case rests on two considerations: how much benefit is awarded to a family with no other income; and how this award is affected by any income the family has, corresponding to the requirements and resources aspects of the benefit.

Requirements are calculated according to scales laid down by law. Income-support payments comprise up to three elements: a personal allowance, which varies according to family size and the ages of any children; premiums for groups of people with special needs, such as families with children, people with disabilities, and people over 60; and help with housing costs. Some of the personal allowances and premiums for 1997/8 are shown in Table 10.1.

The social fund offers additional assistance. There are four types of single payment: budgeting loans for immediate lump-sum needs; crisis loans to meet urgent needs; community-care grants for people facing exceptional problems; and automatic grants for income-support recipients for maternity, funerals, and in exceptionally severe weather. As the names imply, the first two are loans (interest-free), repayable through

Cash benefits

Table 10.1. **Income support rates, 1997/8 (partial listing)**

Types of payment	£ per week
Personal allowances	
Couple (both aged over 18)	77.15
Single householder (aged 25 or over)	49.15
Lone parent (aged 18 over)	49.15
Dependent children	
to September after 11th birthday	16.90[a]
then till September after 16th birthday	24.75[a]
then till day before 19th birthday	29.60[a]
Premiums	
Family	10.80
Family (lone parent)	15.75
Pensioner	
Single	19.65–26.55
Couple	29.65–38.00
Disability	
Single	20.95
Couple	29.90
Severe disability	
One person who qualifies	37.15
Couple (both qualify)	74.30
Disabled child	20.95
Carer	13.35

[a] Child benefit and child benefit increase are, in effect, deducted from these rates.

reduced weekly benefit. The scheme is small (about £250 million in 1996/7 compared with £18 billion on income support).

The treatment of income and capital. The underlying principle is that all income is included unless it is specifically 'disregarded'. Though the regulations are complex (Tolley 1996: ch. 4), the following income is *ignored* for the purposes of establishing entitlement: £5 per week for each claimant; or up to £10 per week for a couple; or £15 per week for elderly or disabled recipients; or £25 per week for a single parent. Certain other types of income may be disregarded, including certain education and training payments and some social-security benefits—for example, the mobility component of disability living allowance.

Disregards apart, *all* income is included in family resources, in particular child benefit and the major national-insurance benefits. For income-support purposes the relevant magnitude is 'net' earnings after tax and national-insurance contributions, and after allowing for limited work expenses, including fares. The ability to deduct these expenses contrasts sharply with the rules applicable for income-tax purposes.

Complications arise in defining the types of income which are disregarded or included, in the interactions when families have several different sources of income, and in the calculation of work expenses. In addition, any capital owned by the individual or family may affect entitlement. The value of an owner-occupied house is ignored entirely. Other capital, including savings, redundancy payments, and some tax rebates, is ignored if it does not exceed an upper limit (£3,000 in 1997/8). Benefits are reduced for recipients with savings between £3,000 and £8,000. Individuals with more than £8,000 (in 1997/8) in savings are not normally eligible for benefit.[1]

A family's benefit is calculated as the difference between its requirements and its resources. If requirements are estimated at £120 and resources at £40 per week, benefit will normally be £80. At the margin an extra pound of earnings therefore costs £1 of benefit, in economic terms a 100 per cent implicit tax rate. Thus the implicit tax on disregarded income is 0 per cent; on most other income, including most national-insurance benefits, it is 100 per cent. Income support can therefore be thought of as 'topping up' family income from whatever source to bring it up to a basic minimum.

HOUSING BENEFIT is administered by local authorities and provides means-tested assistance with rent and local taxation for tenants. Total spending on it in 1996/7 was £12 billion (Table 7.5). For individuals in receipt of income support, benefit is normally equal to the full amount of rent. Otherwise, the value of the benefit depends on the claimant's gross income (including that of his or her spouse), household size, and the amount of rent. Where family income exceeds a specified limit, 65 per cent of 'excess' income is subtracted from the rent in calculating benefit.

FAMILY CREDIT is aimed at the working poor. It is payable to a low-income family with at least one dependent child, and where at least one adult in the family works for at least sixteen hours per week. Spending on family credit in 1996/7 was slightly over £2 billion (Table 7.5). The maximum credit depends on family size. There is an adult credit (£47.65 in 1997/8), plus an additional, age-related credit per child, which are paid in full to families whose net income is below a prescribed amount (£77.17 in 1997/8). Benefit is reduced by 70 per cent of the excess of family net income over the prescribed amount. An award will normally be made for twenty-six weeks, and once made will not be affected by any increase in income during the period. Recipient families are automatically entitled to the same variety of additional benefits as those receiving income support.

CHILD BENEFIT, which replaced child tax allowances and family allowances from 1979 (Chapter 2, Section 6), cost £7 billion in 1996/7 (Table 7.5). Child benefit consists of a tax-free weekly payment (£11.05 for the first child (£17.10 in a lone-parent family) and £9.00 for each subsequent child in 1997/8), where a child for these purposes is under 16, or under 19 if in full-time education. When a child lives with both parents, the mother has title to the benefit.

   In contrast with the former combination of child tax allowances and family allowances, child benefit is administratively much less cumbersome, and is worth the same to everyone, whatever her income. Schemes of this sort exist in many countries—for surveys, see the Further Reading.

---

[1] For a person in long-term residential care, the upper limit for savings is £16,000; benefit is reduced where savings are between £12,000 and £16,000.

Cash benefits

Other schemes range over health benefits (free prescriptions); benefits for the disabled and handicapped; employment and job-training benefits; help for the elderly (e.g. meals on wheels); legal aid; and help for the homeless. There are at least fifty schemes of this sort (see the Further Reading).

2. Theoretical arguments for state intervention

2.1. Arguments for intervention

EFFICIENCY AND SOCIAL JUSTICE. Non-contributory benefits cover three broad categories of people. First are those whose national insurance (despite compulsory membership) leaves them in poverty. Such people are eligible also for income support. Secondly there are those without national-insurance cover because they have exhausted their entitlement or because they never had any (e.g. a school leaver, or a recently divorced woman with no recent contributions). Such individuals have to rely on income support and, where relevant, child benefit. Finally, there are those whose reason for poverty is not covered by national insurance—for example, the parent of a large family in low-paid work, who has to rely on child benefit and family credit.

None of these categories can readily be dealt with by private insurance; and none except the first can be helped by raising national-insurance benefits or by extending their coverage. Much poverty is associated with children and/or high housing costs, neither of which is an insurable risk. Two conclusions emerge: *private* insurance is not possible in most of these cases; nor is extending *national* insurance a complete answer.

The state could, of course, do nothing, and let people face the risk of starvation, but even ignoring equity arguments this would have a variety of *efficiency* costs including social unrest/crime among those facing starvation; the death by starvation of dependants including children (the future labour force); and the fact that malnutrition causes poor health, thereby raising health-care costs and lowering the capacity of adults to work and of children to absorb education. These costs (cf. the nineteenth-century national-efficiency arguments in Chapter 2, Section 2.1) give efficiency grounds for publicly provided income support.

From the viewpoint of social justice, libertarians incline towards private charity where poverty is caused by a non-insurable risk. However, various difficulties (Chapter 4, Section 4.1), including the free-rider problem, are likely to cause voluntary giving to be inefficiently low even by libertarian standards. Thus writers such as Friedman and Hayek do not oppose subsistence payments out of public funds, though they favour every inducement to encourage people to work (the modern incarnation of 'less eligibility' (Chapter 2, Section 1.1)). Socialists, in contrast, argue for generous benefits paid on the basis of need, to advance their egalitarian objectives.

Thus there are solid arguments of both efficiency and social justice for public provision of subsistence benefits on a non-insurance basis. Whether benefits should be above subsistence and, if so by how much, has no definitive answer (Chapter 6, Section 2).

CRITERIA FOR ASSESSING REDISTRIBUTIVE SCHEMES. How effective are non-contributory benefits in achieving the objectives listed at the start of the chapter? This question was tackled for national-insurance benefits (and will be for health care, education, and housing) in terms of their efficiency and equity. But for redistributive schemes the argument is illuminated by three somewhat different criteria which cut across the efficiency/equity distinction.

The level of benefits. Does the scheme give recipients a socially acceptable standard of living—that is, does it achieve the poverty-relief objective? This involves, first, *money benefits*: does the scheme pay enough to allow people to buy an adequate consumption bundle? Secondly, the issue of *stigma*: for any given level of money support a person's living standard (in utility terms) is reduced to the extent that he feels stigmatized by receiving benefit.

Targeting. In Weisbrod's (1969) terminology, targeting has two aspects.

- Vertical efficiency is concerned with avoiding leakages—that is, benefits should go *only* to those who need them. This reduces the cost of the scheme, but may involve high implicit tax rates and the poverty trap (Section 3.2).

- Horizontal efficiency is concerned with avoiding gaps—that is, benefits should go to *all* the poor. Failure can arise either because *eligibility rules* prevent some needy groups from applying, or because *take-up* is less than 100 per cent.

The cost criterion embraces the benefits themselves and also the cost of administration. These three criteria interact in important ways which emerge in subsequent discussion. Cost constrains the freedom to have high benefits. There is an important interaction between cost and the level of benefit: as we shall see, increasing, say, income support by x per cent is likely to increase cost by much more than x per cent. A further interaction is between cost and targeting: again it transpires that reducing the rate at which benefits are withdrawn as family income rises disproportionately affects costs.

2.2. The simple analytics of targeting

Having established targeting as one of the central aims of cash benefits (i.e. the *why* of targeting), it is helpful before proceeding to discuss the *how* (see the Further Reading). There are three basic approaches: via an *income test*, where the amount of benefit is directly related to individual or family income; or via *indicators* of poverty, where benefits are based on easily observable characteristics which are highly correlated with poverty—for example, ill health, old age, or the presence of children in the family. A third possibility is *self-targeting*.

Cash benefits

TARGETING VIA AN INCOME TEST. The idea is simple: poor people are identified by the fact that they have low incomes. The major advantage of this approach is that, at its best, it can target benefits very tightly.

Income-testing, however, has important costs. First, it can create major disincentives to work effort and saving. The central economic issue (discussed in detail in Chapter 11, Section 2.2) concerns the shape of the income distribution—that is, how many poor people there are relative to the number of potential taxpayers. If there are many people in extreme poverty and a small tax base, the tax rates necessary to finance poverty relief create labour-supply disincentives for taxpayers. There will also be disincentives for recipients: if benefits are to be kept in the hands of the poor (which is necessary to meet fiscal constraints), they must be clawed back rapidly as the income of recipients rises. At its extreme, as discussed in Section 3.1, benefit is withdrawn pound for pound with recipients' marginal earnings. This implicit tax rate creates an obvious labour-supply disincentive.

A second problem is that assessing income can be intrusive and hence stigmatizing, particularly if the income unit is the family or extended family rather than the individual, so that the determination of eligibility requires all family members to reveal their income. Thirdly, measuring income is administratively demanding.

INDICATOR-TARGETING uses indicators of poverty which can be measured more easily than income (the classic article is by Akerlof 1978). The idea is best illustrated by example. Assume:

- only redheads are poor;
- all redheads are poor;
- there is no hair-dyeing technology.

In these circumstances it is theoretically possible completely to eliminate poverty, as defined by the poverty line, by paying a redhead benefit; additionally, because benefits go *only* to the poor, expenditure is minimized; and because identification is easy, administrative demands are small.

These results follow, first, because having red hair is a necessary condition for poverty (the first assumption); thus targeting is horizontally efficient; were this not the case, a redhead benefit would leave gaps by failing to cover poor people who did not have red hair. It is also a sufficient condition (the second assumption); targeting is therefore vertically efficient; were this not the case, benefits would 'leak out' to redheads who were not poor. Thus having red hair is perfectly correlated with poverty. Furthermore, having red hair is wholly exogenous to the individual (the third assumption), thus minimizing deleterious incentives. Thus the ideal indicators are:

- highly correlated with poverty, to ensure accurate targeting;
- beyond the control of the individual, to minimize disincentives; and
- easy to observe, to assist administration.

Indicator-targeting can have significant advantages over income-testing. Disincentives for recipients are weaker (since only the income effect works against labour supply). Where the indicator is easily observable (e.g. the number of children in a family), it is less demanding administratively. Thirdly, as discussed shortly, it is possible, with care, to use an indicator which facilitates self-targeting.

There are disadvantages, however. Gaps in coverage arise because some individuals with incomes below the poverty line may not have the relevant characteristics (i.e. the indicators are not completely horizontally efficient). And there may be leakages because some people may possess the necessary characteristics but not be poor (i.e. the indicators are not completely vertically efficient).

SELF-TARGETING. In some circumstances, it is possible to improve targeting by creating an incentive structure under which the choices of claimants act as a signalling device. Two approaches are usefully distinguished.

Price subsidies. This approach subsidizes a carefully chosen bundle of goods consumed disproportionately by the poor. If, for example, only poor people eat black bread, it is possible to offer it at subsidized prices. Other examples include services which have a higher-quality higher-priced substitute, such as public transport. Though analytically valid, the number of commodities which (*a*) have a negative income elasticity of demand, *and* (*b*) form a significant fraction of the consumption of the poor, is very limited.

Conditional benefits. This approach conditions benefit on specific actions by the recipient. One example is 'workfare', where an unemployed person is awarded benefit only so long as she undertakes some form of work or training. This has the advantage that it benefits *all* who come forward and *only* those who come forward; and the only people who claim are those who genuinely cannot find higher paying work. Workfare has these beneficial incentive effects because it imposes costs on recipients in one of two ways: it makes it difficult or impossible for a person to receive benefit while continuing to work unofficially—that is, it 'taxes away' the person's earnings from other work; and, where people are using benefit, in effect, to subsidize their leisure, it 'taxes away' their leisure. In both cases, workfare reduces the individual's replacement rate—in the first case by the reduction or elimination of unofficial earnings, in the second by the forgone leisure—and thus increases the incentive to find work. In principle, the only people who claim benefit are those for whom unemployment benefit plus workfare is genuinely the least-bad option.

There are two potential disadvantages. First, targeting may be imperfect: there are gaps (for instance, because some genuinely poor people are physically unable to work), and leakages (for instance, because public-works employment may crowd out some other wage work) (for a survey, see Ravallion 1991; Ravallion and Datt 1995). Secondly, not everyone agrees that this approach contributes to social justice. Workfare is another manifestation of the nineteenth-century concept of 'less eligibility' (Chapter 2, Section 1.1). The Victorian debate about the balance between incentive effects, on the one hand, and the dignity of the individual, on the other, clearly continues into the present.

Workfare, from one perspective, seeks the beneficial effects of less eligibility whilst trying to minimize the affront to individual dignity.

3. Assessment of non–contributory benefits

3.1. Income support

LEVEL. Are benefits high enough to relieve poverty? With an absolute definition (Chapter 6, Section 2.1) the answer is generally yes: nobody starves; and the level of income support in 1995 was over twice the real value of its 1948 predecessor (UK DSS 1995a: tables 4.1, 5.3). However, there has been concern about hypothermia among the elderly, rising numbers of people sleeping on the streets, and rising numbers suffering multiple deprivation. The problem was serious enough for the 1997 Labour government to introduce a new Social Exclusion Unit, chaired by the Prime Minister, to coordinate policy across departments.

The social fund has been heavily criticized (see Bennett 1996): it works within a fixed budget; most of the payments are loans; and most awards involve local discretion. Though the last aspect is, up to a point, inevitable in a scheme designed to meet exceptional needs, the former two are not. As a result, it is argued, the social fund fails in a significant number of cases to meet the poverty-relief objective, in that take-up is well below 100 per cent.

A separate but equally important issue is whether benefits are high enough not just to *relieve* immediate poverty but to *prevent* it in the longer term (cf. preventive medicine).[2] Again, there is a question mark. Spending cuts in the mid-1990s affected relief to people caring for Alzheimer sufferers. Such benefits, by keeping families together, have obvious social benefits; they are also much cheaper than paying for residential care. Benefits for lone parents are similarly cost effective if, by keeping families together, they keep young people out of (very costly) jail.[3]

TARGETING is concerned with both horizontal and vertical efficiency.

Horizontal efficiency. The eligibility rules for income support are broad, reflecting its status as a benefit of last resort. The USA has no comparable scheme for non-aged adults without children. Income support from that point of view does well.

However, as discussed in Section 3.4, a sizeable proportion of eligible recipients do not receive benefit—that is, take-up is incomplete. On the supply side, some eligible applicants might not be awarded benefit: an official may impose a harsh interpretation on regulations or be unaware of certain entitlements. Such difficulties cannot entirely be

---

[2] In many ways this is the poverty-relief analogue of dynamic efficiency.
[3] See, e.g. Polly Toynbee, 'Poverty by a Thousand Cuts', *Independent*, 25 Nov. 1996, p. 15.

avoided, but there is little evidence of systematic discrimination in the enforcement of rules (e.g. by race) in the award of benefit.[4]

Take-up can be incomplete also for demand-side reasons, in that an unknown number of eligible people do not apply for benefit. Three sets of theories seek to explain why: ignorance, inconvenience, and stigma. It is not surprising that many people are ignorant of their entitlement under the benefit system, notwithstanding considerable efforts to make information more available and easier to understand.

Inconvenience is concerned with the cost to the applicant of making a claim, including the time spent filling in forms, and the need to answer potentially embarrassing questions about income and family circumstances. Some writers (Nichols and Zeckhauser 1982; Blackorby and Donaldson 1988) argue that such costs may be deliberate, to avoid the worst problems of adverse selection and moral hazard. The underlying argument is that the imposition of costs on claimants assists the operation of self-targeting.

Stigma in its pure form arises if individuals feel that, if they receive certain benefits, they will be labelled as belonging to a socially rejected group. Hence there is a psychological cost to claiming benefit additional to the convenience costs just discussed.

Vertical efficiency concerns the extent to which benefit is withheld from those who do not need it. Viewed narrowly, income support scores well. Once a recipient family has used up its small disregard (Section 1), it normally loses £1 of benefit for every pound of additional net earnings, which, in effect, imposes a 100 per cent implicit tax rate on earnings. This targets benefits very tightly indeed.

Figure 10.1 shows in stylized form the combination of leisure and income available to a recipient of income support with an initial endowment at *b* of 24 hours of leisure. The line *ab* shows her earning opportunities. Suppose a scheme is now introduced under which income is not allowed to fall below *Oc*. This is shown by the line *cde*. An individual choosing 24 hours of leisure will receive an income of *Oc=be*. If she works, the first £5 (say) of net earnings is disregarded, and spendable income rises above the income-support level, as shown by the line *eg*. But, once her disregards are exhausted, she loses benefit pound for pound with earnings, and so her spendable income is fixed, as shown by the dotted line *fg*. This is equivalent to an implicit marginal tax of 100 per cent, in the sense that all extra earnings are 'taxed away' by the loss of benefit: it is impossible for recipients to raise their net disposable income; it also removes all financial incentive to work. Where people work solely to earn money, the budget constraint collapses to the two segments *af* and *ge*. No one who works only for money will choose a point on the segment *fg* (since at point *g* the individual has the same income as at *f*, but more leisure). If a person receives £120 in income support, which is lost pound for pound with earnings above £5, then *fg* covers earnings from £5 to at least £125. This strong potential labour supply disincentive is the price of targeting benefit tightly on those in need—in short, vertical efficiency through means testing is inherently in conflict with labour-supply incentives.

---

[4] However, the rules themselves might be discriminatory (e.g. towards women). There have been claims in the past of racial discrimination in the UK (CPAG 1984) and the USA (Barr and Hall 1975).

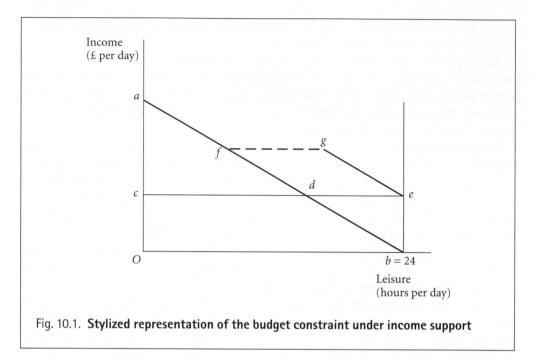

Fig. 10.1. **Stylized representation of the budget constraint under income support**

The labour-supply disincentive is one of the major economic criticisms of income support. An individual who works only for money will choose either to be on the segment *af* (i.e. earning enough to be off income support), or at a point on the line *ge* (i.e. earning under £5 per week). By its very construction, income support almost forces people into one of two extreme categories, of being fully self-sufficient or almost completely dependent on the state, a conjecture supported by US evidence (Barr and Hall 1981). There is no real provision for people who, though not self-sufficient, are able at least partly to support themselves. Such people are rarely apparent because the system almost forces them into full dependence. The very fact of targeting benefits tightly brings about one of the worst features of income support—its tendency to be strongly divisive between the self-supporting and the dependent. The qualitative direction of the disincentive is clear; but there is controversy about its empirical magnitude, to which we return in Section 3.4.

COST. Expenditure has risen sharply over the years largely—though by no means wholly —because of rising unemployment and other reasons for non-participation. When national insurance was introduced in 1948 it was thought that eventually everyone would be self-supporting through work or insurance, and that national assistance (as it was then called) would dwindle. But over time the number of recipients grew, as did the complications.

Administrative costs have also risen. In 1995/6 they amounted to 9 per cent of benefit expenditure for income support and nearly 37 per cent for the social fund; the comparable figure for the national-insurance retirement pension was 1.1 per cent (UK DSS

1997: fig. 12). Are these benefits affordable? The answer must be yes, since they are actually paid. But the possibility of enhancing the scheme is clearly limited.

THE SCOPE FOR IMPROVEMENT is reduced by interactions between the three criteria. First, could benefits be increased? Suppose a family of given size receives £100 per week, which is reduced pound for pound with earnings (disregards are ignored for simplicity). Doubling benefit from £100 to £200 would roughly double the cost of benefits to existing recipients (i.e. by assumption those earning less than £100 per week); but, in addition, more people (by assumption those earning between £100 and £200) would become eligible. Another possible improvement would be to reduce the rate at which benefits are withdrawn as earnings rise. This would increase the transfer receipts of families with other income; and it might reduce stigma, in as much as means-testing (the main cause of stigma) could be reduced. Unfortunately, the room for manœuvre in this direction is also limited. In the example just discussed, with a 100 per cent implicit tax rate only those earning below £100 are eligible; with a 50 per cent rate anyone earning below £200 is eligible. Halving the tax rate, like doubling the benefit level, raises costs both by increasing benefits to existing recipients and by increasing the number of potential beneficiaries. The increase in costs associated with either change is accentuated by the shape of the UK's income distribution. The number of people with incomes between 1 and 1.5 times the income support level is large, correspondingly reducing the scope for increasing benefits.

3.2. Other income-related benefits

HOW THE POVERTY TRAP ARISES

The poverty trap can arise also for people who do not receive income support, but a variety of other benefits. To illustrate with an oversimplified example, someone earning a extra pound could lose (say) 20 pence in income tax, 10 pence in national-insurance contributions, 30 pence in family credit, and 25 pence in various forms of assistance with housing costs, giving a total marginal tax rate of 88 pence.[5]

When discussing the measurement of poverty (Chapter 6, Section 2.3), the three important questions concerned how many people were poor (the 'head count'), by how much they fell below the poverty line (the 'poverty gap'), and for how long they remained there. In the case of the poverty trap, analogously, we need to ask how high are implicit tax rates; how many people do they affect; and for how long do they apply or not apply?

How high are implicit tax rates? The empirical literature is discussed in Section 3.4. Many individuals/families face marginal rates of close to (and in limited cases exceeding) 100 per cent. The ill-effects of such tax rates are twofold. First, low-income families cannot raise their net income. The effect is striking. From official figures (UK DSS

---

[5] In reality, as discussed in Section 3.4, the loss of (say) family credit will take account of the other deductions.

Cash benefits

1995*b*: table 1.8), if the pre-tax wages of a family (married couple with children aged 13 and 16) rose from £50 to £200 per week, spendable income after all taxes and benefits and net of housing costs rose from £146 to £155—that is, an increase in weekly earnings of £150 increased weekly income by less than £10. The second ill-effect is that high tax rates bring about a strong substitution effect against work effort, and so are potentially a major labour-supply disincentive. For fuller discussion of the resulting poverty trap, see Parker (1995).

A complete analysis, however, must take account of several complications. The first is the complexity of the benefit formulas. The more benefits are introduced, the greater the variation in implicit tax rates. In the past, at the point at which entitlement to free school meals was lost, the tax rate in 1982 could reach nearly 300 per cent—that is, an extra pound of earnings could cost nearly £3 in taxes and lost benefit (UK Treasury and Civil Service Committee 1983*b*: 201). In addition, the interactions between different benefits in calculating entitlement to each is complex. The structure of implicit tax rates facing any particular family will depend both on its size and composition, and on the precise mix of benefits it receives; and further complications arise where tax rates are determined by the actual operation of the system, which may differ substantially from the scheme on paper.[6]

This brings us to a second set of complications. It is not enough to analyse the case of a 'typical' family. To assess the impact of the poverty trap we also need to know *how many* families face such rates—that is, how many families of different sizes and types there are at each income level; which benefits they actually receive (the take-up question); and which margin we are discussing, that for the primary or a secondary earner. The empirical literature is discussed in Section 3.4.

MITIGATING FACTORS

The third complication concerns the *length of time* over which people face or do not face these tax rates. Here, fortunately, there are mitigating factors, the most important of which are the existence of fixed period awards, and the fact that most benefits are uprated annually.

THE LOGIC OF FIXED-PERIOD AWARDS. Family credit (and hence also the benefits to which it is a 'passport', such as free school meals and free prescriptions) is awarded for six months, during which the authorities need not be informed of any increases in family income. A family which is awarded £30 a week receives a book of twenty-six vouchers for £30 each, which can be cashed week by week.[7]

The main reason why benefit is awarded for six months is the administrative convenience of not having to reassess a family each time its income changes. This administrative

---

[6] Barr and Hall (1975) found that in 1967 in almost all major US cities the measurement of income by welfare caseworkers reduced the implicit tax rates embodied in Aid to Families with Dependent Children considerably below the 100% rate specified in the regulations.

[7] For a detailed assessment of family credit, see Martin Evans (1996*b*).

practice has a substantial impact on implicit tax rates. Any increase in earnings which occurs during an award period does not result in any immediate loss of benefit, and so the marginal tax rate is zero, at least in the short run. And, even if an increase in earnings is permanent, so that benefits at some future date are assessed on the basis of a higher income, any loss of benefit which occurs not at the time of the increase in earnings, but only later, is likely at least partly to be discounted, and hence to be less of a disincentive.

Conventional presentation of the poverty trap shows that a family earning an extra pound could lose up to, say, 80 pence in benefit. This figure must now be reinterpreted. It is certainly the case that family A will receive 80 pence less benefit than family B if its earnings are one pound higher. Thus the high implicit tax rates apply cross-sectionally. Our interest, however, is the impact on family A's benefits of an increase in its earnings. This is a time-series question, and from this perspective the poverty trap is mitigated in two ways: because of fixed-period awards, an increase in earnings may cause no loss of benefit, at least in the short run; in addition, benefits will generally have been uprated by the end of the award period, taking some of the sting out of reassessment. The moral of the story is the important economic impact of administrative practice.

FORMAL ANALYSIS. The effect of fixed-period awards in reducing the perceived tax effect of the withdrawal of benefits merits more formal analysis (non-technical readers can skip the equations). Consider the value of an income stream of £1 per year subject to a tax rate, t. In perpetuity this is worth

$$P = \int_0^\infty (1-t)e^{-rv}dv = \frac{1-t}{r} \tag{10.1}$$

where v = time, and r can be interpreted either as the rate of interest or as a marginal rate of time preference (both interpretations will be discussed).

If no tax is imposed until the end of the current award period (here till the end of year 1), then the present value of the income stream is P (from equation (10.1)) plus the value of the first year's tax remission, t.

$$P' = P + t = \frac{1-t+rt}{r} = \frac{1-t(1-r)}{r}. \tag{10.2}$$

Comparing equation (10.2) with (10.1) shows that the effect of not levying any tax for the first year is to 'write down' the effect of the tax by a factor $(1-r)$, i.e. the effective burden of the tax is only $(1-r)$ times the nominal burden. Interpreted as a rate of interest, the tax not paid in the first year (£t) can be invested to yield £rt in each successive year, to pay part of each year's tax bill. Interpreted as a rate of time preference, the more heavily the future is discounted, the lower is the perceived burden of the tax.

Equation (10.2) applies strictly only when tax is unpaid for a full year. More generally, suppose that earnings increase when a fraction k, $0 < k < 1$, of the year has already passed. Then only £$(1-k)$ is earned during the current award period, and the present value of the income stream if fully taxed is

Cash benefits

$$P_k = \int_k^\infty (1-t)e^{-rv}\, dv = \frac{1-t}{r}e^{-rk}. \tag{10.3}$$

But, if no tax is levied till the end of the first period, then the present value of the income stream is P_k plus the value of the first year's tax remission:

$$P_k' = P_k + \int_k^1 te^{-rv}\, dv. \tag{10.4}$$

Evaluating and simplifying

$$P_k' = \frac{e^{-rk}}{r} - \frac{te^{-r}}{r}. \tag{10.5}$$

The first term is the present value of an untaxed unit increase in income starting a fraction, k, through the first period; the smaller is k, the larger the value of the pay increase. The second term is the perceived present value of the tax burden where the tax is imposed only after the end of the first period, and is lower the higher is r. Thus the higher the individual's marginal rate of time preference, the greater the tendency for the loss of future benefits to be discounted.

MAJOR IMPLICATIONS. Fixed-period awards have important policy implications. They enable the poor to raise their net income more easily, since benefit need not be lost at the time earnings rise. To that extent, the tendency for families to be trapped in poverty is less acute than the traditional view suggests. Secondly, labour-supply incentives may be improved. Temporary changes in earnings (e.g. overtime at Christmas) will not affect benefits; and even where increases are expected to persist, the tax rate relevant to labour-supply decisions is that *perceived* by recipients, which, from equations (10.2) and (10.5), will depend on their rate of time preference. This is almost certainly high, both because their income is low and because any increase in earnings may only be temporary. A poor worker is unlikely to reject an opportunity to increase his earnings because it might cost him benefit six months later.

There is little systematic evidence on rates of time preference, but inferences are possible. In Canada it normally takes about two months to process a claim for a tax refund. In order to get the money immediately, some people (before the practice was made illegal) would sell their title to a refund for between 30 and 70 per cent of its face value (Community Income Tax Service 1976). The sale of a title to $100 in two months' time for $70 now implies a marginal rate of time preference of 600 per cent per year. From the second term in equation (10.5), $r = 6$ implies

$$t\frac{e^{-r}}{r} = 0.0004t. \tag{10.6}$$

In other words, the perceived tax burden is almost zero. Even with less extreme cases, the tax burden is reduced to under 40 per cent of its nominal value when $r = 100$ per cent, and to under 7 per cent when $r = 200$ per cent. If such rates of time preference are general, the tax effects of delaying the withdrawal of benefits for a few months after earnings have increased are likely to be heavily discounted, thereby considerably reducing the disincentive effect.

In addition to their beneficial impact on (*a*) family poverty and (*b*) labour supply, fixed-period awards have two further advantages. If taxes are fully discounted, the withdrawal of benefit as income rises is analytically equivalent to a lump-sum tax collected at some time in the future, with all the welfare properties of lump-sum taxation. Secondly, fixed-period awards ameliorate the dilemma faced by public policy between the desire to preserve incentives by keeping tax rates low, and the need to reduce costs by targeting benefits tightly on those in need (hence withdrawing benefits rapidly as income rises). Fixed-period awards cushion the impact of high rates of withdrawal, while avoiding the high expenditure which would be involved in substantially reducing them.

3.3. Child benefit

HOW WELL TARGETED? It has been argued that child benefit, because it is not income tested, is poorly targeted. The fallacy with this argument is that it ignores the possibility of indicator-targeting, discussed in Section 2.2.

Having children is highly correlated with poverty and is thus a good indicator. This is no accident. Parents are typically in the younger segments of the population, and thus at a relatively low part of their lifetime earnings trajectory; and the arrival of children frequently reduces second-earner income. For both reasons, family income tends to be low precisely at the time when the demands on that income are high. For life-cycle reasons, families with children *systematically* have low income relative to needs. It is, of course, possible to point to specific high-income families with children; that merely makes the point that child benefit is not *perfectly* targeted. Pointing to exceptions is analogous to arguing that heavy smokers who live into their nineties disprove the ill-health effects of smoking.

This line of argument brings out the point that child benefit, in addition to any re-distributive goals, has an efficiency function as a device which allows families to redistribute to themselves over their lifetime. A similar result could in theory be attained by borrowing, but capital-market imperfections largely rule out that option in policy terms.

TARGETING WITHIN THE FAMILY. Child benefit also assists targeting within the family in two ways. If paid to the mother, the benefit helps to empower women. Secondly, limited systematic evidence and considerable casual empiricism suggest that paying child benefit to the mother improves the targeting of benefits on children.

OTHER ASPECTS. Because targeting is achieved without an income test, the labour-supply disincentive of the benefit is considerably reduced.[8] The incentive, particularly for secondary earners, to work at least part-time is considerably enhanced.

---

[8] There is a disincentive arising via the income effect but, unlike income-testing, none via the substitution effect.

Cash benefits

The administration of an income test is costly, not least because information needs to be updated regularly. Child benefit is administratively cheap because it generally has a single, once-and-for-all information requirement—a birth certificate. Thereafter benefit can be paid automatically for sixteen years. Administrative costs (including single-parent benefit) in 1995/6 were slightly over 2 per cent of benefit spending (UK DSS 1997: fig. 12); as noted earlier, the comparable figure for (income-tested) income support was 9 per cent. For broader discussion of family benefits, see the Further Reading.

3.4. Empirical issues and evidence

The empirical literature on non-contributory benefits is surveyed by Atkinson (1987*a*) and Moffitt (1992). Two issues predominate: their effectiveness in relieving poverty; and their incentive effects.

THE EFFECTIVENESS OF NON-CONTRIBUTORY BENEFITS IN RELIEVING POVERTY

THE LEVEL OF BENEFITS. Are benefits high enough to relieve poverty assuming, initially, that people claim all the benefits to which they are entitled. For the period to 1980, the answer must be a qualified yes. Two points were noteworthy about the level of the main social-assistance benefit: it was set at 100 per cent of a notional poverty line, rather than some fraction; and between 1948 and 1980 it retained its relativity to pre-tax average earnings, and hence rose relative to post-tax earnings (Barr 1981). About 8.4 per cent of GDP was transferred to the lowest income quintile, compared with about 10 per cent in Sweden and Germany, and 4.8 per cent in the USA (Smeeding *et al.* 1990: table 2.3). As a result, Beckerman (1979) found that cash benefits reduced the number of people below the social-assistance poverty line from 22.7 per cent of the population before all transfers to 3.3 per cent, and reduced the poverty gap from £5.9 billion per year to £0.25 billion.[9]

In the mid-1980s, there was a strategic change of direction, in which two sets of changes interacted. First, benefits were increasingly uprated with prices rather than earnings; thus the incomes of recipients fell relative to the rest of the population. As a result, reliance on income-tested assistance grew. Secondly, the underlying concept of poverty changed. 'Indeed, it is possible to argue that "poverty" as a state concept of commitment disappeared' (Martin Evans 1998: 299). The government argued that it made no sense to measure poverty by comparing people's incomes with the level of income support, since improved benefits by definition led to more measured poverty. As a result, official statistics started to count the number of families whose income fell below a fraction of mean or median household income. A commonly used definition was the EU standard of 50 per cent of mean income. An extreme interpretation is that policy,

---

[9] The problems of defining and measuring poverty are discussed in Chapter 6, Section 2.

at least for the decade after 1985, was concerned not with eliminating poverty but with alleviating it. For these and other reasons, as discussed in Chapter 6, Section 2.3, the poverty headcount rose sharply in the UK from the late 1970s onwards.

Poverty relief in the USA differs in two strategic ways: the level of benefit can be inadequate because there is no automatic relation between the official US poverty line (which is federal) and benefit levels (which are set by states); and coverage is incomplete because there is no equivalent to income support, for which *anyone* is in principle eligible. The main post-war social-assistance benefit, Aid to Families with Dependent Children (AFDC), became more generous over the 1960s, but after the first oil shock was increasingly restricted: between 1975 and 1984 real AFDC benefits per recipient fell by 18 per cent (for assessments of the system, see Blank 1997*a*: ch. 4; Levy, 1998). Perhaps more fundamentally, AFDC was replaced in 1996 by a new benefit, Temporary Assistance for Needy Families. The new benefit differs from its predecessor in important ways: states have more discretion over benefit design; the federal contribution is a block grant rather than a matching grant; and the federal contribution is fixed in nominal terms so its real value will decline over time (for fuller discussion, see Blank 1997*b* and the Further Reading). Such policy directions will do nothing to reverse the rising US poverty headcounts discussed in Chapter 6, Section 2.3.

Living standards in utility terms depend not only on cash benefits, but also on the extent of stigma. Empirical studies are inconclusive mainly because stigma is not the only influence on take-up (another crucial variable being the extent to which claimants are aware of their potential entitlement). Serious statistical problems arise in attempting to separate two influences so different and so hard to measure (see Warlick 1981; Moffitt 1983; Duncan 1984).

TARGETING 1: HORIZONTAL EFFICIENCY. First, do benefits go to those who need them (i.e. are they horizontally efficient)? This boils down mainly to take-up, of which there are two main measures: the *caseload* take-up rate refers to the proportion of eligible *claimants* who receive benefit; the *expenditure* measure relates to the fraction of total expenditure (assuming hypothetical full take-up) which is actually claimed. Take-up is far from easy to measure (see Atkinson 1989: ch. 11). It has tended to rise over the years, in part as a result of deliberate action. Official estimates suggest that take-up for supplementary benefit (the predecessor to income support) in the 1970s was slightly over 70 per cent (caseload) and 74 per cent (expenditure) (for this and other estimates, see Martin Evans 1998: table 7.19). In 1994/5 around £9 out of every £10 of available benefit was being claimed, and about four out of every five eligible people were claiming. Take-up was lower for the other main means-tested benefits. Caseload take-up for family-income supplement (the predecessor of family credit) was typically around 50 per cent; by 1994/5 it had risen to 82 per cent of available expenditure and 69 per cent by caseload.

Problems, however, remain. At least one-third of eligible pensioners in 1994/5 received no income support, leaving about 25 per cent of potential benefits unclaimed. In addition, given the sharp increase in the number of poor people, though the *rate* of take-up has increased, the *absolute number* of non-claimants has also gone up.

Cash benefits

In the USA, take-up of the main income-tested benefit, Aid to Families with Dependent Children, increased over the 1970s, largely because of positive action by administrators and rights workers. This progress, however, was reversed from the later 1970s onwards (see Sawhill 1988 and Levy 1998).

A separate aspect of horizontal efficiency is the gender implications of targeting. The feminization of poverty was noted in Chapter 6, Section 2.3. In addition, though results are still tentative, Blank (1997*b*) puts forward a number of reasons why the work requirement in Temporary Assistance for Needy Families may affect women particularly: the disproportionate number of welfare recipients who have experienced domestic and sexual abuse (Raphael 1996), creating labour-market impediments; extensive learning difficulties among the welfare population; and health problems among the children of welfare mothers, hindering paid work.

Drawing the threads together, cash benefits may fail to relieve poverty for three sets of reasons: (*a*) the absolute level of benefits may be too low; (*b*) coverage may be inadequate for certain groups, in the sense that they are poor but not eligible for benefit; and (*c*) take-up may be incomplete either (on the demand side) because of ignorance about entitlement, or stigma, or (on the supply side) out of maladministration and/or discrimination. In the UK (*b*) applies in the case of working families and some single-parent families, and (*c*) applies to the elderly. In the USA problems arise under all three heads.

TARGETING 2: VERTICAL EFFICIENCY. The extent to which benefits are restricted to the poor has two aspects: to what extent does income-testing restrict benefits to the poor; and how well targeted are categorical benefits awarded on the basis of non-income criteria?

Income-testing. For three main reasons—rising unemployment, joblessness connected with lone parenthood and disability, and changes in social security policy—there was a dramatic rise in the number of people dependent on means-tested benefits, from 8 per cent of the population in the mid-1970s to almost 21 per cent twenty years later (Martin Evans 1998: table 7.22). In 1994, nearly 30 per cent of children under 5 lived in households receiving income support—clearly the presence of young children is a powerful indicator of poverty.

There are two key questions about income-testing: the issue of implicit tax rates, and the extent to which benefits go to lower income groups. Prior to the 1985 review (Chapter 9, Section 5.1) marginal tax rates of over 100 per cent were common. The review set out to avoid such rates by basing the income test for different benefits on income *net* of income tax, national-insurance contributions, and other cash benefits. However, attempts to reduce the number of people facing rates of 100 per cent or more led inevitably to a sharp increase in the numbers facing marginal rates of between 70 per cent and 100 per cent. The changes introduced after the review reduced the numbers facing rates of 100 per cent or more from 70,000 in 1985 to 5,000 in 1996/7. Nevertheless, about 645,000 tax units in 1996/7 faced marginal tax rates of over 70 per cent, of whom slightly over 100,000 faced marginal rates of over 90 per cent (UK DSS 1997: fig. 34).

To what extent do benefits go to poorer families? In 1995/6, looking at non-retired households, over two-thirds of spending on cash benefits as a whole went to households (adjusted for household size) in the bottom two income quintiles; these benefits made up 57 per cent of the gross income of a household in the bottom quintile and nearly one-quarter of the income of a household in the next quintile. In contrast, the top two quintiles received some 17 per cent of benefit spending, making up 5 per cent of household income in the fourth quintile and 2 per cent of the income of the top quintile (UK Office for National Statistics 1997: table E).

The interpretation of these figures highlights the dilemma discussed earlier—tightly targeted benefits score well in terms of containing costs, but only by trapping people in poverty and giving them little incentive to increasing their earnings. For these and other reasons, Atkinson (1995a: 303) concludes that 'for all the rhetoric about targeting, means testing has not worked, and a major policy aim in Britain should be to reduce dependence on means-tested benefit'.

Indicator-targeting. A second aspect of vertical efficiency is the extent to which benefits can be targeted through non-income criteria. The a priori arguments why child benefit is likely to be well targeted were set out in Section 3.3. The bottom quintile of households receives 33 per cent of all spending on child benefit, more than three times as much as a household in the top decile (UK Office for National Statistics 1997: table E).

Finally, in assessing the effectiveness of income transfers in relieving poverty, we should remind ourselves of major and unavoidable methodological questions. First, there are the many problems in defining the poverty line, the unit of receipt, and the distribution of income within that unit (Chapter 6, Section 2.1). Secondly there is the value placed by recipients on the transfers: the value of cash benefits may be reduced by stigma, and that placed on in-kind transfers may be less than their market price (though see Chapter 4, Section 4.2). Thirdly, and possibly of greatest intractability, there is the incidence of the transfers (Chapter 7, Section 4.1). Calculations assume (because no other procedure is practicable) that a family's pre-transfer income is that which it would have been in the absence of any system of income support. This is, to say the least, a strong assumption. Similarly, it is assumed that benefits paid to those in work, including family credit and child benefit, have no effect on wage rates.

INCENTIVE EFFECTS

When we turn to the incentive effects of cash transfers, the waters are, if anything, even murkier. The incentive effects of unemployment benefit (Chapter 8, Section 3.1) and pensions (Chapter 9, Section 5.1) are closely linked with the present discussion, which is consequently brief. In the context of income-related benefits, the main empirical questions concern their effects on labour supply and on family formation.

LABOUR SUPPLY. Two questions need to be distinguished: do benefits reduce work effort by those already on benefit; and do they encourage people to join? On the first, Barr and

Cash benefits

Hall (1981), in a study of Aid to Families with Dependent Children in 1967, though it was not an explicit study of labour supply, found that recipients responded rationally to the budget constraint they faced, suggesting a negative relationship between benefit levels and labour supply. Levy (1979) showed that attempts to improve labour-supply incentives in the US system may be successful for existing recipients; but labour-supply overall may fall because benefits (being now more attractive) induce non-recipients to decrease their work effort and join the programme. This is precisely the reason (Section 3.1) why lowering the tax rate implicit in income support is likely to be so costly.

On the second question, Moffitt's (1992) survey of income-tested benefits concluded that, though the major US welfare benefits reduce labour supply, the effect is not strong enough to explain the long-term increase in the number of recipients. All such conclusions, however (and particularly numerical estimates of labour-supply elasticities), should be read alongside the caveats in Chapter 8, Section 3.1, about the empirical literature on unemployment benefits. Saunders's (1995: 6) conclusion about Australia applies equally to other countries: 'while there is a good deal of information on how the income . . . tests influence *incentives*, not enough evidence currently exists for Australia on how these translate into actual *behaviour*.'

Other approaches seek to target benefits in ways which rely less on income-testing (see Gramlich 1989).

- *Regulation* involves policing individual behaviour, for example by enforcing job search or by pursuing child support from absent fathers more vigorously. As examples of the latter, in Australia, child support is enforced through the income tax system; the UK Child Support Agency has a similar function.
- *Indicator targeting*. The categorical approach seeks to minimise distortions by paying more generous benefits to groups (e.g. pensioners) with less elastic labour supplies.
- *Self-targeting*. Another approach is to introduce countervailing incentives which encourage self-targeting. As discussed in section 2.2, income support can be conditioned on work or job training.

EFFECTS ON FAMILY FORMATION. Income support may affect family formation in various ways. Bradshaw and Millar (1991) found no evidence to support the contention that women in the UK become pregnant in order to qualify for benefit. There has been a long-running debate in the USA about whether the welfare system gives families an incentive to split up. In particular, it has been argued that the sharp rise in the number of black female-headed households after 1960 was causally related to the increase in real benefits under Aid to Families with Dependent Children. Conclusions vary widely. Honig (1974, 1976) found a positive relationship between benefit levels and the proportion of female-headed families, with a stronger effect for non-white families. Barr and Hall (1981), using 1967 data, found that race exerted no independent effect on welfare dependency (though this does not rule out the possibility that black and white family formation were equally affected by increasing benefit levels). Yet other studies have failed to find any significant effects. The literature is surveyed by Atkinson (1987*a*) and Moffitt (1992).

Once more, care is needed in interpreting aggregate results. As mentioned earlier, disproportionate numbers of welfare recipients—at least in the USA—suffer domestic and sexual abuse. To the extent that that is the case, it can be argued that an *advantage* of the benefit system is that it makes it possible for families to break up.

3.5. Conclusion

The UK's income distribution, like that in almost all industrialized countries, is heavily skewed towards lower incomes. We want to support the poor (the level criterion), but the income distribution makes it inevitable that benefits must be withdrawn fairly rapidly if limited resources (the cost criterion) are to be targeted on the most needy. This focus can be achieved in various ways: benefit can be withdrawn as family income rises, either immediately (income support) or eventually (family credit); or it can be removed when an individual's status changes (e.g. the loss of unemployment benefit upon resumption of work, or loss of child benefit when a child reaches the age of 16). Whatever the method, a poverty trap in one form or another is largely inevitable, an observation which brings us naturally to Chapter 11.

FURTHER READING

The most comprehensive and up-to-date summaries of the institutions of non-contributory benefits are in Tolley (1996) (which includes references to legislation); this work is published annually. For a survey of social assistance in the OECD countries, see Eardley *et al.* (1996*a*, *b*). Family benefits are surveyed by Ditch *et al.* (1997) and Kamerman and Kahn (1997).

The analytics of targeting are discussed by Weisbrod (1969), Akerlof (1978), Besley and Kanbur (1993), Atkinson (1995*a*: ch. 12; 1995*b*), and Sen (1995*b*). For empirical discussion, see Grosh (1994) and Ravallion and Datt (1995). See also World Bank (1990) for compendious discussion of the practicalities of poverty relief.

For assessment of non-contributory benefits in the UK, see particularly Martin Evans (1996*a*, *b*; 1998); see also Commission on Social Justice (1994: 245–65), Parker (1995), Bennett (1996), and Oppenheim and Harker (1996), and, for more general discussion, Rowntree Foundation (1995). For US discussion, see Burtless (1990), Danziger *et al.* (1994), and Blank 1997*a*: chs. 4 (assessment) and 7 (directions for reform); 1997*b*). Family benefits are assessed by Atkinson (1995*a*: ch. 12). For international comparison, see Smeeding (1997) and Danziger and Jännti (forthcoming), and, for a European perspective, Atkinson (1995*a*: ch. 14). On problems and policies in the reforming former-Communist countries, see Sipos (1994) and World Bank (1996: ch. 4). On poverty and inequality, see also the Further Reading to Chapter 6.

Moffitt (1992) surveys the labour-supply incentives of welfare benefits in the USA; for European discussion, see Atkinson and Mogenson (1993). Effects on family formation are discussed by Bradshaw and Millar (1991). Raphael (1996) discusses the disproportionate amount of domestic and sexual abuse experienced by welfare recipients.

CHAPTER 11

Strategies for reform

If a free society cannot help the many who are poor, it cannot save the few who are rich.

(John F. Kennedy, 1961)

1. Approaches to income support

The last three chapters discussed the cash side of the welfare state in some detail. This chapter considers more generally the pros and cons of different forms of income support. It is a discussion not of specific reform proposals, but of different *strategies*. The starting point is how most usefully to identify the poor. Chapter 10, Section 2.2, distinguished two approaches.

- Benefits can be conditioned on *income* (i.e. means-tested), the archetypal example being the sort of negative income tax discussed in Section 2, below.
- Alternatively, they can be conditioned on the *characteristics* of recipients. The resulting categorical schemes award benefit on the basis of indicators such as being unemployed, sick, or retired. This so-called 'Back-to-Beveridge' strategy is discussed in Section 3.

Section 4 considers mixed strategies. Section 5 summarizes the major conclusions to emerge from Chapters 8 to 11.

The distinction between categorical and non-categorical schemes is important. The former stress the *causes* of poverty, and institute programmes for specific groups. Historically, it was thought that most people would be self-supporting through work, or through insurance against income loss due to unemployment, sickness, or old age; and that the few who fell outside these groups could be categorized into the disabled, the blind, etc. Underlying this approach is the distinction between the 'deserving' poor (e.g. widows with young children) and the 'undeserving'. Such thinking lay behind the Poor Law, and permeated much of the 1930s New Deal legislation in the USA. The Beveridge Report (1942: 124–5), though liberal in its attitude, distinguished eight 'reasonable' causes of poverty.

Non-categorical schemes, in contrast, regard recipients as a spectrum which includes the self-supporting, the very poor, and a large number in between. Such schemes concentrate on *outcome* rather than cause, and classification is made only in terms of need. The approach is attractive because there are few gaps through which 'difficult' cases can fall, but it has the disadvantage of requiring a means test in one form or another.

A common thread throughout the chapter is that there are no easy solutions to poverty in countries with relatively large numbers of people with low incomes. This is not an argument against increased redistribution, but a warning that it will not be brought about without an awareness of the difficulties involved.

2. Income-testing: The negative income-tax approach

2.1. The idea

Negative income taxation is the archetype of cash support conditioned on an income test. This section sets out the analytics of such schemes. Section 2.2 discusses large-scale negative income taxation, and Section 2.3 how a small-scale scheme could be part of a package of wider reform.

THE PRINCIPLE is outlined in terms of a simple income-tax system shown in Figure 11.1*a* by the line *OBA*: individual income is tax free up to £*B*; thereafter it is taxed at *t* per cent. Suppose that $B = £4,000$ and $t = 35$ per cent. The simplest negative income tax is shown by the line G_0BA: if an individual's income is above £4,000, he pays tax of 35 per cent of the excess over £4,000; if it is below £4,000 he *receives* 35 per cent of the shortfall below £4,000. Someone with an income of £4,500 pays 35 per cent of £500, i.e. £175; someone with an income of £3,500 receives £175. More generally, it is possible to have a different tax rate above and below the break-even income (shown by the line G_1BA), and a higher break-even point for larger families.

Formally, the simplest negative income tax relates the individual's tax bill, T (positive or negative), to his income, Y, as

$$T = t(Y - B) \qquad (11.1)$$

where t is the tax rate applied above and below the break-even income, B, as shown by the line G_0BA. It is often more useful to think of the system in a different way: an individual with zero income receives 35 per cent of the amount by which his income falls below £4,000, i.e. £1,400; from equation (11.1) it is entirely equivalent to give *everyone* a transfer of £1,400, and to tax *all* other income at 35 per cent. Thus

$$T = tY - G \qquad (11.2)$$

where $G = tB$ is a lump-sum transfer to the individual, who then pays tax at a rate, t, on all his other income, Y. Similarly, an individual could be given a larger transfer, say G_1 in

Cash benefits

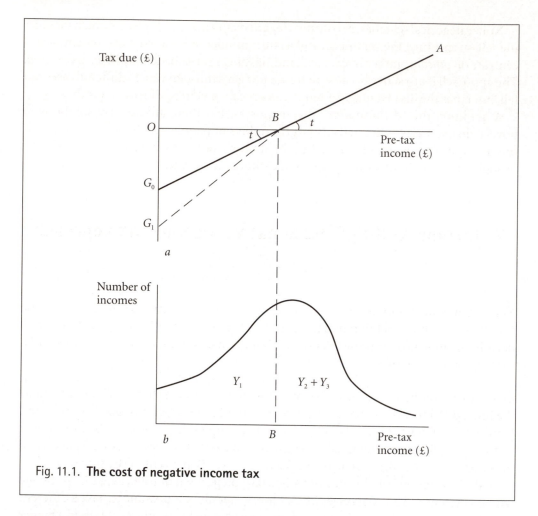

Fig. 11.1. **The cost of negative income tax**

Figure 11.1*a*, and taxed at 50 per cent on the first £*B* of his income and 35 per cent thereafter. A scheme which gives everyone a lump sum and taxes all other income goes under the generic name of a *guaranteed-income scheme*. Equations (11.1) and (11.2) show that guaranteed-income schemes and negative income taxes are analytically identical. Such arrangements have been given various names: minimum-income guarantee, reverse income tax, basic-income guarantee, and social-dividend schemes. Though their administration is different, all are completely identified by two features: the size of the transfer, *G*, to an individual with no income, and the tax structure applied to any other income.

AN EXAMPLE of the guaranteed-income approach is a scheme (the tax-credit scheme) put forward by the UK government in the early 1970s.[1] It proposed weekly payments (at 1972 prices) of £4 per single person, £6 per couple, and £2 per child; all other income was to

---

[1] For the proposals, see UK Treasury and DHSS (1972), for assessments, Prest (1973), UK Select Committee on Tax Credit (1973), and Barr and Roper (1974), and, for a counter-view, Atkinson (1973).

be taxed at 30 per cent, with higher rates for the highest incomes. For people with low earnings the tax credit was greater than their tax liability, thus raising take-home pay above gross pay. Certain groups were excluded—notably, the self-employed and people below the poverty line, the latter because they almost certainly already received some sort of poverty relief, thereby (it was argued) complicating the administration of cash assistance if they received some of their income as tax credit and the rest in other forms of income transfer. The implications of such small-scale schemes are taken up in Section 2.3.

2.2. An assessment of large-scale negative income-tax schemes

Negative income-tax schemes have attracted widespread support (see the Further Reading): from libertarians because cash transfers are compatible with market allocation, and so can loosen what they see as the stranglehold of in-kind transfers under the welfare state, and from socialists because the scheme guarantees everyone at least a minimum income as a right of citizenship and without a means test. Additionally, it is claimed that negative income tax will boost take-up, reduce stigma, and, by bringing all individuals under a single umbrella, enable government to be better informed about the economic condition of the population. Possibly the most important claims are that negative income tax can solve two major problems—the poverty trap, and the failure of the welfare state to redistribute more income.

Why then, despite such widespread support, has no country adopted a large-scale scheme? The short answer, with an income distribution like that in almost all countries, is its cost. This implies a large increase in tax rates, which aggravates the poverty trap and/or creates labour-supply disincentives.

ISSUES OF COST

A useful starting point is the distinction between a small-scale scheme, which offers a low guaranteed income like G_0 in Figure 11.1a, and a large-scale scheme giving a higher transfer like G_1. Under the first, the cost is not large, and no high tax rates are necessary; but the guaranteed income is low, so no substantial help is given to the poor, and the need for additional benefits remains. If negative income tax is the sole anti-poverty device, it is necessary to have a high guaranteed income like G_1. This raises problems of cost, as illustrated in Figure 11.1. The intercept, G_0, and slope, t, of negative income tax completely characterize the position of an individual or family. But the cost of the scheme and its redistributive strength depend *both* on the tax/benefit function *and* on the size distribution of income. The society shown in Figure 11.1b contains many poor people with income less than B, and relatively few rich people; consequently, the cost of the scheme shown in Figure 11.1a will be higher, because of the larger number of net beneficiaries relative to net contributors, than in a richer country (i.e. one in which the left-hand tail, Y_1, is smaller).

Cash benefits

THE LOGIC OF THE COST ISSUE. Estimates for 1972 (Barr 1975) suggest that a scheme which paid a universal transfer equal to the poverty line, would require an average tax burden of between 50 and 60 per cent. Atkinson (1983: 275) illustrates the point: if the guaranteed income for an average family is x per cent of average income, and if income tax currently raises y per cent of average income for purposes other than income support, then the average income tax rate must be $x+y$. With plausible values for x and y (Atkinson suggests 35 per cent and 15 per cent), the *average* rate of *income* tax (i.e. ignoring all indirect taxes, etc.) is at least 50 per cent.

Why are large-scale schemes so costly? The intuitive answer is that 'ordinary' income tax has to raise revenue to finance benefits *only* (or largely) for poor people, whereas negative income tax pays benefit to *everyone*. The resulting increase in taxation can be viewed in two ways: either because higher gross benefit payments require higher taxation; or because higher taxes are necessary to claw back benefits paid to rich people. The effect of universal benefits is to raise at least some marginal tax rates, even if the average tax rate (inclusive of benefits) is unchanged.

It is necessary, however, to dig deeper. Consider the society shown in Table 11.1 with five poor individuals (assumed to have no income) and ten rich people (whose income is £10,000 per year) as shown in rows 1 and 2. The tax base (i.e. pre-transfer personal income) is £100,000 (line 3), and the tax threshold £4,000 under income tax and £0 under negative income tax (row 4). The poverty line, by assumption, is £4,000 per year (row 5). Under 'ordinary' income tax (columns 1 and 2), £4,000 is transferred to each of the five poor individuals in the form of 'welfare' benefits; rich individuals receive no transfer (row 6a). The total cost of the scheme is £20,000 (row 7), requiring a tax rate on income above the threshold of $33\frac{1}{3}$ per cent (rows 8 and 9); post-transfer incomes of poor and rich are £4,000 and £8,000, respectively (row 10). Under an otherwise identical negative income tax (columns 3 and 4), both poor *and* rich receive a transfer of £4,000 (row 6b). The cost of the scheme is £60,000, requiring a tax rate on all income of 60 per cent (rows 7–9). Post-transfer incomes of rich and poor are identical to the income tax case: poor individuals have £4,000; rich individuals each receive £4,000 but have to pay £6,000 in tax, leaving a net income of £8,000. The introduction of a negative income tax with a uniform tax rate has had no effect on post-transfer incomes but, by tripling the cost of income support, has tripled the average tax rate (row 11) to ensure that rich individuals still pay £2,000 net tax despite receiving an initial transfer of £4,000.

However, Table 11.1 to some extent hides the fact that negative income tax may not increase taxation per se, so much as *replace implicit by explicit taxation*.[2] There are two cases. In the first, both the level of benefits and their coverage remain unchanged under negative income tax, as in Table 11.1. Identical recipients receive identical benefits; total net expenditure is unchanged; no increase in net revenue is necessary; and nobody's post-transfer income has changed. Negative income tax has produced an exact mimic of the previous system by a different administrative mechanism: nothing has been done to relieve poverty; and the poverty trap and labour-supply disincentives are unchanged. The only

---

[2] See the Glossary.

Table 11.1. **Hypothetical effect of negative income tax on tax rates**

Basic economic data	'Ordinary' income tax and benefits		Negative income tax	
	Poor individual (1)	Rich individual (2)	Poor individual (3)	Rich individual (4)
Assumptions				
1. Number of individuals	5	10	5	10
2. Pre-transfer income of each individual (per year)	£0	£10,000	£0	£10,000
3. Tax base (=total pre-transfer personal income)	10 × £10,000 = £100,000	10 × £10,000 = £100,000	10 × £10,000 = £100,000	10 × £10,000 = £100,000
4. Tax threshold	£4,000	£4,000	£0	£0
5. Poverty line (per year)	£4,000	£4,000	£4,000	£4,000
6a. Cash transfer to each *poor* individual under income tax	£4,000	£0		
6b. Guaranteed income to *all* individuals under negative income tax			£4,000	£4,000
Implications				
7. Total cost of income support (row (1) × row (6))	5 × £4,000 = £20,000	5 × £4,000 = £20,000	15 × £4,000 = £60,000	15 × £4,000 = £60,000
8. Total taxable income (from rows (3) and (4))		10 × (£10,000 − £4,000) = £60,000		10 × £10,000 = £100,000
9. Tax rate on taxable income (from rows (7) and (8))		£20,000/£60,000 = $33\frac{1}{3}$%		£60,000/£100,000 = 60%
10. Post-transfer income	£4,000	£4,000 + $(1 - \frac{1}{3})$ £6,000 = £8,000	£4,000	£4,000 + (1 − 0.6)£10,000 = £8,000
11. Average tax rate on personal income (from rows (7) and (3))	£20,000/£100,000 = 20%	£20,000/£100,000 = 20%	£60,000/£100,000 = 60%	£60,000/£100,000 = 60%

Note: it is assumed that
1. taxation is levied only to finance cash transfers;
2. there are no transactions costs.

Cash benefits

difference is that in Table 11.1 someone whose income rises from £0 to £10,000 under income tax will (*a*) lose £4,000 via implicit taxation, and (*b*) pay an additional £2,000 in explicit income tax; under negative income tax he pays £6,000 in explicit tax. The only effect of negative income tax in this case is to make *all* withdrawal of benefit part of *explicit* taxation. From one perspective this is a difference more of form than of substance; from another it forecloses the possibility of minimizing incentive effects through devices like fixed-period awards (Chapter 10, Section 3.2), or—as discussed in Section 3—the conditioning of benefits not on income but, for example, on health or employment status.

A second, and very different, case arises where net benefits and/or coverage are increased by negative income tax. This raises the net income of at least some poor people; but net expenditure rises, necessitating an increase in taxes over and above the replacement of implicit by explicit taxation.

The logic of what is happening is seen most easily in terms of two hypothetical states of the world, in which benefits are paid *only* to the poor (state A) or to *everyone* (state B). Then:

1. *Total tax revenue*: gross expenditure, and hence on a revenue-neutral basis also gross tax revenues, must be higher in state B than in state A.

2. *Average tax rate* (ATR): if tax revenues are greater in state B then ATR must be higher.

3. *Marginal tax rates* (MTR): if ATR is higher, then MTR must be higher for at least some groups. There are two polar cases: *either* the increase in MTR is concentrated wholly on the poor, in which case (*a*) the poverty trap is institutionalized, and (*b*) there is a potential labour-supply problem for the poor; *or* the increase in MTR is concentrated wholly on the rich, in which case (*a*) the poverty trap is in principle 'solved', but (*b*) there is a potential labour-supply problem for the rich.

Thus negative income tax inevitably increases explicit tax rates.

FORMAL ANALYSIS. The cost of any scheme is the tax/benefit function in Figure 11.1*a* weighted by the income distribution in Figure 11.1*b* (non-technical readers can skip the equations). Thus:

$$C = AG - \int_0^\infty t(Y)D(Y)dY \tag{11.3}$$

where:

G = the guaranteed income per individual/family,
A = the total number of individuals/families,
Y = personal income,
$t(Y)$ is the tax function (given in Figure 11.1*a* by the tax parameter, t), and
$D(Y)$ is the distribution of pre-tax income (given in Figure 11.1*b*).

Any issue of cost boils down to an empirical question about the elements of equation (11.3). For a given population, A, guaranteed income, G, and tax function, $t(Y)$, the cost of the scheme and its redistributive strength depend on the size distribution of pre-tax personal income $D(Y)$, and in particular on the relative size of the left-hand tail of Figure 11.1b.

Within this framework it is possible (see Barr 1975) to estimate the cost of different tax regimes—'ordinary' income tax and two variants of negative income tax. Each of the systems comprises two elements—gross expenditure and gross revenue. For income tax, gross expenditure consists of total spending on cash benefits, S, and all remaining expenditure, R, out of income tax revenue. R, in other words, is the required surplus of income tax over expenditure on cash benefits. Under a large-scale negative income tax, S is omitted (since all existing cash benefits are, by assumption, abolished), and gross expenditure consists of R and the cost of the guaranteed income payments, AG in equation (11.3). On the revenue side, total personal income, Y, is split into three components: Y_1 is the income of 'poor' individuals/families with pre-transfer income below the tax threshold (i.e. the left-hand tail of Figure 11.1b); Y_2 is income below the tax threshold of families whose total income exceeds the tax threshold (equivalent to the personal allowances under income tax); and Y_3 is income above the tax threshold. Formally,

$$Y_1 = \int_0^B D(Y)\,dY$$

$$Y_2 + Y_3 = \int_B^\infty D(Y)\,dY \tag{11.4}$$

where B is the income-tax threshold. Attention is focused on a very simple form of the tax function, $t(Y)$, in equation (11.3), with tax rates t_1 and t_2 applying, respectively, to income above and below the tax threshold.

Income tax is shown by the line OBA in Figure 11.2. Gross expenditure consists of cash benefits, S, plus the required surplus, R. On the revenue side, income below the tax threshold, $Y_1 + Y_2$, is not taxed (i.e. $t_1 = 0$); income above the threshold, Y_3, is taxed at the basic rate of income tax (including national-insurance contributions), $\bar{t}$. Thus a simplified version of income tax is

$$C_1 = S + R - \bar{t}Y_3 \tag{11.5}$$

where, by definition, $C_1 = 0$.

Dual-rate negative income tax consists on the expenditure side of the gross cost of the guaranteed income, AG (replacing existing cash benefits, S), and the required surplus, R. On the revenue side, taxes are levied at rates t_1 and t_2 on the relevant parts of the tax base, as shown by the line GBC in Figure 11.2. Dual-rate negative income tax is constructed so as to keep benefits in the hands of the poor by ensuring that all benefits are taxed away

Cash benefits

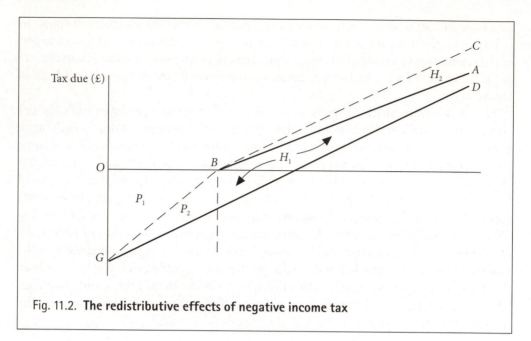

Fig. 11.2. **The redistributive effects of negative income tax**

by the time the tax threshold, B, is reached. A benefit of £80 and a threshold of £100 implies that $t_1 = 80/100 = 0.8$, i.e. the restriction

$$t_1 = \frac{G}{B} \tag{11.6}$$

and the cost of the system is

$$C_2 = AG + R - \frac{G}{B}(Y_1 + Y_2) - t_2 Y_3. \tag{11.7}$$

Compared with income tax, the poor gain an amount related to the area P_1 in Figure 11.2.[3] Since all benefits are taxed away by the time the tax threshold is reached, the rich are invariant between the two systems if the tax rate on income above the threshold remains unchanged. But, as drawn, the dual-rate scheme imposes a higher rate than income tax above the tax threshold (i.e. BC has a steeper slope than BA), so the rich lose an amount related to the area H_2. Benefits remain in the hands of the poor.

Single-rate negative income tax is a special case where the same tax rate is levied on all income. Thus $t_1 = t_2$, and from equation (11.7)

$$C_3 = AG + R - t_2 Y \tag{11.8}$$

where by definition (from Figure 11.1*b* and equation (11.4))

$$Y = \int_0^\infty D(Y)\,dY = Y_1 + Y_2 + Y_3. \tag{11.9}$$

---

[3] Understood as weighted by the appropriate section of the income distribution.

If the constraint of revenue neutrality is relaxed, this system is illustrated by the line GD in Figure 11.2. Income below the tax threshold is now taxed at the lower rate, t_2, so in comparison with income tax the poor gain an amount related to the area $P_1 + P_2$. As drawn, the rich gain H_1.[4] In this scheme, therefore, some benefit spills over to the rich, a result which remains true even if the single tax rate is chosen to ensure revenue neutrality.

A final and important point is the relation between the tax rate t under the single-rate scheme and the dual rates t_1 and t_2, on the assumption that the schemes cost the same. From equations (11.7), (11.8), and (11.9) the tax yields under the two schemes are equal if

$$tY = t_1(Y_1 + Y_2) + t_2 Y_3. \tag{11.10}$$

Hence the relation between the single and dual rates is given by

$$t = \theta t_1 + (1 - \theta)t_2 \tag{11.11}$$

where

$$\theta = \frac{Y_1 + Y_2}{Y}. \tag{11.12}$$

Two important implications follow from equation (11.11). First, t can be thought of as the marginal rate applied to all income, *or* as a weighted average of the dual rates, *or*, more generally, as the average of any set of marginal rates with the same tax yield. Secondly, if t_1 is higher than t_2 (which is likely if the poverty trap is a problem), then t is higher the larger is θ: put another way, t is higher the smaller is Y_3 as a proportion of total income—that is, the lighter the upper tail of the income distribution.

MAJOR IMPLICATIONS. The foregoing apparatus demonstrates some earlier results more precisely. Equation (11.6) shows that under the dual-rate scheme the tax rate, t_1, on low income rises in parallel with the level of benefits. Thus negative income tax recreates the poverty trap in another form. The first conclusion, therefore, is that *with the dual-rate scheme (which keeps all benefits in the hands of the poor) the more successfully poverty is alleviated, the more serious becomes the problem of the poverty trap*. The situation is no different from that under the present benefit system.

The solution to the poverty trap is to withdraw benefits more slowly, in which case the break-even income rises above the tax threshold. This is the case under the single-rate scheme, which lowers the marginal tax rate on the poor. But, from equation (11.7), if the poor pay lower taxes on Y_1, then the rich pay lower taxes on Y_2. It follows, on an equi-cost basis, that more revenue will have to be collected from Y_3. Thus, for a given guaranteed income, *the poverty trap can be alleviated only by increased taxation of the rich*. This, as we shall see, can cause labour-supply problems.

The last result is emphasized by equation (11.11), which shows that the average tax rate t (whether thought of as a single rate of tax applied to all income, or as the

[4] Again weighted by the appropriate section of the income distribution.

Cash benefits

weighted average of a set of marginal rates) will be higher the smaller is Y_3 as a proportion of the tax base. This gives rise to a fundamental (but often overlooked) conclusion—that for a given level of benefit *it is the shape of the income distribution which 'creates' the poverty trap—changing the system of cash transfers will not solve the problem so long as benefits are conditioned on income.*

Negative income tax thus increases tax rates at some or all levels of income: it institutionalizes the poverty trap and/or leads to higher tax rates on incomes above the poverty line. In a country with the UK's income distribution, the level of benefit and its cost can be reconciled only by the imposition of punitive taxation. This raises two consequential problems: the vertical efficiency[5] of negative income tax, as we shall see shortly, is not high despite the presence of high tax rates; and there is potentially a serious labour-supply problem.

CONSEQUENTIAL ISSUES

LABOUR SUPPLY. It is possible to draw on two sets of evidence (see the Further Reading to Chapter 8). Econometric studies broadly confirm the conclusions of attitude surveys that the labour supply of primary workers is wage inelastic. This might be taken to suggest that the introduction of a negative income tax would have no substantial effect on work effort, but several major caveats are necessary. First, labour-supply estimates, being based on actual data, are derived for the most part from tax rates between 25 and 40 per cent; their conclusions are therefore valid only for tax rates within this range. The pitfalls of making predictions outside the range of data on which estimates are based are well known. Secondly (see the references on labour supply in the Further Reading to Chapter 8), the supply elasticity of secondary workers (married women, teenagers, people past retiring age) can be substantial. Finally, there is the effect of perceptions on behaviour. The withdrawal of means-tested benefits as income rises can impose a 100 per cent implicit tax. Negative income taxation makes the tax explicit; and, if taxation is thereby made more visible, labour-supply disincentives might be strengthened.

A second source of evidence is a series of negative income-tax experiments in the USA in the years after 1968. The main one, informally called the New Jersey Experiment, involved more than 1,300 families, who received a guaranteed income between 50 and 125 per cent of the poverty line, and faced tax rates of between 30 and 70 per cent. The experiment spawned a vast literature (see the Further Reading). The consensus, broadly, is that the prime-aged men reduced their labour supply by up to 10 per cent, their spouses by somewhat more, and single women heading families by up to 30 per cent in the longer-lasting schemes, in which the labour-supply responses of participants were not muted by the limited duration of the experiment (see Burtless 1986).

REDISTRIBUTIVE EFFECTS. Negative income taxation has implications for both horizontal and vertical redistribution. A large-scale scheme paying benefits equal to the poverty line may

---

[5] Vertical efficiency is defined in Chapter 10, Section 2.1.

improve horizontal efficiency in two ways: it can increase take-up; and it can reduce stigma, because there is no longer a benefit system for the poor and a tax system for the non-poor, but one system in which everyone is treated similarly.

On vertical efficiency, negative income tax scores less well. At first glance it might appear that by benefiting the poor at the expense of the non-poor, it is strongly redistributive. This is not necessarily so. The cost of negative income tax, as we have seen, depends *inter alia* on the size distribution of income. So too does the redistributive strength of any particular scheme, simply because a 1 per cent increase in the average tax rate raises more revenue for redistribution to the poor the greater the proportion of taxpayers who are non-poor.

Virtually all countries have an income distribution heavily skewed towards lower incomes. With such an income distribution, negative income tax will not be a strong redistributor for two reasons.[6] First, as benefits are increased, the average tax rate has to be raised to finance them. Secondly, there are many people with low incomes and relatively few with high incomes; the tax increase necessary to finance a high guaranteed income therefore falls substantially on those with low and average incomes, thus clawing back a substantial proportion of the benefit to the poor. In consequence, the redistributive effects, though not trivial, are muted.

CONCLUSION 1. Given (*a*) the shape of the UK income distribution, (*b*) current benefit levels, and (*c*) the fact that labour supply is potentially endogenous, two results follow:

- A universal negative income tax will be very costly; this will necessitate high tax rates which are likely to cause labour-supply problems.
- Negative income taxation will not be a strong redistributor.

2.3. The role of a small-scale negative income tax

Given this conclusion, there are three potential ways forward: a small-scale negative income tax in combination with other forms of income support; the 'Back-to-Beveridge' approach discussed in the next section; and schemes which combine the two approaches (Section 4).

THE APPROACH. A small-scale scheme will not solve poverty, and is therefore relevant to poverty relief only if it makes other redistributive schemes more effective. The starting point is the tax-credit proposals described in Section 2.1. The scheme proposed a weekly tax credit, with all other income taxed at 30 per cent;[7] but it would have excluded the self-employed and, more importantly, the poor. The scheme was feasible and would have been implemented but for the election of February 1974. From official evidence (UK Select Committee on Tax Credit 1973: ii. 424), it would have been fiscally possible to make

---

[6] Barr (1975) demonstrates the case in the UK.
[7] Except that those with higher incomes would have paid a higher marginal tax rate.

the scheme universal. This lends support to the proposition that a small-scale negative income tax is financially feasible if the guaranteed income is chosen to supplement existing arrangements rather than to supplant them. For this purpose a guarantee equal to the 'cashed-out' value of the income-tax personal allowance would suffice.[8]

How useful would such a scheme be? We saw in Chapter 6, Section 2.3, that one of the major difficulties in identifying and counting the poor lies in the fact that the income-tax authorities know little about them. The key feature of a universal negative income-tax scheme is not that it would help the poor directly (because the guaranteed income would be small), but that for the first time the great bulk of the population would be brought under the tax authority's umbrella. This would make it possible to use computers to search out the poor (discussed shortly), thereby increasing the take-up of other benefits. The strategy is to use a universal negative income tax not to *solve* poverty, but to enhance the effectiveness of benefits aimed specifically at the poor.

A scheme of this sort, as well as improving take-up, would alleviate the poverty trap in two ways. First, the guaranteed income being universal, all other cash benefits become devices only for 'topping up' income, rather than mechanisms for total income support. This has the important advantage that the tax implicit in, for example, income support will apply over a shorter range of income. Suppose a family receives £100 in income support; under the present system (ignoring disregards) it faces a 100 per cent implicit tax on the first £100 of its net earnings. But if its weekly guaranteed income was £60 it would receive only £40 in income support, and so face a 100 per cent tax rate on only the first £40 of net earnings. As a second improvement, fixed-period awards (Chapter 10, Section 3.2) would further reduce the poverty trap. A family in receipt of a £60 guaranteed income, if awarded housing benefit of £40 per week for six months, would receive £100 per week *irrespective of changes in income*. Thus, by the back door, one is able to achieve the desirable result of paying a larger guaranteed income to families with low incomes. For a detailed proposal of a scheme of this type, see Parker (1989).

ADMINISTRATIVE ASPECTS. It would be highly desirable if existing means-tested benefits were rationalized. This should include standardizing the definition of income used in assessing different benefits; standardizing eligibility requirements (e.g. by extending the current system whereby families receiving income support or family credit are automatically entitled to various other benefits); merging some benefits; and, where possible, making use of fixed-period awards.

Work is also needed on computerizing the tax and benefit systems to enable a universal negative income tax to be used as a search device to seek out the poor. Such development work should ideally be compatible with the move towards self-assessment for income tax in the UK.[9]

---

[8] For example, if the tax threshold is £4,000 per year and the tax rate 25%, the cashed-out value of the personal allowance is £1,000.

[9] For detailed discussion of self-assessment, see Barr *et al.* (1977).

THE RESULTING SCHEME. Anyone could apply for benefit at any time. In addition, the tax authorities could combine their knowledge of (in theory) *everyone's* income to compile at the end of each tax year a list of all tax units with income below some specified amount. This list would be passed to the Department of Social Security. Everyone on the list would have a low income; but not everyone would be poor (e.g. a highly paid person who had started working in the UK only during the last month of the tax year would (legitimately) have a low income for tax purposes, but would not be poor). The Department of Social Security would weed out the non-poor by sending each tax unit on the list an application form for benefit (completion of which would be *voluntary*). The result, almost certainly, would be improved take-up rates.

CONCLUSION 2. The only feasible role for a pure negative income-tax scheme is not as a major redistributor of income, but as a *search device* to discover low-income families, in order to increase take-up rates. For this purpose, the guaranteed income need be no higher than the cashed-out value of current income-tax allowances; thus costs are not excessive, minimizing problems with the poverty trap.

3. Indicator-targeting: The 'Back–to–Beveridge' approach

3.1. The idea

Negative income taxation seeks to raise low incomes by paying benefits conditioned on income. The so-called 'Back-to-Beveridge' strategy makes benefits conditional on other characteristics—for example, being unemployed, ill, or retired, or having children. In its pure form, the approach is based wholly on indicator targeting, with no means testing at all.

Indicator-targeting was discussed in Chapter 10, Section 2.2. The ideal indicators are (*a*) highly correlated with poverty, to ensure accurate targeting, (*b*) exogenous to the individual, to minimize disincentives, and (*c*) easy to observe, to assist administration.

What does the approach imply in practice? Empirically, the major correlates of poverty are unemployment; ill health; large families; single-parent families; old age; and high housing costs; in developing economies, geographical location (i.e. place of residence) or being landless may also be highly correlated with poverty (see Lipton and Ravallion 1995). Benefits paid to people in these categories would embrace a majority of the poor. How exogenous are these characteristics?

- The endogeneity of the level and duration of unemployment is highly controversial (Chapter 8, Section 3.1).

Cash benefits

- With ill health, the problem is less acute because genuine ill health is costly to the individual, and because, if administrative capacity allows, policing is possible through certification procedures.

- The incidence of large families is exogenous with respect to benefits unless decisions to have children are influenced by the existence of family benefits; and, similarly, the occurrence of single-parent families is exogenous unless the decision by parents to separate is substantially influenced by the benefit system (see the discussion in Chapter 10, Section 3.4, of the empirical literature on family formation). A crucial issue in this context is whether having children/separating is more strongly endogenous than labour supply.

- Turning to old age, reaching retirement age is entirely beyond the individual's control. Individuals may choose voluntarily to defer retirement, but this works in the 'right' direction by increasing labour supply.

- Housing costs are far from exogenous under any system which, like housing benefit, bases assistance on *actual* costs. Matters could be improved if assistance were related to a regional index of *average* housing costs (see Chapter 14, Section 5.2).

Particularly where administrative capacity is limited, good indicators are pregnancy, infancy, and school attendance by young children. Such characteristics are not *necessarily* associated with poverty, but the correlation is generally high; there are no major problems of endogeneity (the existence of benefits for very young children is not usually a *primary* motive for pregnancy); and the characteristics are easily observed. In such cases, direct in-kind transfers are both well targeted and non-transferable, particularly because there is a 'captive' target. Pregnant women and infants benefit from nutritional programmes such as free orange juice at maternity clinics and medical check-ups; schoolchildren can be given free milk, meals, and health checks. Such programmes are aimed at a precise, and largely captive group, and they are not readily tradeable. More generally, targeted family support, particularly for nutritional and medical purposes, can be a useful instrument (for further discussion, see Grosh 1994). Another possible indicator is visible old age. Such benefits would empower the elderly (disproportionately women), thereby, through grandmother's discretion, offering family support.

Some comments on indicator-targeting are necessary. First, the strategy offers the possibility of sidestepping the poverty trap by concentrating the entire loss of benefit on a change of category (e.g. accepting a job, or regaining health). Exogeneity in this context is clearly crucial.

Secondly, some individuals with incomes below the poverty line will fall outside the characteristics just described (i.e. the characteristics are not completely horizontally efficient). For this group at least, a residual income-tested scheme would be necessary. There will also be people within the six categories (hence qualifying for benefit) whose pre-transfer income is above the poverty line (i.e. the categories are not completely vertically efficient). For this reason there is a case for making all benefits taxable in the same way as earned income.

Finally, it should be noted that the indicator approach can, at least in part, be organized through the institutions of social insurance (as currently for unemployment, ill health, and old age), but does not have to be (e.g. child benefit). The issue of whether some forms of income support are organized through social insurance therefore remains open.

3.2. A practical example

The Meade proposals are a practical example of the indicator approach. Meade (1978) argues that the existing system fails to prevent poverty because the main national-insurance benefits and child benefit are below the poverty line defined by supplementary benefit/income support, thus violating a key Beveridge principle. His proposed reforms concentrate on rectifying this problem. They are: (*a*) raising all national-insurance benefits to the poverty line defined by income support; (*b*) paying child benefit at the income-support level; (*c*) paying additional benefits (to one-parent families, people with disabilities, etc.); and (*d*) phasing out many means-tested benefits. Income tax should be harmonized with the reformed system: in particular, (*e*) the income-tax threshold should be raised to the poverty line.

Proposals of this sort can alleviate the poverty trap in two ways. First, the major benefits are at or above the poverty line, thus reducing the number of people receiving income support and facing its 100 per cent implicit tax. Secondly, these benefits are not affected by changes in income, but only by a change in the recipient's category—for example, the loss of unemployment benefit upon resumption of work. This does not remove the poverty trap so much as sidestep it by concentrating the entire tax effect on the change in status.

The resulting advantages are twofold. Families are not trapped in poverty (an equity gain). Secondly, the arrangements will have beneficial incentive effects (an efficiency gain), since the criteria on which benefits are awarded are largely exogenous to recipients (or, at least, are more exogenous than labour supply).

4. Mixed strategies

Sections 2 and 3 discussed the two strategies for the most part in isolation. As a guide to practical policy, however, neither on its own is likely to succeed. Benefits conditioned on income generally run into problems of high tax rates, with consequent problems of disincentives and administrative cost; and pure categorical schemes face intractable problems of gaps in coverage, benefits 'leaking' to the non-poor, and problems with defining and administering borderline cases. Targeting, as Atkinson (1995*b*) points out, is a matter of some subtlety and has a number of different dimensions.[10] The most likely path

---

[10] For references on the analytics of targeting, see the Further Reading to Chapter 10.

for reform is a judicious combination of the two approaches. Schemes of this sort start from a small-scale negative income tax, superimposed on which are additional benefits for specific groups such as people who are unemployed or old, and for families with children.

The main purpose of this chapter has been to set out the logic of different strategies for reform, so no attempt is made here to go beyond a brief listing of some proposals. Dilnot *et al.* (1984) advocate a substantial integration of income taxation with benefits, whereby virtually all national-insurance benefits and child benefit are replaced by a series of income-tested benefits with a high rate of withdrawal (in some instances over 80 per cent) at low incomes. The package, though clearing up some of what Dilnot *et al.* regarded as the worst difficulties of present arrangements, had its severe critics (Piachaud 1984; O'Kelly 1985), not least over its administrative feasibility.

The proposals of the Basic Income Research Group (Parker 1989) are more obviously a negative income tax. The scheme has several variants. The most promising pays a guaranteed income roughly equal to the cashed-out value of income-tax allowances, upon which are superimposed more or less the existing structure of social-insurance benefits. Some versions have the additional desirable characteristics that benefit is invariant to age (if below pensionable age), sex, marital status, and employment status, thus minimizing distortions in respect of labour-market decisions and family formation. The use of social-insurance benefits as part of the scheme is seen as transitional, pending the introduction of a large-scale scheme. In many ways this scheme is a universal negative income tax whose intercept varies with the characteristics of recipients, and hence is very much a blend of the two approaches.

Perhaps the most fully articulated mixed scheme is by Atkinson (1995a: ch. 15). He argues (p. 300) that 'it is a mistake to see basic income as an *alternative* to social insurance . . . It is more productive to see [it] as complementary . . . I would see [the] partnership between social insurance and basic income not just as a transitional compromise, but as an alternative conception of basic income' (emphasis in original).

What Atkinson calls the Participation Income scheme is, in essence, a negative income-tax scheme—but one in which benefit is conditioned on some form of participation. Participation is interpreted broadly. A person is eligible if she is working (employed or self-employed), retired, unable to work because of ill health, unemployed and available for work, engaged in education or training, caring for young, old, or disabled dependants, or undertaking approved types of voluntary work.

On the benefits side, the scheme pays a participation income to everyone aged 18 or over who participates in one or more of these ways; and it pays a basic income to all children in place of child benefit. People would also continue to be eligible for social-insurance benefits. On the taxation side, all income, including all social-insurance benefits, is taxed, the only exception being a disregard on the first £10 of weekly earnings (early 1990s prices). Thus the participation income and social-insurance complement and reinforce each other—an explicit mix of the negative income-tax approach and the indicator-targeting approach, with the advantages of both, but few of the disadvantages.

5. Conclusion: Cash benefits

This section brings together the main conclusions of Part 2. The aims of cash benefits were set out in Chapter 1, Section 2.2. Their achievement requires two sorts of mechanism. *Self-help* is necessary for people who are self-supporting on a lifetime basis but need a system of income-smoothing or insurance to iron out discontinuities. *Vertical redistribution* is necessary for those who are unable to support themselves over their lifetime as a whole. Thus the welfare state has both a 'piggy-bank' function and a 'Robin Hood' function.

The menu of methods of self-help includes private insurance and state activity, the latter in the form of social insurance or through transfers out of current tax revenues. Vertical redistribution can be achieved by private charity, or through publicly organized transfers out of tax revenues (note that actuarial insurance cannot systematically redistribute from rich to poor). The respective merits of these methods can be summarized as follows.

ACTUARIAL VERSUS SOCIAL INSURANCE. The private market cannot always supply the efficient quantity and type of insurance against all causes of income loss.

1. Because non-insurance may cause an externality, there is an efficiency argument for making some forms of insurance compulsory (Chapter 8, Section 2.1).

2. Private insurance in several important areas will be inefficient or non-existent: unemployment is an uninsurable risk, mainly because of moral hazard (Chapter 8, Section 2.2); and so, in the context of pensions, is inflation (Chapter 9, Section 3.1). This gives an efficiency justification for public provision of unemployment compensation and, at a minimum, underwriting on a PAYG basis of the indexation component of pension schemes. The efficiency arguments for public provision of sickness benefits and the smaller national-insurance benefits are weaker.

Social insurance was discussed in Chapter 5, Section 4.2. It can deal with risks which market failures prevent actuarial insurance from covering. It can also adapt to changing social and economic circumstances. These can occur because some risks (unemployment, retirement) are in important respects social constructs, the nature of which has changed over time; they can also arise because technical advances (e.g. genetic screening) can create new uninsurable conditions.

PENSION FINANCE. No definitive answer is possible.

1. Theoretical and empirical analysis of the effects of pension schemes on saving and labour supply have produced conflicting results (Chapter 9, Section 5.1).

2. Moving national insurance pensions on to a funded basis will not by itself solve the problems of pension finance caused by demographic change (Chapter 9, Section 5.1).

Cash benefits

The important policies are those which increase national output directly: through investment in new technology and improvements in the quality of labour (both of which increase productivity per worker); and through increased labour-force participation, including lower unemployment, increased participation by women, and—highly effective—later retirement.

3. The choice between PAYG and funding depends mainly on views about income redistribution and policy flexibility (Chapter 9, Sections 3.2 and 5.3).

THE INSURANCE PRINCIPLE—is it possible, necessary, or desirable? It is *possible* for the state to create institutions similar to private, actuarial insurance, e.g. the original Beveridge concept of flat-rate contributions based on average risk, giving entitlement to flat-rate benefits. For non-insurable risks (unemployment, inflation), these merely mimic private institutions but are not true insurance. It does not follow that actuarial institutions (i.e. with risk-related premiums) are *necessary*. If membership is compulsory, it is possible, without the likelihood of substantial inefficiency, to impose a pooling solution in which premiums are not based on individual risk (Chapters 5, Section 3.2, and Chapter 8, Section 3.1).

It is an open question whether adherence to the contributory principle in a state scheme is desirable (Chapter 8, Section 3.1). Social assistance has the advantage of flexibility, since entitlement to benefit does not depend on a contributions record; the corresponding disadvantages are that benefits conditioned on income may be stigmatizing, and can cause a poverty trap (Chapter 10, Section 3). Contributory schemes, while less flexible, may have advantages because they sidestep the poverty trap (Chapter 11, Section 3); because individuals might perceive contributions differently from taxes, with correspondingly different labour-supply effects; and because recipients might feel less stigmatized by benefits conditioned on previous contributions rather than an income test.

VERTICAL REDISTRIBUTION. In part because of the free-rider problem, redistribution through private charity is likely to be suboptimal even from a libertarian perspective and *a fortiori* from a Rawlsian or socialist viewpoint (Chapter 4, Section 4.1). Thus at least some publicly organised redistribution through the tax system can be justified under any theory of society, though with considerable disagreement about how much (Chapter 4, Sections 2.2 and 4.4). Any such redistribution will be constrained by the size distribution of income (Chapter 11, Section 2.2).

NATIONAL INSURANCE IN THE UK. Present arrangements (*a*) are social insurance not run on an actuarial basis (Chapter 8, Section 3.1), and (*b*) (subject to qualifications) redistribute over the life cycle, and from rich to poor, young to old, and men to women (Chapter 8, Section 3.2, and Chapter 9, Section 5.2). Because the scheme is compulsory, (*a*) and (*b*) can be argued to cause no *major* inefficiency apart from a potential labour-supply disincentive—an issue on which evidence to date is inconclusive (Chapter 8, Section 3.1).

272

NON–CONTRIBUTORY BENEFITS IN THE UK. There has been a major move towards income-tested benefits since the late 1970s (Chapter 10, Section 3.4).

1. Income support is withdrawn rapidly as the income of recipients rises, thereby containing costs and targeting benefits on those with the lowest incomes. The price of these advantages is the poverty trap, which makes it difficult for families to increase their standard of living, and therefore creates a labour-supply disincentive (Chapter 10, Section 3.1).

2. Families not in receipt of income support may also face a poverty trap arising out of the withdrawal of other benefits for which entitlement is determined by an income test. Awarding benefit for a fixed period can mitigate the worst labour-supply effects, but the complexity of the existing system makes firm conclusions difficult (Chapter 10, Section 3.2).

REFORM

1. Benefits conditioned on income (whether means-tested explicitly or in the form of a large-scale negative income tax) suffer from the necessity of high tax rates to finance them. This causes a poverty trap with major efficiency and equity costs.

2. For this reason large-scale negative income-tax schemes cannot solve poverty on their own. Their cost is a consequence not of the negative income-tax mechanism *per se* but of (*a*) the existing size distribution of income, (*b*) the poverty line chosen, and (*c*) the empirical fact that labour supply is not exogenous (Chapter 11, Section 2.2).

3. Benefits conditioned on indicators other than income can circumvent some of these difficulties, particularly if the criteria are exogenous to the recipient and highly correlated with poverty. Such indicator-targeting offers some hope of improvement (Chapter 10, Section 2.2, and Chapter 11, Section 3). The most hopeful route for reform is a careful blend of the two approaches (Chapter 11, Section 4).

4. Reform is likely to be hampered by the political difficulties which can beset even small changes (Prest 1983), and by the major difficulties of theory, measurement, and methodology (Chapter 8, Section 3.1, Chapter 9, Section 5.1, and Chapter 10, Section 3.4) which face empirical work.

What are the implications for policy of these largely technical arguments? The preferred libertarian methods of voluntary private insurance and voluntary charity rather fall by the wayside. Private insurance will frequently be inefficient, sometimes because, with complex, long-term contracts, consumers might be badly informed, but more often because of technical problems on the supply side. Libertarians might therefore concede an element of compulsion in view of the externality caused by non-insurance (Chapter 8, Section 2.1), and allow in addition a limited role for non-actuarial, tax-financed transfers to raise to subsistence those incomes which remain low despite private charity. This will be especially relevant to non-insurable risks. Libertarians criticize national insurance as exceeding the scope necessary to achieve this limited purpose, thereby curtailing the freedom of taxpayers to make their own decisions.

Socialists favour public organization of cash transfers, financed by progressive taxation; benefits should be awarded on the basis of need, and should be above subsistence so as to reduce inequality. Whether insurable risks are dealt with out of tax revenues or by social insurance is an area of debate. However, many socialists abhor means-testing, partly because of the poverty trap and partly as a legacy of the Poor Law. In the absence of a universal guaranteed income, this brings us back to insurance, at which point there is some convergence between socialist and liberal views.

FURTHER READING

There is a huge literature on negative income taxation. For a government proposal, see UK Treasury and DHSS (1972), for a range of other proposals, Christopher *et al.* (1970) (tending to the libertarian), Meade (1972) (a cogent liberal appeal), and, for a detailed proposal, Parker (1989). In the US context, see Tobin *et al.* (1967), Christopher Green (1967), Tobin (1968), and Aaron (1973). On the costs of negative income tax, see Barr (1975) and Atkinson (1989: ch. 16).

One of the best accounts of the US negative income-tax experiments, including details of the experimental design and an analysis of the labour-supply responses, can be found in the contributions to Pechman and Timpane (1975); for an account of the experiments in rural areas, see Palmer and Pechman (1978). The official findings from the New Jersey experiment on labour supply are presented in Watts and Rees (1977). For a survey of the large literature on the incentive effects of the experiments, see Burtless (1986).

On the case for 'Back to Beveridge', see Meade (1978: ch. 13) and UK Treasury and Civil Service Committee (1983*a*). On targeting issues more generally, see the Further Reading to Chapter 10.

Reform proposals can be found in Dilnot *et al.* (1984), Parker (1989), Atkinson (1995*a*: ch. 15), Brittan (1995: ch. 13), and Field (1996*b*).

Part 3
BENEFITS IN KIND

CHAPTER 12

Health and health care

Risk varies inversely with knowledge.
(Irving Fisher, 1930)

That any sane nation, having observed that you could provide for the supply of bread by giving bakers a pecuniary interest in baking for you, should go on to give a surgeon a pecuniary interest in cutting off your leg, is enough to make one despair of political humanity.
(George Bernard Shaw, 1911)

1. Introduction to benefits in kind

THE QUESTIONS. Three intellectual threads run through this book: the social-welfare maximization problem, issues of social justice, and problems of definition and measurement. The discussion of cash benefits was concerned mainly with the first two; in the case of benefits in kind the third assumes special importance. Many of the arguments about health care and education turn crucially on the measurement of private and social costs and benefits, and also on the extent to which it is reasonable to assume perfect information.

In part because of these problems, the issues raised by benefits in kind are particularly complex. It is therefore unfortunate that health care and education are bedevilled by emotional polemics, most of which confuse aims and methods. The main purpose of these chapters is not to give the 'right' answer, but firmly to establish the right battleground.

Chapters 12–14 look at health care, education, and housing. Each chapter has a common outline. After a brief introduction (Section 1), the aims of policy are discussed in Section 2 and the theoretical arguments about state intervention in Section 3. Policy analysis concentrates on assessment of the current UK system (Section 4) and possible reform strategies in the UK and elsewhere (Section 5). The conclusions are set out in Section 6. Many of the theoretical arguments, particularly as they apply to health care and education, are very similar. The theoretical sections of Chapters 12 and 13 are written to bring out the parallels rather than to be repetitive.

Given the size of the topics, the three chapters are inevitably eclectic. The main questions asked are: how efficient/just is a competitive market for health care/

education/housing likely to be; to what extent would public production and allocation be more efficient/just; and would any mixed system perform better than either of the pure cases? Several important issues receive little mention, including the detailed finances of health care and education (see Glennerster 1997 and the Further Reading).

NON-ECONOMIC ARGUMENTS. To clarify the approach, it is useful to remind ourselves of earlier discussion of flawed arguments. Bad economic arguments about state intervention are generally of two sorts: either they fail to understand the nature and limitations of market allocation; or they confuse aims and methods. A common libertarian position is that health care is an 'ordinary' commodity which (like any other) should be distributed in accordance with income, tastes, and relative prices; if we do not like the distribution of health care or education, we should change the distribution of income. It is argued below that this is a mistake of the first kind.

Arguments which confuse aims and methods were discussed in Chapter 4, Section 7.2. The view that 'health care/education/housing are basic rights and therefore should be provided by the state' is illogical because the words 'and therefore' simply do not follow from the initial premiss. If health care, etc., are basic rights, then so is food, which is provided well enough by the private sector. For the same reason, the argument that 'health care, etc. should be publicly provided because otherwise the poor could not afford them' does not stand up. Poverty may justify cash transfers but is not, without considerable qualification, a justification for public provision.

The same arguments can be viewed from the political perspectives discussed in Chapter 3. Many socialists believe that health care, education, and housing should be provided collectively. This view is tenable as a value judgement, but the consequent policies will be unsuccessful unless they go with rather than against the grain of economic theory. It is argued here that health care can successfully be provided publicly, mostly without direct charge; but the same cannot be said of housing. Libertarians argue that virtually all goods, including health care, education, and housing, should be supplied privately, because collective provision is both inefficient and a violation of individual liberty. This view, again, is workable in practice only if it accords with economic theory. Markets can fail entirely (unemployment insurance) or be inefficient (many forms of health-care insurance)—devout hopes are not enough. Liberals reject both lines of argument because each makes the *method* of provision (market or state) a primary *aim*. It is argued in Chapter 4, Section 7.2, that a better approach is to choose aims on the basis of personal values and ideology, and then to select on technical grounds whichever method best achieves them.

INSTITUTIONS. The institutions of the National Health Service (NHS) are described in Section 4.1. During the early part of the chapter virtually no institutional knowledge is necessary. As a good approximation, the NHS is financed out of central government revenues, and health care (with minor exceptions) is provided publicly and without charge, both for treatment by a general practitioner (i.e. family doctor) and for hospital in- and out-patient treatment. Most hospital doctors and nurses in the NHS are paid a salary. Family doctors are paid in a complex way reflecting *inter alia* the numbers and ages of their patients. Throughout the NHS there is relatively little fee-for-service. Alongside the NHS is a small private sector.

2. Aims

2.1. Concepts

Social welfare is maximized by the joint pursuit of efficiency[1] and social justice (or equity). This section outlines the meaning of these ideas as they apply to the health sector and then turns to the more difficult problem of measuring them.

The starting point is the obvious, but often overlooked, distinction between health and health care. The primary objective of health policy, it can be argued, is to improve people's health. Health, however, derives from many sources, including (*a*) overall living standards, including the level of income and its distribution, (*b*) individual choice, for example about diet (plenty of fruit and vegetables) and life style (exercise, avoiding smoking, etc.), (*c*) the general external environment (e.g. pollution), (*d*) the individual environment, such as the type of job (or *having* a job), (*e*) the quality and availability of health care, and (*f*) a person's inheritance (e.g. physical and emotional strength). Medical treatment is thus only part of the story. Health policy should look at all of (*a*)–(*e*), not just at health care narrowly defined; policy, for example, should include action on food quality and public education about the health benefits of diet and life-style decisions as well as the resourcing and management of the NHS.

Efficiency is as important here as elsewhere. If we spent nothing on health, some people would die unnecessarily of trivial complaints; if we spent the whole of national income on health care, there would be no food and we would all die of starvation. The optimal quantity lies somewhere between—in principle where the value gained from the last health intervention is equal to the marginal value which would be derived from the alternative use to which the resources involved could be put. This is the quantity X^* in Figure 4.1.

Allocative efficiency (sometimes referred to in discussions of health and education as *external efficiency*) is concerned with producing the quantity, quality, and mix of health interventions (including preventive care and health education) which bring about the greatest improvement in health. External efficiency relates both to the overall size of the health sector as a proportion of gross domestic product (the macro-efficiency aim in Chapter 1, Section 2.2) and to the way resources are divided between alternative uses within the health sector (the micro-efficiency aim). Separately, productive efficiency (Chapter 4, Section 2.1) (sometimes referred to as *internal efficiency*) is concerned, for example, with running medical institutions as efficiently as possible.

---

[1] The concept of efficiency is defined in Chapter 4, Section 2.1.

Equity is more elusive.[2] Le Grand (1982: 14–15) distinguishes four definitions of equity in consumption: equality of public expenditure; equality of use—that is, individuals with the same need should consume the same quantity; equality of cost—that is, *ceteris paribus* individuals should face the same 'price' for the service (including such factors as forgone earnings, time, etc.); and equality of outcome. Two definitions are of particular interest. Equality of utilization implies that everyone in a given condition should receive the same quantity; the problem is that people differ in the extent to which they choose to consume health care or education. Equality of outcome implies an unequal allocation such that everyone enjoys an equal state of health or level of educational attainment. Whether or not such an aim is thought desirable, it is not fully feasible.

To avoid some of these difficulties equity will be defined as a form of *equality of opportunity*, as described in Chapter 6, Section 3.1 (especially equation (6.18)). This does not mean that individuals can necessarily obtain as much health care as they want (since health-care resources are scarce, no system can satisfy everyone's wants). But it does mean that any individual should receive as much health care as anyone else in the same medical condition, regardless of any factors which are thought to be irrelevant—for example, income. The same is true, *mutatis mutandis*, for education.

Problems remain, however. Le Grand (1996) assesses health systems in terms of their efficiency, equity, and administrative feasibility and concludes that no rationing device can simultaneously satisfy all three. Hence evaluation of any system will depend on the relative weights accorded each of the criteria.

Once we have decided the efficient level of health activities and their equitable distribution, the remaining question is who should pay for them—that is, to what extent is it appropriate to finance health care progressively? This is the issue of vertical equity discussed in Chapter 4, Section 4.1. It was argued in Chapter 4, Section 7.2, that if, for example, health care is allocated efficiently by the market, then equity aims are generally best achieved through cash transfers. But where health care is publicly produced and allocated for *efficiency* reasons, it may be appropriate to finance it out of progressive taxation; if so, it is possible, though not inevitable (Section 4.3), that in-kind transfers will redistribute from rich to poor.

2.2. Measuring costs and benefits

The concept of efficiency is well understood. But attempts to make it operational by measuring costs and benefits must of necessity be rough and ready because of serious measurement problems, particularly in quantifying benefits. The total cost of the NHS and its component parts is readily available (Table 12.1). The costs of different types of treatment are harder to establish, *inter alia* because of the familiar problem of apportioning overheads and the need to distinguish short- and long-run marginal costs, but these problems are not insurmountable.

[2] See Chapter 4, Section 4, and Chapter 6, Section 3.1. See also Le Grand (1991*b*, 1996) and Culyer and Wagstaff (1993).

MEASURING BENEFITS faces three major problems.

Health is hard to measure. Health care is only an *input*; the output is improved health. Expenditure on health care can be estimated, but health itself is hard to measure except in terms of broad indicators such as infant mortality, life expectancy, and estimates of the burden of disease.

Causality is complex. To what extent is any improvement in health *caused* by medical care? A patient's complete recovery could be due entirely to the treatment she has received; or it could be due, wholly or in part, to her natural recuperative powers. The influence of intangible factors (the 'will to live') is crucial, but impossible to measure. Similarly, improvements in health outcomes (e.g. life expectancy) may be due to improved diet, reduced smoking, cleaner air, and the like. If such factors are ignored, we will tend to overestimate the benefits of health care.

Improved health is hard to value. The difficulties are illustrated by the extensive literature on valuing human life (see the Further Reading). Such attempts are sometimes regarded as immoral. But all sorts of policies affect the risks faced by individuals, and hence the number of deaths. Many accident victims would be saved if they could receive medical attention rapidly; nevertheless, we do not have casualty departments on every corner, nor ambulances constantly patrolling the streets. Thus we are not prepared to spend infinite sums of money to save one life. The question therefore arises of how much we should be prepared to spend to reduce the risk of death by 1 per cent or, more generally, to reduce the extent or duration of ill health.

The measurement problems are obvious once we realize that the benefits of improved health are twofold. There are (or may be) *output benefits*—that is, the increased output/income of the individual whose affliction is reduced or removed. This is hard enough to measure. In addition, there are intractable problems in measuring the *utility benefits* arising from any reduction in the physical and emotional suffering of the patient and his or her family.

ASSESSING EFFICIENCY is therefore problematical. There are three approaches: cost-benefit analysis, cost-effectiveness analysis, and cost-utility analysis. Cost-benefit studies are limited by the difficulties of measuring health benefits. Cost-effectiveness analysis considers a specific medical condition, and examines the costs of alternative forms of treatment. Thus it avoids the need to measure benefits; major difficulties remain, however, because evidence on the effectiveness of most medical treatment is scant (only about 25 per cent of current health interventions have been tested in double-blind trials).

Cost-utility analysis looks not at the *health* benefits of treatment but at the *utility* benefits, based round the idea of a Quality Adjusted Life Year (QALY). A QALY starts from the premiss that the outcome of medical care should be measured in terms not only of the quantity of extra life it produces, but also of its quality. Though measuring quality inevitably involves subjective judgement (e.g. of *how much* a restriction in mobility reduces the quality of life), QALYs have the merit of incorporating subjective values explicitly and systematically. QALYs look at the extra years (adjusted for quality) resulting from treatment, and divide them by its cost. Some forms of treatment represent an inefficient use of resources—for example, the treatment is unpleasant, it does not extend life by much, and the time remaining is full of pain and discomfort. Other types of treatment, in contrast, are underused. One example is a hip replacement: it is not expensive; and, though it does not prolong life, it considerably improves its quality. For further discussion, see Williams (1985) (the classic article) and Wagstaff (1991), and for discussion of an alternative measure, Healthy Year Equivalents, Bleichrodt (1995) and Culyer and Wagstaff (1995).

The conclusion to which this leads is simple but depressing. The efficiency aim for health is clear enough in principle (and the same will turn out to be true for education), but measurement problems make definitive empirical answers unlikely, if not impossible. The definition of equity is more elusive but, as we shall see in Section 4.3, empirical work has made some headway.

3. Methods

3.1. Theoretical arguments for intervention 1: Efficiency

This section looks at how the aims discussed in Section 2 might be achieved, in particular *why* the state intervenes (Sections 3.1 and 3.2) and *how* in theory it might intervene so as jointly to maximize efficiency and equity (Section 3.3).

Private markets allocate efficiently only if the *standard assumptions* hold—that is, perfect information, perfect competition, and no market failures such as external effects (Chapter 4, Section 3.2, and the Appendix to Chapter 4, paras. 5–17). The underlying question is why health care is 'different' from equally vital commodities like food.

INFORMATION PROBLEMS

Does medical care conform with the standard assumptions (Arrow 1963; Culyer 1971a)? First, are individuals perfectly informed about the nature of the product (in analytical terms, is their indifference map well defined)? The answer, clearly, is no. Many people are unknowingly ill, particularly the elderly, and those with ailments such as diabetes and hypertension, which can be largely without symptoms in their early stages. In addition, individuals are often ignorant about which types of treatment are available, and about the outcome of different treatments, which is often probabilistic. Furthermore, what little the patient knows is generally learnt from the provider of medical services; and many types of treatment (e.g. setting a broken leg) are not repeated so that much of what a patient learns is of little future use.

There are other areas (hi-fi, used cars) where the consumer has to rely on the supplier for information. But in these cases it is usually possible to buy information (e.g.

consumer magazines, or a report by the Automobile Association), and legislation offers increasing consumer protection.[3] With medical care:

- Much (though not all) the information is technically complex, so that a person would not necessarily understand the information even were it available.
- Mistaken choice is costlier and less reversible than with most other commodities.
- An individual generally does not have time to shop around if his condition is acute (contrast the situation with a car repair, which can be left until the car owner has enough information and can afford the repair).
- Consumers frequently lack the information to weigh one doctor's advice against another's.
- Health and health care have strongly emotive connotations—for example, ignorance may in part be a consequence of fear, superstition, etc.

To a considerable extent, therefore, consumers are poorly informed both about the quantity of treatment they need and the quality of the care they receive; and even if information were available, health care is inherently a technical subject, so that there is a limit to what consumers could understand without themselves becoming doctors. The problem is exacerbated by the existence of groups who would not be able to make use of information even if they had it, such as victims of road accidents.

Ignorance is not necessarily evidence of inefficiency. Information may be costly, and its acquisition therefore inefficient if the resulting gain is small. Some degree of ignorance may well be optimal, though certainly less than would prevail under a private health-care market.

If consumers are to make rational choices, they need to have the necessary information, and also the power to enforce their decisions. Efficiency therefore requires equal power, in the sense that there should be no constraint on the ability of individuals to consume health care (or education) apart from differences in their money income—that is, people may have different incomes, but there should be no discrimination. This assumption was presented in Chapter 4, Section 3.2, as a precondition of perfect competition, but the issue is closely related to perfect information and so fits naturally into the discussion at this point. In the context of health care and education, power consists largely of knowledge about their uses and benefits; knowledge about one's rights in respect of the NHS and the educational system; and the ability and confidence to be articulate. It is somewhat implausible to imagine that this is the state of affairs for all consumers, though in the final analysis the issue is empirical.

Because of imperfect information and unequal power, consumers will choose inefficiently, though there is room for debate about the extent of the problem (this is one of the key issues in any discussion of health care). It is also not clear whether the result will be under- or over-consumption. If the 'true' marginal private valuation in Figure 12.1 is shown by the curve *MPV*, consumer ignorance can result in demand curves *D1*

---

[3] It has been suggested that a consumer magazine about medicine might be called *Which Doctor?*

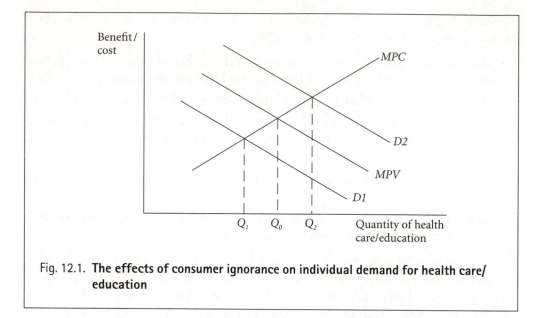

Fig. 12.1. **The effects of consumer ignorance on individual demand for health care/ education**

(under-consumption) or *D2* (over-consumption). In addition, where knowledge and power are systematically related to socioeconomic status, there is also inequity (Section 3.3).

What solutions exist? The provision of information on a scale sufficient for rational individual choice may be too costly, in which case decisions about treatment must be delegated to doctors. Minimal intervention takes the form of regulation—for example, only individuals with approved qualifications are allowed to practise medicine. But where the information problem is serious, the performance of the market may be so inefficient that more extensive state involvement, either through substantial regulation of private production, or through public production and allocation, might be a better solution. We return to this issue in Section 4.2.

A separate issue is whether consumers are adequately informed about prices (formally, whether their budget constraint is well defined). Here, again, it can be argued that most consumers are ignorant of what a particular form of treatment 'should' cost; and, because a great deal of medical care is not repeated, information often has no future use. Nor would it help if consumers were well informed about prices. Rational choice requires simultaneous knowledge *both* of prices *and* of the nature of the product (i.e. of both budget constraint and indifference map); knowledge of prices without adequate information about different types of treatment will not ensure efficiency.

The result is inefficiency of the type discussed above, and summarized in Figure 12.1. If the *only* problem were inadequate information about prices, the appropriate intervention would be regulation, either in the form of a published price list or through price controls. But where information about the nature of the product is imperfect, ignorance about prices adds further weight to the argument for more substantial state involvement.

INSURANCE PROBLEMS

The third information assumption—knowledge about the future—clearly fails with health care, as stressed in Arrow's (1963) classic article. Patients do not know when, or how much, health care they will demand; they lack information about the probabilities of different outcomes for different types of treatment, and about the relative efficiency of different providers of health care; and they consume health-care services infrequently, often at a time when their judgement and ability to acquire information are small. The problem of uncertainty is therefore serious.

In many instances the market solution is insurance (Chapter 5). The real issue, therefore, is whether the private market can supply medical insurance efficiently. This, we saw in Chapter 5, Section 3.1, requires five technical conditions to hold: the probability of needing treatment (see equation (5.12)) must be independent across individuals, and less than one; it must be known or estimable; and there must be no substantial problem of adverse selection or moral hazard (the last three conditions adding up to perfect information on the part of the insurance company). The extent to which these hold for health care is discussed *inter alia* by Arrow (1963) and Pauly (1974, 1986); for a summary, see Culyer (1993).

Looking at the first condition, the probabilities of different individuals requiring treatment are independent except during major epidemics.

Secondly, the probability of requiring treatment of a particular type is less than one for ailments like appendicitis or a broken leg. But the condition fails for chronic medical problems (e.g. diabetes) arising before a policy is taken out. Also—a big future problem—it will fail as developments in genetic screening, by improving knowledge of future health problems, create more and more uninsurable conditions (Barr 1995).[4] The libertarian solution is insurance starting before birth. More realistically, perhaps, President Clinton in 1997 foreshadowed regulation preventing insurance companies discriminating on the basis of genetic tests.

Thirdly, the probabilities relevant to medical insurance are generally estimable. However, problems arise with policies whose benefits are a long time in the future, clouding knowledge of the relevant risks—for example, long-term incapacity to work (Burchardt and Hills 1997: ch. 5) and residential-care insurance, discussed in Chapter 9, Section 3.1.

Finally, problems arise of both adverse selection and moral hazard (Chapter 5, Section 3.2).

ADVERSE SELECTION occurs where an individual can conceal from the insurance company that he is a bad risk. In this situation equilibrium can be inefficient, unstable, or non-existent. Akerlof (1970: 492–3) asks why Americans over 65 cannot easily buy medical insurance, and concludes 'that as the price [of insurance] rises the people who insure themselves will be those who are increasingly certain that they will need the insurance; for error

---

[4] A related (but different) point is that treatment of long-term illness is generally expensive, so that competitive pressures act to reduce premiums at the expense of long-term coverage.

in medical check-ups, doctors' sympathy with older patients, and so on make it much easier for the applicant to assess the risks involved than the insurance company'. Summers (1989), more broadly, argues that, if employees know better than their employers whether they are likely to have high medical bills, the employers providing good medical benefits will disproportionately attract employees with health problems, thus discouraging the provision of fringe benefits.

Notwithstanding debate about the magnitude of the problem (see Pauly 1986), there is evidence about the instability of pooling equilibria (see Chapter 5, Section 3.2) in the face of competitive pressures: Blue Cross/Blue Shield, the main US non-profit insurer, originally practised community rating (charging everyone in a locality the same premium), but was forced by competitive pressures from commercial insurers to adopt experience rating (related to the risk of individual subscribers).

MORAL HAZARD can arise in two generic ways: patients may be able to influence either the probability of requiring medical treatment, or its cost. Taking the probability issue first, individuals with full insurance might take fewer health precautions; this is the problem (case 2 in Chapter 5, Section 3.2) addressed by Pauly (1974, 1986). Secondly, both the decision to consult one's family doctor and pregnancy can be matters of *choice* which lead to the consumption of medical services. Elective medical care of this sort (case 3 in Chapter 5, Section 3.2) is not well covered by voluntary policies: some risks are un-insurable in private markets, at least for voluntary individual policies.

Moral hazard arises also through the *third-party payment* problem (case 4 in Chapter 5, Section 3.2). The problem arises because (*a*) the insurance company is largely divorced from the decisions of doctor and patient, and (*b*) the doctor is paid a fee for service. At its simplest, suppose medical insurance covers all costs. Health care is then 'free' to the patient; and the supplier is not constrained by the patient's ability to pay. Patient and doctor both face zero *private* costs, even though the *social* costs of health care are positive and frequently large, and both have an incentive to consume all health care which yields *any* private benefit. The result is over-consumption, i.e. Q_1, greater than the efficient outcome, Q^*, in Figure 12.2.

Matters, however, can be more complex. The doctor is an agent for *two* principals—the patient and the insurance company. As a result, 'the relation between health care and health outcomes is so loose that performance guarantees cannot be given to either principal; this is a kind of information asymmetry that faces both ways and that is perhaps even shared by the agent him- or herself' (Blaug, 1997, p.10; for fuller discussion, see Blomqvist 1991).

One additional, and separate, problem requires discussion—that of transactions costs. We saw earlier (equation (5.17)) that insurance, even if efficient on the supply side, can be provided at a price which the individual is prepared to pay only if his degree of risk aversion is sufficient to cover the insurance company's administrative costs and normal profit. If transactions costs are too high, some risk-averse individuals will choose not to insure. This is not *per se* inefficient if high transactions costs are unavoidable. But it is inefficient if an alternative system could avoid them—for example, private

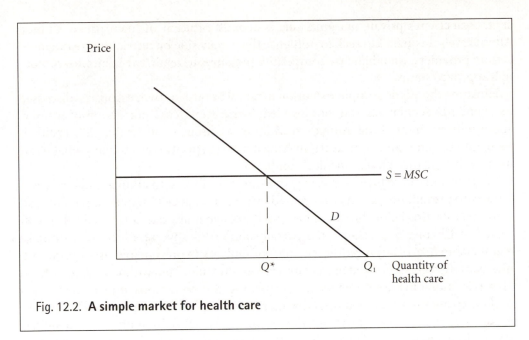

Fig. 12.2. **A simple market for health care**

health-care insurance in the USA has high accounting costs; these are avoided by the NHS, which rarely has to send patients a bill.

The theory thus predicts that conventional medical insurance will face two sets of problems:

- *Gaps in coverage* arise for risks such as chronic and congenital illness, the medical needs of the elderly, and primary health care.
- *Inefficiency* occurs in various forms, particularly over-prescription of medical care as a result of third-party incentives.

The first set of difficulties, plus the problem which arises if transactions costs are high, all lead to *under-consumption*. Third-party payments cause *over-consumption*.

SOLUTIONS. There are two lines of attack on these problems: market solutions, and the adoption of different forms of intervention. As discussed in Chapter 5, Section 3.2 (see also Pauly 1986; Ellis and McGuire 1993), insurance companies have adopted various devices to contain costs in the face of the third-party payment problem. To reduce demand, insurers can limit coverage: premiums can rise disproportionately with the degree of cover sought; and there can be less-than-full cover through deductibles (where the insured person pays the first $X of any claim) and coinsurance (where the insured person pays x per cent of any claim). Such devices reduce the demand for treatment. None is a complete solution: deductibles, except for small claims, do nothing to face individuals with the *marginal* cost of treatment; and, with a coinsurance rate of, say, 20 per cent, the patient's private marginal cost is only 20 per cent of marginal social cost. Alternatively, insurers can seek to influence the supply side by restricting treatment to certain providers, who then face competitive pressures to retain the insurance company's approved status.

However, there is no complete solution to moral hazard for two reasons. As discussed in Chapter 5, Section 3.2, the root problem is the imperfect information of insurers about the behaviour of the insured. In addition, as discussed in Section 2.2, 'health' is hard both to define and to measure, making it hard to specify contractually what treatment is covered for different medical conditions.

Intervention can reduce inefficiency in a number of ways. Insurance could be compulsory to prevent the externalities caused by non-insurance (Chapter 8, Section 2.1), with cover starting before birth to cope with the congenitally and chronically ill. As discussed in Chapter 5, Section 3.2, a partial solution to adverse selection is to make membership (e.g. of an employer scheme) compulsory to prevent low risks opting out. Alternatively, regulation could prevent insurance companies from withholding cover from high-risk individuals, simultaneously regulating the conditions under which they could increase premiums. Compulsory membership of national, provincial, or work-related systems of social insurance in various industrialized countries has a similar effect. Moral hazard would have to be left to dubiously effective devices like coinsurance, or to different types of insurance, like health maintenance organizations (discussed in Section 5).

Most industrial countries (the USA is an outlier) do not use private insurance as the primary method of financing health care. Two models predominate. Social insurance (as defined and discussed in Chapter 5, Section 4.2) abandons the model of actuarial insurance because it does not fit health care very well. Alternatively, medical care can be financed via the tax system.

THE REMAINING ASSUMPTIONS

The assumption of equal power was discussed earlier. The next step is to consider the applicability of perfect competition—that is, whether the markets for inputs like skilled manpower and drugs are competitive. Doctors, it is argued, do not act like the profit-maximizing monopolists of elementary textbooks, but rather pursue several goals. It is suggested that a doctor's reputation depends more on the assessment of her fellow professionals than on direct evaluation by the consumer, and that the approval of colleagues is more easily achieved in the development of more advanced techniques (e.g. heart transplants). Thus, there can be a bias towards certain glamorous types of health care. Doctors' behaviour is then determined jointly by this type of motive and by their economic environment. As we have seen, doctors may not face the costs of their production decisions, but are reimbursed by insurance companies. There is no budget constraint facing doctors individually; and on aggregate they are constrained only by the willingness of consumers or employers to pay insurance premiums. These arguments, if true, point towards oversupply of health care generally. In addition, the *composition* of that supply may be distorted in favour of glamorous areas, and against low-prestige activities (e.g. general practice, occupational health).

What solutions exist for this non-competitive behaviour? At a minimum, regulation is required on standards (e.g. doctors must have approved qualifications), plus perhaps some regulation of prices and possibly also monitoring of doctors' activities. Another potential solution is the libertarian approach (see the Further Reading) of removing entry barriers to medical practice, thereby enhancing competitiveness on the supply side and largely removing the need for state intervention of the type just described. This solution may be more apparent than real. The advantages of competition are that it increases consumer choice and minimizes costs. As we saw in Chapter 4, Section 3.2, however, an increase in the range of choice is desirable only where consumers are sufficiently well informed to make choices, which is frequently not the case with health care; and, if competitive forces push down prices, consumers, for the same reason, are unable to assess whether quality has declined, and if so whether they want the lower-quality product at the lower price. The counter-argument to the proponents of market systems for health care is that *the advantages of competition are contingent on perfect information.*

The conclusion is that supply-side deviations from competitive behaviour may cause inefficiency; but removing restrictions to competition is unlikely *on its own* to improve economic welfare.

The remaining assumptions concern externalities and increasing returns to scale. The literature on health care distinguishes two sorts of externality: 'caring' externalities, such that my utility is reduced if you receive less health care than I think you should (these are a matter more of the *distribution* of health care than the efficiency of its production (see Section 3.2)); and technological externalities.[5] The latter arise mainly via communicable diseases (e.g. if I am vaccinated against polio I benefit, and also confer a benefit on you because you cannot now catch polio from me). In the context of today's medical technology, these externalities, though real, are only a small fraction of the total value of health care. It is a standard proposition that technological external benefits, if uncorrected, cause under-consumption by creating a divergence between private and social benefits. The problem can be solved in a variety of ways, the most relevant here being regulation (e.g. making vaccination compulsory) or a Pigovian subsidy. Externalities are not *per se* a justification for public production and allocation.

It is sometimes argued that health care is subject to increasing returns to scale (Chapter 4, Section 3.2, and Figure 4.4). Were this the case, health care would be a natural monopoly which, if uncorrected, would lead to under-consumption. However, the range of output over which health care exhibits increasing returns to scale is small even with today's large-scale technology, so the problem is unlikely to arise except, possibly, in sparsely populated areas.

---

[5] On the definition and effects of externalities, and possible remedies, see Chapter 4, Section 3.2, and/or the Appendix to Chapter 4, para. 15.

For all these reasons, according to Blaug (1997, p. 4): 'the thrust of [Arrow's (1963)] essay was to show that health care markets *invariably* fail and that the best we can do is to minimise the consequences of market failure . . . what we can never do is entirely to eradicate the inherent inefficiencies of resource allocation in health' (emphasis added).

3.2. Theoretical arguments for intervention 2: Equity

HORIZONTAL EQUITY was discussed in Chapter 4, Section 4.3, in terms of perfect information (which is necessary for rational decisions) and equal power (which is necessary to enforce those decisions). Both may be lacking for consumers of health care (and of education). Equity issues arise most acutely where these problems systematically affect the lower socioeconomic groups most strongly (a likely occurrence if information is costly to acquire). Thus lower-income individuals may have less information relevant to choices about health; in addition, they may be less able to make use of any information they acquire. In such cases intervention in the following forms may improve equity as well as efficiency.

Regulation would be concerned with the professional qualifications of doctors and nurses, with drugs, and with medical facilities in both public and private sectors.

Where imperfect information causes under-consumption, a subsidy might be applied either to prices (e.g. free medical prescriptions) or to incomes. In most circumstances price subsidies are cheaper (Lindsay 1969): if the price of health care is subsidized, consumption will increase via both income *and* substitution effects; with an income subsidy only the income effect operates, so a larger subsidy is generally needed to bring about a given increase in consumption.

Where problems of inadequate information and inequality of power are serious, efficiency and equity may jointly be maximized by public allocation and/or production. In broad terms this depends on two factors: whether the private or public sector is more efficient at producing health care; and whether monitoring of standards is more effective in one sector or the other. This issue is discussed in Section 3.3.

VERTICAL EQUITY concerns the extent to which health care does or should redistribute from rich to poor. We saw in Chapter 7, Section 4, that (subject to various caveats) publicly provided health care is redistributive if (rich) individual R pays more tax contributions to its cost than (poor) P where each consumes the same quantity, and also if R consumes twice as much as P but pays more than twice as much in contributions. Why might this be thought desirable—why, in other words, might people care about the distribution of health care? A formal explanation is given by the voting model discussed in Chapter 4, Section 4.2. Suppose R's utility rises both with his own consumption and with P's. In particular, suppose that R's utility rises with 'good' consumption by P (e.g. health care or education) but falls with P's 'bad' consumption, e.g. beer and karaoke. This is a consumption externality of the type described by equation (4.15). It might, therefore, be rational for R to offer P a transfer of health-care costing, say, £300 but a cash transfer of only

£100 (since P might spend the latter on 'bad' consumption). Given these offers, P might prefer the in-kind transfer to the lower cash amount (see Figure 4.5). If the difference between the two offers is sufficiently large, both rich *and* poor might vote for compulsory in-kind transfers of health care.

It is worth delving more deeply into the nature of the consumption externality. 'Good' consumption by the poor can raise the utility of the rich for two entirely different reasons. The rich might vote for transfers of health care for reasons of efficiency/self-interest. They might believe that a healthier workforce fosters economic growth; or that increased health care for the poor raises their productivity and/or reduces the cost of caring for them; or that such transfers prevent social unrest. This is the 'national-efficiency' argument (Chapter 2, Section 2.1) which gives rise to the Marxist interpretation of the welfare state (Chapter 3, Section 5.3). A completely different explanation is that some rich individuals care about the distribution of health care for reasons of *altruism* (Lindsay 1969).

Thus, alongside efficiency arguments for public production and allocation, there may be powerful equity motives making it politically easier to make transfers in kind. The rich may favour them for either selfish or altruistic reasons; and the poor may prefer them, either because the in-kind transfer is considerably more generous than the cash offer, and/or because they feel less stigmatized by receiving benefits in kind than in the form of means-tested cash transfers.

The voting model explains why *some* transfers of health care take place. But is the amount transferred *optimal*? This was discussed in Chapter 4, Section 4.4. Libertarians support in-kind transfers (if at all) only as *voluntary* action by the rich, but not as a result of coercion by the poor via the ballot box (Chapter 4, Section 4.1); they therefore argue that redistribution under the existing system is greater than optimal. Socialists support in-kind transfers for their own sake, because they increase equality, and argue that redistribution of health care is almost certainly suboptimal.

THE ROLE OF GIVING. Previous discussion suggested two reasons for intervention to enhance equity: inadequacies of information or power may justify intervention to improve horizontal equity; and consumption externalities can explain in-kind transfers. The role of giving raises a third set of arguments. The analysis so far has treated health care as a commodity to which the standard economic arguments apply. But most societies, for generally accepted ethical reasons, decree that certain commodities, which in principle are readily marketable, should be excluded from the usual economic calculus. Thus, there is a free market for the purchase and sale of cattle but, in most countries, no similar market for babies, for wives, or for slaves. Titmuss (1970) argues that, for ethical and philosophical reasons, there should similarly be no market for blood, which should be donated to recipients. This, he argues, is a morally superior method of distribution.

Two questions arise: how valid are Titmuss's views about blood; and do the arguments generalize to other commodities? Whether blood should be given rather than allocated by the market is ultimately one of social values, so that no answer is unambiguously right or wrong. But Titmuss's views are rightly respected on moral grounds, and also because certain characteristics of blood make its allocation as a gift both feasible and (arguably) also efficient. The reasons for the latter view are threefold: the opportunity cost of the act of giving blood (e.g. the time and discomfort) is small; and that of losing a pint of blood effectively zero; furthermore, blood donation can create an altruistic externality, in as much as donors often experience a utility gain, not from the act of giving but from the thought of the benefit the blood will confer on others. These considerations together suggest that the marginal social cost of blood is likely to be low, and may be zero. In this case giving might be both morally superior *and* efficient.

This makes blood a special case, so that it is dangerous indiscriminately to generalize the notion of giving into areas like health care and education (a mistake of which Titmuss himself was never guilty). The main reason is that the marginal social cost of, for example, health care is positive and often large. It is, therefore, an economic commodity. If a doctor spends more time with one patient, she will have less time to spend with others; and resources devoted to health care are at the expense of other uses (contrast the case of blood, the giving of which has virtually no opportunity cost to the donor, and which (*pace* Dracula) has no non-medical uses).[6] Thus, voluntary giving of health care and education, even if regarded as morally superior, will generally run into major allocative problems which do not arise with blood (though see Sugden 1984).

3.3. Types of intervention

Sections 3.1 and 3.2 discussed *why* the state might intervene. The next question is *how* best it might do so. Since the aim is jointly to maximize efficiency and equity, they are discussed together. Three types of regime are considered: market production and allocation (with or without income transfers); public production and allocation; and intermediate strategies. The analysis of market production is closely linked to the issue of 'privatization' discussed in Chapter 4, Section 6, which should be read alongside this section (see especially Table 4.1, which is referred to extensively).

Medical technology used to be cheap, so that health care could be treated as a basic right like voting privileges; but costly advances are making this approach unsustainable.

The policy of meeting medical need, which once entailed little social waste, now threatens to cause considerable waste, largely through the provision of services that are medically needed (the benefit to the patient is positive), demanded (because marginal cost to the patient is zero or very low), and supplied (because providers are fully reimbursed or are indifferent between low- and high-benefit care), but that provide benefits worth less . . . than social cost.   (Aaron 1981a: 25)

Advances in medical technology, by increasing the range of feasible medical interventions, contribute to rising medical spending. Thus macro-efficiency (i.e. expenditure on health care as a proportion of national income) has become increasingly important in all industrial economies (Section 4.1). It is therefore more than usually important to be dispassionate in considering methods of allocation.

---

[6] Though resources used in *processing* and *storing* blood do have alternative uses and hence a positive opportunity cost.

PURE MARKET PROVISION. Some writers (see the Further Reading) argue that health care is similar to food. On the demand side, consumers have preferences which they should be allowed to translate into their utility-maximizing consumption pattern. Supply will adjust to these preferences more efficiently if it is competitive. Government intervention destroys the fit between demand and supply, and the destruction is greatest if intervention takes the form of public production. Writers of this ilk favour privatization to the greatest extent possible—that is, ideally row 1 in Table 4.1, or for low-income families row 2.

We saw in Section 3.1 that health care comes nowhere near conformity with the standard assumptions, so that unrestricted market allocation is not a theoretically promising approach. But analysis of the pure market case is important to an understanding of the problems raised by health care. To focus the argument, discussion concentrates on two simple cases, initially assuming away non-competitive supply-side behaviour, and concentrating on problems of imperfect information on the demand side of the product market and the supply side of the insurance market.

Case 1. Assume initially that there is no insurance, so that consumption is constrained by price. In the presence of consumer ignorance (and to some extent also because of unequal power) the demand curve is not properly defined, but 'wobbly', as shown in Figure 12.1, so that the market-clearing quantity can be above or below the optimum. Uncorrected externalities lead to under-consumption, and non-competitive supply-side behaviour to under- or over-consumption, depending on what it is that doctors seek to maximize. The result is inefficiency in the total volume of resources (i.e. macro-inefficiency), possibly substantial, though with no clear presumption of its direction, and also micro-inefficiency (i.e. the allocation of resources to different types of health care). There is also considerable inequity; the distribution of health care is determined by inequalities in the income distribution; and these inequalities are heightened if knowledge and power are correlated with income, and also by the absence of insurance and perfect capital markets. The overall result is likely to be *under-consumption* of health care.

Case 2. Assume that the insurer pays all bills in full. Consumption is no longer constrained by price, and is therefore determined mainly by the supplier; as a result, the indeterminacy of the patient's demand curve is less important. On the supply side, the doctor has no incentive to ration demand to the efficient quantity Q^* in Figure 12.2. Both patient and doctor can behave as though the cost of health care were zero, leading to *over-consumption* Q_1.[7] There is also inequity, since some individuals are unable to buy insurance (the old, the chronically ill, etc.), and others cannot afford insurance premiums which over-consumption has raised to an inefficiently high level.

These arguments, it should be noted, do not necessarily apply on the input side. There is no reason why many material inputs should not be privately produced—for example, food products (the NHS does not grow its own vegetables), drugs, beds, towels,

---

[7] There might be some pressures to economy—e.g. from employers who pay health-care insurance premiums on behalf of their employees.

Benefits in kind

X-ray machines, and so on. Some inputs of services might also be privately produced (e.g. food or laundry), provided that the costs of quality control are not excessive.

MIXED PUBLIC/PRIVATE INVOLVEMENT. To what extent might health care be based on mixed public/private involvement so as to avoid the worst problems of pure private provision? The desirability of such a package depends on two factors: would it be more efficient/ equitable than any other method including the NHS; and might it be politically more acceptable than NHS-type arrangements (as might be the case, for instance, in the USA)?

Production. The supply of medical treatment in a private market is crucially influenced by fee for service and third-party payments. Thus, as we saw above, the market output, Q_1 in Figure 12.2, exceeds the efficient output, Q^*. Third-party payments create a divergence between private and social costs and benefits, and hence cause a particular kind of externality. These, we know, can be dealt with in a number of ways, of which two are of special relevance. First, output could be restricted to Q^* by *regulation*; this would involve policing doctors' decisions, either by administrative means or through the imposition of a budget constraint (e.g. row 3(*b*) in Table 4.1).

Alternatively, it is possible to *internalize the externality* by merging the activities of doctor and insurance company, thereby forcing doctors to face the social marginal cost of the treatment they prescribe. The outstanding example of this approach is the notion of a *health maintenance organization* of the type now widespread in the USA (see the fuller discussion in Section 5.1). The essence of a health maintenance organization in this context is that *doctors* provide the insurance. As a result, the externality is internalized and there is no longer an incentive to over-prescribe. It might be possible by one of these methods to constrain private production to its efficient level.

Finance could be organized in one of two generic ways. One possibility is private finance plus residual state finance. 'Easy' cases (i.e. the insurable conditions of non-poor individuals) are financed by private insurance, subject to regulation in two ways: there would be minimum standards of coverage; and insurance would be compulsory because of the externality caused by non-insurance (see Chapter 8, Section 2.1). Two difficulties arise: non-insurable risks, and the poor. The former, as we saw in Section 3.1, include congenital and chronic health problems, the medical needs of the elderly, visits to general practitioners, and pregnancy. The state could deal with these cases either by subsidizing private insurance premiums, or by paying for treatment through a residual public insurance scheme or out of tax revenues. The poor could be assisted similarly. This approach raises serious problems: there is the difficulty of defining borderlines, both as between the types of health-care problem which qualify for state assistance, and over the income level below which the poor are subsidized; policing would be necessary to prevent oversupply; and the familiar poverty trap (Chapter 10, Section 3) could arise for the poor.

A second possibility is state finance. Here the state pays medical bills through social insurance or out of tax revenues. An analytically equivalent arrangement is compulsory membership of regulated, private, non-profit insurance institutions acting, in effect, as agents of the state. The advantages of this arrangement are twofold: the scheme's compulsory nature makes it possible with no efficiency loss to gear premiums to ability to pay, rather than to risk (Chapter 5, Section 4.1); and its universal coverage (with respect both to individuals and type of illness) avoids problems with borderlines. Such social-insurance institutions, precisely because they are not strictly actuarial (i.e. because premiums are not risk-rated on an individual basis), can avoid the gaps of private schemes (cf. Chapter 8, Section 2.2, for the case of unemployment benefits).

These considerations suggest two coherent mixed strategies. Suppose that health care is *produced* by health maintenance organizations of some kind; that membership is compulsory for all individuals; and that insurance premiums are *financed* by individuals (in the case of the poor out of transfer incomes). This arrangement has the flavour of row 3(*a*) in Table 4.1. Alternatively, suppose health care is produced privately, but not by health maintenance organizations; payment is made by the state (directly, through social insurance, or through regulated medical insurance); and total output or expenditure is controlled by the state either directly or via a global budget constraint. This mechanism (broadly that of Canada) follows the general thrust of row 3(*b*) for health care per se and of row 6 for health-care insurance.

PUBLIC PRODUCTION, ALLOCATION, AND FINANCE. The elements of row 8 in Table 4.1 require separate justification. Consumer sovereignty is appropriate where information is sufficient for rational choice, a process which may be assisted by regulation of quality. In the case of health care, the patient's information is often so imperfect that the individual-consumption decision is best made on his behalf by an agent (column 3). The argument for publicly financed health care (column 4) rests on the problems just discussed of private insurance—namely, the imperfect information of insurance companies (which contributes to the third-party-payment problem), and the fact that not all medical conditions are insurable. The third-party-payment problem can also justify public production as a method of controlling the resulting large and inefficient increases in the output of health care. More formally, the imperfect information of consumers justifies control of *quality*, and that of insurance companies control of *quantity* (column 2). Both forms of policing might be more effective if production itself were public (column 1).

The argument for public production and allocation thus turns in a crucial though complex way on the issue of information. To justify this arrangement, however, it is necessary to show not only that the conditions for market efficiency fail, but also that public production and allocation are less inefficient than other arrangements. The first point is relatively easy to establish, the second less so.

Because of information problems the NHS strategy can be regarded as feasible—an institution which arose historically largely for equity reasons works because it goes with the grain of *efficiency* considerations. The strategy has four cornerstones. Dealing with demand-side problems:

Benefits in kind

- Treatment is decided by doctors, thus addressing problems of consumer ignorance.
- Health care is (mostly) tax financed and (mostly) free at the point of use.

These features avoid gaps in insurance by abandoning the insurance principle even as a fiction; and medical care is made available without stigma. On the supply side:

- There is little fee for service, reducing third-party-payment incentives to oversupply.
- Health care is explicitly rationed, in part by administrative means, and partly by the existence of a budget constraint for the NHS as a whole. The idea, at least in principle, is to restrict consumption to the quantity Q^* in Figure 12.2.

Furthermore, once it is established that public production and allocation are justifiable on efficiency grounds, it is legitimate to finance health care so as to further distributional aims (Chapter 4, Section 7.2). In theory, therefore, the strategy is feasible in both efficiency and equity terms. We turn now to assessment of the practice.

4. Assessment of the UK system of health care

4.1. Institutions

This part of the chapter starts with an overview of the institutions of the National Health Service (NHS) and of private health care, and then attempts to assess the extent to which the NHS meets the aims of efficiency (Section 4.2) and social justice (Section 4.3).

Two points should be made immediately. First, expenditure on the NHS (around 6 per cent of national income in the later 1990s) is low by international standards. However, expenditure has risen since the mid-1970s for several reasons. There was a 'bulge' in the birth rate in 1948 and another in the mid-1960s (Figure 9.1). The number of old people has increased, intensifying the demand on facilities (health spending per person over 85 is about sixteen times that on someone aged 16–44). Costly new techniques have led to increased expectations. The relative price effect has also acted to raise the cost of health-care services by more than the average increase in prices.[8]

A second feature of the NHS, notwithstanding the problems discussed later, is its popularity. In the words of two American commentators, 'the NHS promised high quality medical care to the acutely ill and increasingly delivered on that promise. It unquestionably spared patients the fear of financial ruin from medical bills. As a result, it became and remained one of the most popular institutions in Britain' (Aaron and

---

[8] The relative price effect (also referred to as 'excess medical inflation') measures the extent to which the price of commodities like health care tends to rise faster than prices generally. There are two reasons: first, throughout the economy the price of labour tends to rise faster than the general price level (i.e. real earnings rise); and, secondly, health care has a higher than average direct labour content, about three-quarters of NHS current spending being on directly employed staff. The same, broadly, is true of education. See Baumol (1996).

Schwartz 1984: 14). The major conclusion of a Parliamentary Report (UK House of Commons Social Services Committee 1988: lx) was that the 'strengths of the NHS should not be cast aside in a short term effort to remedy some of its weaknesses'.

THE OPERATION OF THE NATIONAL HEALTH SERVICE

The NHS in England[9] is the responsibility of the Secretary of State for Health, who is answerable to Parliament, and is responsible for the Department of Health. The Department funds District Health Authorities, whose task, historically, has been to organize hospital and community health services in their areas, and family health authorities, whose main responsibility is primary health care, including family doctors, pharmacists, and dentists. Under a major reform (UK DoH 1989) the task of the District Health Authorities changed in 1991 to that of *purchasing* care rather than *providing* it.

Discussion is organized round the four areas highlighted in Table 4.1: the production of health care; the individual consumption decision (i.e. how the system works from the viewpoint of the consumer); finance; and the aggregate production decision (i.e. budget-setting).

PRODUCTION OF HEALTH CARE UNDER THE NHS has a tripartite structure of primary health care, hospitals, and community health care.

Primary health care. The main element is the system of general practitioners (i.e. family doctors). Every individual is registered with a general practitioner (GP), who deals with straightforward complaints and chronic conditions and, when necessary, refers patients to hospital and specialist services. In the latter case the GP acts both as a guide (to steer patients to the appropriate specialist) and as a filter (to prevent trivial complaints being taken to a specialist). GPs also have a role in preventive medicine, including immunization, family planning, and cervical screening. Though publicly funded, they are self-employed on the basis of a contract introduced in 1990.

The other major types of primary medical care are dentistry, pharmaceutical services, and ophthalmic services. Dentists are paid on a fee-for-service basis on an agreed scale, net of the consumer charges they levy (also on an agreed scale). Pharmacists dispense drugs, dressings, etc. as prescribed by doctors for which they are reimbursed on the basis of costs plus a profit margin, but net of the consumer charges discussed below.

Hospitals, together with community health activities, absorb about three-quarters of the resources of the NHS (Table 12.1). In the mid-1990s, the hospital sector in England directly employed over 750,000 people, including 52,000 medical personnel, about 350,000 nurses and 92,000 professional technical staff such as radiographers (UK DoH 1997).

Hospital doctors are paid a salary rather than a fee for service, though, as discussed below, they are able to combine salaried work for the NHS with private practice. As a result

[9] The Secretaries of State for Scotland, Wales, and Northern Ireland are responsible *inter alia* for the NHS in those countries.

Benefits in kind

Table 12.1. **Health, UK, 1996/7 (est.) (£m.)**

National Health Service		
NHS hospitals, community health, etc.	31,623	
NHS Trusts	377	
Family health services	9,771	
Central health services	877	
Administration	345	
Total gross spending		42,987
Charges and capital revenues		−1,864
Total health		41,123
Personal social services		10,104
TOTAL HEALTH AND PERSONAL SOCIAL SERVICES		51,227

Sources: UK DoH (1997: table B1); UK Treasury (1997: table 3.5).

of the 1991 reforms, most hospitals are now self-governing Trusts—independent public corporations run by a board whose membership has to be approved by the Secretary of State. These Trusts finance their current expenditure from contracts with district health authorities and GP fundholders (discussed below). The underlying idea is to encourage competition between such independent Trusts to improve the efficiency of resource use within the NHS (see Glennerster 1997: ch. 10).

Community health services, also often provided by trust-type organizations, have two functions: preventive health services, including health education, health-visiting, screening and vaccination programmes, and maternity and child-welfare clinics; and cooperation with personal social-services departments, so that wherever possible health and social care can be dealt with together.

THE INDIVIDUAL CONSUMPTION DECISION. As a first approximation, all health care under the NHS is free, except for the charges described below. The main source of health care for most people is their GP. Individuals are free to register with any NHS GP in their area who is prepared to add them to his list of patients. Anyone who wishes, for whatever reason, to change to another GP may do so. No charge is made for consultations or for home visits. The GP prescribes treatment or, in more complex or serious cases, refers the patient to an NHS hospital.

Where a GP prescribes drugs, the patient has in principle to pay the pharmacist a fixed charge per item—for example, per bottle of tablets. The charge in 1997 was £5.65, having risen steeply since 1979,[10] though broad classes of people are exempt—for example, children, expectant mothers, old people, certain chronically ill individuals, and people with low incomes (Tolley 1996: ch. 12), representing about 75 per cent of individuals, disproportionately those who make the greatest use of drugs. As in many other countries, the UK's drug bill has increased sharply in recent years.

Individuals are also free to choose their dentist. Charges, though formerly heavily subsidized, are close to economic costs.

[10] A charge of one shilling (5 pence) was introduced in 1952; in early 1979 it was 20 pence.

A patient is usually referred to hospital by his GP, but in emergencies this procedure is bypassed. All hospital treatment under the NHS is free, including test procedures, consultations with doctors, nursing, drugs, and intensive care, whatever the type of complaint and however long the hospital stay. All the facilities of the NHS are available to anyone living in the UK, with the exception of temporary residents (i.e. those staying in the country for less than six months).

FINANCE. The funding of the NHS is discussed in detail by Glennerster (1997: ch. 10). Of the total cost of the NHS shown in Table 12.1, 81 per cent came from general (mainly central government) tax revenues and about 12.5 per cent from national-insurance contributions. Thus close to 95 per cent of the NHS was financed out of taxation, and under 3 per cent from charges (UK DoH 1997: table 2.3).

Hospitals in the past were, for the most part, both financed and managed by the Health District. A key objective of the 1991 reforms was to improve efficiency by separating the finance of health care from its provision. District General Managers now act as purchasing agents on behalf of their resident populations. The intention is that they should buy health care from the most efficient providers, public or private, inside or outside their District. Most hospital care will come from institutions within the District, but money will follow patients treated elsewhere. Thus hospitals receive part of their funding from the District. They also receive income from GPs who act as budget-holders for their patients.

GP fundholding. Under the 1990 Health Service and Community Care Act, as amended, GPs in practices with more than 5,000 patients can elect to become budget-holders, managing the budget for care given by the GP and for simpler types of hospital treatment such as X-rays, pathology tests, and simple surgery. By 1995 over 40 per cent of the population in England were members of fundholding practices. In 1996 a number of experiments were introduced with 'total fundholding', whereby groups of GPs were given a budget to pay for all health care for their patients. GP fundholders make their own contracts with providers and pay them from their own, larger, budget. The underlying idea is that larger numbers of smaller purchasing agents lead to a more competitive environment—certainly fundholding has changed the balance of power, giving GPs greater leverage in pushing for improvements in hospital services (see Section 5.2).

General practitioners' remuneration is complex. Somewhat to simplify, GPs receive three forms of payment. First, there are various allowances, mainly a basic practice allowance to cover running costs. Secondly, they receive a capitation payment of £X for each person on their register, where X is higher for older people. Thirdly, there is a variety of other payments, *inter alia* to encourage certain forms of preventive health care.

GPs work under a contract imposed on them in 1990, which specifies core services, sets targets for the provision of those services, and offers extra payments for the achievement of certain targets, particularly some types of preventive care. A key point, and one to which we return, is that, with few exceptions (notably payments to dentists, and for some types of preventive care to GPs), payment throughout the NHS takes the form more of a *salary* than a fee for service (for details, see Glennerster 1997: ch. 10).

Benefits in kind

THE AGGREGATE PRODUCTION DECISION—that is, setting budget limits. The annual budget for the NHS is determined in the same way as the budget for defence or any other government service, as the result of negotiation between the Treasury and spending departments, as modified by subsequent discussion in Cabinet (Glennerster 1997: chs. 4–6). The figure which emerges is a global budget for the NHS as a whole, which is divided between the relevant Secretaries of State. Within England and Wales, resources are allocated by the Secretary of State to each District according to a population-weighted formula. The procedure is therefore largely one of 'top-down' allocation, substantially constrained by expenditure in previous years. GP budget-holders, like Districts, are cash limited (i.e. they have to operate within a fixed annual budget).

PRIVATE HEALTH CARE

Alongside the NHS is a system of private health care. An individual can consult a GP privately, in which case he pays the GP's fees and the full cost of any drugs; he can be referred to a consultant either through the NHS or privately, whether or not the original consultation with the GP was private; and the consultant can refer him to hospital either through the NHS or privately. Though it has grown somewhat in recent years, the private sector remains small. By the mid-1990s, about 11 per cent of the population had some sort of private medical insurance, up from 4 per cent twenty years earlier. Benefits are only a small fraction of NHS expenditure. Private medical care is used mainly by those wanting the convenience of a private room or (more contentiously) by those faced with a long wait for treatment under the NHS, and only for a narrow range of relatively uncomplicated treatment.

Most private health care is financed by voluntary insurance, which is cheap in the UK for at least four reasons: most patients use an NHS GP even if they see a specialist privately; the NHS provides a back-up if patients present complications beyond the capacity of a private hospital; people with private insurance are usually young and employed (their health-care insurance is often a fringe benefit), and hence low risk; finally, health care is cheaper in the UK than, for example, the USA, not least because UK doctors and nurses are paid less.

The relationship between private health care and the NHS is a source of continuing controversy. NHS hospitals have specialist consultants who are contracted to work for the NHS, but can choose whether to do so full-time or part-time. Most of them elect for the part-time option and practise in their consultative capacity both as part of the NHS and privately.[11] The existence of 'pay beds' within the NHS has aroused the greatest controversy. It is argued that people with money can jump the queue without necessarily paying the full economic cost of treatment, and many regard this as inequitable. Others argue that private patients bring extra income to some consultants, and that to ban private practice by NHS employees would result in large and costly pay demands, and possibly the loss of highly skilled specialists. The issue remains a political football.

---

[11] Consultants choosing the full-time option are allowed to earn up to 10% of their income from private practice.

INTERNATIONAL COMPARISON

Before turning to an assessment of the NHS, it is helpful to have some perspective on the organization and problems of systems elsewhere (see OECD 1992, 1994; Saltman and von Otter 1995; Hurst 1996). In very broad terms, all industrialized countries adopt one of the three models.

- *The quasi-actuarial approach* is characterized by employer-based or individual purchase of private medical insurance, and by private ownership of medical factors of production. The closest approximation (and the only major example among OECD economies) is the USA.
- *Earnings-related social-insurance contributions* are characterized by compulsory coverage financed by earnings-related employee contributions and/or an employer payroll tax, possibly supplemented by tax funding. Such funding regimes are compatible with a larger (Canada) or smaller (Germany) role for the private sector.
- *'Universal' medical care* is characterized by tax funding and public ownership and/or control of the factors of production (e.g. Sweden, the UK).

PROBLEMS. Inspection of the international scene yields two major conclusions: the pervasiveness of regulation in *all* health-care systems; and a dramatic escalation of health-care costs in most countries in the later 1970s and early 1980s, with, for the most part, a subsequent slowdown in the rate of expenditure growth (Abel Smith 1984, 1985; Barr 1992: table 3). Despite the variety of systems, there is considerable similarity in the difficulties they face. The most important arise out of the third-party-payment problem (Section 3.1).

Since fee for service paid by a third party is the most common way of paying doctors, it is not surprising, despite the variety of their institutions, that most countries have at one time or another experienced a dramatic escalation in health expenditures. The point is vital. According to the contributors to McLachlan and Maynard (1982):

The rising costs of medical care and, as a result, the problems of expenditures and cost containment . . . is of major concern in the Federal Republic of Germany.   (p. 235)

. . . moves for a closer control to check the growth of expenditure [on health care in France] which is alarmingly high.   (p. 267)

In the US cost containment is the major driving force behind legislative and private sector health strategies.   (p. 333)

The editors conclude that

however much health systems and policies may seem to differ from country to country all current policies have one major aim, cost containment which is an omnibus description of policies . . . to contain not just *unit* costs but also *total* expenditure in both public and private sectors.   (McLachlan and Maynard 1982: 13, emphasis in original)

Benefits in kind

Of the countries covered by McLachlan and Maynard only two have not suffered a cost explosion: the UK, largely because of parliamentary control of public expenditure;[12] and Canada, which imposes a global budget constraint on the expenditure of its publicly funded scheme.

The situation in the USA is a textbook example. Prior to the 1960s the system was broadly one of private production financed by private health care insurance. But problems arose, and as a response Medicare (for the old) and Medicaid (for the poor) were introduced in the mid-1960s. The modification they introduced was simple: the poor and old continued to receive private treatment, but their medical bills were now paid out of federal/state funds. The effect of these unlimited third-party payments was entirely predictable: public spending on health care rose very sharply to the point where health care became the fourth largest item of federal spending after income support, defence, and debt interest (the classic article is Robert G. Evans 1974; see also Aaron 1991).

There are two possible arguments against the assertion that these cost escalations are caused by inadequately policed third-party payments. Americans might have a greater taste for health care than, say, the British (i.e. demand is higher in the USA); or Americans might suffer more health problems (i.e. need is greater in the USA). If the former, we would expect high-spending countries to enjoy better health; if the latter, that they suffer more illness. Neither phenomenon is the case. In 1997 the USA spent 16 per cent of GNP on health care; the UK spent about 7 per cent of a smaller GDP. Yet in terms of infant mortality and life expectancy health in the USA is no better than in the UK. The US story is taken up in Section 5.1.

SOLUTIONS. Two broad classes of solution—regulation, and the use of incentives—have been adopted to try to contain costs (for fuller discussion, see Barr 1992).

Regulation is both pervasive and inescapable. The logic is simple: expenditure = price × quantity. Successful cost containment must (*a*) control total spending directly, or (*b*) control price *and* quantity, or (*c*) use price control to reinforce an overall spending constraint. Control of medical fees (i.e. price control) with open-ended total budgets only partially contains costs because of the incentive for doctors to increase output to compensate for lost income. This is exactly what happened with Medicare in the USA (Robert G. Evans 1974; Evans *et al.* 1989). Canada, in contrast, managed to avoid the worst of the medicare cost explosion because it adopted both price control *and* a global budget ceiling. European countries, too, have developed systems which combine price and expenditure control (Abel Smith 1984, 1985; OECD 1992, 1994).

Whatever the system, successful methods of restricting supply to around its efficient level all include the imposition of budget limits either on public expenditure (the UK, Sweden) or on insurance disbursements (Canada). This is an important conclusion because the demand for health care will increase in the future not only with advances in medical technology but also because of the problem (Chapter 9, Sections 2, 3.2) of ageing populations in almost all industrialized countries.

---

[12] The ability of the NHS to act as a monopoly buyer is another contributory factor.

Incentives to economy take various forms (see Ellis and McGuire 1993; Barnum *et al.* 1995). The third-party-payment problem arises because health-care providers are reimbursed retrospectively on what is, in effect, a cost-plus basis. The idea of *prospective payment* is becoming increasingly widespread. In one form, each hospital receives a fixed annual global budget which it can spend as it wishes. Other mechanisms, including diagnosis-related groups and health maintenance organizations, are discussed in Section 5.1.

Other forms of incentive have also been tried, including cost-sharing (where the patient pays part of the cost of treatment), privatization, and (particularly in the USA) attempts to increase competition between providers. Though doubts have been expressed (Weisbrod 1983; Fuchs 1988) about uncritical adherence to competition, the European experience suggests that regulated competition may help to contain medical spending (see OECD 1992, 1994).

4.2. Assessment 1: Efficiency

As discussed in Section 2.1, efficiency can be defined in principle but is hard to measure, mainly because of difficulties in measuring (*a*) the benefits of health care as opposed to other activities (the *macro*-efficiency issue), and (*b*) the relative benefits in different areas of health care (*micro*-efficiency). Quantitative work on both is scant, so that relatively little is known about the health gains deriving from different types of intervention. Thus discussion is to some extent a mixture of a priori argument with only a small leavening of empirical evidence.

Assessment of the efficiency, or otherwise, of the NHS is organized under four broad heads: advantages in principle; advantages in practice; criticisms with little validity; and criticisms which are valid. The NHS has at least four efficiency advantages in principle.

1. *Supply-side incentives* to economize arise, first, from the way remuneration is organized. Doctors are not generally paid a fee for service. Thus there is no financial incentive to oversupply (see Gerdttham *et al.* 1992). There is no argument of principle against paying doctors a high salary—the crucial point is that it is not related to medical activity. GPs are paid on the basis of capitation (to contain costs) with some fee for service to encourage particular preventive activities. A pure capitation system gives GPs an incentive to increase the size of their lists, but to decrease the time spent with any one patient. To that extent there is an incentive for GPs either to *undersupply* or to pass patients to the hospital sector. The argument should not be overstated, however, both because of the fee-for-service element to encourage preventive activity, and because a patient who feels she is not receiving adequate attention from her GP can transfer to the list of another doctor, thereby reducing the original GP's income.[13]

A second form of constraint is the NHS budget (a macro-efficiency point), coupled with the control exercised by the NHS over doctors' behaviour and the traditions of the

---

[13] The capitation element of GPs' pay under the NHS thus approximates to a voucher system.

medical profession in the UK. The overall result is that there is no financial incentive to supply excessive medical care, Q_1 in Figure 12.2, rather than the socially optimal quantity, Q^*. This is true both for health care as a whole and for different types of treatment, though with a question mark over the possibility of undersupply by GPs.

2. *The individual-consumption decision.* The decision about treatment is generally made by doctors. This reduces the problem of imperfect information. In addition, the patient is more likely to trust a doctor's decision based on clinical judgement unclouded by financial motives.

3. *Finance* for the most part is out of general taxation, thereby avoiding problems in insurance markets, such as high probabilities of requiring treatment, adverse selection, and moral hazard (Chapter 5, Section 3 and Section 3.1). To the extent that taxes are based on ability to pay there are also equity advantages, discussed below.

4. *Treatment* is mostly free at the point of use. This encourages early diagnosis, reduces the externality problem, and has equity advantages.

The system has advantages also in practical terms.

5. *Macro-efficiency.* The NHS is cheap by international standards. Total medical spending (public and private) in the later 1990s absorbed about 7 per cent of national income; the US figure was about 16 per cent. As discussed earlier, however, there were no corresponding differences in infant mortality or life expectancy. Klein's (1984: 15) argument that 'the NHS seems to be a remarkably successful instrument for making the rationing of scarce resources socially and politically acceptable' remains broadly true.

6. *Micro-efficiency.* We shall see shortly that the NHS is not above criticism for the way it allocates resources to different areas of health care. But it also has advantages. Because of its unified structure and because payment is not generally based on fee for service, the NHS faces fewer adverse incentives than systems based on fee for service; and the unified structure of the NHS enables action to be taken on overall medical priorities (see points 10 and 11 below).

Two criticisms were sometimes made of the NHS, particularly in the USA, which do not hold water.

7. *The NHS is a monopoly.* The first argument is that consumers have no choice. This is not the case. They are free to choose (and change) their GP, to ask for a second opinion, or to opt for private medical care. A different argument is that the NHS devotes too many resources to bureaucracy. In fact, the NHS bureaucracy is low by international standards. Administrative costs in the USA in the late 1980s were about 26 per cent of total current expenditure (Himmelstein and Woolhandler 1986, 1991).[14] The NHS figure in 1987/8 was 2.9 per cent, in part because the NHS devoted virtually no resources to billing patients. Indeed, as discussed below, one of the motivations of the 1991 reforms was to *increase* the amount of management in the NHS in order to improve internal

[14] If US administrative spending had been brought down to the average of countries which fund medical care through social insurance, the resulting savings in 1987 would have been around $50 billion.

efficiency. A third argument is that the NHS is too centralized. Centralization, how-ever, can have positive advantages: it makes it possible to establish priorities; and the NHS can use its powers as a monopsony to negotiate low prices for drugs. In addition, the 1991 reforms gave hospital trusts and GP fundholders considerable autonomy.

8. *Work effort.* Doctors, it is argued, work less hard if they are not paid a fee for ser-vice and/or the best and most innovative individuals will be lost to the profession (this is the issue of *dynamic* efficiency). There are two lines of attack on this position. It assumes uncritically that labour supply is motivated solely by financial gain, but loses plausibility if one allows for non-money wages and a tradition of service. Many professionals—academics, lawyers, and accountants—are paid salaries, yet it is not argued that they should be paid a fee for service. Though difficult to prove, it might be argued that the UK attracts to the medical profession individuals who gain substantial job satisfaction, while countries with private systems attract those with more strongly financial motives. If so, it does not follow that the latter group is either more able or hard-er working. A second counter-argument is that, even if work effort/innovation is sub-stantially motivated by high pay, it might well suffice to base remuneration on high salaries rather than fee for service.

To rebut these arguments is not to say that no criticism is possible.

9. *Macro-inefficiency.* Some commentators argue that too few resources are devoted to the NHS. Budget restrictions have aggravated waiting lists for non-urgent (and some urgent) treatment; and many hospital buildings are old. Pro-market writers argue that the NHS *causes* too few resources to be devoted to medical care; but international com-parison suggests that private systems can lead to excessive production which regulation has only partly curtailed. There are at least two reasons why there is no definitive answer to the funding question: first, the health benefits of different medical interventions are hard, if not impossible, to measure; secondly, 'the optimal level of health funding is a normative question dictated partly by the aggregate tastes and preferences of society' (McGuire 1994: 147). For these and other reasons, there is little *scientific* support for the idea of a major funding crisis in the NHS (see McGuire 1994; Dixon 1997; Harrison *et al.* 1997*a, b*), though rather more *political* support for additional funding, not least to sustain standards in the face of an ageing population.

10. *Micro-inefficiency in the geographical allocation of resources.* The location of NHS facilities is largely a matter of historical accident and over time matched the location and age structure of the population less well. The Resource Allocation Working Party (RAWP) (UK DHSS 1976) made specific proposals for geographical reallocation on the basis of such criteria as the size and demographic structure of the population in an area, health indicators such as local mortality and fertility, and gaps in existing provision. As a result, resources were shifted away from London and the south-east of England. Problems remained, however—notably inequality *within* regions. Under the 1991 reforms, therefore, the RAWP formula was replaced by a sophisticated system of direct allocation of resources from the central Department of Health to Districts (Carr-Hill

et al. 1994; Glennerster 1997: 179–80). There is continuing controversy about whether London still has a disproportionate share of NHS resources (see King's Fund London Commission 1997).

11. *Micro-inefficiency in the allocation of resources to different types of health care.* Enthoven's (1985) book, which had considerable influence on the 1991 reforms, pointed to significant inefficiencies. First, incentives were inadequate and could be perverse: a consultant who treated more patients would get extra work but no extra resources; and, since capital costs were generally paid by the central government, local providers did not face the opportunity cost of capital. Secondly, over-centralization, particularly through national pay agreements, led to staffing problems in high-wage parts of the country like London. Thirdly, there was a lack of accountability: no one knew what anything cost or whether they were keeping within their budget. Fourthly, the system was inflexible—for example, it was hard to close an unwanted hospital.

In addition to action to increase efficiency within the NHS, there is also scope for better coordination between NHS activities and related activities paid from the social-security budget and local-authority budgets. Care for the frail elderly, for example, gives respite to their carers and thus helps to keep older people out of hospital or residential care; similarly, care packages for elderly people waiting to leave hospital can reduce hospital stays, with benefits both for the person concerned and the NHS budget.

Greater efficiency requires two sorts of information:

- Technical information, in particular on the costs and health benefits of different types of treatment.
- Social and political information to generate a set of weights to be applied to relevant non-medical criteria (e.g. whether the patient has dependants).

Information on the first is woeful. The problem is largely intractable because of the major problems (particularly of measuring health and of attributing causality) discussed in Section 2.2; thus progress is likely to be slow and incomplete. That said, a legitimate criticism of the NHS prior to the reforms is that it gathered *too little information* (see Enthoven 1989).

Alongside better management, there is also a role for some competition on the supply side. The 1991 reforms introduced internal markets into the NHS (see Section 5.2, below).

12. *Productive inefficiency* (i.e. internal efficiency) is also not fully achieved. The argument that the NHS has a disproportionate number of bureaucrats does not stand up (point 7). The opposite argument is, if anything, more true. It can be argued that the NHS should devote *more* managerial resources to improving efficiency.

4.3. Assessment 2: Equity

As we saw in Chapter 4, Sections 2.2 and 4.3, equity cannot be defined unambiguously, but depends on political values; in addition (Chapter 6, Section 3.1), the definition of equality is fraught with ambiguities. For present purposes horizontal equity is defined in terms of equality of opportunity in respect of health care, as set out in Section 2.1. Thus individuals A and B with identical medical conditions should receive equal health care unless other relevant differences exist (e.g. one of them has young or old dependants); irrelevant considerations (e.g. that A is rich and B poor) should make no difference. How closely does the NHS approximate this ideal?

13. *The unimportance of income.* The quantity of health care an individual receives is largely (though as we shall see not wholly) unconstrained by her income. No one is denied health care because of poverty; and no one goes in fear of financial ruin as a result of expensive medical treatment. The latter is a particular problem in the USA.

14. *The system accords with British notions of social justice* (McCreadie 1976), and is highly popular politically (Halpern, 1985). A leaked report of a proposal in the late 1980s to introduce significant privatization caused such a political backlash that the 1991 reforms preserved the basic principles of publicly funded and largely publicly produced health care.

15. *The system allows action on the distribution of health care by region*, which, as a result of the policy discussed in point 10, is more equal than previously.

16. *The distribution of health* is controversial. Black's (1980) conclusion that disparities in health across UK socioeconomic groups had widened over the lifetime of the NHS were disputed by Le Grand (1987a). The essence of Le Grand's (1987a; see also Illsley and Le Grand 1987; Le Grand 1989a) argument was that the composition of socioeconomic groups had changed, so that the lowest group in the 1980s was relatively much more disadvantaged compared to the median than the lowest group forty years earlier. Le Grand therefore measured inequality in health outcomes not through data on socioeconomic *groups* but by measuring the Gini coefficient (see Chapter 6, Section 4) for *individual* data on age-at-death. Le Grand (1987a: table 1) concluded that the most equal countries included the UK, The Netherlands, and Sweden; the least equal countries included the USA (measuring mortality inequality in terms of the Gini coefficient, the only country consistently less equal than the USA was Romania).

Recent findings point to a striking relationship between health and socioeconomic variables (Robert G. Evans *et al.* 1994 and, for a cogent survey, Evans 1996). Wilkinson (1996) finds that among developed countries it is not the richest societies which have the best health but the most equal. Smaller income differences raise average life expectancy. Morris *et al.* (1994) find a significant link between loss of employment and mortality. Studies of British civil servants (Marmot *et al.* 1991; North *et al.*, 1993) find that people with less control over their work suffer poorer health outcomes. Not least because of such findings the Labour government elected in 1997 placed renewed emphasis on the links between poverty, inequality and ill-health.

17. *The distribution of health care.* Three issues arise: the empirical facts; the explanation of those facts; and implications for policy. Le Grand (1982: ch. 3) confirms the findings of the Black Report (1980: ch. 4) that the NHS does not achieve equality of use.

Benefits in kind

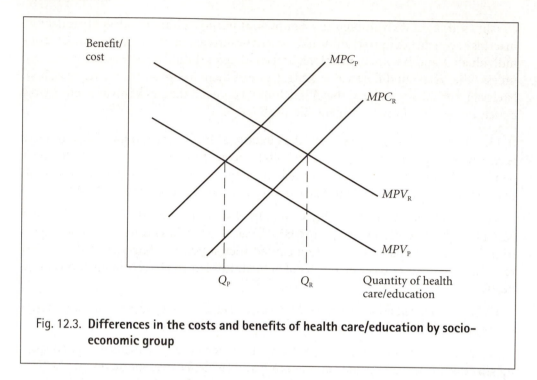

Fig. 12.3. **Differences in the costs and benefits of health care/education by socio-economic group**

'The evidence suggests that the top socioeconomic group receives 40 per cent more NHS expenditure per person reporting illness than the bottom one' (Le Grand 1982: 46).

This result can be explained (see Figure 12.3) in terms of two sets of factors. The *benefits* of health care perceived by the lower socioeconomic groups (MPV_P) may be lower than those of the rich (MPV_R) (e.g. if the poor have worse information); or the poor might rationally place a lower value on health (e.g. smoking might genuinely be a rare pleasure for someone whose life is otherwise miserable); or the actual benefits to poorer people might be lower if doctors treat them with less care than middle-class patients. Probably of greater importance, the poor face higher *costs* of health care. Since treatment is free, the main cost is time. Travel time is generally higher for less advantaged people, who more often have to rely on public transport; and the cost of time is generally higher for the poor, who generally lose pay if they spend a morning in a hospital out-patient clinic, a cost not faced by people on salaries. These factors taken together can explain why in practice Q_R in Figure 12.3 is 40 per cent higher than Q_P.

These results are not universally accepted. Powell (1995) disputes Le Grand's premiss, that equality is *the* objective. Consider the ratio B_R/B_P, where B_R is the benefit going to the rich and B_P that going to the poor. The objectives of the welfare state include:

- Efficiency: for this purpose, $B_R/B_P > 1$ may well be right. For example, one purpose of pensions is to provide income-smoothing, implying that pensions should rise with income.

- Poverty relief: for this purpose B_R/B_P should be less than one; the tighter the targeting the greater the extent to which B_R/B_P should tend to zero.
- Social cohesion, which implies that B_R/B_P should tend to one.

Thus whether $B_R/B_P > 1$ is a problem depends in part on what the objective is. Inequality in the distribution of welfare state benefits is not *necessarily* a sign of failure.

Secondly, various writers, using more disaggregated and more recent data, dispute Le Grand's empirical results. They find that people with lower incomes receive more health care but have poorer health, and conclude that the NHS delivers broadly equal care for equal need on the basis of both cross-section data (Propper and Upward 1992) and time-series analysis (Propper 1995a). That conclusion, however, remains contentious (see the Further Reading). So far as horizontal equity is concerned, Smaje and Le Grand (1997) find that health care is not significantly affected by ethnic factors.

What implications can be drawn from these results? Even if it does not fully achieve the objective of equal treatment for equal need, the NHS can still be an equalizing force. First, the NHS cannot be regarded as a failure unless an alternative system of health care is more equalizing. International comparison offers no strong evidence for such a proposition (Le Grand 1989a).

Secondly, whether or not the NHS is an equalizing force depends not only on the distribution of benefits but also whether expenditure is discussed not in isolation but, more properly, in conjunction with the taxation which finances it (Chapter 7, Section 4.2). The argument is important, and worth spelling out. Suppose that the pre-transfer incomes of poor and rich are 20 and 80; that all income is taxed away by the state to provide free goods and services; and that the rich receive twice as many goods and services as the (equally numerous) poor. As a result, the post-transfer incomes of poor and rich are $33\frac{1}{3}$ and $66\frac{2}{3}$, respectively. From the perspective of expenditure, the rich receive twice as much as the poor, suggesting that public allocation has failed as an equalizing force. But when expenditure and taxation are considered together, the income of the poor has been raised both absolutely from 20 to $33\frac{1}{3}$, and relatively, from one-quarter of that of the rich to one-half. On either count, the system taken as a whole is equalizing.

18. *Redistributive effects of the NHS.* To what extent is the NHS thus financed progressively? In practice, measurement raises almost insuperable problems, *inter alia* because of the difficulty of measuring the incidence of taxes and benefits, but the *logic* is clear (Chapter 7, Section 4.2, as qualified by Chapter 7, Section 4.1). If (rich) individual R contributes on average, say, twice as much as (poor) P in whatever tax is used to pay for the NHS, but receives the same quantity of health care, then the NHS redistributes from rich to poor (i.e. is progressive). But if R contributes twice as much but consumes four times as much as P then the NHS is regressive.

Empirically, the NHS is financed progressively. Propper (1995a: 202) concludes that 'the gainers are those in the lowest six decile groups and women, the losers are those in the top four decile groups and men'.

Additionally, even if the redistributive effect is weak, the NHS is still an equalizing force if it reduces inequality more than any alternative system. International studies (Aaron

1992; Wagstaff and van Doorslaer 1992) find that the NHS scores highly from this perspective. The most plausible conclusion is not that the NHS has failed, but that it may not be as strong an equalizing force as some of its supporters hoped. This suggests that the aims of egalitarians are likely to be served better by keeping and improving the NHS than by replacing it.

5. Reform

5.1. Reform in principle

This section discusses four sets of reform: radical privatization; managed health care; a system of privately produced but publicly funded medical care; and approaches to improving the NHS. Section 5.2 assesses the 1991 NHS reforms, including discussion of quasi-markets.

RADICAL PRIVATIZATION. The failure of virtually all the standard assumptions[15] (Section 3.1) suggests that an unrestricted private market (i.e. rows 1 or 2 in Table 4.1) is likely to be highly inefficient for technical reasons (Section 3.1), and also inconsistent with widely held notions of social justice (Section 3.2). This view, as we saw in Section 4.1, is confirmed by empirical observation. Countries which have adopted careless ad hoc modifications to private health-care systems have typically experienced sharp and unexpected cost increases.

An additional argument concerns the possible effects of any rapid expansion of private medical care in the UK. So long as private treatment is only a marginal activity, it can serve as a useful device for enhancing consumer choice and alleviating excess demand. But if the private sector were to grow beyond a certain (unknown) size, it is possible that 'the most demanding consumers of health care [would] exit from the public sector so diminishing the political voice for more spending in the public sector' (Klein 1984: 23–4). This, it is argued, could lead to a two-tier system—high-quality private care for the better off, and low-quality NHS treatment for the poor. Such an outcome would have two effects. It would shift medical resources from the poor to the rich; whether this is desirable depends on one's definition of social justice. In addition, if the private health-care sector becomes large, it is likely to run into the cost-containment problems faced by other countries (Section 4.1), particularly the USA.

If radical privatization is not the answer, what package of reform might be feasible? The main conclusion of the theoretical discussion in Section 3 is that it is not possible to make health care efficient and equitable by ad hoc tinkering. What is needed is a *strategy*. Since virtually all health care is financed by third parties (i.e. insurers or the taxpayer),

---

[15] i.e. the assumptions necessary for the market to allocate efficiently—see Chapter 4, section 3.2, or the Appendix to Chapter 4, paras. 6–17.

the marginal cost to the consumer is zero, and he will generally demand an inefficiently high quantity, Q_1 in Figure 12.2. The heart of the issue, therefore, is rationing treatment to Q^*. In principle this can be done in two ways: (*a*) by making medical providers face the marginal social cost of health care; or (*b*) by imposing a budget constraint on total expenditure. The next two mixed public/private packages follow these two routes, the first being rather more private than the second. Each is presented only in outline to illustrate the approach; and other examples are, no doubt, possible.

MANAGED CARE. This is the case of private health care and private medical insurance subject to extensive management and regulation. The approach is also being applied in the public sector: in 1997 about three-quarters of US states used managed care for medicaid, and the medicare programme has a stated objective of moving into managed care.

The discussion at the end of Section 4.1 pointed to two complementary approaches to containing costs: regulation, and the use of incentives. Managed care has both ingredients.[16]

- Regulation takes the form of *intensive management* of medical provision. Since the mid-1980s, the USA has increasingly moved from a system in which doctors had free rein to a management-controlled industrial model (Scheffler and Waitzman, forthcoming).

- Incentives are based round *prospective payment*. If expenses are reimbursed *ex post*, medical providers face no risk and no incentive to economize; if, in contrast, they are paid *ex ante* (e.g. a prepayment of $X for a hip replacement), they face strong incentives to use resources carefully. The following institutions translate the idea into practice.

Health maintenance organizations (HMOs). Under this approach, individuals pay a lump-sum annual contribution to a 'firm' of doctors (the HMO), which promises in return to provide the contributor with a comprehensive range of medical services. The doctors provide primary care themselves, and buy in hospital care as necessary. The HMO's income, which consists of the contributions of its members, is used to pay for health care, including the salaries of the doctors. Any surplus (like that of any firm) can be distributed to the doctors as higher pay, or to members as lower contributions, or ploughed back into the HMO to improve its service.

An important theoretical advantage of HMOs is that the doctor provides both health care *and* medical insurance. The HMO is thus analytically equivalent to merging the activities of doctor and insurance company. As discussed in Section 3.3, this internalizes the externality caused by third-party payments, giving doctors an incentive to economize —for example, providing preventive care or early treatment to nip an incipient problem in the bud.

Evidence (Manning *et al.* 1987; Newhouse 1993) suggests that HMOs reduce medical costs, though the extent of the effect may depend on the precise form of HMO

---

[16] Note that, Medicaid apart, regulation is private, rather than imposed by government.

(Hillman *et al.* 1989). Notwithstanding Enthoven's (1989) enthusiasm, it is well not to be too optimistic. First, HMOs may ameliorate one strategic insurance problem—exploding costs—but they do nothing to deal with the other—uninsurable risks. Anecdotal evidence suggests that, as with any prepayment system, attempts are made in the USA to restrict membership to the best risks, an effect which is becoming stronger as the US population ages.[17] Secondly, HMOs do not *necessarily* provide the efficient quantity Q^* in Figure 12.2. Theory suggests that they will provide less than Q_1; but it does not follow that they will provide Q^*.

Diagnosis-related groups (DRGs) are another form of prospective payment. Hospital in-patient cases are classified into different types, and hospitals are paid a fixed price per case, depending primarily on its DRG. Once more, the idea is no panacea. Like any classification system, costs vary *within* each category, giving hospitals an incentive to select cheaper cases of each type. Pressures therefore grew for more refined DRGs. That, however, gave incentives to 'DRG creep', where hospitals classify as 'severe' as many cases as possible (Russell 1989).

Preferred provider organizations (PPOs). Increasingly insurers in the USA and elsewhere give patients an incentive to choose from a limited range of providers, inviting institutions to tender competitively to become such a preferred provider. The idea is to exert downward pressure on price.

Since the mid-1980s the USA has moved aggressively towards prospective payment methods, up to a point moderating the increase in spending (though doing little to address gaps in coverage). HMOs are now the main form of health finance. Medical providers have responded by more intensive management (see, for example, Scheffler *et al.* 1991). The duration of hospital stays has fallen by about 50 per cent, partly because of medical advances, but largely because of financial incentives and consequent managerial pressures. Notwithstanding these changes, the US continues to face problems both with containing costs and with gaps in coverage.

PUBLIC FINANCE OF PRIVATELY PRODUCED MEDICAL CARE. This package of private production, public funding, and extensive regulation embraces more public involvement than the previous one. *Production* of health care is private, fee for service. There is *regulation* of the quality of treatment and, crucially, also its quantity. The latter, as discussed in Section 4.1, could be achieved, as in Canada, through a combination of price control and global spending limits. *Finance* is public (private, non-profit institutions (as in Germany), acting in effect as agents of the state, could achieve the same result). Membership is compulsory. Finance could be arranged in one of two ways. With compulsory insurance, premiums could be income-related with no efficiency loss (Chapter 5, Section 4.1). Alternatively, the state could drop the idea of actuarial insurance because it does not fit health care very well, and finance the scheme from general taxation. The general thrust of these arrangements follows row 3(*b*) of Table 4.1 for health care, and row 6 for health insurance. This is broadly the Canadian system.

---

[17] It is said that some HMOs have offices on the third floor of buildings with no elevator; if you are fit enough to get to the office, you are fit enough to join the HMO.

The approach has two advantages. The problems of private insurance are largely avoided; and the incentive to oversupply, resulting from fee-for-service and third-party payments, is moderated by constraining total expenditure. The strategy rests crucially on effective imposition of a budget constraint, which in turn depends on political will and administrative capacity. Such arrangements can undoubtedly be successful, as, for example, the Canadian system, which works well and is popular (Robert G. Evans *et al.* 1989; Blendon *et al.* 1995).

POSSIBLE IMPROVEMENTS TO THE NHS. The NHS strategy (approximately row 8 in Table 4.1) has powerful advantages. But it also has problems, so that some reforms are desirable.

In macro-efficiency terms, a central question is whether the NHS is underfunded, as manifested, for example, by waiting lists and old hospital buildings. There is no scientific support for this view (point 9). To the extent that there *is* a problem, the solution is to devote more resources to the NHS. There are also problems of micro-efficiency, not least for lack of technical information on the costs and benefits of treatment, and of clearly stated priorities about different types of treatment and different classes of recipient. The solution is to gather more information of the type discussed in point 11. It is in this context that proposals for *internal (or quasi-) markets* offer prospects of improvement. We return to the topic shortly.

As for equity issues, the distribution of medical care by social class is one of the more intractable of the problems discussed. One approach is to reduce the cost of treatment for less-well-off groups—for example by compensating out-patients for transport costs and forgone earnings (as is done already with jurors). This process would be assisted by more general equalizing measures—for example, further income redistribution, and better education. These measures may appear rather pale. It may be that we simply have to accept that inequality in health care, like inequality generally, cannot easily be reduced beyond a certain point. This does not mean that we should not try—merely that we should not expect easy answers. At a minimum we should not forget that the distribution of health care under the NHS, unequal though it might be, is more equal than that in many (if not most) other countries. The balance between realism and complacency is never easy.

Finally, there is growing evidence that a powerful factor in improving health (as opposed to health care) is rising income and greater equality. In that respect progress in health depends on events well outside the health sector.

5.2. The NHS reforms

THE REFORMS. In a rare case of professional unanimity, the great weight of advice to a parliamentary inquiry (UK House of Commons Social Services Committee 1988; see also Barr *et al.* 1989), was to stick to tax funding, and to make efforts to introduce some competition on the supply side. The reforms introduced in 1990 and 1991 attempted to do just that. They left a lot unchanged: the NHS continued to provide comprehensive

Benefits in kind

medical care; access remained universal; medical care continued, for the most part, to be funded out of general taxation and was free at the point of use. There were four major changes:

1. A new contract was imposed on GPs in 1990, designed to improve patients' choice of GP and to give GPs incentives to offer services such as preventive care and minor surgery.

2. Purchasers (Districts and GPs) were separated from providers (hospitals)—that is, demand and supply were separated. The underlying idea (Enthoven 1985) is that Districts are no longer required to *provide* services for their residents but to *buy* care on their behalf. Districts thus change from *providers* to *purchasing agents*. They make contracts with hospitals, and hospitals compete with each other for contracts (cf. preferred providers, discussed in Section 5.1).

3. Large GP practices were given the opportunity to become fundholders—that is, to buy certain types of care on behalf of their patients, the argument (Maynard 1986) being that Districts are too distant from the consumer. Such a move increases the power of GPs relative to consultants and hospitals, thus increasing pressure on hospitals to be efficient. The GP fundholder is, in essence, a form of HMO.

4. Well-managed hospitals were given the option to become self-governing Trusts, with greater autonomy than previously.

The last three changes introduced an internal market (or quasi-market) into the NHS. The shape of the reforms reflects a growing convergence among OECD countries: continued reliance on public funding, political control of total health spending, and the use of managed markets or quasi-markets to foster efficiency on the supply side (on reforms in other countries, see OECD 1992, 1994; Hurst 1996; and the Further Reading).

QUASI-MARKETS. The traditional welfare-state model was based on public funding and public production, usually by a monopoly state supplier. Quasi-markets retain public funding but decentralize demand and supply. This trend has occurred in the NHS, in education (Chapter 13, Section 5), and in other areas. As just mentioned, similar changes are occurring in other countries.

More specifically (Le Grand and Bartlett 1993: ch. 1), quasi-markets are markets in the sense that they introduce market forces. But they differ from the market for, say, food.

- On the supply side, they introduce competition (e.g. between hospitals or schools), but the suppliers are not necessarily private, nor necessarily profit maximizing.

- On the demand side, consumers do not spend cash; their purchasing power is expressed as an earmarked budget (e.g. capitation payments to GPs or to primary schools). This is, in effect, a form of voucher.

- Consumers may make their own choice (e.g. of school), or choice may be made on their behalf by an agent (a GP or District Health Authority).

The argument for competition is that it improves internal (but not necessarily external) efficiency. Though simple in principle, the approach raises strategic questions (for further detail, see the Further Reading) about the NHS reforms.

Incentives for quality. At the heart of the approach is an inherent tension. Either medical providers face the costs of their decisions, or they do not. If they do not, they face no incentives to productive efficiency. But if providers do face the costs of their decisions, downward cost pressures may affect quality, which imperfectly informed consumers may be unable to judge (another example of asymmetric information). Alternatively, GPs (like HMOs) will face incentives to weed out patients who fall into costly groups (another example of cream-skimming). Thus quality control and monitoring of medical outcomes become critical.

Can quality be monitored cost effectively? The question is then whether the purchaser (District or GP) can ensure quality by specifying contracts sufficiently tightly and by monitoring providers. The underlying problem is the difficulty (Section 2.2) of measuring health outcomes, making it hard to decide which supplier offers the most efficient and effective treatment. Management decisions are increasingly based on cost data. This is the wrong variable but, in the absence of outcome data, is all that managers have to go on.

How useful is competition? There are two questions: how much competition results from the reforms; and is such competition desirable? On the first, competition can be exaggerated. The existence of waiting lists points to at least some excess demand, reducing competitive pressures; and competition is limited outside metropolitan areas. Secondly, the benefits of competition are contingent on perfect information (Section 3.1). Patients are certainly not well informed; and the difficulties of measuring quality mean that Districts and GPs, acting as agents, will not be perfectly informed either. Thus Chalkley and Malcomson (1996: 85–6) conclude that

getting hospitals to bid for contracts to provide health services is not . . . like conducting an auction for wheat because the quality . . . of the services to be provided is not easily specified by contract. Taking the lowest bid may simply result in the provision of poor-quality services . . . The key problem . . . is that there are many dimensions of quality that cannot be enforced by contract.

Co-ordination problems. Districts as fundholders (Enthoven 1985) is one potentially coherent approach; GPs as fundholders (Maynard 1986) is another. The 1991 reforms, however, introduced *both* approaches, creating potential coordination problems, since the two groups have different priorities and because the lines of financial control over purchasing are unclear.

BRIEF ASSESSMENT. There are at least three reasons why the large literature on the reforms (see the Further Reading) reaches few strong conclusions. The intractable problems in evaluating the health gains from different interventions have already been discussed. Secondly, the reforms were introduced with a significant increase in NHS funding, making it difficult to disentangle the effects of increased resources from those of the reforms themselves. Thirdly there is the problem of self-selection: Bartlett and Le Grand (1994) argue, for example, that the first wave of hospital trusts were the most entrepreneurial and hence not typical. Notwithstanding strident political claims in the early 1990s, the scientific evidence yields few robust results—hence the brevity of the following discussion of two aspects of the reforms, GP fundholders and hospital Trusts.

GP fundholding. Writers like Glennerster (1994) conclude that decisions are best located at the lowest level (i.e. GPs) where information about consumers is richest. From this perspective, the movement in the years after 1991 towards more GP fundholding (e.g. by allowing smaller practices to become fundholders) is a move in the right direction. Goodwin's (forthcoming) survey is more agnostic, arguing that the evidence on GP fundholding can be used to support both a strong defence and a vitriolic attack. Many non-fundholding practices have achieved equal or higher efficiency gains; and the Audit Commission (UK National Audit Office 1994) concluded that most fundholders were failing to secure the expected benefits for patients. Goodwin concludes that the evidence to assess the true impact of fundholding on transactions costs, equity and quality of care is very poor, and advocates further research.

Hospital Trusts. Hamblin's (forthcoming) survey is also agnostic, not least because, as he points out, if Trusts are more efficient this may not be because they are Trusts, but because of broader trends in NHS organization or medical technology. He questions whether Trusts have increased competition and points out that there is no evidence that Trusts have increased patient choice and some arguments that they are not able to.

Blaug (1997, p. 19) concludes that,

the overwhelming opinion of all health economists who have looked carefully at these quasi-market reforms is that at best they will encourage an evidence-based, cost-conscious health service that may improve outcomes for some patients registered with managerially competent GPs . . . but at worst they will dramatically increase the costs of administration, produce no improvement in health care for the average patient, and may well destroy irremediably the morale of the NHS.

6. Conclusion: Health and health care

Health derives from many sources, including income, diet, and life style and—it is increasingly clear—broader socioeconomic factors (Section 4.3, point 16). Improved health, therefore, depends in part on developments well outside the health sector.

But health care is also important. Yet no system of health care can be perfect—the real issue is to choose the least inefficient and inequitable form of organization. Radical privatization (as defined in Chapter 4, Section 6) is no way of doing so. This conclusion rests not on personal values but on the *technical* nature of health care, and particularly, though not exclusively, on information problems.

Health care conforms only minimally with the assumptions necessary for market efficiency. The imperfect information and unequal power of consumers, externalities, and technical difficulties with private medical insurance cause serious problems on the demand side of a hypothetical private market; non-competitive behaviour by doctors can cause problems with supply, and third-party payments cause inefficiency via both demand and supply (Section 3.1). A priori there is an overwhelming presumption that an unrestricted private market will be highly inefficient, and also inconsistent with widely held notions of social justice. This view is confirmed by empirical observation (Section 4.1). Countries with little public involvement in health care, or which adopted careless ad hoc modifications to private systems, typically experienced sharp, unplanned increases in expenditure. Efficiency requires, at a minimum, considerable regulation and state financial involvement (Section 3.3).

Because of information problems, the NHS strategy has major advantages—an institution motivated largely by equity is successful because it goes with the grain of efficiency arguments. On the demand side, decisions about treatment are made by doctors, alleviating the worst effects of consumer ignorance; the problems of private insurance are resolved by abandoning insurance even as a fiction; and treatment is largely free at the point of use, which reduces the externality problem and goes a long way towards eliminating the influence of income on consumption. On the supply side, doctors are not as a rule paid a fee for service, thus removing incentives to oversupply. Health care is rationed partly by administrative means and partly by the NHS budget. Furthermore, if public production and allocation can be defended on efficiency grounds, it is legitimate to finance health care redistributively for reasons of social justice (Chapter 4, Section 7.2). In theory, therefore, the strategy is feasible in both efficiency and equity terms.

The practice (Section 4) is far from perfect. Many hospital buildings are old, and there are waiting lists for non-urgent (and even some urgent) conditions. There is room for improvement in both external and internal efficiency. The distribution of health care by social class is less equal than many would wish. However, a good deal can be said on the plus side.

- The average quality of health care in the UK is good, in that health standards are not out of line with those in other countries.
- The NHS is cheaper than the health-care system of any comparable country, and considerably cheaper than most.
- Doctors have no financial incentive to over-prescribe and (partly because of this) patients generally trust their doctor.
- The variation in the quality and quantity of treatment by income level is smaller than in most other countries.
- Treatment is free whatever the extent and duration of illness; no one is denied access because of low income; and no one goes in fear of financial ruin.

Benefits in kind

The NHS thus has much to commend it; and many of its remaining problems could largely be resolved by giving it some more resources and by gathering more and better information.

Its advantages notwithstanding, the NHS is not the only system which makes sense. The strategy has, however, served the UK well, is widely popular, and can be drastically changed only at considerable risk of throwing out the baby with the bathwater. Institutions in other countries show that the adoption of a different system is likely to raise problems very similar to those of the NHS, and additional and more intense problems as well. 'Privatization' (whatever its proponents mean by the term) will not solve old problems, and is likely to create new (and probably larger) ones. My preferred reform for the UK, therefore, is to keep the NHS; the principle should be retained, and the system improved within the existing strategy along the lines suggested in Section 5.2.

However, the political economy and the structure of the medical profession in many other countries make it unlikely that they would readily adopt a system of public production. This is especially true of the USA, where the mixed public/private arrangements described in Section 5.1 might be a more satisfactory solution. The Canadian model of publicly funded, privately produced health care has much to offer; and a system based on regulated health maintenance organizations buttressed by income transfers may offer an alternative.

The crucial point is that any system of health care must constitute a genuine *strategy* —ad hoc tinkering is a guaranteed road to disaster. Both theory and international experience point to two effective strategies:

- (mainly) public funding (taxation or social insurance) plus public production; or
- (mainly) public funding plus private production *plus* regulation to contain costs.

At a strategic level the problems a country faces are largely predictable consequences of its chosen health strategy. Consider four broad objectives of a health-care system: (a) equitable access, (b) cost containment, (c) no waiting lists, and (d) consumer choice. A country like the USA, with largely private funding, faces the problems discussed in Section 3.1, so that its major problems are (a) and (b). In countries like Canada, with public funding of private production, the pressure point is (b). Countries like the UK, with mainly public funding of mainly public production, score well on (a) and (b), but tend to face problems on (c) or (d). There is no perfect solution. The trick is to learn from theory and experience to choose the least bad second-best option.

FURTHER READING

As general reinforcement of the material in this chapter, Le Grand and Vizard (1998) assess health care in the UK from the mid-1970s to the mid-1990s, and Glennerster (1997: ch. 10) analyses the finance of the system.

For general discussion of the economics of health, see Stiglitz (1988: ch. 11). On the nature of health care, including problems with insurance, see Arrow (1963) (the classic article) and Culyer

(1993). Problems with medical insurance are discussed by Pauly (1974, 1986) and Culyer (1993); Barr (1995) discusses the implications of genetic screening for insurance. On equity in health care, see Le Grand (1991*b*) and Culyer and Wagstaff (1993), and on the impossibility of rationing health care in a way which is simultaneously efficient, equitable, and administratively feasible, Le Grand (1996). On the debate over the equity, or otherwise, of the NHS, see Culyer and Wagstaff (1993); Le Grand (1991*b*, 1992, 1995); and Powell (1995). For the distributional effects of benefits in kind more generally, see Evandrou *et al.* (1993).

The case for market provision of health care is set out *inter alia* by Lees (1961), Seldon (1981), and Friedman and Friedman (1980: ch. 4). On the role of giving, the classic work is Titmuss (1970).

On the valuation of human life, see Jones-Lee (1976); for an early critique, see Broome (1978). See also Mooney (1992: ch. 5). On the socioeconomic determinants of health, see Robert C. Evans *et al.* (1994), Wilkinson (1996) and, for a cogent survey, Robert C. Evans (1996). For attempts to quantify the benefits of health care, such as QALYs and similar measures, see Williams (1985), Wagstaff (1991), Bleichrodt (1995), and Culyer and Wagstaff (1995).

For assessment of the NHS, see Le Grand and Vizard (1998). For discussion of health care in an international context, see Schieber *et al.* (1991), Barr (1992), OECD (1992, 1994), Hurst (1996), and Ham (1997). On reform in the USA, see the various essays in Aaron (1996) and Scheffler and Waitzman (forthcoming), on Canada, McArthur *et al.* (1996) and National Health Forum (1997), Australia, Peabody *et al.* (1996) and Podger (1997), and New Zealand, Malcolm and Barnett (1994). For discussion of health in the former-communist countries, see World Bank (1996, Ch. 8) or, more fully, Preker and Feachem (1994) and Shapiro (1993) (a riveting but sobering account of the Russian mortality crisis).

A thoughtful (and sympathetic) discussion of reform within the NHS is by Enthoven (1985). The 1991 reforms are set out in UK DoH (1989). For overviews of the NHS reforms, see Robinson and Le Grand (1994) and Le Grand *et al.* (forthcoming).

The theory and practice of quasi-markets are discussed by Bartlett and Harrison (1993), Propper (1995 *b*, *c*, forthcoming), Glennerster and Le Grand (1995), Chalkley and Malcomson (1996), and Maynard and Bloor (1996). For an international perspective, see Hurst (1996).

GP fundholding is evaluated *inter alia* by Dixon and Glennerster (1995), Glennerster (1994), Glennerster *et al.* (1994), UK National Audit Office (1994), and Goodwin (forthcoming) (the last contains an exhaustive bibliography of studies on fundholding). On hospital Trusts, see Bartlett and Le Grand (1994), and Hamblin (forthcoming).

CHAPTER 13

Education

Man is the most versatile of all forms of capital.

(Irving Fisher, 1930)

All that is spent during many years in opening the means of higher education to the masses would be well paid for if it called out one more Newton or Darwin, Shakespeare or Beethoven.

(Alfred Marshall, 1842–1924)

1. Introduction

The introductory discussion of health (Chapter 12, Section 1), which should be (re)read at this stage, applies equally to education. The role of the public sector in both finance and production is less clear-cut than with many types of cash benefits, particularly for post-primary education. This chapter is concerned mainly with setting out the ground rules for policy analysis, rather than with asserting strong conclusions. The theoretical arguments are very similar to those for health care.

The chapter discusses the aims of education (Section 2), theoretical arguments about state intervention in pursuit of efficiency and equity (Section 3), assessment of the UK education system (Section 4), the range of possible reforms (Section 5), and major conclusions (Section 6).

During the early part of the chapter little knowledge is needed of the institutions described in Section 4.1. Education is compulsory to age 16. Primary (age 5 to 11) and secondary education (age 11 to 18) are provided publicly and without charge. There is also a small private sector. For the most part these are publicly organized, publicly funded institutions. In contrast, university education is privately *produced* but substantially (though decreasingly) publicly *financed*.[1]

---

[1] Chapter 4, Section 6, discusses in detail the distinction between public and private production and finance.

2. Aims

2.1. Concepts

Social welfare is maximized through the pursuit of economic efficiency[2] and social justice (or equity). This section discusses how these concepts apply to education.

The primary objective of education policy is to improve educational outcomes. As discussed in Chapter 12, Section 2.1, good health derives from many sources, of which health care is only one. Good educational outcomes, analogously, derive from many sources, of which formal education is only one: parenting is key; there is increasing evidence of the link between childhood poverty and poor educational outcomes (see Section 4.2, point 3); and natural ability is also part of the story.

What, however, do we mean by 'good educational outcomes'? The primary purpose of education is to transmit knowledge and skills *and*, as important, attitudes and values. Education is not only technical but also cultural: it is essential if the UK (or any country) is 'to be a successful nation in a competitive world, and to maintain a cohesive society and rich culture' (UK National Committee of Inquiry into Higher Education 1997*b*: 7). Part of the objective is to produce agreement about values. As examples, consider the following statements: students should never disagree with their teachers; women should sit in class and just listen; answers get higher marks if they conform with the teacher's ideology. In the West there is strong disagreement with the values contained in such statements, the prevailing value being that what matters is the analytical *content* of the argument, not the gender or status of the *person* making it. Instilling such values is part of the purpose of education. Another part of the objective is to allow diversity. Families will have different views about subject matter, the role of discipline, and the place of religion. Thus, the education package (and hence the meaning of a 'good' education) will depend on the economic, political, and social structure of the country concerned,[3] and will vary far more than the definition of good health.

Achieving this primary objective involves a number of subsidiary ones. Efficiency is important here as elsewhere. If we spent nothing on education, children would all be illiterate; if we spent the whole of national income on education, there would be no food or health care. The optimal quantity clearly lies somewhere between—in principle where the value gained from the last unit of education is equal to the marginal value which would be derived from the alternative use to which the resources involved could be put. This is the quantity X^* in Figure 4.1.

Allocative efficiency (sometimes referred to in discussion of education as *external efficiency*) is concerned with producing the types of educational activities which equip individuals—economically, socially, politically, and culturally—for the societies in which

---

[2] The concept of economic efficiency is defined in Chapter 4, Section 2.1.

[3] See World Bank (1996: ch. 8) for discussion of how education in Communist countries was well suited to the needs of central planning and totalitarian government.

they live. External efficiency applies to the totality of resources devoted to education (the macro-efficiency aim in Chapter 1, Section 2.2), and also to the division of resources between different types and levels of education (the micro-efficiency aim), so as to produce the optimal quantity, quality, and mix. Separately, productive efficiency (Chapter 4, Section 2.1), sometimes referred to as *internal* efficiency, is concerned with running schools and other institutions as efficiently as possible.

Equity is more elusive (see the discussion in Chapter 12, Section 2.1). To sidestep some of these difficulties equity will be defined as a form of *equality of opportunity* (Chapter 6, Section 3.1, especially equation (6.18)). This does not mean that individuals can necessarily obtain as much education as they want. However, it implies that, if individuals A and B have similar tastes and ability, they should receive the same education, irrespective of factors which are regarded as irrelevant—for example, income. This definition of equity at least has the merit that it apportions scarcity in a just way.

Once we have decided the efficient level of production of different types of education and their equitable distribution, the remaining question is how to finance education. This is an issue of vertical equity discussed in Chapter 4, Section 4.1. It was argued in Chapter 4, Section 7.2, that if, for example, education is allocated efficiently by the market then equity aims are generally best achieved through income transfers. But where education is publicly produced and allocated for *efficiency* reasons, it may be appropriate to finance it out of progressive taxation; if so, it is possible, though not inevitable (Section 4.3) that in-kind transfers will redistribute from rich to poor.

2.2. Measuring costs and benefits

Measuring costs, as with health care (Chapter 12, Section 2.2), presents no insurmountable problems. We know the direct costs of the state educational system and its components (Table 13.1). The problem of apportioning overheads is broadly the same as for health care. For people past school-leaving age it is also necessary to include an estimate of forgone earnings.

Measuring benefits faces a series of intractable problems. There are distinct echoes of the discussion of defining and measuring poverty (Chapter 6, Section 2). In both cases, there is no scientifically satisfactory solution.

- *Output cannot be measured.* Since there is no single definition of a 'good' education, there is no unambiguous measure of output. We can measure test scores, but (*a*) such measures are imperfect even in their own terms, and (*b*) educational outputs are much broader than such technical benefits. Education has *consumption benefits*—that is, the enjoyment of the educational process itself; *investment benefits*, including higher pay, job satisfaction and the enjoyment of leisure; and various *external benefits*, including shared values. Most of these are unmeasurable, but that does not make them unreal.

- *Connecting inputs and outputs* (the education production function) *is problematical.* It is possible to measure the quantity of some inputs (teachers' and pupils' time, buildings, equipment). But it is not possible to measure their quality. Nor is it possible to measure other inputs, such as natural ability and the quantity of quality of parenting. Secondly, as just discussed, output can be measured only in terms of test scores. Thirdly, the production function is hard to estimate. Studies typically assume (because no other assumption is available) that schools have a single, narrow objective—maximizing pupils' test scores.

- *Causality cannot be established*. Even if these measurement problems were solved, a further problem remains. As discussed shortly, the 'screening hypothesis' questions the causal link between post-primary education and increased individual productivity. Is an individual productive because she is naturally able, or because she has been well educated?

THE HUMAN CAPITAL MODEL attempts to explain the demand for education in terms of its production and utility benefits. It is argued, in the case of the former, that an individual who acquires more education becomes more skilful and productive. This approach sees education as a form of investment, analogous to improving machinery. From the individual viewpoint, such investment is profitable to the extent that it increases future income by more than its initial costs (including forgone earnings). Empirically there is a strong correlation between an individual's education and his lifetime earnings (see Psacharopoulos and Woodhall 1985: ch. 3). The overall pattern summarized by Blaug (1970: 27) is that 'within a few years after leaving school . . . better educated people earn more than less educated people; their advantage continues to widen with age and . . . the favourable differential persists until retirement'.

Utility benefits arise because the individual may derive utility from the educational process itself (i.e. education might have consumption benefits in the present as well as investment benefits in the future). The individual return to education also includes non-money rewards such as job satisfaction and the enjoyment of leisure.

To clarify the *individual* return to education, it is helpful to set out formally the individual investment decision. The initial assumptions of the simplest human capital model are:

1. Education raises the individual's marginal product in the future and therefore his future money income.

2. This increase in money income is the *only* benefit from education, i.e. we rule out consumption benefits and future non-money returns.

If B_t is the benefit to the individual from an extra year's education, and r is his personal rate of time preference, the *gross present value*[4] (*GPV*) of an additional year of education is

$$GPV = \frac{B_1}{1+r} + \frac{B_2}{(1+r)^2} + \ldots + \frac{B_N}{(1+r)^N}. \tag{13.1}$$

[4] For further discussion of cost-benefit analysis, see Stiglitz (1988: ch. 10), Musgrave and Musgrave (1989: ch. 9), or Cullis and Jones (1998: ch. 6).

Benefits in kind

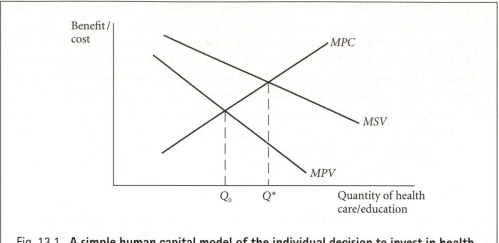

Fig. 13.1. **A simple human capital model of the individual decision to invest in health care/education**

The *net present value (NPV)* is

$$NPV = \sum_{t=0}^{N} \frac{B_t}{(1+r)^t} - C_0 \tag{13.2}$$

where C_0 is the cost of an additional year of education (including forgone earnings). The individual will continue to acquire education so long as $GPV > C_0$—i.e. up to the point where $NPV = 0$. This is the level of education Q_0 in Figure 13.1, where the marginal private value (*MPV*) of education is the marginal gross present value from equation (13.1), and the marginal private cost (*MPC*) is the cost of education to the individual.

Relaxing the second assumption does not change the flavour of the results. Consumption benefits reduce C_0 and non-money returns increase B_t in equation (13.2), thus increasing the quantity of education an individual will choose to acquire.

THE SCREENING HYPOTHESIS. It might seem, therefore, that by measuring the money income benefits (though not the utility benefits) to the individual we can establish a lower bound on the production benefits of education. This is valid if we are prepared to assume that education is *causally* related to increases in individual productivity. This is the strong first assumption made above. In contrast, the screening hypothesis argues that education is *associated* with increased productivity but does not *cause* it.[5]

The screening hypothesis argues, first, that education beyond a basic level does not increase individual productivity and, secondly, that firms seek high-ability workers but

[5] The large literature on this and other aspects of the economics of education is surveyed by Blaug (1976, 1985) and Glennerster (1993). For fuller discussion of screening, see Stiglitz (1975) or, for formal discussion, Hirshleifer and Riley (1992: chs. 8, 11).

are unable, prior to employing them, to distinguish them from those with low ability. The problem is analytically similar to adverse selection in insurance markets (Chapter 5, Section 3.2), or more generally to 'lemons' (Akerlof 1970), in the sense that one side of the market has more information than the other. Individuals therefore have an incentive to make themselves distinctive by some sort of signal. According to the screening hypothesis, post-primary education fills exactly this function: it gives a signal to prospective employers, which it is in the *individuals'* (though not necessarily in society's) interests to acquire. Just as an individual's good health may be due more to a naturally strong constitution than to medical care so, according to this view, is productivity the result of natural ability rather than post-primary education.

There are various counter-arguments. Where education includes professional training (e.g. medicine), there is a direct contribution to productivity. The strong form of the hypothesis also assumes that there is only one type of job. In practice, skills and job characteristics are heterogeneous, so that it is necessary to match workers and jobs, giving education an additional social return as a matching device. Whether there is *some* validity in the hypothesis is an empirical matter. The verdict is undecided and likely to remain so, since individual productivity is determined in part by unmeasurable influences such as natural ability and family background.

The conclusion from the individual viewpoint is that it is possible to measure the money income benefits (but not the utility benefits) *associated* with different levels of education, but the *causal* relationship is less clear. The screening hypothesis leaves the *individual* decision to invest unaffected, and so leads to the same result as the human capital model. But, to the extent that it is true, screening has profound implications for the *socially* optimal level of investment in education, to which we turn next.

EXTERNAL BENEFITS. Setting the screening hypothesis to one side for the moment, education may create benefits to society over and above those to the individual in a number of ways.[6] There is at least one strong external benefit. Education, to the extent that it raises an individual's future earnings, increases her future tax payments; in the absence of any subsidy, an individual's investment in education confers a 'dividend' on future taxpayers.[7]

Does education create external benefits over and above this tax dividend? It is part of the conventional wisdom (Le Grand *et al.* 1992: 74–6) that it does. *Production benefits* arise if education not only makes someone more productive, but also contributes to the productivity of others (your ability to use e-mail increases my productivity as well as your own). Individuals may become more adaptable and better able to keep up with technological change. The economic spin-offs of higher education and a more mobile educated population are relevant in this context. It is not surprising that much 'high-tech' industry is concentrated round clusters of universities—for example, Cambridge (Massachusetts) and Cambridge (England). Education lies at the heart of recently developed theories of endogenous growth (see Romer 1993). Measuring these benefits

---

[6] The theory of externalities is discussed in Chapter 4, Section 3.2, and the Appendix to Chapter 4, para. 15.

[7] This line of argument can be used to justify a subsidy for any type of investment which raises future income. That is precisely what usually happens through the tax system in the case of business investment.

is difficult, not least because it is hard to separate the effects of education from other determinants of productivity, such as natural ability and the quantity and quality of capital equipment.

Education may also have broader benefits. First, there are *family benefits*. Schools viewed as a child-minding institution can create output benefits by enabling parents to work in the market sector (thereby raising their output and earnings) or in the household sector (thereby raising their output but not their earnings). Schools can also create utility benefits by enabling parents to enjoy more leisure. The value of these child-minding benefits can be measured by what parents would be prepared to pay a child-minder. Education may also create *cultural benefits* external to the recipient in at least two ways. A common cultural experience (music, art, literature) may foster communication generally, both at the time and in the future. In addition, there may be neighbourhood effects; the mechanics of taking children to school, parent–teacher associations, etc. bring people into contact and may foster shared attitudes locally. Education in this context is part of the socialization process, as a device which fosters shared values and social cohesion.

These effects, however, can go both ways. Education encourages questioning attitudes and so, it might be argued, can create negative cultural benefits (Grosvenor Square, Paris, and Berkeley in 1968). If education raises expectations unduly, the result could be individuals who are discontented with their job, with possible ill effects on their productivity.

The previous paragraph is intended merely as a caution against blindly *assuming* that education has positive external benefits. If there are potential costs as well as benefits, the issue must be resolved empirically. Again, however, measurement problems make definitive answer impossible. Estimates of private rates of return are suspect because, of necessity, they omit all non-money returns. Estimates of the social rate of return are doubly suspect: they omit non-money returns and (since no other procedure is possible) they also ignore the screening problem.

The externality argument is strong in presumptive terms, but wholly satisfactory empirical verification is still lacking. Because of the 'tax-dividend' point, there is an unarguable external benefit, but it is not possible to show how much.

If education (*a*) increases individual productivity and (*b*) creates external production benefits, then the amount of education chosen by an individual in a market system, Q_0 in Figure 13.1, will generally be less than the optimal amount, Q^*, an issue discussed in more detail in Section 3.1. However, if the claims of the screening hypothesis are valid, then education leads to (but does not *cause*) an increase in individual income, but does not raise output. In this case individuals may acquire *more* education than is socially efficient.

RATE-OF-RETURN STUDIES, despite these difficulties, have attempted to measure the benefits of education. The rate of return, r_0, is that rate of interest which equates the present value of the stream of future benefits in equation (13.2) to the initial cost of acquiring an additional unit of education. In other words, r_0 is the rate of interest which reduces the *net* present value of additional education to zero. It is vital to distinguish the private rate of return (which determines individual decisions) from the social rate (which is the relevant variable for public policy).

Two conclusions tend to emerge from empirical studies.[8] The rate of return is highest for primary education, and then declines; and the private rate of return exceeds the social rate at all levels of education (mainly because in all countries education subsidies reduce costs to the individual but not to society). These results must be heavily qualified. First, they are based on *money* returns. No account is (or can be) taken of the consumption value of education, nor of its non-money returns. Where these factors are present, empirical estimates *understate* both private and social benefits to an unknown extent. Secondly, such estimates can measure only the *association* between education and earnings. But to the extent that the screening hypothesis is true the causal link is weakened, in which case the measured social (though not the private) benefits of postprimary education will be *overstated* by an unknown amount. The estimation of rates of return, in short, is a heroic undertaking.

THE RELATIONSHIP BETWEEN EDUCATION AND ECONOMIC GROWTH, for these and other reasons, remains unclear. Output growth depends on the increase in the quantity and quality of the capital stock; on the increase in quantity and quality of the labour force; and on a variety of non-economic factors. Education affects only one of these, the quality of the labour force. The problem is to separate the quantitative effect of this variable given the influence of all the others. Despite much work, progress has been scant (see Psacharopoulos 1984 and Psacharopoulos and Woodhall 1985: ch. 2 for surveys). About the only firm conclusion to emerge is the unsurprising one that no country has experienced a substantial degree of economic development without first achieving a level of basic literacy in a substantial proportion of its population. Beyond this, little has been established, notwithstanding Denison's (1962, 1967, and 1969) classic works or the promise of the new growth theories (Romer 1993).

To sum up:

Human capital theory has failed to resolve the difficulties . . . that appeared at the very outset, such as the relative impact on individual earnings of endowed ability, acquired ability and educational attainment, on the one hand, and quantity and quality of formal schooling . . . on the other. The so-called screening . . . hypothesis has never been convincingly tested . . . and screening throws cold water on any belief that the social rate of return on educational investment can provide governments with an investment criterion for educational spending. Nothing new has been said since 1970 on so central a concept as the externalities of education and even production function estimates of education—the relationship between school resources and student achievement—has made little progress.   (Blaug, 1997, p. 6)

[8] See Psacharopoulos (1973, 1980) and Psacharopoulos and Woodhall (1985: chs. 3, 5) for international comparison. For recent UK evidence, see the Education Department's submission to the Dearing Committee (UK NCIHE 1997*d*) and Glennerster (1998: table 3.8).

3. **Methods**

3.1. Theoretical arguments for intervention 1: Efficiency

The arguments about the conformity of education with the standard assumptions in many ways parallel those for health care (see the discussion in Chapter 12, Section 3.1), so discussion is brief.

PERFECT INFORMATION. Do consumers of education have perfect information about the nature of the product (i.e. are indifference maps well defined); about prices (i.e. do they know their budget constraint); and about the future? Knowledge of the nature of the product is certainly not perfect. Children (the immediate consumers) are not well informed. In a market system decisions are therefore left to parents, at least for early education. But parental preferences can cause inefficiency in two ways: they might themselves have imperfect information; or they might not consider the child's best interests but those of the family as a whole, themselves included. The issue is further complicated by the particular difficulty in defining 'the product'.

Such complexities can make rational decisions difficult. In addition, consumers of education are likely to differ in the extent of their confidence and articulateness (the issue of unequal power). The result of these factors is inefficiency, though both its extent and direction (see Figure 12.1) are open to debate. But it is likely that imperfect information leads to under-consumption, particularly by the lowest socioeconomic groups (see Section 3.2).

Solutions can take several forms. In contrast with health care, the market itself might supply information—for example, advisory centres, or a 'Good Schools Guide' which included relevant performance indicators. But it can be argued that, where children or their families have imperfect information and/or where families cannot be relied on to act in their best interests, there is an efficiency argument for intervention, particularly in the form of regulation. This would embrace mandatory school attendance (discussed below), and the establishment of minimum standards and inspection to ensure conformity with those standards. Only if the information problem is regarded as major is there an argument on this account for public production and allocation.

A second issue is the extent to which consumers or their families are well informed about prices. If education were privately produced, this information would be provided by the market. But, as with health care, it should be remembered that improved knowledge of prices increases efficiency only where consumers are well informed also in other respects. If intervention on efficiency grounds were thought necessary, it would take the form of publishing a list of school fees, or regulating them.

The problem of information about the future is minor. Parents know that their children will need education at least until minimum school-leaving age. In a market system they would make financial provision for their children's education out of current income, out of savings, or, if they were uncertain of their future income or lifespan, by taking out an endowment policy, the proceeds of which could be used to pay school fees in the future. Uncertainty (as opposed to poverty) raises no substantial problems in this context.

PERFECT COMPETITION. The proposition that the advantages of a competitive market for health care are contingent on perfect information (Chapter 12, Section 3.1) is equally applicable here. But the information problem is perhaps less severe for education, so this section is not concerned with the desirability of competition but its feasibility. Two issues arise: the supply of education; and the supply through the private market of finance for education. There is no reason why schools in cities should not act competitively. But a rural school may have a local monopoly and, if run to maximize profits, would under-provide. The standard solution is price regulation (Chapter 4, Section 3.2).

Education finance raises different issues, which recur in later discussion of higher education. From an efficiency viewpoint we do not normally worry if an individual cannot afford more than x units of a good. If a student cannot afford smoked salmon and therefore buys none, there are no efficiency implications. But if an individual cannot afford an adequate diet and becomes malnourished, there are efficiency losses as well as equity costs. Similar losses arise if an individual cannot afford to buy the socially efficient amount of education—for example, basic literacy, numeracy, and computer skills. With perfect capital markets, children could finance their own education by borrowing against their future earnings. But capital markets are not perfect; students seeking to borrow money can usually offer only human capital as collateral, whereas lending institutions require physical capital or financial wealth. In a pure market system this would result in under-consumption, giving an efficiency (as well as a possible equity) justification for intervention. This could take several forms: the state could act as guarantor for loans made by private institutions to children for educational purposes; it could provide loan finance itself; or it might choose to subsidize education.

MARKET FAILURES. Education is not a public good;[9] nor does it generally face increasing returns to scale. But we saw in Section 2.2 that education can create a variety of external benefits, both productive and cultural. The strength of these effects is hard to measure, but they cannot on that account be ignored. Intervention can involve regulation in the form of compulsory attendance at school until age 16 to prevent under-consumption (see the analogous argument for compulsory membership of an unemployment insurance scheme in Chapter 8, Section 2.1); and an appropriate Pigovian subsidy could in principle achieve a similar effect.

3.2. Theoretical arguments for intervention 2: Equity

HORIZONTAL EQUITY relates to perfect information (to assist rational choice) and equal power (to enforce that choice). Both may be lacking for consumers of education. A

---

[9] See the definition of public goods in the Appendix to Chapter 4, paras. 13, 14.

major equity issue arises where these problems are greater for individuals in lower socioeconomic groups (which is likely if information is costly to acquire). Thus parents with little education may have less information than better-educated parents in making decisions about their children; in addition, they may be less able to make use of any information they do acquire. In such cases intervention may improve equity as well as efficiency.

Regulation would be concerned with the professional qualifications of teachers, minimum physical facilities, school attendance, and, possibly, curricula. Where imperfect information causes under-consumption, a subsidy might be applied either to prices or to incomes. Income subsidies usually take the form of cash transfers, but education vouchers (Section 5) can be thought of as a form of tied transfer; so too can student educational grants.

Where inadequate information and inequality of power are serious problems, efficiency and equity may both be increased by public allocation and/or production, depending on whether (*a*) the private or public sector is more efficient at producing education and (*b*) regulation of standards is more effective in one sector or the other. The issue is discussed in Section 3.3.

VERTICAL EQUITY concerns the extent to which education does or should redistribute from rich to poor. As discussed in Chapter 7, Section 4, publicly provided education, subject to caveats, is redistributive if (rich) individual R pays more taxes to pay for education than (poor) P where each consumes the same quantity, and also if R consumes twice as much as P but pays more than twice as much in contributions. The voting model in Chapter 4, Section 4.2, offers an explanation of why this might happen. If R's utility rises with P's 'good' consumption (education for P's children) but falls with P's 'bad' consumption, we have a consumption externality of the sort described by equation (4.15). In those circumstances, it might be rational for R to offer an in-kind transfer of education worth £1,000, but to make a cash offer of only £200 (since P might spend the latter on 'bad' consumption). If the difference between the two offers is large enough, P might prefer the in-kind offer to the lower cash amount (see Figure 4.5).

Analogous to the arguments about health care, the rich may have an interest in the education of the poor for two reasons. They might support transfers of education for reasons of efficiency/self-interest: a well-educated workforce might foster economic growth, and/or might reduce social unrest. This is the 'national-efficiency' argument (Chapter 2, Section 2.1) which gave rise to the Marxist interpretation of the welfare state (Chapter 3, Section 5.3). Alternatively, rich individuals might care about the distribution of education for altruistic/equity reasons.

Thus efficiency arguments for public production and allocation may be reinforced by equity motives which make it politically easier to make transfers in kind. The rich may favour them for selfish or altruistic reasons; and, if the offer is sufficiently generous, the poor might also prefer in-kind transfers.

The voting model offers an explanation of why *some* transfer of education takes place. But is the amount transferred *optimal*? As discussed in Chapter 4, Section 4.4, libertarians support in-kind transfers only as *voluntary* action by the rich, but not as a result of government failure in the face of coercive electoral behaviour by the poor (Chapter 4, Section 5). They therefore argue that redistribution under the current system is greater than optimal. Many socialists support in-kind transfers for their own sake (particularly in the case of education) because they increase equality, and argue that redistribution is almost certainly suboptimal.

3.3. Types of intervention

Sections 3.1 and 3.2 discussed *why* the state might intervene. The next issue is *how* best it might do so. The theoretical arguments raised by education largely parallel those for health care. The main differences are that the problem of information (though not of equal power) may be less acute; that problems with private insurance are not relevant; and that the issues of imperfect capital markets (and probably also of external effects) are more important.

PURE MARKET PROVISION (i.e. rows 1 or 2 of Table 4.1). Critics of public provision (see the Further Reading) ideally wish to see education produced, allocated, and financed privately. But because they recognize some of the difficulties described earlier, their policy proposals (Section 5.1) are of private production, with mixed public/private finance and some regulation.

The argument against market production and allocation of pre-university education is the failure of many of the assumptions necessary for market efficiency. Regulation can be justified by imperfect information and unequal power, and the presence of externalities and local monopolies. Subsidies can be justified by externalities, and subsidies or the provision of loan guarantees (or of loans themselves) by capital market imperfections. The issue of public production rests largely on the extent of information problems. It should be clear that a pure market system is likely to be highly inefficient, and also inequitable to the extent that knowledge, power, and access to capital markets are correlated with socioeconomic status. Unrestricted market provision of pre-university education is theoretically implausible and, in practice, does not exist in any country.

MIXED PUBLIC/PRIVATE INVOLVEMENT (e.g. row 4(*a*) in Table 4.1). The issue is whether it is possible to devise an efficient and equitable package whereby the state regulates education and subsidizes it wholly or in part, but where production takes place in the private sector. This is the way universities operate in many countries, and proposals to extend these arrangements to schools ('voucher' schemes) are discussed in Section 5.1.

Several ingredients are necessary for this approach to be efficient and equitable. The state would have to regulate education in one or more of the following areas: mandatory school attendance to some minimum age; course content; minimum qualifications for teachers; certification of schools (i.e. would an individual need permission to start a school?); inspection to ensure an adequate quality of service; and fee levels (i.e. should schools be allowed to charge what they liked?). Though the principle of regulation is accepted, commentators disagree as to how far it should go.

Subsidies to education can be justified in both efficiency and equity terms. In a libertarian world, individuals pay for the private benefits they receive from education, but are subsidized to the extent that external benefits are thereby conferred upon others.[10] This degree of subsidy might, however, be insufficient. Individuals from lower socioeconomic groups might face imperfect capital markets; in addition they (and their families) might systematically have poorer information about the benefits of education and/or be reluctant to incur large debts. Any resulting tendency to under-consumption suggests a larger subsidy than the externality argument implies, and maybe a 100 per cent subsidy, at least for school education. Additionally, if the subsidy is only partial, it may be necessary on both efficiency and equity grounds for the state to provide loan capital.

Private production is likely to be efficient only if quality is adequately monitored. Libertarians dispute this view, arguing that dissatisfied parents can move their child to another school, and that if a private school has a bad reputation it will go out of business. This argument has two weaknesses. Parents may not have enough information to realize that their child is being badly educated or, if they do, may not have the confidence to do anything about it. Secondly, education is not a repeatable experiment. It is true that a restaurant which provides bad service will go out of business; its former clients will have suffered nothing worse than a bad meal, and can spend the rest of their lives going to better restaurants. Education, in contrast, is largely a once-and-for-all experience; a child who has had a year of bad education may never recover. In addition, a child may face high emotional costs (changing friends, etc.) in changing school. A more apt analogy is a restaurant whose food is so bad that it might cause permanent ill health.

Finally, private-consumption decisions are likely to be efficient and equitable only if families have sufficient information, and if they use it in the child's best interests. The issue of whether the state or the family is better qualified to make educational decisions in the name of an individual child is controversial to say the least. Some parents, maybe disproportionately in the higher socioeconomic groups, are capable of more informed decisions than the state; others make poorer decisions. If the quality of parental choice is systematically related to socioeconomic status and the effect is strong, then private allocation can be argued to be less equitable than state allocation, irrespective of the balance of argument about efficiency. It is not surprising that the advocates of parental choice almost invariably belong to the higher socioeconomic groups.

PUBLIC PRODUCTION, ALLOCATION, AND FINANCE (i.e. row 8 in Table 4.1). Is public funding, together with public production and allocation, less inefficient and inequitable than the sort of arrangements just described? The allocation issue should be argued on the basis of perceptions about imperfect information and social cohesion, and that of public production on whether it is, or is not, likely to be more efficient than the private market. These issues, we have seen, turn crucially on the answers to two questions.

---

[10] Note that this approach is logically incompatible with the screening hypothesis (Section 2.2).

- Do parents on average make better or worse decisions than the state about their children's education?
- If the quality of parental choice varies systematically with socioeconomic status, how do we weigh the relative claims of middle-class children and their parents to be allowed private choice, against those of children in lower socioeconomic groups, whose interests might be served better by the state?

The answer to the first question is empirical. The answer to the second depends on political stance. Libertarians argue that state allocation interferes with parental freedom and therefore reject it. To socialists the aim of equality is paramount; the claim of children from poorer families therefore takes priority, and state allocation is preferred. Liberals try to recognize the claims of both groups. This involves a system either of public allocation which takes account of stated parental preferences or of parental choice subject to careful scrutiny.

The a priori arguments about the provision of education are more finely balanced than those about health care.[11] But it is fair to say that the failures of the assumptions necessary for market efficiency are sufficiently strong to make public production, allocation, and finance of school education a tenable strategy. To the extent that this is the case on efficiency grounds, it is appropriate to finance education redistributively for reasons of social justice (Chapter 4, Section 7.2).

Finally, since education is not a homogeneous whole, it is necessary to ask whether the same answers apply to all types of education. Should there be one set of answers for compulsory education and another for education beyond the minimum school-leaving age; should some types of education be free and others not; are market solutions more applicable to higher education than to school education; should higher education be financed in part by loans and, if so, on what terms should the loan be made or repaid? These and other questions are discussed in Section 5.

4. Assessment of the UK Educational System

4.1. Institutions

This section describes the operation of school education (public and private) and higher education under the four heads of Table 4.1—that is, production, the individual-consumption decision, finance, and the aggregate production decision. The efficiency and equity of the system are assessed in Sections 4.2 and 4.3, respectively.[12]

---

[11] It is therefore curious that the educational systems of different countries vary much *less* than their systems of health care. In particular it is surprising from an *economic* point of view that school education in the USA is publicly produced, allocated, and financed (i.e. row 8 in Table 4.1).

[12] Though the analytical arguments apply to the entire UK, Scottish educational institutions differ significantly from those in the rest of the country, the difference in education being much larger than for cash benefits, health care, and housing. Institutional discussion is limited, for the most part, to the system in England and Wales.

Benefits in kind

Public expenditure on education roughly doubled in real terms between 1960 and 1976, when it reached a peak of nearly 7 per cent of gross national product. The increase was partly the result of increased birth rates in the late 1940s and mid-1960s; partly because expectations about educational standards rose; and partly because of the relative price effect.[13] Thereafter, public spending on education declined to 4.7 per cent at the end of the 1980s—a cut unparalleled even under the 'Geddes axe' of the 1920s or the Great Depression of the 1930s (Chapter 2, Section 3). Spending rose somewhat over the 1990s to around 5 per cent in 1996/7. Even adjusting for increased private spending and demographic change, there was a significant dip in the 1980s (for fuller discussion, see Glennerster 1998). In contrast, real spending per pupil in the USA increased by 75 per cent between 1970 and 1990 (Burtless 1996d).

THE OPERATION OF SCHOOL EDUCATION

The ultimate responsibility for education in England and Wales[14] rests with the Secretary of State for Education, who is responsible for the Education Department and is accountable to Parliament. Under the Department are over 100 Local Education Authorities (LEAs). Since 1988, schools may opt out of LEA control and be under the direct jurisdiction of the Department for Education. In addition, a few schools are run by voluntary bodies, mostly religious, but most of the running costs are paid by the LEA. There is also a small private sector. Universities are not part of the legal framework established by the 1944 Education Act (Chapter 2, Section 5.1), nor are they the responsibility of LEAs. They are therefore discussed separately.

Schools are inspected by a central body, the Office for Standards in Education, headed by Her Majesty's Chief Inspector of Schools, which is independent of the Secretary of State (see UK DfEE 1997a: ch. 17). The inspectorate, which visits schools and publishes reports, is an important source of quality control by a central body of a locally provided service, a feature almost entirely lacking in the NHS. As a separate aspect of quality control, the 1992 Education Act required schools to publish data on the examination performance of their pupils, leading to the publication of so-called league tables.

THE PRODUCTION OF PRIMARY, SECONDARY, AND FURTHER EDUCATION. Education for the under-fives has been given increasing priority in recent years, public spending on such education rising to £1.5 billion in 1996/7. The objective is that by the later 1990s all children will be eligible from age 4 onwards. All children receive compulsory primary education from age 5 to 11, usually at schools provided by LEAs. Secondary education is provided by LEAs, and to a limited extent by opted-out schools, for children aged 11 to 19 years. It is free, and compulsory up to 16 years. Most teachers are employed by the LEA and paid on an agreed national scale. Total public expenditure on primary and secondary education in 1996/7 (Table 13.1) was £19.5 billion.

[13] See Chapter 12, note 8.

[14] The Secretaries of State for Scotland and Northern Ireland are responsible *inter alia* for education in those countries.

The third arm of the statutory system is further education, which covers the vocational, cultural, social, and recreational needs of everyone over school-leaving age who is not in full-time secondary or higher (i.e. university) education. The system provides education relevant to people's working lives, and is often dovetailed with the practical training provided by industry. A second function is to provide for people's leisure. This involves a huge variety of courses, for most of which charges are levied. Since 1993, the funding of further education has been the responsibility of the central Further Education Funding Council.

This is not the place to discuss further education in detail, but one development in particular should be noted. A policy of rationalization in the late 1950s culminated in a report (UK Department of Education 1966) which provided for polytechnics (which were then part of the LEA further-education sector) to offer degree courses, leading to rapid expansion of degree courses by polytechnics, with standards supervised by a national body, the Council for National Academic Awards. Under the 1988 Education Reform Act, polytechnics became independent of LEA control, receiving their funding from central government through a new body, the Polytechnics and Colleges Funding Council. In 1992 the funding of universities and polytechnics was unified under the Higher Education Funding Council, and the technical distinction between university and polytechnic abolished. In the rest of the chapter, polytechnics are discussed alongside universities as part of a unified higher-education sector.

THE INDIVIDUAL-CONSUMPTION DECISION. A child normally attends a local primary school, and then proceeds to a local comprehensive school. Children normally take the General Certificate of Secondary Education (GCSE) in up to ten subjects, both arts and sciences, at about the age of 16. At that stage many children leave school; by the later 1990s about 8 per cent of children left school with no GCSE qualification at all. The next step on the educational ladder is so-called Advanced Level (A level), taken at about the age of 18, usually in three or four subjects. The number of students staying on till 18 increased sharply over the 1990s. Universities do not normally admit students unless they have two or three A levels or the equivalent.

Issues of individual choice arise in at least three ways. First, there is the decision to continue education beyond the minimum leaving age. This is the individual investment decision discussed in Section 2.2, to which we return later. Second is the extent to which parents can choose which school their child attends. The 1944 Education Act allowed parents considerable discretion, but often the exercise of this choice conflicted with attempts by the LEA to balance numbers and quality of intake across schools within their jurisdiction. Partly to assist parental choice, the 1988 Education Reform Act gave the Secretary of State for Education wide powers to determine the size of each school.

A third aspect of individual choice is the extent to which parents and their children have (or should have) any influence over the LEA and the teaching profession in the running of schools. After many years of debate (see UK Department of Education 1977), legislation in 1986 extended parental representation on schools' governing bodies. A major change under the 1988 Education Reform Act was the introduction of a national

Benefits in kind

Table 13.1. **Education, UK, 1996/7 (est.) (£m.)**

Under fives		1,469
Schools		19,469
Further education		4,985
Higher education		5,001
Student support		3,010
of which:		
Mandatory student awards[a]	2,008	
Student loans (gross)	750	
Student loan repayments	−69	
Other	321	
Miscellaneous educational services and administration		<u>2,917</u>
TOTAL EDUCATION		36,851

[a] England and Wales.

Sources: UK DEE (1997a: annex A); UK Treasury (1997: table 3.5).

curriculum, which applies to all state schools. The Act specifies 'attainment targets' at ages of 7, 11, 14, and 16. The national curriculum specifies programmes of study to achieve these targets, and also establishes a system of assessment.

FINANCE. Spending on schools absorbed about half of the education budget in 1996/7 (Table 13.1). Since few charges are levied, basic education is financed mainly by the state out of tax revenues. Historically, in contrast with the NHS, most expenditure took place at a local level. By the mid-1990s, however, about three-quarters of education spending (schools, further education, and higher education) came from central sources, with about 10 per cent each from local authorities and private spending (Hills 1995). There are also limited sources of non-governmental finance: schools are able to raise funds through their own efforts to pay for 'extras'; and the voluntary sector contributes to the cost of some schools.

THE AGGREGATE PRODUCTION DECISION (i.e. setting budget limits). In the past most decisions about educational expenditure were a more or less complex mix of decisions at central and local levels. Since 1991, however, the bulk of education finance, and hence the aggregate production decision, has been a central government responsibility (Glennerster 1997: chs. 4–6).

Over the years there have been major controversies. The heated debate over the place, if any, of private education is discussed shortly. The most recent controversy concerns the Education Reform Act 1988, which introduced far-reaching changes: introducing a national curriculum; allowing schools to choose to be controlled by central rather than local government (opting out); decentralizing day-to-day management decisions (local management of schools); and introducing an element of voucher funding within the state system (open enrolment and formula funding). These are included in the discussion of quasi-markets in Section 5.1.

336

PRIVATE SCHOOLS

Alongside the state sector a small number of private schools (often confusingly called 'public' schools) provide day and residential education. In the mid-1990s, private schools catered to slightly over 6 per cent of all school pupils and about 18 per cent of 16–18 year olds (in both cases about the same as a decade earlier) and absorbed about 20 per cent of state spending on state schools. The existence of a private sector is controversial. Private schools over the years have come under heavy attack. It is argued that they cream off scarce resources of academically gifted children and teachers, and of finance, making it difficult for state schools to maintain high standards; and, through their hold on recruitment to key positions, that they perpetuate and accentuate economic and social divisions. The counter-arguments centre on their high quality, the beneficial effects of competition, and the freedom of parents to choose their favoured education.

The finance of private schools is complex. The bulk of their income comes from fees, though many have income from private endowments and from appeals to former pupils. They also benefit from tax expenditures. Their charitable status gives them tax advantages such as exemption from paying VAT on fees, and exemption from income tax and corporation tax. Private schools can also receive direct assistance. Under the 1902 Education Act so-called direct grant schools received financial assistance from central government if they took a specified number of children from the state sector. This scheme was abolished in 1976. From 1981, under the assisted-places scheme, central government paid for some gifted children from the state sector to be educated at private schools. In 1995 there were about 35,000 beneficiaries. The Labour government elected in 1997 announced that the scheme would be wound up.

HIGHER EDUCATION

Higher education comprises what used to be two sets of institutions: polytechnics (discussed earlier) and universities. Polytechnics, formerly under LEA control, became independent under the 1988 Education Reform Act. Universities have always been independent, self-governing bodies. The formal distinction between universities and polytechnics disappeared in 1992.

THE INDIVIDUAL-CONSUMPTION DECISION for UK students is relatively straightforward. Universities offer places on the basis of academic qualifications, usually A levels. Students do not have a right to a place; they are carefully selected, and the drop-out rate is low by international standards. The tuition fees of UK full-time undergraduates at a UK university were paid from public funds until 1998, when a tuition fee was foreshadowed.

Until 1998, British undergraduate students in full-time higher education were also eligible for a maintenance grant to cover living costs. The system was introduced in 1962 after a government inquiry (UK Department of Education 1960). The grant varied according to where the student studied and whether or not he continued to live in the parental home, and was generally means-tested on parental income. Students from the best-off families received no grant. Where students received less than the full amount, parents were expected to make a parental contribution to bring the student's income up to the full grant.

In its early days the system worked well. Over the years, however, fiscal constraints plus rising student numbers put the system under pressure. Partly for that reason, top-up loans were introduced in 1990. The grant system is assessed later (Section 4.3, point 10) and the loan proposal in Section 5.2, which also discusses reforms suggested by the Dearing Committee (UK NCIHE 1997a, b). Higher education is thus subsidized for UK students, particularly undergraduates. Overseas students are not generally eligible for public funding. They pay full tuition fees and must finance their own living costs.

FINANCE. With hindsight, the 1960s were something of a golden age for UK higher education (the same was true in the USA). The Anderson Report (UK Department of Education 1960) advocated generous maintenance grants; and the Robbins Report (UK Committee on Higher Education 1963), whose importance to higher education has been compared with that of the 1944 Education Act to general education, recommended sharp expansion of student numbers. As a result, higher education in the 1960s and early 1970s was generously funded from tax revenues, with few questions asked. Universities received much of their funding through the University Grants Committee (UGC), which divided government grants between universities, acted as a general link and a buffer between the Education Department and the universities, and formulated a national policy for higher education. The Committee was an attempt to reconcile public funding with the independence of universities. The good times drew to a close in the mid-1970s. Tax funding declined in real terms; and the UGC gave increasing 'guidance' about how money should be spent (see Kogan and Kogan 1983).

The Education Reform Act 1988 greatly extended central planning of higher education. From 1992, universities in England were funded by the Higher Education Funding Council for England (HEFCE), with separate bodies for the other parts of the UK. Whereas the UGC gave *grants* (albeit with increasing strings attached), HEFCE awards *contracts*. Universities 'bid' to teach N students at a price of £X, each. As a result, they receive public funds from three main sources: income from HEFCE; students' tuition fees (which—at least until the late 1990s—were paid from tax revenues, not by the student); and research funds, channelled largely through the Research Councils. Universities also increasingly earn money in the private sector: from the fees of privately funded UK students and of overseas students; from privately funded research activity; from a variety of commercial activities; and (in some cases) from their own endowments.

A further change, introduced in 1991 (UK DES 1991), was the separation of funding for teaching and research (previous arrangements covered academic salaries on the assumption that 40 per cent of an academic's time was for research). Research funding became more selective, based on a four-yearly Research Assessment Exercise (see HEFCE 1997a, and, for international comparison, Bourke 1997).

In 1996/7 direct public expenditure on universities was £5 billion, plus an additional £3 billion on student support (Table 13.1).

THE AGGREGATE-PRODUCTION DECISION. In the 1960s and early 1970s, somewhat to oversimplify, higher-education institutions decided how many students to admit and the state made available sufficient funds to make this possible. There was a major expansion of the university sector in the aftermath of the Robbins Report; at the same time, as discussed earlier, there was an increase in degree opportunities at polytechnics. After 1975 these policies were to some extent reversed, or at any rate halted. In 1990 only 14 per cent of the relevant age group started full-time degree courses. As well as restricting the *size* of the higher-education sector, there was also growing government influence on its *composition*. What used to be virtually untied transfers to higher education became increasingly like tied grants.

The dramatic expansion in student numbers between 1990 and 1995 requires explanation.

- In 1990 the then Secretary of State for Education, Kenneth Baker, established a target of a 30 per cent participation rate by the turn of the century.
- From 1991, teaching and research were funded separately. Thus expansion, being based only on teaching costs, became cheaper.
- Each university was given a contract to teach N students, funded at the full estimate of teaching costs.
- Universities were allowed to attract students in excess of N. For such students, they were paid a lower sum. Since this was the only way cash-strapped universities could get any more money, they expanded rapidly—so rapidly that in 1996 government reimposed limits on student numbers.

Thus participation doubled to 30 per cent (the good news), so that the UK moved from an élite system of higher education in 1960 to a mass system by 1995. However (the bad news), funding failed to keep pace, leading by 1997 to an average 30 per cent reduction in the real resources universities received per student compared with 1990.

Thus, higher education is subject not only to the ordinary government budgetary process on aggregate expenditure, but also to an element of control over the disposition of public funds.

In short, the production and finance of school education in the state sector are both public (approximating row 8 of Table 4.1). Private schools approximate to row 1, with elements of row 2. In the higher-education sector, production is private and finance for UK students partly public (row 2), but with increasing elements of row 4(*b*).

4.2. Assessment 1: Efficiency

The measurement problems discussed in Section 2.2 create enormous problems for the assessment of external efficiency. Much of the argument is, therefore, of necessity a priori. Efficiency advantages and disadvantages are more finely balanced than with health care—one person's 'sign of a civilized society' is another's 'society is going to the dogs'. Discussion of efficiency therefore concentrates on seven areas, with no attempt at division into advantages and disadvantages.

1. *The individual consumption decision* is substantially influenced by the state and the teaching profession both centrally and locally. Children must attend school until they are 16; the LEA can influence (or in some cases control) the choice of school; and state schools are bound by the national curriculum. These constraints mitigate to some extent the problem of imperfect information, but at the expense of consumer sovereignty. As discussed earlier (Section 3.3), there is heated debate about whether the LEA or the parent is better able to make decisions in the child's interests (see David Green 1991).

2. *Primary and secondary education is free*, or nearly so, and higher education is subsidized. Such subsidies avoid the externality problem and have equity advantages. However, according to the screening hypothesis (Section 2.2) they are inefficient, at least for university education; as discussed in points 10 and 11, below, they may also be inequitable so far as university education is concerned.

3. *Macro-efficiency: schools.* Measurement problems (Section 2.2) make it impossible to quantify on a scientific basis the efficient volume of resources to devote to education. It is generally agreed that good health is due at least as much to factors outside the health sector as to the availability of health care per se. Similarly—and perhaps the only strong result to emerge—educational achievement depends on many more factors than schooling, including the quantity and quality of parenting, poverty, family size, and the influence of television and neighbourhood. Glennerster (1998: table 3.13) reports a cross-section study of all secondary schools in 1995 which shows a striking relation between child poverty (measured by the fraction of children in the school receiving free school meals) and poor examination performance (see also Peter Robinson 1997).

An early urban US study (Burkhead *et al.* 1967) found that variations in test scores depended almost entirely on factors unrelated to the school system—for example, family income and the character of the neighbourhood. Jencks (1972) reached two even stronger conclusions: that differences in educational inputs offered no explanation of differences in educational attainment; and that differences in educational attainment made no independent contribution to explaining disparities in income. UK studies, similarly, found that what went on in schools explained between 5 per cent (Rutter *et al.* 1979) and 10 per cent (Mortimore *et al.* 1988) of differences in pupil achievement. These results suggest that attempts to equalize the distribution of educational inputs may do little to reduce inequality.

Hanushek (1996*b*) concludes that increases in spending in the USA have not led to commensurate improvements in test scores. Given the complex connection between the two, it is wrong to imagine that increased inputs (i.e. money) *necessarily* lead to improved outcomes. Controversy continues, and definitive resolution is a long way off. For surveys, see Hanushek (1986; 1996*a*, *b*), Burtless (1996*d*), and Card and Krueger (1996).

4. *Micro-efficiency: schools.* Having asked (but failed to answer) the question 'are we spending the right amount on education?', we need next to ask the other half of the external-efficiency question: 'are we doing the right thing with educational resources?' Here some answers are possible, but only in terms of examination performance.

An international study of achievements in mathematics and science (Keys *et al.* 1996) makes it possible to compare achievements over time (are UK educational standards slipping?) and across country (is Europe keeping up with the Asian 'tigers'?). The study puts the UK at about the middle of industrialized countries for mathematics achievements, but close to the top in science results at ages 9 and 13. Glennerster (1998) discusses the considerable difficulty of interpreting these and similar results.

About the only body of work which addresses external efficiency explicitly is a series of studies by Prais (drawn together in Prais 1995) which compares the school achievements and industrial training of UK children with those elsewhere in Europe. He finds that UK education and training put employers at an international competitive disadvantage, the deficiency being particularly acute for average and below-average children. Not least for these reasons, the Labour government elected in 1997 published a White Paper (UK DfEE 1997*b*) proposing measures to raise the quality of school education.

5. *Macro-efficiency: higher education.* In the late 1980s I argued (Barr 1989*a*: ch. 1) that the UK higher-education sector was too small, with 14 per cent of the age group going to university, far short of the comparable figure in most other industrial countries. By the mid-1990s, as discussed earlier, participation had increased to 30 per cent. The problem was then different—that of quality—given real cuts in funding per student. As an illustration, each university teacher on average had responsibility for 40 per cent more students in 1996 than in 1989 (UK Committee of Vice-Chancellors and Principals 1996: 4). The suggestion (though again quantification is impossible) is that there is a powerful efficiency case for more resources for higher education, a case all the stronger because of international competition.

6. *Micro-efficiency: higher education.* A separate issue is whether higher education is subject to excessive central planning. The argument against present arrangements is that the division of public funds between different higher-education institutions is centrally decided. Such a process is inevitably bureaucratic. The UGC came under increasing criticism: its decisions were attacked, and so was the way it made those decisions—that is, both the outcome *and* the process were questioned. In addition, there was an increasingly burdensome paper chase (see Barnes and Barr 1988: ch. 3). Such planning continues under HEFCE. In 1997 each UK university was told how many home and EU students it could accept and what fee it could charge—that is, a 'market' in which price and quantity were determined by the central planner. Section 5.2 argues that such central planning is neither necessary nor desirable, particularly for a mass higher education system.

7. *Administrative efficiency.* The schools' inspectorate (UK DES 1986) found that many schools suffered shortages of equipment and neglected buildings, and that in some instances management was ineffective. Knight (1983) argued that localities

gather too little detailed cost data, and do not make the best use of the data they have. This was part of the reason for local managements of schools, whereby schools faced the marginal costs of their decisions but, at the same time, were better informed of school-specific realities. Universities, too, have had problems of administrative efficiency.

4.3. Assessment 2: Equity

As discussed in Chapter 4, Sections 2.2 and 4.3, equity is hard to define and depends in part on political perspective. Following Section 2.1, horizontal equity is taken to imply that children A and B should have an equal *opportunity* (as defined in Chapter 6, Section 3.1) to acquire an education of equal quality and duration, irrespective of whether, for example, A comes from a middle-class family and B from a lower socioeconomic group. Equality of opportunity, as discussed in Chapter 6, Section 3, does not necessarily imply equality of outcome for at least three reasons: A may be luckier than B; they may have different tastes where (and the proviso is crucial) both have perfect information; and A may be more 'able' than B, where such differences are not related to educational and other circumstances earlier in their lives.

8. *The role of income.* The intention of the 1944 Education Act and subsequent policies, including action following the Robbins Report, was that access to education should not be constrained by family income. This aim has not been fully achieved for either schools or higher education. Though no fees are charged, school attendance still involves parental expenditure—for example, on uniforms or sports gear (Bull 1980); and the Education Reform Act 1988 allows schools to charge for individual music tuition and for some outside-hours activities. In addition, many children leave school at 16 not because they want to or because they do not have the ability to proceed further, but because their family needs their earnings. School education after age 16 (for which maintenance grants are very limited), like health care under the NHS, is not 'free', but imposes a cost in forgone earnings which bears disproportionately on the lower socio-economic groups. This disproportion has major implications (discussed below) for university attendance.

9. *Access to school education* has improved significantly since the late 1960s. Academic achievement, once almost exclusively the preserve of the better-off, has become more widespread. The fraction of children leaving school without qualifications fell from 44 per cent in 1970/1 to 6 per cent in 1993/4; the numbers gaining one or more passes at A level doubled (Glennerster 1998: table 3.5; and, as measured by the ability to achieve at least some passes at GCSE, the class gradient at 16 had largely been levelled (ibid., table 3.11). Glennerster explains these outcomes in terms of two sets of factors. First, labour-market developments increased the demand for skills. Secondly, education policies in the 1960s included the abolition of the 11 plus examination (which separated 'academic' children from others on the basis of an examination

at age 11) and introduced comprehensive schools, whereby children with a wide ability range congregated in the same school. These two changes, together with raising the school-leaving age to 16 in the early 1970s, reduced supply-side barriers to progress up the education ladder. Equally, the peer-group effects of comprehensive schools acted to break down demand-side constraints—notably the view of post-compulsory education as something to which only the élite could and should aspire. Educational outcomes are becoming more equal across socioeconomic groups also in other countries (see Mills *et al.* 1996).

Access improved in other ways. Girls' achievements improved unambiguously. In 1980/1 boys did better at A level; by the mid-1990s the situation had reversed; and by the mid-1990s women slightly outnumbered men at university (UK Office for National Statistics 1996; Glennerster 1998: table 3.7). The achievements of ethnic minority children also improved. The general pattern was a tendency to do less well in primary school, but to catch up later, in some instances surpassing the performance of white pupils (Sammons 1995; Glennerster 1998).

The fact that access has improved does not, however, mean that all is well. Middle-class parents can better exercise choice within the state sector, both directly and by moving to areas with good schools (what former Education Minister, Kenneth Clarke, referred to as 'selection by mortgage'), and some increase their choice further by sending their children to private schools. At this point the conflict between equity and individual freedom is at its sharpest.

Pupils from better-off backgrounds cluster in the same schools, leaving other schools with disproportionate numbers of pupils from poorer backgrounds (Walker and Walker 1997; West *et al.* 1997). This is not surprising. As discussed in Section 5.1, a major component of the move towards quasi-markets was to give parents greater choice and to face schools with more competition. Chapter 12 discussed at length the problems which arise when private medical insurers attempt to screen out all but the best risks. Glennerster (1991) argues that schools face similar pressures. We know that (*a*) performance is determined largely by socioeconomic background, and (*b*) schools in greater demand can attract more pupils and hence more funds. A school achieves (*b*) by maximizing the examination results of its pupils; it does that at minimum cost by selecting students from higher socioeconomic backgrounds. Just as medical insurers seek healthy clients, schools seek potentially high-achieving pupils.

The incentives for schools are clear, but the outcome is inequitable. It is also inefficient, because it wastes talent. A countervailing incentive is to target more resources on pupils from poorer backgrounds (analogous to paying doctors a higher capitation allowance for chronically ill or elderly patients). Such an instrument, the educational needs component of central-government grants to local authorities, existed but was downgraded in 1993 (West *et al.* 1995; see also West 1997). The Labour government elected in 1997 announced its intention to take action. It also announced the abolition of the assisted places scheme, which awarded tax-funded scholarships at private schools to pupils from poorer backgrounds.

Benefits in kind

10. *Access to higher education.* As with school education, access has improved. Participation by students from the lower socioeconomic groups rose slightly, from 23 per cent of full-time undergraduates in 1986 to 28 per cent in 1995.[15] Over the same period, women's participation rose from 42 per cent to 52 per cent of undergraduates.

Improvements over the longer term represent more of an improvement than is apparent from the raw statistics. The point is identical to that for health care (Chapter 12, Section 4.3, point 16): 'the unskilled manual group may form a low percentage of students but there are far fewer people in that position to start with' (Glennerster, 1998: 59). For that reason, disparities should be measured not by data on groups but by data on individuals. Hellevick and Ringen (1995), comparing the cohort born in the 1960s with that of the 1930s, found that inequality in educational achievement halved, as measured by the Gini coefficient applied to individual data. Glennerster (1998: table 3.11) reaches a similar conclusion: in 1974 children with professional and managerial parents were overrepresented among degree-holders by a factor of 2.7 relative to their overall numbers in the population; by 1990, the disproportion had fallen to 1.4.

As with school education, these improvements are not grounds for complacency. Disparities can still be striking: a study based on UK postcode areas found that half of young people in the best-off neighbourhoods (and 70 per cent in some) were likely to enter higher education, compared with 10 per cent in the poorest (HEFCE 1997*b*).

What can be said about causes? A central point is that participation in higher education is largely determined earlier in the educational system—notably, by the decision to stay at school and get A levels. In 1993 only 16 per cent of 18–19 year olds from the lowest socioeconomic groups achieved two A levels or equivalent; of those, a very high proportion, 47 per cent, went on to higher education (UK NCIHE 1997*b*: table 7.2). Action on access thus requires action outside higher education to ensure improved staying-on rates in school. Such action includes improved information about the value of education, improved quality in schools, assistance with forgone earnings past school-leaving age, and policies to make it easier for people to enter higher education later in their career (e.g. through part-time options).

A second set of causes lies within the higher-education system itself. The role of tax-funded maintenance grants in this context should not be overlooked. When the system was first introduced in the early 1960s (see UK Department of Education 1960), the intention was to pay students from poorer backgrounds a grant to cover living costs, thereby, it was hoped, removing impediments to access to higher education. The system, in reality, had three major problems.

(a) *Student poverty*: the real value of the grant fell over the 1970s and 1980s, so that its purchasing power in 1989 was 25 per cent below its 1962 level. The full grant became too low to support a typical student; and many students did not receive even that limited amount because the parental-contributions system worked badly. About half the students entitled to a parental contribution received less than the assessed amount, and the shortfall was substantial; students whose parents

---

[15] i.e. people from groups IIIm, IV, and V (UK NCIHE 1997*b*: table 7.1).

gave less than supposed, received only £53 of every £100 of assessed parental contribution (Barr and Low 1988: 31–4). As a result, one student in thirteen in the early 1980s remained below the poverty line, even when income from all sources was included (ibid., table 6).

(b) *Parental wealth*: though many students are poor, their parents, typically, are not. Le Grand (1982: table 4.1) found that public expenditure on university education for the average student from socioeconomic group 1 was 5.5 times that for a child from the lowest socioeconomic group. Barr and Low (1988) report that, compared with the population at large, students are twice as likely to come from high-income families (the top 40 per cent), and over three times as likely to come from the highest incomes (the top 12.5 per cent).

(c) *The cost of the system*: when account is taken of the taxpayer contribution to tuition fees and living costs, the UK taxpayer made one of the largest contributions of any country (UK DES 1988: chart 6), and continued to do so even after the 1990s expansion. Higher education is therefore expensive in public-expenditure terms. Until 1990 the result was to impede access by keeping the system small; thereafter, access was impeded more by the parsimonious living standards implied by the combination of grant and loan.

How should these findings be interpreted? Several issues arise. First, differential access to education *could* in principle be caused entirely by exogenous differences in tastes and abilities, in which case no issue of inequality arises.[16] A person would be brave (or foolish) to argue that this is the whole explanation. But to the extent that it is part of the story, a simple observation of outcomes tends to overstate inequality. Secondly, if this inequality is genuine, should we be concerned about it? Is education the engine of economic prosperity or the plaything of the rich? If the former, it is appropriate to be concerned about its distribution on efficiency as well as equity grounds. If the latter (i.e. if the screening hypothesis holds), post-compulsory education may have no *social* benefits, thereby diminishing the importance of the efficiency question. But, since education confers *private* benefits, its distribution, if inequitable, remains a proper concern. Thirdly, it is necessary to remind ourselves that a different system of education would not *necessarily* be more egalitarian. As with the NHS, it is not enough to argue that the present system is imperfect; it is also necessary to suggest an alternative which will do better. If none can be found, egalitarian goals must be pursued by other means.

These caveats notwithstanding, it is hard to resist the conclusion that the distribution of education is influenced by inequalities in society. Individuals from less fortunate backgrounds have less information about the value of education, and less of the *savoir-faire* necessary to make the best use of 'the system'. They have lower incomes, and are therefore less able to afford the earnings forgone by continuing education. Nor should it be forgotten that education is an investment which, like all investments, takes time to

---

[16] Murphy (1981) sums up the issue neatly: 'though no necessary relationship exists between class *disparity* in education and class *inequality* in education, educational commentators have conventionally taken the existence of one to indicate the existence of the other' (p. 182, emphasis added).

pay off; but the pursuit of long-run goals requires *hope*; and hope, too, is distributed unequally by social class. The expectations of children are formed largely on the experience of their parents, whose lives may give little encouragement to long-run optimism. For all these reasons, children from low-income families tend to receive education of a lower quality, and to avail themselves of a smaller quantity. There is inequality in education, and the inequality is much greater than in health care.

11. *Redistributive effects of the educational system.* We have seen (Chapter 7, Section 4.2, as qualified by Chapter 7, Section 4.1) that education is financed progressively even if (rich) individual R consumes (say) twice as much education as (poor) individual P, so long as R (or her parents) pays more than twice as much as B in the taxes which pay for education. For the system as a whole, educational expenditure on a child of a family in socioeconomic group 1 (henceforth for short a 'rich' child) is about 50 per cent higher than that for a 'poor' child—that is, one in the lowest socioeconomic group (Le Grand 1982: table 4.1). Thus the system is financed progressively if on average the tax contribution towards education of an individual in the highest socioeconomic group exceeds that of someone in the lowest by more than 50 per cent. As with the NHS (see the discussion in Chapter 12, Section 4.3), this is likely if we are prepared to assume that education is financed out of taxation generally—that, if all public expenditure on education were withdrawn, there would be, for example, a reduction in income tax, or an equi-proportionate reduction in all taxes, rather than a reduction of a regressive tax.

In contrast with the NHS, however, matters cannot be left there. The picture for different parts of the educational system must be discussed; and so must its intergenerational impact. The ratio of public expenditure on 'rich' children to 'poor' for education as a whole is about 1.5. For secondary education after age 16, for further education, and for university education, the ratios are approximately 1.75, 3.5, and 5.5, respectively (Le Grand 1982: table 4.1). It is possible, subject to the caveats in the previous paragraph, to argue that post-compulsory secondary education might still be progressive; but the finance of further education is at best proportional, and that of universities almost certainly regressive. A similar conclusion was reached, for similar reasons, by Hansen and Weisbrod (1969, 1978) for the heavily subsidized system of public higher education in California.

The regressivity of university finance is compounded by noting that education has major intergenerational aspects. One of the main conclusions of Atkinson *et al.* (1983) is that nearly half of their sample of poor people came from poor parents. In part, this is because children of poor parents tend to have lower-quality education, and less of it. Thus the taxes of poor families contribute to consumption by the rich of a university education which helps to keep them rich.

5. Reform

Section 5.1 looks at four sets of reforms for schools: radical privatization, voucher schemes, possible improvements within the existing system, and assessment of the 1988 Education Reform Act. Section 5.2 discusses the reform of higher education.

5.1. School education

RADICAL PRIVATIZATION. Section 3.1 discusses the failure of many of the standard assumptions.[17] A priori we would therefore expect an unrestricted private market for school education (i.e. row 1 or 2 in Table 4.1) to be inefficient for technical reasons (Section 3.1), and also inconsistent with widely held views of social justice (Section 3.2). Complete privatization offers no solution, so it is not surprising that no advanced country has a system of school education which remotely approximates a pure private market. It is more useful to ask whether any mixed public/private package offers hope of improvement.

VOUCHER SCHEMES FOR SCHOOL EDUCATION. The idea is that parents receive an education voucher for each child—that is, a tied grant which can be 'spent' by parents at a school of their choice. There are many variants (see the Further Reading), of which two best illustrate the mechanism.

The Friedman proposal (1962; see also Maynard 1975) has three defining characteristics.

- The value of the voucher is the average cost of a place in a state school, or a proportion of that cost.
- 'Topping-up' is allowed (i.e. if the voucher does not fully cover fees, parents can top it up out of their own pockets).
- Parents and schools are unconstrained: parents can spend the voucher at any school, public or private, and schools have complete freedom in their choice of pupils and organization of waiting lists.

The Jencks' scheme (1970) is very different.

- The basic voucher covers the full average cost of state education.
- Topping-up is not allowed, but low-income parents receive a compensatory increment to the basic voucher, thereby diverting resources to schools with disproportionate numbers of children from poor backgrounds.
- Schools where demand exceeds supply are constrained in that they must allocate at least half of their places by ballot.

Thus the Jencks scheme has more of an equalizing effect on expenditure. Both Friedman and Jencks are concerned with consumer sovereignty and efficiency, but Jencks's scheme places more emphasis on distributional goals.

The essence of the voucher idea is that education is at least in part produced in the private sector, with intervention to increase efficiency and equity by subsidy (i.e. the voucher) and regulation (e.g. compulsory school attendance, minimum standards, and, in some schemes, restrictions on topping-up and the allocation of places). The

---

[17] i.e. the assumptions necessary for the market to allocate efficiently—see Chapter 4, Section 3.2, or the Appendix to Chapter 4, paras. 6–17.

Benefits in kind

Friedman scheme is therefore a mixture of rows 1 and 2 of Table 4.1 (because parents can choose their child's school, and are free to top up the voucher) and row 4(*a*) (since education up to a certain age is compulsory). The Jencks scheme is a combination of row 2 and line 4(*b*), the latter because the 'no-topping-up' rule imposes a constraint on total output.

Voucher schemes, it is argued, increase efficiency, enhance consumer sovereignty, and reduce the risk of political indoctrination. Parents choose their child's school; and education is privately produced and competitive, so that schools are responsive to parental demand. Proponents also claim as an advantage that voucher schemes avoid the situation where parents who send their children to private schools receive no tax relief in respect of costs from which they thereby relieve the state system.

To opponents of voucher schemes, their efficiency advantages are debatable and their equity effects almost certainly deleterious. The efficiency issue, as we saw in Section 3.1, hinges on whether parents are sufficiently well informed to police the standards of their child's school and, if not, whether a publicly organized inspectorate will be more effective with public or private production. In equity terms, it is argued that voucher schemes will increase inequalities in the distribution of education (both quantity and quality) by social class, though less so in the case of a Jencks type of scheme than under the Friedman proposals. Vouchers might well have advantages for middle-class families, but only at the expense of less well-informed choices by lower socioeconomic groups. The equity issue therefore turns on the relative weight given to the claims of the two groups. Finally, voucher schemes are criticized because privately produced education is likely to reduce social cohesion.[18]

Empirical evidence is scant. A small early experiment with vouchers in the USA is described by Blaug (1984). Vouchers worth £1,100 per child per year were introduced for nursery education in England and Wales in 1996. The scheme was problematical, less for reasons inherent in the voucher mechanism than because it was badly designed (see UK House of Commons Education and Employment Committee 1997). It was wound up by the new Labour government a year later. According to Bosanquet (1983: 170), 'voucher schemes have not shown a robust Hayekian will to evolve. They have not been a socially selected institution which has grown.'

POSSIBLE IMPROVEMENTS WITHIN THE EXISTING SYSTEM. The strategy of public production, regulation, and finance (row 8 in Table 4.1), at least for school education, is common to all industrialized countries. The evidence on the efficiency of the UK system is scant (Section 4.2), so discussion of reform is concerned mainly with equity. The first issue is that imperfect information arises differentially by social class. Partly as a result, the *quality* of school education varies with socioeconomic status. Attempts to increase the information available to working-class parents are unlikely to have much impact. A more plausible approach, where disadvantage is geographically concentrated, is to

---

[18] As a graphic illustration of differences of opinion about what constitutes a good education, note the chasm between 'reduce social cohesion' here and 'reduce the risk of political indoctrination' in the previous paragraph.

strengthen efforts to increase the resources available to primary and secondary schools with disproportionate numbers of disadvantaged children.

The information problem is also one of the causes of the unequal distribution of the *quantity* of education (see Bennett *et al.* 1992). In addition to better information, children from poor families might be induced to consume more education by a grant, probably income related, for those who continue with education/training after the minimum school leaving age.

QUASI-MARKETS AND THE 1988 EDUCATION REFORM ACT. Another approach to reform within the existing system is the development of quasi-markets (Glennerster 1991; Will Bartlett 1993). As explained in Chapter 12, Section 5.2, the basic idea is to retain public funding but to increase efficiency and responsiveness by introducing market forces *within* the state system. The 1988 Education Reform Act includes provisions specifically designed to do this (see Glennerster 1996, 1997: ch. 12, for fuller discussion), reinforced by a 1992 Act requiring schools to publish the examination performance of their pupils, leading to the publication of league tables. It is useful to draw out the different strands of quasi-markets as they apply to education.

Competition. The argument for competition is that it improves efficiency. As with health care (Chapter 12, Section 5.2), optimism should not be uncritical. Problems include imperfect consumer information on the demand side and local monopoly on the supply side. In addition, as discussed in Section 4.3, point 9, competition gives schools incentives to recruit students from better-off backgrounds, analogous to medical insurers seeking healthy clients, so as to maximize the school's examination performance, hence (given the publication of league tables) maximizing demand for places. Such competition causes inefficiency and, by, restricting the choices of children from poorer backgrounds, is also inequitable. Competition thus creates two contradictory pressures: towards the efficient use of resources; and towards 'cream-skimming'.

Local management of schools allows individual schools to manage their current resources as they wish (the same freedom does not apply to capital spending), thus, it was intended, allowing them to respond to competitive pressures. As discussed earlier (Section 4.2, point 6) in the context of higher education, the argument for decentralized management is that it improves efficiency. Local managers have better information than managers at the LEA or the Education Department. In addition, if management is central, information flows become distorted by local managers so as to maximize their freedom. Empirical evidence from the USA (Chubb and Moe 1990) supports the view that decentralized schooling systems produce better results, measured in terms of educational outcomes.

Opting-out. Under the 1988 Act, a simple majority of a ballot of parents, together with the approval of the Secretary of State, can take the school into what is called 'grant maintained status'. The school is then run by an independent governing body, responsible to the Secretary of State, with representatives of parents, teachers, and the locality. The school's property is transferred from the LEA to the governing body, which also becomes the employer of the teachers. By 1995 about 1,000 schools (out of a total of about

25,000) had opted out. Such schools are the responsibility of the central Education Department rather than the LEA, and are centrally funded out of resources recovered from the LEA.

How should such freedom be interpreted? According to one view, opting-out is a device to improve the freedom of schools by giving parents and governors countervailing power in the face of inefficient LEA governance. However, opted-out schools are controlled by central government in broadly the same way as under the LEA, so that it is not clear how much additional freedom actually results.

A second view is that opting-out is a step towards vouchers. Schools receive a per capita grant; and parents have a measure of choice (see the discussion of open enrolment, below) to choose their child's school. As Glennerster *et al.* (1991: 396) point out, this is a short step from genuinely independent schools financed by vouchers. The route to such reform would be twofold: to encourage large numbers of schools to opt out; and then to allow genuine independence.

The counter-argument (view 3) is that opting-out is a device to centralize control by breaking LEA control. A bureaucratic theory of government (Chapter 4, Section 5) predicts that once the Education Department has acquired control it will be reluctant to let it go; and the argument is reinforced by the reluctance of the Treasury to hand large sums of taxpayer money to independent private institutions. According to Glennerster *et al.* (1991: 397), 'the potential powers handed to a centralist government are disturbing'.

Open enrolment and formula funding. Under open enrolment parents, within limits, can choose to which school to send their child, though (Section 4.3, point 9) middle-class parents are more effective in using this freedom. Formula funding introduced a capitation element into school finance, since any pupil signing on at a state school triggers a payment by the LEA to the school; thus schools which attract more pupils receive more resources. To that extent, as with vouchers, school finance is determined in part by parental choice rather than bureaucratic decision.

The national curriculum can be viewed in very different ways. In its favour, first, it can be regarded as regulating education markets, analogous to managed health care. Secondly, and complementary, is the view that the national curriculum increases equality of opportunity by spreading best practice. The assessment targets are outcome measures against which school performance can be measured. Where a school does badly, action can be taken to raise the standards of the lowest achievers.

A very different view, thirdly, is that the national curriculum exemplifies a centralizing tendency and interferes with the individual/family-consumption decision. As discussed in Section 2.1, there cannot be agreement about what constitutes a 'good' education, so that the family is best at making choices about a child's education. Schools wishing to experiment, which was possible under the old system subject to *local* agreement, now require *central* agreement from the Secretary of State. The only parents with real freedom are those who can afford private education (private schools are not bound by the national curriculum). The national curriculum, according to this view, reduces efficiency, equity, and individual freedom.

A fourth view, drawing on the experience of other countries, is that the national curriculum politicizes education achievement, since politicians will not like to see large numbers of pupils failing the tests. 'If politicians can influence the unemployment figures, why not assessment standards?' (Glennerster *et al.* 1991: 396).

5.2. Higher education

Policy reform in higher education (discussed at the end of this section) rests on the answers to two sets of theoretical questions: how useful are market forces in higher education; and how should any system of student loans be designed?

MARKET FORCES IN HIGHER EDUCATION

Applying the quasi-markets idea to higher education involves government giving less money to *universities* and more to *students*—for example, as vouchers. Two questions are central (for fuller discussion, see Barnes and Barr 1988: chs. 1, 5, 6): are students capable of making informed choices; and how useful is competition?

CONSUMER SOVEREIGNTY, as discussed in Chapter 4, Section 3.2, is more useful (*a*) the better is consumer information, (*b*) the more cheaply and effectively it can be improved, (*c*) the easier it is for consumers to understand available information, (*d*) the lower are the costs of choosing badly, and (*e*) the more diverse are consumer tastes. There are good reasons for optimism in applying these criteria to higher education. First, information is available, and more can be made available. There are already 'good universities guides', and universities increasingly publish detailed information on the Internet. Secondly, students can, for the most part, understand and evaluate that information. The process is easier because going to university can be anticipated (contrast finding a doctor to deal with injury after a road accident), so that the student has time to acquire the information and advice she needs. Thirdly, though the costs of mistaken choice can be large, it is not clear that a central planner would do better; moreover, the move towards modular degrees, allowing students to change subjects and, increasingly, institutions, reduces those costs. It should be noted, fourthly, that students make choices already.

Finally (item (*e*), above), consumer tastes are diverse, degrees are becoming more diverse, and change is increasingly rapid. For all these reasons, students are more capable than central planners of making choices which conform with their own needs and those of the economy. In contrast, attempts at manpower planning are even more likely than hitherto to be wrong because of the increasing complexity of post-industrial society. Consumer sovereignty can thus be regarded as more useful for higher education than for schools.

COMPETITION AND REGULATION. In a simple-minded vouchers model, institutions compete for students; those which attract large numbers flourish and expand, those which fail to attract students go to the wall. Universities, however, are not the conventional firms of economic theory: they do not make a homogeneous product; they do not maximize profit; and the 'product' is not well defined. Thus red-in-tooth-and-claw competition is not the best environment for higher education. It is a huge mistake, however, to think that this is the only approach to competition. At the other extreme, government, as in the UK in the late 1990s, could decide how many students would study which subjects at which university, and issue vouchers accordingly. Such a regime simply mimics central planning.

Thus vouchers should be thought of as a continuum, from 0 per cent constrained (law of the jungle) to 100 per cent constrained (pure central planning) or anywhere in between. There are a variety of constraints for policy-makers to consider.

- *Protecting subjects*. Accounting, law, economics, etc. can look after themselves. If a subject like classics needed protection, some vouchers could be tied to the subject.

- *Protecting institutions* could be organized similarly. For reasons of regional balance there could be vouchers tied to universities in particular parts of the country.

- *Protecting individuals*. This type of regime does not, as is commonly supposed, have to penalize students from poorer backgrounds. It would be possible—and desirable—to offer larger vouchers to students from poorer backgrounds (for the use of vouchers, more generally, as a redistributive device, see Le Grand 1989b).

- *Protecting quality*. Would competition degrade quality? There are, of course, incentives in that direction (e.g. grade inflation); but there are also adverse incentives in a non-competitive environment—for example, for academics to write books rather than look after their students. Indeed, one of the stronger arguments in favour of competition is that it gives institutions a strong incentive to look after students. One way to protect standards is to monitor quality and publish the results. There is a clear regulatory role to ensure the prompt publication of accurate performance data. Once published, such data would enable potential students to vote with their feet (see Cave *et al.* 1992).

In short, vouchers allow intervention to foster both educational and distributional objectives. The degree of competition is a policy variable; different answers are possible for different subjects; and the system can be as redistributive as desired. Market forces are useful in higher education; and central planning is neither feasible nor desirable.

STUDENT LOANS

Loans can be organized in different ways.[19] Conventional loans such as mortgages or bank overdrafts generally have fixed repayments of £X per week. Income-contingent repayments, in contrast, are expressed as a fraction of the borrower's income. They can take two generic forms.

---

[19] This section draws heavily on two submissions, jointly with Iain Crawford, to the UK National Committee of Inquiry into Higher Education (the Dearing Committee), subsequently published as Barr (1997) and Barr and Crawford (1998a). See also Barr (1989a, 1991).

- With *income-contingent loans*, repayment ceases once the loan plus interest has been repaid; thus no-one repays more than he has borrowed.
- With a *graduate tax*, repayments continue for life, or until retirement. High-earning graduates may therefore repay more than they have borrowed.

OBJECTIVES. Given the problems of higher education discussed in Sections 4.2 and 4.3, any loan system should:

- *Promote access*, both for equity reasons and for efficiency, to minimize the waste of talent. Improved access requires that loans have income-contingent repayments and *also* that any loan entitlement is large enough to allow students an adequate standard of living.
- *Restore quality*, both through more resources and through the development of a system which allows universities to respond to student and employer demand.
- *Contain taxpayer cost*. The taxpayer cannot shoulder the major burden of mass system, not least because of the need to promote access earlier in the educational system.
- *Liberate private funds* by devising a loan mechanism which allows students to borrow from the private sector.

CAPITAL MARKET IMPERFECTIONS. Because of major capital-market imperfections, mortgage loans create problems on both sides of the market. On the demand side, they are risky from the student's viewpoint and so are likely to deter applicants, particularly from poorer backgrounds. This is inefficient, because it wastes talent, and inequitable.

The government has argued (UK DES 1988: chart J) that relatively poor people will borrow to buy a house, so why not to buy a degree? Apart from the tax advantages, when someone buys a house (*a*) he knows what he is buying, since he has lived in a house all his life, (*b*) the house is unlikely to fall down, and (*c*), at least until the early 1990s, the value of the house is likely to go up. When people borrow for a degree (*a*) they are imperfectly informed about the nature of the product (particularly if they come from a family with no graduates), (*b*) there is a high risk (or at least a perceived high risk) of failing the degree, and (*c*) though the *average* private return to a degree is positive (UK NCIHE 1997*b*: ch. 6), there is considerable variance around it. For all three reasons, borrowing to buy a degree is more risky than borrowing to buy a house, and the risks are likely to be greater for people from poorer backgrounds and for women.

Long-term loans are risky also to the lender. There is no collateral (contrast the case of lending for house purchase), since slavery is illegal. In addition, students are better informed than lenders, whether they aspire to careers in financial markets or the arts (another example of asymmetric information).

Friedman (1962) was clear about these capital-market imperfections. He pointed out that

353

the device adopted to meet the corresponding problem for other risky investments is equity investment plus limited liability on the part of shareholders. The counterpart for education would be to 'buy' a share in an individual's earning prospects; to advance him the funds needed to finance his training on condition that he agree to pay the lender a specified fraction of his future earnings.   (p. 103)

On that basis he advocated loans from government, in return for which

the individual . . . would agree to pay to the government in each future year a specified percentage of his earnings in excess of a specified sum for each $1,000 that he received . . . The payment could easily be combined with payment of income tax and so involve a minimum of additional administrative expense.   (p. 105)

Thus Friedman, starting from the benefit principle (he who benefits should pay), ends up advocating a graduate tax (in the sense described above). A different approach starts from a predisposition towards free, tax-financed education, abandoning that model only because of its regressiveness when applied to higher education. Glennerster *et al.* (1968: 26) point out that

in the United Kingdom, higher education is now financed as a social service. Nearly all the costs are borne out of general taxation . . . But it differs radically from other social services. It is reserved for a small and highly selected group . . . It is exceptionally expensive . . . [And] education confers benefits which reveal themselves in the form of higher earnings. A graduate tax would enable the community to recover the value of the resources devoted to higher education from those who have themselves derived such substantial benefit from it.

Thus the benefit principle and the ability-to-pay approach, despite their very different starting points, lead to identical policy prescriptions—income-contingent repayments.

PROBLEMS WITH THE 1990 LOAN SCHEME. The government introduced a loan scheme in 1990. Loans are disbursed by the Student Loans Company (SLC), which also collects repayments. Loans carry a zero real interest rate—that is, they incorporate an interest subsidy. Borrowers normally repay in sixty equal monthly instalments.[20] Repayment can be deferred if the graduate's income is below 85 per cent of national average earnings. The source of funds is the taxpayer.

The argument against this scheme is simple. It completely fails to achieve *any* of the objectives set out earlier.

- Its mortgage-type repayments harm access.
- It provides no additional resources for universities, hence does nothing to restore quality.
- It is hugely and unnecessarily costly in public-expenditure terms: students borrow public money; loans carry an interest subsidy; deferments slow the repayment flow; and defaults are a growing problem.
- It mobilizes no private funding at all.

---

[20] Borrowers repay over sixty months if they have taken out between one and four loans and over eighty-four months if they have taken out five or more loans. For fuller detail, see Tolley (1996: ch. 18).

All this was both predictable and predicted (Barr 1989*a*: ch. 4; 1989*b*, 1991).

AN INCOME-CONTINGENT LOAN SCHEME. An alternative scheme (Barr 1989*a*, 1997; Barr and Crawford 1998*a*) was designed explicitly to achieve the objectives set out earlier. To that end, loans should have two central characteristics: they should have income-contingent repayments and, to the maximum extent possible, should derive from private-sector sources. To do so:

- Income-contingent repayments should be implemented by piggy-backing student loan repayments onto National Insurance Contributions (NICs). Repayments are collected by the tax or national-insurance authorities. Income contingency is thus automatic.
- Repayments are collected at source: thus they are secure; thus they can be spread over a long period; thus weekly repayments are low; thus students can afford to pay a market interest rate. Private lenders want to make secure loans at market interest rates. The scheme gives them exactly that.

To what extent could loans be privately funded? Suppose the SLC wishes to lend £2 billion (roughly the 1998 level of annual spending on student grants plus loans). Empirical evidence (Barr and Falkingham 1996) suggests that, if repayments are collected alongside NICs, about 80 per cent of lending to students is repaid in the long run (the unpaid part being mainly the result of low earnings). Thus, provided that loans pay a satisfactory interest rate, the private market would provide up to £1.6 billion for each £2 billion of lending to students. The Treasury pays only the remaining £400 million, rather than the whole of student borrowing. The new owners of the debt are entitled to the loan repayments of the graduates. The financial market bears the risk of loan repayments falling short of £1.6 billion.[21]

ADVANTAGES. These arrangements fulfil the objectives set out earlier.
Promoting access.

- Repayments are fully income contingent and hence automatically affordable.
- Increasing the loan entitlement to 120 per cent of present arrangements would deal with student poverty and simultaneously allow the abolition of parental contributions.
- Loans could (and should) be extended to currently excluded groups, such as part-time and postgraduate students.
- Some of the savings could (and should) be channelled earlier in the educational system. As discussed in Section 4.3, point 10, the major impediment to access to higher education is low staying-on rates in school by children from poorer backgrounds.

---

[21] For fuller discussion of how to bring in private resources, see Barr (1997).

Benefits in kind

Restoring quality. In sharpest contrast with the post-1990 arrangements, the scheme brings in private resources which could be used to restore quality. One way in which this could happen is for part of the loan to be used to pay a contribution to fees.

Containing taxpayer cost. Savings arise for several reasons.

- There is less deferment and hence a faster repayment stream. If repayments are income contingent, they can start at a lower income than the post-1990 scheme, thus collecting repayments from a dense part of the income distribution and reducing deferment. Under the 1990 system, in contrast, nearly half of all graduates deferred repayment in 1995/6.[22]

- The scheme has no interest subsidy. This is possible because repayments are fully income contingent, thus protecting low earners.[23] The repayment mechanism is sufficiently secure that students could borrow at only a fraction above base rate.

- Low default rates—the default rate for NICs is around 1.5 per cent.

Liberating private funds. The taxpayer savings just listed arise if loans are not privatized. It is precisely those advantages (strong repayment stream, no interest subsidy, and a low default rate) which attract the private sector. If loans come mainly from private sources, the savings to the taxpayer are larger and sooner. If 1998 public spending on student support were converted into a loan, the SLC would lend about £2 billion per year. If loans were properly designed, private funds could bring in around £1.5 billion, *immediately* and *every year*.

Market interest rates are central. With interest subsidies, loans are costly to the taxpayer and are therefore rationed. Market interest rates make it possible (*a*) to offer larger loans, hence improving students' living standards, and (*b*) to use some of the saved taxpayer resources for better targeted action on access. This is another example (the case of housing is discussed in Chapter 14) of how *price* subsidies (in this case the subsidized interest rate) can end up hurting the very people they are intended to help. Paradoxical though it sounds, market interest rates, when combined with targeted *income* subsidies, assist access.

A POLICY STRATEGY

THE UK STORY. Reform in the UK starts from one central fact—higher education has moved from an élite system with a 5 per cent participation rate in 1960 to a 30 per cent mass system in 1995. This expansion has three principal implications.

The need for a wide-ranging loan system. Public funding of a high-quality system is possible for an élite system. It is not possible, politically or fiscally, for a mass system. Thus public funding must be supplemented by private funding. In principle, private funds can

---

[22] 62% of graduates deferred in the first year in which repayment was due; the figure for all graduates was 47% (UK SLC 1996).

[23] It is possible to give additional protection to students with low earnings to prevent debt spiralling upwards (see Barr 1997).

derive from four sources (see Barr 1993)—family resources, student earnings while a student, employers, and students' future earnings. The first three are only partial answers. Excessive reliance on family resources is inequitable (Section 4.3, point 10); and earning activities compete with study and leisure. Employer contributions cannot be pushed too far without becoming a tax on graduate employment. In a mass system the only source of funding which is large and not grossly inequitable is a loan of the sort described above which allows students to borrow against their future earnings.

Price differentiation. With an élite system it was possible, at least as a polite myth, to assume that all universities were of equal quality, that degrees were worth the same whichever university conferred them, and hence that universities could, broadly, be funded equally. With a mass system that myth is no longer sustainable. The characteristics, the quality, and the costs of different degrees at different institutions will vary more widely than hitherto.

If all universities are funded at the level of the internationally competitive universities, the result is inefficient, wasteful, unaffordable, and politically unsustainable. Alternatively, if all institutions are funded at an average level, the quality of the internationally competitive institutions cannot be sustained, while lower-quality institutions are overfunded; the latter result is wasteful and gives no incentive to improve. Finally, if all institutions are funded at a low level, the best universities are even more disadvantaged—like expecting Manchester United to compete in Europe on Torquay United's wage structure—and the average quality also suffers.

In theory, differential funding could be determined by an all-knowing central planner. In practice, the problem is far too complex for that. Universities need to be able, at least at the margin, to set their own fees.

Central planning of higher education is no longer feasible or desirable. Forty years ago, universities in England and Wales offered a fairly homogenous product: a three-year degree in a limited range of subjects. This was appropriate for a more static and less-technological era. Today, however, more people receive more education and training, and the labour market requires learning to be a continuing experience. Thus there are more students; the training they require is more diverse; and it is changing and will continue to change. The task has become vastly too complex for central planning any longer to be possible (Section 4.2, point 6). Nor, as discussed earlier, is central planning desirable.

To repeat earlier discussion, what is being suggested is *not* a free-for-all. Government still has an important role. It contributes to funding, engages actively in promoting access, determines the degree of competition, and ensures that regulation relating to quality is in place and enforced.

AN EMERGING INTERNATIONAL CONSENSUS. In the second half of the 1980s writers in different countries were converging on similar conclusions about the design of loan systems—particularly the centrality of income-contingent repayments—through similar reasoning in the face of similar problems (for discussion of the UK proposals just discussed, together with proposals in Australia, New Zealand, Sweden, and the USA, see Barr

1991). In the late 1990s, a consensus is growing about broader aspects of higher education finance.

- *Element 1.* There should be a continuing taxpayer subsidy to universities.
- *Element 2.* Separately, there should be a mechanism for targeting taxpayer subsidies at *particular* students to promote access. However, the *generality* of students should contribute, because of the private benefits they receive.
- *Element 3.* Fees need to vary across universities, reflecting diversity of activity and cost. Within a regulatory framework, each university should determine its own fee level and structure.
- *Element 4.* Students should be able to pay fees and living costs via a system of loans—that is, there should be no up-front fees. Those loans should have income-contingent repayments (the 1980s consensus).

All Western countries face (*a*) pressures towards rising participation in higher education and (*b*) fiscal constraints which will become increasingly severe for demographic and other reasons. Thus:

- *Element 5.* Loans should be constructed so that the bulk of lending to students comes from private sources, *or* the government accounts should be organized in a way which reflects the fact that current spending on student loans is not like spending on grants, but will mostly be repaid. Given international statistical conventions, this element requires careful technical attention (for fuller discussion, see Barr 1997).

THE REPORT OF THE DEARING COMMITTEE. The wide-ranging report (UK NCIHE 1997*a*, *b*) was published in July 1997. Its unambiguous endorsement of the principle of income contingency was warmly received. Its other recommendations, however, were controversial: a flat-rate fee of £1,000 per student per year; and continuation of existing arrangements (50 per cent loan/50 per cent grant and parental contribution) for living costs, except that the loan would become income contingent.

The fee proposal was attacked by some who thought it wrong to charge *any* fee and by others (Barr and Crawford 1998*b*) because the proposal did not go far enough—the flat-rate nature of the fee, in essence, enshrining continued central planning. The maintenance proposals were also criticized, and the government announced the intention to replace the remaining grant by a loan from 1998.

The crystal ball remained murky in early 1998. For contemporary assessment of the report and the government's response, see Barr and Crawford (1998*b*).

6. Conclusion: Education

Educational outcomes derive from many sources, including family income, the quality of parenting, and natural ability (Section 4.2), and thus depend not only on classroom activity but on much broader factors. Conceptual and measurement problems make the area highly controversial, and controversy is compounded by differences over the meaning of a 'good' education, which includes not only technical matters but also attitudes and values (Section 2.1).

So far as school education is concerned, many of the assumptions necessary for market efficiency fail, the main problems being imperfect information, imperfect capital markets, and external effects. From an equity viewpoint, the most important problem is that knowledge about the operation and value of education is likely to be correlated with socio-economic status. Substantial public involvement is therefore essential (Section 3.3), although, because the information problem is less acute than with health care, the theoretical arguments about public production (as opposed to regulation and finance) are rather more finely balanced. It is, therefore, not surprising that no advanced country has a system of school education which even remotely approximates a pure private market. State-school systems universally are publicly regulated and financed; they are also all publicly produced. To the extent that this strategy is valid on efficiency grounds, it is legitimate for education to be financed in accordance with distributional goals (Chapter 4, Section 7.2).

The practice of education in the UK is far from unblemished. The conclusion on the efficiency of the system is that we simply do not know (Section 4.2); and, because measurement problems are so intractable (Section 2.2), it is unlikely that it will ever be possible to collect the information necessary to produce definitive answers. However, with little increase in real resources, educational achievement has increased and access has improved in terms of gender, ethnicity, and social class. Access, however, is far from equal; nor is it as equal as in many other industrial countries. The rich receive higher-quality school education and make considerably more intensive use of the system, particularly of higher education. The latter difference cannot be explained entirely by differences in tastes and ability. Additionally, though it can be argued that about four-fifths of educational expenditure is financed progressively or proportionately, the finance of the university sector is almost certainly regressive. For this sector at least, the hopes of the founders of the welfare state have not been met.

The performance of the educational system is thus more mixed than that of the NHS. But its critics have to show not that it is less than wholly efficient or equitable (which is not in dispute), but that a more market-oriented solution would do better. So far as school education is concerned, opponents of the broad thrust of existing arrangements have yet to prove their case. The advocates of a mixed public/private system of school education offer only limited evidence in support of their views. The efficiency effects of vouchers for schools are unclear a priori and not proven empirically. In equity terms they are likely to increase inequalities in the distribution of education, and in particular to benefit the middle class at the expense of lower socioeconomic groups (Section 4.3).

Reform of higher-education finance, including a well-designed loan scheme (Section 5.2), would open up capital markets to allow investment in human capital and make it possible to restore erosions in quality (both micro-efficiency gains). Loans can also improve equity by reducing the regressivity of higher-education finance, and by freeing resources to promote access. Loans, however, are far from a complete answer. The regressivity of university finance has two roots: the extent of tax finance; and the fact that too few children from poorer backgrounds go to university. Loan schemes address the first root but do little to eradicate the second. Increasing university attendance by working-class children requires not only expansion of higher education, but also, and importantly, action to improve equity within the school system.

The essential first step towards equality of opportunity is thus to reduce inequalities in the quantity and quality of school education by social class in the ways described in Section 5.1. But there might be limits to the extent to which this can be achieved solely within the confines of the educational system. To the extent that inequalities in education are the result of broader inequalities, progress in the former will depend in part on improvements in the latter. International comparison suggests that the UK record in education, in contrast with health care, leaves considerable room for improvement.

FURTHER READING

As general reinforcement of the material in this chapter, see Glennerster (1997: ch. 12; 1998). The first analyses the finance of education; the second assesses the UK educational experience from the mid-1970s to the mid-1990s.

The case for market provision of education is set out by Lees (1961), Friedman and Friedman (1980: ch. 6), Seldon (1981), and Minford (1984); for a critique, see Bosanquet (1983: chs. 11, 12).

For general texts on the economics of education, see Blaug (1970), Johnes (1993) (a UK text), Cohn and Geske (1990) (a US text), and, for a collection of major articles, Cohn and Johnes (1994). For shorter surveys, see Stiglitz (1988: ch. 15) or Glennerster (1993). On the vast literature on the theory of human capital and its applications, see Blaug (1970: ch. 1) for an excellent introduction; the classic work is Becker (1975). The screening literature is surveyed by Blaug (1976, 1985) and Hirshleifer and Riley (1992: chs. 8, 11). For a survey of economic aspects of education, see Psacharopoulos and Woodhall (1985). See also the Further Reading on the theoretical literature on information problems at the end of Chapter 5.

For the relationship (or lack of it) between educational inputs, educational attainment, and the distribution of income, see Jencks (1972), Hanushek (1986, 1996a, b), Card and Krueger (1996), and Burtless (1996d) in a US context, and Bennett et al. (1992) for a UK study. Contrasting views of the UK educational system and various voucher schemes are contained in Friedman (1962: ch. 6), Jencks (1970), Maynard (1975), Friedman and Friedman (1980: ch. 6), and Bosanquet (1983: ch. 12); for US discussion, see also Coons and Sugarman (1978); for a summary of the voucher issue and an assessment of practical experience, see Blaug (1984). For discussion of quasi-markets in education, see Glennerster (1991) and Bartlett (1993).

The detailed financial institutions of education are analysed by Glennerster (1997: ch. 12); for the detailed institutions of student finance, see Tolley (1996: ch. 18). Le Grand (1982) discusses distributional aspects, and Le Grand and Robinson (1984) look at the possibility of privatizing different parts of the welfare state. On additional discussion of the class bias in educational attendance and attainment, see Le Grand (1987b).

The 1988 Education Reform Act is discussed by Glennerster (1991, 1996, 1997: ch. 12, 1998), Glennerster et al. (1991), and West et al. (1997). For broader discussion of reform of education as a whole, see UK National Commission on Education (1993) and Commission on Social Justice 1994: ch. 4). Distributional effects of education are discussed by Evandrou *et al.* (1993) and Glennerster *et al.* (1995).

Problems and policies for the education sectors in the former-Communist countries are discussed by Laporte and Schweitzer (1994); see also World Bank (1996: ch. 8).

For discussion of higher education in the UK, see Farmer and Barrell (1982), Barnes and Barr (1988), Barr (1989*a*, 1991, 1997), and Barr and Crawford (1996, 1998*a*, *b*). For international discussion, see Barr (1989*a*: ch. 3), Albrecht and Ziderman (1992), Edwin G. West (1994), World Bank (1994*b*), and Chapman (1997). Institutions in other countries are described in UK NCIHE 1997*c*). For compendious background and official recommendations, see UK NCIHE 1997*a*, *b*) and UK DfEE (1998*a*, *b*) for higher education, and UK Further Education Funding Council (1997) and UK DfEE (1998*c*) on further education.

CHAPTER 14

Housing

An Englishman's home is his tax haven.
(The Economist, 1979)

1. Introduction

This chapter argues that housing is the least successful part of the welfare state, largely because (with the wisdom of hindsight) it is apparent that policy-makers blurred the distinction between aims and methods. In part by historical accident the post-war Labour government chose a method of achieving its health-care objectives which broadly accords with the predictions of economic theory. It is therefore not surprising that health care in the UK, by and large, has worked well. Housing policy, in contrast, went wrong, not because its aims have been inappropriate, but because historically methods were chosen which were unable to achieve them. The resulting problems are entirely predictable. The system misallocates housing. Poor people can be homeless or overcrowded. At the same time, owner-occupiers and people fortunate enough to occupy local-authority housing face incentives to consume inefficiently large quantities, so that the system simultaneously creates overoccupation and underoccupation, and at the same time subsidizes the rich. Policy since 1980 has begun to address some of the worst problems.

The main questions are concerned with the efficiency and equity of different ways of organizing the housing market. A number of important matters are not discussed, including inner-city problems and the planning of land use (on which see the Further Reading). The aims of housing policy are discussed in Section 2. Section 3 discusses in principle whether housing as a commodity accords with the standard assumptions[1] and, where it does not, what type of intervention might be appropriate. The conclusion is that economic theory offers no strong arguments for public production of housing, and powerful arguments against general subsidies of house *prices* as opposed to subsidies of individual/family *incomes*. Section 4 assesses the practice, looking in

---

[1] i.e. the assumptions necessary for the market to allocate efficiently—see Chapter 4, Section 3.2, and/or the Appendix to Chapter 4, paras. 6–17.

particular at the inequities and inefficiencies resulting from past and present policies. This sets the scene for discussion of reform in Section 5.

2. Aims

A Conservative White Paper (UK DoE 1971) listed three objectives of housing policy.

1. A decent home for every family at a price within their means.[2]

2. A fairer choice between owning a home and renting one.

3. Fairness between one citizen and another in giving and receiving help towards housing costs.

A subsequent Green Paper under a Labour government (UK DoE 1977*a*: para. 2.16) added six further aims.

4. A better balance between investment in new houses and the improvement and repair of older houses.

5. Housing costs should be a reasonably stable element in family finances.

6. Increased scope for mobility in housing.

7. A reasonable degree of priority in access for people in housing need who in the past have found themselves at the end of the queue.

8. The necessity to safeguard the independence of tenants.

9. The necessity to ensure that the housing needs of groups such as frail elderly people, the disabled, and the handicapped are met.[3]

Various of these goals reappear, more recently, in UK DoE (1997). It is helpful for subsequent discussion if some order is imposed on these objectives. Efficiency in the context of housing arises in three ways: the size and quality of the housing stock, tenure neutrality, and mobility.

THE SIZE AND QUALITY OF THE HOUSING STOCK must be efficient. Housing faces the same trade-off as, for example, health care: clearly it is inefficient to spend nothing on housing; equally, if the whole of national income were devoted to accommodation, there would be no resources for the production of food and health care. The optimal quantity lies somewhere in between—in principle where the value placed on the marginal unit of housing equals the marginal social cost of the resources used. This is the quantity Q^* in Figure 14.1 (see Chapter 4, Section 2.1, and the Appendix to Chapter 4, paras. 2–4). Part of this aim is captured by objective 4, above.

---

[2] More recently, the official aim was expressed similarly, as 'To bring a decent home within the reach of every family' (UK DoE 1997: 19).

[3] For further discussion of objectives, see Hills (1991: ch. 2; 1998).

Benefits in kind

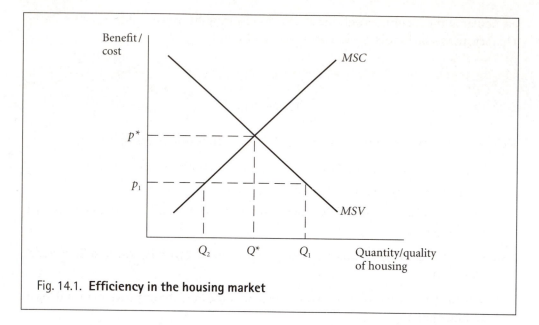

Fig. 14.1. **Efficiency in the housing market**

TENURE NEUTRALITY (captured by objective 2) exists when competitive markets leave individuals (on average and in the long run) financially indifferent between buying accommodation and renting it, with no artificial distortions (e.g. via the tax system) of their relative costs. An approximate example of tenure neutrality in the UK is the choice between buying a television or renting one. The concept, which has both efficiency and equity implications, is important and requires careful explanation (non-technical readers can skip the equations).

Formal analysis. Consider the flow of housing services[4] (net of maintenance costs) $R_1, R_2, \ldots, R_N$ for a rational individual with a constant rate of time preference, r. The present value of the benefit stream is

$$PVB = \sum_{t=1}^{N} \frac{R_t}{(1+r)_t} \qquad (14.1)$$

To simplify, let $R_t = R$ for all t. Then in perpetuity[5]

$$PVB = \frac{R}{r} \qquad (14.2)$$

---

[4] i.e. the value placed by occupants on housing of a given quality/type, as measured by the annual rent they would be willing to pay. The concept of the flow of services from physical wealth is discussed in Chapter 6, Section 1.1.

[5] The easiest way to prove equation (14.2) is to express the flow of benefits in continuous terms. Then

$$PVB = \int_0^\infty Re^{-rt}dt = \frac{R}{r}\left[e^{-rt}\right]_0^\infty = \frac{R}{r}.$$

For exposition of the present value formula, see Stiglitz (1988: ch. 10) or Cullis and Jones (1998: ch. 6).

and the individual will buy the house only if $R/r > P$ where P is the purchase price. On the cost side, consider the individual decision whether to buy the house outright, or to borrow P at the market rate of interest, i. Suppose, for simplicity, that for the duration of the mortgage she repays interest only (i.e. repayments are iP per period); at the end she repays the principal. The present value of the stream of costs is

$$PVC = \sum_{t=1}^{N} \frac{iP}{(1+r)^t} + \frac{P}{(1+r)^{N+1}}. \tag{14.3}$$

Assume that N is large (so that the second term on the right-hand side of equation (14.3) drops out); and that i and P are constant. Then

$$PVC = \frac{iP}{r}. \tag{14.4}$$

Equations (14.2) and (14.4) have been derived via assumptions which are purely analytical. At this stage two important *behavioural* assumptions are introduced. Assume, first, that the market for housing is competitive for both purchase (so that $PVB = P$ in equation (14.2)) and rental, so that R (the flow of housing services per period) equals the competitive market rent R_c at the margin. Hence equation (14.2) becomes

$$PVB = \frac{R_c}{r} = P. \tag{14.5}$$

The second assumption is that capital markets are perfect; thus $i = r$. Two important results follow. First, from equation (14.5)

$$\frac{R_c}{i} = P \Rightarrow R_c = iP \tag{14.6}$$

that is, *there is an economic relationship between the market rent, R_c and the purchase price, P,* i.e. between the flow and the stock prices. Thus there is no artificial incentive to rent or buy. Secondly, from equation (14.4)

$$PVC = P. \tag{14.7}$$

Equation (14.7) shows that the cost of borrowing and the purchase price are equal; *a rational individual is indifferent between taking out a mortgage or making an outright purchase—* there is no artificial incentive to borrow.

Implications. Equations (14.6) and (14.7) show that tenure neutrality requires two conditions: a competitive market for purchase and rental; *and* a perfect capital market, in the sense that mortgage finance should be available competitively and on a non-discriminatory basis. In practice, matters are complicated, *inter alia* by uncertainties about future rates of inflation, which may cause unforeseen variations in real interest rates and house prices. These factors make the relationship between purchase price, rent, and borrowing costs more complex than equations (14.6) and (14.7) suggest. But the meaning of the condition remains unchanged: even in a world of uncertainty, tenure neutrality implies an undistorted economic relationship between purchase price and annual rent, and requires perfect capital markets.

MOBILITY (objective 6) arises out of the fixed location of housing. The issue does not occur with food, for example. If an individual moves to another part of the country, he simply buys his food in a different shop. But he cannot take housing with him, nor buy it off a supermarket shelf. It is therefore important that the housing market is sufficiently flexible to prevent persistent excess demand—a desirable aim for many reasons, and certainly in the context of mobility, because excess demand could hinder an individual who lives in area A from taking a job in area B.

Turning to distributional issues, the definition of horizontal equity, as we have seen (Chapter 4, Section 4.3, and Chapter 6, Section 3.1), is elusive. For housing it can refer to a minimum standard, or to equality of cost, equality of subsidy, or equality of final outcome. All are different, and all lead to different results. For present purposes, as with health care and education, horizontal equity is defined in terms of equality of opportunity and minimum standards.

EQUALITY OF OPPORTUNITY, as defined in Chapter 6, Section 3.1, refers to access to housing of at least some minimum standard, analogous to the implicit but widely accepted aim for food, that everyone should have a healthy diet such that no one starves. Equality of opportunity applies in two ways: access to adequate housing generally (this is the 'decent home for every family' in objective 1, and also includes objectives 7 and 9); and access to different tenures—that is, tenure neutrality expressed in objective 2. If the price of different tenures or access to capital markets favours the better off, then issues of equity as well as efficiency arise.

MINIMUM STANDARDS (objectives 1 and to some extent 8) can be justified on efficiency grounds by imperfect information and by certain types of externality, and on equity grounds if information and power are systematically correlated with income (Chapter 4, Sections 3.2 and 4.3). They might also be necessary to protect children. There is considerable disagreement as to where the minimum standard should be set (see Section 5.2).

VERTICAL EQUITY. Once the efficient quantity/quality of housing and its equitable distribution have been decided, the remaining question is how housing should be financed. This concerns vertical equity, expressed in objectives 3 and 5, and also in the second part of objective 1 ('at a price within their means'). The quotation is important. Vertical equity can be pursued *either* by reducing 'price' (e.g. health care) *or* by increasing 'means' (e.g. food). It was argued in Chapter 4, Section 7.2, that in general the former is appropriate to achieve vertical equity only where there exist *efficiency* grounds for subsidy or for public production and allocation; in their absence, the latter policy (i.e. cash transfers) will generally contribute more to efficiency and social justice.[6] The extent of vertical redistribution will depend largely on political perspective (Chapter 4, Section 2.2).

3. Methods

3.1. The simple theory of the housing market

One of the key characteristics of housing is its durability. A family of four may over its lifetime spend £200,000 on food. But consumption, expenditure, and (crucially) production take place on a day-by-day basis, so supply can respond fairly rapidly to changes in demand. It is possible to make a loaf which lasts for two days; but it is not possible to build a two-day house—for example, out of cardboard.[7] Though the consumption of housing *services* occurs on a daily basis, the *stock* (i.e. the building itself) can last a lifetime. New building is therefore only a small proportion of the existing housing stock, and so total supply can increase only slowly (in the UK at an annual average of less than 2 per cent (Hills 1991: table 1.2)). Thus short-run supply is highly inelastic, even though it may be elastic in the long run. The best representation of the housing market is therefore by a disequilibrium stock-adjustment model.

The left-hand diagram in Figure 14.2 shows the market for the stock of housing; the right-hand diagram, the *flow* of new housing (i.e. net additions to the housing stock). No distinction is made between accommodation for rent and for owner occupation. The curve D_1 shows the demand for housing at different prices, given the prices of other goods, the level of income and its dispersion, and the size and demographic structure of the population. The curve SRS_1 is the highly inelastic *short-run* stock supply of housing. The curve S in the right-hand diagram shows the supply schedule for new housing as a function of its price, based on two simplifications. First, building activity empirically depends less on current prices than on expectations about future prices; secondly, current completions depend on past decisions. The model at its simplest assumes that completions this period are a function of the stock price last period (Muth 1960; Whitehead 1974; Ray Robinson 1979). The net addition to the stock of housing in any period is total completions minus losses through depreciation and demolition.

With demand shown by D_1 in Figure 14.2 and stock supply by SRS_1, the initial equilibrium housing stock is Q^*. The price p^* serves two functions: it clears the market for

---

[6] Note the theoretical caveat in Chapter 4, Section 7.2, that the optimal taxation approach can give a different result. The taxation necessary to finance income transfers may cause a substantial labour-supply disincentive. If so, it may be possible to improve both efficiency and equity by subsidizing the *prices* of goods consumed by the poor if (*a*) such goods are consumed only (or mainly) by the poor, and (*b*) the consumption of such goods is not strongly complementary to leisure. Since neither condition applies to housing, the argument, even as a theoretical proposition, is not of immediate relevance.

[7] Such dwellings do exist in some developing economies. But they are largely ruled out in industrial economies by prevailing attitudes, by legally binding minimum standards, and often also by the climate.

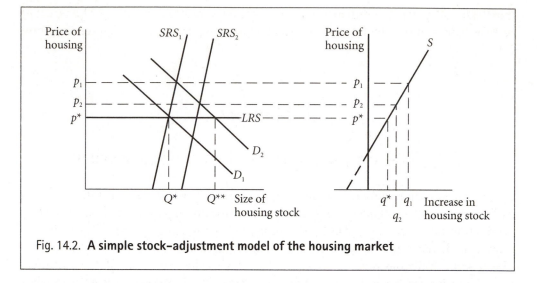

Fig. 14.2. A simple stock–adjustment model of the housing market

the stock of housing; and it induces new building (q^* in the right-hand diagram) just sufficient to offset losses through depreciation. Thus the net stock of housing is exactly maintained, and the market remains in equilibrium. Now suppose that there is an increase in demand, shown by an outward shift in the demand curve to D_2. The stock price rises to P_1, so additions to the stock-one period later rise to q_1 in the right-hand diagram. Since this exceeds the rate of depreciation q^*, the net stock of housing increases, as shown by the new short-run stock supply curve SRS_2. The new stock price is p_2, lower than p_1 but still higher than the equilibrium price p^*. Net additions to stock therefore continue until the price returns to p^*. With demand shown by D_2, this occurs with a housing stock of Q^{**}. *Long-run* supply can therefore be represented by the curve *LRS*.

In practice, the market for a number of reasons is unlikely to converge smoothly to a new equilibrium. It is more realistic to think of the housing market as in continual disequilibrium as the result of shocks, but generally tending towards equilibrium. Nevertheless, the stock-adjustment model is useful because it illustrates the behaviour of a market where supply is inelastic in the short run but elastic over a longer period (for a survey, see L. Smith *et al.* 1988).

3.2. Theoretical arguments for intervention 1: Efficiency

The rest of Section 3 discusses the theoretical arguments for public involvement in housing. We know (Chapter 4, Section 3.2) that the market allocates resources efficiently only if the standard assumptions hold—that is, perfect information, perfect competition, and no market failures such as external effects, public goods, or increasing returns to scale. The argument in this section considers the nature of housing as a commodity, and in particular the extent to which these assumptions hold; Section 3.3 looks at equity arguments.

PERFECT INFORMATION. Are individuals well informed about the nature of the product—that is, are their indifference maps well defined? If an individual inspects a house, does he thereby acquire full information about its qualities? For many characteristics (e.g. size and location), the answer is yes; but most house-buyers have highly imperfect information on technical matters like rising damp. This does not necessarily imply state intervention, because market institutions (e.g. surveyors) have developed to supply information. Furthermore, housing, from the viewpoint of the consumer, is not as highly complex a commodity as health care (Chapter 12, Section 3.1), so that consumers generally understand the information they acquire. To that extent, market institutions deal more effectively with information problems with housing than with health care.

A second question is whether consumers are adequately informed about prices (formally, whether their budget constraint is well defined). This is the case for homogeneous commodities which are bought repeatedly (e.g. food), so that information is regularly updated. Where a good is bought infrequently but is homogeneous (e.g. train fares) out-of-date information can speedily be rectified. Housing, in contrast, is both an irregular purchase (taken to include renting) and highly heterogeneous, so that buyers will not have perfect knowledge. Again, however, the market has developed institutions such as estate agents and realtors to improve consumer information; or the buyer can commission a professional valuation from an independent expert.

The third information assumption concerns knowledge about the future. One problem is uncertainty about whether one's house will be destroyed—for example, by fire. The market solution is house-structure insurance, which is efficient because it conforms with the technical conditions necessary for private insurance (Chapter 5, Section 3). Other forms of uncertainty (e.g. a decline in property values, either generally or in one's locality), are not directly insurable; but by renting rather than buying, the worst of such risks can be transferred to the landlord.

Though none of the information assumptions holds fully, the problems which arise are those which the market itself is often able to solve. The role of the state in this context is to regulate minimum standards for the surveying and valuation professions, and for house-insurance policies.

PERFECT COMPETITION. Because housing is durable, its short-run supply elasticity is low. As a result, an increase in demand (e.g. from D_1 to D_2 in Figure 14.2) can cause a short-run, sharp increase in price from p^* to p_1, though in the long run, as new houses are built, the price will tend to return to p^*. The fact that house prices and rents can change substantially in the short run may cause equity problems (discussed below), but—like the sharp rise in coffee prices after a bad harvest—is neither uncompetitive nor inefficient. Thus it can be argued that the supply of housing displays no *major* violations of the competitive assumption.

Competition can, however, fail in two ways: the assumption of equal power; and the issue of perfect capital markets. The equal-power assumption can be violated with rented accommodation because, in brief, a 'house' over time becomes a 'home', thus giving the landlord an element of monopoly power. Consider an individual who moves to a new area. At least in principle, he faces a competitive market, so that he pays a rent (say £100 per week) equal to his marginal valuation of the property. But, once he has moved in, the house, for at least three reasons, becomes over time that mystical thing, a home. This is first because of the pictures and other personal effects he puts up (which features could all be transferred if he moved). Secondly, he (or his landlord) might redecorate or improve the house; this is investment in physical capital, which raises the value of the property. Thirdly (and crucially), he learns about the area (the best school, the best bakery), and makes friends. These last are investments in human capital. They do not raise the value of the property; nor are they transferrable if he moves elsewhere.

These factors, and especially the third, raise the marginal value (MV) of the house to the individual—that is, MV (home) $> MV$ (house). Ignoring inflation, the individual would be prepared to pay a higher rent (say £125) to stay there, both to protect his investment in human capital, and to avoid the substantial transactions costs (search time, removal expenses, etc.) of moving elsewhere.[8] At a rent of £100 he is intra-marginal, and this gives the landlord monopoly power,[9] though its strength is an empirical question.[10] If the problem is thought to be serious, the simplest solution is regulation, not via rent control but through a tribunal with the power to reduce rents if a landlord exploits his monopoly by raising the rent to £125, when new tenancies for similar property are fetching only £110.

In the case of owner-occupiers the assumption of perfect competition applies not only to the housing market per se but also to capital markets. As we have seen (equations (14.6) and (14.7)), both conditions are essential for tenure neutrality. But capital markets in practice may be (and often are) far from perfect—for example, if lending institutions refuse loans to all but the safest cases. Intervention could take the form of public provision of loan finance, or of loan guarantees—that is, the state would indemnify lending institutions against losses incurred if an individual defaulted on repayments. Such intervention could have equity as well as efficiency advantages.

THE REMAINING ASSUMPTIONS. Externalities[11] arise in several ways. Houses which are structurally unsafe or fire hazards threaten their occupants and neighbours, the fire hazard point being recognized in local by-laws as long ago as the Middle Ages. Similarly, a house with improper sanitation creates public-health hazards (Chadwick 1842,

---

[8] On the general topic of mobility in the context of housing transactions costs, see Venti and Wise (1984).

[9] A similar phenomenon can occur with owner-occupiers. An individual buys a house as a marginal decision. Over time it becomes a home, and its marginal value to the individual rises, and can often exceed the market price of the house (proof: try knocking on people's doors and asking if they would agree to sell their house at its market price plus moving costs, etc.). It is therefore iniquitous that governments can compulsorily purchase houses at their market price. Such an action steals from the individual the difference between MV (home) and MV (house)—it is a theft of the value of comfort, habit, and of the human capital the individual has built up in the locality. Setting measurement problems to one side, the equitable compensation for compulsory purchase should in principle be that sum for which the individual would agree to move voluntarily. This would include not only the value of the garage which he has added (i.e. physical capital), but also his accumulation of human capital.

[10] There may be an element of monopoly power in the opposite direction, since landlords also face costs if a tenancy changes hands.

[11] See Chapter 4, Section 3.2, and the Appendix to Chapter 4, para. 15.

discussed in Chapter 2, Section 1.2). One solution is to subsidize the maintenance of building standards. But the aim in this case is not so much to encourage building quality as to ensure that it does not fall below a minimum level. This might be achieved more directly through regulation of minimum standards of individual dwellings.

A related but different phenomenon is that housing can create a spatial externality. This arises in one form if I build a factory in my back garden, which imposes costs on my neighbours as an eyesore and a general reduction in the amenities they enjoy. There is a conflict between my freedom to do what I like on my land, and the freedom of others to be unaffected by my activities. This problem can sometimes be resolved by the market, if property rights are unambiguously assigned and enforceable (Coase 1960). Another solution is a Pigovian 'eyesore tax', though this faces serious measurement problems. The most direct intervention is regulation of land use in the form of zoning and planning controls, though with room for disagreement as to their extent—for example, should I be allowed to paint my house psychedelic orange?

A different type of spatial externality arises out of slums. A slum landlord (particularly if subject to rent control) faces incentives to reduce expenditure on his property (see Section 4.2), which then deteriorates, thereby reducing the value of surrounding property. Slum neighbourhood characteristics generally dominate attempts at improvement by any *individual* landlord because he cannot find tenants prepared to pay a rent high enough to cover the costs of improvement. Once the slum process has started, it tends to continue, creating *inter alia* a public-health problem. Two solutions are possible. If the houses are worth saving, subsidies (e.g. improvement grants) can lead to 'gentrification' and are therefore justifiable in efficiency terms. If the houses are not worth saving, because they are old or their density exceeds minimum standards, regulation in the form of planning controls may be appropriate (see Gauldie's (1974: 279–80) description of how Birmingham in the nineteenth century purchased both houses and factories in areas it wished to improve).

A further problem, with the same analytical characteristics as externalities, arises if the private discount rate exceeds the social discount rate. In such cases, private markets tend to under-invest in terms of both quantity and quality. This gives rise to one of the few efficiency arguments for financial assistance with housing costs in the form of a general *price* subsidy.

The issue of public goods[12] arises over the provision of parks and open space. Though it is possible to practise exclusion (i.e. to charge for admission to parks), the marginal cost of an extra user is zero if the park is not full. Thus the efficient price is zero, in which case private developers have no incentive to provide the efficient quantity of public open space, and may have no incentive to provide any at all. The most direct solution, again, is regulation in the form of planning controls—for example, that at least x per cent of any development should be public open space.

Amenities such as sewers, drains, water, and the distribution (though not the production) of domestic gas and electricity face increasing returns to scale. If, for example,

---

[12] See Chapter 4, Section 3.2, and the Appendix to Chapter 4, paras. 13, 14.

electricity is supplied to a particular area, it is obviously cheaper to run a main cable down a whole street with a branch to each house than to supply each house separately. The solution is regulation—in this case that all property developments should include provision of these services.

Before proceeding, it is worth spelling out a number of complexities implicit in earlier discussion. First, housing is a heterogeneous commodity, so that there is not a single market, but a series of interrelated ones. Secondly, the longevity of housing, and its consequent nature as a capital asset, mean that the operation of the housing market is related to the availability of finance, and hence to capital markets. Thirdly there is the problem of indivisibilities, both in terms of the 'lumpiness' of much housing expenditure and in changing the quality of a given dwelling. Fourthly, changing house can involve substantial transactions costs in both financial and utility terms. None of these features necessarily prevents housing markets from operating efficiently, but they may well prevent them from operating quickly (as shown in the stock-adjustment model in Section 3.1) and/or may necessitate regulation. Policy design needs to take account of these factors. For further discussion of the nature of housing, see MacLennan and Gibb (1993).

The conclusion is that efficiency is likely to be enhanced by regulation in a variety of forms; by limited subsidies for specific reasons; and by public provision of loan finance or loan guarantees. It should be noted that none of the efficiency arguments points towards either public production of housing or state allocation to the individual.

3.3. Theoretical arguments for intervention 2: Equity

HORIZONTAL EQUITY raises two issues: access to housing; and access to capital markets. The latter can be dealt with briefly. Capital-market imperfections bear disproportionately on the lower socioeconomic groups. The problem is less that the poor are charged a higher interest rate (which would be justifiable on efficiency grounds to the extent that they were worse risks), than that those with lower and/or fluctuating incomes may not be able to borrow at *any* interest rate. Public intervention in the form of loans or loan guarantees may therefore be desirable to enhance tenure neutrality for equity as well as efficiency reasons.

Turning to access to housing per se, the crucial assumptions for horizontal equity (Chapter 4, Section 4.3) are perfect information (to enable consumers to make rational decisions) and equal power (to enable them to enforce those decisions). If these assumptions hold, there is little reason for the state to intervene. The question we need to ask, therefore, is why the state might wish to encourage or force people to consume more or better housing than they would voluntarily choose. Several reasons have been suggested. Individuals, it is argued, may not accurately perceive the benefits of housing (i.e. an aspect of imperfect information), and may therefore consume less than is efficient. If this problem disproportionately afflicts the lower socioeconomic groups, we have equity as well as efficiency grounds for intervention. Whether this is in fact the case is an empirical question, and a crucial one. But it can be argued that imperfect information is not a *major* problem with housing—poor people live in sub-standard accommodation less because they misperceive the benefits of housing than because they cannot afford anything better. A second argument is that individuals may accurately perceive the value of housing to themselves, but fail to take account of the effects of their decisions on others—for example, the public-health argument. This problem is real and, where it affects the poor disproportionately, again gives equity as well as efficiency grounds for intervention.

In either case, what intervention is appropriate? One form involves regulation of building standards and of land use generally. Alternatively, the state could seek to encourage consumption through subsidies applied either to prices or to incomes. The problems of price subsidies for housing (discussed in Section 4) suggest that regulation will usually be more satisfactory.

VERTICAL EQUITY involves intervention either via income redistribution, allowing individuals to make their own consumption decisions, or through direct transfers of housing. Consumption externalities (Chapter 4, Section 4.2) offer one explanation of in-kind transfers: the utility of a representative rich individual, R, rises with his own consumption, rises with the 'good' consumption (e.g. housing) of a representative poor man, P, but falls with P's 'bad' consumption. In this situation, R might agree to an in-kind transfer to P of housing worth, say, £1,000, but offer a cash transfer (which might be spent on 'bad' consumption) of only £200, in which case both rich and poor might prefer the in-kind transfer (see Figure 4.5).

The rich might also favour this approach for other reasons, including their own self-interest. They might believe that good housing improves the health and productivity of the workforce or that good housing prevents social unrest (Chapter 3, Section 5.3). Another argument (discussed by Culyer 1971*b*) is that housing is such an important part of community welfare that individuals should be compelled to consume at least some minimum quantity. This is the 'merit-good' argument (Chapter 4, Section 4.2) in its pure form. The poor may prefer direct transfers of housing either because of the generosity of the in-kind transfer in comparison with the cash offer they would otherwise receive, or because they feel less stigmatized by receiving benefits in kind than in the form of means-tested cash transfers. For all these reasons it may be politically easier to transfer housing in kind.

3.4. Types of intervention

The preceding two sections considered *why* the state intervenes. This section discusses in principle *how* best it might do so (i.e. the question of method).

PURE MARKET PROVISION, according to the theoretical analysis, is likely to be inefficient and inequitable. Many of the assumptions necessary for efficiency can fail: landlords may have monopoly power, exposing tenants to potential exploitation; capital markets may be imperfect; and housing creates a wide range of external effects. If these problems disproportionately affect the lower socioeconomic groups, there is also a problem of horizontal equity; and, in the absence of redistributive policies, inequalities in the distribution of income would lead to wider inequalities in the distribution of housing than most people would like. Proponents of a free market for housing (Hayek 1960: ch. 22; Friedman 1962: 178–80) pointed to undoubted problems with housing in the UK. They were correct in attributing some of them to inappropriate intervention. But advocacy of unrestricted markets is implausible; a better solution is not to adopt a 'hands-off' policy, but to choose more effective policy instruments.

MIXED PUBLIC/PRIVATE PROVISION involves the design of a theoretical package of regulation and subsidy such that private production and allocation is efficient and equitable. Such a scheme (whose policy aspects are discussed in Section 5) would involve the following ingredients.

Regulation on the supply side would include minimum standards, *inter alia* because of the public-health externality; planning of land use (because of spatial and other externalities); regulation of professional standards for surveyors and valuers (thus improving information about the quality of housing); and regulation of landlords, as a counterweight to any monopoly power they acquire in the long run.

Finance. There is a strong case for public provision of loan finance or loan guarantees if capital markets are imperfect, not least to encourage tenure neutrality. In addition, price subsidies may be appropriate in strictly limited cases: in the presence of slum-type externalities; where there is a divergence between private and social discount rates; and possibly on equity grounds if short-run supply inelasticity causes financial hardship (though the latter subsidy should be of limited duration).

The arguments of principle suggest that state intervention along these lines could achieve efficiency and horizontal equity. Three major theoretical conclusions emerge. First, information problems are not overriding. Individuals (with professional assistance if necessary) generally have sufficient information about the quality and price of housing to make rational decisions. In the case of housing, much more than with health care (Chapter 12, Section 3.1), one can argue that consumer sovereignty is useful. Secondly, there is an efficiency justification for *general* price subsidies only if the private discount rate is thought to be inefficiently high. Together with the first point, this suggests powerful advantages if prices are kept at their efficient level, p^* in Figure 14.1, and vertical equity aims pursued through cash transfers (Chapter 4, Section 7.2).[13] Thirdly, the theory offers no efficiency justification for public production of housing (as opposed to regulation of private supply). This is not an argument against public production. But, taken together with the previous two points, it suggests that the aims set out in Section 2 are more likely to be achieved if housing is allocated via efficient prices, supported by income transfers. If untied cash transfers are politically unacceptable, or if the untied

---

[13] Though see note 6 above.

transfer necessary to raise the consumption of housing to the desired level is too expensive, cash transfers could be tied to expenditure on housing. The kernel of the argument is its suggestion that *the UK's housing difficulties are not a market-allocation problem but an income-distribution problem.* In other words, as argued in Sections 4 and 5, the technical nature of housing makes it more like food than like health care.

PUBLIC PRODUCTION AND ALLOCATION to the individual at a zero or subsidized price (i.e. less than p^* in Figure 14.1) are theoretically defensible for health care (Chapter 12, Section 3.3). Precisely the same theoretical considerations suggest that this approach is unlikely to work well with housing. First, there are problems with allocating accommodation to individuals by administrative decision. When faced with efficient prices, consumers are likely to make better decisions than housing administrators for two sets of reasons: because they have better information about their own tastes and requirements; and because tastes about housing vary widely across individuals. Both aspects contrast sharply with health care (Chapter 12, Section 3.1).

A second problem arises if prices are inefficiently low. Unless the demand for housing is completely price inelastic, any subsidy of rents/prices greater than justified for efficiency reasons (e.g. p_1 instead of p^* in Figure 14.1) will raise demand to Q_1. One or both of two consequences follow: if supply increases to Q_1, the result is a housing stock larger than the efficient quantity/quality Q^*; and, if it remains at Q^*, the result is excess demand—for example, waiting lists, immobility and/or homelessness, as discussed in Section 4.

The theoretical arguments therefore suggest that a strategy of public allocation of housing by administrative decision at a subsidized price will be inefficient and inequitable.

4. Assessment of UK housing institutions

4.1. Institutions

Public intervention in housing is far-reaching and diverse. It involves regulation, subsidy, and public production and allocation, though with considerable variation between different types of tenure—owner occupation, the local-authority rental sector, housing associations, and private rented accommodation. Because of the complexity of these institutions it is impossible to give a comprehensive picture (see the Further Reading). This section seeks to sketch out the main institutional features. Section 4.2 assesses the extent to which different parts of the housing market meet the aims discussed in Section 2; the housing market as a whole is discussed in Section 4.3. Throughout, housing is taken to include flats, apartments, etc.

Benefits in kind

HOUSING AS A WHOLE

THE HISTORICAL BACKGROUND is probably more relevant in housing than to any other part of the welfare state. Government involvement at a national level began in the second half of the nineteenth century (Chapter 2, Section 1.2) mainly out of concern with public health. Legislation established two powers: to set minimum standards for new houses, and to demolish unsafe or unhealthy dwellings. These simultaneously increased the cost of housing and reduced its supply. As a result, many families could not pay the market rent of minimum standard accommodation.[14] The main response in the nineteenth century was private philanthropy.

By the early twentieth century this approach was increasingly regarded as unsatisfactory. Two solutions were discussed: provision by local authorities of housing for the poor at subsidized rents; and income subsidies for the poor. The latter policy commanded little support at the time, partly for ideological reasons and partly for lack of a suitable administrative structure to distribute income transfers. The Housing and Town Planning Act 1919 (the Addison Act) imposed on local authorities the duty of remedying housing deficiencies in their area (Chapter 2, Section 3.1). Wartime exigencies had already led to the imposition of rent controls in 1915. The rejection of income subsidies at a time of acute housing shortage thus led over a four-year period to the adoption of two sets of policies: rent (i.e. price) subsidies in the form of rent control, and public provision of housing. These policies continued in various forms during the inter- and post-war periods.

CENTRAL- AND LOCAL-GOVERNMENT RESPONSIBILITIES. Central-government policy is formulated by the Department of the Environment. Housing itself is provided by local authorities, housing associations, and private landlords (for rent) and by private builders (for purchase). Local authorities have a general responsibility for meeting housing need in their area, including the clearance of individual unfit dwellings, the exercise of planning controls to enforce minimum standards, and the building, managing, and letting of housing.

PLANNING of the quantity, quality, and location of housing is conducted by local authorities in consultation with central government. Once an overall plan has been approved, its detailed implementation is the responsibility of the local authority. Any proposal to construct a new development or modify an existing one must be approved by the local authority. Unsuccessful applicants can appeal to the Minister, who has the power to reverse local decisions.

PUBLIC EXPENDITURE on housing in 1996/7 (Table 14.1) was £4 billion. That figure, however, is very narrow. It omits income transfers like housing benefit (Table 7.5) and also

---

[14] See the evidence presented in UK Royal Commission on the Housing of the Working Class (1885). This was, and still is, the last Royal Commission on housing in the UK, though see National Federation of Housing Associations (1985) (and its follow-up, Inquiry into British Housing 1991) for a non-governmental attempt, chaired by HRH The Duke of Edinburgh, to fill the gap.

Table 14.1. **Public expenditure on housing, UK, 1996/7 (est.) (£m.)**

Central-government subsidies to local authorities	1,051
Other central-government subsidies	221
Other housing and central-government administration	1,915
Support for social housing	279
Housing corporations	519
TOTAL HOUSING	3,985

Source: UK Treasury (1997: table 3.5).

Table 14.2. **Public expenditure (more broadly defined) on housing, UK, 1996/7 (est.) (£m.)**

Current spending		
General current subsidies	682	
Housing revenue account (surplus)	−1,194	
Other current spending	397	
Net current spending[a]		−115
Capital spending		
Gross spending, local authorities	3,160	
Gross spending, housing associations	1,836	
Capital receipts	−2,279	
Net capital spending[a]		2,717
Housing benefit		
Local authority tenants	5,499	
Other tenants	5,743	
Mortgage interest	927	
Northern Ireland	254	
Total housing benefit		12,423
Other		
Mortgage interest tax relief	2,634	
Capital gains tax relief on main residence	2,000[b]	
Other	242[c]	
	4,876	
TOTAL PUBLIC EXPENDITURE ON HOUSING		19,901

[a] Great Britain.
[b] Estimated figure.
[c] Net current and capital spending in Northern Ireland.

Source: Hills (1998: table 5A.1), which includes data back to 1973/4.

implicit spending in the form of tax concessions to owner-occupiers (i.e. tax expenditures, discussed in Chapter 7, Section 1.1).[15] Table 14.2 gives a more complete picture. Net current spending has essentially fallen to zero; capital spending, after deducting capital receipts (mainly from selling public housing), was £2.7 billion. Housing benefit (Chapter 10, Section 1), somewhat over £12 billion, is now the dominant government intervention in the housing market, representing a major shift over the years from general subsidies (i.e. subsidized rents) towards income transfers. Tax advantages for

[15] It also omits the transfer to tenants resulting from rent control, which exemplifies a more general phenomenon—regulation as a form of implicit taxation/expenditure; for an analysis, see Prest (1985).

owner occupiers, albeit declining, remain substantial. Mortgage interest relief in 1996/7 was £2.6 billion. Thus total public spending on housing was around £20 billion (for further discussion, see Hills 1998). Given this vast expenditure, what has been achieved?

THE QUANTITY AND QUALITY OF HOUSING. Since the 1970s there has been no *general* housing shortage (Hills 1998: table 5.9). Average housing conditions improved unambiguously. The numbers living at high density (one or more person per room) fell from 22 per cent of the population in 1971 to 13 per cent in 1994 (Hills 1997: 68). As discussed later, however, these gains have not been spread evenly: people on low incomes continue to face a greater likelihood of living at high density and there are more people living on the streets.

TENURE patterns shifted dramatically. Between 1950 and 1995, owner occupation rose from 30 per cent to 67 per cent of all houses, while renting from private landlords fell from 52 per cent to 9 per cent. Local-authority lettings, having peaked at over 30 per cent, were under 20 per cent in 1995 (Hills 1998: table 5.11). As discussed later, tenure has become increasingly polarized.

Because the tenures are organized so differently, they are discussed separately, using the same four heads as health care and education (see also Table 4.1)—production, the aggregate-production decision, the individual-consumption decision, and finance.

THE OWNER-OCCUPIED SECTOR

PRODUCTION of owner-occupied housing is by private individuals or property developers, subject to planning controls, and to considerable regulation of minimum standards of design and materials. The aggregate production decision is private, though again tempered by the need to obtain planning permission and by more general land policies.

THE INDIVIDUAL-CONSUMPTION DECISION is private in the sense that individuals can choose which house they want to buy. But decisions are generally constrained by the availability of mortgage finance, which, as we shall see, is a greater problem for some people than others.

FINANCE for house purchase is generally private, though with subsidies through tax relief. Those subsidies have declined over the years.[16] Prior to 1976 all interest rates were deductible at the individual's full marginal tax rate, thus giving the greatest benefit to those (*a*) with larger mortgages and (*b*) paying higher tax rates. Such an arrangement was highly regressive: the best off, facing high tax rates (as high as 83 per cent on earnings in the 1970s), were given almost interest-free loans. By 1998 individuals could deduct only

---

[16] Both the *quantity* of interest and the *rate* at which it can be deducted have fallen. Tax relief was restricted to the first £25,000 of any mortgage in 1976 and raised to £30,000 in 1983, at which level it has since been frozen. Tax relief was restricted in 1991 to the then basic rate of income tax of 25%, and thereafter reduced in stages to 15% in 1995/6 and to 10% in 1998/9.

10 per cent of their interest repayments on the first £30,000 of a mortgage, with equivalent assistance to individuals below the tax threshold.[17] With a 10 per cent interest rate, tax relief is rather like a lump-sum subsidy worth £300 per year. As discussed in Section 5, phasing out mortgage interest relief, representing a movement from price subsidies towards income subsidies, is entirely desirable. A second tax advantage is that no capital-gains tax is charged on the increase in the real value of an individual's main residence (for discussion of the taxation of housing, see Hills 1991: chs. 11, 12).

These reliefs require explanation. Businesses pay tax on their net profits. Analogously, a landlord pays tax on his *net* rent—that is, the excess of gross rent receipts over total costs, including maintenance and repair costs and any interest costs on borrowed money. Historically, if the landlord rented the house to himself (i.e. was an owner-occupier), he would pay tax on a similar sum. He would have imputed to him the gross rent he would receive if he rented the house to someone else; from this he could deduct maintenance costs and mortgage interest payments. So long as an owner-occupier paid tax on this imputed income, it was entirely proper for mortgage interest to be deductible. But over time the income imputed to individuals was eroded, partly by inflation, partly because rent control made it difficult to estimate market rents, and partly because the tax was politically unpopular. It was abolished in 1962. It is thus open to debate whether the transfer to owner-occupiers is the deductibility of mortgage interest or the non-taxation of imputed housing income. Whichever measure of tax advantages is used, owner-occupied housing is favourably treated—though less so than formerly—relative to other forms of saving, with important implications for tenure neutrality (see Section 4.3, point 23).

These tax advantages are a form of price subsidy. In addition, housing benefit (Chapter 10, Section 1) offers poor homeowners an income subsidy.

LOCAL-AUTHORITY HOUSING

PRODUCTION. Local-authority housing is publicly designed and planned, though its construction may be contracted out to private builders. The aggregate production decision rests in principle with local authorities. The size of the sector has declined sharply since 1980 as a result of deliberate policy—notably because the Housing Act 1980 gave tenants the right to buy at a discount the local-authority property in which they lived. Between 1980 and the mid-1990s about 1.7 million local-authority dwellings were sold this way, representing about one-quarter of the 1980 stock (see Forrest and Murie 1990; Hills 1991).

THE INDIVIDUAL-CONSUMPTION DECISION. Local authorities have a statutory duty to meet housing need. Families signal their demand by asking to be put on an authority's waiting list. In practice, however, few people are able to acquire a local-authority tenancy unless

---

[17] This is administratively simple. An individual who pays £100 gross mortgage interest sends the lender £90; the lender receives the remaining £10 from the tax authorities.

they are homeless. In large measure, therefore, the individual-consumption decision is beyond both the individual and the local authority.

FINANCE. Historically, the rent of tenants in local-authority housing was heavily subsidized. The details, however, are a morass which will be touched on only briefly (for fuller discussion, see Hills 1991: ch. 7, and Glennerster 1997: ch. 13). Each local authority has a *Housing Revenue Account,* which shows all expenditure and revenue on a cash-flow basis, including interest payments on past loans, and subsidies from central and local government. In the past, there was a requirement that the account should balance on a current basis, with important implications: by 'pooling' its rent income a local authority could spread the high costs of new building across the whole of its housing stock; similarly, the interest charges to the Housing Revenue Account were the average 'pooled' interest rates paid by the local authority on its historical borrowing. Rents in a given local authority therefore depended on two factors: the average age of the housing stock (which determined the historic cost of building, and hence interest charges); and the extent of subsidy from central and local government.

Alongside price subsidies, local-authority (and private) tenants are eligible also for housing benefit (Chapter 10, Section 1), i.e. an income subsidy. The basic idea, in the words of an earlier debate, is 'to subsidize people rather than houses'; poor tenants in local-authority and private rented accommodation receive assistance in paying their rent. Such assistance is higher the lower the family's income, the higher its housing costs, and the larger the family size.

Local-authority housing subsidies were reformed in 1990 under the 1989 Local Government and Housing Act. Two changes stand out: each local authority's Housing Revenue Account was 'ring fenced', so that local authorities could no longer subsidize the Account from other sources; and the calculation of central-government grant was changed so as to reduce the advantage of local authorities with an older housing stock. The overall result of the changes was twofold. First, subsidies to different local authorities became somewhat more systematic: subsidies were divided into a housing-benefit element covering the cost of income subsidies to poorer tenants, and a housing element covering the cost of price (i.e. rent) subsidies. Secondly, the extent of price subsidy declined from around 44 per cent in the later 1970s to 15 per cent in the later 1980s (Hills 1991: table 3.3), continuing to decline over the 1990s (as Table 14.2 shows, current spending had fallen to zero by 1996/7), tipping the balance from *general* subsidies towards subsidies to individuals. Section 5 argues in favour of such a substitution of income subsidies for price subsidies.

HOUSING ASSOCIATIONS

Governments from the 1960s onwards sought to diversify sources of housing for poorer tenants.

PRODUCTION. Housing associations are in some ways intermediate between public and private housing—another example of a private institution acting, in effect, as an agent of the state. In theory, therefore, the production decision is private, though in practice heavily constrained by the availability of finance and, for older housing, by decisions by a local rent officer. The Conservative governments of the 1980s sought to tip the balance towards housing associations as the main providers of low-rent accommodation. By 1995/6, some 136,000 households lived in housing-association accommodation, compared with 415,000 in local-authority dwellings (UK DoE 1997: figure 2*b*).

THE INDIVIDUAL-CONSUMPTION DECISION. In principle the individual-consumption decision is private, in that individuals are free to apply for housing-association accommodation. As discussed in Section 4.2, however, rent subsidies lead to excess demand. Thus the individual-consumption decision may be frustrated.

FINANCE, like that of local-authority housing, is complex. In 1974 a housing-association grant was established to offer *capital* grants to housing associations at the start of a new scheme. The amount of this Housing Association Grant (HAG) was calculated to reduce interest repayments on new housing to a rent fixed by a local rent officer. In theory the idea is to pay the rent subsidy not as current spending (as with local-authority housing) but through an *endowment* which pays the subsidy in perpetuity. The strategic flaw in the system was that calculations were based on nominal values prevailing at the time the capital grant was made, so that, as prices rose, the real rent fell below those for comparable dwellings in other sectors.

The Housing Act 1988 sought to rectify the problem by changing the basis on which the grant was calculated. In particular, from 1989 the capital subsidy became a fixed proportion of the total cost of housing, with private capital intended to cover the rest.[18] Rents are fixed not by a rent officer but by the housing association itself. These arrangements apply to activities from 1989 onwards, those in the previous paragraph to pre-1989 activities. Thus the extent of capital subsidy depends on the historical accident of when the house was built. For further detail, see Hills (1991: ch. 8) and Glennerster (1997: ch. 13).

THE PRIVATE RENTED SECTOR

PRODUCTION of new housing for private rental is in principle decided by property developers, subject to planning controls and regulation of minimum standards. Total supply is determined privately, including decisions about building new rental property, and also whether new or existing stock is used for private rental or sold for owner occupation.

THE INDIVIDUAL-CONSUMPTION DECISION is private in the sense that individuals can choose whether to seek a private tenancy. But choices are severely constrained by the

---

[18] Since 1988 there has been about £10 billion of private investment in social housing (UK DoE, 1997: para. 2.13).

availability of such accommodation, for which, as we shall see, there has been considerable excess demand in some areas.

THE FINANCE of private rented accommodation is private, subject to two major qualifications: poor tenants are eligible for housing benefit as described above; and private tenancies starting before 1988 still offer security of tenure and are subject to rent control. Rent control was first introduced in 1915. Its history and institutions are complex (see Chapter 2, Section 3.1, and the Further Reading). Two points are crucial: rent control is an implicit price subsidy; and it is not financed by the taxpayer, but is a transfer from landlord to tenant. Since 1988 new tenancies have been deregulated.

CONCLUSION

A key conclusion is the historical pervasiveness of subsidies. The first point is their *scale*. From Table 14.2, public expenditure (including tax expenditures) on housing in 1996/7 was about £20 billion (expenditure on the National Health Service in England was £41 billion (Table 12.1)). Secondly, much of this expenditure historically was on *price* subsidies, though the balance between price subsidy and income subsidy tipped substantially after 1980. The analysis of Section 3.2 suggests, in strategic terms, that such a move was desirable.

There is no general housing shortage; and housing quality has improved. Yet many families live in poor housing, and homelessness is a growing problem. This suggests that the housing stock is misallocated, causing both inefficiency and inequity. The next two sections seek to explain how this has come about.

4.2. Problems in individual parts of the housing market

This section is concerned not with the detailed workings of different parts of the housing market, but with the overall pattern. The conclusion is that the substantial problems of the system conform strikingly with the predictions of economic theory.

THE OWNER-OCCUPIED SECTOR has major efficiency problems.

1. *Under-occupation*. Price subsidies to owner-occupiers, mainly in the form of tax reliefs, lead to over-consumption and under-occupation. The theory is simple. If house prices are p_1 rather than p^* in Figure 14.1, demand will be Q_1, greater than the efficient quantity/quality, Q^*, unless price elasticity is zero. As an empirical matter this is not the case: though not without their econometric difficulties, estimates agree that the elasticity of housing demand is greater than zero with respect to both prices and incomes (Byatt *et al.* 1973: ch. 2; King 1980). Furthermore, since the subsidy is paid out of tax revenues (rather than by private builders), supply will increase to Q_1. In practical terms the main effect is over-consumption. People tend to live in larger/higher-quality hous-

ing than they would if prices were set at p^*. This is partly because at a subsidized price they choose to consume more housing services (a consumption motive). There is also an asset motive, to the extent that housing is treated more favourably than other forms of private asset accumulation. The result, historically, has been a tendency to under-occupation. Though the incentive is now weaker for new house-buyers, the effects of past housing decisions remain.

2. *Tax reliefs artificially raise the return to housing.* Housing was formerly treated more favourably than other forms of saving available to individuals; thus a disproportionate share of limited savings was attracted to housing finance. The effect has been reduced by reducing the tax advantages to housing and also through tax concessions for other forms of saving.

There are also serious equity criticisms.

3. *Access to mortgage finance is unequal.* Lending policies of building societies and banks generally exclude individuals with low or irregular earnings and those without sufficient savings to pay the initial deposit on a house. This disproportionately affects the lower socioeconomic groups, thereby causing inefficiency, and also inequity which is only partially mitigated because many local-authority tenants have been able to buy the property they formerly rented. The result is a housing market which is largely segmented, with poorer families restricted for the most part to rented accommodation.

4. *The tax reliefs to owner occupation are regressive.* Individuals with higher incomes generally have larger mortgages. In the past they also received tax relief at a higher rate. In 1983/4, mortgage interest relief was nearly twelve times as high, on average, for mortgage-holders with incomes over £20,000 per year as for those with income under £5,000 (*Hansard*, 3 Feb. 1984). In 1989/90 tax advantages continued to be higher for the best off (Hills 1991: ch. 14). The reduction in this type of tax advantage over the 1990s (note 16) greatly reduced such regressivity. Capital-gains tax relief is also regressive: individuals with higher incomes tend to own larger houses and so make larger capital gains. Prima facie both forms of tax relief go mainly to the better off.

5. *Tax capitalization.* A partial counter-argument to the regressivity of tax reliefs is that they are capitalized. As a result, house prices are higher than they would otherwise be, thereby depriving owner-occupiers of the benefit of the tax concessions. The argument is best illustrated by example. Suppose that mortgage repayments consist only of interest, and that an individual wants to buy the largest house she can afford with mortgage repayments of £400 per month. In a world with no tax reliefs, suppose she can buy a house costing £100,000. If tax relief at 50 per cent is introduced, she can now afford monthly repayments of £800 (because the government pays half), and so can buy a house costing £200,000. But if the supply of housing is totally inelastic, her extra purchasing power (together with that of other similarly placed individuals) will double house prices, leaving her in exactly the same position as before. Thus the introduction of tax relief does not benefit new house-buyers, but only existing homeowners, who make large capital gains.

Benefits in kind

In practice, however, the long-run supply of housing is not completely inelastic, so house prices in the previous example would not rise by 100 per cent. Thus tax reliefs do benefit owner-occupiers, though probably by less than the tax expenditure figures suggest.[19] The regressivity argument therefore stands. A different argument follows from the observation that the real burden of income tax rose fairly steadily from 1948 until the mid-1980s. This suggests that an *increasing* amount of tax relief has been capitalized, an argument strengthened by the gradual erosion and eventual abolition of the taxation of imputed income. As a result, the tax system can be argued to have exerted not a once-and-for-all effect on house prices, but a fairly steady upward pressure. The effect has been to confer capital gains on earlier house-buyers at the expense of more recent purchasers who have experienced, at worst, a decline in house prices in response to the decline in their tax advantages.

The conclusion on vertical equity is that various tax reliefs worth some £4.5 billion in 1996/7 have benefited mainly the better off, though probably by less than the figures in Table 14.2 suggest; and to the extent that capital gains have accrued disproportionately to earlier buyers, redistribution has also been arbitrary.

LOCAL-AUTHORITY AND OTHER SOCIAL HOUSING. In efficiency terms there is little theoretical justification for price subsidies (Section 3.2). Yet local-authority rents in the early 1970s covered on average only 40 per cent of the historic cost of housing. As Table 14.2 shows, that is no longer the case, but problems still arise as an inheritance of the old system.

6. *Subsidized rents lead to over-consumption/under-occupation.* If rents are shown by $p_1 < p^*$ in Figure 14.1, people will wish to consume quantity/quality $Q_1 > Q^*$. Local-authority and housing-association tenants will demand a larger/higher-quality house than they would if they had to pay an efficient rent, p^*, which reflects the marginal social cost of housing. The crucial point for efficiency (given that demand, empirically, is price elastic) is that the *marginal* cost of rented accommodation should be p^*. Since administrative allocation is not, in practice, fully efficient (see point 10 below), subsidized rents create an incentive to over-consumption/under-occupation.

7. *Excess demand.* As another aspect of the same problem, subsidized rents lead to excess demand for housing from local authorities and housing associations, thereby contributing to overcrowding (usually in the other sectors) and to homelessness.[20] If rents in Figure 14.1 are shown by p_1, people will demand Q_1. If local authorities increased the supply of housing to Q_1 demand would be satisfied, but only at the expense of over-investment in housing (since $Q_1 > Q^*$). In practice this has not happened. As a result, there is excess demand, as manifested by waiting lists in most areas; people want local-authority or housing-association accommodation (or want larger or higher-quality housing) but are unable to obtain it. Frequently they are unable to move into the

---

[19] If supply is not totally elastic, landowners and property developers will also benefit from the tax concessions.

[20] A rough association has been remarked between administrative allocation schemes and homelessness, and between market allocation and overcrowding.

owner-occupied sector, because they cannot afford to do so, and/or because of inequalities in access to mortgage finance (point 3 above); nor can they always find suitable private rented accommodation; before 1988 because rent control led to excess demand in that sector (point 15 below), since then because of the cost of unregulated tenancies. Two results follow. Families who already have social housing but want more spacious accommodation (e.g. because their family has grown) suffer overcrowding; and families still on the waiting list suffer from low-quality (often private rented) accommodation and/or from overcrowding (e.g. if they are living with family or friends), or from homelessness (which almost doubled between 1979 and 1995), temporary accommodation, or sleeping in the street (Hills 1998: table 5.10).

Points 6 and 7 taken together show that (unless there is *over-investment* in housing, i.e. Q_1 in Figure 14.1), inefficiently low rents can *simultaneously* cause underoccupation, overcrowding, and homelessness. The proponents of price subsidies had unimpeachable aims; but the method they chose is questionable, to say the very least.

8. *Labour immobility* is a further consequence of excess demand, in that existing tenants may be unable to take up work in a different locality because they would have to go on the waiting list in the new area. Immobility is reinforced, for the reasons given in point 7, by the inability of many local-authority tenants to find accommodation in other sectors of the housing market. Lomas (1974) and Shankland *et al.* (1977) describe how unemployed people in local-authority housing in Inner London were unable for this reason to move to areas with better job prospects. A more general study by Hughes and McCormick (1981) concluded that local-authority tenants had lower migration rates (except for moves within a locality) than owner-occupiers.

9. *Hard-to-let* property results largely from charging rents on the basis of 'pooled' historic costs (Section 4.1). Its existence is telling evidence that not only absolute rents, but also rent *differentials* for different properties were inefficiently small. Efficiency requires that if house P ('penthouse') is four times as attractive as house T ('terrace') in terms of quantity and quality, then its rent should be about four times as high. Because of rent pooling this is not the case in many localities. Furthermore, a family on the waiting list knows that, if it accepts house T, it is unlikely subsequently to be able to transfer to P. For this reason, and because the rent of T is not sufficiently lower than the rent of P, the family is likely to refuse T in the hope of later being offered P. Consequently, T is hard to let. This occurs only because rent *relativities* are inefficiently small. In the owner-occupied sector, in contrast, relative prices are determined by the market, even if absolute prices are subsidized. Thus long-run problems of hard-to-sell are minimal.

Local-authority housing and other social housing can also cause inequity.

10. *Access to social housing in a given area can be arbitrary.* The first source of the problem is the imperfect knowledge of housing administrators, who cannot have complete information about the circumstances of individuals on the waiting list. Inequity arises, secondly, if housing allocation is influenced by extraneous considerations like racial

prejudice; and some survey evidence suggests that the least desirable local-authority housing tends to be occupied by the most disadvantaged people (P. Harrison 1985). A third source of mismatch between need and housing allocation arises over time. A needy family in the past may quite properly have been given local-authority housing; but if the family's income rose substantially over the years, it was possible neither to evict it nor to raise its rent to an efficient level.[21]

Local-authority and other social housing can thus fail to be allocated to those in greatest need. The result is arbitrariness, and hence horizontal inequity. Because of excess demand, the system benefits those who obtain social housing at the expense of those on the waiting list, with no guarantee that the former group is necessarily the more needy.

11. *Regional inequality in access to social housing* arises because waiting lists vary by region. Some authorities, for historical reasons, have a large housing stock, but demand may be relatively low, e.g. because of out-migration. Elsewhere the situation is reversed. Thus it is easier to obtain local-authority housing in some parts of the country than in others.

12. *Redistribution via price subsidy* has been arbitrary in at least three ways. Consider two areas A and B. A's housing stock for historical reasons is older than B's but of equal quality. The determination of rents on the basis of historic cost implies that rents in A will be lower than in B, even if tenants in the two areas have the same average income. To that extent, redistribution is thus arbitrary by region. Secondly, within a given area, the fact that housing costs are pooled can imply, depending on the precise method of rent-setting, that tenants in newer (and hence higher-cost) housing are subsidized by those in older accommodation. The result of these two effects is that redistribution by income level can easily be arbitrary. The move away from price subsidies towards income subsidies described in Section 4.1 has reduced this form of arbitrariness: in the late 1980s, low-income tenants benefited most (because of the importance of housing benefit); above the lowest incomes, the distribution of subsidy varied little with income (Hills 1991: figures 14.1, 14.3). Finally, because there is excess demand, families with local authority or housing association tenancies benefit at the expense of those on the waiting list. The overall result has been described as redistribution by luck.

13. *Redistribution via income subsidies* is progressive. Housing benefit is paid to low-income families, and is withdrawn as family income rises.

The conclusion is that the shifting balance from price subsidies towards income subsidies will act over time to improve vertical equity.

THE PRIVATE RENTED SECTOR. Many problems in this sector can be attributed to rent control (a form of implicit price subsidy), and to the fact that many individuals in regulated tenancies enjoy security of tenure.

---

[21] For a particularly lurid example of the problem which used to exist, see 'Council House Tenant's Rolls-Royce', *The Times*, 10 Feb. 1983.

14. *Rent controls lead to over-consumption/under-occupation.* The argument is similar to that in point 6. Rent control reduces rents to $p_1 < p^*$ in Figure 14.1. Since demand is price elastic, people consume more and/or higher-quality accommodation, Q_1, than they would at the efficient rent, p^*. The result, for tenants who are able to find regulated private rented accommodation, is over-consumption/under-occupation. At a minimum it is likely to reduce the downward adjustment which would normally be expected in the later stages of a family's life cycle.

15. *Excess demand* is a related consequence which aggravates overcrowding and homelessness. The argument is similar to that in point 7. Assume for the moment (the assumption is relaxed in point 16) that the supply of rented accommodation is Q^*. If rents in Figure 14.1 are shown by p_1, people will demand $Q_1 > Q^*$. The result is excess demand. Many families want private rented accommodation (or want larger/higher-quality accommodation) but are not able to find any. Frequently they are not able to move into the owner-occupied sector because of unequal access to mortgage finance etc. (point 3), nor into social housing because of the existence of waiting lists (point 7). Thus individuals who already have private rented accommodation, but want more space as their family grows, experience overcrowding; and families without accommodation may suffer homelessness.

The previous two points are accentuated by the fact that the price subsidy implicit in rent control is paid not from public funds, but by the landlord. This can have two effects.

16. *Reduction in quantity supplied.* The standard argument is that if controls reduce rents from p^* to p_1 in Figure 14.1, landlords will respond by reducing the supply of private rented accommodation from its optimum level, Q^* to Q_2, thereby accentuating excess demand. This argument is naïve even in theory. A more realistic picture is given by the stock-adjustment model in Section 3.1 (see Figure 14.2). Suppose that the market rent in long-run equilibrium is p^*. If demand increases from D_1 to D_2, the short-run equilibrium rent rises to p_1. In the absence of rent control, new houses are built at a more rapid rate, q_1 in the right-hand part of the diagram, a process which continues until the total stock has increased to Q^{**} restoring equilibrium rents to p^*. If rents, instead, are held at p_2, new construction will be slower (q_2 in the right-hand diagram), but in the long run the housing market still returns to equilibrium, restoring rents to p^*. The theoretical conclusion, therefore, is that rent controls do not reduce long-run supply *so long as controlled rents exceed the long-run equilibrium* (though not necessarily the short-run equilibrium). Only if rents are held below their long-run equilibrium, p^*, does the conclusion of the naïve model hold.

Empirical investigation is complex and hampered by data problems. But there is consensus that for most (though not all) of the period since 1915 rents have been held below their long-run equilibrium; and that this has acted to reduce the supply of private rented accommodation, but is not the sole explanation of the dramatic decline in the private rented sector.

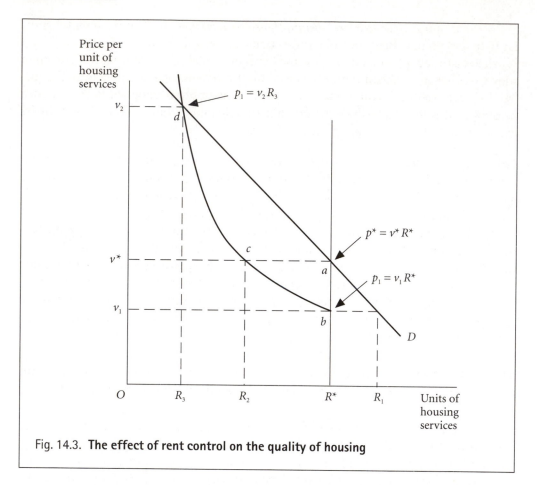

Fig. 14.3. The effect of rent control on the quality of housing

17. *Reduction in quality supplied.* The fact that rent control is a subsidy from land-lord to tenant is argued also to have reduced the *quality* of private rented accommodation below its optimum. The theoretical argument is shown in Figure 14.3.[22] A house yields a flow of services, of which some are fixed (e.g. its size) and some variable (its state of decoration and repair); taken together these services determine quality. The price of each unit of service, v, is measured on the vertical axis, and their quantity, R, on the horizontal axis. When the rental market is in long-run equilibrium, the market rent, p^*, is shown in Figure 14.3 by the rectangle Ov^*aR^*, i.e. $p^* = v^*R^*$ shown at point a. If rents are restricted to $p_1 < p^*$, the landlord's receipts are reduced to the rectangle Ov_1bR^*, and the implied price per unit of service to v_1 as shown at point b.

A possible response by landlords, while observing the restriction of their receipts to p_1, is to reduce costs and hence to increase their profits by reducing the quality of the house by cutting expenditure on repairs and maintenance. The line bcd is a rectangular hyperbola; it therefore shows all combinations of v and R which yield the same revenue (i.e.

22 This approach is taken from Culyer (1980: ch. 10).

rent) as the rectangle Ov_1bR^*. Suppose the landlord reduces quality to R_2. His receipts are shown by the rectangle $Ov^*cR_2 = Ov_1bR^*$. However, at this implied price per unit of service, v^*, there will be excess demand (at price v^*, demand will be R^*, supply R_2). The market-clearing quantity is R_3, with an implied price per unit of service v_2. The landlord can obtain his required return at any price at or above v^*, hence at any quality at or below R_2. If legislation on minimum standards prevents him from lowering quality to R_3 (but allows him to lower it below R_2), he will still obtain his required return, but there will be excess demand for rented accommodation.

The theoretical conclusion is that rent control creates incentives to reduce the quality of housing, but the reduction in quality may not prevent excess demand. Empirically, the average quality of housing in the private rented sector is dramatically lower than in the other tenures, the prevalence of dwellings which are unfit, lacking in amenities, or in serious disrepair being markedly higher than for other tenures (Hills and Mullings 1990: table 5.19). Though causality is hard to establish, there is a strong implication that rent control has been a contributory, though not necessarily the only, factor.

18. *Labour immobility* is a consequence of rent control to the extent that it creates excess demand. A tenant who leaves a controlled property may find no accommodation at a similar rent, and is therefore less likely to move. This reinforces the immobility caused by local-authority waiting lists (point 8 above), though its quantitative magnitude is smaller, partly because the sector is smaller, and partly because relatively few people in the controlled private rented sector are members of the labour force.

Equity effects can be listed more briefly.

19. *Access to regulated tenancies is arbitrary*, first, because only people whose tenancy pre-dates the 1988 Act benefit from controlled rents. In addition, it was the most needy who found it hardest to obtain such accommodation. Because of security of tenure, landlords chose tenants so as to minimize risk, which tended to exclude those who imposed the greatest costs. These, disproportionately, were people in greatest housing need—for example, large families with low incomes, and individuals with personal handicaps.

20. *Minimum standards are enforced least* in private rented accommodation, whose average standard (point 17) is lower than in the other sectors. This quality differential disproportionately affects the lowest socioeconomic group (point 25).

21. *The redistributive effects of rent control may be arbitrary*. Not all landlords are rich and not all tenants poor. The transfer from landlord to tenant can therefore be distributionally arbitrary in individual cases, even though on average it is probably progressive because most tenants in the regulated rental sector are poor.

22. *Redistribution via income subsidies*, as with local-authority housing, is progressive.

4.3. Housing as a whole:
Tenure neutrality and the distribution of housing

This section discusses three aspects of the housing market as a whole: the relative subsidy to the different tenures, equality of access to different tenures (which are two aspects of tenure neutrality), and the distribution of housing.

23. *The relative subsidy to different tenures is unequal.* The subsidy to owner occupation is analysed by Ray Robinson (1979: 129–30) drawing on Rosenthal (1975). A renter and a homeowner have pre-tax money incomes Y_R and Y_O, respectively, and live in identical houses with the same market value, P. The owner-occupier receives an imputed income from his house of iE, where i is the (uniform) rate of return on capital and E his equity holding in his house. The two are assumed to have equal total (money plus imputed) incomes. Thus:

$$Y_R = Y_O + iE. \tag{14.8}$$

The renter (ignoring maintenance costs, etc.) is assumed to pay a competitive market rent, iP. If we now introduce tax at a constant rate t on money income, but not on imputed income or mortgage interest payments, the disposable income (net of tax and housing costs) of the renter is

$$YD_R = (1-t)Y_R - iP. \tag{14.9}$$

For the owner-occupier, income after tax and housing costs is

$$YD_O = (1-t)Y_O - i(P-E) + ti(P-E) \tag{14.10}$$

where $(P-E)$ is the size of the mortgage, $i(P-E)$ the mortgage interest payment, and $ti(P-E)$ the mortgage tax relief. Comparing the disposable incomes of the two individuals by subtracting equation (14.9) from (14.10) gives

$$YD_O - YD_R = (1-t)(Y_O - Y_R) + (1-t)iE + tiP. \tag{14.11}$$

We know from equation (14.8) that $Y_O - Y_R = -iE$; hence substituting into equation (14.11) the first two right-hand terms cancel and

$$YD_O - YD_R = tiP. \tag{14.12}$$

The advantage to the owner-occupier, ceteris paribus, is tiP, the tax relief on the imputed income from his house.

The difference between the tax relief on imputed income and that on mortgage interest payments is more than a technicality in two important respects. First, the relief on imputed income, iP, is related to the current market value of the house and will therefore rise as P appreciates, whereas mortgage interest payments, $i(P_O - E)$, and hence the associated tax relief, are related to the initial purchase price, P_O, and so remain constant or decline over time. Thus, for any particular house, the tax base is increased more by restoring the taxation of imputed housing income than by abolishing mortgage interest relief, since $iP > i(P_O - E)$ and the difference increases over time.[23] A second difference is that taxation of imputed income applies not just to individuals with a mortgage (who could offset their interest payments against their imputed income), but to all owner-occupiers, including the 50 per cent (largely the elderly) without a mortgage.

Is the tax relief on imputed income, tiP, or on mortgage interest, $ti(P_O - E)$, the better measure of the transfer to homeowners? As so often, the answer depends on what is being compared with what. The tax relief on imputed income shows the advantage of owner occupation relative to renting; and the tax relief on mortgage interest measures the advantage relative to investment in other consumer durables like cars, interest payments for which receive no tax concessions. On either measure, this type of transfer has been reduced sharply over the 1990s.

To these reliefs, however measured, is added the transfer to owner-occupiers due to the exemption from capital-gains tax. The value of this relief has declined since 1984, when extensions to the indexation of capital gains reduced the impact of the tax on non-housing assets. It is possible at least approximately to measure the *actual* value of this relief; but it is much harder to measure the concession relative to 'true' capital gains, given the well-known difficulties of choosing an appropriate base for the tax. A complete measure of the tax benefit to owner-occupiers would have to resolve the ambiguities of all the various tax reliefs, as well as considering the extent to which they are capitalized in house prices (point 5).

Transfers to local-authority tenants can be discussed more briefly. The subsidy can be measured by comparing the actual rent (net of housing benefit) with *either* the historic cost of housing *or* the notional competitive market rent. The latter is the more appropriate in economic terms (Rosenthal 1977; Ray Robinson 1979: 132–3; Piggott 1984) though much harder to measure. The former is more relevant to public expenditure, and is therefore the figure used in official publications. On either measure, the transfer declined to the point where current transfers to local-authority housing in the mid-1990s were negligible (Table 14.2).

The transfer due to rent control is the difference between the controlled rent (again net of housing benefit) and the market rent, though with ambiguity as to whether the comparison should be with the short-run equilibrium rent (p_1 in Figure 14.2) or the theoretical long-run equilibrium, p^*. Since 1988 this transfer, too, has declined.

Though conceptually it is all but impossible to disentangle an unambiguous definition of equality of subsidy, there is agreement that owner occupation has been favoured relative to the other tenures. Owner-occupiers built up substantial wealth over the post-war period, in part through their own contributions. But they also received two forms of transfer: from taxpayers generally (because of the non-taxation of mortgage interest and capital gains), and from savers. The latter transfer results from the redistributive effects of unanticipated inflation, which led to periods of negative real interest rates; and

---

[23] The widening difference is offset only in part by the tendency for P_O to increase as individuals move to a larger house.

Benefits in kind

Table 14.3. **Household tenure by income quintile, Great Britain, 1994 (%)**

Income quintile	Owner-occupier	Local-authority tenants	Housing-association tenants	Other
Bottom quintile	34	45	7.6	14
Second quintile	55	33	4.5	9
Third quintile	75	15	3.2	6
Fourth quintile	86	7	1.4	6
Top quintile	92	2	0.2	6
ALL	68	20	3.4	8

Note: Percentages may not add up because of rounding.

Source: Hills (1998: table 5.12), which includes data back to 1974, calculated from General Household Survey raw data files.

mortgage repayments for many individuals fell as a proportion of their income. Over the same period, tenants had to pay rising rents and built up no housing wealth.

24. *Access to different tenures is unequal.* This is a second aspect of tenure neutrality. Access to owner occupation is restricted by capital-market imperfections, to the detriment of the worst off (point 3). The allocation of local-authority housing is marred by the way tenants are selected from the waiting list (point 10); and regional inequalities cause further problems (point 11). Excess demand for private rented accommodation and risk-averting behaviour by landlords together create arbitrariness in access to regulated tenancies, with particular difficulties for those in greatest housing need (point 19).

As a result, tenure has become increasingly polarized, with the better off heavily over-represented among owner-occupiers. In 1994, over 50 per cent of households in the bottom income quintile lived in social housing, compared with 2 per cent in the top quintile (Table 14.3); the equivalent figures in 1974 were 44 per cent and 18 per cent, respectively (Hills 1998: table 5.12). At first glance this suggests that social housing is increasingly well targeted. That interpretation is disastrously wrong because it looks at housing in isolation. In practice, polarization is not just by housing tenure but is also geographical and sociological.

Experience with large purpose-built estates not just in Britain, but elsewhere in Europe, shows that concentrating the unemployed, single parents, teenagers, and those dependent on state benefits in particular areas not only disproportionately increases housing management and social service costs, but also makes it harder for people to solve their own problems.   (Hills 1997: 71; for fuller discussion, see Power 1997)

Tenure neutrality is thus achieved in terms of neither equality of subsidy nor equality of opportunity. In both respects, the system tends to work to the advantage of the better off, with an added element of arbitrariness. Whitehead's (1980: 112) conclusion remains true, that

'fiscal neutrality and 'appropriate' incentives are not obtained: between consumers, between different types of investment, within housing, between housing and other assets, or between consumption, saving and investment. Horizontal inequalities between tenures are particularly common and, especially for people living in the private rental sector, assistance helps to exacerbate the strong vertical inequities of the system.'

25. *The distribution of housing.* Housing conditions overall have improved greatly over the years. But the lowest-income quintile has experienced a decline in both the quantity and quality of housing, as measured by the incidence of crowding, missing amenities, and the lack of central heating (Hills 1998: table 5.19). The extreme case of shortage of space is homelessness. To an even greater extent than overcrowding, homelessness, temporary accommodation, and sleeping rough in city streets have afflicted the lowest socioeconomic groups. These problems reached a peak in the early 1990s, since when there has been some improvement.

5. **Reform**

5.1. The debate over reform

An early reform proposal by Nevitt (1966) (see also National Federation of Housing Associations 1985) advocated tenure-neutral taxation together with a unified system of subsidies for all tenures, under which poor families receive assistance scaled to their housing need, and better-off families receive no subsidy at all. The scheme suggested in Section 5.2 is in many ways similar.

Donnison and Ungerson (1982) suggest a scheme which pays the full cost of housing for low-income families, the benefit to be withdrawn as family income rises. The problem with this proposal is its expense. If it were financed through the abolition of mortgage interest relief, the package would resemble the scheme in the previous paragraph. Lansley (1982) advocates a universal, flat-rate (i.e. non-means-tested) housing allowance based on family size and an index of regional housing costs, where the allowance covers the full cost of minimum standard accommodation. Conceptually, this scheme is a form of negative income tax, and so raises the problems discussed in Chapter 11. Its universal nature makes it immensely costly, and therefore requires a sharp increase in tax rates (on these and other proposals, see Glennerster 1997: ch. 13, and Hills 1991: ch. 16).

The USA has also seen its fair share of reform proposals, concerned particularly with improving the housing conditions of the poor. Most schemes focus on income subsidies rather than public production of housing at subsidized rents. Bradbury and Downs (1981) (especially the chapter by Aaron) discuss a series of experiments on the feasibility of housing allowances in twelve cities funded by the US Department of Housing and Urban Development. For more recent discussion, see Caplin *et al.* (1997).

5.2. Designing a system for a brand new country

This section discusses how housing finance in the UK might be reformed, assuming that we are designing a system for a hypothetical brand new country. Section 5.3 considers how such a system might be implemented in practice. The two aspects of reform are discussed more fully by Hills (1991: chs. 16, 17).

REGULATION is essential. First, there would be minimum standards for individual dwellings, partly because of the public health externality and also (though more arguably) on the grounds of horizontal equity. Minimum standards to protect the poor 'for their own good' (i.e. the merit-goods argument discussed in Chapter 4, Section 4.2) should not be accepted uncritically. If they are set at a level higher than is justified on *efficiency* grounds, the cost of minimum standard housing will (*a*) be inefficiently high for those who would rationally choose housing of lesser (but still efficient) quality, and (*b*) be beyond the reach of those with lower incomes. Given its longevity, there are enough unavoidable problems over the affordability of housing without aggravating them unnecessarily (though with the best of motives) by setting standards which can worsen the housing problem to the detriment particularly of the poor. It can be argued that the only *equity* justification for minimum standards is the protection of children and possibly also the elderly.

Zoning and planning controls over land use would be concerned with housing density (because of the public-health externality); the separation of residential housing from factories (because of the spatial externality); and the provision of amenities such as public open space (which has public good attributes) and water, gas, electricity, and sewerage (for reasons of public health, and because their distribution displays increasing returns to scale). Thirdly, there would be some regulation of private landlords to prevent exploitation of monopoly power over tenants (see Section 3.2), and to protect tenants against arbitrary eviction. This type of regulation is necessary for the fulfilment of the 'equal-power' assumption (Chapter 4, Section 3.2), thereby increasing both efficiency and horizontal equity. Finally, it may be necessary to regulate the professional standards of surveyors and valuers to ensure adequate consumer information about the quality and price of housing (cf. hygiene laws for food).

PRODUCTION of housing would be subject to the relevant regulation; it could take place in either or both public and private sectors. In terms of allocative efficiency the issues of public/private production of the housing stock and its ownership are less important than its *price*. The UK is an outlier in the extent to which local government is involved in managing housing (Power 1993), and there is increasing support for more decentralized forms of management, not least to give residents greater voice. Options include 'arm's-length companies' (Inquiry into British Housing 1991) or introducing a financial regime which gives greater incentives to private landlords to provide social housing.

FINANCE. Three issues are important: the supply of mortgage finance; the price of housing; and vertical equity. *The supply of loan finance* should remain in the private sector, but with the addition of some sort of loan guarantee for individuals who have difficulty in obtaining an adequate mortgage in the private sector; and all mortgages would be fully indexed to the real value of the initial loan. These interventions would make access to capital markets more equitable, and would aid tenure neutrality; the supply of mortgages would not be artificially restricted; and there would be no arbitrary transfer from savers to mortgage-holders.

House prices (both purchase price and rent) would be market prices with only three possible exceptions. There would be price subsidies in respect of a limited number of externalities—for example, to prevent the spread of slums and/or to encourage 'gentrification' (see UK DoE 1985). Subsidies of this type are likely to be small in amount, and would apply only to a limited proportion of the total housing stock. The only argument for a *general* price subsidy is if it is believed that the private discount rate systematically exceeds the social discount rate. These two forms of subsidy perform an efficiency function.

The third exception is that it may be necessary for equity reasons to subsidize rents to prevent hardship if housing demand in an area rises, thereby (because short-run supply is inelastic) causing rents to rise sharply. These subsidies could be implemented in various ways: as additional income transfers to poor tenants in high-rent areas; or as a price subsidy paid by the *state* to prevent the contraction of private supply (measured in quantity and quality) resulting from rent control. Rent control is probably the least attractive method, and should be adopted, if at all, only as a temporary expedient;[24] and it is essential that controlled rents equal or exceed the long-run equilibrium, p^* in Figure 14.2, though they should obviously be below the (temporarily high) short-run market-clearing rent. This last solution has the disadvantages that it is likely to slow adjustment to the higher level of demand (point 16), and also has arbitrary distributional effects (point 21).

The adoption of market prices implies the removal of all price subsidies except in the cases just discussed. For owner occupation this should ideally take the form of taxing imputed housing income. If this is not possible for administrative or political reasons, there should be no mortgage interest tax relief. In either case it would be necessary to apply capital gains tax, indexed in some sensible way, to owner-occupied houses. There would be no subsidies from central and local revenues to local-authority housing, and local authorities would pay market interest rates on borrowed funds. In the private sector there would be no rent control except, possibly, in the circumstances just discussed, in which case it should be strictly limited as to time and place. House prices and rents, in short, would be *market* prices, subject to long-run modification only for very specific reasons.

Income transfers would be the main vehicle for pursuing vertical equity. There would be one system applying to all tenures. Consider first the transfer to a householder with

---

[24] Though this was the intention in 1915. Income tax was also originally intended to be temporary.

no income. He would receive £X per week, related to family size. In strict efficiency terms the subsidy would not vary regionally, so as to leave migration decisions undistorted. But housing costs vary so substantially in different areas that this policy conflicts with equity considerations. It can therefore be argued that the income subsidy should be higher in areas with higher *average* housing costs (ideally the transfer should not be directly related to a family's *actual* housing costs because this would interfere with marginal decisions). The transfer could be untied (i.e. paid in cash), or tied to expenditure on housing if this were necessary for political or other reasons (e.g. to protect children). The transfer would be reduced as family income increased, and above a certain income would cease entirely.

A veil is deliberately being drawn over the size of the transfer and its relation to family income. But the scheme is undoubtedly feasible in purely *financial* terms. Public expenditure (broadly defined) on housing in 1996/7 was around £20 billion (Table 14.2), by no means all of it well targeted. The scheme just described uses this sum to pay an income-related (i.e. better-targeted) transfer. It follows as a proposition in pure logic that on a revenue-neutral basis the poor on average must benefit at the expense of the non-poor.[25]

THE INDIVIDUAL-CONSUMPTION DECISION. Individuals would make a utility-maximizing decision constrained by their income (including the housing transfer) and subject in all tenures to the (generally) market price/rent of housing.

These proposals may sound abhorrent to those who regard market allocation of housing as inequitable. Such readers are asked to bear with the argument, and invited to remember the aims of housing policy outlined in Section 2; to acknowledge (at least in part) the magnitude of the failure of the system to achieve them (Section 4); and to consider the advantages of the scheme outlined above, advantages in terms of efficiency and, possibly even more, in terms of horizontal and vertical equity.

In efficiency terms, market prices, modified if at all only for the three reasons discussed, avert incentives to under-occupy, thereby avoiding many of the forces contributing to overcrowding and homelessness. Owner-occupiers have no incentive to buy a large house as an artificially inflated asset; and the existence of market (or modified market) rents prevents systematic excess demand in both rental sectors, thus avoiding the worst of the problems discussed in Section 4.2. Waiting lists would no longer be a permanent part of the landscape, though it would be desirable for local authorities to have some housing under their control for emergency cases, and also because housing markets take time to adjust. Additionally, market pricing together with indexed mortgages result, at least approximately, in tenure neutrality.

The system also contributes substantially to horizontal equity. Access to mortgage finance would be more equal; arbitrariness in the allocation of rented accommodation in both

---

[25] The point in the income distribution at which people would receive less assistance than under the arrangement in place in the late 1990s would depend on the precise details of the transfer.

public and private sectors would be reduced; and regional inequalities in access to social housing would be less important because there would be approximate neutrality between social housing and the other tenures. Access to housing would be determined not by administrative decision but by individual choice; and the distribution of housing by income level could be adjusted via the size of the housing transfer and its relation to family income.[26]

In terms of vertical equity the housing transfer is unambiguously progressive. In comparison with the present system, transfers would go to those in greatest need, with no subsidy at all for the well off. As a result, access to housing for the poor would be increased; for the rich it would be reduced. Additionally, the indexation of loans for house purchase eliminates the arbitrary transfer from savers to mortgage-holders.

In terms of cost, the system would either be cheaper because individuals who were not poor would no longer receive subsidies; or, if it were not cheaper, but revenue neutral, would be more cost effective, because benefits would be focused more systematically.

5.3. How to get from here to there

In the first edition (1987) of this book, this section pointed out that the sorts of change just discussed—taking housing policy in a very different direction from previously—would set in train a series of long-run adjustments in all sectors of the housing market, implying that change should be phased in gradually. Much of that reform has now happened. Discussion here is thus concerned more with how to proceed, broadly, along the lines of policy since the mid-1980s (for a more detailed set of rather similar proposals, see National Federation of Housing Associations 1985, and Inquiry into British Housing 1991).

Adjustment problems can be particularly acute in the owner-occupied sector. If tax reliefs for owner-occupiers are removed too rapidly, the effect is capitalized in house prices. This can (and has) led to 'negative equity', whereby someone with a £100,000 mortgage ends up with a house worth only £90,000. The gradual phasing-out of mortgage interest relief (note 16) is therefore undoubtedly the right approach for economic as well as for political reasons. The removal of capital-gains tax relief can also be phased in fairly easily, by bringing into tax only the real gains arising after some date subsequent to legislation (i.e. only gains arising *after* the market has at least partly adjusted to the withdrawal of mortgage tax relief).

The withdrawal of price subsidies for local-authority housing has taken place, accompanied by enlargement of housing benefit. The same, broadly, is true of the removal of rent control for tenancies beginning after 1988. In both cases there is controversy about whether housing benefit is generous enough, particularly for people above the income-support level. The main losers have been tenants with incomes too high to qualify for housing benefit.

[26] Another result is that council-house sales would be less controversial. On the supply side, state intervention in mortgage markets would make owner occupation more generally available; on the demand side, tenure neutrality would remove the financial advantages of owner occupation relative to renting.

Thus far the strategy sounds simple. Major difficulties remain, however (Hills 1997), with echoes of problems discussed in earlier chapters.

- The move towards income subsidies aggravates the poverty trap, in as much as the transfer is reduced as family income rises. Improvement, if any, depends on more general reform of income support along the lines discussed in Chapter 11.
- Polarization of housing aggravates broader social problems. Improvement includes action well outside the housing sector. Progress, in health and education, similarly, depends on progress more broadly.
- The management of social housing is a continuing problem. Improvement will almost certainly involve more decentralized management, with echoes of quasi-markets in health care and education.

6. Conclusion: Housing

Housing fails in various ways to conform with the conditions necessary for an unrestricted private market to be efficient. The specific failures justify substantial regulation, price subsidies for strictly limited reasons, and public provision of loan finance or loan guarantees. The theoretical discussion in Sections 3.2 and 3.3 suggests that state intervention along these lines would improve efficiency and horizontal equity.

Three conclusions follow (Section 3.4). First, in sharp contrast with health care, the information problems which arise are of a type which the market itself is able to solve; individuals (with professional advice if necessary) are generally able to make rational choices. Secondly, the efficiency justification for *general* price subsidies is highly qualified. This point, together with the first, implies that there are powerful advantages to keeping prices at the level dictated by efficiency, and seeking to achieve distributional objectives through cash transfers. Thirdly, no efficiency justification emerges for public production of housing (as opposed to regulation of private supply). This is not an argument *against* public production. But the three points taken together suggest that the aims of housing policy (Section 2) are more likely to be achieved if housing is allocated through individual consumption decisions, subject to regulation on minimum standards and efficient prices, and supported by income transfers.

UK housing institutions (Section 4.1), characterized by substantial and pervasive subsidies, have historically been strongly at variance with this model. Until the late 1980s, owner-occupiers received considerable tax relief; local-authority rents were subsidized in a number of ways and private-sector rents were often reduced by rent control.

Many of these institutions date from decisions made during and just after the First World War (Chapter 2, Section 3.1). For the reasons discussed in Section 3, there is no efficiency justification for such large subsidies, nor for their application to such a large proportion of the housing stock. The result (Section 4.2) is that price subsidies in each sector of the housing market created excess demand, which reinforced excess demand in the other sectors. In consequence, there is evidence simultaneously of under-occupation, overcrowding, and homelessness; the quantity and quality of the regulated private rental stock has deteriorated; labour mobility is hindered; and the system is decidedly not tenure neutral. The system also performs badly in terms of horizontal equity. Access to mortgage finance favours the higher socioeconomic groups; and access to rental accommodation in both public and private sectors has a strong arbitrary element. The redistributive effects of housing finance can also be perverse. The tax advantages to owner-occupiers have been regressive. The distributional impact of price subsidies to tenants in social housing and (in a very different way) to households living in regulated private rented accommodation are largely arbitrary. Income subsidies to households in rented accommodation are progressive, but take-up and administration are still patchy.

These problems are predictable consequence of price subsidies introduced mainly to increase equity.[27] The conclusion is clear. The use of price subsidies *only* for equity reasons is a confusion of aims and methods which is almost bound to cause inefficiency and inequity (Chapter 4, Section 7.2). In the absence of an efficiency justification, price subsidies are likely to cause excess demand and/or over-consumption unless demand can be rationed efficiently by administrative means. This is possible with health care but works less well with housing. In the latter case, equity (as well as efficiency) aims are more likely to be achieved by income subsidies. No policy-maker starting from scratch with the vast sum currently spent on housing would choose to spend it in the manner described in Section 4.1.

Changes since the mid-1980s have moved in the right direction: the tax concessions for owner occupation have been reduced, though owner occupation continues to receive favourable treatment; and there has been a major change in balance away from price subsidies for social housing, with higher rents accompanied by greater spending on housing benefit. Major problems remain, however: housing is polarized, with ill effects for broader social policy, and social housing is poorly managed.

In the strategy for reform in Section 5.2, drawing on the theoretical discussion of Section 3 and the policy analysis of Section 4, the state retains wide regulatory powers over individual dwellings and over land use generally; there is also regulation to prevent private landlords from abusing their power. The production of housing, subject to regulation, can be private, public, or both. Housing finance should be reformed in three ways. First, the state would take action to improve access to capital markets. Secondly, with only limited exceptions, house prices and rents should continue to move towards market-clearing prices. Thirdly, the revenue thereby released should be used to pay income-related transfers.

The result would come closer than existing arrangements to tenure neutrality, reducing under-occupation, overcrowding, immobility, and homelessness. Vertical equity

---

[27] Many other countries avoid at least some of these problems. It is noteworthy that a major US study of priorities for the 1980s in both foreign and domestic policy (Pechman 1980) had a chapter on health care, another on education, another on the environment (pollution, safety, etc.). But in a volume of 500 pages there was scarcely a mention of housing (or of food).

would be improved because subsidies are systematically related to income; and those with above-average incomes would no longer be subsidized at all.

These arrangements approximate more closely to the case of food than to the National Health Service. The implied suggestion is that difficulties with housing are more an income-distribution problem than a market-allocation problem. The strategy is chosen *not* for ideological reasons, but because it is more likely to achieve the aims set out in Section 2. The National Health Service strategy of free provision via administrative decision works well for health care, for the reasons given in Chapter 12; it does not work well for housing. Individuals have diverse tastes about housing, and can generally make better decisions than housing administrators because they have better information than officials (contrast the case of health care). The nature of housing as a commodity thus approximates more closely to food than to health care. This *technical* observation is the basis of the reforms proposed in Sections 5.2 and 5.3. As with reform in other sectors, the UK needs a *strategy* for the reform of housing finance, not just ad hoc tinkering.

It is important, in conclusion, to be clear what I am *not* saying. I am not arguing for the abolition of subsidies to social housing, nor simply for the abolition of rent control, nor even for the abolition of all housing subsidies. What is being suggested, quite simply, is that over time *price* subsidies should be replaced by *income* subsidies in all sectors of the housing market.

FURTHER READING

As general reinforcement of the material in this chapter, Hills (1998) assesses the UK housing experience from the mid-1970s to the mid-1990s, and Glennerster (1997: ch. 13) analyses the finance of housing.

On the historical background, see Gauldie (1974), UK DoE (1977*b*: ch. 1), Ray Robinson (1979: ch. 6), and Swenarton (1981). On the quantity and quality of the housing stock, see National Federation of Housing Associations (1985: ch. 2), Inquiry into British Housing (1991), and Hills (1998). On housing benefit, see the Further Reading to Chapter 10. For analytical discussion of financial aspects, see Hills (1991) and Glennerster (1997: ch. 12). On planning of land use, see Thornley (1993), and, on urban policy more generally, Atkinson and Moon (1994).

The best discussions of housing economics, both theoretical and with a review of empirical evidence, are by Hills (1991) and Muth and Goodman (1989). For a simple introduction, see Le Grand *et al.* (1992: ch. 4) and, for a survey, L. Smith *et al.* (1988).

For assessment of the UK situation, see Malpass and Means (1993), Whitehead (1997), and Hills (1998). For US discussion, see Caplin *et al.* (1997).

The most complete early proposal for reform is by Nevitt (1966). An inquiry chaired by HRH The Duke of Edinburgh (National Federation of Housing Associations 1985) and a second inquiry (Inquiry into British Housing 1991) reached similar conclusions; see also Hills (1991: chs. 16, 17).

Part 4
EPILOGUE

CHAPTER 15

Conclusion

A democratic capitalist society will keep searching for better ways of drawing the
boundary lines between the domain of rights and the domain of dollars. And it can
make progress. To be sure, it will never solve the problem, for the conflict between
equality and economic efficiency is inescapable. In that sense, capitalism and democracy are really a most improbable mixture. Maybe that is why they need each
other—to put some rationality into equality and some humanity into efficiency.

(Arthur M. Okun, 1975)

1. Arguments for a welfare state

1.1. Theory

The UK welfare state is the outcome of diverse forces over nearly four centuries of
developing social policy. Two aspects, in particular, stand out from the historical discussion in Chapter 2: debates about ideology (which are taken up in Chapter 3), and the
welfare state's functional purposes, notably economic efficiency (Chapters 4 and 5).
Ideological aims vary widely. To libertarians (Chapter 3, Section 2) the primary goal is
individual freedom, which is best achieved by unrestricted private markets. Empirical
libertarians such as Hayek and Friedman therefore espouse minimal intervention and
oppose all but the most austere welfare systems, whose purpose is limited to poverty relief.
Marxists (Chapter 3, Section 4.2) regard the market system by its very nature as incompatible with their primary aim of meeting need. They therefore reject it, and give the state
a primary role in production and allocation. Marxists have mixed feelings about the welfare state (Chapter 3, Section 5.3). In part it accords with their aim of meeting need and
is therefore to be applauded; yet it serves also to support a capitalist system which they
regard as inherently unjust.

Liberals take a more eclectic view. The utilitarian aim (Chapter 3, Section 3.1) is the
maximization of total welfare, leaving open the question of whether it is to be achieved
by private markets, by public production and allocation, or by a mix of the two. Rawls

Epilogue

(Chapter 3, Section 3.2) argues that goods, liberty, and opportunity should be distributed equally unless any other arrangement is to the advantage of the least well off. Again, the issue of how this is best achieved is left open. For the purposes of this book, the single feature which above all distinguishes liberal theories is the treatment of private property as an issue which is contingent, not dogmatic—that is, the treatment of private property is not an end in itself but a means towards the achievement of stated aims (see Okun 1975).

Society has functional as well as ideological goals, notably the achievement of economic efficiency, as defined in Chapter 4, Section 2.1. Where there is a trade-off between efficiency and social justice, their relative weights will vary between libertarians, liberals, and Marxists. But an increase in efficiency which does not impair social justice is an unambiguous gain under *any* of these theories of society (Chapter 4, Section 2.2).

Efficiency can be achieved as an outcome of a market-clearing process, notably in a competitive environment with no market failures and, importantly, with no significant information failures (Chapter 4, Section 3.2). Similar conditions are necessary if insurance is to be efficient: at least some individuals must be risk averse (Chapter 5, Section 2.1), and there must be no technical problems with privately supplied insurance (Chapter 5, Section 3). These conditions, referred to collectively as the *standard assumptions*, must all hold if the market is to be relied on to allocate efficiently.

The distinction between *aims* and *methods* is crucial. The ideological and functional aims of policy can be encapsulated in large measure in the twin goals of economic efficiency and social justice. Once the aims have been chosen, the next step is to select methods to achieve them, including (Chapter 4, Section 3.1) no state intervention at all; intervention in the form of cash transfers; or interference with the market mechanism through regulation, through financial involvement, and/or through public production. The approach can be summarized in two statements: (*a*) the proper place of ideology is in the choice of aims, particularly the definition of social justice and its trade-off with economic efficiency; (*b*) once these aims have been agreed, the choice of method should be treated as a *technical* issue.

Whether a good is better produced publicly or privately should be decided on the basis of which method more closely achieves specified aims; and a major purpose has been to give a rationale in any situation for choosing the method(s) most likely to do so. This was given in the form of two propositions (Chapter 4, Section 7.2).

- If the standard assumptions hold, market allocation will be efficient; in this case social justice should generally be pursued via income transfers (e.g. so that poor people can buy food at market prices).

- Suppose the standard assumptions fail in a way that justifies public production and allocation on *efficiency* grounds; social justice may then appropriately be pursued through transfers in kind (e.g. free medical care under the National Health Service).

Whether a particular commodity should be publicly or privately produced is thus contingent on its technical characteristics—that is, a liberal approach in the sense described above (for libertarian and Marxist counter-arguments, see Chapter 4, Section 7.3). The welfare state should not be judged in dogmatic terms, but should be supported only if it contributes more than alternative arrangements to the achievement of agreed policy objectives.

1.2. Policy

Chapter 1 started with two questions: what theoretical arguments justify the existence of the various parts of the welfare state; and, given these arguments of principle, how well do the British and other systems perform? The answers are summarized in Chapter 4, Section 7, for the underlying theory, Chapter 11, Section 5, for cash benefits, and the concluding sections of Chapters 12, 13, and 14 for health care, education, and housing, respectively, so only the most important conclusions are set out here.

The aims of cash benefits (Chapter 1, Section 2.2) include the relief of poverty (about which there is general agreement) and, more controversially, the protection of accustomed living standards and the reduction of inequality. Their achievement requires mechanisms to foster self-help and vertical redistribution.

SELF-HELP is necessary for an individual (or family) who is self-supporting over his lifetime, but who needs a system of income smoothing and insurance to facilitate redistribution from himself at one time (e.g. when working) to himself at another (e.g. when unemployed or retired). The answer in principle is voluntary private insurance. This, however, is not a tenable strategy (Chapters 8 and 9). On the demand side, non-insurance imposes external costs on various groups including taxpayers, giving an efficiency reason for making insurance compulsory (Chapter 8, Section 2.1). On the supply side, the private market is unable for technical reasons to provide the efficient quantity and type of insurance against all causes of income loss; in particular, unemployment and inflation are not insurable risks.

Several important results follow. There are strong efficiency grounds for public provision of unemployment compensation (Chapter 8, Section 2.2) and, at at a minimum, underwriting the indexation component of retirement pensions (Chapter 9, Section 3.1). For these benefits at least, public involvement, whatever the form it takes, will not (because it cannot) be actuarially related to individual risks. For the major risks covered by the state scheme, adherence to strict actuarial principles is neither possible (except as a mimic of private institutions) nor necessary, and only arguably desirable. Various reforms of the insurance system are possible, but a substantial return to voluntary private insurance and pure, private, funded pensions is not one of them (Chapters 8, Section 3.1, and Chapter 9, Section 5.1). Social policy requires that individuals are protected against income loss; but strict adherence to market supply enables them to acquire protection only where risks are insurable. This puts the cart before the horse by making

Epilogue

social policy subservient to *technical* considerations. A bridge is needed between the two sets of issues.

VERTICAL REDISTRIBUTION is relevant to those who cannot support themselves over their lifetime. In principle it can be organized through private charity or by the state. Partly because of the free-rider problem, redistribution through private charity is likely to be suboptimal even by libertarian standards, and even further below the Rawlsian or socialist optimum (Chapter 4, Section 4.1). Redistribution through the tax system may therefore be justified in both efficiency and equity terms (Chapter 10, Section 2) under any theory of society, though with considerable disagreement as to how much redistribution is desirable (Chapter 4, Section 4.4) or feasible (Chapter 11). The overall success of cash benefits in practice is also controversial (Chapter 8, Section 3, Chapter 9, Section 5, and Chapter 10, Section 3). The UK has a wide-ranging system of insurance benefits whose effect, albeit imperfectly, is redistributive from rich to poor; these are buttressed by assistance benefits organized on a national basis, for which *everyone* is potentially eligible. Many other countries have less comprehensive systems (Chapter 2, Section 6). Nevertheless, poverty remains (Chapter 10, Section 3.4). Indeed, poverty in the UK and the USA increased over the 1980s and 1990s.

Reform can follow one of two strategies. Benefits can be conditioned on income by an explicit means test or through a negative income tax (Chapter 11, Section 2), though this approach can easily aggravate the poverty trap.[1] Alternatively, it may be possible to sidestep the worst of the poverty trap by adopting the 'Back to Beveridge' approach (Chapter 11, Section 3), under which benefits are conditioned on carefully chosen characteristics of recipients, such as being unemployed or retired, or having children. The most hopeful reform strategy is through a judicious combination of the two approaches (Chapter 11, Section 4).

BENEFITS IN KIND. The theoretical discussion of public involvement in health care and education is set out in the early parts of Chapters 12 and 13, respectively. The issues are complex, not least because of intractable measurement problems (Chapter 12, Section 2.2, and Chapter 13, Section 2.2). There are strong a priori arguments suggesting that unrestricted private markets for health care and education (Chapter 12, Section 3, and Chapter 13, Section 3) will be inefficient, and also inequitable to the extent that information, power, and access to capital markets are correlated with socioeconomic status. The precise form of public involvement has two aspects. The *allocation* issue rests crucially on whether individuals or 'experts' (doctors, teachers, etc.) are better informed and/or better able to act in the interests of consumers. The question of *production* depends largely on whether quality/quantity can be monitored more effectively with production in the public or private sector. The theoretical arguments for public production and allocation of health care and school education (Chapter 12, Section 3.3, and Chapter 13, Section 3.3), though not irrefutable, are strong, largely because of information problems, particularly in the case of health care.

---

[1] See the Glossary.

The National Health Service is not above criticism, but it has powerful advantages (Chapter 12, Section 4). In comparison with other countries, the system is cheap, yet health outcomes in the UK are close to the average for advanced countries. Theoretical argument and international comparison both suggest that radical 'privatization' (whatever its advocates mean by the term) will not solve old problems, and is likely to create new and larger ones. The evidence for the UK, overwhelmingly, is that the National Health Service should be retained, and improvement sought within the existing strategy by increasing its resources, gathering and using more and better information, and continuing experiments with quasi-markets. This is not to say that public production is the only possible model. Other countries with different political traditions and different medical structures have adopted other sensible *strategies* of mixed public/private provision—for example, private production and public funding subject to a budget constraint, as in Canada (Chapter 12, Section 5).

The educational system fares less well (Chapter 13, Section 4). Notwithstanding improvements over the years, middle-class children continue to receive a disproportionate share of educational resources in terms of both quantity and quality, at both school and university level. It is open to question to what extent these features are *necessarily* an indictment of the present system. Opponents have to show not that the state sector is imperfect (which is not in dispute), but that a more market-oriented system would do better. Vouchers for school education (Chapter 13, Section 5.1) offer no such prospect. Their efficiency effects are unclear a priori and unproven empirically; in equity terms they are likely to benefit middle-class children more than other groups. In sharp contrast, the introduction of market forces, supported by a well-designed loan system, would greatly benefit higher education (Chapter 13, Section 5.2).

Housing is the one major area where the welfare state has performed badly historically, not through choosing controversial aims (Chapter 14, Section 2), but by adopting methods which were unlikely to achieve them. The theoretical arguments (Chapter 14, Section 3) support a substantial efficiency role for the state through widespread regulation, limited price subsidies for very specific reasons, and intervention in the market for loans. There is little necessity for public production of housing, and no justification for state allocation to the individual. Equity objectives are thus likely to be met most effectively by market or near-market prices and regulation, supported by income transfers.

The historical strategy, however, has been based on price subsidies (Chapter 14, Section 4.1), with substantial public production allocated by administrative means. The system worked badly. Price subsidies throughout the housing market led to excess demand and misallocation (Chapter 14, Section 4.2), with problems simultaneously of underoccupation, overcrowding, immobility, and homelessness; the quantity and quality of the private rental housing stock declined; and the system is nowhere near tenure neutral. The distributional effects of the subsidies has also been largely perverse (Chapter 14, Section 4.3): owner-occupiers (mainly in the higher socioeconomic groups) benefit disproportionately; and the redistributive impact of rent control and remaining rent subsidies is arbitrary. The reforms set out in Chapter 14, Section 5, therefore adopt a strategy in which *price* subsidies (i.e. mortgage-interest relief, subsidized local-authority rents, and rent control) are gradually replaced by *income* subsidies. Changes in that direction since the mid-1980s, though not without problems, have been steps in the right direction.

One of the most important points I have tried to convey is that the approach to housing (and to the other areas) is advocated *not* for ideological reasons but because it would have substantial advantages in terms of efficiency and, possibly even more, of social justice. Housing and health care are equally important from the viewpoint of *social* policy; but there are substantial differences in their *technical* natures. As a result, they require different solutions.

1.3. Why have a welfare state?

This book has asserted the powerful arguments in favour of the welfare state: it addresses major issues of market failure; it achieves equity objectives which many people support; and it contributes to important non-economic objectives such as social integration. Virtually all parts of the welfare state address all three aspects. Education from a functional perspective is a form of investment in the next generation of workers and citizens, and, provided 'free', it acts also to help the poor and enhance social cohesion; analogous arguments apply to health care. Publicly provided income transfers, similarly, have an efficiency role where the private market is unable to supply insurance (e.g. against unemployment) even to individuals able to support themselves on a lifetime basis.

Several important conclusions emerge. First, to the extent that the welfare state has a substantial functional aspect, opposition by writers such as Hayek and Friedman is misplaced. The single theoretical issue which, more than any other, divides their arguments from those in this book is their failure to take account of the major implications of information problems, which affect consumers of increasingly complex products, and also arise in important ways in insurance markets. Information problems of this sort greatly strengthen the efficiency case for the welfare state. The debate with libertarians (Chapter 4, Section 7.3), surprisingly, turns out to be at least as much technical as ideological. As a result, it is less public involvement *per se* which should be a matter for controversy, than its precise form and the choice of its distributional objectives.

This theoretical conclusion is supported by recent history. A British study concluded that 'the welfare state, and indeed welfare itself, is very robust. Over the thirteen years from 1974 to 1987, welfare policy successfully weathered an economic hurricane in the mid-1970s and an ideological blizzard in the 1980s. The resources going to public welfare were maintained; [and] welfare indicators continued to show a steady improvement' (Le Grand 1990: 350). In the USA, 'the Reagan era ended with the welfare state substantially intact, though somewhat frayed around the edges. It is now tilted more toward its middle-class beneficiaries than it was a decade ago, but the broad contours remain essentially as they have evolved since the 1930s, when the welfare state began' (Peterson 1991: 133). An international study concluded: 'Popular perceptions notwithstanding, the degree of welfare state roll-back, let alone significant change, has so far been modest' (Esping-Andersen 1996a: 10).

Once the welfare state's efficiency role is understood, these findings should not be surprising. The argument is not diminished by the fact that it can explain only part of the variation across countries. The major efficiency role of social institutions makes them relevant to the population at large, not just to the poor. The welfare state is much more than a safety net; it is justified not simply by any redistributive aims one may (or may not) have, but because it does things which private markets for technical reasons either would not do at all, or would do inefficiently. We need a welfare state of some sort for efficiency reasons, and would continue to do so even if all distributional problems had been solved.

That said, the welfare state is not—even in principle—a complete solution. It may make unemployment more bearable, but it does little to reduce the number of people out of work; nor does it improve working conditions for those in employment; and many people—for example, women, ethnic minorities—are underprivileged for reasons not directly connected with poverty. There is room for debate about the nature of these problems and about appropriate ameliorative action, but little disagreement that each is a legitimate concern of public policy. Their omission is not because they are unimportant but because (with the exception of unemployment) economics has little to say about them.

2. A changing world: Debates

Notwithstanding strong arguments supporting the general idea of the welfare state, there is major and continuing debate round two broad sets of questions.

- Is the welfare state desirable, particularly in terms of its effects on incentives and on economic growth?
- Even if desirable, is a welfare state any longer feasible, given the challenges discussed in Chapter 1, Section 3, of demographic and social change, and global and political pressures?

2.1. Is the welfare state desirable?

MISTAKEN OBJECTIVES? Libertarians, espousing freedom and choice, criticize the welfare state's emphasis on equality and security. Since these are matters of fundamental value judgements, the opposite view is equally plausible. Libertarians also argue that the welfare state is a threat to individual freedom. The validity of this view depends on two factors: the weight given to freedom compared with other objectives; and how freedom is defined (to a Libertarian, freedom means absence of coercion, to a socialist it includes an element of security (Chapter 3, Section 4.2)).

Epilogue

AN INHERENTLY MISTAKEN ENTERPRISE? Libertarians attack the welfare state on theoretical grounds, arguing that it is not possible to have a large purposeful collective enterprise. In many ways this is an appeal to the coordination/information-processing problems which beset central planning. The first counter-argument is that the welfare state is not a monolith, but comprises many smaller components. Secondly, many of these components are publicly *financed* but privately and competitively *produced*—welfare does not have to be state welfare. Thirdly, where market failures are severe, state action, albeit imperfect, may produce the least-bad outcomes.

Libertarians also attack the practice as inefficient and ineffective in terms of the services it provides. As already indicated, imperfect state action may be the least-bad way. Furthermore, a major thrust of modern policy is to introduce competition on the supply side, as exemplified by the discussion of quasi-markets in Chapters 12, Section 5.2, and Chapter 13, Section 5.1, *precisely* to improve internal incentives to efficiency.

DAMAGING TO ECONOMIC GROWTH? The argument is that the welfare state harms growth because the level of welfare-state spending is too high or (separately) because its rate of growth is too rapid. In consequence, high or rising levels of taxation create a drag on economic growth (see the Further Reading).

It is not controversial to argue that beyond a certain point taxation harms growth. What *is* controversial is (*a*) where that point is, and (*b*) the precise mechanism by which welfare-state spending might reduce growth. The issue remains disputed territory. As Atkinson's (1995*a*: ch. 6) survey makes clear, the argument is far from simple.

- For most of the post-war period, spending on the welfare state in Germany has been higher than in the UK, yet German economic growth has been faster.[2]
- If the charge is that the *level* of welfare-state spending is too high, then, as Atkinson (1995*a*: 123) points out, 'the Welfare State is no more than a co-defendant with other elements of the state budget'.
- Causation can be problematic. Do countries with higher spending reduce their growth rate, or do countries with lower growth and more poverty need to spend a larger fraction of GDP alleviating poverty?
- Looking at aggregates can obscure other key influences on growth, notably the detailed structure—and hence the incentive effects—of benefits. Benefits awarded without an income test, for example, may cost more but have less powerful adverse incentives.

For these and other reasons, Solow, in an assessment of cross-country comparative analysis (1994: 51, quoted by Atkinson 1995*a*: 124), concluded: 'I do not find this a confidence-inspiring project. It seems altogether too vulnerable to bias from omitted variables, to reverse causation, and above all to the recurrent suspicion that the experiences

---

[2] In the early 1990s, for example, UK welfare state spending was around 23% of GDP; in Germany, just prior to unification, it was 27.5% of GDP.

of very different national economies cannot be explained as if they represented different "points" on some well-defined surface'.

Even if it could be shown conclusively that the welfare state *does* reduce growth, that is not the end of the argument. The welfare state has benefits as well as costs—increased security, reduced poverty, increased investment in human capital, to name but a few. If the benefits sufficiently outweigh the costs, the project should proceed. In concrete terms, people may prefer to trade a small amount of growth for increased security, the slight reduction in growth being in some ways analogous to an insurance premium. The fact that this argument cannot be pushed too far does not make it less valid.

DAMAGING INCENTIVE EFFECTS? Writers like Murray (1984: ch. 12) argue that social benefits, far from being the cure to social ills, are part of their *cause*. According to this argument, which echoes nineteenth-century British debates about poverty relief (Chapter 2, Section 1.1), social assistance is too generous, thereby creating a 'culture of poverty'. The counter-view (Marmor *et al.* 1990; Levy 1998) is that labour-market behaviour, crime, and single parenthood are far too complex to be explained only—or even mainly—by the incentives offered by social benefits.[3]

A more sophisticated argument (Lindbeck 1997*a*) is that over an extended period the existence of social benefits changes social norms. To paraphrase his argument, a typical person in (say) the 1930s felt stigmatized by the need to rely on benefits; in the early post-war period, partly because of deliberate policy, stigma (Chapter 10, Section 3.1) was felt less acutely; by the 1980s benefits were regarded as an entitlement—not something to be avoided if at all possible but, along with wages and the tax system, part of a person's budget constraint. In economic terms, in the 1930s a pound of income transfers was worth less in utility terms than a pound of earnings; by the 1980s, according to Lindbeck, the difference was much smaller, with predictable effects on behaviour.

2.2. Is the welfare state sustainable?

Even if we conclude that none of these problems applies with major force, and hence that the welfare state is desirable, it is still necessary to discuss whether it is any longer feasible.

COMPATIBLE WITH A GLOBAL ECONOMY? As discussed in Chapter 1, Section 3, the core of the globalization argument is that, because of technological change, much economic activity has become 'dematerialized'—that is, takes the form of computer-transmitted information. As a result, national boundaries become porous, making competition global and thus reducing the freedom of any country to conduct an independent economic policy. The argument is important. Many activities are genuinely becoming more global, as exemplified by growing commercial activity over the Internet. But the implications for the welfare state are not necessarily apocalyptic.

---

[3] For discussion of these issues in a UK context, see Murray (1990), which includes responses by British commentators.

Epilogue

The world is not wholly global. Though global competition is powerful, it is not all-powerful. Not all goods are tradeable. Nor are all factors mobile: labour mobility is reduced both by choice (people prefer to stay with their language, culture, and family) and because of constraints such as immigration controls. For these and other reasons, Burtless (1996*b*) concludes that the globalization of the US economy explains less than one-fifth of the large increase in inequality in the USA since 1970.

The Western countries can adapt. It is vital to keep two issues logically separate:

- What should be the *scale* of the state's activities—that is, the level of public spending on income transfers, health care, education, and the like?
- What is the appropriate *structure* of activity—that is, the public/private mix?

The first is largely a matter of budgetary balance—a macroeconomic issue. The second is microeconomic. It is concerned with which activities are most efficiently privately funded and/or privately produced and which are not. The distinction is important: a budgetary crisis is *not* a ground for privatization.

Globalization means that countries—for instance, in South East Asia—with low social spending, can exert competitive pressures on OECD countries. That, however, is not an argument for dismantling the welfare state, still less for radical structural change such as privatization. Rather, it is an argument for some reduction in the scale of some welfare-state activities. For this reason as well as for demographic ones governments in virtually all the OECD countries have tried to restrain welfare-state spending (UK DSS 1993).

The newly industrialized countries may also adapt. A third reason why globalization is not the death knell for the welfare state is that in all the industrialized countries, social spending has been a superior good: as incomes have risen, electorates have voted to increase the share of such spending in GDP. In some countries the process has perhaps gone too far,[4] but that does not mean is that the premiss is flawed. Unless the countries of East Asia are very different, rising incomes and the weakening of extended family ties will lead to demands for rising social expenditures (David Phillips 1992).

A plausible outcome of global competition, therefore, is some convergence between the OECD countries and their Asian competitors. Competition will continue to exert downwards pressure on wage costs and on the generosity of social benefits in the OECD; and over time rising incomes will lead to increased social spending in the newly industrializing countries.

DEMOGRAPHICALLY SUSTAINABLE? Rising life expectancy and falling birth rates in many countries result in an ageing population. The facts are not in dispute. As discussed in Chapter 9, Section 5.1, however, a whole range of policies can address the problem: increasing the quantity and quality of capital; increasing labour-force participation; more generous immigration policies; and—most powerful of all—raising the age of retirement.

---

[4] Government failure is discussed in Chapter 5, Section 5.

A CRISIS OF THE WELFARE STATE? Esping-Andersen (1996*a*) argues that political and other institutions are enormously important for managing potential conflict between efficiency and distributional objectives. He goes on to argue that during the 1950s and 1960s, and in some countries longer, it was possible to pursue distributional objectives with little efficiency cost because there was a consensus of acquiescence to wage restraint in return for full employment (see also Atkinson and Mogensen 1993; Blank 1994). That consensus, it can be argued, was what underpinned the early success of Keynesian policies, providing a positive-sum solution to the trade-off between growth and equity. According to this view, institutions have become more fragmented. Because of changes in social norms and a weakening of some institutions, the trade-off between growth and equity had by the 1990s become less favourable than formerly. What has emerged is a zero-sum trade-off.[5]

Though the issue is of critical importance, it does not counsel despair. It is un-arguable that parts of the system require change—generous tax-funded pensions are more feasible the fewer the number of pensioners (Chapter 9); similarly, free, tax-funded university education is possible with an élite system but not with the mass system required by modern technology (Chapter 13). In these areas, as elsewhere, the welfare state is adapting:

- There is particular emphasis in many countries on improving the incentive structure of the benefit system.
- The generosity of some benefits is being reduced (UK DSS 1993), for both economic and, in some countries, political reasons.
- Other reforms, such as raising the age of retirement, are part of the menu of options.

The welfare state will continue to adapt in the future. Some of those adaptions can be foreseen.

- Demographic and global change will continue to create pressure to contain total spending. In consequence, pensions and health care will continue to face resource constraints, creating upward pressure on the age of retirement.
- Not least because of labour-market trends, inequality will be a continuing problem. A consequence will be pressures more carefully to distinguish the insurance function of cash benefits from their redistributive function. This may lead to social insurance becoming more actuarial; more generally, pensions will, up to a point, become more individualized. Such moves, if well designed, could (*a*) facilitate labour-market flexibility and (*b*) enable women, in the face of more fluid family structures, to have their own pension entitlement.
- There will be mounting pressure for new insurance instruments (public, private, or mixed) to cover contingencies such as requiring residential care in old age.

[5] For theoretical discussion of how social customs can influence economic outcomes, see Akerlof (1980).

Epilogue

- New lending instruments will emerge. Income-contingent loans, ideally drawing on private-sector funds, will increasingly pay for part of the costs of post-compulsory education and training. In the face of labour-market developments, especially reduced job security and the increasing prevalence of part-time work, there will also be pressure for more flexible lending for house purchase.

In all these points, the word 'adapt' is key. To criticize the welfare state as though it were set in tablets of stone is to make the same mistake as Marxists in criticizing capitalism—it ignores the fact that both the market system and state institutions adapt. The welfare state faces *problems*; as a result, its institutions *adapt*; this does not mean that there is a *crisis*. The proper debate is about the form and extent of adaptation.

POLITICALLY SUSTAINABLE? The survival of the welfare state depends on its political as well as its economic sustainability. Libertarians argue that the state takes on tasks (e.g. the abolition of poverty) which are impossible, that failure undermines the state, and, to that extent, that the welfare state contains the seeds of its own political demise. The exact opposite can be asserted. It is the welfare state which has made capitalism, with all its attendant benefits of economic growth, politically feasible, as the quote by Arthur Okun at the head of the chapter suggests. Failure to address poverty can be destabilizing and hence politically damaging—a key problem in many of the reforming former Communist countries.

Libertarians also argue that the welfare state leads to the formation of powerful interest groups. This is true. It is also true that capitalist lobbies create powerful interest groups, such as employers' organizations, Chambers of Commerce, and the like. These, it can be argued, are all desirable activities within democratic pluralist societies.

In the face of all these controversies, it is not surprising that there is a flourishing political debate about whether the UK or other countries can afford a welfare state. The easy complacency of earlier years about the continued growth of social spending has been replaced by discussion of whether or not there is a crisis in welfare. The argument in this book is that the discussion should not be about *whether* there should be a welfare state, but about its precise form and its distributional objectives. Glennerster reaches a similar conclusion. He points out two crucial facts. First, the level of taxation and social spending, though high in all the Western industrial economies, varies widely and is not correlated in any obvious way with economic performance. These facts contradict the simple view that the present scale of the welfare state or something rather larger or smaller is incompatible with a substantial capitalist sector. Secondly, fifty years ago, 'in a ravaged economy, when real incomes were less than half what they are today, people voted for what came to be called the welfare state, and paid the price, and voted to continue affording it' (Glennerster 1997: 298).

This brings out a final point—that the future of the welfare state depends not only on economic feasibility, but also very much on what people, through the political process, decide that they want.

None of the ideas in this book has been intended as a detailed blueprint, but more as an illustration of an approach which has been, throughout, to entertain moderately egalitarian aims while avoiding dogmatism about methods. The result shows how, with care, it is possible to create institutions both within the welfare state and more broadly which contribute to a society characterized simultaneously by economic efficiency and social justice.

FURTHER READING

For a classic defence of the mixed economy, see Okun (1975). For early discussion of the 'crisis in welfare' by libertarians, see Harris and Seldon (1979), and Seldon (1981), and by Marxists, see Ginsburg (1979) and Gough (1979). For more recent discussion, see Esping-Anderson (1996*b*) and Glennerster (1997: ch. 15).

Murray (1984) and Marmor *et al.* (1990) offer two opposing views of the effects of the welfare state on individual behaviour; see also Lindbeck (1997*a, b*). The effects of the welfare state on growth rates are discussed by Lindbeck *et al.* (1993) and Drèze and Malinvaud (1994); see also the symposium on the Swedish welfare state in the *Economic Journal*, 106/439 (Nov. 1996) 1725–79.

REFERENCES

Aaron, Henry J. (1973), *Why is Welfare so Hard to Reform?* (Washington: The Brookings Institution).

—— (1981*a*), 'Economic Aspects of the Role of Government in Health Care', in J. van der Gaag, and M. Perlman (eds.), *Health, Economics, and Health Economics* (Amsterdam: North Holland).

—— (1981*b*), 'Policy Implications: A Progress Report' in Bradbury and Downs (1981), 67–111.

—— (1982), *Economic Effects of Social Security* (Washington: The Brookings Institution).

—— (1991), *Serious and Unstable Condition: Financing America's Health Care* (Washington: The Brookings Institution).

—— (1992), 'Equity in the Finance and Delivery of Health Care', *Journal of Health Economics*, 11/4 (Dec.), 467–71.

—— (1996) (ed.), *The Problem That Won't Go Away: Reforming US Health Care Financing* (Washington: The Brookings Institution).

—— and Burtless, Gary (1984) (eds.), *Retirement and Economic Behavior* (Washington: The Brookings Institution),

—— and Pechman, Joseph A. (1981), *How Taxes Affect Economic Behavior* (Washington: The Brookings Institution).

—— and Schwartz, William B. (1984), *The Painful Prescription: Rationing Hospital Care* (Washington: The Brookings Institution).

—— Bosworth, Barry P., and Burtless, Gary T. (1989), *Can America Afford to Grow Old?* (Washington: The Brookings Institution).

Abel Smith, Brian (1964), *The Hospitals, 1800–1948* (London: Heinemann).

—— (1984), *Cost Containment in Health Care* (Occasional Papers in Social Administration No. 73; London: Bedford Square Press).

—— (1985), 'Who is the Odd Man Out?: The Experience of Western Europe in Containing the Costs of Health Care', *Health and Society*, 63/1: 1–17.

—— and Townsend, Peter (1965), *The Poor and the Poorest* (London: Bell and Sons).

Akerlof, George A. (1970), 'The Market for "Lemons": Qualitative Uncertainty and the Market Mechanism', *Quarterly Journal of Economic*, 84 (Aug.) 488–500.

—— (1978), 'The Economics of "Tagging" as Applied to the Optimal Income Tax, Welfare Programs and Manpower Planning', *American Economic Review*, 68: 8–19.

—— (1980), 'A Theory of Social Custom of Which Unemployment May Be One Consequence', *Quarterly Journal of Economics*, 94 (June), 749–75.

Albrecht, Douglas, and Ziderman, Adrian (1992), *Deferred Cost Recovery for Higher Education: Student Loan Programs in Development Countries* (World Bank Discussion Paper 137; Washington: The World Bank).

Altmeyer, A. J. (1966), *The Formative Years of Social Security* (Madison: University of Wisconsin Press).

Andreoni, J. (1989), 'Giving with Impure Altruism: Applications to Charity and Ricardian Equivalence', *Journal of Political Economy*, 97: 1447–58.

—— (1990), 'Impure Altruism and Donations to Public Goods: A Theory of Warm-Glow Giving', *Economic Journal*, 100: 464–77.

Apps, Patricia F. (1981), *A Theory of Inequality and Taxation* (Cambridge: Cambridge University Press).

—— and Rees, Ray (1996), 'Labour Supply, Household Production and Intra-family Welfare Distribution', *Journal of Public Economics*, 60: 199–219.

Arrow, Kenneth F. (1963), 'Uncertainty and the Welfare Economics of Medical Care', *American Economic Review*, 53: 941–73; repr. in Cooper and Culyer (1973: 13–48) and Diamond and Rothschild (1978: 348–75).

—— (1973*a*), 'Some Ordinalist–Utilitarian Notes on Rawls's *Theory of Justice*', *Journal of Philosophy*, 70 (May), 245–63.

—— (1973*b*), 'Higher Education as a Filter', *Journal of Public Economic*, 2: 193–216.

Ashenfelter, Orley, and Layard, Richard (1986) (eds.), *Handbook of Labor Economics*, (Amsterdam: North Holland).

Atkinson, Anthony B. (1970), 'On the Measurement of Inequality', *Journal of Economic Theory*, ii. 244–63; repr. in Atkinson (1980), 23–43 (including a non-mathematical summary).

—— (1973), *The Tax Credit Scheme and the Redistribution of Income* (London: Institute for Fiscal Studies).

—— (1980) (ed.), *Wealth, Income and Inequality* (2nd edn., Oxford: Oxford University Press).

—— (1983), *The Economics of Inequality* (2nd edn., Oxford: Oxford University Press).

—— (1987*a*), 'Income Maintenance and Social Insurance', in Alan J. Auerbach, and Martin S. Feldstein (eds.), *Handbook of Public Economics*, ii (Amsterdam: North Holland), 779–908.

—— (1987*b*), 'On the Measurement of Poverty', *Econometrica*, 55: 749–64.

—— (1989), *Poverty and Social Security* (Brighton, Sussex: Harvester Press).

—— (1995*a*), *Incomes and the Welfare State: Essays on Britain and Europe* (Cambridge: Cambridge University Press).

—— (1995*b*), 'On Targeting Social Security', in van de Walle and Nead (1995), 25–68.

—— (1996), 'Seeking to Explain the Distribution of Income', in Hills (1996*b*), 19–48.

—— (1997), 'Bringing Income Distribution in from the Cold', *Economic Journal*, 107/441: 297–321.

—— and Bourguignon, François (forthcoming) (eds.), *Handbook on Income Distribution* (Amsterdam: North Holland).

—— and Micklewright, John (1989), 'Turning the Screw: Benefits for the Unemployed 1979–1988' in Andrew Dilnot, and Ian Walker (eds.), *The Economics of Social Security* (Oxford: Oxford University Press), 17–51.

—— —— (1991), 'Unemployment Compensation and Labour Market Transitions: A Critical Review', *Journal of Economic Literature*, 29/4 (Dec.), 1679–727.

—— —— (1992), *Economic Transformation in Eastern Europe and the Distribution of Income* (Cambridge: Cambridge University Press).

—— and Mogensen, Gunnar V. (1993), *Welfare and Work Incentives: A North European Perspective* (Oxford: Oxford University Press).

—— and Stiglitz, Joseph E. (1980), *Lectures on Public Economic* (London and New York: McGraw-Hill).

—— Maynard, Alan K., and Trinder, Chris (1983), *Parents and Children* (London: Heinemann).

—— Rainwater, Lee, and Smeeding, Timothy M. (1995), *Income Distribution in OECD Countries: Evidence from the Luxembourg Income Study* (Social Policy Studies No. 18, Paris: OECD).

References

Atkinson, R., and Moon, G. (1994), *Urban Policy in Britain: The City, the State and the Market* (London: Macmillan).

Auerbach, Alan J., and Kotlikoff, Laurence J. (1990), 'Demographics, Fiscal Policy and US Saving in the 1980s and Beyond', in Lawrence H. Summers (ed.), *Tax Policy and the Economy*, iv (Cambridge, Mass.: MIT Press).

—— *et al.* (1989), 'The Economic Dynamics of Ageing Populations: The Case of Four OECD Economies', *OECD Economic Studies* (Spring), 97–130.

Baldwin, Sally, and Falkingham, Jane (1994), *Social Security and Social Change* (Hemel Hempstead: Harvester Wheatsheaf).

Ballard, Charles L., Shoven, John B., and Whalley, John (1985), 'General Equilibrium Computations of the Marginal Welfare Costs of Taxes in the United States', *American Economic Review*, 75/1: 128–38.

Banks, J., and Tanner S. (1996), 'Savings and Wealth in the UK: Evidence from Micro-Data', *Fiscal Studies*, 17/2 (May), 37–64.

—— Dilnot, Andrew, and Low, Hamish (1996), 'Patterns of Financial Wealth-Holding in the United Kingdom', in Hills (1996*b*), 321–47.

Barnes, John, and Barr, Nicholas (1988), *Strategies for Higher Education: The Alternative White Paper* (Aberdeen University Press for the David Hume Institute, Edinburgh, and the Suntory-Toyota International Centre for Economics and Related Disciplines, London School of Economics).

Barnum, Howard, Kutzin, Joseph, and Saxenian, Helen (1995), 'Incentives and Provider Payment Methods', *International Journal of Health Planning and Management*, 10: 23–45.

Barr, Nicholas A. (1975), 'Negative Income Taxation and the Redistribution of Income', *Oxford Bulletin of Economic and Statistics*, 37/1 (Feb.), 29–48, as revised in 38/2 (May 1976), 147.

—— (1979), 'Myths My Grandpa Taught Me', *Three Banks Review*, 124 (Dec.), 27–55.

—— (1981), 'Empirical Definitions of the Poverty Line', *Policy and Politics*, 9/1: 1–21.

—— (1985), 'Economic Welfare and Social Justice', *Journal of Social Policy*, 14/2 (Apr.), 175–87.

—— (1989*a*), *Student Loans: The Next Steps* (Aberdeen University Press for the David Hume Institute, Edinburgh, and the Suntory-Toyota International Centre for Economics and Related Disciplines, London School of Economics).

—— (1989*b*), 'The White Paper on Student Loans', *Journal of Social Policy*, 18/3 (July), 409–17.

—— (1991), 'Income-Contingent Student Loans: An Idea Whose Time has Come', in G. K. Shaw (ed.), *Economics, Culture and Education: Essays in Honour of Mark Blaug* (Aldershot: Edward Elgar), 155–70.

—— (1992), 'Economic Theory and the Welfare State: A Survey and Interpretation', *Journal of Economic Literature*, 30/2: 741–803.

—— (1993), 'Alternative Funding Resources for Higher Education', *Economic Journal*, 103/418 (May), 718–28.

—— (1994*a*), 'The Role of Government in a Market Economy', in Barr (1994*c*), 29–50.

—— (1994*b*), 'Income Transfers: Social Insurance', in Barr (1994*c*), 192–225.

—— (1994*c*) (ed.), *Labor Markets and Social Policy in Central and Eastern Europe: The Transition and Beyond* (New York and Oxford: Oxford University Press for the World Bank (also available in Hungarian, Romanian, and Russian)).

—— (1995), 'Genetic Screening and Insurance', in *Third Report: Human Genetics: The Science and Its Consequences*, ii. *Minutes of Evidence, House of Commons Science and Technology Committee, Session 1994–95*, HC 41-IV (London: HMSO), 242–7.

—— (1997), 'Student Loans: Towards a New Public/Private Mix', *Public Money and Management*, 17/3 (July–Sept.), 31–40.

—— and Crawford, Iain (1996), *Student Loans: Where Are We Now?* (Welfare State Programme, Discussion Paper No. WSP/127; London: London School of Economics).

—— —— (1998a), 'Funding Higher Education in an Age of Expansion: Submission to the National Committee of Inquiry into Higher Education', *Education Economics*, 6/1: 45–70.

—— —— (1998b), 'The Dearing Report and the Government's Response: A Critique', *Political Quarterly*, 69/1 (Jan.–Mar.), 72–84.

—— and Falkingham, Jane (1996), *Repayment Rates for Student Loans: Some Sensitivity Tests* (Welfare State Programme, Discussion Paper No. WSP/127; London: London School of Economics).

—— and Hall, Robert E. (1975), 'The Taxation of Earnings Under Public Assistance', *Economica*, 42/168 (Nov.), 373–84.

—— —— (1981), 'The Probability of Dependence on Public Assistance', *Economica*, 48/190 (May), 109–23.

—— and Low, William (1988), *Student Grants and Student Poverty* (Welfare State Programme, Discussion Paper No. WSP/28; London: London School of Economics).

—— and Roper, John F. H. (1974), 'Tax-Credits: An Optimistic Appraisal', *Three Banks Review*, 101 (Mar.), 24–45.

—— and Whynes, David (1993) (eds.), *Issues in the Economics of the Welfare State* (London: Macmillan).

—— James, Simon R., and Prest, Alan R. (1977), *Self-Assessment for Income Tax* (London: Heinemann).

—— Glennerster, Howard, and Le Grand, Julian (1989), 'Working for Patients? The Right Approach?', in *Resourcing the National Health Service: The Government's White Paper: Working for Patients* (House of Common Social Services Committee, Session 1988–9, HC 214-I; London: HMSO), 17–22; repr. in *Social Policy and Administration*, 23/2 (Aug.), 117–27.

Barry, Brian (1973), *The Liberal Theory of Social Justice* (Oxford: Oxford University Press).

Bartlett, Donald, and Steele, James (1992), *America: What Went Wrong?* (Kansas City, Miss.: Andrews & McMeel).

Bartlett, Will (1993), 'Quasi-Markets and Educational Reforms', in Le Grand and Bartlett (1993), 125–153.

—— and Harrison, Lyn (1993), 'Quasi-Markets and the National Health Service Reforms', in Le Grand and Bartlett (1993), 68–92.

—— and Le Grand, Julian (1994), 'The Performance of Trusts', in Robinson and Le Grand (1994), 54–73.

Baumol, William (1996), 'Children of the Performing Arts, The Economics Dilemma: The Climbing Costs of Health Care and Education', *Journal of Cultural Economics*, 20/3: 183–206.

—— and Blinder, Alan (1997), *Economics: Principles and Policy* (New York: Harcourt Brace).

Bean, Charles (1994), 'European Unemployment: A Survey', *Journal of Economic Literature*, 32/2 (June), 573–619.

Becker, Gary (1975), *Human Capital* (2nd edn., Cambridge, Mass.: National Bureau of Economic Research).

—— (1983), 'A Theory of Competition among Pressure Groups for Political Influence', *Quarterly Journal of Economics*, 98 (Aug.), 371–400.

—— (1985), 'Public Policies, Pressure Groups, and Dead Weight Costs', *Journal of Public Economics*, 28 (Dec.), 329–47.

References

Beckerman, Wilfred (1979), 'The Impact of Income Maintenance Payments on Poverty: 1975', *Economic Journal*, 89: 261–79.

Beenstock, Michael, and Brasse, Valerie (1986), *Insurance for Unemployment* (London: Allen & Unwin).

Bennett, Fran (1996) (ed.), *Out of Pocket: The Failure of the Social Fund* (London: Family Welfare Association).

Bennett, Robert, Glennerster, Howard, and Nevison, Douglas (1992), 'Investing in Skill: To Stay On or Not To Stay On', *Oxford Review of Economic Policy*, 8/2: 130–45.

Bentham, Jeremy (1789), *An Introduction to the Principles of Morals and Legislation* (London: Payne).

Besley, Timothy, and Kanbur, Ravi (1993), 'Principles of Targeting' in Michael Lipton, and Jacques van der Gaag (eds.), *Including the Poor* (Washington: The World Bank), 67–90.

Beveridge, William (1944), *Full Employment in a Free Society* (London: Allen & Unwin).

Beveridge Report (1942), *Social Insurance and Allied Services*, Cmd 6404 (London: HMSO).

Bjorklund, Anders, and Holmlund, Bertil (1989), 'Effects of Extended Unemployment Compensation in Sweden', in Bjorn A. Gustafsson, and N. Anders Klevmarken (eds.), *The Political Economy of Social Security* (Amsterdam: North Holland), 165–83.

Black, Douglas (1980), *Inequalities in Health* (the Black Report), Report of a Research Working Group chaired by Douglas Black (Department of Health and Social Security, London), published in Townsend and Davidson (1982).

Blackorby, Charles, and Donaldson, David (1988), 'Cash versus Kind, Self-Selection, and Efficient Transfers', *American Economic Review*, 78: 691–700.

Blake, David (1997), 'Pensions Choices and Pensions Policy in the United Kingdom', in Valdes-Prieto, Salvador (ed.), *The Economics of Pensions* (Cambridge: Cambridge University Press), 277–317.

Blank, Rebecca (1994) (ed.), *Social Protection versus Economic Flexibility* (Chicago: University of Chicago Press).

—— (1997a), *It Takes a Nation: A New Agenda for Fighting Poverty* (Princeton: Princeton University Press).

—— (1997b), 'The 1996 Welfare Reform', *Journal of Economic Perspectives*, 11/1: 169–77.

Blaug, Mark (1970), *An Introduction to the Economics of Education* (London: Penguin).

—— (1976), 'The Empirical Status of Human Capital Theory: A Slightly Jaundiced Survey', *Journal of Economic Literature* (Sept.), 827–56; repr. in Blaug (1987), 100–28.

—— (1984), 'Education Vouchers—It All Depends on What You Mean', in Le Grand and Robinson (1984), 160–76.

—— (1985), 'Where Are We Now in the Economics of Education?', *Economics of Education Review*, 4/1: 17–28; repr. in Blaug (1987), 129–40.

—— (1987), *The Economics of Education and the Education of an Economist* (Aldershot: Edward Elgar).

—— (1997), 'Where Are We Now in British Health Economics?', Presentation to the Twenty-Fifth Anniversary of the UK Health Economists' Study Group (Centre for Health Economics, York: University of York).

Bleichrodt, H. (1995), 'QALYs and HYEs: Under What Conditions Are They Equivalent?', *Journal of Health Economics*, 14/1 (May), 17–37.

Blendon, R. J., Benson, J., Donelan, K., Leitman, R., Taylor, H., Koeck, C., and Gitterman, D. (1995), 'What Has the Best Health Care System? A Second Look', *Health Affairs*, 14/4: 220–30.

Blomqvist, A. (1991), 'The Doctor as Double-Agent: Information Asymmetry, Health Insurance and Medical Care', *Journal of Health Economics*, 10/4 (Nov.), 411–32.

Blundell, Richard (1992), 'Labour Supply and Taxation: A Survey', *Fiscal Studies*, 13/3 (Aug.), 15–40.

—— (1995), 'Tax Policy Reform: Why We Need Microeconomics', *Fiscal Studies*, 16/3 (Aug.), 106–25.

Boadway, R., and Wildasin, D. (1994), 'Taxation and Savings: A Survey', *Fiscal Studies*, 15/3 (Aug.), 19–63.

Boardman, Anthony, and Vining, Aidan (1989), 'Ownership and Performance in Competitive Environments: A Comparison of the Performance of Private, Mixed and State-Owned Enterprises', *Journal of Law and Economics*, 32 (Apr.), 1–33.

Bodie, Zvi (1990), 'Pensions as Retirement Income Insurance', *Journal of Economic Literature*, 28 (Mar.), 28–49.

—— Marcus, Alan J., and Merton, Robert C. (1988), 'Defined Benefit versus Defined Contribution Plans: What Are the Real Tradeoffs?', in Zvi Bodie, John B. Shoven, and David Wise (eds.), *Pensions in the US Economy* (Chicago: Chicago University Press), 139–60.

—— Mitchell, O., and Turner, J. (1996), *Securing Employed-Based Pensions* (Philadelphia: University of Pennsylvania Press).

Booth, Charles (1902), *Life and Labour of the People of London*, 17 vols. (London: Macmillan).

Bosanquet, Nicholas (1983), *After the New Right* (London: Heinemann).

Bosworth, Barry (1996), 'The Social Security Fund: How Big? How Managed?', in Diamond *et al.* (1996) 89–115.

Bourke, Paul (1997), *Evaluating University Research: The British Research Assessment Exercise and Australian Practice* (Commissioned Report No. 56; Australian National Board of Employment, Education and Training, Canberra: Australian Government Printing Service).

Bowley, Marion (1937), *Nassau Senior and Classical Economics*, (London: Allen & Unwin).

Boycko, Maxim, Shleifer, Andrei, and Vishny, Robert (1995), *Privatizing Russia* (Cambridge, Mass.: MIT Press).

Bradbury, K. L., and Downs, A. (1981) (eds.), *Do Housing Allowances Work?* (Washington: The Brookings Institution).

Bradshaw, J., and Millar, J. (1991), *Lone Parent Families in the UK* (UK Department of Social Security Research Report, No. 7; London: HMSO).

Briggs, Asa (1961*a*), 'The Welfare State in Historical Perspective', *Archives européennes de sociologie*, 2/2: 221–59.

—— (1961*b*), *Social Thought and Social Action: A Study of the Work of Seebohm Rowntree, 1917–1954* (London: Longman).

Brittan, Samuel (1995), *Capitalism with a Human Face* (Aldershot and Brookfield, Vermont: Edward Elgar).

Broome, John (1978), 'Trying to Value a Human Life', *Journal of Public Economics*, 9/1: 91–100, and discussion in the same journal, 12/2, (1979) 259–62.

Bruce, Maurice (1972), *The Coming of the Welfare State* (4th edn., London: Batsford).

Buchanan, James M., and Tullock, Gordon (1962), *The Calculus of Consent* (Ann Arbor, Mich.: University of Michigan Press).

Buhmann, Brigitte, Rainwater, Lee, Schmaus, Guenther, and Smeeding, Timothy (1988), 'Equivalence Scales, Well-Being, Inequality, and Poverty: Sensitivity Estimates across Ten Countries, Using the Luxembourg Income Study (LIS) Database', *Review of Income and Wealth*, 34/2: 115–42.

Bull, D. (1980), *What Price Education?* (Poverty Pamphlet 48; London: Child Poverty Action Group).

References

Burchardt, Tania, and Hills, John (1997), *Private Welfare Insurance and Social Security: Pushing the Boundaries* (York: Joseph Rowntree Foundation).

Burkhead, J., Fox, T. G., and Holland, J. W. (1967), *Input and Output in Large City High Schools* (New York: Syracuse University Press).

Burtless, Gary (1986), 'The Work Response to a Guaranteed Income: A Survey of Experimental Evidence', in Alicia H. Munnell (ed.), *Lessons from the Income Maintenance Experiments* (Federal Reserve Bank of Boston), 22–52.

—— (1987), 'The Adequacy and Counter-Cyclical Effectiveness of the Unemployment System', Testimony to the Committee on Unemployment and Means, US House of Representatives, 15 Dec. 1987.

—— (1990), 'The Economist's Lament: Public Assistance in America', *Journal of Economic Perspectives*, 4: 57–78.

—— (1996a), 'Trends in the Level and Distribution of US Living Standards: 1973–1993', *Eastern Economic Journal*, 22/3 (Summer), 271–90.

—— (1996b), 'Rising US Income Inequality and the Growth in World Trade', *Tokyo Club Papers*, 9: 129–59.

—— (1996c), 'The Folly of Means Testing Social Security', in Diamond *et al.* (1996), 172–80.

—— (1996d) (ed.), *Does Money Matter?: The Effect of School Resources on Student Achievement and Adult Success* (Washington: The Brookings Institution).

Byatt, I. C. R., Holmans, A. E., Laidler, D. E. W., and Nicholson, R. J. (1973), 'Income and the Demand for Housing', in Michael Parkin (ed.), *Essays in Modern Economics* (London: Longman).

Caplin, Andrew, Chan, Sewin, Freeman, Charles, and Tracy, Joseph (1997), *Housing Partnerships: A New Approach to a Market at a Crossroads* (Cambridge, Mass.: MIT Press).

Card, David, and Freeman, Richard (1993), *Small Differences that Matter: Labor Markets and Income Maintenance in Canada and the United States* (Chicago: University of Chicago Press).

—— and Krueger, Alan (1996), 'School Resources and Student Outcomes: An Overview of the Literature and New Evidence from North and South Carolina', *Journal of Economic Perspectives*, 10/4: 31–50.

Carr-Hill, R., Hardman, G., Martin, S., Peacock, S., Sheldon T. A., and Smith, P. (1994), *Formula for Distributing NHS Revenues Based on Small Area Use of Hospital Beds* (Centre for Health Economics, York: University of York).

Castles, Frances (1996), 'Needs-Based Strategies of Social Protection in Australia and New Zealand', in Esping-Andersen (1996b), 88–115.

Cave, Martin, Dodsworth, Ruth, and Thompson, David (1992), 'Regulatory Reform in Higher Education in the UK: Incentives for Efficiency and Product Quality', *Oxford Review of Economic Policy*, 8/2: 79–102.

Chadwick, Edwin (1842), *Inquiry into the Sanitary Condition of the Laboring Population of Great Britain* (London: HMSO).

Chalkley, Martin, and Malcomson, James M. (1996), 'Contracts and Competition in the NHS', in Culyer and Wagstaff (1996), 65–87.

Chand, Sheetal K., and Jaeger, Albert (1996), 'Aging Populations and Public Pension Schemes', IMF Occasional Paper 147; Washington: The International Monetary Fund).

Chapman, Bruce (1997), 'Conceptual Issues and the Australian Experience with Income Contingent Charges for Higher Education', *Economic Journal*, 107/442 (May), 738–51.

Chaudhuri, Shubham, and Ravallion, Martin (1994), 'How Well Do Static Indicators Identify the Chronically Poor?', *Journal of Public Economics*, 53: 367–94.

Christopher, A., *et al.* (1970), *Policy for Poverty* (Research Monograph 20; London: Institute of Economic Affairs).

Chubb, J. W., and Moe, T. M. (1990), *Politics, Markets and America's Schools* (Washington: The Brookings Institution).

Coase, Ronald H. (1960), 'The Problem of Social Cost', *Journal of Law and Economics*, 3 (Oct.), 1–44.

Cohn, E., and Geske, T. G. (1990), *The Economics of Education* (3rd edn., Oxford: Pergamum Press).

—— and Johnes, G. (1994), *Recent Developments in the Economics of Education* (Aldershot: Edward Elgar).

Collard, David (1983), 'Economics of Philanthropy: A Comment', *Economic Journal*, 93/371 (Sept.), 637–8.

Commission on Social Justice (1994), *Social Justice: Strategies for National Renewal* (London: Vintage).

Community Income Tax Service (1976), *Annual Report* (Winnipeg, Manitoba).

Coons, J., and Sugarman, S. (1978), *Education by Choice: The Case for Family Control* (Berkeley and Los Angeles: University of California Press).

Cooper, Michael H., and Culyer, Anthony J. (1973) (eds.), *Health Economics* (London: Penguin).

Corry, Dan (1997) (ed.), *Public Expenditure: Effective Management and Control* (London: Dryden Press).

Coulter, Fiona, Cowell, Frank, and Jenkins, Stephen (1992), 'Equivalence Scale Relativities and the Extent of Inequality and Poverty', *Economic Journal*, 102/414 (Sept.), 1067–82.

Cowell, Frank A. (1995), *Measuring Inequality* (2nd edn., Hemel Hempstead: Prentice Hall/Harvester Wheatsheaf).

CPAG (1984): Child Poverty Action Group, *Double Discrimination: Racism in Social Security* (London: Child Poverty Action Group).

Crosland, Anthony (1956), *The Future of Socialism* (London: Cape).

Cullis, John, and Jones, Philip (1998), *Public Finance and Public Choice* (2nd edn., Oxford: Oxford University Press).

Culyer, Anthony J. (1971*a*), 'The Nature of the Commodity "Health Care" and its Efficient Allocation', *Oxford Economic Papers*, 23: 189–211, repr. in Cooper and Culyer (1973: 49–74).

—— (1971*b*), 'Merit Goods and the Welfare Economics of Coercion', *Public Finance*, 4/546–72.

—— (1980), *The Political Economy of Social Policy* (Oxford: Martin Robertson).

—— (1993), 'Health Care Insurance and Provision', in Barr and Whynes (1993), 153–75.

—— and Wagstaff, Adam (1993), 'Equity and Equality in Health and Health Care', *Journal of Health Economics*, 12: 431–57.

—— —— (1995), 'QALYs versus HYEs: A Reply to Gafni, Birch, and Mehrez', *Journal of Health Economics*, 14/1 (May), 39–45.

—— —— (1996) (eds.), *Reforming Health Care Systems: Experiments with the NHS: Proceedings of Section F (Economics) of the British Association for the Advancement of Science, Loughborough 1994* (Cheltenham and Brookfield, Mass.: Edward Elgar).

Dalton, H. (1920), 'The Measurement of the Inequality of Income', *Economic Journal*, 30: 348–61.

Daniel, Caroline (1997), 'Socialists and Equality', in Franklin (1997), 11–27.

Daniels, N. (1975) (ed.), *Reading Rawls* (Oxford: Basil Blackwell).

Danziger, Sheldon, and Gottschalk, Peter (1995), *America Unequal* (New York: Russell Sage Foundation; Cambridge and London: Harvard University Press).

References

Danziger, Sheldon, and Jännti, Markus (forthcoming), 'Income Poverty in Advanced Countries', in Atkinson and Bourguignon (forthcoming).

—— Sandefur, Gary, and Weinberg, Daniel (1994), *Confronting Poverty: Prescriptions for Change* (Cambridge, Mass.: Harvard University Press).

Dasgupta, Partha (1993), *An Inquiry into Well-Being and Destitution* (Oxford: Oxford Unviersity Press).

—— and Maskin, Eric (1986), 'The Existence of Equilibrium in Discontinuous Economics Games I and II', *Review of Economic Studies*, 53: 1–41.

Davis, O. E., and Whinston, A. (1965), 'Welfare Economics and the Theory of Second Best', *Review of Economic Studies*, 32/89 (Jan.), 1–14.

Deininger, Klaus, and Squire, Lyn (1996), 'A New Data Set Measuring Income Inequality', *The World Bank Economic Review*, 10/3: 565–91.

Denison, Edward F. (1962), *The Sources of Economic Growth in the United States and the Alternatives Before Us* (New York: Committee for Economic Development).

—— (1967), *Why Growth Rates Differ: Postwar Experience in Nine Western Countries* (Washington: The Brookings Institution).

—— (1969), 'The Contribution of Education to the Quality of Labor: Comment', *American Economic Review* (Dec.), 935–43.

Derthick, Martha (1979), *Policymaking for Social Security* (Washington: The Brookings Institution).

Desai, Meghnad (1979), *Marxian Economics* (Oxford: Basil Blackwell).

Diamond, Peter (1995), 'Government Provision and Regulation of Economic Support in Old Age' in Bruno, Michael and Pleskovic, Boris (eds.), *Annual Bank Conference on Development Economics* (Washington: The World Bank), 83–103.

—— (1996a), 'Proposals to Restructure Social Security', *Journal of Economic Perspectives*, 10/3: 67–88.

—— (1996b), 'Insulation of Pensions from Political Risk', in Salvador Valdes-Prieto (ed.), *The Economics of Pensions: Principles, Policies and International Experience* (Cambridge: Cambridge University Press), 33–57.

—— (1998), 'Macroeconomic Aspects of Social Security Reform', *Brookings Papers on Economic Activity*, 1998/2, 1–87.

—— and Hausman, Jerry A. (1984), 'Individual Retirement and Savings Behavior', *Journal of Public Economics*, 23: 81–114.

—— and Rothschild, Michael (1978) (eds.), *Uncertainty in Economics: Readings and Exercises* (New York: Academic Press).

—— Lindeman, David, and Young, Howard (1996) (eds.), *Social Security: What Role for the Future?* (Washington: The Brookings Institution).

Dicks-Mireaux, Leslie, and King, Mervyn (1994), 'Pension Wealth and Household Savings: Tests of Robustness', *Journal of Public Economic*, 23: 115–39.

Dilnot, Andrew, Kay, John, and Morris, Nick (1984), *The Reform of Social Security* (Oxford: Oxford University Press, for the Institute for Fiscal Studies, London).

—— Disney, Richard, Johnson, Paul, and Whitehouse, Edward (1994), *Pensions Policy in the UK: An Economic Analysis* (London: Institute for Fiscal Studies).

Disney, Richard (1996), *Can We Afford to Grow Older?* (Cambridge, Mass.: MIT Press).

—— and Webb, Steven (1991), 'Why Are There So Many Long-Term Sick in Britain?', *Economic Journal*, 101: 252–62.

Ditch, J., Barnes, H., and Bradshaw, J. (1997), *European Observatory on National Family Policies: Synthesis Report 1996* (European Commission/University of York).

Dixon, Jennifer (1997), 'The British NHS—A Funding Crisis?', *Eurohealth*, 3/1 (Spring), 36–7.

—— and Glennerster, Howard (1995), 'What Do We Know about Fundholding in General Practice?', *British Medical Journal*, 311: 727–30.

Donnison, David, and Ungerson, Clare (1982), *Housing Policy* (London: Penguin).

Douglas, P. H. (1925), *Wages and the Family* (Chicago: University of Chicago Press).

—— (1939), *Social Security in the United States: An Analysis of the Federal Social Security Act* (New York: McGraw-Hill).

Downs, Anthony (1957), *An Economic Theory of Democracy* (New York: Harper & Row).

Drèze, Jacques H., and Malinvaud, E. (1994), 'Growth and Employment: The Scope for a European Initiative', *European Economy*, 1: 77–106.

Duncan, G. J. (1984) (ed.), *Years of Poverty, Years of Plenty* (Michigan: Institute for Social Research).

Dunleavy, Patrick (1985), 'Bureaucrats, Budgets and the Growth of the State: Reconstructing an Instrumental Model', *British Journal of Political Science*, 15: 299–328.

—— (1991), *Democracy, Bureaucracy and Public Choice* (Hemel Hempstead: Harvester Wheatsheaf).

Eardley, Tony, Bradshaw, Jonathan, Ditch, John, Gough, Ian, and Whiteford, Peter (1996a), *Social Assistance in OECD Countries: Synthesis Report* (London: HMSO; Paris: OECD).

—— —— —— —— —— (1996b), *Social Assistance in OECD Countries: Country Reports* (London: HMSO; Paris: OECD).

Ehrenberg, Ronald, and Smith, Robert (1994), *Modern Labour Economics* (5th edn., New York: Harper Collins).

Elliott, Robert F. (1990), *Labour Economics: A Comparative Text* (Maidenhead: McGraw-Hill).

Ellis, Randall P., and McGuire, Thomas G. (1993), 'Supply-Side and Demand-Side Cost Sharing in Health Care', *Journal of Economic Perspectives*, 7/4: 135–51.

Engen, Eric, Gale, William, and Scholz, John Karl (1994), 'Do Savings Incentives Work?', *Brookings Papers on Economic Activity*, 1994/1: 85–180.

Enthoven, Alain C. (1985), *Reflections on the Management of the National Health Service: An American Looks at Incentives to Efficiency in Health Services Management in the UK* (London: Nuffield Provincial Hospitals Trust) (a summary is contained in *The Economist*, 22 June 1985, pp. 19–20).

—— (1989), 'What Can Europeans Learn from Americans?', in US HCFA (1989), 49–63.

Esping-Anderson, Gøspa (1990), *The Three Worlds of Welfare Capitalism* (Cambridge: Polity Press).

—— (1996a), 'After the Golden Age? Welfare State Dilemmas in a Global Economy', in Esping-Andersen (1996b), 1–31.

—— (1996b) (ed.), *Welfare States in Transition: National Adaptations in Global Economies* (London: Sage).

Estrin, Saul (1994), 'The Inheritance', in Barr (1994c), 53–76.

—— and Laidler, David (1995), *Introduction to Microeconomics* (4th edn., London and New York: Harvester Wheatsheaf).

European Commission (1991), *Final Report on the Second European Poverty Programme 1985–1989* (Brussels: European Commission).

Evandrou, Maria, Falkingham, Jane, Hills, John, and Le Grand, Julian (1993), 'Welfare Benefits In Kind and Income Distribution', *Fiscal Studies*, 14/1 (Feb.), 57–76.

References

Evans, Martin (1996a), 'Fairer or Fowler? The Effects of the 1986 Social Security Act on Family Incomes', in Hills (1996b), 236–61.

—— (1996b), *Giving Credit Where It's Due? The Success of Family Credit Reassessed* (Welfare State Programme, Discussion Paper No. WSP/28; London: London School of Economics).

—— (1998), 'Social Security: Dismantling the Pyramids?', in Glennerster and Hills (1998), 258–307.

Evans, Robert, G. (1974), 'Supplier-Induced Demand: Some Empirical Evidence and Implications', in M. Perlman (ed.), *The Economics of Health and Medical Care* (London: Macmillan) 162–73.

—— (1996), 'Health, Hierarchy and Hominids—Biological Correlates of the Sociological Gradient in Health', in Culyer and Wagstaff (1996), 35–64.

—— Lomas, Jonathan, Barer, Morris, L., *et al.* (1989), 'Controlling Health Expenditures: The Canadian Reality', *New England Journal of Medicine*, 320/9: 571–7.

—— Barer, Morris L., and Marmor, Theodore R. (1994) (eds.), *Why Are Some People Healthy and Others Not? The Determinants of Health of Populations* (New York: Aldine).

Falkingham, Jane (1989), 'Dependency and Ageing in Britain: A Re-Examination of the Evidence', *Journal of Social Policy*, 18/2: 211–33.

—— and Hills, John (1995a), 'Lifetime Incomes and the Welfare State', in Falkingham and Hills (1995b), 108–36.

—— —— (1995b) (eds.), *The Dynamic of Welfare: The Welfare State and the Life Cycle* (Hemel Hempstead: Prentice-Hall / Harvester Wheatsheaf.

—— and Johnson, Paul (1995), 'Funding Pensions over the Life Cycle', in Falkingham and Hills (1995b), 204–17.

Farmer, M., and Barrell, R. (1982), 'Why Student Loans Are Fairer Than Grants', *Public Money*, 2/1 (June), 19–24.

Feinstein, C. H. (1972). *Statistical Tables of National Income, Expenditure and Output of the UK, 1855–1965* (Cambridge: Cambridge University Press).

Feldstein, Martin S. (1974), 'Social Security, Induced Retirement and Aggregate Capital Accumulation', *Journal of Political Economy*, 82: 905–26.

—— (1996), 'The Missing Piece in Policy Analysis: Social Security Reform', *American Economic Review*, 86/2 (May), 1–14.

Field, Frank (1996a), *How to Pay for the Future: Building a Stakeholders' Welfare* (London: Institute of Community Studies).

—— (1996b), *Stakeholder Welfare* (London: Institute for Economic Affairs).

Finer, S. E. (1952), *The Life and Times of Sir Edwin Chadwick* (London: Methuen).

Fischer, Claude, S., Hout, Michael, Jankowski, Martin, Lucas, Samuel R., Swidler, Ann, and Voss, Kim (1996), *Inequality by Design: Cracking the Bell Curve Myth* (Princeton: Princeton University Press).

Fisher, Irving (1930), *The Theory of Interest* (New York: Macmillan).

Flanagan, Robert J. (1987), 'Efficiency and Equality in Swedish Labor Markets', in Barry P. Bosworth, and Alice M. Rivlin (eds.), *The Swedish Economy* (Washington: The Brookings Institution).

Forrest, R., and Murie, A. (1990), *Selling the Welfare State: The Privatisation of Public Housing* (London: Routledge)

Foster, James E. (1984), 'On Economic Poverty: A Survey of Aggregate Measures', *Advances in Econometrics*, 3: 215–51.

Franklin, Jane (1997) (ed.), *Equality* (London: Institute for Public Policy Research).

Fraser, Derek (1984), *The Evolution of the British Welfare State* (2nd edn., London: Macmillan).

Freeden, M. (1978), *The New Liberalism: An Ideology of Social Reform* (Oxford: Oxford University Press).

Fretwell, David, and Jackman, Richard (1994), 'Labor Markets: Unemployment', in Barr (1994c), 160–91.

Friedman, Milton (1962), *Capitalism and Freedom* (Chicago: University of Chicago Press).

—— and Friedman, Rose (1980), *Free to Choose* (London: Penguin).

Fuchs, Victor R. (1988), 'The "Competition Revolution" in Health Care', *Health Affairs*, 7/3: 5–24.

—— (1996) (ed.), *Individual and Social Responsibility: Child Care, Education, Medical Care, and Long-Term Care in America* (National Bureau of Economic Research Conference Report Series; Chicago and London: University of Chicago Press).

Galal, Ahmed, *et al.* (1994), *Welfare Consequences of Selling Public Enterprises: An Empirical Analysis* (New York: Oxford University Press).

Gale, William (1998), 'The Effects of Pensions on Wealth: a Re-Evaluation of Theory and Evidence', *Journal of Political Economy*, August, forthcoming.

—— and Scholz, John Karl (1994), 'IRA's and Household Saving', *American Economic Review* (Dec.), 1233–60.

Gauldie, E. (1974), *Cruel Habitations: A History of Working-Class Housing, 1780–1918* (London: George Allen & Unwin).

George, Victor, and Wilding, Paul (1994), *Welfare and Ideology* (Hemel Hempstead: Harvester Wheatsheaf).

Gerdttham, Ulf-G., *et al.* (1992), 'An Econometric Analysis of Health Care Expenditure: A Cross-Section Study of the OECD Countries', *Journal of Health Economics*, 11/1 (May), 63–84.

Gilbert, Bentley B. (1973), *The Evolution of National Insurance in Great Britain* (London: Michael Joseph).

Gilmour, Ian (1992), *Dancing with Dogma* (Hemel Hempstead: Simon & Schuster).

Ginsburg, N. (1979), *Class, Capital and Social Policy* (London: Macmillan).

Gintis, H., and Bowles, S. (1982), 'The Welfare State and Long-Term Economic Growth: Marxian, Neoclassical and Keynesian Approaches', *American Economic Review*, Papers and Proceedings, 72/1: 341–5.

Glennerster, Howard (1991), 'Quasi-Markets for Education?', *Economic Journal*, 101/408 (Sept.), 1268–76.

—— (1992), *Paying for Welfare: The 1990s* (Hemel Hempstead: Harvester Wheatsheaf).

—— (1993), 'The Economics of Education: Changing Fortunes', in Barr and Whynes (1993), 176–99.

—— (1994), *Implementing GP Fundholding* (Milton Keynes: Open University press).

—— (1995), *British Social Policy since 1945* (Oxford: Blackwell Publishers).

—— (1996), 'Vouchers and Quasi Vouchers in Education', in M. May, E. Brunsdon, and G. Craig (eds.), *Social Policy Review*, No. 8 (London: Social Policy Association).

—— (1997), *Paying for Welfare: Towards 2000* (3rd edn., Hemel Hempstead: Prentice Hall/Harvester Wheatsheaf).

—— (1998), 'Education: Reaping the Harvest?', in Glennerster and Hills (1998), 27–74.

—— and Hills, John (1998) (eds.), *The State of Welfare II: The Economics of Social Spending* (2nd edn., Oxford: Oxford University Press).

References

Glennerster, Howard and Le Grand, Julian (1995), 'The Development of Quasi Markets in Welfare Provision in the UK', *International Journal of Health Services*, 25/2: 203–18.

—— Merrett, Stephen, and Wilson, Gail (1968), 'A Graduate Tax', *Higher Education Review*, 1/1: 26–38.

—— Power, Anne, and Travers, Tony (1991), 'A New Era for Social Policy: A New Enlightenment or a New Leviathan?', *Journal of Social Policy*, 20/3 (July), 389–414.

—— Matsaganis, Manos, Owens, Pat, and Hancock, Stephanie (1994), 'GP Fundholding: Wild Card or Winning Hand?', in Robinson and Le Grand (1994); 74–107.

—— Falkingham, Jane and Barr, Nicholas (1995), 'Education Funding, Equity and the Life Cycle' in Falkingham and Hills (1995*b*), 137–49.

Goodin, Robert, and Le Grand, Julian (1987), *Not Only the Poor: The Middle Classes and the Welfare State* (London: Allen & Unwin).

Goodman, Alissa, Johnson, Paul, and Webb, Steven (1997), *Inequality in the UK* (Oxford: Oxford University Press).

Goodwin, Nick (forthcoming), 'GP Fundholding: A Review of the Evidence', in Le Grand *et al.* (forthcoming).

Gordon, David M. (1969), 'Income and Welfare in New York City', *Public Interest*, 16 (Summer), 64–88.

Gordon, Margaret (1988), *Social Security Policies in Industrial Countries: A Comparative Analysis* (Cambridge: Cambridge University Press).

Gordon, Michael S., Mitchell, Olivia S., and Twinney, Marc M. (1997) (eds.), *Positioning Pensions for the Twenty-First Century* (Philadelphia: University of Pennsylvania Press).

Gordon, Robert J. (1997), 'The Time-Varying NAIRU and its Implications for Economic Policy', *Journal of Economic Perspectives*, 11/1: 11–32.

Gorovitz, S. (1975), 'John Rawls: A Theory of Justice', in A. de Crespigny and K. R. Minogue (eds.), *Contemporary Political Philosophers* (London: Methuen), 272–89.

Gottschalk, Peter (1993), 'Changes in Inequality of Family Income in Seven Industrialized Countries', *American Economic Review*, 2: 136–42.

—— (1997), 'Inequality, Income Growth and Mobility: The Basic Facts', *Journal of Economic Perspectives*, 11/2 (Spring) 21–40.

—— and Smeeding, Timothy M. (1997), 'Cross-National Comparisons of Earnings and Income Inequality', *Journal of Economic Literature*, 35/2 (June), 633–87.

—— —— (forthcoming), 'Empirical Evidence on Income Inequality in Industrialized Countries', in Atkinson and Bourguignon (forthcoming).

Gough, I. (1979), *The Political Economy of the Welfare State* (London: Macmillan).

Gramlich, Edward M. (1989), 'Economists' View of the Welfare System', *American Economic Review*, 79/2 (May), 191–6.

—— (1996), 'Different Approaches for Dealing with Social Security', *Journal of Economic Perspectives*, 10/3: 55–66.

Green, Christopher (1967), *Negative Taxes and the Poverty Problem* (Washington: The Brookings Institution).

Green, David (1991) (ed.), *Empowering the Parents: How to Break the Schools Monopoly* (London: Institute of Economic Affairs).

Gronbjerg, K., Street, D., and Suttles, G. D. (1978), *Poverty and Social Change* (Chicago: University of Chicago Press).

Grosh, Margaret (1994), *Administering Targeted Social Programs in Latin America: From Platitudes to Practice* (Washington: The World Bank).

Grubel, H. G., and Maki, D. R. (1976), 'The Effects of Unemployment Benefits on US Unemployment Rates', *Weltwirtschaftliches Archiv*, 112: 274–97.

Gruber, Jonathan (1997), 'The Consumption Smoothing Benefits of Unemployment Insurance', *American Economic Review*, 87/1(Mar.), 192–205.

Halpern, S. (1985), 'What the Public Thinks of the NHS', *Health and Social Service Journal*, 6 June, pp. 702–4.

Ham, Chris (1997), 'Primary Managed Care in Europe', *British Medical Journal*, 314: 457.

Hamblin, Richard (forthcoming), 'NHS Trusts: The Evidence So Far', in Le Grand *et al.* (forthcoming).

Hamnett, Chris, and Seavers, Jenny (1996), 'Home-Ownership, Housing Wealth and Wealth Distribution in Britain', in Hills (1996*b*), 348–73.

Hannah, Leslie (1986), *Inventing Retirement* (Cambridge: Cambridge University Press).

Hansen, W. Lee, and Weisbrod, Burton A. (1969), 'The Distribution of Costs and Direct Benefits of Public Higher Education: The Case of California', *Journal of Human Resources*, 4/2 (Spring), 176–91.

—— —— (1978), 'The Distribution of Subsidies to Students in California Public Higher Education: Reply', *Journal of Human Resources*, 13/1 (Winter), 137–9.

Hanushek, Eric A. (1986), 'The Economics of Schooling: Production and Efficiency in Public Schools', *Journal of Economic Literature*, 23/3: 1141–77.

—— (1996*a*), 'Measuring Investment in Education', *Journal of Economic Perspectives*, 10/4: 9–30.

—— (1996*b*), 'School Resources and Student Performance', in Burtless (1996*d*), 43–73.

Harberger, Arnold C. (1962), 'The Incidence of the Corporation Income Tax', *Journal of Political Economy*, 70/3 (June), 215–40.

Harris, Jose F. (1972), *Unemployment and Politics, 1886–1914* (Oxford: Oxford University Press).

—— (1977), *William Beveridge: A Biography* (Oxford: Oxford University Press).

Harris, Ralph, and Seldon, Arthur (1979), *Over-Ruled on Welfare* (Hobart Paperback No. 13; London: Institute of Economic Affairs).

Harrison, A. H., Dixon, J., New, B., and Judge, K. (1997*a*), 'Is the NHS Sustainable?', *British Medical Journal*, 314: 296–8.

—— —— —— —— (1997*b*), 'Can the NHS Cope in the Future?', *British Medical Journal*, 314: 139–42.

Harrison, J. (1978), *Marxist Economics for Socialists* (London: Pluto).

Harrison, P. (1985), *Inside the Inner City* (rev. edn., London: Penguin).

Hattersley, Roy (1987), *Choose Freedom: The Future for Democratic Socialism* (London: Michael Joseph).

Hay, J. R. (1975), *The Origins of the Liberal Welfare Reforms 1906–1914* (London: Macmillan).

Hayek, Friedrich A. (1944), *The Road to Serfdom* (London: Routledge; Chicago: Chicago University Press).

—— (1945), 'The Use of Knowledge in Society', *American Economic Review*, 35: 519–30.

—— (1960), *The Constitution of Liberty* (London: Routledge & Kegan Paul; Chicago: Chicago University Press).

—— (1976), *Law, Legislation and Liberty*, ii. *The Mirage of Social Justice* (London: Routledge & Kegan Paul).

Heckman, James J. (1993), 'What Has Been Learned about Supply in the past Twenty Years?', *American Economic Review*, 83/2 (May), 116–21.

References

HEFCE (1997*a*): Higher Education Funding Council for England, *The Impact of the 1992 Research Assessment Exercise on Higher Education Institutions in England* (Bristol: Higher Education Funding Council for England).

—— (1997*b*), *The Influence of Neighbourhood Type on Participation in Higher Education* (Bristol: Higher Education Funding Council for England).

Hellevick, O., and Ringen, S. (1995), 'Class Inequality and Egalitarian Reform', Oxford, Department of Applied Social Studies.

Hellwig, Martin (1987), 'Some Recent Development in the Theory of Competition in Markets with Adverse Selection', *European Economic Review*, 31: 319–25.

Hemming, Richard (1984), *Poverty and Incentives* (Oxford: Oxford Univeristy Press).

Hey, John (1989) (ed.), *Current Issues in Microeconomics* (London: Macmillan).

Hicks, John R. (1946), *Value and Capital* (2nd end., Oxford: Oxford University Press).

Higgins, Joan (1981), *States of Welfare: Comparative Analysis in Social Policy* (Oxford: Basil Blackwell and Martin Robertson).

Hillman, Alan L., Pauly, Mark V., and Kersten, Joseph J. (1989), 'How Do Financial Incentives Affect Physicians' Clinical Decisions and the Financial Performance of Health Maintenance Organizations?', *New England Journal of Medicine*, 321/2: 86–92.

Hills, John (1990) (ed.), *The State of Welfare: The Welfare State in Britain since 1974* (Oxford: Oxford University Press).

—— (1991), *Unravelling Housing Finance* (Oxford: Oxford University Press).

—— (1995), 'Funding the Welfare State', *Oxford Review of Economic Policy*, 11/3: 27–43.

—— (1996*a*), 'Introduction: After the Turning Point', in Hills (1996*b*), 1–16.

—— (1996b) (ed.), *New Inequalities: The Changing Distribution of Income and Wealth in the United Kingdom* (Cambridge: Cambridge University Press).

—— (1998), 'Housing: A Decent Home with the Reach of Every Family?', in Glennerster and Hills (1998), 122–88.

—— with Gardiner, Karen (1997), *The Future of Welfare: A Guide to the Debate* (Rev. edn., York: Joseph Rowntree Foundation).

—— and Mullings, Beverly (1990), 'Housing: A Decent Home for All at a Price within their Means?', in Hills (1990), 135–205.

Himmelfarb, Gertrude (1984), *The Idea of Poverty: England in the Early Industrial Age* (London: Faber).

Himmelstein, David, U., and Woolhandler, Steffie (1986), 'Cost without Benefit: Administrative Waste in US Health Care', *New England Journal of Medicine*, 314/7: 441–5.

—— —— (1991), 'The Deteriorating Administrative Efficiency of the US Health Care System', *New England Journal of Medicine*, 324/18: 1253–7.

Hirshleifer, J. (1980), *Price Theory and Application* (2nd edn., Hemel Hempstead: Prentice Hall).

—— and Riley, John G. (1992), *The Analytics of Uncertainty and Information* (Cambridge Surveys of Economic Literature; Cambridge and New York: Cambridge University Press).

Hobsbawn, E. J. (1964), *Labouring Men* (London: Weidenfeld & Nicolson).

Hobson, J. A. (1908), *The Problem of the Unemployed* (4th edn., London: Methuen).

—— (1909), *The Crisis of Liberalism: New Issues of Democracy* (London: King & Son).

Hochman, Harold, and Rodgers, James (1969), 'Pareto Optimal Distribution', *American Economic Review*, 59/4: 542–57.

Holzmann, Robert (1997), 'Pension Reform, Financial Market Development, and Economic Growth: Preliminary Evidence from Chile', The IMF Staff Papers, 44/2: 149–78.

Honig, Marjorie (1974), 'AFDC Income, Recipient Rates, and Family Dissolution', *Journal of Human Resources*, 9: 303–22.

—— (1976), 'AFDC Income, Receipient Rates, and Family Dissolution: A Reply', *Journal of Human Resources*, 11: 250–9.

Horn, M. (1996), *The Political Economy of Public Administration* (Cambridge: Cambridge University Press).

Hughes, G., McCormick, B. (1981), 'Do Council Housing Policies Reduce Migration between Regions?', *Economic Journal*, 91/364 (Dec.), 919–37.

Hume, David (1770), 'Enquiry Concerning the Principles of Morals', in *Essays and Treatises on Several Subjects* (London: Cadell).

Hurst, Jeremy (1996), 'The NHS Reforms in an International Context', in Culyer and Wagstaff (1996), 15–34.

Illsley, Raymond, and Le Grand, Julian (1987), *The Measurement of Health Inequality* (Welfare State Programme, Discussion Paper No. WSP/12; London: London School of Economics.

Inman, Robert P. (1987), 'Markets, Governments and the "New" Political Economy', in Alan J. Auerbach and Martin S. Feldstein (eds.), *Handbook of Public Economics*, ii (Amsterdam: North Holland), 647–777.

Inquiry into British Housing (1991), *Second Report* (York: Joseph Rowntree Foundation).

Jarvis, Sarah, and Jenkins, Stephen P. (1997), 'Low Income Dynamics in 1990s Britain', *Fiscal Studies*, 18/2: 123–42.

Jencks, Christopher (1970), *Education Vouchers: A Report on the Financing of Elementary Education by Grants to Parents* (Cambridge, Mass.: Cambridge Center for the Study of Public Policy).

—— (1972), *Inequality: A Reassessment of the Effect of Family and Schooling in America* (New York: Basic Books; London: Allen Lane).

Johannson, Per-Olov (1991), *An Introduction to Modern Welfare Economics* (Cambridge and New York: Cambridge University Press).

Johnes, Geraint (1993), *The Economics of Education* (London: Macmillan).

Johnson, Paul, and Falkingham, Jane (1992), *Ageing and Economic Welfare* (London: Sage).

—— and Rake, Katherine (1997), 'The Case of Britain', in *Pension Systems and Reforms—Britain, Hungary, Italy, Poland, Sweden: Final Report* (Budapest: European Commission's PHARE ACE Programme, Research Project P95-2139-R), 25–50.

—— and Stears, Gary (1996), 'Should the Basic State Pension be a Contributory Benefit?', *Fiscal Studies*, 17/1: 105–12.

Jones, Andrew M., and Posnett, John W. (1993), 'The Economics of Charity', in Barr and Whynes (1993), 130–52.

Jones-Lee, M. (1976), *The Value of Life: An Economic Assessment* (Oxford: Martin Robertson).

Kaim-Caudle, P. (1973), *Comparative Social Policy and Social Security: A Ten-Country Study* (Oxford: Martin Robertson).

Kaldor, Nicholas (1955), *An Expenditure Tax* (London: Allen & Unwin).

Kamerman, Sheila B., and Kahn, Alfred J. (1997), 'Investing in Children: Government Expenditures for Children and their Families in Western Industrialized Countries', in Giovanni Andrea Cornia and Sheldon Danziger (eds.), *Child Poverty and Deprivation in the Industrialized Countries 1945–95* (New York and Oxford: Oxford University Press), 91–121.

Karoly, Lynn A., and Burtless, Gary (1995), 'Demographic Change, Rising Earnings Inequality and the Distribution of Personal Well Being, 1959–89', *Demography*, 32/3: 379–405.

References

Katznelson, Ira (1978), 'Considerations on Social Democracy in the United States', *Comparative Politics*, 11: 77–99.

Kay, John, and King, Mervyn A. (1990), *The British Tax System* (5th edn., Oxford: Oxford University Press).

Keys, Wendy, Harris, Sue, and Fernandes, Cres (1996), *Third International Mathematics and Science Study* (Slough: National Foundation for Educational Research).

King, Mervyn A. (1980), 'An Econometric Model of Tenure Choice and Demand for Housing as a Joint Decision', *Journal of Public Economics*, 14/2 (Oct.), 137–59.

—— (1983), 'An Index of Inequality: With Applications to Horizontal Equity and Social Mobility', *Econometrica*, 51: 99–115.

King's Fund London Commission (1997), *Transforming Health in London* (London: King's Fund Institute).

Klein, Rudolf (1984), 'Privatisation and the Welfare State', *Lloyds Bank Review*, 151 (Jan.), 12–29.

Kneen, Pat, and Travers, Tony (1994), *Implementing the Council Tax* (York: Joseph Rowntree Foundation).

Knight, B. (1983), 'Accounting for Educational Priorities', *Public Money*, 3/3 (Dec.), 37–40.

Kogan, M., and Kogan, D. (1983), *The Attack on Higher Education* (London: Kogan Page).

Kotlikoff, Laurence J. (1989*a*), 'On the Contribution of Economics to the Evaluation and Formation of Social Insurance Policy', *American Economic Review*, 79/2 (May), 184–90.

—— (1989*b*), *What Determines Savings?* (Cambridge, Mass.: MIT Press).

Lachman, Desmond, Bennett, Adam, Green, John H., Hagemann, Robert, and Ramaswamy, Ramana (1995), *Challenges to the Swedish Welfare State* (Occasional Paper 130; Washington: The International Monetary Fund).

Lansley, Stewart (1982), *Housing Policy: New Policies for Labour* (London: Labour Housing Group).

Laporte, Bruno, and Schweitzer, Julian (1994), 'Education and Training', in Barr (1994*c*), 260–87.

Laski, Harold (1967), *A Grammar of Politics* (5th edn., London: Allen & Unwin).

Layard, Richard, Nickell, Stephen, and Jackman, Richard (1991), Unemployment (Oxford: Oxford University Press).

Lazear, Edward (1986*a*), 'Retirement from the Labor Force', in Ashenfelter and Layard (1986), i. 305–55.

—— (1986*b*), 'Incentive Effects of Pensions', in David A. Wise (ed.), *Pensions, Labor and Individual Behavior* (Chicago: University of Chicago Press).

Le Grand, Julian (1982), *The Strategy of Equality* (London: George Allen & Unwin).

—— (1984), 'Equity as an Economic Objective', *Journal of Applied Philosophy*, 1/1: 39–51.

—— (1987*a*), 'Inequalities in Health: Some International Comparisons', *European Economic Review*, 31: 182–91.

—— (1987*b*), 'The Middle-Class Use of the British Social Services', in Goodin and Le Grand (1987), 91–107.

—— (1987*c*), 'Measuring the Distributional Impact of the Welfare State: Methodological Issues', in Goodin and Le Grand (1987), 17–33.

—— (1989*a*), 'An International Comparison of Distribution of Ages-at-Death', in J. Fox (ed.), *Health Inequalities in European Countries* (London: Gower), 75–91.

—— (1989*b*), 'Markets, Welfare and Equality', in Le Grand and Estrin (1989), 193–211.

—— (1990), 'The State of Welfare', in Hills (1990), 338–62.

—— (1991*a*), *Equity and Choice: An Essay in Applied Philosophy* (London and New York: HarperCollins).

—— (1991*b*), 'Equity in the Distribution of UK National Health Service Resources', *Journal of Health Economics*, 10/1 (May), 1–9.

—— (1992), 'The Distribution of the Health Care Revisited', *Journal of Health Economics*, 10: 239–45.

—— (1995), 'The Strategy of Equality Revisited: Reply', *Journal of Social Policy*, 24/2: 187–91.

—— (1996), 'Equity, Efficiency and Rationing of Health Care' in Culyer and Wagstaff (1996), 150–63.

—— and Bartlett, Will (1993) (eds.), *Quasi-Markets and Social Policy* (London: Macmillan).

—— and Estrin, Saul (1989) (eds.), *Market Socialism* (Oxford: Oxford University Press).

—— and Robinson, Ray (1984) (eds.), *Privatisation and the Welfare State* (London: George Allen & Unwin).

—— and Vizard, Polly (1998), 'The National Health Service: Crisis, Change or Continuity?', in Glennerster and Hills (1998), 75–121.

—— Dixon, Jennifer, and Mays, Nicholas (eds.) (forthcoming), *The NHS Internal Market: A Review of the Evidence* (London: King's Fund Institute).

—— Propper, Carol, and Robinson, Ray (1992), *The Economics of Social Problems* (3rd edn., London: Macmillan).

Lees, Dennis S. (1961), *Health through Choice* (London: Institute of Economic Affairs).

Leimer, Dean R., and Lesnoy, Selig D. (1982), 'Social Security and Private Saving: New Time-Series Evidence', *Journal of Political Economy*, 90: 606–42.

Letwin, William (1983) (ed.), *Against Equality* (London: Macmillan).

Levy, Frank (1979), 'The Labor Supply of Female Household Heads, or AFDC Work Incentives Don't Work Too Well', *Journal of Human Resources*, 14/1 (Winter), 76–97.

—— (1998), *Dollars and Dreams: The Changing American Income Distribution* (2nd edn., New York: Russell Sage Foundation).

Lindbeck, Assar (1994), *Turning Sweden Round* (Cambridge, Mass.: MIT Press).

—— (1997*a*), 'Incentives and Social Norms in Household Behavior', *American Economic Review*, 87/2 (May), 370–7.

—— (1997*b*), 'The Swedish Experiment', *Journal of Public Literature*, 35 (Sept.), 1273–319.

—— Molander, P., Persson, T., Petersson, O., Sandmo, A., Swedenbord, B., and Thygesen, N. (1993), 'Options for Economic and Political Reform in Sweden', *Economic Policy*, 17: 29–64.

Lindsay, Cotton M. (1969), 'Medical Care and the Economics of Sharing', *Economica*, 36: 351–62; repr. in Cooper and Culyer (1973), 75–89.

Lipsey, Richard G., and Lancaster, Kelvin (1956), 'The General Theory of Second-Best', *Review of Economic Studies*, 24/63 (Jan.), 11–32.

Lipton, Michael, and Ravallion, Martin (1995), 'Poverty and Policy' in J. Behrman and T. N. Srinavasan, *Handbook of Development Economics*, iii (Amsterdam: North Holland).

Lomas, G. (1974), *The Inner City* (London: London Voluntary Service Council).

Lorenz, M. C. (1905), 'Methods of Measuring the Concentration of Wealth', *Publications of the American Statistical Association*, 9: 209–16.

Lucas, Robert E. (1987), *Models of Business Cycles* (Oxford: Basil Blackwell).

McArthur, William, Ramsay, Cynthia, and Walker, Michael (eds.) (1996), *Health Incentives: Canadian Health Reform in an International Context* (Vancouver: The Fraser Institute).

McCreadie, C. (1976), 'Rawlsian Justice and the Financing of the National Health Service', *Journal of Social Policy*, 5/2 (Apr.), 113–30.

References

McDaniel, P. R., and Surrey, S. S. (1984), *International Aspects of Tax Expenditures: A Comparative Study* (Deventer: Kluwer).

McDonagh, O. (1960), 'The Nineteenth Century Revolution in Government: A Reappraisal Reappraised', *Historical Journal*, 2.

McGuire, Alistair (1994), 'Is There Adequate Funding of Health Care?', in Culyer and Wagstaff (1996), 134–49.

Mackenzie, G. A., Gerson, Philip, and Cuevas, Alfredo (1997), *Pension Regimes and Saving* (Occasional Paper 153; Washington: International Monetary Fund).

McLachlan, Gordon, and Maynard, Alan K. (1982) (eds.), *The Public/Private Mix for Health* (London: The Nuffield Provincial Hospitals Trust).

Maclennan, Duncan, and Gibb, Kenneth (1993), 'Political Economy, Applied Welfare Economics and Housing in the UK', in Barr and Whynes (1993), 200–24.

Maki, D. R., and Spindler, Z. A. (1975), 'The Effect of Unemployment Compensation on the Rate of Unemployment in Great Britain', *Oxford Economic Papers*, 27: 440–54.

Malcolm, L., and Barnett, P. (1994), 'New Zealand's Health Providers in an Emerging Market', *Health Policy*, 29: 85–90.

Malpass, P., and Means, R. (1993) (eds.), *Implementing Housing Policy* (Buckingham: Open University Press).

Mandel, E. (1976), 'Introduction' to Karl Marx, *Capital*, i (London: Penguin).

Manning, Willard G., Newhouse, Joseph P., Duan, Naihua, Keeler, Emmett B., Liebowitz, Arleen, and Marquis, Susan M. (1987), 'Health Insurance and the Demand for Medical Care: Evidence from a Randomized Experiment', *American Economic Review*, 77/3 (June), 251–77.

Marmor, Theodore, Mashaw, Jerry, and Harvey, Philip (1990), *America's Misunderstood Welfare State: Persistent Myths, Enduring Realities* (London: HarperCollins: New York: Basic Books).

Marmot, M. G., Davey Smith, G., Stanseld, S., Patel, C., North, F., Head, J., White, I., Brunner, E., and Feeney, A. (1991), 'Health Inequalities among British Civil Servants: The Whitehall II Study', *The Lancet*, 8 June, 337, pp. 1387–93.

Marsh, D. (1980), *The Welfare State* (2nd edn., London: Longman).

Marshall, Thomas H. (1975), *Social Policy in the Twentieth Century* (4th edn., London: Hutchinson).

Maynard, Alan K. (1975), *Experiment with Choice in Education* (London: Institute of Economic Affairs).

—— (1986), 'Performance Incentives in General Practice', in *Health Education and General Practice* (London: Office of Health Economics).

—— and Bloor, Karen (1996), 'Introducing a Market to the United Kingdom's National Health Service', *New England Journal of Medicine*, 334/9, 29 February, pp. 604–8.

Meade, James E. (1952), 'External Economies and Diseconomies in a Competitive Situation', *Economic Journal*, 62: 54–67.

—— (1972), 'Poverty in the Welfare State', *Oxford Economic Papers*, 24: 289–326.

—— (1978), *The Structure and Reform of Direct Taxation* (London: Institution for Fiscal Studies and George Allen & Unwin).

Megginson, William, Nash, Robert C., and van Randenborgh, Matthias (1994), 'The Financial and Operating Performance of Newly Privatized Firms: An International Empirical Analysis,' *Journal of Finance*, 49/2: 403–52.

Menscher, S. (1967), *Poor Law to Poverty Program* (Pittsburgh: University of Pittsburgh Press).

Merrett, Stephen (1979), *State Housing in Britain* (London: Routledge & Kegan Paul).

Mesa-Lego, Carmelo (1990), *Economic and Financial Aspects of Social Security in Latin America and the Caribbean: Tendencies, Problems and Alternatives for the Year 2000* (World Bank, Latin American and the Caribbean Region, Technical Department, Human Resources Division, Report No. IDP-095; Washington).

Milanovic, Branko (1998), *Income, Inequality and Poverty during the Transition from Planned to Market Economy* (Washington: The World Bank).

Miliband, Ralph (1969), *The State in a Capitalist Society* (London: Weidenfeld & Nicolson).

Mill, John Stuart (1863), *Utilitarianism* (London: Parker, Son & Bourn).

Miller, David (1976), *Social Justice* (Oxford: Oxford University).

Mills, C., Jonsson, J. O., and Muller, W. (1996), 'A Half Century of Educational Openness? Social Class, Gender and Educational Achievement in Sweden, Germany and Britain', in R. Erickson and J. O. Jonsson (eds.), *Can Education Be Equalized? The Swedish Case in Comparative Perspective* (Boulder, Colo.: Westview Press).

Minford, Patrick (1984), 'State Expenditure: A Study in Waste', supplement to *Economic Affairs* (London: Institute of Economic Affairs).

Mishra, Ramesh (1981), *Society and Social Policy* (London: Macmillan).

Mitchell, Olivia S., and Fields, Gary S. (1981), 'The Effects of Pensions and Earnings on Retirement: A Review Essay' (Working Paper 772; Cambridge, Mass.: National Bureau of Economic Research).

Moffitt, Robert A. (1983), 'An Economic Model of Welfare Stigma', *American Economic Review*, 73: 1023–35.

—— (1992), 'Incentive Effects of the US Welfare System: A Review', *Journal of Economic Literature*, 30/1 (Mar.), 1–61.

Mooney, Gavin (1992), *Economics, Medicine and Health Care* (2nd edn., Hemel Hempstead: Wheatsheaf Books.

Morris, J. K., Cook, D. G., and Shaper, A. G. (1994), 'Loss of Employment and Mortality', *British Medical Journal*, 308 (6937), 30 April, pp. 1135–9.

Mortensen, Dale T. (1986), 'Job Search and Labor Market Analysis', in Ashenfelter and Layard (1986), ii. 849–919.

Mortimore, P., Sammons, P., Stall, L., Leiris, D., and Ecob, R. (1988), *The Junior School Project: Understanding School Effectiveness* (Research and Statistics Branch; London: Inner London Education Authority).

Mueller, Dennis C. (1989), *Public Choice II* (Cambridge: Cambridge University Press).

—— (1997), *Perspectives on Public Choice* (Cambridge: Cambridge University Press).

Munnell, Alicia, and Yohn, Fredrick (1992), 'What Is the Impact of Pensions on Savings?' in Zvi Bodie and Alicia Munnell (eds.), *Pensions and the Economy: Sources, Uses, and Limitations of Data* (Philadelphia, Pa.: Pension Research Council and University of Pennsylvania Press).

Murphy, J. (1981), 'Class Inequality in Education: Two Justifications, One Evaluation but No Hard Evidence', *British Journal of Sociology*, 32/2 (June) 182–201.

Murray, Charles (1984), *Losing Ground: American Social Policy, 1950–1980* (New York: Basic Books).

—— (1990), *The Emerging British Underclass* (London: Institute of Economics Affairs).

Musgrave, Richard A., and Musgrave, Peggy B. (1989), *Public Finance in Theory and Practice* (5th edn., London and New York: McGraw-Hill).

Muth, R. F. (1960), 'The Demand for Non-Farm Housing', in A. C. Harberger (ed.), *The Demand for Durable Goods* (Chicago: University of Chicago Press).

References

—— and Goodman, Allen C. (1989), *The Economics of Housing Markets* (London and New York: Chur).

Myers, R. J. (1965), *Social Insurance and Allied Government Programs* (New York: Irwin).

Myles, John (1996), 'When Markets Fail: Social Welfare in Canada and the United States', in Esping-Andersen (1996*b*), 116–40.

National Federation of Housing Associations (1985), *Inquiry into British Housing: Report* (London: National Federation of Housing Associations).

National Health Forum (1997), *Canada Health Action: Building on the Legacy*, i, ii: *Synthesis Reports and Issues Paper* (Ottawa: National Health Forum).

Nevitt, Adella A. (1966), *Housing, Taxation and Subsidies* (London: Nelson).

Newfield, Jack (1978), *Robert F. Kennedy: A Memoir* (New York: Berkley Publishing Corporation).

Newhouse, Joseph P. (1993), *Free for All: Lessons from the RAND Health Insurance Experiment* (Cambridge, Mass.: Harvard University Press).

Nichols, Albert L., and Zeckhauser, Richard J. (1982), 'Targeting Transfers through Restrictions on Recipients', *American Economic Review* (Papers and Proceedings), 72: 372–7.

Nisbet, R. (1974), 'The Pursuit of Equality', *The Public Interest*, 35 (Spring), 103–20; repr. in Letwin (1983), 124–47.

Niskanen, William A. (1971), *Bureaucracy and Representative Government* (Chicago: Aldine Atherton).

North, F., Syme, S. L., Feeney, A., *et al.* (1993), 'Explaining Sociological Differences in Sickness Absence: The Whitehall II Study', *British Medical Journal*, 306, 6 Feb., p. 363.

Nozick, Robert (1974), *Anarchy, State and Utopia* (Oxford: Basil Blackwell).

O'Donnell, Owen, and Propper, Carol (1991), 'Equity and the Distribution of UK National Health Service Resources', *Journal of Health Economics*, 10: 1–21.

OECD (1990): Organization for Economic Cooperation and Development, *Health Care Systems in Transition: The Search for Efficiency* (Paris: OECD); also published as US HCFA (1989).

—— (1992), *The Reform of Health Care: A Comparative Analysis of Seven OECD Countries* (Paris: OECD).

—— (1994), *The Reform of Health Care Systems: A Comparative Analysis of Seventeen OECD Countries* (Paris: OECD).

O'Kelly, Rory (1985), 'The Future of Social Security' (Submission by the Fabian Society to the Labour Party's National Executive Committee; London: The Fabian Society).

Okin, S. M. (1989), *Justice, Gender and the Family* (New York: Basic Books).

Okun, Arthur M. (1975), *Equality and Efficiency: The Big Tradeoff* (Washington: The Brookings Institution).

Oppenheim, Carey, and Harker, Lisa (1996), *Poverty: The Facts* (3rd edn., London: Child Poverty Action Group).

Orshansky, Molly (1965), 'Counting the Poor: Another Look at the Poverty Problem', *Social Security Bulletin*, 28: 3–29.

Palmer, J. L., and Pechman, J. A. (1978) (eds.), *Welfare in Rural Areas: The North Carolina–Iowa Income Maintenance Experiment* (Washington: The Brookings Institution).

Parker, Hermione (1989), *Instead of the Dole: An Enquiry into Integration of the Tax and Benefit System* (London: Routledge).

—— (1995), *Taxes, Benefits and Family Life: The Seven Deadly Traps* (Research Monograph 50; London: Institute of Economic Affairs).

Pauly, Mark V. (1974), 'Overinsurance and Public Provision of Insurance: The Roles of Moral Hazard and Adverse Selection', *Quarterly Journal of Economics*, 88: 44–62.

—— (1986), 'Taxation, Health Insurance and Market Failure in the Medical Economy', *Journal of Economic Literature*, 24 (June), 629–75.

Peabody, John W., Bickel, Stephen R., and Lawson, James S. (1996), 'The Australian Health Care System: Are the Incentives Down Under Right Side Up?', *Journal of the American Medical Association*, 276/24 (Dec.), 1946–50.

Peacock, Alan T., and Shannon, Robin (1968), 'The Welfare State and the Redistribution of Income', *Westminster Bank Review* (Aug.), 30–46.

—— and Wiseman, Jack (1967), *The Growth of Public Expenditure in the United Kingdom* (rev. edn., London: George Allen & Unwin).

Pechman, Joseph A. (1980) (ed.), *Setting National Priorities: Agenda for the 1980s* (Washington: The Brookings Institution).

—— (1985), *Who Paid the Taxes, 1966–85* (Washington: The Brookings Institution).

—— and Timpane, P. Michael (1975) (eds.), *Work Incentives and Income Guarantees: The New Jersey Negative Income Tax Experiment* (Washington: The Brookings Institution).

—— Aaron, Henry J., and Taussig, Michael K. (1968), *Social Security: Perspectives for Reform* (Washington: The Brookings Institution).

Pelling, Henry (1979), *Popular Politics and Society in Late Victorian Britain* (2nd edn., London: Macmillan).

Pelzmann, Samuel (1976), 'Towards a More General Theory of Regulation', *Journal of Law and Economics*, 19 (Aug.), 211–40.

Pen, Jan (1971), 'A Parade of Dwarfs (and a Few Giants)', extract from *Income Distribution* (London: Penguin); repr. in Atkinson (1980: 47–55).

Peterson, Wallace C. (1991), *Transfer Spending, Taxes and the American Welfare State* (Boston, Mass.: Kluwer).

Phillips, Anne (1997), 'What has Socialism to do with Sexual Equality?', in Franklin (1997), 101–21.

Phillips, David (1992) (ed.), *Ageing in East and South-East Asia* (Sevenoaks: Edward Arnold).

Phlips, Louis (1988), *The Economics of Imperfect Information* (Cambridge and New York: Cambridge University Press).

Piachaud, David (1981), 'Peter Townsend and the Holy Grail', *New Society*, 10 Sept., pp. 419–21.

—— (1984), 'The Means Test State', *New Socialist* (Oct.), 53–4.

—— (1987), 'Problems in the Definition and Measurement of Poverty', *Journal of Social Policy*, 16/2: 147–64.

—— (1993), 'The Definition and Measurement of Poverty and Inequality', in Barr and Whynes (1993), 105–29.

Piggott, John (1984), 'The Value of Tenant Benefits from UK Council House Subsidies', *Economic Journal*, 94/374 (June), 384–9.

—— and Whalley, John (1985), *UK Tax Policy and Applied General Equilibrium Analysis* (Cambridge: Cambridge University Press).

—— —— (1986) (eds.), *New Developments in Applied General Equilibrium Analysis* (Cambridge: Cambridge University Press).

Pinker, Robert (1979), *The Idea of Welfare* (London: Heinemann).

Podger, Andrew (1997), 'Health Reform in Australia in an International Perspective,' *Canberra Bulletin of Public Administration*, Special Supplement: Health Economics Forum, 83: 20–2.

References

Posner, Richard A. (1975), 'The Social Costs of Monopoly and Regulation', *Journal of Political Economy*, 83 (Aug.), 807–27.

Powell, M. (1995), 'The Strategy of Equality Revisited', *Journal of Social Policy*, 24/2: 163–91.

Power, Anne (1993), *Hovels to High Rise: State Housing in Europe since 1850* (London: Routledge).

—— (1997), *Estates on the Edge: The Social Consequences of Mass Housing in Northern Europe* (London: Macmillan).

Prais, S. G. (1995), *Productivity, Education and Training: An International Perspective* (Cambridge: Cambridge University Press).

Preker, Alexander, and Feachem, Richard G. A. (1994), 'Health and Health Care' in Barr (1994*c*), 288–321.

Prest, Alan R. (1968), 'The Budget and Interpersonal Redistribution', *Public Finance*, 23: 80–98.

—— (1973), 'Proposals for a Tax-Credit System', *British Tax Review*, 1: 6–16.

—— (1983), 'The Social Security Reform Minefield', *British Tax Review*, 1: 44–53.

—— (1985), 'Implicit Taxes: Are We Taxed More than We Think?' *Royal Bank of Scotland Review*, 147 (Sept.), 10–26.

—— and Barr, Nicholas A. (1985), *Public Finance in Theory and Practice* (7th edn., London: Weidenfeld & Nicolson).

Propper, Carol (1995*a*), 'For Richer, for Poorer, in Sickness and in Health: The Lifetime Distribution of NHS Health Care', in Falkingham and Hills (1995*b*), 184–203.

—— (1995*b*), 'Agency and Incentives in the NHS Internal Market', *Social Science and Medicine*, 40: 1683–90.

—— (1995*c*), 'Regulatory Reform of the NHS Internal Market', *Health Economics*, 4: 77–83.

—— (1996), 'Market Structure and Prices: The Responses of Hospitals in the UK National Health Service to Competition', *Journal of Public Economics*, 61: 307–35.

—— and Upward, Richard (1992), 'Need, Equity and the NHS: The Distribution of Health Care Expenditure 1974–87', *Fiscal Studies*, 13/7 (May), 1–21.

Psacharopoulos, George (1973), *Returns to Education: An International Comparison* (Amsterdam: Elsevier).

—— (1980), *Education and Income* (World Bank Staff Working Paper No. 402; Washington: The World Bank).

—— (1984), 'The Contribution of Education to Economic Growth: International Comparisons', in J. Kendrick (ed.), *International Productivity Comparisons and the Causes of the Slowdown* (Cambridge, Mass.: Ballinger).

—— and Woodhall, Maureen (1985), *Education for Development: An Analysis of Investment Choices* (Oxford: Oxford University Press).

Quah, D. (1996), *The Invisible Hand and the Weightless Economy* (Occasional Paper No. 12; London: London School of Economics, Centre for Economic Performance, May).

Radford, R. A. (1945), 'The Economic Organisation of a POW Camp', *Economica*, NS 12/48 (Nov.), 189–201.

Raphael, Jody (1996), *Prisoners of Abuse: Domestic Violence and Welfare Receipt* (Chicago: Taylor Institute).

Ravallion, Martin (1991), 'Reaching the Rural Poor through Public Employment: Arguments, Evidence and Lessons from South Asia', *World Bank Research Observer*, 6/12 (July), 153–75.

—— (1996), 'Issues in Measuring and Modeling Poverty', *Economic Journal*, 106 (Sept.), 1328–44.

—— and Datt, Gaurav (1995), 'Is Targeting through a Work Requirement Effective?', in van de Walle and Nead (1995), 413–44.

—— van de Walle, Dominique, and Gautam, Madhur (1995), 'Testing a Social Safety Net', *Journal of Public Economics*, 57/2 (June), 175–99.

Rawls, John (1972), *A Theory of Justice* (Oxford: Oxford University Press).

Rees, Ray (1989), 'Uncertainty, Information and Insurance' in Hey (1989), 47–78.

Ricardo, David (1817), *On the Principles of Political Economy and Taxation* (London: Murray).

Rimlinger, G. (1971), *Welfare Policy and Industrialisation in Europe, America and Russia* (New York: Wiley).

Robbins, Lionel C. (1977), *Political Economy Past and Present: A Review of Leading Theories of Economic Policy* (London: Macmillan).

—— (1978), *The Theory of Economic Policy in English Classical Political Economy* (2nd edn., London: Macmillan).

Robinson, Peter (1997), *Literacy, Numeracy and Economic Performance* (London: London School of Economics, Centre for Economic Performance).

Robinson, Ray (1979), *Housing Economics and Public Policy* (London: Macmillan).

—— and Le Grand, Julian (1994) (eds.), *Evaluating the NHS Reforms* (London: King's Fund Institute).

Robson, Mark (1995), 'Taxation and Household Saving: Reflections on the OECD Report', *Fiscal Studies*, 16/1 (Feb.), 38–57.

Robson, William A. (1976), *Welfare State and Welfare Society* (London: George Allen & Unwin).

Romer, Paul (1993), 'Ideal Gaps and Object Gaps in Economic Development', *Journal of Monetary Economics*, 32: 338–69.

Rosa, Jean-Jacques (1982) (ed.), *The World Crisis in Social Security* (Paris: Fondation Nationale d'Économie Politique; San Francisco: Institute for Contemporary Studies).

Rose, M.E. (1972), *The Relief of Poverty 1834–1914* (London: Macmillan).

Rosenthal, L. (1975), 'The Nature of Council House Subsidies', Ph.D. thesis (University of Essex).

—— (1977), 'The Regional and Income Distribution of Council House Subsidy in the United Kingdom', *The Manchester School*, 45: 127–40.

Rothschild, Michael, and Stiglitz, Joseph E. (1976), 'Equilibrium in Competitive Insurance Markets: An Essay on the Economics of Imperfect Information', *Quarterly Journal of Economics*, 90: 629–49.

Rowntree, B. Seebohm (1901), *Poverty: A Study of Town Life* (London: Longman).

—— (1941), *Poverty and Progress: A Second Social Survey of York* (London: Longman).

—— and Lavers, G. R. (1951), *Poverty and the Welfare State* (London: Longman).

Rowntree Foundation (1995), *Inquiry into Income and Wealth* (York: The Joseph Rowntree Foundation).

Russell, Louise B. (1989), *Medicare's New Hospital Payment System: Is It Working?* (Washington: The Brookings Institution).

Rutter, M., Maughan, B., Mortimore, P., and Ouston, J. (1979), *Fifteen Thousand Hours: Secondary Schools and their Effects on Children* (London: Open Books).

Sainsbury, Diane (1994) (ed.), *Gendering Welfare States* (London: Sage).

Saltman, R., and von Otter, C. (1995) (eds.), *Implementing Planned Markets in Health Care* (Milton Keynes: Open University Press).

Sammons, P. (1995), 'Gender, Ethnic and Socio-Economic Differences in Attainment Progress: A Longitudinal Analysis of Student Achievement over Nine Years', *British Educational Research Journal*, 21/4: 465–85.

References

Samuelson, Paul A. (1954), 'The Pure Theory of Public Expenditures', *Review of Economics and Statistics*, 36/4 (Nov.), 387–9.

—— (1958), 'An Exact Consumption-Loan Model of Interest with or without the Social Contrivance of Money', *Journal of Political Economy*, 66/6 (Dec.), 467–82.

Saunders, Peter (1995), 'Improving Work Incentives in a Means-Tested Welfare System: The 1994 Australia Social Security Reforms', *Fiscal Studies*, 16/2: 45–70.

Sawhill, Isabel V. (1988), 'Poverty in the US: Why Is It So Persistent?', *Journal of Economic Literature*, 26: 1073–119.

Scheffler, Richard, and Waitzman, Norman (forthcoming), *The Health Workforce of the Future* (Berkeley and Los Angeles: University of California Press).

—— Sullivan, Sean D., and Ko, Timothy Hauchung (1991), 'The Impact of Blue Cross and Blue Shield Plan Utilization Management Programs, 1980–1988', *Inquiry*, 28: 263–75.

Schieber, George J., Poullier, Jean-Pierre, and Greenwald, Leslie M. (1991), 'Health Care Systems in Twenty-Four Countries', *Health Affairs*, 10/3: 22–38.

Schottland, C. I. (1963), *The Social Security Program in the United States* (New York: Appleton-Century-Crofts).

Seldon, Arthur (1981), *Wither the Welfare State* (London: Institute of Economic Affairs).

Sen, Amartya K. (1970), 'The Impossibility of a Paretian Liberal', *Journal of Political Economy*, 78/1 (Jan.–Feb.), 152–7.

—— (1973), *On Economic Inequality* (Oxford: Oxford University Press).

—— (1976), 'Poverty: An Ordinal Approach to Measurement', *Econometrica*, 46: 437–46.

—— (1982), *Choice, Welfare and Measurement* (Oxford: Oxford University Press).

—— (1983), 'Poor, Relatively Speaking', *Oxford Economic Papers*, 35: 153–69.

—— (1985), *Commodities and Capabilities* (Amsterdam: North Holland).

—— (1987), *The Standard of Living* (Cambridge: Cambridge University Press).

—— (1992), *Inequality Reexamined* (Oxford: Oxford University Press).

—— (1995*a*), *Mortality as an Indicator of Economic Success and Failure* (Innocenti Lectures; Florence: UNICEF).

—— (1995*b*), 'The Political Economy of Targeting', in van de Walle and Nead (1995), 11–24.

—— and Williams, Bernard (1982) (eds.), *Utilitarianism and Beyond* (Cambridge: Cambridge University Press).

Shankland, G., Willmott, P., and Jordan, D. (1977), *Inner London: Policies for Dispersal and Balance* (Department of the Environment, London: HMSO).

Shapiro, Judith (1993), 'The Russian Mortality Crisis and Its Causes', in Anders Aslund (ed.), *Russian Economic Reform at Risk* (London and New York: Pinter).

Shorrocks, A. F. (1983), 'Ranking Income Distributions', *Economica*, 50/197 (Feb.), 3–17.

Simons, Herbert (1938), *Personal Income Taxation* (Chicago: University of Chicago Press).

Sipos, Sándor (1994), 'Income Transfers: Family Support and Poverty Relief', in Barr (1994*c*), 226–59.

Smaje, Chris, and Le Grand, Julian (1997), 'Ethnicity, Equity and the Use of Health Services in the British National Health Service', *Social Science and Medicine*, 45/3: 485–96.

Smeeding, Timothy (1997), *Financial Poverty in Developed Countries: The Evidence from LIS. Final Report to the UNDP* (Working Paper No. 155; Luxembourg: Luxembourg Income Study).

—— O'Higgins, Michael, and Rainwater, Lee (1990) (eds.), *Poverty, Inequality and Income Distribution in Comparative Perspective: The Luxembourg Income Study* (Washington: The Urban Institute; Hemel Hempstead: Harvester Wheatsheaf).

Smith, Adam (1776), *An Inquiry into the Nature and Causes of the Wealth of Nations* (repr. Oxford: Oxford University Press, 1976).

Smith, L., Rosen, C., and Fallis, G. (1988), 'Recent Developments in Economic Models of Housing Markets', *Journal of Economic Literature*, 26: 29–44.

Smith, Stephen (1992), 'Taxation and the Environment: A Survey', *Fiscal Studies*, 13/4 (Nov.), 21–57.

Solow, Robert M. (1994), 'Perspectives on Growth Theory', *Journal of Economic Perspectives*, 8: 45–54.

Spencer, Herbert (1884), *The Man versus the State* (New York: Appleton).

Steel, D., and Heald, D. (1984) (eds.), *Privatizing Public Enterprises* (London: Royal Institute of Public Administration).

Stephens, John D. (1996), 'The Scandinavian Welfare State: Achievements, Crisis and Prospects', in Esping-Andersen (1996*b*), 32–65.

Stevens, J. (1993), *The Economics of Collective Choice* (Boulder, Colo.: Westview).

Stevens, R. B. (1970) (ed.), *Statutory History of the United States: Income Security* (New York: McGraw-Hill).

Stigler, George (1971), 'The Theory of Economic Regulation', *Bell Journal of Economics and Management Science*, 2 (Spring), 137–46.

Stiglitz, Joseph E. (1975), 'The Theory of Screening, Education and the Distribution of Income', *American Economic Review*, 65: 283–300.

—— (1983), 'Risk, Incentives and Insurance: The Pure Theory of Moral Hazard', *Geneva Papers on Risk and Insurance*, 8/26: 4–33.

—— (1987), 'The Causes and Consequences of the Dependence of Quality on Price', *Journal of Economic Literature*, 25/1: 1–48.

—— (1988), *The Economics of the Public Sector* (2nd edn., New York and London: Norton).

—— (1989), 'The Economic Role of the State' in Arnold Heertje (ed.), *The Economic Role of the State* (Oxford: Basil Blackwell).

—— (1993*a*), *Information and Economic Analysis* (Oxford: Oxford University Press).

—— (1993*b*), *Economics* (2nd edn., New York: Norton; see also http://www.wwnorton.com/college/econ/stec2.htm).

—— (1997), 'Reflections on the Natural Rate Hypothesis', *Journal of Economic Perspectives*, 11/1: 3–10.

Stock, James H., and Wise, David A. (1988), 'The Pension Inducement to Retire: An Option Value Analysis' (Working Paper No. 2660; Cambridge, Mass.: National Bureau of Economic Research).

Strachey, John (1936), *The Theory and Practice of Socialism* (London: Gollancz).

Sugden, Robert (1982), 'On the Economics of Philanthropy', *Economic Journal*, 92/366 (June), 341–50.

—— (1983*a*), 'On the Economics of Philanthropy: Reply', *Economic Journal*, 93/371 (Sept.), 639.

—— (1983*b*), *Who Care? An Economic and Ethical Analysis of Private Charity and the Welfare State* (Occasional Paper 67; London: Institute of Economic Affairs).

—— (1984), 'Reciprocity: The Supply of Public Goods through Voluntary Contributions', *Economic Journal*, 94/376 (Dec.), 772–87.

Summers, Lawrence H. (1989), 'Some Simple Economics of Mandated Benefits', *American Economic Review*, 79/2 (May), 177–83.

References

Surrey, S. S., and McDaniel, R. R. (1985), *Tax Expenditures* (Cambridge, Mass.: Harvard University Press).

Sutherland, Holly (1997), 'Women, Men and the Redistribution of Income', *Fiscal Studies*, 18/1: 1–22.

Sweezy, Paul (1942), *The Theory of Capitalist Developement* (London: Dennis Dobson).

Swenarton, Mark (1981), *Homes Fit for Heroes: The Politics and Architecture of Early State Housing in Britain* (London: Heinemann).

Tawney, R. H. (1953), *The Attack and Other Paper* (London: Allen & Unwin).

—— (1964), *Equality* (4th edn., London: George Allen & Unwin).

Taylor, Alan J. (1972), *Laissez-faire and State Intervention in Nineteenth-Century Britain* (London: Macmillian).

Thane, Pat (1982), *The Foundations of the Welfare State* (London: Longman).

Theil, Henri (1967), *Economic and Information Theory* (Amsterdam: North Holland).

Thornley, Andy (1993), *Urban Planning under Thatcherism: The Challenge of the Market* (2nd edn., London: Routledge).

Thurow, Lester C. (1971), 'The Income Distribution as a Pure Public Good', *Quarterly Journal of Economics* (May), 327–36.

Tiebout, Charles (1956), 'A Pure Theory of Local Expenditure', *Journal of Political Economy* (Oct.), 416–24.

Timmins, Nicholas (1996), *The Five Giants: A Biography of the Welfare State* (London: Fontana).

Titmuss, Richard M. (1958), *Essays on 'The Welfare State'* (London: Allen & Unwin; 3rd edn., 1976).

—— (1968), *Commitment to Welfare* (London: Allen & Unwin; 2nd edn., 1976).

—— (1970), *The Gift Relationship* (London: Penguin).

Tobin, James (1968), 'Raising the Incomes of the Poor', in K. Gordon (ed.), *Agenda for the Nation* (Washington: The Brookings Institution).

—— Pechman, J., and Mieszkowski, P. (1967), 'Is a Negative Income Tax Practical?', *Yale Law Journal*, 77: 1–27.

Tolley (1996), *Social Security and State Benefits Handbook, 1996–97*, ed. Jim, Matthewman *et al.* (Croydon: Tolley Publishing Company).

Townsend, Peter (1979), *Poverty in the United Kingdom* (London: Penguin).

—— and Davidson, N. (1982), *Inequalities in Health* (London: Penguin).

Tullock, Gordon (1970), *Private Wants, Public Means* (New York: Basic Books).

—— (1971), 'The Charity of the Uncharitable', *Western Economic Journal*, 9: 379–92; repr. in Letwin (1983: 328–44).

—— (1976), *The Vote Motive* (Hobart Paperback No. 9; London: Institute of Economic Affairs).

—— (1987), 'Public Choice', in J. Eatwell, M. Milgate, and P. Newman (eds.), *The New Palgrave, A Dictionary of Economics* (London: Macmillan).

UK Board of Education (1943), *Educational Reconstruction*, Cmd 6458 (London: HMSO).

UK Board of Inland Revenue (1983), *Cost of Tax Reliefs for Pensions Schemes: Appropriate Statistical Approach* (London: HMSO).

UK Commitee of Vice-Chancellors and Principals (1996), *Our Universities, Our Future: Part 4: The Case for a New Funding System—Special Report* (The CVCP's evidence to the National Committee of Inquiry into Higher Education; London: Committee of Vice-Chancellors and Principals).

UK Committee on Higher Education (1963), *Higher Education* (The Robbins Report), Cmnd 2154 (London: HMSO).

UK Department of Education (1960), *Grants for Students* (The Anderson Report), Report of the Committee Appointed by the Minister of Education and the Secretary of State for Scotland, Cmnd 1051 (London: HMSO).

—— (1966), *A Plan for Polytechnics and Other Colleges* (London: HMSO).

—— (1977), *A New Partnership for our Schools* (London: HMSO).

UK Department of Labour (1944), *Employment Policy*, Cmd 6527 (London: HMSO).

UK DES (1986): UK Department of Education and Science (1986), *Report by Her Majesty's Inspectors on the Effects of Local Authority Expenditure Policies on Education Provision in England, 1985* (London: HMSO).

—— (1988), *Top-Up Loans for Students*, Cm 520 (London: HMSO).

—— (1991), *Higher Education: A New Framework*, Cm 1541 (London: HMSO).

UK DfEE (1997a): UK Department for Education and Employment, *The Government's Expenditure Plans 1997–98 to 1999–2000: Departmental Report, Department for Education and Employment*, Cm 3610 (London: HMSO).

—— (1997b), *Excellence in Schools*, Cm 3681 (London: HMSO).

—— (1998a), *The Learning Age: A Rennaissance of a New Britain*, Cm 3790 (London: HMSO).

—— (1998b), *Higher Education for the 21st Century: Response to the Dearing Report* (London: HMSO).

—— (1998c), *Further Education for the New Millennium: Response to the Kennedy Report* (London: HMSO).

UK DHSS (1974): UK Department of Health and Social Security, *Better Pensions Fully Protected Against Inflation*, Cmnd 5713 (London: HMSO).

—— (1976), *Sharing Resources for Health in England: Report of the Joint Resource Allocation Working Party* (London: HMSO).

—— (1985a), *Reform of Social Security*, Cmnd 9517 (London: HMSO).

—— (1985b), *Reform of Social Security: Background Papers*, Cmnd 9519 (London: HMSO).

—— (1985c), *Reform of Social Security: Programme for Action*, Cmnd 9691 (London: HMSO).

UK DoE (1971): UK Department of the Environment, *Fair Deal for Housing*, Cmnd 4728 (London: HMSO).

—— (1977a), *Housing Policy: A Consultative Document*, Cmnd 6851 (London: HMSO).

—— (1977b), *Housing Policy: Technical Volume, Part I* (London: HMSO).

—— (1997), *The Government's Expenditure Plans 1997–98 to 1999–2000: Annual Report 1997, Department of the Environment*, Cm 3607 (London: HMSO).

UK DoH (1944): UK Department of Health, *A National Health Service*, Cmd 6502 (London: HMSO).

—— (1989), *Working for Patients*, Cm 555 (London: HMSO).

—— (1997), *The Government's Expenditure Plans 1997–98 to 1999–2000: Departmental Report, Department of Health*, Cm 3612 (London: HMSO).

UK DSS (1993): UK Department of Social Security (1993), *Containing the Costs of Social Security—the International Context*, London: HMSO.

—— (1995a), *The Abstract of Statistics for Social Security Benefits and Contributions and Indices of Prices and Earnings, 1995 Edition* (Department of Social Security, Analytical Services Division, Newcastle).

—— (1995b), *Tax Benefit Model Tables* (Department of Social Security, Analytical Services Division; London: HMSO).

References

—— (1997), *The Government's Expenditure Plans 1997–98 to 1999–2000: Social Security Departmental Report*, Cm 3613 (London: HMSO).

UK Further Education Funding Council (1997), *Learning Works: Widening Participation in Further Education* (the Kennedy Report) (Coventry: Further Education Funding Council).

UK Government (1944), *Social Insurance*, Pt. I, Cmd 6550, and Pt. II (Workmen's Compensation), Cmd 6551 (London: HMSO).

UK Government Actuary's Department (1978), *The Financing of Occupational Pension Schemes*, Evidence of the Government Actuary's Department to the Committee to Review the Functioning of Financial Institutions (London: HMSO).

UK House of Commons Education and Employment Committee (1997), *3rd Report: The Operation of the Nursery Education Voucher Scheme*, Session 1996–97, HC-25 (London: HMSO).

UK House of Commons Social Services Committee (1988), *Fifth Report: The Future of the National Health Service*, Session 1987–88, HC 613 (London: HMSO).

UK National Audit Office (1994), *General Practitioner Fundholding in England* (London: HMSO).

UK National Commission on Education (1993), *Learning to Succeed: A Radical Look at Education Today and a Strategy for the Future*, Report of the Paul Hamlin Foundation National Commission on Education (London: Heinemann).

UK NCIHE (1997*a*) UK National Committee of Inquiry into Higher Education (the Dearing Committee), *Higher Education in the Learning Society: Summary Report* (London: HMSO).

—— (1997*b*), *Higher Education in the Learning Society: Report of the National Committee* (London: HMSO).

—— (1997*c*), *Higher Education in the Learning Society: Appendix 5: Higher Education in Other Countries*, London: HMSO.

—— (1997*d*), *Report 7: Rates of Return to Higher Education* (London: HMSO).

UK Office of Fair Trading (1997), *Report of the Director General's Inquiry into Pensions* (London: HMSO).

UK Office for National Statistics (1996), *Social Trends 1996* (London: HMSO).

—— (1997), *Economic Trends*, No. 520, March (London: HMSO).

UK Pension Law Review Committee (1993), *Pension Law Reform*, Report of the Pension Law Review Committee, Vol. I *Report*, and Vol. II *Research* (London: HMSO).

UK Royal Commission on the Distribution of Income and Wealth (1979), *Report No. 7: Fourth Report on the Standing Reference*, Cmnd 7595 (London: HMSO).

UK Royal Commission on the Housing of the Working Class (1885), *Report* (London: HMSO).

UK Select Committee on a Wealth Tax (1975), *Minutes of Evidence*, Volume II, Session 1974–75, HC 696-II (London: HMSO).

UK Select Committee on Tax Credit (1973), *Report and Proceedings*, Session 1972–73, HC 341-I, 341-II, 341-III (London: HMSO).

UK Student Loans Company (1996), *Annual Report 1996*, Glasgow: Student Loans Company.

UK Treasury (1996), *Financial Statement and Budget Report 1997–98* (London: HMSO).

—— (1997), *Public Expenditure: Statistical Analyses 1997–98*, Cm 3601 (London: HMSO).

UK Treasury and Civil Service Committee (1983*a*), *The Structure of Personal Income Taxation and Income Support*, Third Special Report, Session 1982–83, HC 386 (London: HMSO).

—— (1983*b*), *The Structure of Personal Income Taxation and Income Support, Minutes of Evidence*, Treasury and Civil Service Committee Sub-Committee, Session 1982–83, HC 20-I (London: HMSO).

UK Treasury and Department of Health and Social Security (1972), *Proposals for a Tax-Credit System*, Cmnd 5116 (London: HMSO).

US Advisory Council on Social Security (1938), *Final Report*, S. Doc. 4, 76 Cong. 1 sess. (1939).

US Department of Health and Human Services (1997), *Social Security Programs Throughout the World 1997*, Research Report No. 65 (Washington, DC: US Social Security Administration: Office of Research and Statistics; also available at http://www.ssa.gov/statistics/ssptw97.html).

US Federal Emergency Relief Administration (1942), *Final Statistical Report of the Federal Emergency Relief Administration* (Washington: US Government Printing Office).

US HCFA (1989), *Health Care Financing Review* (Annual Supplement, Office of Research and Demonstrations, Health Care Financing Administration, Washington, DC: Government Printing Office, December); also published as OECD (1990).

US National Resources and Planning Board (1942), *Long Range Work and Relief Policies: Report of the Committee on Long Range Work and Relief to the National Resources Planning Board* (Washington: US Government Printing Office).

US Panel on Poverty and Public Assistance (1995), *Measuring Poverty: A New Approach* (Washington: National Academy Press).

US President's Commission on Income Maintenance Programs (1969), *Poverty Amid Plenty: The American Paradox*, Report of the President's Commission on Income Maintenance Programs (Washington: US Government Printing Office).

US Supreme Court (1978), *City of Los Angeles, Department of Water and Power et al. v. Manhart et al.*, Case No. 76-1810.

Van de Walle, Dominique, and Nead, Kimberly (1995) (eds.), *Public Spending and the Poor: Theory and Evidence* (Washington and London: Johns Hopkins University Press).

Varian, Hal R. (1992), *Microeconomic Analysis* (3rd edn., New York: Norton).

Varian, Hal R. (1996), *Intermediate Microeconomics: A Modern Approach* (4th edn., New York: Norton).

Venti, S. F., and Wise, D. A. (1984), 'Moving and Housing Expenditure: Transactions Costs and Disequilibrium', *Journal of Public Economics*, 23/1–2 (Feb.–Mar.), 207–43.

—— (1990), 'Have IRAs Increased US Saving? Evidence from Consumer Expenditure Surveys', *Quarterly Journal of Economics*, 105/3: 661–98.

Vickers, J., and Yarrow, G. (1988), *Privatization: An Economic Analysis* (London and Cambridge: Mass.: MIT Press).

Wagstaff, Adam (1991), 'QALYS and the Equity-Efficiency Tradeoff', *Journal of Health Economics*, 10: 21–43.

—— and van Doorslaer, Eddy (1992), 'Equity in the Finance of Health Care: Some International Comparisons', *Journal of Health Economics*, 11/4, (Dec.), 361–87.

Walker, Alan, and Walker, Carol (1997) (eds.), *Britain Divided: The Growth of Social Exclusion in the 1980s and 1990s* (London: Child Poverty Action Group).

Warlick, Jennifer L. (1981), 'Participation of the Aged in SSI', *Journal of Human Resources*, 17: 236–60.

Watts, Harold W., and Rees, Albert (1977) (eds.), *The New Jersey Income Maintenance Experiment, ii, Labor Supply Responses* (New York and London: Academic Press).

Weale, Albert (1978), *Equality and Social Policy* (London: Routledge & Kegan Paul).

Weaver, Caroline L. (1982), *The Crisis in Social Security: Economic and Political Origins* (Durham, NC: Duke University Press).

Webb, M. (1984), 'Privatisation of the Electricity and Gas Industries', in Steel and Heald (1984), 87–100.

References

Webb, Sidney, and Webb, Beatrice (1909), *The Break Up of the Poor Law*, Minority Report of the Poor Law Commission, Part I (London: Longman).

Weisbrod, Burton A. (1969), 'Collective Action and the Distribution of Income: A Conceptual Approach', in Joint Economic Committee, *The Analysis and Evaluation of Public Expenditures* (Washington: US Government Printing Office).

—— (1983), 'Competition in Health Care: A Cautionary View', in Jack Meyer (ed.), *Market Reforms in Health Care*, Washington and London: American Enterprise Institute for Public Policy Research).

West, Anne (1997), 'The Way to a Fairer Admissions System', *Parliamentary Brief*, 5/1, (June–July), 17.

—— West, R. and Pennell, Hazel (1995), 'Financing of School Based Education: Changing the Additional School Needs Allowance', *Education Economics*, 3/3: 265–75.

—— Pennell, Hazel, and Edge, Ann (1997), 'Exploring the Impact of Reform on School-Enrolment Policies in England', *Education Administration Quarterly*, 33/2 (Apr.), 170–82.

West, Edwin G. (1970), *Education and the State* (2nd edn., London: Institute of Economic Affairs).

—— (1994), *Britain's Student Loan System in World Perspective* (London: Institute of Economic Affairs).

Whitehead, Christine M. E. (1974), *The UK Housing Market: An Econometric Model* (Farnborough: Saxon House).

—— (1980), 'Fiscal Aspects of Housing', in Cedric Sandford, Christopher Pond, and Robert Walker (eds.), *Taxation and Social Policy* (London: Heinemann), 84–114.

—— (1997), 'Changing Needs, Changing Incentives: Trends in the UK Housing System', in P. Williams (ed.), *Directions in Housing Policy* (London: Paul Chapman Publishing).

Wilensky, Harold L., and Lebeaux, Charles N. (1965), *Industrial Society and Social Welfare* (New York: Free Press; London: Collier-Macmillan).

Wiles, Peter J. D. (1974), *Distribution of Income: East and West* (Amsterdam: North Holland).

Wilkinson, Richard (1996), *Unhealthy Societies: The Afflictions of Inequality* (London: Routledge).

Willetts, David (1992), *Modern Conservatism* (London: Penguin).

Williams, Alan (1985), 'Economics of Coronary Artery Bypass Grafting', *British Medical Journal*, 3 Aug., pp. 326–9.

Willis, J. R. M., and Hardwick, P. J. W. (1978), *Tax Expenditures in the United Kingdom* (London: Heinemann, for the Institute for Fiscal Studies).

Winch, Donald M. (1971), *Analytical Welfare Economics* (London: Penguin).

Wise, David A. (1986) (ed.), *Pensions, Labor and Individual Behavior* (Chicago: University of Chicago Press).

Witte, E. E. (1962), *The Development of the Social Security Act* (Madison: University of Wisconsin Press).

World Bank (1990), *World Development Report: Poverty* (New York: Oxford University Press).

—— (1992), *Poverty Reduction Handbook* (Washington: The World Bank).

—— (1994*a*), *Averting the Old Age Crisis* (New York: Oxford University Press).

—— (1994*b*), *Higher Education: The Lessons of Experience* (Washington: The World Bank).

—— (1996), *World Development Report 1996: From Plan to Market* (New York and Oxford: Oxford University Press).

GLOSSARY

absolute poverty poverty line defined in terms of a subsistence standard of living; as opposed to **relative poverty**

actuarial an actuarial contribution is based on two factors: (*a*) the size of the benefit to be paid if the insured event (e.g. becoming ill) occurs; and (*b*) the probability of the event occurring. The probability needs to take into account mortality, morbidity, inflation, and all other relevant factors. This is the way in which private insurance works

administrative efficiency see **productive efficiency**

adverse selection situation in which an individual who is a poor risk can conceal the fact from the insurance company

Aid to Families with Dependent Children (AFDC) the main US **income-tested benefit** for families with no (or virtually no) other income; replaced from 1996 by Temporary Assistance to Needy Families

allocative efficiency the allocation of scarce resources in such a way that no reallocation can make any individual better off without making at least one other individual worse off. Also referred to as economic efficiency, **external efficiency**, Pareto efficiency, or Pareto optimality

annuity the payment of an income of £*x* per year for life; often given to an individual in exchange for a single, lump-sum payment at the time he retires. See Chapter 5, Section 2.3

building society UK financial institution which lends money to individuals for the purpose of buying a house. The US equivalent, broadly, is a savings and loan association

cardinal utility If utility is *cardinally* measurable we can make statements such as 'A gets twice as much utility from his first ice cream as from his second' or 'B gets the same utility as A from an ice cream'. When utility is measurable only *ordinally* we can say only that A gets *more* utility from his first ice cream than from his second, but not how much more; and it is not possible to make interpersonal comparisons between A's and B's utility. See also **utility**

cash benefits income support in the form of cash, in contrast with benefits in kind like free health care. Cash benefits generally include **social insurance** and **social assistance**

child benefit UK system of weekly, tax-free cash payment of £*x* for each child in the family, generally payable to the mother

collectivist view which gives priority to the achievement of equality or meeting need. Can take various forms including **democratic socialist** or **Marxist**

comprehensive school UK secondary school for pupils of all abilities, generally covering the age range 11–18

contributory benefit benefit payable only to individuals who (*a*) have a **national insurance** contribution record, and (*b*) are unemployed, retired, or suffering from ill health, etc. See also **social insurance** and **non-contributory benefit**

Glossary

cream–skimming attempt by the supplier of services to select the least costly clients; frequently used in connection with medical insurers who face incentives to try to screen out all but the best risks

cross section series of observations on different entities during a single period of time—e.g. the Family Expenditure Survey gathers data on the expenditure patterns of a large number of families in a given week; as opposed to **time series**

democratic socialist view that **collectivist** goals can be achieved within a mixed economy. See also **libertarian, liberal, Marxist**

disregard amount of earnings or other income which is disregarded (i.e. ignored) in calculating the benefit to which an individual or family is entitled

earnings-related benefits benefits which, in contrast with **flat-rate benefits**, are paid as a percentage of previous earnings; thus, individuals with higher previous earnings receive higher benefits

economic efficiency see **allocative efficiency**

efficiency see **allocative efficiency**

engineering efficiency see **productive efficiency**

equity a goal relating to the way in which resources should be distributed or shared between individuals, hence synonymous with **social justice**; see also **horizontal equity** and **vertical equity**. Equity *may* imply equality, but does not have to—see also **libertarian, liberal, collectivist**

estate agent institution to assist with the purchase and sale of property; in the US a realtor

external efficiency synonymous with **allocative efficiency**; often used in the context of health care and education. It means, for example, the allocation of resources so as to maximise the health gain from a given budget or the production of the mix of educational activities which equip individuals—economically, socially, and politically—for the societies in which they live

family credit UK system of supplementing the incomes of low-income working families, introduced in 1988 to replace Family Income Supplement

Family Income Supplement (FIS) see **Family Credit**

flat-rate benefits benefits which, in contrast with **earnings-related benefits**, are paid at a fixed monthly rate (though they may be higher for larger families) and are not related to previous income; thus, for a given family type, all recipients receive the same benefits

funded funded pensions are paid from an accumulated fund built up over a period of years out of contributions of its members. Contrasts with **Pay-As-You-Go** schemes

general practitioner (GP) family doctor

Gini coefficient a measure of the overall inequality in society; it takes on values between zero (when income is distributed equally) and one (when one individual has all the income)

Green Paper consultative document issued by UK central government, inviting discussion and comment; as distinct from a **White Paper**

health maintenance organization (HMO) a 'firm' of doctors, which charges individuals/families an annual premium, in return for which it provides the individual/family with a comprehensive range of medical services. See Chapter 12, Section 5

Higher Education Funding Council for England (HEFCE) a body which finances universities and colleges on the basis of contracts; replaces the former **Polytechnics and Colleges Funding Council** and **Universities Funding Council**. There are similar bodies for the other parts of the UK

horizontal efficiency concerned with ensuring that benefits should go to *all* the poor. Failure can arise either because eligibility rules prevent some needy groups from applying, or because **take-up** is less than 100 per cent. Thus horizontal equity is concerned with avoiding gaps, as opposed to **vertical efficiency**, which is concerned with avoiding leakages

horizontal equity distribution in accordance with equal treatment of equals—e.g. the relative tax treatment of families of different sizes at a given level of income. See also **equity** and **vertical equity**

housing benefit UK system of assistance with rent and local taxation for low-income householders

housing revenue account (HRA) shows housing revenue and expenditure in each local authority on a cash-flow basis

implicit tax rate a tax which arises when a family in receipt of an **income-tested benefit** earns extra income, and as a consequence loses benefit. If benefit is lost pound for pound with earnings, the implicit tax rate is 100 per cent. See Chapter 10, Section 3

income–related benefit see **income-tested benefit**

income support UK system of **means-tested, non-contributory** benefits, for which individuals/families are eligible if their income from all other sources is less than the poverty standard. Replaced **supplementary benefit** in 1988

income-tested benefit benefit awarded to individuals/families with low incomes, and withdrawn as income rises; as distinct from benefits awarded on the basis of other criteria—e.g. having a contributions record. Also referred to as income-related benefit. See also **contributory benefit** and **means-tested benefit**

indexed government bonds an ordinary 10-year bond sold in 2000 for £100 would pay, say, £10 interest per year and repay the £100 loan in 2010. A similar indexed bond makes a lower interest payment, but repays in 2010 not £100, but the initial sum indexed for changes in the price level. If prices double over the period, the bond holder receives £200 plus interest (also indexed) in 2010

internal efficiency see **productive efficiency**

laissez-faire the term is used in this book in its most frequent sense as 'a belief in the efficacy of a free market economy' (Taylor 1972: 11). See also **libertarian**

less eligibility condition that the standard of living of those in receipt of **Poor Law** benefits should be lower than that of the poorest worker

liberal view of property rights and income distribution as contingent matters rather than as items of dogma. Note the confusing ambiguity in the use of the word. In the nineteenth century it was used as a label for classical Liberal thinkers such as Bentham and Nassau Senior; and today a writer like Friedman, in calling himself a liberal, is using the term in the same way. Throughout the book such writers are referred to as **libertarians**

Glossary

libertarian view which gives priority to individual liberty, usually associated with a belief in the free market and **laissez-faire**. See also **liberal** and **collectivist**

Local Education Authority the body which organizes most forms of education at a local level, including building schools and employing teachers

local rates former UK system of local taxation, based on the annual rental value of property

macro-efficiency concerns the proportion of national resources devoted to a particular activity such as health care or education; as opposed to **micro-efficiency**

market failure impediment to the efficient working of the market, in particular externalities, public goods, or increasing returns to scale (see Appendix to Chapter 4, paras. 12–16)

Marxist view that **collectivist** goals are incompatible with capitalism, and can be achieved only under state ownership of major productive resources. See also **libertarian, liberal,** and **democratic socialist**

means test see **means-tested benefits**

means-tested benefits benefits paid to individuals whose income and wealth from all other sources are below a given amount. The term thus embraces both income-testing and wealth-testing

micro-efficiency concerns the division of total medical resources between the different parts of the health-care system, or that of educational resources between different areas of education, etc.; as opposed to **macro-efficiency**

moral hazard situation in which an insured person can affect the insurance company's liability without its knowledge

National Health Service (NHS) UK system under which medical care is (a) provided by the state, (b) financed mainly out of general tax revenues, and (c) supplied to patients mostly without charge

national insurance UK system of **social insurance** in respect (e.g.) of unemployment, ill health, and retirement. See also **contributory benefit**

negative income tax a system in which income support and income taxation are integrated by using the tax system, both to pay benefits to those with low incomes and to levy taxes on those with higher incomes

non-contributory benefit benefit awarded without the need for a contributions record, and financed out of general tax revenues (in contrast with a **contributory benefit**). May be **income-tested**, or awarded on the basis of non-income criteria, e.g. **child benefit**

ordinal utility see **cardinal utility**

Organization for Economic Cooperation and Development (OECD) an organization of the world's advanced industrial countries

original position hypothetical situation (used by the philosopher John Rawls) in which rational negotiators behind the **veil of ignorance** negotiate a just constitution for a country in which they will all have to live

outdoor relief benefits paid under the **Poor Law** to individuals, principally the elderly, who were not required to live in the **workhouse**

Pareto efficiency see **allocative efficiency**

Pareto optimality see **allocative efficiency**

Pay-As-You-Go pensions paid (usually by the state) out of current tax revenues, rather than out of an accumulated fund; contrasts with **funded** schemes

Pigovian subsidy/tax where an activity creates an external benefit, an unrestricted private market will supply an inefficiently small quantity. One way of restoring supply to its efficient level is to pay a so-called Pigovian subsidy. Analogously, a Pigovian tax discourages excessive supply in the present of an external cost. See Chapter 4, Section 3.2 and/or the Appendix to Chapter 4, para. 15

Polytechnics and Colleges Funding Council (PCFC) a body which financed polytechnics and colleges in England and Wales on the basis of contracts from 1990 to 1993, after which it was replaced by the **Higher Education Funding Council for England**

Poor Law UK system for the relief of destitution, from late sixteenth century; it was phased out over the first half of the twentieth century

poverty trap situation in which individuals/families earning an extra £1 lose £1 or more in income-tested benefits, and hence make themselves absolutely worse off. Such people have no financial incentive to work longer hours. As distinct from the **unemployment trap**; see also **implicit tax rate**

productive efficiency the allocation of resources so as to produce the maximum output from given inputs. Also referred to as administrative efficiency, engineering efficiency, or internal efficiency. A component of **allocative efficiency**

progressive taxation tax system in which tax paid as a proportion of income is higher for individuals with higher incomes. See also **proportional taxation** and **regressive taxation**

proportional taxation tax system in which tax paid is the same proportion of income at all income levels. See also **progressive taxation** and **regressive taxation**

quasi-markets used to improve the efficiency of public providers by introducing market forces. But they differ from the market for, say, food: on the supply side, they introduce competition (e.g. between hospitals or schools), but the suppliers are not necessarily private, nor necessarily profit maximizing. On the demand side, consumers do not spend cash; their purchasing power is expressed as an earmarked budget. Consumers may make their own choice (of school), or choice may be made on their behalf by an agent (much medical care)

rates see **local rates**

regressive taxation tax system in which tax paid as a proportion of income is lower for individuals with higher incomes. See also **progressive taxation** and **proportional taxation**

relative poverty poverty line defined relative to the average standard of living—e.g. as a proportion of average income; as opposed to **absolute poverty**

replacement ratio ratio of income when unemployed or retired, to income (post-tax and transfers) when in work

revenue neutral a policy change is revenue neutral if any resulting increase in expenditure is accompanied by a matching increase in taxation

Glossary

SERPS UK State Earnings-Related Pension Scheme

social assistance state benefits paid out of general tax revenues without contribution condition, but usually subject to a **means test**. See also **income-tested benefit**

social dividend scheme form of **negative income tax**

social insurance form of organization, originally modelled on private insurance, under which individuals receive state benefits in respect of (e.g.) unemployment or retirement, often without any test of means or need, on the basis of previous (usually compulsory) contributions. See also **contributory benefit** and **national insurance**

social justice a goal relating to the way in which resources should be distributed or shared between individuals. See also **equity**, **horizontal equity**, and **vertical equity**. For different definitions of social justice, see **libertarian**, **liberal**, and **collectivist**

social security all publicly provided cash benefits. Note that this standard UK usage differs from the narrower US definition of social security as retirement benefits, and the broader EU definition which includes health services. Throughout the book the term is used with its UK meaning

standard assumptions the assumptions under which the market will, in theory, allocate resources efficiently—namely, perfect information, perfect competition, and no **market failures** (see Chapter 4, Section 3.2, or the Appendix to Chapter 4, paras. 5–17)

stigma loss of **utility** because income is received in the form of (usually) **income-tested benefits**, rather than from some more congenial source (e.g. earnings or insurance benefits)

supplementary benefit former UK system of **means-tested**, **non-contributory** benefits, for which individuals/families were eligible if their income from all other sources was less than the poverty standard. Replaced the earlier system of National Assistance in 1966. Replaced in 1988 by **income support**

take–up the number of people receiving a particular benefit as a proportion of those potentially eligible

tax expenditures public expenditure implicit in the granting of tax relief to certain activities—e.g. approved private pension contributions or mortgage interest payments, as opposed to explicit expenditure. See Chapter 7, Section 1.1

tenure neutrality an aim of housing policy, whereby individuals (on average and in the long run) are financially indifferent between buying accommodation and renting it. See Chapter 14, Section 2

third–party–payment problem situation in which the insurance company pays the whole of an individual's (e.g.) medical bill; as a result neither patient nor doctor has an incentive to economize. Technically, a form of **moral hazard**

time series series of observations on a single entity (or aggregate) over several periods—e.g. data on the level of unemployment benefits, the number of people out of work, etc. in a country each year from 1960 to 1980. As opposed to **cross section**

unemployment trap situation in which an individual/family is better off (or little worse off) when unemployed than when in work, and hence has little financial incentive to seek work. This situation arises particularly for those with low earnings and/or with large families. As distinct from the **poverty trap**, under which an individual doing at least some work is given no financial incentive to work longer hours

unfunded see Pay-As-You-Go

Universities Funding Council (UFC) body which financed universities in England and Wales on the basis of contracts from 1990 to 1993, after which it was replaced by the **Higher Education Funding Council for England**

uprating increase in the value of almost all cash benefits, usually at annual intervals, and usually in line with changes in the price level

utility individual well-being or satisfaction. See also **cardinal utility**

veil of ignorance hypothetical situation in which rational individuals in the **original position** have to negotiate a just constitution for a country in which they will all have to live, but *without knowing who they will be* (i.e. whether they will be born as one of the most or least fortunate)

vertical efficiency concerned with ensuring that benefits go *only* to people who need them. This reduces the cost of benefits, but may involve high **implicit tax rates** and the **poverty trap** (see Chapter 10, Section 3.2). Thus vertical equity is concerned with avoiding leakages, as opposed to **horizontal efficiency**, which is concerned with avoiding gaps

vertical equity the extent of redistribution of income, consumption, or wealth from rich to poor. See also **equity** and **horizontal equity**

welfare US usage for **income-tested benefits**. See also **social assistance**

White Paper firm statement of government intent; as distinct from a **Green Paper**

workhouse institution giving work and rudimentary accommodation to the destitute, under the Poor Law

workhouse test condition that recipients of benefits under the **Poor Law** must live in the workhouse

NAME INDEX

Name Index

Culyer, A. J. 113 n., 115 n., 118 n., 121 n., 126, 280 n., 282, 285, 318–19, 373, 388 n.

Dalton, H. 153 n.
Daniel, C. 54, 56
Daniels, N. 51, 53, 59, 64
Danziger, S. 143, 157, 159, 160, 253
Dasgupta, P. 117, 132, 133
Datt, G. 117, 239, 253
Davis, O. E. 99
Deininger, K. 159
Denison, E. F. 327
Derthick, M. 29
Desai, M. 64
Diamond, P. A. 217 n., 228, 231
Dicks-Mireaux, L. 231
Dilnot, A. W. 205, 207, 231, 270, 274
Disney, R. 199, 201, 231
Ditch, J. 40 n., 253
Dixon, J. 305, 319
Donaldson, D. 241
Donnison, D. 393
Doorslaer, E. van 310
Douglas, P. H. 29, 43
Downs, A. 39, 85–6, 87, 101
Drèze, J. H. 415
Duncan, G. J. 249
Dunleavy, P. 93, 102

Eardley, T. 253
Ehrenberg, R. 200
Elliott, R. F. 200
Ellis, R. P. 287, 303
Engen, E. 231
Enthoven, A. C. 306, 312, 314, 315, 319
Esping-Anderson, G. 12, 13, 14, 173, 409, 413, 415
Estrin, S. 60, 70 n., 73 n., 80 n., 101, 102, 109 n., 126
Evandrou, M. 319, 361
Evans, M. 36, 141, 142, 159, 177, 200, 201, 205 n., 221, 228, 231, 232, 244 n., 248, 249, 250, 253, 307, 313
Evans, R. G. 302, 319

Falkingham, J. 200, 213, 228, 231, 355
Farmer, M. 361
Feachem, R. G. A. 319
Feinstein, C. H. 172
Feldstein, M. S. 223–4, 231
Field, F. 228, 231, 274
Fields, G. S. 225
Finer, S. E. 18
Fischer, C. S. 157, 160
Fisher, I. 159, 277, 320
Flanagan, R. J. 198 n.
Forrest, R. 379
Foster, J. E. 142
Franklin, J. 64
Fraser, D. 16, 18, 27, 32, 40, 43
Freeden, M. 20, 43
Freeman, R. 200
Fretwell, D. 198 n.

Friedman, M. 44, 46, 61, 62, 63, 87, 93, 100, 236, 319, 347–8, 353–6, 360, 374
Friedman, R. 63, 319, 360
Fuchs, V. R. 231, 303

Galal, A. 102
Gale, W. 224, 231
Gauldie, E. 24, 371, 400
George, V. 47, 48, 56, 61, 62, 64
Gerdttham, Ulf-G. 303
Geske, T. G. 360
Gibb, K. 372
Gilbert, B. B. 43
Gilmour, I. 62
Ginsburg, N. 57, 64, 415
Gintis, H. 63
Glennerster, H. 6, 14, 35, 37, 43, 167, 170, 177, 182, 278, 298, 299, 300, 306, 316, 318, 319, 324 n., 327 n., 334, 336, 340, 341, 342, 343, 344, 349, 350, 351, 354, 360, 361, 380, 381, 393, 400, 414, 415
Goodman, A. C. 160, 400
Goodwin, N. 316, 319
Gordon, D. M. 38
Gordon, M. 7, 200, 211, 217, 231
Gorovitz, S. 51, 64
Gottschalk, P. 142, 157, 159, 160
Gough, I. 58, 63, 64, 415
Gramlich, E. M. 201, 228, 231, 252
Green, C. 274
Green, D. 340
Gronbjerg, K. 29
Grosh, M. 253, 268
Grubel, H. G. 197
Gruber, J. 196

Hall, R. E. 38, 241 n., 242, 244 n., 252
Halpern, S. 307
Ham, C. 319
Hamblin, R. 316, 319
Hamnett, C. 160, 231
Hannah, L. 209, 225, 231
Hansen, W. L. 346
Hanushek, E. A. 340, 360
Hardwick, P. J. W. 182
Harker, L. 143, 159, 199, 201, 253
Harris, J. F. 22, 43
Harris, R. 415
Harrison, A. H. 305
Harrison, J. 64
Harrison, L. 319
Hart 53
Hattersley, R. 54
Hausman, J. A. 231
Hay, J. R. 19, 22, 43
Hayek, F. A. 11, 46–7, 55 n., 59, 61, 63, 124, 192, 236, 348, 374
Heckman, J. J. 200
Hellevick, O. 344
Hellwig, M. 117
Hemming, R. 199
Hicks, J. R. 159

Name Index

Mishra, R. 43, 57, 63, 64
Mitchell, O. S. 225
Moe, T. M. 349
Moffitt, R. A. 248, 249, 252, 253
Mogenson, G. V. 201, 253, 413
Moon, G. 400
Mooney, G. 319
Morris, C. N. 307
Mortensen, D. T. 82 n.
Mortimore, P. 340
Mueller, D. C. 92, 102
Mullings, B. 389
Munnell, A. H. 231
Murie, A. 379
Murphy, J. 345 n.
Murray, C. 47, 411, 415
Musgrave, P. B. & R. A. 80 n., 323 n.
Muth, R. F. 367, 400
Myers, R. J. 31 n.
Myles, J. 200

Nead, K. 159
Nevitt, A. A. 393, 400
Newfield, J. 134 n.
Newhouse, J. P. 311–12
Nichols, A. L. 241
Nisbet, R. 52, 64
Niskanen, W. A. 93
North, F. 307
Nozick, R. 46, 60, 63, 74

O'Kelly, R. 270
Okin, S. M. 133
Okun, A. M. 11, 68, 98 n., 101, 145, 160, 403, 404, 415
Oppenheim, C. 143, 159, 199, 201, 253
Orshansky, M. 159
Otter, C. von 301

Palmer, J. L. 274
Parker, H. 201, 244, 253, 266, 270, 274
Pauly, M. V. 115 n., 126, 285, 286, 287, 319
Peabody, J. W. 319
Peacock, A. T. 182
Pechman, J. A. 29, 31 n., 182, 274
Pelling, H. 19, 21 n.
Pelzmann, S. 92
Pen, J. 149 n., 160
Peterson, W. C. 408
Phillips, A. 64, 201
Phillips, D. 412
Phlips, L. 82 n., 126
Piachaud, D. F. S. 137 n., 159, 270
Piggott, J. 182, 391
Pinker, R. 14
Podger, A. 319
Posner, R. A. 92
Posnett, J. W. 87 n., 102
Powell, M. 308, 319
Power, A. 392, 394
Prais, S. G. 341
Preker, A. 319

Prest, A. R. 130 n., 167, 179, 182, 195, 201, 256 n., 273, 377 n.
Propper, C. 309, 319
Psacharopoulos, G. 323, 327, 360

Quah, D. 12

Radford, R. A. 73 n.
Rainwater, L. 147, 148
Rake, K. 22
Raphael, J. 250, 253
Ravallion, M. 117, 137, 140 n., 142, 143, 239, 253, 267
Rawls, J. xxvii, 51
Rees, P. M. 91 n., 113 n., 115 n., 118 n., 126, 130 n., 132 n., 274
Ricardo, D. 56
Riley, J. G. 82 n., 126, 324 n., 360
Rimlinger, G. 43
Ringen, S. 344
Robbins, L. C. 17, 43, 46, 60, 64
Robinson, P. 340
Robinson, R. 102, 319, 360, 367, 390, 391, 400
Robson, W. A. 14, 62, 231
Rodgers, S. J. 86, 93, 101
Romer, P. 325, 327
Roosevelt, F. D. 167
Roper, J. F. H. 256 n.
Rosa, J. J. 225
Rose, M. E. 43
Rosenthal, L. 390, 391
Rothschild, M. 115, 124, 126
Rowntree, B. S. 20, 159
Russell, L. B. 312
Rutter, M. 340

Sachs, J. 231
Sainsbury, S. 64, 133, 201
Saltman, R. 301
Sammons, P. 343
Samuelson, P. A. 10, 207, 213
Saunders, P. 252
Sawhill, I. V. 250
Scheffler, R. 311, 312, 319
Schieber, G. J. 319
Scholz, J. K. 231
Schottland, C. I. 43
Schwartz, W. B. 297
Schweitzer, J. 361
Seavers, J. 160, 231
Seldon, A. 319, 360, 415
Sen, A. K. 49, 64, 132, 137 n., 138, 148 n., 152, 159, 160, 253
Shankland, G. 385
Shannon, R. 182
Shapiro, J. 319
Shaw, G. B. 277
Shorrocks, A. F. 151 n.
Simons, H. 132, 159
Sipos, S. 253
Smaje, C. 309
Smeeding, T. 143, 147, 148, 152 n., 157, 159, 160, 248

SUBJECT INDEX

Subject Index

Subject Index